BI 0563961 1

BI 8604057

Play – Its Role in Development and Evolution

Formerly Watts Professor of Psychology at the University of Oxford from 1972 to 1980, Jerome S. Bruner is now G. H. Mead University Professor at the New School for Social Research, New York.

A former Research Associate in the School of Biological Sciences at the University of Sussex, Dr Alison Jolly now works at Rockefeller University, New York.

A former Research Fel
University of St An... **O WEEK LO**
ment of Social Adm...

D1635164

BIRMINGHAM CITY
UNIVERSITY
DISCARDED

Edited by Jerome S. Bruner, Alison Jolly, Kathy Sylva

Play – Its Role in Development and Evolution ^{Mise}

Penguin Books

CITY OF BIRMINGHAM
LIBRARY
POLYTECHNIC

Penguin Books Ltd, Harmondsworth, Middlesex, England
Viking Penguin Inc., 40 West 23rd Street, New York, New York 10010, U.S.A.
Penguin Books Australia Ltd, Ringwood, Victoria, Australia
Penguin Books Canada Ltd, 2801 John Street, Markham, Ontario, Canada L3R 1B4
Penguin Books (N.Z.) Ltd, 182–190 Wairau Road, Auckland 10, New Zealand

First published 1976
Reprinted 1985

This selection copyright © Jerome Bruner, Alison Jolly, Kathy Sylva, 1976
Introduction and notes copyright © Jerome S. Bruner, Alison Jolly, Kathy Sylva, 1976
All rights reserved

Copyright acknowledgements for items in this volume will be found on pp. 705–7

Made and printed in Great Britain by
Hazell Watson & Viney Limited,
Member of the BPCC Group,
Aylesbury, Bucks
Set in Monotype Times

Except in the United States of America, this book is sold subject
to the condition that it shall not, by way of trade or otherwise, be lent,
re-sold, hired out, or otherwise circulated without the
publisher's prior consent in any form of binding or cover other than
that in which it is published and without a similar condition
including this condition being imposed on the subsequent purchaser

CITY OF BIRMINGHAM
POLYTECHNIC LIBRARY

BOOK
No. 0563961

SUBJECT
No. 155.418

Contents

6 Contents

8 Contents

Acknowledgements

We are grateful for the gifts we have received in the form of suggestions about articles on play – it turns out that our friends had hat-fulls of them! We want to express special gratitude to Meg Penning-Rowsell who gathered manuscripts, chose photographs, and dealt with publishers with a competence and cheerfulness that buoyed us even in moments of grave unplayfulness.

Introduction*

Who would dare study play? In fact, there have been many ways in which serious men have tried to grasp this antic topic – historical, literary, clinical, introspective, anthropological, sociological, linguistic, ethological and via controlled experimental methods of the behavioural sciences. We have, in this volume, included all of them, although the principal focus is on the carefully conducted observational or experimental study of play behaviour itself. We must begin, then, with some words of background on the emergence of such studies over the last decades.

The behavioural sciences tend to be rather sober disciplines, tough-minded not only in procedures, but in choice of topics as well. These must be scientifically manageable. No surprise, then, that when scientists began extending their investigations into the realm of early human development they steered clear of so frivolous a phenomenon as play. For even as recently as a few decades ago, Harold Schlosberg (1947) of Brown University, a highly respected psychological critic, published a carefully reasoned paper concluding sternly that, since play could not even be properly defined, it could scarcely be a manageable topic for experimental research. His conclusion was not without foundation, for the phenomena of play cannot be impeccably framed into a single operational definition. How indeed can one encompass so motley a set of capers as childish punning, cowboys-and-Indians, and the construction of a tower of bricks into a single or even a sober dictionary entry?

Fortunately, the progress of research is subject to accidents of opportunity. Once data begin seriously to undermine presuppositions, the course can change very quickly. A decade ago, while Schlosberg's words still reverberated, work on primate ethology began to force a change in direction, raising new and basic questions about the nature and role of play in the evolution of the primate series. On closer inspection, play is not as diverse a phenomenon as had been thought, particularly when looked at in its natural setting. Nor is it all that antic in its structure, if analysed properly. But perhaps most important, its role during immaturity appears to

* Parts of this Introduction appeared in 'Child's Play' by J. S. Bruner in *New Scientist*, 18 April 1974.

be more and more central as one moves up the living primate series from Old World monkeys through Great Apes, to Man – suggesting that in the evolution of primates, marked by an increase in the number of years of immaturity, the selection of a capacity for play during those years may have been crucial. So while play seemed to the methodologically vexed to be an unmanageable laboratory topic, primatologists were pondering its possible centrality in evolution!

A first field finding served to reduce the apparently dizzying variety of forms that play could take. On closer inspection, it turns out that play is universally accompanied in subhuman primates by a recognizab!e form of metasignalling, a 'play face', first carefully studied by the Dutch primatologist van Hooff (p. 130). It signifies within the species the message, to use Gregory Bateson's phrase, 'this is play' (p. 119). It is a powerful signal – redundant in its features, which include a particular kind of open-mouthed gesture, a slack but exaggerated gait, and a marked 'galumphing' in movement – and its function is plainly not to be understood simply as 'practice of instinctive activities crucial for survival'. When, for example, Stephen Miller (1973) set about analysing filmed field records of juvenile play behaviour made by Irven DeVore while studying Savanna baboons in the Amboseli Game Reserve in East Africa, he very quickly discovered that if one young animal did not see the 'metasignal' of another who was seeking to play-fight with him, a real fight broke out with no lack of skill. But once the signal was perceived by both parties the fight was transformed into the universally recognizable clownish ballet of monkeys feigning a fight. They obviously knew how to do it both ways. What was it for, then, play-fighting? And why should the accompanying form of metasignalling have been selected in evolution?

We begin to get a hint of the functional significance of play in higher primates from the pioneering observations of the group led by Jane van Lawick-Goodall (1968) studying free-ranging chimpanzees at the Gombe Stream Reserve in Tanzania. Recall first the considerably longer childhood in chimpanzees than in Old World monkeys – the young chimp in close contact with the mother for four or five years during which the mother has no other offspring, whilst in monkeys the oestrus cycle ensures that within a year new young are born, with the rapidly maturing animals of last year's crop relegated to a peer group of juveniles in which play declines rapidly.

Observation and play

David Hamburg (1968) of Stanford, a psychiatrist-primatologist working at Gombe Stream, has noted the extent to which young chimpanzees in the first five years spend time observing adult behaviour, incorporating observed patterns of adult behaviour into their play. Van Lawick-Goodall

(1968) has a telling observation to report that relates this early observation-cum-play to adult skilled behaviour – an observation that deepens our understanding of the function of early play. Adult chimps develop (when the ecology permits) a very skilled technique of termiting, in which they put mouth-wetted, stripped sticks into the opening of a termite hill, wait a bit for the termites to adhere to the stick, then carefully remove their fishing 'instrument' with termites adhering to it which they then eat with relish. One of the young animals, Merlin, lost his mother in his third year. He had not learned to termite by $4\frac{1}{2}$ nearly as well as the others, though raised by older siblings. For the young animals appear to learn the 'art of termiting' by sitting by the mother, buffered from pressures, trying out in play and learning the individual constituent acts that make up termiting, and without the usual reinforcement of food from catching: learning to play with sticks, to strip leaves from twigs and to pick the right length of twig for getting into different holes. These are the constituents that must be combined in the final act and they are tried out in all manner of antic episodes.

Merlin, compared to his age mates, was inept and unequipped. He had not had the opportunity for such observation and play nor, probably, did he get the buffering from distraction and pressure normally provided by the presence of a mother (p. 224). This would suggest, then, that play has the effect of providing practice not so much of survival-relevant instinctive behaviour but, rather, of making possible the playful practice of subroutines of behaviour later to be combined in more useful problem-solving. What appears to be at stake in play is the opportunity for assembling and reassembling behaviour sequences for skilled action. That, at least, is one function of play.

Moratorium on frustration

This function suggests a more general feature of play. It is able to reduce or neutralize the pressure of goal-directed action, the 'push' to successful completion of an act. There is a well-known rule in the psychology of learning, the Yerkes-Dodson law, that states that the more complex a skill to be learned, the lower the *optimum* motivational level required for fastest learning. Play, then, may provide the means for reducing excessive drive and frustration. The distinguished Russian investigator Lev Vygotsky (p. 549), in a long-lost manuscript published a few years ago, reports an investigation in which young children could easily be induced not to eat their favourite candy laid before them, when that candy was made part of a game of 'Poison'. And years before, Wolfgang Köhler (1925) had reported that when his chimps were learning to stack boxes to reach fruit suspended from the high tops of their cages, they often lost interest in eating the fruit when they were closing in on the solution. It is no surprise, then, to find results indicating that prior play with materials improves children's problem-solving with those materials later.

Sylva, Bruner and Genova (p. 244) worked with children aged three to five who had the task of fishing a prize from a latched box out of reach. To do so, they had to extend two sticks by clamping them together. The children were given various 'training' procedures beforehand, including demonstration of the principle of clamping two sticks together, or practice in fastening clamps on single sticks, or an opportunity to watch the experimenter carry out the task. One group was simply allowed to play with the materials. They did as well in solving the problem as the ones who had been given a demonstration of the principle of clamping sticks together and better than any of the other groups. The table (below) summarizes the differences between the groups (each thirty-six in number, equally divided between 3-, 4-, and 5-year-olds) in terms of number of spontaneous solutions with no aid from the experimenter.

Prior training	Per cent spontaneous solution
Play with materials	39
Observation of complete solution	41
Observation of components of solution	17
Instructed manipulation of materials	20
No training	8

The difference between the 'play' group and the 'observe solution' group is insignificant, and both are better than all the other groups. In fact, what was striking about the play group was their tenacity in sticking with the task so that even when they were poor in their initial approach, they ended by solving the problem. What was particularly striking was their capacity to resist frustration and 'giving up'. They were playing.

The young are more inventive

There are comparable results with primates below man where the pressure is taken off animals by other means – as by semi-domestication achieved by putting out food in a natural habitat, a technique pioneered by Japanese primatologists (see Itani, 1958). It appears to have the effect of increasing innovation in the animals studied. Japanese macaques at Takasakiyama have taken to washing yams, to separating maize from the sand on which it is spread by dropping a handful of the mix into sea-water and letting the sand sink. And once in the water, playing in this new medium to the edge of which they have been transplanted, the young learn to swim, first in play, and then begin swimming off, migrating to near islands. In all of these activities, it is the playful young who are centrally involved in the new enterprises, even if they may not always be the innovators of the new 'technologies'. But it is the young who are game for a change, and it is this gameness that predisposes the troop to change its ways. The fully adult males are often the most resistant or, at least, the most out of touch, because the novelties are being tried out in the groups playing around the mother from which the big males are absent. Jean-Claude Fady (p. 328), the French primatologist, has shown that even ordinarily combative adult males will co-operate with each other in moving heavy rocks under which food is hidden – if the pressure is taken off by the technique of semi-domestication.

Ample early opportunity for play may have a more lasting effect still, as Corinne Hutt (p. 202) has shown. She designed a super-toy for children of three to five years old, consisting of a table with a lever, buzzer, bells and counters, different movements of the lever systematically sounding buzzers, and turning counters, etc. Children first explore its possibilities, then having contented themselves, often proceed to play. She was able to rate how inventive the children were in their play, dividing them into non-explorers, explorers, and inventive explorers, the last group carrying on all the way from initial exploration to full-blown play. Four years later, when the children were aged seven to ten, Hutt and Bhavnani (p. 216) tested them on a creativity test designed by Mike Wallach and Nathan Kogan in the United States, as well as on some personality tests.

The more inventive and exploratory the children had been initially in playing with the super-toy, the higher their originality scores were four years later. The non-exploring boys in general had come to view themselves as unadventurous and inactive and their parents and teachers considered them as lacking curiosity. The non-exploratory and unplayful girls were later rather unforthcoming in social interaction as well and more tense than their originally more playful mates. Early unplayfulness may go with a lack of later originality.

Obviously, more studies of this kind are needed (and are in progress). But the psychiatrist Erik Erikson, reporting in his Godkin Lectures at Harvard in 1973 on a thirty-year follow-up of children earlier studied, has commented that the ones with the most interesting and fulfilling lives were the ones who had managed to keep a sense of playfulness at the centre of things.

Play has rules

Consider play now from a structural point of view as a form of activity. Rather than being 'random' it is usually found to be characterized by a recognizable rule structure.

New studies by the psycholinguist Catherine Garvey (p. 570) show how three- to five-year-old children, playing in pairs, manage implicitly even in their simplest games to create and recognize rules and expectancies, managing the while to distinguish sharply between the structure of make-believe or possibility and the real thing.

Here is an example, one in which the rule is to respond identically:

First child	*Second child*
Bye Mommy.	
	Bye Mommy.
Bye Mommy.	
	Bye Daddy.
You're a nut.	
	No I'm not.

In other rounds, a complement rule prevails, and the expected response is indeed 'Bye Daddy' in reaction to the first child's 'Bye Mommy'. The rules also specify recognition of the situation in which the play is set, as in the example:

I have to go to work.
You're already at work.
No I'm not.

But, withal, children at this age are quite aware of the line between fantasy and reality, as in the following example when one child sits down on a three-legged stool with a magnifying glass at its centre:

I've got to go to the potty.
(Turns to him) Really?
(Grins) No, pretend.

Amusing though these protocols may be, they reveal a concise, almost grammatical quality in the interchanges and an extraordinary sensitivity on the part of the children to violations of implicit expectancies and codes.

It is hardly surprising then that different cultures encourage different forms of play as 'fitting'. Ours tend, in the main, to admire play and games of 'zero sum', one wins what the other loses. The anthropologist Kenelm Burridge (p. 364) contrasts our favourite form with a typical ritual food-exchange game of 'taketak' among the Tangu in New Guinea, a tribe that practises strict and equal sharing. The object of their game is to achieve equal shares among the players – not to win, not to lose, but to tie. It is reminiscent of a game reported years ago by James Sully (see Vygotsky, p. 537). He tells of two sisters, five and seven, who played a game they called 'Sisters', a game with one rule: equal shares for each player, no matter what – in their case quite unlike life! We are only at the beginning of studying the functions of play in fitting children to their culture, but there are already some classic studies.

If the rule structure of human play and games sensitizes the child to the rules of culture, both generally and in preparation for a particular way of life, then surely play must have some special role in nurturing symbolic activity in general. For culture is symbolism in action. Does play then have some deep connection with the origins of language? One can never know. Yet we have already noted the extraordinary combinatorial push behind play, its working out of variations. Play is certainly implicated in early language acquisition. Its structured interactions and 'rules' precede and are a part of the child's first mastery of language. Our own studies at Oxford on language acquisition suggest that in exchange games, in 'peek-a-boo' (p. 277), and in other structured interactions, young children learn to signal and to recognize signals and expectancies. They delight in primitive rule structures that come to govern their encounters. In these encounters they master the idea of 'privileges of occurrence' so central to grammar, as well as other constituents of language that must later be put together.

One set of episodes from our studies illustrate how play serves as a vehicle for language acquisition. Nan at nine months has begun to signal in an exchange game when she gives an object to her mother, using *Kew* (a version of 'Thank You'). She has not yet learned the language code for giving and receiving, although she has learned the rules for the game. In three months, the demonstrative *Look* has replaced *Kew* in the giving phase, and *Kew* has moved into its correct receiving position in the sequence. Nan has used the correct serial order in the play to sort out the right order in the language that accompanies the play.

(Nine months, two weeks) Give-and-take game. Child offers book to Mother and then withdraws it when Mother reaches for it, with the Child showing great excitement. Hands book to Mother, saying *Kew* when Mother takes it.

(Ten months, two weeks) Child plays with blocks. Says *Kew* when offering block to camera operators. Not observed ever to say *Kew* when receiving block or any object. Give-and-take game always involves Nan saying *Kew* when handing block to Mother.

(Twelve months, two weeks) Mother hands Child ring. Now Child says *Kew* when receiving. Three minutes later Child hands Mother a toy postbox, a favourite. Child says *Look* when handing.

Indeed, there is a celebrated and highly technical volume by Ruth Weir (p. 609) on language play in a 2½-year-old child, *Language in the Crib*, in which she reports on the language of her son Anthony after he had been put to bed with lights out. He pushes combinatorial activity to the limit, phonologically, syntactically and semantically, often to the point at which he reproves himself with an adult 'Oh no, no'.

Much more is being learned about play than we would have expected a decade ago. We have come a long way since Piaget's brilliant observations on the role of play in assimilating the child's experience to his personal schema of the world, as preparation for later accommodation to it (p. 166). A new period of research on play is under way. Nick Blurton-Jones (p. 352) has shown that Niko Tinbergen's ethological methods can be applied to children at play as readily as to chimps in the forest. The new work begins to suggest why play is the principal business of childhood, the vehicle of improvisation and combination, the first carrier of rule systems through which a world of cultural restraint is substituted for the operation of impulse.

It is, of course, self-evident that such research raises deep questions about the role of play in our own society. Although we do not yet know how important play is for growing up, we do know that it is serious business. How serious it is can perhaps be exemplified by citing a study done on children's laughter by Alan Sroufe and his colleagues (1972) at Minnesota. They find that those things most likely to make a child laugh when done by his mother at a year are most likely to make him cry when done by a stranger.

Aims and structure of this book

Our purpose in collecting these papers in book form was principally to bring together a body of literature emphasizing the crucial role of play in the development of the individual human child as well as in the evolution of the primate order. Many of the articles have appeared in specialized journals usually accessible only to the advanced student of animal or human behaviour. Some of them also appeared originally in a foreign language and are presented here for the first time in translation. In selecting the articles to be included, we sifted through a very much larger collection and in the course of that exercise allowed ourselves to recognize the biases that were operating initially in the backs of our minds and, eventually, at the focus of our consciousness. We should in fairness to the reader try to make those biases clear.

The first of them was that we were interested in exploring the emergence of evolutionary trends in the primate order as these reflect themselves in the play of human beings. In consequence, each section of the book contains papers that are comparative in intent. In some instances, this comparative treatment yields something approaching a parallelism throughout the primate order, as for example in rough-and-tumble play. In others, as in the emergence of symbolic play, the result is to highlight striking discontinuities in play patterns that emerge when language becomes a factor in the regulation and indeed in the content of play. In yet other instances, the issue of the comparative development of play remains properly ambiguous, since in most instances play is to be understood in the context of the adaptation of a given species to its habitat. An obvious instance of this is to be found in the extent to which and the manner in which older juveniles play with the young infants of their species, in some instances this pattern being prominent both in the juvenile male and female, whilst in others it is restricted to the female juvenile. Such 'mothering' patterns in play inevitably reflect the role of the adult male and the female of the particular species in the care of the young. In any case, the object of the comparative exercise is to throw into bold relief the fact that play, whatever its nature, must be thought of not only in an evolutionary perspective, but also in relation to the adaptation of a particular species.

This brings us to a second principle of selection or bias. Play among humans inevitably reflects the culture in which it occurs or indeed the subcultural condition (such as poverty) in which individuals find themselves within a culture. Particularly in the later sections of the book, we have tried to emphasize the rich connection that exists between play and human culture and have favoured articles in our selection that elucidated that connection.

A third principle of selection was what might be called a canon of relevance. We chose papers that were broad in their perspective, however technical or literary they might be. In consequence, then, the reader will find sections in which technical reports of primate symbolic play live side-by-side with deeply intuitive accounts of play written by poets like W. H. Auden or historians like Huizinga. We make no apology for this practice, for in our view Simone de Beauvoir must be counted not only an artist, but a masterful ethologist of the conditions of her own fantasy life. If it has turned out to be the case that we have included more technical papers than literary ones, it is simply because it is our belief that the technical literature is both less accessible and less well known to the general reader than the works of our great literary artists.

We must admit to one other bias. We have been struck in exploring the literature on play in animals and man alike with the formal parallelism that exists in the rule-bound structure of play and in the rule-bound structure of language. We unashamedly confess to entertaining the plausible hypothesis that the evolution of play might be a major precursor to the emergence of language and symbolic behaviour in higher primates and man. In consequence there is a quite rich representation in the sections that follow of papers exploring the structure of language play and examining the language-like nature of play. This will be found particularly in work by Vygotsky, Reynolds, Bruner, Garvey, Weir and others. We would not be surprised if over the coming decade the powerful techniques of linguistic analysis emerged as a major tool for unravelling what on the surface seems like an antic disorder in play activity.

The last of the biases of which we are aware – and reviewers will doubtless find others – is that we have excluded much of the literature on play therapy and, in general, on psychoanalytic interpretations of play. We would plead that our bias is not so much ideological or theoretical, but rather that it comes out of the conviction that the psychoanalytic interpretation of play and its incorporation in doctrines of play therapy are by now very much part of the common culture. Freud's great formulations of play as a displacement of instinctual activity, the notion that one can 'work' through internal tensions and conflicts by playing them out in a therapeutic situation, and allied views of the instinctual origin of symbolic forms through transformations in fantasy, all of these are well known to the general reader. We have not excluded the new insights of psychoanalytic writers, as the reader will find in perusing Erik Erikson's paper (p. 688). We can perhaps best guide the reader to other sources of material in this sphere by citing a collection of readings by Herron and Sutton-Smith (1971) which contains a good sample from this literature. The reader is also directed to the classic book by Winnicott (1971) on the role of play in fantasy. Jerome Singer's recent volume (1973) can also be recommended in this connection.

Perhaps the best way of alerting the reader to other ways of conceiving of the role of play in human life as well as its role in evolution is to cite two excellent volumes that have in recent years tried to synthesize the literature on the subject. One is Susanna Millar's *The Psychology of Play* (1968) and the other is M. J. Ellis's new book *Why People Play* (1973). These provide a synoptic view of the field, but neither of them attempts to give the reader a sampling of the prime literature. And that is our principal objective.

We must say a word now as to the audience we have in mind when collecting these papers and in editing them for this volume. As always, one is caught in the conflict between the desire to inform those who are already knowledgeable in the study of human behaviour in a professional way and at the same time to make the literature accessible to the general reader – whether the general reader be professionally concerned with human development as teacher or physician or counsellor or whether he or she be a parent interested in what underlies the startling capers of the young. Indeed, we even had in mind the reader freshly returned from a visit to the zoo who might be wondering why so much of the energies of the young of all species is turned into such evident jackanapes. Because we were caught in this inevitable conflict, we have tried to edit the papers in such a way that they could be enjoyed by the general reader and yet contain sufficient description of research methods and data analysis to satisfy the technical student of animal or human behaviour. We have edited some papers to illustrate one particular approach or empirical finding, occasionally at the expense of other emphases. We hope we have not done an injustice to our authors in so doing.

At the beginning of each section of the book, and also before certain articles, we have provided introductory remarks to put particular papers in broader perspective or to summarize details about method. These sections will, we hope, redress some of the deletions we have made in the papers, but also help the lay reader bring the issues into balance. In virtually all instances we have rather drastically curtailed descriptions of statistical procedures employed, in the full expectation that the more technical reader, once interested, can turn to the relevant journal or book for the fuller treatment.

We began by warning the reader that psychologists and other students of behaviour are often given to an excessive sobriety in dealing with play. We have perhaps been guilty of this endemic shortcoming of our profession, but not entirely so!

Oxford
1 August 1974

References

BATESON, G. (1955), 'A theory of play and fantasy', *Psychiatric Research Reports*, 2, pp. 39–51. (And see this volume, p. 119.)

BLURTON-JONES, N. G. (1967), 'An ethological study of some aspects of social behaviour of children in nursery school,' in D. Morris (ed.), *Primate Ethology*, Weidenfeld & Nicolson. (And see this volume, p. 352.)

BRUNER, J. S. (1974), 'The ontogenesis of speech acts', paper presented at the School of Epistemics, University of Edinburgh, 21 May 1974.

BURRIDGE, K. O. L. (1957), 'A Tangu game', *Man*, June 1957. (And see this volume, p. 364.)

ELLIS, M. J. (1973), *Why People Play*, Prentice Hall, Englewood Cliffs, New Jersey.

ERIKSON, E. H. (1973), Godkin Lectures at Harvard University.

FADY, J.-C. (1970), 'Co-opération et communication chez les primates', *Rev. Comport. Anim.*, Vol. 4, No. 4, pp. 41–9. (And see this volume, p. 328.)

GARVEY, C. (1974), 'Some properties of social play', *Merrill-Palmer Quarterly*, Vol. 20, No. 3, pp. 163–80. (And see this volume, p. 570.)

HAMBURG, D. (1968), 'Evolution of emotional responses: Evidence from recent research on non-human primates', *Science and Psychoanalysis*, No. 12, pp. 39–54.

HERRON, R. E., and SUTTON-SMITH, B. (1971), *Child's Play*, Wiley, New York.

HOOFF, J. A. R. A. M. VAN (1972), 'Possible primate homologues of laughter and smiling', in R. A. Hinde (ed.), *Non-Verbal Communication*, Cambridge University Press. (And see this volume, p. 130.)

HUTT, C. (1966), 'Exploration and play in children', *Symp. Zool. Soc. London*, No. 18. (And see this volume, p. 202.)

ITANI, J. (1958), 'On the acquisition and propagation of a new food habit in the natural group of the Japanese monkey at Takasakiyama', *Primates*, No. 1, pp. 84–98.

KÖHLER, W. (1926), *The Mentality of Apes*, Routledge & Kegan Paul.

LAWICK-GOODALL, J. VAN (1968), 'The behaviour of chimpanzees', *Anim. Behav. Monog.*, No. 1, pp. 165–301. (And see this volume, p. 222.)

MILLAR, S. (1968), *The Psychology of Play*, Penguin.

PIAGET, J. (1951), *Play, Dreams and Imitation in Childhood*, Routledge & Kegan Paul. (And see this volume, p. 166.)

SCHLOSBERG, H. (1947), 'The concept of play', *Psych. Rev.*, No. 54, pp. 229–31.

SINGER, J. L. (1973), *The Child's World of Make-Believe*, Academic Press, New York.

SROUFE, L. A., and WUNSCH, J. P. (1972), 'The development of laughter in the first year of life', *Child Development*, No. 43, pp. 1326–44.

SULLY, J., quoted in L. S. Vygotsky, 'Play and its role in the mental development of the child', *Soviet Psychology*, Vol. 3, No. 5, 1933, pp. 62–76. (And see this volume, p. 537.)

SYLVA, K., BRUNER, J. S., and GENOVA, P. (1974), 'The relationship between play and problem-solving in children three to five years old'. (And see this volume, p. 244.)

VYGOTSKY, L. S. (1933), 'Play and its role in the mental development of the child', *Soviet Psychology*, Vol. 3, No. 5. (And see this volume, p. 537.)

WEIR, R. H. (1962), *Language in the Crib*, Mouton, The Hague. (And see this volume, p. 609.)

WINNICOTT, D. W. (1971), *Play and Reality*, Tavistock Publications.

Part One

The Evolutionary Context

A Why Play Evolved in Animals and Man

Nature and Uses of Immaturity

To understand the nature of any species fully, we need to know more than the ways of its adults. We need to know how its young are brought from initial, infantile inadequacy to mature, species-typical functioning. Variation in the uses of immaturity tells much about how adaptation to habitat is accomplished, as well as what is likely to happen given a change in habitat. The nature and uses of immaturity are themselves subject to evolution, and their variations are subject to natural selection, much as any morphological or behavioural variant would be.

One of the major speculations about primate evolution is that it is based on the progressive selection of a distinctive pattern of immaturity. It is this pattern of progressive selection that has made possible the more flexible adaptation of our species. Too often this pattern is over-explained by noting that human immaturity is less dominated by instinct and more governed by learning.

Because our ultimate concern is with the emergence of human adaptation, our first concern must be the most distinctive feature of that adaptation. This feature is man's trait, typical of his species, of 'culture using', with all of the intricate set of implications that follow. Man adapts (within limits) by changing the environment, by developing not only amplifiers and transformers for his sense organs, muscles and reckoning powers, as well as banks for his memory, but also by changing literally the properties of his habitat. Man, so the truism goes, lives increasingly in a man-made environment. This circumstance places social burdens on human immaturity. For one thing, adaptation to such variable conditions depends heavily on opportunities for learning, in order to achieve knowledge and skills that are not stored in the gene pool. But not all that must be mastered can be learned by direct encounter. Much must be 'read out' of the culture pool, things learned and remembered over several generations: knowledge about values and history, skills as varied as an obligatory natural language or an optional mathematical one, as mute as using levers or as articulate as myth telling. Yet, though there is the gene pool, and though there exist direct experience and the culture as means for shaping immaturity, none of these directly prepares for the novelty that results when man alters his environment. That flexibility depends on something else.

Yet it would be a mistake to leap to the conclusion that, because human immaturity makes possible high flexibility in later adjustment, anything is possible for the species. Human traits were selected for their survival value over a 4–5-million year period, with a great acceleration of the selection process during the last half of that period. There were crucial, irreversible changes during that final man-making period – recession of formidable dentition, doubling of brain volume, creation of what Washburn and Howell (1960) have called a 'technical-social way of life', involving tool and symbol use. Note, however, that *hominidization* consisted principally of adaptations to conditions in the Pleistocene. These preadaptations, shaped in response to earlier demands of the habitat, are part of man's evolutionary inheritance. This is not to say that close beneath the skin of man is a naked ape, that 'civilization' is only a 'veneer'. The technical-social way of life is a deep feature of the species adaptation.

But we would err if we assumed *a priori* that man's inheritance places no constraint on his power to adapt. Some of the preadaptations can be shown to be of no present use. Man's inordinate fondness for fats and sweets no longer serves his individual survival well. And human obsession with sexuality is plainly not fitted for survival of the species now, however well it might have served to populate the upper Pliocene and the Pleistocene. But note that the species responds typically to these challenges by technical innovation rather than by morphological or behavioural change. This is not to say that man is not capable of controlling or, better, transforming behaviour. Whatever its origin, the incest taboo is a phenomenally successful technique for the control of certain aspects of sexuality – although its beginning among the great apes (van Lawick-Goodall, 1968) suggests that it may have a base that is rooted partly in the biology of propinquity, a puzzling issue. The technical innovation is contraception, which dissociates sexuality from reproduction. What we do not know, of course, is what kinds and what range of stresses are produced by successive rounds of such technical innovation. Dissociating sexuality and reproduction, for example, may produce changes in the structure of the family be re-defining the sexual role of women, which in turn may alter the authority pattern affecting the child, etc. Continuous, even accelerating, change may be inherent in such adaptation. If this is so, then there is an enormous added pressure on man's uses of immaturity for instruction. We must prepare the young for unforeseeable change – a task made the more difficult if severe constraints imposed by human preadaptations to earlier conditions of life have created rigidities.

Evolution of educability

Le Gros Clark's (1963) *échelle des êtres* of the primates runs from tree shrews through the prosimian lorisformes, lemuriformes, and related forms through the New World and Old World monkeys, through the hylobates such as the gibbon, through the great apes, through the early hominids like *Australopithecus* and *Homo habilis* and other small-brained predecessors, terminating in the modern form of *Homo sapiens* with his 1300-cubic-centimetre brain. Closing the gap between great apes and modern man is, of course, a complex and uncertain undertaking, particularly where behaviour is concerned, for all that remains are paleontological and archaeological fragments, and little by way of a behaviour record. But there are inferences that can be made from these fragments, as well as from the evolution of primate behaviour up to the great apes. Enough is known to suggest hypotheses, though no conclusions. Such an *échelle des êtres* is bound to be only a metaphor since contemporary species are only approximations to those that existed in the evolutionary tree. But it can tell us something about change in the primate order. We propose to use it where we can to make inferences, not so much about preadaptations to earlier conditions that characterize our species, but rather more to assess crucial changes that have been recurring in immaturity. My interest is in the evolution of educability.

I am not primarily a student of pre-human primates. I have brought the materials of primate evolution together to understand better the course of human infancy and childhood, its distinctiveness or species typicality. I propose to go back and forth, so to speak, between primate phylogeny and human ontogeny, not to establish any shallow parallel between the two, but in the hope that certain contrasts will help us see more clearly. If indeed the fish will be the last to discover water, perhaps we can help ourselves by looking at some other species.

Specifically, I should like to look at several issues whose resolution might be of particular help. The first of these has to do with the nature and evolution of social organization within a species and how this may affect the behaviour of the immature. The second has to do with the structure of skill and how the evolution of primate skill almost inevitably leads to tool using. We must then pause to consider the nature of tool using and its consequences. That matter in turn leads us directly to the roles of both play and imitation in the evolution of educability. Inevitably, we shall deal with that distinctly human trait, language: what it is and how its emergence drastically alters the manner in which we induct young into the species.

My emphasis throughout is principally on the evolution of intellect – problem solving, adaptation to habitat, and the like. But it will soon be apparent that, to use the jargon (Bloom, 1956), one cannot easily separate the cognitive from the conative and the affective. I have been told that the Chinese character for *thinking* combines the character for *head* and the character for *heart*. Pity it does not also include the character for *others* as well, for then it would be appropriate to what will concern us. At the end, I try to deal with the question of what can be done better to equip the young for coping.

Any species depends, as we know from the work of the last half century (e.g. Mayr, 1963), on the development of a system of mutuality – a set of mechanisms for sharing a habitat or territory, a system of signalling that is effective against predators, dominance relations that are effective without being pre-empting (Chance, 1967), a system of courtship with matching mating releasers (Tinbergen, 1953), etc. There is, at the lower end of the primate line, a considerable amount of rather fixed or linear structure about such mutuality. Behaviour repertoires are limited in prosimians and in monkeys, and the combinatorial richness in their behaviour is not great (see Jolly, 1966), though one can make a case for their goodness of fit to habitat conditions (as Hinde, 1971, recently has). Even where there is, within a given species, an increased variety in behaviour produced by enriched or more challenging environments – as in the contrast between urban and forest-dwelling rhesus monkeys (Singh, 1969) or among Japanese macaques tempted by new foods introduced in their terrain (Itani, 1958) – the difference is not towards variability or loosening of social structure, but towards the incorporation of new patterns into the species-typical social pattern. Action patterns that are altogether fixed prevail; and *play*, that special form of violating fixity, is limited in variety, early and short-lived, and irreversibly gone by adulthood – a matter to which I shall return.

There are notably fixed limits for the young of these species; and as the animal grows from infant to juvenile to adult – transitions usually marked by conspicuous changes in appearance and coat colour – social induction into the group is effected rapidly, usually by the quick response of a young animal to the threat of attack by an older animal in the troop. The sharply defined oestrous receptivity of the adult female almost assures that the young animal will be rejected and made virtually self-sufficient within a year. It is this sharply defined receptivity that also creates a scarcity economy in sexual access and leads to such a close link between male dominance and sexual access – perhaps the most notable source of linear, tight social structure virtually throughout the monkeys and prosimians. The comfort-contact system of mother and infant, involving not only initial nursing but also hair holding and grasping by the young for protection in flight and for sheer comfort, is obviously of great importance in prosimians, New World and Old World monkeys. But as Dolhinow and Bishop (1970) have remarked, we must be careful about exaggerating it. Harlow's (e.g. 1959) pioneering studies do show that a macaque made solely dependent on a terry-cloth or wire-mesh mother surrogate is more backward than one dependent on a real mother. Yet, for all that, twenty minutes of play daily with peers in a play cage obliterates the difference between the three groups – another of Harlow's (Harlow and Harlow, 1962) findings. Note by way of contrast that a three-year-old chimpanzee deprived of a mother modelling the skilled act of fishing for termites seems not to be able to master the act later, even if among peers who are succeeding.

Loosening the primate bond

Probably the first step toward loosening the initially tight primate bond is the development of what Chance (1967) has referred to as an 'attentional structure' within the group. Rather than behaviour patterns leading to constant interaction and mutual release of agonistic patterns, there is instead a deployment of attention in which the dominant animal is watched, his behaviour is anticipated, and confrontation is avoided. One of the major things that induction into a tightly organized Old-World monkey group means, then, is an enormous investment in attention to the requirements of the troop – mating, dominance, food foraging, etc. There is, so to speak, little attentional capacity left for anything else.

The great apes represent a crucial break away from this pattern toward a far more relaxed one, and as we shall see in a moment, the effect on the young is striking. All three of the great ape species are virtually free of predators. None of them defends a territory. None of them has a troop structure nearly as well defined and rigidly maintained as, say, the least rigid Old-World species, if such a phrase makes sense. In the gorilla, the orang-utan, and the chimpanzee, male dominance does not preclude copulation between a subdominant male and a female in the presence of the dominant male. It is even difficult, in fact, in the case of chimpanzee and orang-utan to define a dominant male in the monkey sense (cf., e.g., Goodall, 1965; Reynolds, 1965; Schaller, 1964). Indeed the route to dominance may even involve a superior technological skill. Note the increased deference paid to a male in the Gombe Stream Reserve who had learned to produce an intimidating din by banging two discarded tin cans together (van Lawick-Goodall, 1968). Thus, too, while oestrous marks the period of maximum receptivity in which the female initiates sexual activity, her availability to a male may in fact continue even into the first two months of pregnancy (Reynolds, 1965). Doubtless the achievement of a 600–700-cubic-centimetre brain in great apes also contributes to the further evolution of cerebral control of sexual behaviour of which Beach (1965) has written. The spacing of infants is over three years apart, on average, and the bond between mother and infant, particularly in the chimpanzee, remains active for as long as five years (van Lawick-Goodall, 1968).

One concomitant of the change is the decline in fixed patterns of induction into the group. There is much less of what might be called training by threat from adults or actual punishment by adults of a juvenile who has violated a species-typical pattern. The prolonged infant–mother interaction includes now a much larger element of play between them, often initiated by the mother and often used to divert an infant from a frustration-arousing situation.

What appears to be happening is that, with the loosening of fixed bonds, a system of reciprocal exchange emerges, the structure of which is at first difficult to describe. In any case, the system makes it possible for chimpanzee and gorilla groups to encounter groups of conspecifics in their range without fighting; indeed, in the case of the more flexibly organized chimpanzees, such encounters may even include sexual relations between groups and an exchange of members (Reynolds, 1965; van Lawick-Goodall, 1968). There can be little doubt that primate evolution is strongly and increasingly characterized by such reciprocal exchange. The trend probably pre-dates the emergence of hominids. In a recent article, Trivers (1971) said,

> During the Pleistocene, and probably before, a hominid species would have met the preconditions for the evolution of reciprocal altruism: long life span, low dispersal rate; life in small, mutually dependent, stable, social groups (Lee and DeVore, 1968; Campbell, 1966); and a long period of parental care. It is very likely that dominance relations were of the relaxed, less linear form characteristic of the baboon (Hall and DeVore, 1965) [p. 45].

As Gouldner (1960) reminded us a decade ago and as new studies on remaining hunter-gatherers reassert (Lee and DeVore, 1968), there is no known human culture that is not marked by reciprocal help in times of danger and trouble, by food sharing, by communal nurture of the young or disabled, and by the sharing of knowledge and implements for expressing skill. Lévi-Strauss (1963) posited such exchanges as the human watershed and classified them into three types: one involving the exchange of symbols and myths and knowledge; another involving the exchange of affectional and affiliative bonds, including the exchange of kin women in marriage to outside groups for political alliances, with this rare resource preserved by an incest taboo; and finally an exchange system for goods and services. The pressures in such primate groups would surely select traits consonant with reciprocity, leading to self-domestication by the selection of those capable of 'fitting in'. The incessant aggressiveness of the linear pattern would wane gradually.

What accompanies these changes is a marked transformation in ways of managing immaturity. The maternal buffering and protection of the young not only lengthens materially but undergoes qualitative changes. Several of these have been mentioned: a much prolonged period dominated by play: increased participation in play by adults, especially though not exclusively, by the mother; decline in the use of punishment and threat as modes of inducting the young into the pattern of species-typical interactions. The most important, I believe, is the appearance of a pattern involving an enormous amount of observation of adult behaviour by the young, with incorporation of what has been learned into a pattern of play (Dolhinow and Bishop, 1970; Hamburg, 1968; Hayes and Hayes, 1952; Köhler, 1925; Reynolds, 1965; Rumbaugh, 1970; van Lawick-Goodall, 1968; Yerkes and Yerkes, 1929).* Though psychologists are chary about using the term imitation because of the difficulty of defining it, virtually all primatologists comment on the enormous increase in imitation found in chimpanzees in contrast to Old World monkeys (where there is genuine doubt whether imitation in any common-sense meaning of the term occurs at all). After its first appearance at about 17 months of age, this pattern of observing and imitating takes up much of the time of infants and young juveniles – watching social interaction, watching the care of the young, watching copulation, watching agonistic displays, watching instrumental or tool behaviour. Such observation requires free attention on the part of the young; and, indeed, the incorporation of observed behaviour in play occurs most usually during the more relaxed periods in the life of the group. It was Köhler (1925), in his classic *The Mentality of Apes*, who commented initially on the intelligent rather than the mechanical or slavish nature of imitative behaviour in anthropoids – how the sight of another animal solving a problem is used not to mimic but as a basis for guiding the observer's own problem solving or goal striving. He used the term 'serious play' (p. 157), and the literature since the early 1920s bears him out (e.g., Dolhinow and Bishop, 1970; Hamburg, 1968). In a word the chimpanzee adult serves not only as a buffer or protector or 'shaper' for the young but as a model – though there is no indication of any intentional modelling or of behaviour that is specifically 'demonstrational'.

To summarize briefly, the emergence of a more flexible form of social bonding in primate groups seems to be accompanied by the emergence of a new capacity for learning by observation. Such learning indeed may be necessary if not sufficient for transmission of culture. But that gets ahead of the argument still to be made; for there is still an enormous gap to be

* It should be noted carefully that in certain crucial ways, both mountain and lowland gorilla are exceptions to what is described here. For some interesting speculations about the lack of curiosity and imitativeness in the gorilla as related to his undemanding habitat and food supply as well as to his lack of need for co-operative efforts, see Yerkes and Yerkes (1929), Rumbaugh (1970), and particularly Reynolds (1965).

accounted for between the behaviour of a grouping of great apes, however flexible, and the mode of structuring of a human society, no matter how simple it may be.

Observational learning

There are many facets to observational learning (I cautiously continue to avoid the term *imitation*). There is ample evidence that many mammals considerably less evolved than primates can benefit from exposure to another animal carrying out a task; for example, the classic study of cats by Herbert and Harsh (1944) demonstrates improvement in escape from a puzzle box by cats who have seen other animals escape – and the more so if the cats observed were still inexpert at the task. Whether they are learning the possibility of getting out of the box, the means for doing so (by displacing a bar), or whatever, observation helps. So too with *Macaca fuscata*, the Japanese macaque, where the young animals learn to eat what the mother eats by eating what she leaves (Itani, 1958; Kawamura, 1959); or the naïve, cage-reared *patas* monkey transported to a habitat and released in a natural troop, who learns from the group by following it in search of food.

But this is quite different from the sort of 'serious play' to which Köhler (1925) referred. Consider an example:

I would call the following behaviour of a chimpanzee imitation of the 'serious play' type. On the playground a man has painted a wooden pole in white colour. After the work is done he goes away leaving behind a pot of white paint and a beautiful brush. I observe the only chimpanzee who is present, hiding my face behind my hands, as if I were not paying attention to him. The ape for a while gives much attention to me before approaching the brush and the paint because he has learned that misuse of our things may have serious consequences. But very soon, encouraged by my attitude, he takes the brush, puts it into the pot of colour and paints a big stone which happens to be in the place, beautifully white. The whole time the ape behaved completely seriously. So did others when imitating the washing of laundry or the use of a borer [pp. 156–7].

I consider such behaviour to be dependent on two important prerequisites both amenable to experimental analysis:

The first is the ability to differentiate or abstract oneself from a task, to turn around on one's own performance and, so to speak, see oneself, one's own performance as differentiated from another. This involves self-recognition in which one, in some way, is able to model one's *own* performance on some selected feature of another's performance. This phenomenon in linguistics is known as *deixis*: as in learning that when I say *I*, it is not the same as when you say *I*, or that *in front* of me is not the same as *in front* of you or *in front* of the car (cf. Miller and Johnson-Laird*). It is a

* G. Miller and P. Johnson-Laird, *Presuppositions of Language*. In preparation.

deep problem in language learning, and though it seems cumbersome and abstract in a discussion of hominid evolution, it may be amenable to demonstration. Indeed I believe that the excellent study by Gallup (1970) indicates that there is a large gap between such Old World monkeys as the stumptailed macaque and the chimpanzee: the latter can recognize his mirror image and guide self-directed behaviour by it (e.g. inspecting by touch a spot on the forehead seen in the mirror); the former cannot. The macaque, as a matter of fact, seems able only to attack or threaten its mirror image or to ignore it. These findings are surely not proof of the emergence of deictic capacities in the ape, but they do suggest a crucial trend for guiding one's own behaviour by feedback other than, so to speak, from action proper. Learning by observation is one instance of that class.

The second prerequisite for observation learning is a form of skill I now examine: *construction of an action pattern by the appropriate sequencing of a set of constituent sub-routines to match a model* (Lashley, 1951). Observing the development of skilled, visually directed manipulatory activity in human infants and children, one is struck repeatedly by the extent to which such activity grows from the mastery of specific acts, the gradual perfecting of these acts into what may be called a modular form, and the combining of these into higher-order, longer-range sequences. Flexible skilled action may almost be conceived of as the construction of a sequence of constituent acts to achieve an objective (usually a change in the environment) while taking into account local conditions. As the Russian neurophysiologist Bernstein (1967) has put it, one can almost conceive of an initial skilled act as a motoric hypothesis concerning how to change the environment along a desired parameter. The flexibility of skill consists not only of this constructive feature but also of the rich range of 'paraphrases' that are possible: for a skilled operator, there are many different ways of skinning a cat: and the word 'paraphrase' is not amiss, for there is in this sense something language-like about skill, the kind of substitution rules that permit the achievement of the same objective (meaning) by alternative means.

If one compares the manipulatory activity of a child (or of a young chimpanzee) and a prosimian, such as a loris, the most striking difference is precisely the extent to which manual activity of human and chimpanzee is constructed of components to meet the properties of the task. The wide range of combinations in the use of the component gestures that go into the making of the final prehension – relatively independent movement of fingers, of hand, of wrist, etc. – is striking. But as Bishop (1964) pointed out, prosimians use virtually the same grip for a variety of activities: taking hold of a branch, grooming, taking a piece of fruit, etc. My own informal observation on slow loris confirms this. The grip is adapted to the task by changing the orientation of the whole hand, by altering speed or force, etc.

Napier (1962) has noted how the development of flexibility is facilitated morphologically by the evolutionary selection of phalangeal flexibility, and change in the hamate and trapezium with emergence of power and precision grips, but I part company with Napier in that it is *not* so much a change of manual morphology that separates baboon from ape from man, but the nature of the *programme* that controls the use of the hands. (See photo inset.)

Imitation as 'serious play' – incorporating what is observed into behaviour that is not mere mimicry but is directed intelligently to an end – must of course depend on 'matching to model', on constructing behaviour in the manner we have just examined, and must be concerned with the kind of deictic anchoring that permits one to distinguish and relate what is analogous in my behaviour and in that of another member of the species.

Effect of tools

We must consider now the question of tools and their use, and what effect this evolutionary step may have had on the management of immaturity. We might begin with its first emergence in chimpanzees, but before we do, it is worth considering initially a speculation by DeVore (1965) on the emergence of bipedalism and the freeing of hands. According to this speculation, and it can be nothing more, two contradictory selection pressures operated on the emerging protohominid. The first was for bipedal locomotion and easy standing, freeing the hands. The second was for a larger brain to provide the more flexible programming for the hands (as discussed above). Bipedalism, involving stronger impact on the pelvic girdle, led to selection of a smaller bony aperture of the birth canal to assure greater structural strength of the pelvis. If a bigger-brained creature is to get through a smaller canal, there is required, of course, a smaller initial brain size and, therefore, greater initial immaturity (the human brain grows from approximately 335 to 1300 cubic centimetres during development).* To assure the larger brain, the argument goes, there had also to be a recession in such apelike features as a heavy prognathous jaw as a base for effective dentition. En route, there is a critical point where the basic adaptation of the hominid must change.

So we may begin with the fact that tool using at its first appearance in apes comes before that point: it is an optional and not an obligatory adaptation. Chimpanzee survival does not depend on the use of sticks for fishing termites or on the use of crushed leaves as drinking or grooming sponges.

---

*For an excellent account of the changes that occur during this enlargement, making possible greater flexibility of connection and possibly better memory storage, see Altman (1967). Some of the same changes during this period of expansion also occur as a result of challenging environments (Bennett, Diamond, Krech, and Rosenzweig, 1964) and in the course of phylogeny (Altman, 1967).

As Jane Lancaster (1968) put it in a closely reasoned article on tool use, there is 'a major change from the kind of tool use that is incidental to the life of a chimpanzee to the kind that is absolutely essential for survival of the human individual' [p. 62]. Yet, in spite of the absence of 'obligatory pressures', chimpanzees use tools optionally in an extraordinary variety of ways: for eating, drinking, self-cleaning, agonistic displays, constructing sleeping platforms, etc. Nor is it some accident of morphology:

The hands of monkeys and apes are equally suited to picking up a stick and making poking or scratching movements with it but differences in the brain make these much more likely behaviour patterns for the chimpanzee [p. 61].

I would like to make the rather unorthodox suggestion that in order for tool using to develop, it was essential to have a long period of optional, pressure-free opportunity for combinatorial activity. By its very nature, tool using (or the incorporation of objects into skilled activity) required a chance to achieve the kind of wide variation upon which selection could operate.

Dolhinow and Bishop (1970) made the point most directly. Commenting first that 'many special skills and behaviours important in the life of the individual are developed and practised in playful activity long before they are used in adult life' [p. 142], they then note that play 'occurs only in an atmosphere of familiarity, emotional reassurance, and lack of tension or danger' [p. 142]. Schiller (1952) reported, 'with no incentive the chimpanzee displayed a higher variety of handling objects than under the pressure of a lure which they attempted to obtain' [p. 186]. He reported, actually, that attempting to direct play by reinforcing chimpanzees for play behaviour had the effect of inhibiting play.

Functions of play

Play appears to serve several centrally important functions. First, it is a means of minimizing the consequences of one's actions and of learning, therefore, in a less risky situation. This is particularly true of social play, where, by adopting a play face or a 'galumphing gait' (Miller, 1973) or some other form of metacommunication (Dolhinow and Bishop, 1970), the young animal signals his intent to play. Now, so to speak, he can test limits with relative impunity:

There are many rules of what can and cannot be done in a troop, and most of these are learned early in life, when the consequences of violating them are less severe than later on [Dolhinow and Bishop, 1970, p. 148].

Second, play provides an excellent opportunity to try combinations of behaviour that would, under functional pressure, never be tried.

The tendency to manipulate sticks, to lick the ends, to poke them into any available hole are responses that occur over and over again in captive chimpanzees. These responses are not necessarily organized into the efficient use of sticks to probe for objects, but they probably form the basis of complex motor patterns such as termiting [Lancaster, 1968, p. 61].

Or in van Lawick-Goodall's (1968) account:

With the fruit, Figan devised a game of his own: lying on his back, he spins a *Strychnos* ball round and round, balancing it on his hands and kicking gently with his feet, like a circus bear . . . Toys like this are not always at hand, but then the youngsters seem just as content to play with stones, leaves, or twigs. They may throw them, rub them over their bodies, pull leaves off stems, break and bend twigs, or poke them into holes in the ground. This form of play may be of tremendous importance in developing dexterity in manipulating objects. As the chimps grow older this skill becomes invaluable not only in routine activities such as nest-making and food-gathering, but also in the most specialized field of tool use [pp. 36–7].

And even in captivity, this same tendency to incorporate objects into manipulative patterns goes on undiminished, as one may judge from this report by Caroline Loizos (1967) of a young female chimpanzee habituating to and then 'mastering in play' a tennis ball:

I bounce a tennis ball in front of the cage several times so that she hears as well as sees it and place it inside on the floor. She backs away, watching ball fixedly – approaches with pouted lips, pats it – it rolls. She backs hurriedly to the wall. Hair erection . . . J. pokes at it from a distance, arm maximally extended, watching intently; looks at me; pokes ball and immediately sniffs finger . . . She dabs at ball and misses; sniffs finger; she backs away and circles ball from a distance of several feet, watching it intently. Sits and watches ball . . . (pause of several minutes) . . . walks around ball. J. walks past the ball again even closer but quite hurriedly. She lifts some of the woodwool in the cage to peer at the ball from a new angle, approaches ball by sliding forward on stomach with arms and legs tucked underneath her, so that protruded lips are very close to ball without actually touching it. Withdraws. Pokes a finger towards it and sniffs finger . . . returns to ball, again slides forward on stomach with protruded lips without actually connecting. Pokes with extended forefinger, connects and it moves; she scurries backwards; more dabs at it with forefinger and it moves again (but not far because of the woodwool in that area of the cage). J. dabs, ball rolls and she follows, but jumps back in a hurry as it hits the far wall. She rolls the ball on the spot with her finger resting on it, then rolls it forward, watching intently the whole time. She dabs again – arm movement now more exaggerated, flung upwards at end of movement. Tries to pick ball up between thumb and forefinger very gingerly . . . fails. Rolls it towards her, sniffs with lowered head. Picks it up and places it in front of her – *just* touches it with lips – pushes it into straw with right forefinger – touches it with lower lip pushed out, pokes, flicking up hand at end of movement, but backs away as it rolls towards her. Bites at own thumb. Dabs at it with lips, pulls it towards her and backs away. Examines own lip, squinting down, where it touched ball. Picks at it with forefinger and covers ball as it rolls (walking on all fours, with head down to watch ball as it rolls along at a point approximately under her belly). Pushes with outside knuckles. Stamps on it, dabbing at it with foot. Sits on it, rolls it with foot; carries it gingerly with hand and puts it on shelf, climbing up to sit beside it. It drops down – she holds it in one hand and pats it increasingly hard with the other. Holds it in right hand, picks at stripe on ball with her left. Rolls it between two hands. Rolls it between hand and shelf. Holds and pats; bangs it on shelf. Holds and *bites*, examining ball after each bite. Ball drops from shelf and she pats at it on ground with right hand. Lies on her back, balances ball on her feet, holding it there with hands; sits up, holds ball under chin and rolls it two or three times round back of neck and under chin. It rolls away and she chases it immediately and brings it back to shelf. Lies on back and holds it on feet. Presses it against teeth with her feet and bites – all fear appears to be gone – lies and bites at ball held in feet, hands. Rolls it in feet, hands. Climbs to ceiling, ball drops and she chases it at once, J. makes playface, rolls and tumbles with ball, around, over, under ball, bangs it; rolls it over her own body [pp. 194–5].

Various writers (Dolhinow and Bishop, 1970; Loizos, 1967; van Lawick-Goodall, 1968) are convinced that the mastery of complex tool skills among subhuman anthropoids depends not only on observation learning but also on whether or not they take place in the close setting of the infant–mother interaction. Reference was made in passing to one of the infants in the Gombe Stream Reserve, Merlin, who lost his mother at age three and was 'taken over' by older siblings. He mastered neither termiting nor nest building, skills that apparently require repeated observation.

Van Lawick-Goodall (1968) made it clear in her detailed reporting why such repeated opportunity to observe and play is necessary; mastery of a complex skill like termiting is a complex process of mastering *features* of the task – a non-mimicking approach – and then combining the mastered features. There is, for example, mastery of pushing a stick or grass into an opening, though initially this will be done without regard to appropriate rigidity of the probe or appropriate diameter, or appropriate length. It will be played with as a past skill once mastered – as Flint (2·8 years, who had started at play termiting) pushing a grass stalk though the hairs of his leg. And sheer repetition will provide the familiar routinization that permits an act to be combined with other acts to meet the complex requirement of a stick of a particular diameter and rigidity, pushed in a particular way, withdrawn at a particular angle at a certain speed, etc. A comparable set of observations on human infants by Wood, Bruner and Ross* shows the

---

* D. Wood, J. S. Bruner and G. Ross, *Modelling and Mastery in Construction Task*. In preparation.

importance of skill to three–five-year-olds in enabling them to benefit from demonstrations of how to put together an interlocking set of blocks to make a pyramid. Unless the child can master the subroutines, the demonstration of the whole task is about as helpful as a demonstration by an accomplished skier is to a beginner. As with the young chimps, so too with the young children: they take selectively from the demonstration those features of performance that are within the range of their capacity for constructing skilled acts. They are helped, but the process is slow.

One very crucial feature of tool skills in chimpanzees as in humans is the trying out of variants of the new skill in different contexts. Once Köhler's (1925) ape Sultan had 'learned' to use a stick to draw in food, he tried using it very soon for poking other animals, for digging, and for dipping it through an opening in a cesspool. Once Rana had learned to climb up stacked boxes to get a suspended piece of fruit, she rapidly tried her new climbing routine on a ladder, a board, a keeper, and Köhler himself – most often forgetting the fruit in preference for the combinatory activity *per se*. Nor is this a response to the boredom of captivity, since the same variant exploration is to be found in the Gombe Stream animals studied by van Lawick-Goodall (1968) – one of the most ingenious instances being the use of a twig as an olfactory probe by the juvenile female Fifi, an accomplished termiter:

On three occasions [she] pushed a long grass stalk, right into my trouser pocket, subsequently sniffing the end, when I prevented her feeling there with her hand for a banana. Each time there was in fact a banana there, and she followed me whimpering until I gave it to her [p. 206].

It is probably this 'push to variation' (rather than fixation by positive reinforcement) that gives chimpanzee manipulation such widespread efficacy – such opportunism as dipping sticks into beehives for honey (Merfield and Miller, 1956), using sticks for clubbing lizards and rodents (Köhler, 1925), and using branches for striking at or throwing at big felines (Kortland and Koöij, 1963). The ecological significance of this wide potential repertory is attested to by observations of Kortland and his collaborators (Kortland, 1965; Kortland and Koöij, 1963; Kortland and van Zon, 1969). They have reported striking differences between forest-dwelling chimpanzees from the rain forest of the Congo and Guinea and those from the Guinea savanna. An animated, dummy leopard was placed in the path of the chimpanzees. Forest apes broke and brandished branches and swung them in horizontal orbit at the dummy. The only hit was by one animal, punching the dummy in the face from in front. Savanna apes warmed up with such sabre rattling, but then attacked the dummy *from the rear* with strong vertical blows with the heaviest available branch and scored violent hits – 'showing both tactical co-operation between the actual assailants and vocal support by the onlookers' [Kortland and van Zon, 1969, p. 12]. These authors suggest that open country prevents arboreal escape and thus poses for the animals a problem in tool manipulation that calls for great flexibility in adapting tools to local constraints.

The play aspect of tool use (and, indeed, complex problem solving in general) is underlined by the animal's loss of interest in the goal of the act being performed and by its preoccupation with means – also a characteristic of human children. Consider the following episode:

Hebb recounted how a chimpanzee he tested solved problems for banana slice incentives. On one particular day, she arranged the banana slice rewards in a row instead of eating them! Apparently, she had solved the problems for their own sake. 'I was out of bananas, but I offered her another problem . . . she solved the problem: opened the correct box and put a slice of banana into it. I took it out and then set the box again . . . I ended up with thirty slices of banana' [Rumbaugh, 1970, p. 56].

A far cry from reinforcement in any conventional sense!

Köhler's (1925) account contains an interesting happening. He gave a handful of straw to one animal who tried to use it to draw in an out-of-reach piece of fruit. Finding the straw too flexible, the animal doubled it up, but it was too short, so he abandoned the effort. Modification is systematic, most often directed to features relevant to the task, and is combinatorial. It follows first constructions or first efforts at copying a model. But it appears first in play, not in problem solving.

Play in relation to tool use

I have described these play activities at great length because I believe them to be crucial to the evolution of tool using – steps that help free the organism from the immediate requirements of its task. Play, given its concomitant freedom from reinforcement and its setting in a relatively pressureless environment, can produce the flexibility that makes tool using possible. At least two laboratory studies, one by Birch (1945) and the other by Schiller (1952), indicate the necessity of initial play with materials in order for them to be converted to instrumental ends. They both used problems involving the raking in of food with sticks of varying length – before and after an opportunity to play with sticks. Few succeeded before play. Observed during play, Birch's animals were seen to explore increasingly over three days the capacity of the sticks to lengthen an arm. When put back into the test situation, all of these animals solved the problem within half a minute. Perhaps, as Loizos (1967) has suggested, it is the very exaggeration and lack of economy of play that encourage extension of the limits.

Looked at logically, play has two crucial formal patterns: one consists of a function and its arguments; the other, an argument and the functions into which it can fit. A ball or a stick are fitted into as many acts as possible; or an act, climbing, is performed on as many objects to which it can be applied appropriately. This pattern, I would speculate, is close to one of the universal structures of language, predication, which is organized in terms of topic and comment:

John has a hat
John is a man
John jumps the fence, or

Brush the hat
Wear the hat
Toss the hat.

It is interesting that the language play after 'lights out' of the three-year-old, reported by Ruth Weir (1962) in her remarkable book *Language in the Crib*, takes precisely such a form. And I will not be the first to comment that the simultaneous appearance in man of language and tool using suggests that the two may derive from some common programming capacities of the enlarging hominid nervous system.

Another feature of play that is crucial to tool use is the feature referred to by Barsh (1972) as *dissociation* – 'the ability to anticipate the potential component parts of an object' for use in a new arrangement. It is a question that occupied Köhler (1925) in terms of the ability of his animals to 'dissolve visual wholes' of great visual firmness. A Russian investigator, Khroustov (1968), performed a most elegant experiment on tool using in a chimpanzee, showing to what degree these animals are capable of such dissociation. Fruit was to be extracted from a narrow tube, and sticks of appropriate diameter were provided. The animal succeeded, and knowing the capability of the species, we are not surprised. The experimenter then provided a wood plaque too wide for the job. After inspecting it, the animal broke it along the grains to obtain a stick of appropriate size. Khroustov then painted a false set of grain lines on a plaque at right angles to the true grain. The animal, using them to guide a first splintering attempt and failing, looked more closely for the true grain and used it.

To summarize once again, the great ape possesses manipulative subroutines that are practised, perfected and varied in play. These are then put together clumsily and selectively to meet the requirements of more extended tasks, very often in response to observing an adult in a stable and relaxed setting. The imitation observed is akin to imitation by a child of an adult speech model: the child's output is *not* a copy of the adult's; it has its own form even though it is designed to fill the same function. These initial acts are then modified in a systematic manner to fulfil further requirements of the task. The acts themselves have a self-rewarding character. They are varied systematically, almost as if a play to test the limits of a new skill. A baboon living in the same habitat as the chimpanzee is as eager to eat termites as is the latter; yet he shows none of these capacities even though he is seen to observe the chimpanzee exercising them often. He too is equipped with a good pair of hands. Note that there is an association between play and tool use, and that the natural selection of one, tools, led to the selection of the other as well, in the evolution of the hominids and man.

Adults as models

Neither among chimpanzees nor in the infinitely more evolved society of hunter-gatherers is there much direct intervention by adults in the learning of the young. They serve principally as models and as sources of the necessary affection (Bruner, 1965). Among the primates, there is very little intentional pedagogy of any kind. Hinde (1971) recently reviewed the literature and concluded as follows:

On the whole, the mothers of nonhuman primates seem not to teach their infants. In a number of species, a mother has been seen to move a little away from her infant and then to wait while it crawled after her (e.g., Howler monkeys, Carpenter, 1934; rhesus, Hinde, Rowell and Spencer-Booth, 1964; gorilla, Schaller, 1963; chimpanzees, van Lawick-Goodall, 1968): this has the effect of encouraging the infant to walk, but can hardly be called teaching. However, it is clear that infants learn a great deal from their mothers, especially in the context of avoidance and food-getting behaviour. Even avoidance of snakes differs between laboratory and wild-reared monkeys and may depend in part on parental example (Joslin, Fletcher and Emlen, 1964). It has been shown in the laboratory that monkeys can learn to avoid situations or responses that are seen to cause pain to other individuals (Child, 1938; Hansen and Mason, 1962; Hall, 1968), and to accept food that other individuals are seen to take (Weiskrantz and Cowey, 1963). In nature, the infant's proximity to its mother ensures that it becomes rapidly conditioned by her fear responses and that its feeding behaviour is influenced by her (e.g., Baldwin, 1969). In the patas monkey (Hall, 1965), Japanese macaque (*Macaca fuscata*) (Kawamura, 1959), and chimpanzee (van Lawick-Goodall, 1968), the young eat fragments that their mothers drop, as well as being especially likely to feed at the same food sources. Although by the time they are one year old, Japanese macaques are acquainted with all the types of food used by the troop, it is difficult to make them take new types of food in the laboratory. Apparently learning from the mother is normally important (Kawamura, 1959). Schaller (1963) records an infant gorilla removing food from its mother's mouth and eating it, and one case of a mother breaking off a stem for its infant to eat.

Imitation, principally of the mother, is important for the development of tool-using behaviour in wild-living chimpanzees (Goodall, 1964; van Lawick-Goodall, 1968); and the development of actions by imitation has also been recorded in hand-reared individuals (Hayes and Hayes, 1952; Kellogg, 1968). In the latter case, the actions may be used for social communication (Gardner and Gardner, 1969, 1971).

In squirrel monkeys, food-catching skill is learned by younger juveniles from older ones, rather than from their mothers (Baldwin, 1969). However it is by no means always the younger animals that learn food habits from older ones. Under natural conditions, young animals investigate new objects more than do older individuals, and this may lead to a transfer of feeding habits from younger to older animals. Thus, among the Japanese macaques, new foods tended to be accepted first by juveniles, and their use then diffused through the colony via their mothers and then the mothers' younger offspring and consorts (Itani, 1958). Although diffusion sometimes occurs in the opposite direction (Frisch, 1968), kinship ties are probably always important (Kawamura, 1959; Tsumori, 1967) [p. 32].

There may, however, be something like 'tutor proneness' among the young – an increased eagerness to learn from adults. One study now in progress suggests how such tutor proneness may come about. Rumbaugh, Riesen and Wright (1972) are training chimpanzees and orang-utans under the following conditions. One group receives tutoring modelling on a variety of tasks; each task is presented on each new encounter in the form of a new embodiment of the problem. A second group gets the same problems, but each time in the same form, so that this group is essentially repeating. The third group is presented the materials used by the others, but the human tutor model neither presents them as tasks nor models the solutions as in the first two instances. The tasks are mechanical puzzles, packing fitted containers within each other, searching for a hidden object, transporting an object to another part of the room, extracting candy from a container, etc. The reward is some combination of task completion and the tutor's approval. A preliminary finding of this work-in-progress is of particular interest. The apes in the more challenging first condition are the ones most likely to wait for the tutor to provide a clue before beginning on their own.

Does it then require a certain level of challenge and novelty to create tutor proneness in primates? Schaller (1964) remarked of the gorillas he observed in the Congo:

Why was the Australopithecus, with the brain capacity of a large gorilla, the maker of stone tools, a being with a culture in the human sense, while the free-living gorilla in no way reveals the marvellous potential of its brain? I suspect that the gorilla's failure to develop further is related to the ease with which it can satisfy its needs in the forest. In its lush realm there is no selective advantage for improvement ... The need for tools ... is more likely in a harsh and marginal habitat where a premium is placed on an alert mind ... [p. 232].

And the same view was voiced by Yerkes and Yerkes (1929) in their classic work on the great apes, as well as by Vernon Reynolds (1965) who, in a penetrating article on the comparative analysis of selection pressures operating on chimpanzees and on gorilla, concluded:

Finally, we may briefly consider the contrast in temperaments between these two anthropoid species. Comparative behaviour studies in the past often stressed this difference. Tevis (1921), for instance, wrote, 'In mental characteristics there is the widest difference between the two apes that we are considering. The chimpanzee is lively, and at least when young, teachable and tameable. The gorilla, on the other hand, is gloomy and ferocious, and quite untameable' (p. 122). It is possible to suggest an explanation for this contrast between the morose, sullen, placid gorilla, and the lively, excitable chimpanzee. The difference seems to be most clearly related to the difference in social organization and foraging behaviour. The herbivorous gorilla is surrounded by food: the more intensively it feeds, the slower it travels; its survival needs are easily met, and it is protected from predators by the presence of powerful males. Here there is no advantage to any form of hyper-activity except in threat displays and the charge of the big male, which is a hyper-aggressive behaviour form. Chimpanzee survival, on the other hand, depends heavily on the fluidity of social groups and the ability to communicate the whereabouts of food by intense forms of activity (wild vocalizing and strong drumming). Moving rapidly about the forest, meeting up with new chimpanzees every day, vocalizing and drumming, and locating other chimpanzees by following their calls, are the basic facts of chimpanzee existence. Here an advantage may be seen in having a responsive, expressive, and adaptable temperament. Hyper-activity is the chimpanzee norm in the wild, and with it goes a volatile temperament [p. 704].

But here we encounter a seeming contradiction. The evolutionary trend we have been examining seems to have placed a major emphasis on a combination of developments: a relatively pressure-free environment with its concomitant increase in play, exploration and observation; and at the same time, a certain challenge in the requirements of adaptation to a habitat. (Play in young gorillas and orang-utans in the wild, by the way, is not nearly as elaborate as in the chimpanzee [cf. Reynolds, 1965; Rodman, 1972; Schaller, 1963; Yerkes and Yerkes, 1929], and in neither of these species is there much challenge from the habitat.)

I believe that Desmond Morris (1964) has a resolution for this apparent dilemma – that, on the one hand, a non-pressureful habitat seems crucial and, on the other, challenge is significant. He made the distinction between two modes of adaptation to habitat *specialist* and *opportunist* – the squirrel versus the rat, certain exclusively forest-dwelling monkeys like the vervet or green versus the adaptable rhesus (cf. Hinde, 1971). Non-specialists depend on high flexibility rather than on morphology or behavioural specialization. Aristarchus said it well and provided Isaiah Berlin (1953) with a famous book title: 'The fox knows many things; the hedgehog knows one big thing.'

One can only speculate that the evolution of intellectual processes in the primate stock from which man descended was in the direction of opportunism and away from specialism. It could be argued, indeed, that the original stock, as far as intellect goes, was closer to chimpanzee than to either of the contemporary pongids, though Rumbaugh (1970) believed that in certain forms of intellectual performance there are striking parallels between man and orang-utan. The argument for opportunism seems in fact essential to account for the rapid fanning out of the evolved species to such a variety of habitats.

Instructional interaction between adults and young

What can be said of 'instruction' of the young in the protohominids and early man? Alas, nothing definite. But contemporary 'simple' societies, hunter-gatherers, provide certain clues. No matter how constraining the ecological conditions, there is among such people an expansion in adult–child instructional interaction, both quantitatively and qualitatively, of a major order. Although one cannot reconstruct the Pleistocene hunter-gatherer by reference to such isolated hunter-gatherers as the contemporary !Kung Bushmen, their practices do suggest something about the magnitude of the change. !Kung adults and children play and dance together, sit together, participate in minor hunting together, join in song and story-telling together. At frequent intervals, moreover, children are the objects of intense rituals presided over by adults – minor, as in the first haircutting, or major, as when a boy kills his first Kudu buck and undergoes the proud but painful process of scarification. Children also are playing constantly at the rituals, with the implements, tools and weapons of the adult world. However, in tens of thousands of feet of !Kung film prepared by the Marshalls (see Bruner, 1966), one virtually never finds an instance of teaching taking place outside the situation where the behaviour to be learned is relevant. Nobody teaches away from the scene, as in a school setting. Indeed, there is nothing like a school.

Often the adult seems to play the role of inducting the young into novel situations that, without the presence of a protecting and familiar adult, would be frightening – as in extended trekking, in witchcraft ceremonials, and in many other spheres where the child comes along and participates to the limit that he is able. This induction to the margin of anxiety, I believe, starts very early. A study by Sroufe and Wunsch (1972) provides a hint of just how early that may be. The study sets out to explore what makes human infants laugh. From four months (when laughing first appears in reliable and recognizable form) into the second year of life, the sufficient stimulus for laughter becomes increasingly distal – at first being principally tactile and close visual (e.g., tickle plus looming), with incongruities following later, as when the mother adopts an unusual position such as crawling on all fours. Note, however, that at all ages the capers most likely to produce laughter when performed by the mother are the ones most likely to produce tears when performed by a stranger. The mother seems able to bring the young, so to speak, to the edge of terror. King (1966) has suggested that this feature of mothering is universal; that among birds as well as mammals, the presence of the mother reduces fear of novel stimuli and provides the assurance necessary for exploratory behaviour. But it is only among humans that the adult *introduces* the novel, inducts the young into new, challenging, and frightening situations – sometimes in a highly ritualistic way, as with the *rites de passage*.

There is little question that the human young (and the young of the primates generally) are quite ready to be lured by the novel, given even the minimum adult reassurance. 'Neophilia' is what Desmond Morris (1967) calls it. Such readiness for novelty may even be attested to by a superiority, at least among the great apes and man, of the young over and old in detecting or extracting the rules and regularities in new situations. At least one laboratory study, Rumbaugh and McCormack (1967), has even found a *negative* correlation between age and the ability to master learning-set problems – tasks that have a common principle but a new embodiment on each presentation, like 'pick the odd one when two are alike and one is different'.* But note that it is in man only that adults arrange play and ritual for children that capitalize on this tendency.

It is obvious that the play and ritual in which young and adult humans are involved are saturated heavily with symbolism. Though the kind of mastery play I have been at some pains to describe in the preceding discussion is still a feature of human play, there is added to it now an extraordinary range of play forms that have as their vehicle the use of *symbols* and *conventions* – two terms that will concern us in due course. Not only are sticks, so to speak, used as arrows or spears or even as novel and unusual tools,

*Rumbaugh (1970) commented in a recent review of the learning capacities of great apes:

It is frequently observed, however, that an animal that excels in learning when young remains excellent *if* frequently worked with as it grows to adulthood (at least 8 years of age) and beyond. Might it be the case that early experience in some manner determines the avenues along which intelligent behaviour will be manifest. If early experiences are with formal test and learning situations, will the animal's adaptability be maximally manifest as an adult in the context of that order [p. 65]?

they may be used now in a symbolic way that transcends utility – as horses, for example, when put between the legs (Vygotsky, 1933) or giant trees when propped up in the sand. The prop or 'pivot' or toy (it is difficult to name the stick) is not used as a *utilitandum* (as, say, Khroustov's chimpanzee used a separated splinter to poke food out of a tube) but as a point of departure from the present perceptual situation. Though the stick must have some feature that is horselike (it must at least be 'go-between-the-leggable'), it must now also fit into an imaginary situation. It is for this reason that the great Russian psychologist Vygotsky used the term pivot: the stick is a pivot between the real and the imagined.

Once the symbolic transformation of play has occurred, two consequences follow. Play can serve as a vehicle for teaching the nature of a society's conventions, and it can also teach about the nature of convention *per se*. David Lewis (1969) defined a convention as an agreement about procedure, the procedure itself being trivial, but the agreement not. We drive to the right, or we exhibit a red light to port and a green to starboard. And it is evident immediately that a linguistic-cultural community depends on an easy and fluent grasp of convention on the part of its members. Symbolic play, whatever function it may serve for the individual child in working through his own problems or fulfilling his wishes at the fantasy level, has an even more crucial role in teaching that child fluency with rules and conventions.

As for pre-training in the particular system of conventions of the society, let me give an instance from an exotic culture. The reader can provide instances closer to home. This one is from Dolhinow and Bishop's (1970) review:

> In New Guinea the Tangu engage in a ritual food exchange in which strict equivalence is maintained (Burridge, 1957). Equivalence is determined by mutual agreement between trading partners. The Tangu children play a game called taketak in which the object of the game is equivalence, just as in the food exchange ritual of the adults, and in both cases the outcome or equivalence is decided upon by mutal agreement. There is no winner or loser; the object is to tie.

A fuller description of this game is on p. 364.

Using symbolic means: language

Having gone this far into symbolic play, I now turn to language in order to be more precise about what is involved when symbolic means are used for preparing the human young for culture. Higher primate skill, as I have described it, has about it certain language-like properties. Skilled action, like language, has paraphrases and a kind of grammar. But there is also a communicative function of language; and it is this function, in all probability, that determines many of its design features (cf. Hockett, 1960). I have emphasized the similarity between action and the structure of language in order to propose a critical hypothesis: The initial use of language is probably in support of and closely linked to action. The initial structure of language and, indeed, the universal structure of its syntax are extensions of the structure of action. Syntax is not arbitrary; its cases mirror the requirements of signalling about action and representing action: agent, action, object, location, attribution and direction are among its cases. Whatever the language, the agent-action-object structure is the form soon realized by the young speaker. Propositions about the evolution of language are justly suspect. I offer this hypothesis not on the basis of evolutionary evidence but on developmental grounds. For what the child himself shows us is that initial development of language follows and does not lead his development of skill in action and thought. It is only *after* a distinction has been mastered in action that it appears in initial language; and when it first does so, it is referenced by paraphrase of previously learned words or phrases (cf. Slobin, 1971). Piaget (1967) put it succinctly; 'language is not enough to explain thought, because the structures that characterize thought have their roots in action and in sensorimotor mechanisms that are deeper than linguistics' [p. 98].* And, to use Cromer's (1968) words: 'once certain cognitive abilities have developed, we find an active search ... for new forms. Suddenly, forms (and words!) which the child has been exposed to for years become a part of his own speech' [p. 219].

At the onset of speech, then, language is virtually an outgrowth of the mastery of skilled action and perceptual discrimination. These abilities sensitize and almost drive the child to linguistic development. De Laguna (1963, originally published 1927) remarked that the most likely evolutionary explanation of language lies in the human need for help, crucial to the 'social-technical way of life' that is distinctly human (cf. Washburn and Howell, 1960). De Laguna went on:

> Once we deliberately ask the question: What does speech do? What objective function does it perform in human life – the answer is not far to seek. Speech is the great medium through which human co-operation is brought about. It is the means by which the diverse activities of men are co-ordinated and correlated with each other for the attainment of common and reciprocal ends [p. 19].

Having said that much, we must next note that with further growth, the major trend is a steadfast march *away* from the use of language as an

*This is not to say that once a language has been mastered to a certain level (unfortunately, not easily specifiable), it cannot then be used to signal properties of action and events that up to then had *not* been mastered by the child. It is in this sense that language can in fact be used as a medium for instruction (see Bruner, Greenfield, and Olver 1966).

adjunct of action or as a marker for representing the immediate experience. If in the beginning it is true (Bloch, p. 107, cited in De Laguna, 1963, originally published 1927, pp. 89–90) that 'a substantive does not denote simply an object but all the actions with which it is in relation in the experience of the child', it is soon the case that language in the human comes increasingly to be free of the context of action. Whereas 'to understand what a baby is saying, you must see what the baby is doing', nothing of the sort is true for the adult. This brings us to the famous De Laguna dictum, the implications of which will concern us for the remainder of this article.*

The evolution of language is characterized by a progressive freeing of speech from dependence on the perceived conditions under which it is uttered and heard, and from the behaviour which accompanies it. The extreme limit of this freedom is reached in language which is written (or printed) and read. For example, it is quite indifferent to the reader of these words, under what physical conditions they have been penned or typed. This represents, we repeat, the extreme limit of the process by which language comes to be increasingly independent of the conditions of its use [p. 107].

We need not pause long on a comparison of language as it is acquired and used by man and by chimpanzee – notably by the chimpanzee Washoe (Gardner and Gardner, 1971; Ploog and Melnechuk, 1971). For one thing, Washoe's language acquisition is not spontaneous, and she can be seen from the film record to be both reluctant and bored as a language learner. There is neither the play nor the drive of the human child, the *Funktionslust* (Bühler, 1934), that keeps the child exploring and playing with language. The young chimpanzee's grammar is tied perpetually to action. The nominatives and the attributives of early childhood speech, naming objects and attributing properties to them, are lacking and never seem to appear in Washoe. The evident delight of Matthew (Greenfield, May and Bruner, 1972) in the use of such nominatives as 'airplane', 'apple', 'piece', and 'cow, is quite as important as the fact that these holophrases were used in a context of action. Roger Brown (1970, 1971) has commented that virtually all of the two-sign and three-sign 'utterances' in Washoe's use of American sign language were either 'emphasizers' of action (*Hurry open*), 'specifiers' of action (*Listen dog*, at sound of barking), or indicated agents for action (*You eat, Roger Washoe tickle*). David McNeill (1972) put it concisely: Washoe's grammar can be characterized by the single proposition:

$$s \ldots p^n$$

*For excellent accounts of the process of decontextualization in language, see Werner and Kaplan (1963) and Luria and Yudovich (1956). Both of these volumes provide rich documentation and interesting commentary on the point.

or, 'statement that raises a predicated action to a higher level', a grammatical form not spontaneously present in human adult speech.* In a word, chimpanzee use of a taught form of human speech is strongly tied to action, beyond which it tends not to go either spontaneously or by dint of teaching effort.

On the other hand, the development of language in humans not only moves in the direction of becoming itself free of context and accompanying action, it also frees the attention of the user from his immediate surroundings, directing attention to what is being said rather than to what is being done or seen. In the process, language becomes a powerful instrument in selectively directing attention to features of the environment represented by it.

With respect to the first of these, language processing goes on in its very nature at different levels. We process the phonological output of a speaker, interpret his syntax, hold the head words of imbedding phrases until the imbedded phrase is completed and the tail is located to match the head word, etc. At the same time, we direct attention to meanings and to references. The acts of language, argue Miller and Johnson-Laird (see Footnote, p. 35), by their very performance free attention from control by immediate stimulation in the environment. One might even argue that the requirement of organizing what one experiences into sentence form may impose upon experience itself a certain cast – the classic arguments of Humboldt (1836) and Benjamin Lee Whorf (1956). Once language captures control of attention, the swiftness and subtlety of attention change come to match the swiftness and subtlety of linguistic manoeuvring. Language permits search specifications to be set in such a fashion as to fulfil any question that may be asked. The eye-movement records collected by Yarbus (1967) provide stunning illustration of the tactics of the language user: how, while guiding his eye movements by physical features of a picture or scene, he manages at the same time to pick up the features that answer questions he is entertaining – looking now to pick up the ages of people, now to judge their furniture, now to see what they are doing, etc.

To summarize then, though language springs from and aids action, it quickly becomes self-contained and free of the context of action. It is a device, moreover, that frees its possessor from the immediacy of the environment, not only by pre-emption of attention during language use but by its capacity to direct attention towards those aspects of the environment that are singled out by language.

---

*McNeill also made the cogent point that perhaps (as with Premack, 1971) chimpanzees can be taught a human-like syntax, a not uninteresting point; but they seem not to acquire it as children do, by a process not so much of detailed learning or imitation as of spontaneous constructions of grammatical utterances most often exhibiting initial grammatical rules not present in the adult speech to which they are exposed.

I have gone into this much detail regarding early language because it is a necessary preliminary to a crucial point about the management of immaturity in human culture. I have commented already on the fact that in simple, hunter-gatherer societies, there is very little formal teaching outside the sphere of action. The child is not drawn aside and told how to do it; he is shown while the action is going on, with language as an auxiliary and as a marker of action – an aid in calling attention to what is going on that is relevant. Over and beyond that, the principal use of language was probably some mix of guiding group action and giving shape to a belief system through myths and incantations, as Susanne Langer (1969) has long proposed. I rather suspect that increasing technology imposed an increasing demand on language to represent and store knowledge in a fashion to be helpful outside the immediate context of original use. L. S. B. Leaky* suggested that once stone instruments came to be made to match a pattern rather than by spontaneous breaking, as in fabricating an Acheulean pebble tool with a single-face edge, *models* could be fashioned and kept. He has found excellent, obsidian-grained hand axes at Olduvai that appear never to have been used; he speculates that they were 'models for copy', with a religious significance as well.

But an inert model is a poor thing; it is, in effect, an end state, something to be attained with no intervening instruction concerning means. Language does better than that, and it is interesting to see the extent to which magic becomes mixed with practice and imitation in a primitive technology. A good example is afforded by the boat building and inter-island navigation of the pre-literate Puluwat Islanders in the Marshalls, recently described in rich detail by Gladwin (1970) in a book entitled *East is a Big Bird*. Theirs is a system in which East is marked by Altair at horizon elevation, distance by a common-sense speed-estimating method, with distance 'logged' by noting the supposed parallax of islands at different distances over the horizon. Final homing on an island is accomplished by noting the direction of end-of-day nesting flights of boobies and frigate birds. And the lot is peppered with sundry omens given by weeds and sea turtles and the feel of things. I happen to be a navigator myself. I am impressed not only that the system works but that it is genuinely a *system*; it ties together means and ends. The framework of the system can be *told*; however, without language it would be impossible, for the ingredients of the system involve reference to the absent or invisible, to the possible, to the conditional, and even (I suspect) to the knowingly false (the white lies all navigators must tell to keep the trustful sailors trusting). There must have been hunting systems and seasonal marking systems of this sort, representable outside the setting

*L. S. B. Leaky, personal communication, April 1966.

of action, in use by very early man – probably much earlier than heretofore suspected (cf. Marshack, 1972).

Increasingly, then, language in its decontextualized form becomes a-mong human beings the medium for passing on knowledge. And, of course, the emergence of written language – a very recent innovation from an evolutionary point of view – gives this tendency still further amplification. Once this mode of transmitting knowledge has become established, the conditions for the invention of school – a place where teaching occurs – are present. School is a very recent development in evolutionary terms, even in historical terms. I explore now some of the consequences of these de-velopments for our mode of dealing with, informing, and shaping the immature.

From 'knowing how' to 'knowing that'

As soon as schools, pedagogues, and the storing of decontextualized in-formation received legitimacy – and it was probably the written word that accomplished this legitimization – the emphasis shifted from *knowing how* to *knowing that*. Even growth becomes re-defined in accordance with the shift – the adult 'having' more knowledge, that is, 'knowing about' more things. We have even come to define the needs of infancy in these terms, as 'the need for experience' (rather than, as Bowlby, 1969, noted, in terms of the need for love and for predictability). Knowledge in some way becomes a central desideratum. And when, as in the United States, attention turns to the children of the under-privileged and the exploited, their difficulty is likely to be, and indeed in this case was, attributed to 'cultural depri-vation'. Hence, an 'enriched environment' was prescribed much as if the issue were avitaminosis.* Dewey (1916) referred early to this diagnosis as the 'cold-storage' ideal of knowledge and, of course, attacked it vigor-ously.

But this is too simple, for in fact there is great power inherent in de-contextualized knowledge – knowledge represented in a form that is relatively free from the uses to which it is to be put or to which it has been put in the past.† It is not too serious an over-simplification to say that it is precisely such a process of reorganizing knowledge into formal systems that frees it of functional fixedness. By using a system of notation that re-defines

*For a discussion of these problems in childhood as reflecting the growth of skills for surviving under hopeless conditions, see Bruner (1970), Cole and Bruner (1971), and Denenberg (1970).

†For a fuller discussion of the nature of thought processes employing formal and functional modes of organizing knowledge, the reader is referred to Bruner, Goodnow, and Austin (1956); Polanyi (1958); Popper (1954); Bartlett (1958); and Piaget's (1971) striking little volume on structuralism.

functional requirements in formal terms, far greater flexibility can be achieved. Rather than thinking in terms of 'hammers', with all of their associated conventionalized imagery, one thinks instead in terms of force to be applied in excess of a certain level of resistance to be overcome. It is, in effect, the way of science to render the problem into this form in order to make the solving of *particular* problems mere instances of much simpler general problems and thereby to increase the range of applicability of knowledge. Why should the Puluwatan navigator struggle with such a set of complexities as I have described, when all it gets him is competence over a few hundred miles of ocean, and a shaky competence at that! He would be more accurate and more general, as well as more flexible, if he learned to take the elevation of a heavenly body, note the time, and reduce the sight to the easily solved spherical triangle of the western navigator. Such a system would serve him anywhere.

But there are two problems (at least!) in this ideal of efficient formal knowledge rather than implicit knowledge, to use Polanyi's (1958) phrase. The first grows out of the point already made about skill and its de-emphasis. That de-emphasis comes out of what I believe to be a misplaced confidence in the ease with which we go from *knowing that* to *knowing how*. It is not easy; it is a deep and perplexing problem. Let me call it the effectiveness problem. Just as deep is a second problem: it may well be that the message of decontextualization and formal structure is implicitly anti-fantasy and anti-play. Call this the engagement problem. The two together – effectiveness and engagement – bring us to the heart of the matter.

With respect to effectiveness, it is probably a reasonable hypothesis that as technology advances, the effector and the energy components of industrial activity become increasingly remote from human empathy; neither the arm nor the hand any longer give the models for energy or for artificing. Energy and the tool kit become, for planning purposes, black boxes, and the major human functions are *control* and the *organization* of work. There is a spiral. It becomes possible to talk about the conduct of work almost without reference to skill or vocation – wheat production and steel production and gross national product and energy production and balance of payments. With work and competence presented in that mode, the young become more and more remote from the nature of the effort involved in running a society. Vocation, competence, skill, sense of place in the system – these become more and more difficult for the young to fathom – or, for that matter, for the adult. It is difficult for the child to say what he will do or what he will 'be' as an adult. Effectiveness becomes elusive.

For while the new technological complexity produces an enormous increase in production processes and distribution processes, it produces no increase either in the number or in the clarity of comprehensible vocations.

Production and distribution, in high technology, do not provide an operator with an opportunity to carry through from the initiation of a recognizable problem to its completion, or to see plainly how his task relates to the cycle from task initiation to task completion. Intrinsic structure and reward are removed. The result is what Norbert Wiener (1950) long ago called 'work unfit for human production'. The industrial revolution removed the worker from the home. Its technological elaboration made the worker's work away from home incomprehensible to the young and the uninitiated – the latter often a worker himself. The greatest tribute to technique decontextualized from vocation, carried to an extreme where it becomes fascinating, is the *Whole Earth Catalogue*. Even the counter-culture reaches a point where it is without vocations but offers only spontaneity as a contrast to over-rationalized 'vocationless' work.

School, separated from work which itself has grown difficult to understand, becomes its own world. As McLuhan (1964) insists, it becomes a medium and has its own message, regardless of what is taught. The message is its irrelevance to work, to adult life. For those who wish to pursue knowledge for its own sake, this is not upsetting. But for those who do not or cannot, school provides no guide – only knowledge, the relevance of which is clear neither to students nor to teachers. These are the conditions for alienation and confusion. I would urge that when adult models become incomprehensible, they lose the power either to guide or to inspire. I do not mean to settle the question here as to whether present adult models are in fact totally irrelevant to the problems of those entering society now. I will, however, return to it later.

Bronfenbrenner (1970) in his book on child rearing commented on the accelerating trend towards generational separation in technical cultures. The self-sealing peer culture, the denigration of adult ideal figures, the counter-culture committed to protest and romanticized ideals – these are by now familiar instruments of separation. But I believe them to be symptoms of the struggle to adjust to a social-technical order that changes at a rate faster than comprehension of it can be achieved and widely transmitted. This, you recall, is the problem with which we started: How can a system for preparing the immature for entry into the society deal with a future that is increasingly difficult to predict within a single lifetime? Many of the means for inducting the young into the social group, a heritage of the evolution of man's capacity for culture, appear to become ineffective under such conditions when such rapid change becomes the rule. Observation and imitative play, demonstration in context of skilled problem solving, induced tutor proneness, an effective teaching microcosm in the form of an extended family or a habitat group, and the concept of vocation – are all seemingly threatened. Yet I wonder.

I do not propose to become gloomy. Surely human culture and our species are in deep trouble, not the least of which is loss of heart. But much of the trouble is real: We are degrading the biosphere, failing to cope with population, permitting technology to degrade individuality, and failing to plan. Many of the experimental and often radical efforts of the young represent, I believe, new variants of ancient, biologically rooted modes by which the young characteristically work through to maturity. And a great many of these efforts are in response to the new conditions we have been at such pains to describe – a rate of change faster than can be transmitted intergenerationally with concomitant likelihood of disastrous consequences. Let me conclude with a closer analysis of this point and, in so doing, come to what was referred to above as the problem of engagement.

Problem of engagement

A great many of the world's schools are conventional and dull places. They do not foster much productive play and little of what Jeremy Bentham (1840), in his *Theory of Legislation*, called 'deep play' and condemned as irrational and in violation of the utilitarian ideal. By deep play, Bentham meant play in which the stakes are so high that it is irrational for men to engage in it at all – a situation in which the marginal utility of what one stands to win is clearly less than the marginal disutility of what one stands to lose. Bentham proposed, good utilitarian that he was, that such play should be outlawed. But as the anthropologist Geertz (1972) commented in his close analysis of cockfighting in Bali, 'despite the logical force of Bentham's analysis men do engage in such play, both passionately and often, and even in the face of law's revenge' [p. 667]. Deep play is playing with fire. It is the kind of serious play that tidy and even permissive institutions for educating the young cannot live with happily, for their mandate from the society requires them to carry out their work with due regard for minimizing chagrin concerning outcomes achieved. And deep play is a poor vehicle for that.

What strikes me about the decade just past is the enormous increase in the depth of play in adolescence and, by reflection downward into lower age groups, among the young. Willingness to risk future preferment by dropping out of the system that is designed to qualify one for the future, in return for a season of communal mutuality – surely the balance of utility to disutility is not Benthamite. Such wagers are highly dangerous for the lives of the individuals involved in them. (Note that Russian roulette is the worst bargain to be had in deep play.) When one finds deep play, the inference must be that there are deep and unresolved problems in the culture. There always are, but that does not mean that one should not look carefully at what these are and what they signify for the future.

There is ample reason to believe that the present forms of deep play point to a thwarted, backed-up need for defining competence, both individually and socially, to oneself and to others. Recall that in most previous cultural eras, adults provided challenge and excitement and a certain sense of muted terror for the young by induction into rituals and skills that had momentous consequences. Engagement was built into the system. One knew the steps to growing up, both ritually and in terms of skill.

If adult life ceases to be comprehensible, or begins to be less a challenge than a drag, then engagement is lost – but only for a while. I have the impression of something new emerging. What takes the place of the deposed, incomprehensible, or worn-out competence figure, the classical adult image of skill? At first, of course, protest-withdrawal figures will – the pop figures of rock and the Timothy Leary prophets who offer an intravenous version of competence via subjectivity. I believe that gradually there is emerging a new form of role bearer – the *intermediate generation* – adolescents and young adults who take over the role of acting as models. They exist visibly in context. Their skills and vocation are proclaimed, miniaturized to appropriate size, and personalized. I should like to propose that such an intermediate generation is a response to the crisis of a change rate that goes faster than we can transmit from generation to generation.

Lest we go too rapidly, consider the pointlessness of an inter-generation in a society *with* continuity. Turnbull's (1961) account of a Pygmy group in Africa serves well:

When a hunting party goes off there are always people left in the camp – usually some of the older men and women, some children, and perhaps one or two younger men and women. The children always have their own playground, called bopi, a few yards off from the main camp . . .

There were always trees for the youngsters to climb, and this is one of the main sports even for those not yet old enough to walk properly. The great game is for half a dozen or more children to climb to the top of a young tree, bending it down until its top touches the ground. They then all leap off at once, and if anyone is too slow he goes flying back upward as the tree springs upright, to the jeers and laughter of his friends.

Like children everywhere, Pygmy children love to imitate their adult idols. This is the beginning of their schooling, for the adults will always encourage and help them. What else is there for them to learn except to grow into good adults? So a fond father will make a tiny bow for his son, and arrows of soft wood with blunt points. He may also give him a strip of a hunting net. A mother will delight herself and her daughter by weaving a miniature carrying basket. At an early age, boys and girls are 'playing house'. . .

They will also play at hunting, the boys stretching out their little bits of net while the girls beat the ground with bunches of leaves and drive some poor tired old frog in toward the boys. . . And one day they find that the games they have been playing are not games any longer, but the real thing, for they have become adults. Their hunting is now real hunting; their tree climbing is in earnest search of inaccessible honey; their acrobatics on the swings are repeated almost daily, in other forms, in the pursuit of elusive game, or in avoiding malicious forest buffalo. It happens so gradually that they hardly notice the change at first, for even when they are proud and famous hunters their life is still full of fun and laughter [pp. 128–9].

The transition is gradual, its excitement increased from time to time by rituals. But technological societies move away from such gradualism as they become increasingly developed. Indeed, the Protestant ethic made very early a sharp separation between what one does when young and what one does later, with the transition very sharply defined. In the western tradition there grew a puritan separation of the 'works of the adult' and 'the play of babes'. But it was clear to both sides what the two were about. Now 'the play of the babes' has become separate from, dissociated from, the adult community and not understood by that community any better than the young comprehend or accept the ideals of the adult community.

A place is made automatically, perhaps for the first time in our cultural tradition, for an intermediate generation, with power to model new forms of behaviour. Their power comes precisely, I think, from the fact that they offer deep play, that irresistible charisma that so disturbed the tidy Jeremy Bentham. They are modelling new life styles to fit better what is perceived as the new and changing conditions, new changes that they claim to be able to see – perhaps rightly, perhaps not – more clearly than those who had adapted to something still earlier. The great question is whether the intermediate generation can reduce the uncertainty of growing up under conditions of unpredictable change, and can serve as purveyors of effectiveness as well as of engagement.

I do not think that intermediate models are a transitory phenomenon. I believe that we would do well to recognize the new phenomenon and to incorporate it, even make it easier for the young adult and later juvenile to get more expert at it. Nobody can offer a blueprint on how an intermediate generation can help ready the less mature for life in an unforseeably changing world. It is not altogether a comfortable problem either, for the way of cultural revolutions and Red Guards (both composed of intermediates) can only inspire caution. But letting the young have more of a hand in the teaching of the younger, letting them have a better sense of the dilemmas of society as a whole, these may be part of the way in which a new community can be helped to emerge. What may be in order is a mode of inducting the young by the use of a more communal system of education in which each takes responsibility for teaching or aiding or abetting or provoking those less able, less knowledgeable, and less provoked than he.

It was in the universities that these current matters first surfaced – a long way from the high savannas of East Africa where we began our quest for an understanding of immaturity and its uses. One becomes increasingly shaky the closer one comes to man in his contemporary technological society. I would only urge that in considering these deep issues of educability we keep our perspective broad and remember that the human race has a biological past from which we can read lessons for the culture of the present. We cannot adapt to everything, and in designing a way to the future we would do well to examine again what we are and what our limits are. Such a course does not mean opposition to change but, rather, using man's natural modes of adapting to render change both as intelligent and as stable as possible.

(From *American Psychologist*, Vol. 27, No. 8, August 1972.)

References

ALTMAN, J. (1967), 'Post-natal growth and differentiation of the mammalian brain, with implications for a morphological theory of memory', in G. C. Quarton, T. Melnechuk, and F. O. Schmitt (eds), *The Neurosciences: A Study Program*, Vol. 1, Rockefeller University Press, New York.

BALDWIN, J. D. (1969), 'The ontogeny of social behaviour of squirrel monkeys (Saimiri sciurea) in a semi-natural environment', *Folia Primat.*, No. 11, pp. 35–79.

BARSH, R. (1972), 'The evolution of tool use', unpublished research paper, Center for Cognitive Studies, Harvard University.

BARTLETT, F. C. (1958), *Thinking: An Experimental and Social Study*, Basic Books, New York.

BEACH, F. (1965), *Sex and Behavior*, Wiley, New York.

BENNETT, E. L., DIAMOND, M. C., KRECH, D., and ROSENZWEIG, M. R. (1964), 'Chemical and anatomical plasticity of the brain', *Science*, No. 146, pp. 610–19.

BENTHAM, J. (1840), *The Theory of Legislation*, Weeks, Jordan, Boston, U.S.A.

BERLIN, I. (1953), *The Hedgehog and the Fox*, Simon & Schuster, New York.

BERNSTEIN, N. (1967), *The Co-ordination and Regulation of Movements*, Pergamon Press.

BIRCH, H. G. (1945), 'The relation of previous experience to insightful problem-solving', *J. Comp. Physiol. Psychol.*, No. 38, pp. 367–83.

BISHOP, A. (1964), 'Use of the hand in lower primates', in J. Buettner-Janusch (ed.), *Evolutionary and Genetic Biology of Primates*, Vol. 2, Academic Press.

BLOCK, S. C. (1972), 'Early competence in problem-solving,' in K. Connolly and J. S. Bruner (eds), *Competence in Early Childhood*, (CIBA Foundation Conference), Academic Press.

BLOOM, B. (ed.) (1956), *Taxonomy of Educational Objectives*, McKay, New York.

BOWLBY, J. (1969), *Attachment and Loss*, Vol. 1, Hogarth Press.

BRONFENBRENNER, U. (1970), *Two Worlds of Childhood, U.S. and U.S.S.R.*, Allen & Unwin.

BROWN, R. W. (1970), 'The first sentence of child chimpanzee', in *Psycholinguistics: Selected Papers by Roger Brown*, Free Press, New York.

BROWN, R. W. (1971), 'Are apes capable of language?', *Neurosciences Research Program Bulletin*, Vol. 9, No. 5.

BRUNER, J. S. (1965), 'The growth of mind', *Amer. Psychol.*, No. 20, pp. 1007–17.

BRUNER, J. S. (1966), *Toward a Theory of Instruction*, Harvard University Press.

BRUNER, J. S. (1970), *Poverty and Childhood*, Merrill-Palmer Institute, Detroit.

BRUNER, J. S., GOODNOW, J. J., and AUSTIN, G. A. (1956), *A Study of Thinking*, Wiley, New York.

BRUNER, J. S., GREENFIELD, P. M., and OLVER, R. R. (1966), *Studies in Cognitive Growth*, Wiley, New York.

BRUNER, J. S., and KOSLOWSKI, B. (1972), 'Preadaptation in initial visually guided reaching', *Perception*, No. 1.

BÜHLER, K. (1934), *Sprachtheorie*, Jena.

BURRIDGE, K. O. L. (1957), 'A Tangu Game', *Man*, pp. 88–9. (And see this volume, p. 364.)

CARPENTER, C. R. (1934), 'A field study of the behavior and social relations of Howling monkeys', *Comp. Psychol. Monog.*, No. 10, pp. 1–168.

CHANCE, M. R. A. (1967), 'Attention structure as the basis of primate rank orders', *Man*, No. 2, pp. 503–18.

CLARK, W. E. LE GROS (1963), *The Antecedents of Man: An Introduction to the Evolution of the Primates*, Harper & Row, New York.

COLE, M., and BRUNER, J. S. (1971), 'Cultural differences and inferences about psychological processes', *Amer. Psychol.*, No. 26, pp. 867–76.

CROMER, R. F. (1968), 'The development of temporal reference during the acquisition of language', unpublished doctoral dissertation, Department of Social Relations, Harvard University.

DENENBERG, V. H. (ed.) (1970), *Education of the Infant and the Young Child*, Academic Press.

DEVORE, I. (1965), *The Primates,* Time-Life Books, New York.

DEWEY, J. (1916), *Democracy and Education*, Macmillan, New York.

DOLHINOW, P. J., and BISHOP, N. (1970), 'The development of motor skills and social relationships among primates through play', *Minn. Symp. Child Psychol.*

GALLUP, G. G., JR. (1970), 'Chimpanzees: Self-recognition', *Science*, No. 167, pp. 86–7.

GARDNER, B. J., and GARDNER, R. A. (1971), 'Two-way communication with an infant chimpanzee'. In A. M. Schrier and F. Stollnitz (eds), *Behavior of Nonhuman Primates*, Vol. 4, Academic Press.

GEERTZ, C. (1972), 'Deep play: Notes on the Balinese cockfight', *Daedalus*, No. 101, pp. 1–38. (And see this volume, p. 656.)

GLADWIN, T. (1970), *East is a Big Bird*, Harvard University Press, Cambridge.

GOODALL, J. (1965), 'Chimpanzees of the Gombe Stream Reserve', in
I. DeVore (ed.), *Primate Behavior: Field Studies of Monkeys and Apes*, Holt,
Rinehart & Winston, New York.

GOULDNER, A. (1960), 'The norm of reciprocity: A preliminary statement',
American Sociological Review, No. 25, pp. 161–78.

GREENFIELD, P., MAY, A. A., and BRUNER, J. S. (1972), *Early Words*,
(A film), Wiley, New York.

HALL. K. R. L. (1965), 'Behavior and ecology of the wild Patas monkey
(*Erythrocebus patas*) in Uganda', *J. Zool.*, No. 148, pp. 15–87.

HALL, K. R. L., and DeVORE, I. (1965), 'Baboon social behavior', in
I. DeVore (ed.), *Primate Behavior: Field Studies of Monkeys and Apes*,
Holt, Rinehart & Winston, New York.

HAMBURG, D. (1968), 'Evolution of emotional responses: Evidence from recent
research on non-human primates', *Science and Psychoanalysis*, No. 12, pp. 39–54.

HARLOW, H. F. (1959), 'Love in infant monkeys', *Sci. American*, No. 200,
pp. 68–74.

HARLOW, H. F., and HARLOW, M. K. (1962), 'The effect of rearing conditions
on behavior', *Bulletin of the Menninger Clinic*, No. 26, pp. 213–24.

HAYES, K. J., and HAYES, C. (1952), 'Imitation in a home-raised chimpanzee',
J. Comp. Physiol. Psychol., No. 45, pp. 450–59.

HERBERT, M. J., and HARSH, C. M. (1944), 'Observational learning in cats',
J. Comp. Physiol. Psychol., No. 37, pp. 81–95.

HINDE, R. A. (1971), 'Development of social behavior', in A. M. Schrier and
F. Stollnitz (eds), *Behavior of Nonhuman Primates*, Vol. 3, Academic Press.

HOCKETT, C. D. (1960), 'The origins of speech', *Sci. American*.

HUMBOLDT, W. VON (1836), *Ueber die Verschiedenheit des menschlichen
Sprachbaues*, Berlin. (Facsimile ed., Bonn 1960.)

ITANI, J. (1958), 'On the acquisition and propagation of a new food habit in
the natural group of the Japanese monkey at Takasakiyama', *Primates*, No. 1,
pp. 84–98.

JOLLY, A. (1966), *Lemur Behavior: A Madagascar Field Study*, University of
Chicago Press.

KAWAMURA, S. (1959), 'The process of subculture propagation among
Japanese macaques', *Primates*, No. 2, pp. 43–54.

KHROUSTOV, G. F. (1968), 'Formation and highest frontier of the implemental
activity of anthropoids', in *Seventh International Congress of Anthropological
and Ethnological Sciences*, Moscow, pp. 503–9.

KING, D. L. (1966), 'A review and interpretation of some aspects of the
infant–mother relationship in mammals and birds', *Psychological Bulletin*,
No. 65, pp. 143–55.

KÖHLER, W. (1925), *The Mentality of Apes*, Routledge & Kegan Paul.

KORTLAND, A. (1965), 'How do chimpanzees use weapons when fighting
leopards?', *Yearbook of the American Philosophical Society*, pp. 327–32.

KORTLAND A., and KOÖIJ, M. (1963), 'Protohominid behaviour in primates',
in J. Napier and N. A. Barnicot (eds), *The Primates*, Symposia Zoological
Society, London.

KORTLAND, A., and VAN ZON, J. C. J. (1969), 'The present state of research on the dehumanization hypothesis of African ape evolution', *Proceedings of the International Congress of Primatology*, No. 3, pp. 10–13.

LAGUNA, G. A. DE (1963), *Speech: Its Function and Development*, Indiana University Press. (Orig. publ. 1927.)

LANCASTER, J. B. (1968), 'On the evolution of tool-using behavior', *American Anthropologist*, No. 70, pp. 56–66.

LANGER, S. (1969), *Philosophy in a New Key*, Harvard University Press. (Revised edition: orig. publ. 1942.)

LASHLEY, K. S. (1951), 'The problem of serial order in behavior', in L. A. Jeffress (ed.), *Cerebral Mechanisms in Behavior: The Hixon Symposium*, Wiley, New York.

LAWICK-GOODALL, J. VAN (1968), 'The behavior of free living chimpanzees in the Gombe Stream Reserve', *Anim. Behav. Monog.*, No. 1, pp. 165–301. (And see this volume, p. 222.)

LEE, R. B., and DEVORE, I. (eds) (1968), *Man the Hunter*, Aldine, Chicago.

LEVI-STRAUSS, C. (1968), *Structural Anthropology*, Allen Lane.

LEWIS, D. (1969), *Convention*, Harvard University Press.

LOIZOS, C. (1967), 'Play behaviour in higher primates: a review,' in D. Morris (ed.), *Primate Ethology*, Weidenfeld & Nicolson.

LURIA, A. R., and YUDOVICH, F. Y. (1959), *Speech and the Development of Mental Processes in the Child*, Staples Press.

MARSHACK, H. (1972), *The Roots of Civilization*, McGraw-Hill, New York.

MAYR, E. (1963), *Animal Species and Evolution*, Harvard University Press.

MCLUHAN, M. (1964), *Understanding Media*, Routledge & Kegan Paul.

MCNEILL, D. (1972), 'Comments', in K. Connolly, and J. S. Bruner (eds), *Competence in Early Childhood*, (CIBA Foundation Conference), Academic Press.

MERFIELD, F. G., and MILLER, H. (1956), *Gorilla Hunter*, Farrar, Straus, New York.

MILLER, S. N. (1973), 'Ends, means and galumphing: Some leitmotifs of play', *American Anthropologist*, No. 75.

MORRIS, D. (1964), 'The response of animals to a restricted environment', *Symp. Zool. Soc.*, No. 13, pp. 99–118.

MORRIS, D. (ed.) (1967), *Primate Ethology*, Weidenfeld & Nicolson.

NAPIER, J. R. (1962), 'The evolution of the hand', *Sc. American*, No. 107, pp. 56–62.

PIAGET, J. (1967), *Six Psychological Studies* (ed. D. Elkind), Random House, New York.

PIAGET, J. (1971), *Structuralism*, Routledge & Kegan Paul.

PLOOG, D., and MELNECHUK, T. (1971), 'Are apes capable of language?', *Neurosciences Research Program Bulletin*, No. 9, pp. 600–700.

POLANYI, J. (1958), *Personal Knowledge*, University of Chicago Press, Chicago.

POPPER, K. (1954), *Nature, Mind and Modern Science*, Hutchinson.

PREMACK, D. (1971), 'On the assessment of language competence in the chimpanzee', in A. M. Schrier, and F. Stollnitz (eds), *Behavior of Nonhuman Primates*, Vol. 4, Academic Press.

REYNOLDS, V. (1965), 'Behavioral comparisons between the chimpanzee and the mountain gorilla in the wild', *American Anthropologist*, No. 67, pp. 691–706.

RODMAN, P. (1972), 'Observations of free-ranging orang-utans in Borneo', colloquium talk at the Center for Cognitive Studies, Harvard University.

RUMBAUGH, D. M. (1970), 'Learning skills of anthropoids', in *Primate Behavior*, Vol. 1, Academic Press.

RUMBAUGH, D. M., and McCORMACK, C. (1967), 'The learning skills of primates: A comparative study of apes and monkeys', in D. Stark, R. Schneider, and J. H. Kuhn (eds.), *Progress in Primatology*, Fischer, Stuttgart.

RUMBAUGH, D. M., RIESEN, A. H., and WRIGHT, S. C. (1972), 'Creative responsiveness to objects: A report of a pilot study with young apes', privately distributed paper from Yerkes Laboratory of Psychobiology, Atlanta, Georgia.

SCHALLER, G. (1963), *Mountain Gorilla*, University of Chicago Press, Chicago.

SCHALLER, G. (1964), *The Year of the Gorilla*, Collins.

SCHILLER, P. H. (1952), 'Innate constituents of complex responses in primates', *Psych. Rev.*, No. 59, pp. 177–191.

SINGH, S. D. (1969), 'Urban monkeys', *Sci. American*, No. 221, pp. 108–15.

SLOBIN, D. (1971), 'Cognitive prerequisites of language', in W. O. Dingwall (ed.), *Developmental Psycholinguistics: A Survey of Linguistic Science*, University of Maryland Linguistics Program, College Park.

SROUFE, L. A., and WUNSCH, J. P. (1972), 'The development of laughter in the first year of life', *Child Development*, No. 43, pp. 1326–44.

TINBERGEN, N. (1953), *The Herring Gull's World: A Study of the Social Behaviour of Birds*, Collins.

TRIVERS, R. (1971), 'The evolution of reciprocal altruism', *Quart. Rev. Biol.*, No. 46, pp. 35–57.

TURNBULL, C. (1961), *The Forest People*, Simon & Schuster, New York.

VYGOTSKY, L. S. (1933), 'Play and its role in the mental development of the child', *Soviet Psychology*, Vol. 3, No. 5, pp. 62–76. (And see this volume, p. 537.)

WASHBURN, S. L., and HOWELL, F. C. (1960), 'Human evolution and culture', in S. Tax (ed.), *The Evolution of Man*, University of Chicago Press.

WEIR, R. H. (1962), *Language in the Crib*, Mouton, The Hague. (And see this volume, pp. 609.)

WERNER, H., and KAPLAN, B. (1963), *Symbol Formation*, Wiley, New York.

WHORF, B. L. (1956), *Language, Thought and Reality: Selected Writings*, (ed. J. B. Carroll), M.I.T. Press, Cambridge, U.S.A.; Wiley, New York.

WIENER, N. (1950), *The Human Use of Human Beings; Cybernetics and Society*, Houghton Mifflin, Boston, U.S.A.

YARBUS, A. L. (1967), *Eye Movements and Vision*, Plenum Press, New York.

YERKES, R. M., and YERKES, A. W. (1929), *The Great Apes: A Study of Anthropoid Life*, Yale University Press, New Haven, U.S.A.

The Play of Animals:
Play and Instinct

Karl Groos, Professor of Philosophy at the University of Basle, was fascinated by inherited instinctual patterns 'necessary in the animal's struggle for life and preservation of the species'. He noted the appearance of play in higher orders and hypothesized that animals with complex forms of adaptation required youthful play to practise a variety of behaviours for which inherited instinct might not be wholly adequate.

Such advancement of the evolution of intelligence as we have been considering is favoured also by play, as I believe. I trace the connection as follows: A succession of important life tasks is appointed for the adult animal of the higher orders as for primitive man, some of the principal being as follows:

1. Absolute control of its own body. Grounded on this fundamental necessity are the special tasks, namely:

2. Complete control over the means of locomotion for change of place, characteristic of the species, as walking, running, leaping, swimming, flying.

3. Great agility in the pursuit of prey, as lying in wait, chasing, seizing, shaking. Equal fitness for escaping from powerful enemies, as fleeing, dodging in rapid flight, hiding, etc.

4. Special ability for fighting, especially in the struggle with others of the same kind during courtship, etc.

After the foregoing discussion there can be no doubt that instinct plays a part in all this adaptation for the struggle for life and preservation of the species, so necessary in man and other animals. Further – and here I again come into touch with the end of the last chapter – it would be entirely in harmony with other phenomena of heredity if we found that these instincts appear at that period of life when they are first seriously needed. Just as many physical peculiarities which are of use in the struggle for the female only develop when the animal needs them; just as many instincts that belong to reproduction first appear at maturity; so the instinct of hostility might first spring up in the same manner only when there is real need for it; and so it might be supposed with other instincts in connection with the related activities. The instinct for flight would only be awakened by real danger, and that of hunting only when the animal's parents no longer nourished it, and so on. What would be the result if this were actually the case – if, in other words, there were no such thing as play? It would be necessary for the special instincts to be elaborated to their last and finest details. For if they were only imperfectly prepared, and therefore insufficient for the real end, the animal might as well enter on his struggle for life totally unprepared. The tiger, for instance, no longer fed by his parents, and without practice in springing and seizing his prey, would inevitably perish, though he might have an undefined hereditary impulse to creep upon it noiselessly, strike it down by a tremendous leap, and subdue it with tooth and nail, for the pursued creature would certainly escape on account of his unskilfulness.

Without play practice it would be absolutely indispensable that instinct should be very completely developed, in order that the acts described might be accurately performed by inherited mechanism, as is also the case with such instinctive acts as are exhibited but once in a lifetime. Even assuming this possibility, what becomes of the evolution of higher intelligence? Animals would certainly make no progress intellectually if they were thus blindly left in the swaddling-clothes of inherited impulse; but, fortunately, they are not so dealt with. In the very moment when advancing evolution has gone so far that intellect alone can accomplish more than instinct, hereditary mechanism tends to lose its perfection, and the 'chiselling out of brain predisposition' by means of individual experience becomes more and more prominent. And it is by the play of children and animals alone that this carving out can be properly and perfectly accomplished. So natural selection through the play of the young furthers the fulfilment of Goethe's profound saying: 'What thou hast inherited from the fathers, labour for, in order to possess it.'

At this point the full biological significance of play first becomes apparent. It is a very widespread opinion that youth, which belongs, strictly speaking, only to the higher orders, is for the purpose of giving the animal time to adjust itself to the complicated tasks of its life to which its instincts are not adequate. The higher the attainment required, the longer the time of preparation. This being the case, the investigation of play assumes great importance. Hitherto we have been in the habit of referring to the period of youth as a matter of fact only important at all because some instincts of biological significance appear then. Now we see that youth probably exists for the sake of play. Animals cannot be said to play because they are young and frolicsome, *but rather they have a period of youth in order to play*; for only by so doing can they supplement the insufficient hereditary endowment with individual experience, in view of the coming tasks of life. Of course this does not exclude other grounds, physiological ones, for instance, for the phenomenon of youth; but so far as concerns the fitting of the animal to his life duties, play is the most important one.

I may now briefly recapitulate. Our leading question seems to be as to the play of the young. That once adequately explained, the play of adults would present no special difficulties. The play of young animals has its origin in the fact that certain very important instincts appear at a time when the animal does not seriously need them. This premature appearance cannot be accounted for by inherited skill, because the inheritance of acquired characters is extremely doubtful. Even if such inheritance did have a part in it, the explanation by means of selection would be most probable, since the utility of play is incalculable. This utility consists in the practice and exercise it affords for some of the more important duties of life, inasmuch as selection tends to weaken the blind force of instinct, and aids more and more the development of independent intelligence as a substitute for it. At the moment when intelligence is sufficiently evolved to be more useful in the struggle for life than the most perfect instinct, then will selection favour those individuals in whom the instincts in question appear earlier and in less elaborated forms – in forms that do not require serious motive, and are merely for purposes of practice and exercise – that is to say, it will favour those animals which play. Finally, in estimating the biological significance of play at its true worth, the thought was suggested that perhaps the very existence of youth is largely for the sake of play.

The animals do not play because they are young, but they have their youth because they must play.

(From *The Play of Animals*, D. Appleton, New York, 1898, first published in Basle, 1896.)

The Play of Man:
Teasing and Love-Play

Professor Groos extends to man his thesis that play is practice for more serious behaviours. He documents teasing and love-play as the playful forms of instinctual adult behaviours, and explores the basis for the pleasure all of us find in play.

Teasing

The fighting instinct of mankind is so intense that playful duels, mass conflicts, single combats, and contests do not satisfy it. When there is no occasion for an actual testing of their powers, children and adults turn their belligerent tendencies into a means of amusement, and so arise those playful attacks, provocations, and challenges which we class together under the general name of teasing. The roughest if not the earliest form of such play is that of bodily attack, such as is often observed among animals. A female ape which Brehm brought to Germany loved to annoy the sullen house dog.

When he had stretched himself as usual on the greensward, the roguish monkey would appear and, seeing with satisfaction that he was fast asleep, seize him softly by the tail and wake him by a sudden jerk of that member. The enraged dog would fly at his tormentor, barking and growling, while the monkey took a defensive position, striking repeatedly on the ground with her large hand and awaiting the enemy's attack. The dog could never reach her, though, for, to his unbounded rage, as he made a rush for her, she sprang at one bound far over his head, and the next moment had him again by the tail.

We all know how children delight in just such teasing. To throw an unsuspecting comrade suddenly on his back, to box him or tickle and pinch him, to knock off his cap, pull his hair, take his biscuit from his hand, and if he is small hold it so high that the victim leaps after it in vain – all this gives the aggressor an agreeable feeling of superiority, and he enjoys the anger or alarm of his victim. When I was in one of the lower gymnasium classes our singing on one occasion was suddenly broken into by a shrill scream. One of the pupils had found a pin which he energetically pushed into an inviting spot in the anatomy of the boy in front of him. The culprit could only say in palliation of his offence that he did it 'without thinking', which excuse was received rather incredulously. Schoolboys often pull out small handfuls of one another's hair, and it is a point of honour not to display any feeling during the process. Becq de Fouquières records an ancient trick of this kind, consisting of a blow on the ear in conjunction with a simultaneous fillip of the nose. Cold water is a time-honoured instrument of torture. To duck the timid bather who is cautiously stepping into the pond, to empty a pitcher on a heedless passer-by, to place a vessel full of water so that the inmate of a room will overturn it on opening the door – these are jokes familiar wherever merry young people are found. The lover of teasing naturally seeks such victims as are defenceless against him, especially those who are physically weak or so situated as to be incapable of revenge. Yet there are ways of annoying the strong and capable. A good-natured teacher is apt to be the subject of his pupils' pranks, though in this case they seldom take the form of physical assaults. It is not an unheard-of thing, however, for a paper ball to hit his head or for his seat to be smeared with ink or perhaps with glue.

Youths and grown men are little behind the children in such jests. There is, for instance, the christening on board ship in honour of crossing the line which Leopold Wagner thinks is derived from the ancient religious ceremony celebrated on passing the pillars of Hercules. Tossing in a blanket, which made such a lasting impression on Sancho Panza, was known to the Romans by the name of *sagatio*. Such rough sports were practised in the time of the Roman emperors by noble youths. Suetonius relates of Otho that the future emperor as a young man often seized, with his companions, upon weak or drunken fellows at night, and tossed them on a soldier's mantle (*distento sago impositum in sublime jactare*). In popular festivities fighting with pigs' bladders is a fruitful source of amusements to which tickling with a peacock's feather is a modern addition, and lassoing with curled strips of paper which cling about the neck. Students make a speciality of such pranks. A favourite one was crowding, when the streets had only a narrow pavement for pedestrians, while in bad weather the rest of the road was a mass of unfathomable mud; another was to deal a hard blow on the high hat of some worthy Philistine, plunging him suddenly into hopeless darkness, or tracing a circle on the bald head of a toper asleep over his wine, etc. In an inn in Giessen there is still in existence a bench through whose seat a nail projects when a hidden cord is pulled – a pleasant surprise for the unsuspecting guest who reclines upon it. On entering the gymnasium I was initiated in an aesthetic little practice which is of ancient date and serves as an instance of the coarse jesting that is so common there. One of the company secretly fills his mouth with beer and reclines on two chairs. With a handkerchief spread over his face he plays the part of The Innkeeper's Daughter. They all sing the familiar song, and two accomplices play the role of two of the peasants while the novice is asked to be the third. The veil is thus twice withdrawn from the daughter's face, and twice replaced without any suspicious revelations, but when the innocent third lover arrives he is greeted with the stream of stale beer full in the face.

Turning now to other forms of teasing than direct bodily annoyance, we find again that children very early understand it. When the pretence is made of great alarm at his beating with a spoon or banging a book or at a sudden cry, a child as young as two years old shows great delight, and will repeat the performance with a roguish expression. From this time on, to cause sudden fright is a favourite method of gratifying the taste for teasing. The ghostly manifestations which terrify each generation in turn can often be traced to some mischievous urchins.

I remember a joke played on a geographical professor at the gymnasium who, as he carelessly opened a closet door, was confronted by a skeleton which had been used in the previous lecture. Students could hardly subsist without the ancient trick of stuffing the clothes of a 'suicide', and placing the figure on the floor of their victim's room with a pistol lying near, or hanging it by a rope to the window frame, to give the late home-comer a genuine scare. In Athenäus we find a beautiful instance of readiness to meet such a trick. King Lysimachus, who took delight in teasing his guests, one day at a banquet threw a skilfully made artificial scorpion on to the dress of one Bithys, who recoiled; but, quickly recovering himself, said to the rather penurious king: 'My lord, it is now my turn to frighten you; I beseech you give me a talent.'

A common and early developed form of teasing is the deception which imparts to the perpetrator a feeling of intellectual superiority. Children display this in their tender years principally by pretending that they are going to do forbidden or improper things, as revolt against authority. When the little girl observed by Pollock was twenty-three months old she often declined to kiss her father good-night. She turned from him as if annoyed or indifferent, to make a *fausse sortie*, and then called him back and gave the kiss. Sigismund's boy often exhibited a 'kind of humorous defiance of authority', such as grasping at a light standing near him, but not so that it could burn him, and looking slyly at his father. Older children have innumerable tricks of this kind. A sort of game is to strike on a table with a spoon or on the floor with a card and repeat the formula 'He can do little who can't do this, this', and pass the stick or spoon to the next neighbour with the left hand. The uninitiated who attempt to do this usually pass it with the right hand and are much puzzled when told that they are wrong. There is much of this element, too, in the games of magic which children are so fond of. For examples of it among adults it is only necessary to turn again to the old jokes of students. In a university town a merchant, Karl Klingel, was roused in the middle of the night by a ring at the bell. The visitor was a student named Karl, who pretended to think that the name on the sign was a signal for him. 'Mystification,' says Goethe in *Wahrheit und Dichtung*,

is and ever will be amusement for idle people who are more or less intelligent. Indolent mischievousness, selfish enjoyment of doing some damage is a resource to those who are without occupation or any wholesome external interests. No age is entirely free from such proclivities.

Moreover, one whole day in every year is given over to this jesting deception. The civilized world over the first of April is fool's day. Wagner thinks that this custom arose from the change of the new year from the vernal equinox to 1 January, thus giving to the customary exchange of New Year's gifts the character of jests, and to those who should forget the change of time the appearance of fools. So they are called *Aprilnarren, poisson d'Avril*, April fools, and in Scotland gowks.

Memory forms another important division of our subject. The child's natural impulse is easily aroused by new and striking peculiarities – for instance, he soon learns by example to stammer, to talk through his nose, to imitate any other defect without at first intending to tease. When his mimicry is laughed at he attempts intentional caricature, yet we are not to suppose from this that he would never do so alone. As a rule, though, it is the amusement of adults which stimulates him to improve on his former efforts. And as soon as he perceives that his victim is annoyed his mimicry becomes teasing. At school this sort of teasing attacks unmercifully any little weakness or peculiarity, such as a halting or limping gait, stammering or lisping speech, a strange accent or foreign pronunciation. All these become the objects of ridiculous exaggeration even in the presence of older persons if they show no signs of disapproval. In our club in the high school there was a boy who ran his words together in a comical fashion, and from imitating his manner of speech we constructed a formal language, some words of which still survive in the memories of his contemporaries. The most important sphere of this sort of imitation is that of pictorial art, where the caricaturist seeks to amuse by his exaggerated representations of familiar peculiarities. Children attempt this too. Their efforts are at first, of course, the grossest deformities with projecting ears, huge noses, etc., which they label with the name of some comrade whom they wish to annoy, but later when they have learned to draw they achieve some creditable caricaturing. I well remember our portrait of a French teacher who had two deep lines from the base of his nose to the corners of his mouth, forming with his long nose the letter M. Such pictures are, of course, not to be classed with methods of teasing unless the intention is to show them to the subject, which is by no means always the case, and unless their *raison d'être* is something less than serious malice or hatred. There is always a charm in wielding, under the safe refuge of anonymity, these effective weapons against the mighty of the earth. What has not the nose of Napoleon III, for instance, suffered in this way!

Love-play

Is there such a thing as playful application of the sexual impulse? Views of this subject differ widely, and the remarks on it of animal observers show that many hesitate to use the term 'play' in this connection. Wundt says:

The distinction has been made between fighting play and love-play, and such actions and expressions as, for instance, the cooing of doves, the calls of singing birds, etc., have been interpreted as wooings. But these wooings are quite seriously intended by the bird, and I do not think that we can regard them as in any sense playful.

On the other hand, others can be cited who assure us that most observers agree in ascribing to singing birds, besides their regular courtship, arts of song and flight, actions which have all the marks by which Wundt himself characterizes play – namely, enjoyment, repetition and pretence. However, we shall find that it is in man that play with the function in question is most clearly exhibited and, as its connection with art has already been referred to, it will be sufficient to dwell on one aspect of it here – namely, its relation to poetry. However derogatory it may be considered to condition poetic art on such stimuli, the fact is incontestable that, deprived of their influence, the tree of poetry would be stripped of its verdant living dress.

On the other hand, we must avoid the older and more common error of speaking about the 'sweet sportiveness of love' without distinguishing between what is really playful and what is quite seriously meant. It is true that such popular usages of speech have not become general without some foundation in fact, and it may prove interesting to inquire how this one arose. We find the element of truth in the popular feeling by comparing the subject under discussion with eating and drinking, which are also sensuous pleasures. Why do we not hear so much of play in their exercise? Evidently there is a difference. While in eating and drinking, so far as directed by hunger, the real end, the preservation of life, is always in view, the real end of lovers' dalliance, namely, the preservation of the species, is far in the background. It is true that we sometimes eat and drink for the enjoyment it gives, as well as to satisfy hunger and renew our strength, yet the practical bearing of the act is so closely and inseparably connected with it that only under very special circumstances can we speak of it as playful. It is quite otherwise with the caresses and the traffic of love. Here the practical results are so far removed and the things in themselves are so enjoyable that such language is quite justified.

Birds have many familiar courtship arts which are hereditary (the isolated adult bird displays almost as much capacity in this direction as does one reared with his kind), but mammals exhibit much less of it. In relation to man there is a theory that sex grounds all art (of this we shall speak later), but a scientific system of comparative courtship of the various human races does not exist; nor, indeed, have we systematic observations of any one people. It is therefore impossible to affirm whether there are such things as instinctive gestures, expressions, caresses, etc., which all human beings recognize as sexual stimuli. From the little that is known it seems probable that the number of such tokens is not great – even the kiss is by no means general! We can only be sure of a universal tendency to approach and to touch one another, and of a disposition to self-exhibition and coquetry as probably instinctive, and of the special forms which these tendencies take under the influence of imitation and tradition as secondary causes. Caressing contact may then be regarded as a play when it is an end in itself, which is possible under two conditions: first, when the pursuance of the instinctive movements to their legitimate end is prevented by incapacity or ignorance; and, second, when it is prevented by an act of will on the part of the participants. Children exhibit the first case, adults often enough the second.

It is generally known that children are frequently very early susceptible to sexual excitement, and show a desire for contact with others as well as enjoyment of it, without having the least suspicion of its meaning. Keller gives a beautiful and touching example of this in his *Romeo und Julia auf dem Dorfe*:

On a tiny plot of ground all covered with green herbs the little lass lay down upon her back, for she was tired, and began to croon some words in a monotonous way, while the boy sat near her and joined in the song, almost wishing to follow her example, so weary and languid he felt. The sun shone into the open mouth of the singing girl, gleaming on her teeth so dazzlingly white and shining through the full red lips. The boy noticed this, and taking her head in his hands he examined the little teeth curiously and cried, 'Guess how many teeth you have?' She reflected for a moment, as though making a careful calculation, and then said with conviction, 'A hundred.' 'No; thirty-two,' he answered; 'but wait till I count again.' Then he counted aloud, but as he did not make thirty-two he had to begin over several times. The little girl kept still for some time, but as the zealous enumerator seemed never to get any nearer the end of his task she shook him off at last and cried, 'I will count yours.' So the boy stretched himself on the grass with the girl above him, throwing his head back while she counted 1, 2, 7, 5, 2; but the task was too hard for the little beauty, and the boy had to teach and correct her, so she too had to begin over and over again. This play seemed to please them better than any they had had that day. But at last the little girl slid down by the side of her small instructor, and the children slept together in the bright sunshine.

From such tender, unconscious premonitions we pass to more strongly marked love-plays, for which the services of a special instructor are usually necessary, as in the somewhat peculiar relation of the boy Rousseau to the little Goton who played the part of teacher in their private interviews:

Elle se permettait avec moi les plus grandes privautés, sans jamais m'en permettre aucune avec elle; elle me traitait exactement en enfant: ce qui me fait croire, ou qu'elle avait déjà cessé de l'être ou qu'au contraire elle l'était encore assez elle-même pour ne voir qu'un jeu dans le péril auquel elle s'exposait.

Often, too, children show the same sort of preference, all unconscious of its import, towards particular favourites among their grown-up friends, enjoying the pleasure of contact for its own sake. 'The pretty girl,' says Mantegazza,

whom Nature has endowed with the power to awaken longings and sighs at her every step, often does not realize that in the swarm of her admirers there are boys scarcely yet past their childhood, who secretly kiss any flower on which she may chance to look, who are happy if they may steal like a thief into the room where the beauty has slept and may kiss the carpet that her foot has pressed; . . . and how seldom does she suspect, as her fingers play with the locks of the little fellow whose head rests on her knee, that his heart is beating audibly under her caressing touch!

Perez cites Valle's account of a ten-year-old boy who was in love with his older cousin.

Elle vient quelquefois m'agacer le cou, me ménacer les côtes de ses doigts longs. Elle rit, me caresse, m'embrasse; je la serre en me défendant et je l'ai mordue une fois. Elle m'a crié: Petit méchant! en me donnant une tape sur la joue un peu fort, etc.

This feeling may be involved in some of the positions and movements of tussling boys. Schaeffer has remarked in a short paper that in the belligerent plays of boys, especially ring fighting, 'the fundamental impulse of sexual life for the utmost extensive and intensive contact, with a more or less clearly defined idea of conquest underlying it', plays a most conspicuous part. I do not believe that this is the rule, yet I am convinced that Schaeffer's view is more often correct than would appear at a first glance, and especially so when the contestants are on the ground and laughingly struggle together.

Lastly, we must notice the absorbing friendships between children of the same sex. Here, too, the instinct, robbed of its proper aim, may assume a sportive, playful air. Even among students, friendships are not rare in which the unsatisfied impulse plays its part all unknown to the subjects.

I suppose the general playfulness of the foregoing instances might be called in question on the ground that there is no consciousness that it is all a play, no sham activity. Yet we refer complacently enough to other things which display quite as little of such subconsciousness as play. Indeed, the rule is that it is absent from mental play, and, moreover, this is a case that more closely concerns the emotions. The plays which involve subjective sham activity overlap to a great extent the sphere of the objective ones where the man or animal takes pleasure in action which has no necessary actual aim, yet without being conscious of having turned aside from the life of cause and effect. If we admit that the boy careering aimlessly about is playing because he enjoys the movement for its own sake, or that gourmands who eat without hunger, and merely to tickle their palates, are playing, then we must also call it play when the child takes pleasure in the sexual sensations arising from touch stimuli without knowing that his activity, on account of the exclusion of their proper end, is all a sham.

With adults the subjective side of play is more prominent, especially when the proper end of the instinctive impulse for contact is held in abeyance by the will of the participants. Here belongs the dalliance of engaged couples. It is no play, of course, when the lovers, on the first revelation of their common feeling or after a long separation, indulge in a passionate embrace. But when in their daily intercourse that manifold trifling begins which is too familiar to need description, I see no reason why it should not be called play with touch stimuli. The more naïve the period or social class the more common this is. In the free intercourse of the sexes in medieval baths the jesting caresses must often have been quite rough. While many of the pictorial representations of such bathing scenes are doubtless exaggerated, still they could not have been pure inventions. The description by the Florentine Poggio (1417) of Swiss bathing customs bears them out. He expressly says:

It is remarkable to see how innocent they are; how unsuspiciously men will look on while their wives are handled by strangers, . . . while they gambol and romp with each other and sometimes without other company; yet the husbands are not disturbed nor surprised at anything because they know that it is all done in an innocent, harmless way.

In feudal times it was the custom for noble gentlemen to be served in the bath by young women, to be washed by them, and afterward rubbed. At the spinning *fêtes* the young couples 'played', as a Christmas piece has it, with all sorts of hand clasping and stroking. But the most remarkable proceeding of this kind was the 'lovers' night of continence', observed in various countries, including France, Italy and Germany, by knightly devotees whose lady permitted them to pass one night at her side, trusting to their oath and honour not to take advantage of her kindness. This strange custom, so shocking to our ideas of propriety, was doubtless derived from similar practices of very ancient origin among the peasantry, the chastity of whose girls was rarely violated in spite of the utmost intimacies. It is interesting to find an ethnological analogue to this among the Zulus. According to Fritsch, the custom of *Uku-hlobonga* obtains there,

in which the young bachelors join the maidens of the neighbourhood, and these latter choose their mates, each according to her pleasure. The rejected swains have to bear the scorn of the whole company, while the chosen ones recline with their sweethearts, and an imitation of the sexual function is gone through with. Yet, as a rule, the girl by force and threats prevents anything more serious!

The psychological standpoint

Here in the first place we are called upon to apply a psychological criterion to playful activity. Wundt, in his lectures on the human and animal soul, suggests three such criteria: first, the pleasurable effect; second, the conscious or unconscious copying of useful activities; and third, the reproduction of the original aim in a playful one. As I have said before, I do not regard the second of these – namely, imitation – as universally a mark of play. Wundt says that an animal can play only when certain memories which are accompanied by pleasurable feeling are renewed, yet under aspects so transformed that all painful effects vanish and only agreeable ones remain; the simple and spontaneous play of animals being, so to speak, association plays. Thus the dog, at the sight of another dog which displays no unfriendly feeling towards him, just as naturally feels a disposition to the agreeable exercise of his awakened powers as to fight with his fellows. Kittens which for the first time try to catch a moving ball, are not playing according to this view, and only play when the action is repeated for the sake of the pleasure it gives. I shall return to this conception, which includes more than simple imitation in its ordinary sense. I feel that I have not succeeded in conveying all that Wundt means in the passage cited from. However, if I understand him aright, he attempts in the last edition of his published works to explain imitation in quite another way. Thus he gives that name to the play of young dogs which, without having seen it done, seize a piece of cloth in the teeth and shake it violently, because such play exhibits the playful activity of former generations. This is a hardly justifiable use of the word, and I think it better to admit at once that imitation, as commonly understood, is not a criterion of play.

The case is entirely different with the 'apparent aim' or sham activity. It is undeniable that, objectively considered, such play appears to be detached from the real, practically directed life of the individual, and Wundt, too, understands it so. No one plays to attain what is a real object of effort outside of the sphere of play. All the objects of play lie within its own bounds, and even games of chance keep in view the aim to promote strong excitement in the parties to the wager until the decision. Since, then, we must consider sham activity as a genuine projection from earnest life, it becomes a universal criterion. This is not contradicted by the fact that playful activity is of great value to the individual, since the value of the play is not the player's motive.

The question respecting the illusion-working character of playful activity is much more difficult to meet, if the psychical processes of the playing subject are kept in view, and the inquiry is pressed as to whether the actual sham quality of the play is reflected in his mental states. Here it must be emphasized that actual consciousness of fulfilling a merely ideal purpose, of being engaged in sham occupation, is not at all essential to imitative play, and is wanting altogether in experimentation and fighting plays. Consequently it too fails as a universal criterion of play. Later we shall inquire whether in much play the objective sham character may not influence the psychic condition of the player in another way.

There remain, then, as general psychological criteria of play, only two more of the elements popularly regarded as essential – namely, its pleasurableness and the actual severance from life's serious aims. . . In short, activity performed for its own sake.

I proceed after this introduction to inquire into the character of the pleasure derived from play. It is the most universal of all the psychological accompaniments of play, resting as it does on the satisfaction of inborn impulses. The sensorimotor and mental capacities (of the latter, attention pre-eminently), fighting and sexual impulses, imitation and the social instincts press for discharge, and lead to enjoyment when they find it in play. To this simple statement of fact we must subjoin the not unimportant consideration which Baldwin has suggested in his preface to *The Play of Animals*. He distinguishes two distinct kinds of play: one 'not psychological at all', and exhibiting only the biological criterion of practice for, not exercise of, the impulse; and the other, which is psychological as well and involves conscious self-deception. The situation, he says, is like that displayed in many other animal and human functions which are at once biologic and instinctive, as well as psychologic and intelligent; for example, sympathy, fear and bashfulness. This last statement is unquestionable, but there is room for doubt whether the previous assumed difference exists. Baldwin's grounds for the distinction seem to me to be inconclusive, in that conscious self-deception is by no means the only nor the most universal psychic accompaniment of play, the most elementary of them all being the enjoyment derived for the satisfaction of an instinct, which makes play an object for psychology, where conscious self-deception is out of the question. But the further question is suggested whether the biological conception of play has not a still deeper grasp than the psychological, and to this extent the proposed distinction is of value.

It may be assumed of young animals, and probably of children, that the first manifestations of what is afterwards experimentation, fighting and imitative play, etc., is rarely conscious, and consequently we cannot assert with assurance that it is pleasurable. Therefore the biological but not the psychological germ of play is present. It was in this sense that I intended my previous remarks to the effect that actual imitation was not an indispensable condition of play, while repetition possibly could be considered so, since the impulsive movements must be repeated frequently and at last performed for the sake alone of the pleasure derived from them, before play ensues. This marks the psychological limits of play.

To make the relation clearer, let us take the grasping movement as an example. The child at first waves his hands aimlessly, and when his fingers chance to strike a suitable object they clutch at it instinctively. From a purely biological point of view this is practice of an instinct, and play has already begun. Psychologically, on the contrary, it is safer to defer calling the movements playful until through repetition they acquire the character of conscious processes accompanied by attention and enjoyment. This distinction, I think, is a proper one, and it enables the biologist to pursue the idea further than the psychologist would be justified in doing. Therefore I cannot recognize any activity as playful in the most complete sense which does not exhibit the psychological criterion as well. Examples of such plays may be found scattered all through the systematic parts of this work, and at the beginning of the section on contact plays.

In examining somewhat more closely the nature of the feeling of pleasure which springs from the satisfaction of an inborn instinct we may assume as a general law that it is threefold: first, there is pleasure in the stimulus as such; then in the agreeableness of the stimulus; and, third, in its intensity. The first is due to the fact that a set of hereditary impulses press for such expression; it is superfluous to attempt to prove that there are special stimuli inherently pleasurable; it is only the third class, then, that need demand our attention, and this we have repeatedly encountered in our excursions into the various departments of play. It would be well worthwhile to devote a monograph to the investigation of its meaning and grounds in the light of the literature of the past. Probably a variety of causes would be brought to light, among which, however, the influence of habit would be prominent, since attention and enjoyment would need constantly stronger stimuli. The most valuable contribution to the subject seems to me that of Lessing in pursuance of Du Bos's idea. He says that the violent emotion produced by the feeling heightened reality is the occasion of the pleasurable effect. But whence comes this feeling? Its origin is sufficiently clear in movement-play, where intense stimulus is connected with the violent exertion of physical powers; but how is it with receptive play? In the eighteenth century it was said, on the ground of Leibnitz's psychology, that what we regard as receptive play was the soul's spontaneous activity. The strong emotion resulting betokened a development of force which is always a satisfaction. This view quite naturally lends itself to modern psychological terms now that we can put our finger on the strong internal motor processes involved; yet it is limited by observation, which shows that intensive stimuli taking possession of us, so to speak, in spite of ourselves, are not invariably cherished as pleasures. Only when we voluntarily seek the strong feeling, and gladly yield ourselves to it so that the emotion it produces is in a measure our own work, do we enjoy the result. The conditions are the same as with the pleasure in power displayed in violent movement plays, and they may be treated together.

Among the many inborn necessities which ground our pleasure in play we find again that three is the number emphasized by psychology – namely, the exercise of attention, the demand for an efficient cause, and imagination. As regards attention, I have already said in the biological discussion that it seems calculated to lend a definite meaning to the vague idea of a general need for activity. The examples of practice in attention which were introduced in the section on experimentation with the higher mental powers were chosen with a view to illustrating mental tension, and special stress was laid on the fact that, apart from these limitations, attention is of the widest and most comprehensive significance. Indeed, fully developed play in the psychological sense is scarcely conceivable without the simultaneous exercise of motor or theoretic attention. From the first sensory and motor play of infants, straight through to aesthetic enjoyment and artistic production, its tension is felt, and when the opportunity is not afforded for its satisfactory exercise a pitiable condition of boredom ensues, the unendurableness of which Schopenhauer has so exhaustively described.

The desire to be an efficient cause also has a motor and a theoretic form. We demand a knowledge of effects and to be ourselves the producers of effects, and it is through this motor form that the theoretic, if not exactly originated, is at least perfected. Hence the root idea of causal connection depends on volition, and Schopenhauer, in referring force to the will, has only expressed in his metapysical way an established psychological fact. This motor impulse finds expression in the joy in being a cause, which I regard as so essential to play, and in conjunction with attention is probably the source of the impulse for activity of which I have spoken. We must bear in mind all the forms of pleasure connected with movement, and especially motor experimental play, where, besides the mere enjoyment of motion in itself, there is the satisfaction of being oneself the originator of it, the joy-bringing sense of being a cause. Use of the sensory apparatus is a source of the same pleasure, since here, too, a motor condition is involved, and is accompanied with consciousness of its own activity; and when the inner imitation which we have described is also included, the connection with external movement is of course still closer. And in any case joy in being a cause is well-nigh universal, since in play no purpose is served apart from the act itself as impelled by inner impulse, which thus appears in the character of an independent cause more than in any other form of activity.

This joy in being a cause is susceptible of varied modification. In violent movements, and even in the receptive enjoyment of intense stimuli, it is converted into pleasure in the mere possession of power, and is proportionate to the magnitude of the results. It appears also in the form of emulation when a model is copied, and in imitative competition, the pleasure of surpassing others arises with enjoyment of pure success and victory, which, as we have seen, results as well from overcoming difficulties as from the subjugation of foes. All these ideas have been so often encountered in the systematic part of our work that merely directing them to their natural conclusions is all-sufficient here.

Of imagination, however, we must speak in greater detail in regard to its illusion-making power, which again brings us to the sham occupation recognized as such by the doer in a partly subjective manner. I am careful to limit this statement because it is evident that only a simple form of the phenomenon, and not its whole content, is present in such reflex forms of consciousness.

In many games there is a veritable playing of a role in which the players, like actors, are quite conscious all through the pretence that they are only 'making believe'. It is a genuine conscious state in which, on the one hand, the illusion is perfect, while on the other there is full knowledge that it is an illusion. Konrad Lange has called this condition one of conscious self-deception, a term which most aptly conveys the idea of the strange contradiction of inner processes. He limited the use of the term, however, to plays that depend on the imitative arts, while I have advanced the view in my *Play of Animals* that it is even more clearly exhibited in such fighting and hunting plays as are conducted independently of models, than in actual imitative play. But when it comes to human play I am forced to admit that speech discloses conscious self-deception in the imitative play of children where it might be doubtful in the case of animals.* Still I have other points of controversy with Lange. If imitation includes the conscious repetition of our own previous acts, as it may be an extension of the definition, then we are warranted in assuming conscious self-deception only with it. Thus, in fighting play, for instance, clear consciousness of playing a role can ensue only when previous experience has taught the players what are the serious manifestations of the fighting instinct. If, however, the narrower use of the word is adopted, illusion is more extensive than imitation, and, furthermore, the latter may exist without the former.

When, as I said before, there is a clear consciousness of sham activity, we may subscribe essentially to Lange's theory, with its oscillation between reality and appearance, since the enjoyment of illusion does alternate with the impression of reality. His figure of the swinging pendulum should not be taken too literally as implying measured regularity in the succession of states.† The essence of his meaning is that in self-illusion which is conscious, even the moments of most absolute abandon are followed by other moments of readjustment, and this is undeniably the case. Think, for instance, of the laughter of romping boys which serves to reassure the combatants by its implication that, in spite of appearances to the contrary, the fight is only playful.

But this does not fully explain the illusion of the players. Just as in aesthetic enjoyment we are for a long time entirely surrendered to the illusion without consciously recognizing the fact, so we find in play, and especially that of children, absorption and self-forgetfulness so complete that no room is left for the idea of oscillation. And when the illusion is so strong and so lasting, as is sometimes the case with little girls nursing their dolls, or with little boys playing soldier or robber, they can no more be said to see through the illusion than to alternate between it and reality. My own contribution to the solution of the problem is set forth in my earlier work in the section on hypnotic phenomena, more exhaustively than is possible here, where the points of view are so much more varied. I therefore content myself with the following partial elucidation:

If we may not assume consciousness of the illusion in complete absorption, nor yet any true alternative with reality, we are forced to the conclusion that the appearance produced by play differs essentially from the reality which it represents, and is incapable of producing genuine deception. Now this postulate seems to be borne out in a very obvious and striking

* Children show conscious self-illusion very clearly when they play something like this: 'Now I am playing that I am papa and have shot a lion.' etc.

† Note, however, the rhythmic action of attention, which frequently admits of 'coming to' at relatively regular intervals.

manner by the fact that sham activity and the pretended object are evidently symbolic, since they are never perfect duplicates of reality. Towards the most perfect imitation the playing child entertains feelings quite different from those called forth by a living creature. How, then, is there positive deception? But closer examination shows us that the solution is not so simple. If such external distinctions alone separated playful illusion from actual deception, the force of the former would inevitably decline as this difference increased. But the facts indicate exactly the contrary, as we may see illustrated by the little girl who takes a sofa pillow for a doll; the illusion is at least quite as great as when the toy is a triumph of imitative art. The child actually approaches the hypnotic state when she says that the pillow is a lady on the sofa, and chats with her. Though there is of course no actual deception, the reason for it must be looked for elsewhere than in any external difference from reality.

I believe its true basis to be the feeling of freedom which is closely connected with joy in being a cause. Not the clear idea, 'This is only pretence', but a subtle consciousness of free, voluntary acceptance of the illusion stamps even the deepest absorption in it with the seal *ipse feci* as a safeguard from error. If we accept E. von Hartman's aesthetic principle that to the consciousness which is sunk in illusion the apparent I is different from the real I of ordinary waking consciousness, then in illusion play the real I is supplanted by the apparent I. Yet pleasurable feelings which belong properly to the obscured real I may come over into the sphere of the apparent I and lend it to a specific character. As in the contemplation of beauty, enjoyment of sensuous pleasure passes into the sphere of apparant feeling, and lends to the object that regal brilliance which characterizes pure beauty, so in the wider field of illusion play, genuine pleasure in the voluntary transference to that world of appearances which transcends all the external aims of play, enters into the sham occupation and converts it into something higher, freer, finer, lighter, which the stress of objective events cannot impair. This effect of the feeling of freedom may advantageously be made the subject of personal observation. Before going to sleep at night it is easy to call up all sorts of faces and forms before the closed eyes and play with them, but as soon as the wearied consciousness lets slip the sense of being the cause of it all, we shrink from these phantoms, and playful illusion takes a serious turn.

Finally, through the feeling of freedom, the recreation theory attains a special psychological significance which is quite generally recognized. As soon as the individual has progressed far enough to realize the seriousness of life (and this probably happens in an unreflective sort of way to children too young to go to school) the liberty of play signifies to him relief from this pressure. The more earnest is a man's life, the more will he enjoy the refuge afforded by play when he can engage in sham occupations chosen at will, and unencumbered by serious aims. There he is released from the bondage of his work and from all the anxieties of life.

(From *The Play of Man*, translated by Elizabeth L. Baldwin, Heinemann, 1901.)

Psychology and Phylogeny

Konrad Lorenz presents a philosophical disquisition on curiosity, adaptation to varied circumstances, and openness to domestication where domestication entails the capacity for learning how to cope with patterns imposed from outside by man. At the apex of non-specialization, man requires a long period of youthful curiosity. But curiosity is not enough; there must be exploration which is a feature-extraction activity, and play which is an exercise in trying out new things in new settings. The Lorenz essay is a particularly succinct justification of the role of play in maintaining openness in higher species.

Specialization in non-specialization and curiosity

Arnold Gehlen (1940) refers to man as the 'deficient organism', expressing the opinion that human beings – owing to the lack of special morphological adaptations – have been driven to the production of tools, weapons, clothes and the like. This is not considered in biological terms – there is no such thing as a non-adapted organism, or at least where such occur they are individuals bearing lethal factors and doomed to succumb. Gehlen also overlooks the fact that the *brain* with its enormous size, represents a very tangible special morphological adaptation. Nevertheless, his tenet contains something fundamentally correct and important: an organism with pronounced, specialized morphological adaptations would never have been able to evolve into man. Perhaps we might have a clearer view of the significance of the *lack* of special adaptations if we change our standpoint and consider the *versatility* of an organism lacking special adaptations. Take, for example, a comparison of some fairly closely related rodents with extensive specializations in different directions: the jerboa (running adaptation), the flying squirrel (climbing and flying adaptation), the mole rat (adaptation for subterranean life) and the beaver (swimming adaptation) with a non-specialized rodent (the Norway rat). The latter greatly exceeds any of the four specialists in the three activities for which the given specialist is *not* specialized, and exceeds it even more in ultimate biological success – number of individuals and distribution of the species. If we now compare purely physical (i.e. completely non-intellectual) activities of *man*, with respect to versatility, against those of mammals of roughly the same size, we find that human beings are by no means as fragile and deficient as one might think. For example, if one sets the following three tasks – walking 22 miles in one day; climbing 15 feet up on a rope; and swimming 15 yards under water at a depth of 12 feet, accurately picking up a number of objects from the substrate (all activities which a quite unsportive armchair human being – such as myself – can perform without difficulty) – *there is no single mammal which can make the same performance.*

In addition, the lack of special adaptations in body structure is always accompanied by extremely characteristic *behavioural* versatility. Highly-specialized organs always require a central nervous system differentiated in the same direction, incorporating *instinctive motor patterns* and usually even more highly specialized *innate releasing mechanisms* which direct each instinctive motor pattern towards its specially defined object. Non-specialists, on the other hand, only possess a few instinctive motor patterns with a small degree of differentiation and thus with a *far more general range of applicability* than the wonderfully differentiated patterns of a specially adapted organism. Even less specialized and selective are the innate releasing mechanisms, which set the unspecialized instinctive motor patterns in operation. With an inexperienced young animal, these mechanisms respond repeatedly in a great variety of environmental situations. It is *exploratory, latent learning* which directs the performance of the pattern towards *specific*, appropriate objects. In order to illustrate this, I shall take from the class of the birds two extreme types – one specialist and one non-specialist. It is no chance effect that the former is the most stupid and the latter one of the cleverest of birds.

In the environment of the great crested grebe (*Podiceps cristatus* Pontopp), almost everything to which the bird responds (the water-surface, the prey, the nest-site, etc.) is already predetermined down to the smallest detail in the inexperienced young bird by highly specialized innate releasing mechanisms, which elicit equally special instinctive motor patterns with a wonderful degree of adaptation. The bird does not need to learn much additional information – in fact it *cannot.* For example, the innate releasing mechanisms for prey-catching and eating require the movement of the fish, and the bird never learns to eat a sufficient quantity of dead fish, even when these are utterly fresh and would be physiologically quite adequate for the metabolic requirements. Adaptability in the bird's behaviour is largely restricted to path-conditioning, which serves in the location of places and situations in which the innate action and response patterns 'fit'. By contrast, there is virtually nothing predetermined in the behaviour of a young raven (*Corvus corax* L.), with the exception of a few instinctive behaviour patterns with great versatility of application. These patterns are employed with *all unknown objects.* The raven first approaches such an object with an extremely high level of *flight motivation.* The raven literally spends several days carefully eyeing the object before approaching it. The first active interaction is very commonly represented by a powerful blow with the beak; the raven instantly flees and observes the effect of this action from an elevated perch. Only when these security measures have carefully been applied does the bird begin to try out the instinctive motor patterns of *predation*. The object is turned in every direction with prising movements of the beak, it is grasped in the claws, pecked with the beak, plucked, torn to pieces if possible, and – finally and without fail – concealed. Living animals are always approached from behind by the young raven and with even greater care than for inanimate objects. It may take weeks before the approach is close enough to permit a vigorous jab with the beak. If the animal then flees, the raven immediately follows with increased courage and kills it, if it can. However, if the animal actively attacks, the raven withdraws and soon loses interest. The innate releasing mechanisms which elicit all this trial-and-error behaviour have an extraordinarily low degree of selectivity. It is only with the handling of living animals that there are evidently mechanisms available to tell the inexperienced raven 'which is the back and which the front'. The oriented attack on the back of the head and the eyes of other animals also seems to be directed by innate orienting mechanisms. But this more or less completely exhausts the innate instinctive equipment which the raven possesses for interaction with the extra-specific environment. The rest is achieved by exploratory learning and the overpowering *greed* for new objects (curiosity). The strength of this curiosity is demonstrated by the following fact: when all the strangest attractants – raw eggs and living grasshoppers – failed, I could always lure my ravens into their cage by placing my *camera* inside . . . an object which they were never allowed to investigate for obvious reasons. With our mongoose, my brother's doctorate diploma played the same role for similar reasons.

The undoubtedly great survival value of this curiosity behaviour is doubtless based on the fact that the animal quite generally treats *everything* as being of potential biological significance. As we have seen, there is a series of treatment ranging from that appropriate to predators, to that suitable for prey and food, and this exists until thorough self-conditioning has taught the animal whether a given object is significant as predator, prey or food . . . or of no significance at all. Objects which the raven has 'rendered intimate' through the application of all motor patterns concerned with predators, prey and foods and which have been 'set aside' as of no significance (to use Gehlen's fitting expression) can be *returned to* at any later date. For example, objects which have acquired an indifferent status in this way can be employed to cover a food-morsel for concealment, or may simply be used as perches.

The method of inquisitive experimentation with all possibilities has the automatic consequence that such specialists in non-specialization can maintain an existence in a *wide range* of environments, since they find sooner or later everything which they need to survive. On bird-inhabited islands, the raven leads a life very similar to that of skuas and other such parasites upon the great colonies of sea-birds, feeding upon eggs, offspring and transported food. In the desert, on the other hand, a raven lives just like a vulture, sailing along in thermal up-currents and searching for afflicted animals. Finally, in Central Europe the raven exists as a predator of small animals and insects.

Among the mammals, the Norway rat (*Epimys norvegicus* L.) is the prototype of a non-specialized creature of curiosity. One of its most prominent characteristics is the tendency towards inquisitive 'learning-by-heart' of all possible *pathways* in a given area – in particular escape pathways leading back to its retreat. In this case, too, 'return' to pathways which had originally been set aside as insignificant can be very neatly demonstrated. The expression *latent learning* is particularly appropriate here. Within the canal system of a maze, the rat at first crawls along *all* of the pathways, but later ceases to use those 'which lead to nothing'. However, if one later slightly alters the conditions (e.g. by changing the site of the food-area), it becomes evident that the animal has by no means forgotten what it has 'filed'. The most efficient revised pathways are not learned afresh; the rat can, when so required, make use of its latent knowledge. With the rat, the biological success of an unspecialized creature of curiosity is particularly evident. This animal literally occurs everywhere where civilized man has travelled. It lives in the holds of ships just as in the canals of big towns; it thrives in farmers' barns, and it can even live independently of man, occurring on islands as the only terrestrial mammal. Everywhere it is found, the rat behaves as if it were a specialist in its element.

All higher vertebrates which are *cosmopolitan* are typical unspecialized creatures of curiosity, and man is undoubtedly one of their number. Human beings also construct their 'significant environment' through active, dialectic interaction with the extra-specific environment, and thus we are also able to adapt to such a wide variety of environmental conditions that many authors are of the opinion that one can no longer refer to a human 'environment' in the sense understood by von Uexküll (1909). However, I merely wish to demonstrate the close fundamental *relationship* between this active, dialectic construction and dismemberment of the environment and the curiosity behaviour of the animals mentioned.

The most outstanding and essential character of curiosity behaviour is its *objectivity*. On observing a raven with a novel object, first conducting exploratory 'security measures' and then trying out one after the other all the instinctive motor patterns concerned in predation, one is at first inclined to think that the bird's entire activity is ultimately to be interpreted as *appetitive behaviour* for food-uptake. However, it can easily be shown that this is not the case. In the first place, the inquisitive investigation is at once abandoned when the raven is genuinely hungry: it immediately turns to an already familiar food-source. Young ravens exhibit their most intensive phase of curiosity behaviour immediately after fledging, i.e. at a time when the youngsters are still fed by their parents. If they become hungry, they follow the parental bird (or human foster-parent) in an insistent manner, and they *only* exhibit interest for unknown objects when they are satiated. Secondly, when the raven is moderately, though still demonstrably, hungry, the appetite for unknown objects prevails over that for the best available food. If one offers a tit-bit to a young raven actively engaged in investigating an unknown object, the tit-bit is almost always ignored. In human terms, this means: the bird does not *want* to eat, it wants to *know* whether the particular object is 'theoretically' edible. The young raven conducting its 'investigations' is not motivated to eat, and in the same way a young Norway rat repeatedly dashing back to the entrance of its retreat from various points within its range is not motivated to flee. This very *independence* of the exploratory learning process from momentary *requirements*, in other words from the *motive of the appetite*, is extremely important. Bally (1945) regards it as the major characteristic of *play* that behaviour patterns really belonging in the area of appetitive behaviour are performed 'in a field released from tension'. As we have seen, the field released from tension – a *sine qua non* for all curiosity behaviour just as for play – is an extremely important common feature of the two kinds of behaviour!

Independence of a momentary drive goal governing the animal's actions has the effect that *different* properties of the object relevant to different drive goals are simultaneously 'rendered intimate' and 'filed'. These 'files' remain as engrams in the animal's central nervous system, evidently arranged according to objects. It is only objectivating recognition of the objects – requiring the entire arsenal of perceptual constancy phenomena – which permits the animal to 'return' to objects and exploit their latently learned properties. This demonstrably occurs when an appetite occurs in a serious functional context. Through this process of learning the properties attached to *things*, independently of the momentary physiological condition and requirements of the organism, curiosity behaviour has an *objectivating function in the most literal and important sense of the word. It is only through curiosity behaviour that objects come to exist in the environment of an animal as in that of man.* In this sense, Gehlen is quite right in stating that man constructs his environment himself, since his environment is an objective one! However, this is also true of all unspecialized creatures of curiosity, though to a lesser extent.

A second constitutive property of curiosity behaviour lies in the fact that the organism *does* something in order to *experience*. In fact, this behaviour incorporates no more and no less than the principle of the *question*. An organism which 'constructs objects' through its curiosity behaviour, determining the properties inherent in an object by means of its own, active efforts, to some extent maintains a *dialectic* relationship to extra-subjective reality. And this – as Baumgarten (1950) correctly emphasized – is one of the most important characteristics of mankind.

From this dialectic interaction with objects, man has developed a function which, like language, is scarcely indicated even in the highest animals. When a human being works on an object, this function is based on the fact that *in the course of* this activity, the 'response' of the object is continuously registered and that further activity is steered accordingly. For example, when a nail is being hammered into something, each blow of the hammer must compensate for the unnoticeable lateral deviation imparted to the nail by the previous blow. Anybody not familiar with animals, who – despite exaggerated ideas of the peculiarity of man – habitually imagines higher animals to be far more similar to man than they are, does not generally realize that the ability for such activity regulated through continuous observation of the success is almost completely lacking even among anthropoid apes.

This is particularly evident in the chimpanzee's crate-piling activity. The animal places one crate on top of the other, but never straightens them up; the most that happens is that when one crate overlaps considerably on one side, the next may possibly be placed somewhat further to the opposite side in compensation. That is all. The foremost achievement in this direction so far known was exhibited by Köhler's chimpanzee Sultan, which gnawed at a detached wooden wall-strip until it could be inserted into the hollow of a bamboo-tube in order to extend its sectional 'fishing-rod'. The chimp repeatedly tested to see whether the strip of wood was thin enough, and continued to gnaw until this was actually the case. However, in order to manufacture a genuine tool, such as a hand-axe, incomparably greater differentiation of continuous success-control of behaviour is necessary. In fact, it seems that this intimate connection between action and recognition, between *praxis* and *gnosis*, requires a *special central organ* which only man possesses – in the *Gyrus supramarginalis* of the temporal lobe of the brain. If this area of the brain, which (significantly) also incorporates the 'speech centre', is damaged, the human being exhibits – in addition to speech disruption – certain omissions in activity and recognition ('*apraxia*' and '*agnosia*'). It has not yet been possible (Klüver, 1933) to demonstrate the existence of similar centres in monkeys, nor to provoke similar omissions.

Although I have, in the foregoing, contrasted the raven and the rat (as typical unspecialized creatures of curiosity) with the great crested grebe (as an instinct and organ specialist), this does not mean that curiosity behaviour is completely lacking in other, somewhat more highly specialized organisms. The role played by *curiosity learning* is dependent not only on the lack of specialization, but also upon the general level of differentiation of the central nervous system. A young orang-utan greatly exceeds the raven and the rat in the achievements of its exploratory learning, although this species is extremely highly specialized in certain directions. Assume that one is observing a young anthropoid ape – preferably a chimpanzee – performing its magnificently logical object-directed curiosity behaviour, which exhibits the character of *play* even more than that of the raven or rat. One would be repeatedly amazed by the fact that, for all this remarkably intelligent – almost creative – experimentation, nothing *more* emerges than the knowledge as to which nuts can be cracked, which branches can be climbed and (at the most) which stick is best suited for fishing for objects. When I observe how such a young animal plays with building blocks or places boxes inside one another, I am repeatedly struck with the suspicion that these creatures were, in the distant past, once of *much higher intelligence* than they are today, and that in the course of their specialization they have *lost* abilities which now only appear as a silhouette in the young animals' play!

One thing in fact fundamentally distinguishes the curiosity behaviour of *all* animals from that of man: it is restricted to a brief developmental phase in young animals. What the raven acquires in early life with its so human-like experimentation soon rigidifies into conditioned patterns which are later so invariable and adaptable that they are scarcely distinguishable from instinctive behaviour. The need for novelty gives way to a pronounced aversion to all unknown things. An adult raven, and not just a really old one, which is forced to make a basic change in its environment is quite incapable of finding its way in the new situation and falls into a neurotic fear state in which it is even unable to recognize a well-acquainted keeper. A raven which has just reached maturity behaves in such a situation very much like a man suffering from senile dementia. A senile man, whose loss of adaptability is inconspicuous as long as he is in familiar surroundings, immediately exhibits extensive dementia when forced to change his surroundings. In order to avoid misunderstandings, it must be explicitly emphasized that it is not learning ability itself which has been eradicated, but the positive orientation to the unknown. For example, an old raven is perfectly able to learn that a given novel situation is dangerous from a single, unpleasant experience. But this learning process only occurs subject to the immediate compulsion of a quite specific, biologically relevant situation. Old rats or old anthropoid apes do actually behave in a more plastic manner than old ravens, but in principle the gulf between the young and the old animal is the same.

In reply to Herder's question, 'What does the animal most similar to man – the ape – lack that prevented it from becoming man?', we can now provide two quite specific answers. Although spatial representation and insight are already present to an almost human degree of development, although the obligate bond between spatial intention and action existing in other animals is broken, and although there is a true dialectic, inquisitive, objectivating interaction with the environment (at least in the young animal) . . . the anthropoid ape *lacks*: *firstly* the intimate reciprocal relationship between action and recognition (praxis and gnosis), which permits activity continuously controlled by success and which can apparently only be ensured by the appropriate human centre in the *gyrus supramarginalis*, so that the ape also lacks a basic precondition for speech; *secondly*, in the fully-grown, mature Pongid, there is almost complete absence of curiosity behaviour which in human beings remains active up to the onset of senility. Only the human being continues to *develop* up to old age.

Domestication and openness to surroundings

The domestication of certain animal species is the oldest biological experiment conducted by mankind. For this reason alone, this experiment is better suited than any for aiding the synthesis between evolutionary and genetic theory. One commonly uses the term 'domesticated' for a race of animals when it is distinguished from the free-living ancestral type on a number of typical, hereditary characters which have been developed in the course of domestication. Almost all domestic animals exhibit mottling, shortening of the extremities and the skullbase; reduction in tautness of the connective tissue (leading to formation of flabby lobes, drooping ears, reduction in muscular tonus and the like), a tendency to fattening, and – above all – a quite general and considerable increase in the range of variation of species characteristics. In the expression of these, and many other, characters of domestication, even widely different domestic animals show remarkably extensive parallels. For example, hybridization experiments show that even with species belonging to separate families (e.g. the Muscovy duck, *Cairina moschata* L., and the mallard, *Anas platyrhynchos*), mottling, drooping belly and other characters are based on homologous hereditary loci. One might possibly be inclined to think that similar environmental conditions (e.g. limitation of freedom of movement; scarcity of air and light; imbalanced, vitamin-impoverished and yet copious food, etc.) have favoured homologous mutations. However, this would definitely seem to be a false assumption; instead the blame for appearance of these characters seems to be exclusively due to the removal of natural selection. According to Herre's observations, the Northern European reindeer (*Rangifer tarandus*) seems to exhibit virtually all the typical domestication characteristics, although admittedly in less extreme form. This, despite the fact that this animal lives in its original environment and in complete freedom. Its environmental conditions differ from those of the wild form in (not even thorough) protection from wolves and a certain selection of breeding stags; the Laps in fact castrate the strongest stags in order to reduce their animosity.

Other organisms which are, so to speak, 'self-domesticated' (the cave-bear and man) demonstrate that close confinement and deficiency phenomena are not responsible for the production of the described changes in the hereditary complement. The cave-bear would appear to have been the 'Lord of the Earth' at the time of its greatest distribution, as man is now. It is, in any case, difficult to imagine that any other carnivore was at that time dominant over the powerful cave-bear. And this species in fact exhibited, in the apparent heyday immediately prior to its disappearance, typical domestication characteristics. In the 'Drachenhöhle' (dragon's cave) near Mixnitz in Steiermark, there were many cave-bear skeletons heaped together which exhibited virtually all of the changes which the domestic dog has undergone in the process of domestication. There are giant bears alongside dwarf ones, long-legged animals with a markedly greyhound-like head alongside some whose shortened skulls are strikingly reminiscent of bulldogs, and whose abbreviated legs are similar to those of a dachshund. One needs little palaeobiological imagination to picture the possessors of these skulls as having dangling ears and spotty coats when they were alive.

The fact that man also exhibits genuine domestication characteristics was, interestingly enough, first noticed by Schopenhauer. He clearly states that the blue eyes and the light skin of the European are 'far from natural' and that they are 'analogous to white mice, or at least to white horses'. It is especially noteworthy that there is a fine biological sense expressed in the words 'at least'! Eugen Fischer pointed out a long, long time ago that the kind of pigment-distribution found in the blue or grey human eye does not occur in one single free-living animal species, and yet is found in exactly the same form in almost *all* domestic animals. It is, no doubt, unnecessary to expound further on the predominant occurrence of typical domestication characteristics in modern man. Anybody who has eyes to see such things sees them as a self-evident fact of life, and nobody would doubt their inherent identity with those exhibited by animals.

It is quite certain that a number of domestication-induced changes belong among the pre-conditions for human evolution, which are lacking in modern anthropoid apes. The most important among them is the developmental inhibition referred to by Bolk as *retardation* or *foetalization*, which fixates juvenile characteristics of the wild form as persistent adult characters. I can see no reason why one should not employ the term *neoteny*, which is otherwise usually used in biology, for the described phenomena – at least for some of these. The reduction of the facial skeleton relative to the brain capsule; the relative shortness of the extremities; flabby ears; short hair and curling of the tail together provide sufficient examples for persistence of juvenile bodily characteristics of the wild form in the domesticated dog, and for domestic ruminants if the last feature is replaced by 'lack of horns'. Bolk (1926) and other authors have indicated a really convincing number of adult human characteristics which exhibit extensive parallels to those of young, and even foetal, anthropoid apes. The head proportions; the curvature of the vertebral column and – above all – the pelvic organs; the distribution of hair; and the relative paucity of pigment, can be given as examples of neotenous characters.

But far more important for the problem of human evolution are neotenous features in *behaviour*. In many extensively domesticated animals, the fighting drive of the adult male is greatly reduced, as is the full manifestation of sexual dimorphism seen in the wild form. If a boar, a bull or a stallion were tame and yet just as aggressive as the wild-living equivalent he would be extremely dangerous and quite useless as a farm animal. However, the domestic animal whose usefulness is most dependent upon neoteny of its behaviour patterns is the *dog*. Its literal fidelity and attachment to a given person doubtless stem from the drives which – in the free-living form – are related *to the mother*, and perhaps later to the leader of the pack. A hand-reared jackal, dingo or wolf behaves towards a human being just like a domestic dog during the first years of life. However, the keeper is later disappointed to see how his charge becomes independent in a quite un-doglike fashion, even though the adult animal still exhibits a certain degree of collegial friendship towards his master. I find it utterly stunning that the dog owes his most important characteristic (fidelity to his master), just as man owes his constitutive *openness to surroundings*, to domestication-induced behavioural neoteny.

In fact, this continuous, inquisitive communication with extra-subjective reality – recognized as one of the constitutive characters of human beings by Gehlen, and accepted as such in this essay – is quite definitely a persistent juvenile characteristic! Inquisitive play also persists in extremely neotenous domestic animals such as the dog! The fact that Gehlen, who extensively discusses morphological neoteny in his book, did not notice the close relationship between neoteny and persistent inquisitive behaviour is a result of his lack of knowledge of the inquisitive behaviour of young 'specialists in non-specialization'. He believed that an animal learns only

Fig. 1. Wild animals and corresponding domesticated derivatives. *a.* crucian carp and veil-tailed goldfish. *b.* wild and domestic goose. *c.* wild and domestic chicken. *d.* wolf and domestic dog. Note the shortening of all skeletal structures and the retarded nature of locomotor organs in the domesticated forms.

under the pressure of immediate biological necessity, as was maintained by many contemporary investigators of the conditioned reflex. All purely material research conducted by a human scientist is pure inquisitive behaviour – appetitive behaviour *in free operation*. In this sense, it is *play behaviour*. All scientific knowledge – to which man owes his role as master of the world – arose from playful activities conducted in a free field entirely for their own sake. When Benjamin Franklin drew sparks from the leash of his kite, he thought no more about the possibility of a lightning conductor than Hertz thought about the possibilities of radio when investigating electric waves. Anybody who has seen in his own activities the smooth transition from inquisitive childhood play to the life-work of a scientist could never doubt the fundamental identity of play and research. Nietzsche states that the inquisitive child (completely departed from the nature of a full-grown, completely animal chimpanzee) is *hidden* within the 'true human being'; but in fact it completely *dominates* him!

(From *Studies in Animal and Human Behaviour*, translated by Robert Martin, Methuen, 1971.)

References

BALLY, G. (1945), *Vom Ursprung und von den Grenzen der Freiheit*, Schwabe, Basle.

BAUMGARTEN, E. (1950), 'Versuch über die menschlichen Gesellschaften und das Gewissen', *Studium Generale*, No. 10.

BOLK, L. (1926), 'Vergleichende Untersuchungen an einem Fetus, eines Gorilla und eines Schimpansen', *Z. für Anat.*, No. 81.

GEHLEN, A. (1940), *Der Mensch, seine Natur und seine Stellung in der Welt*, Berlin.

KLÜVER, H. (1933), *Behavior Mechanisms in Monkeys*, Chicago.

UEXKÜLL, J. VON (1909), *Umwelt und Innenleben der Tiere*, Springer, Berlin.

Modelling How and Why Play Works

Introduction

This paper will attempt to explain certain psychological and evolutionary aspects of 'play' behaviour in animals.

In an adult animal, behaviour which tends to produce immediate, measurable advantages for the individual (such as energy, time, space, material, increased survival probability, dominance rights, or access to mates) is termed adaptive, since such behaviour appears to make a direct contribution towards maintenance, survival or reproduction. The theory of natural selection provides a mechanism for the evolution of adaptive behaviour. Consequently, reported behaviour patterns which do not seem to possess consequences measurable in physical, energetic, or demographic units tend to be dismissed as epiphenomena or, alternatively, to be attributed to inadequate or inaccurate observation. In particular, a well-known behavioural phenomenon which has never been explained satisfactorily in adaptive terms is the play behaviour of young animals. For example, in domestic cats (*Felis catus*), 1–6-month-old kittens chase, capture, manipulate, fight with, and flee from littermates, inanimate objects, or prey, and in doing so exhibit sequences and combinations of behaviours which would be inefficient if measured with respect to actual predation and in terms of conventional adaptive currency (Ewer 1968; Leyhausen 1973b). In the playchases of young rhesus macaques (*Macaca mulatta*) the animals often adopt 'inefficient' gaits such as gambolling or staggering, which are restricted to the play context. The animals may also playfight, attempting simultaneously to bite and not be bitten; the bites tend to be inhibited and not to cause serious injury, the interactions are prolonged and quiet, and gestures of threat and submission are absent. Special communicative patterns accompany these behaviours (Symons, 1973). Young ravens (*Corvus corax*) exhibit complex sequences of motor and manipulatory behaviour, hanging upside down from perches or picking up sticks and carrying them in their talons (Gwinner, 1966). When an 8-month-old human infant has attained rough competence in visually guided reaching, he holds the cup to look at it, he shakes it, he bangs it on his high chair, he drops it over the edge, and before long he manages to fit the object into every activity into which it can be put (Bruner, 1973a).

For other examples, see Ewer, 1968, Loizos, 1967, Muller-Schwarze, 1971, and Nice, 1943.

Animal play, which may be defined as persistent manipulative or loco-motor experimentation with objects, with the environment, with one's own body, and/or with other organisms, includes repeated re-structuring of functioning behavioural procedures, behaviour which appears to maximize inefficiency and instability, prolonged fights in which attack engenders attack though the chance of injury is small, and puzzling variations of hunting, fighting, and escape routines which could never serve to capture prey, to injure or drive off a rival, or to flee from a predator. Hypotheses concerning play often attempt to explain how these seemingly uneconomical behaviour patterns could evolve. It has frequently been suggested, for example, that play may serve to rehearse, perfect, and lend flexibility to adaptive responses and to gather information, but such 'practice' or 'information' hypotheses fail to explain why playful practice and information-gathering, as distinct from specific, rote practice and information-gathering (Beach, 1945; Bruner 1973a, 1973b) should be necessary in development. As Loizos (1966) has argued, why must the formal structure of practice be 'playful' – exaggerated, disequilibrial, variational and combinatorial – in order to be effective? It is not necessary to play in order to practise. And if play provides information about the environment, why does the animal not use a more economical way of acquiring this information? Are there types of practice or information which can be obtained only as a result of 'playful' learning? 'Practice' and 'information' hypotheses appear to lack a precise definition of a play-specific learning mechanism, i.e. a learning mechanism whose operation requires the animal to perform motor behaviour which is structurally (formally) playful.

Lack of a demonstrated play-specific learning mechanism is by no means the only difficulty associated with the study of play. A second difficulty is the following: it has often been suggested that play may provide a source of increased behavioural variability, generating novel, innovative and possibly useful acts which may be propagated to other individuals by observational learning. But the existence of innovative potential in a population of animals capable of observational learning is no guarantee that such potential will be favoured by natural selection. If, for example, non-innovative animals immediately 'steal' all discoveries via observational learning, innovative activity will not be evolutionarily rewarding to the innovators, and play may be counter-selected. Hypotheses which attempt to explain the evolution of innovative play must account for this difficulty and must also justify the assumption that play can be equated with innovative potential.

The purpose of this paper is to answer some mechanistic and evolutionary questions about play behaviour. A discussion of models of learning will suggest why, when, and under what circumstances learning must be playful in form in order to be effective. The evolutionary questions will be investigated using mathematical models of the evolution of innovative play.

Play and learning

In human children, play with the components (objects as well as actions performed on objects) of a mechanical problem has been shown experimentally to constitute effective preparation for solution (Sylva, Bruner and Genova, this volume). The play-trained children in this experiment appeared especially productive and organized in their learning. They used information from failures and from hints, and they began with simple means but progressed systematically towards more complex ones. A possible interpretation of these results is that the play experience enabled the children to construct an internal model or description (Arbib, 1972; Bruner, 1973a; Gregory, 1969; Minsky and Papert, 1972) of the objects and of the kinds of actions that could and could not be performed with them. This model would serve as an economical representation of the information gathered and could be used to make predictions and to generate hypotheses in the course of the solution process, allowing the children to solve the problem in a systematic and purposeful way. This interpretation of the experimental results suggests that play might constitute a mechanism for experimentation with the external world or with one's own body, such that information especially helpful in description-building would result from the interaction. If this supposition is correct, experiments would be designed to produce information for autonomous playful generic learning, defined as learning which involves the extraction of a predictive description (rule, model, hypothesis, or coding system) from a set of self-generated examples.

The two basic tenets of this view of play are that the organism is building or modifying an internal model of itself or of its environment and that it must perform motor or manipulative 'experiments' in order to produce the necessary information. Arbib (1972) draws a parallel between biological problems solved by an animal which is an autonomous generic learner and certain problems in engineering. The brain, whether in adjusting for the growth of the body or in learning to interact with new objects in the environment, is seen as building and changing its internal models, continually solving what engineers call the *identification problem*: 'to use repeated experiments upon the input–output behaviour of a system to build up a state-variable description [model] for a system which yields similar behaviour'. Engineers can derive optimal learning strategies for the solution of simple identification problems and have written computer programmes which use these strategies to experiment with real objects such as aircraft. In these experiments, the computer can be linked electronically (via radio or radar) to the control panel of the airplane and can actually 'fly' the machine in a series of experimental manoeuvres, obtaining feedback from each experiment through the communications link. This feedback is generated by sensors located in the aircraft. Of course, the models constructed in such experiments are still very simple; no completely general, automatic model-building procedure currently exists in engineering. But since play itself may be a component of model-building behaviour in animals, analogous to the computer-controlled experiments performed by identification systems in engineering, these programmes, present and future, could serve as simple functional models of playful learning by experimentation. If this analogy is correct, the behaviour of engineering identification systems should tend to be playful in form, and play could be viewed as optimal generic learning by experimentation. Pending experimental demonstration of such learning in the play of animals other than humans, play could be provisionally defined as behaviour formally resembling optimal learning by experimentation but not serving immediate adaptive goals such as maintenance, survival or reproduction. It remains to define what is meant by the 'behaviour' of an engineering identification system and to demonstrate that the behaviour of some such system is playful in form.

The observable 'behaviour' of an identification procedure consists of appropriate test signals applied to the object of the experiment (i.e. to the thing or process being modelled). These signals can be monitored and their forms studied. The resulting behaviour of the object can also be observed. If the computer containing the identification programme were contained in the head of a humanoid robot and the test signals were transmitted to the object through mechanical manipulations performed by the robot, closer outward resemblance to animal behaviour would result, but functionally and mathematically the programme would be identical to other computer-based identification procedures.

It is important to recognize that the computer-controlled experimental apparatus described can also function as a control system for an object once a model of that object has been experimentally devised. Programmes which perform control tasks with objects whose properties have already been modelled are standard in engineering, and such a control programme could easily be added to our computer's repertory. Following this alteration, the computer-controlled system would be able to perform 'purposeful', 'task-oriented' acts with the object whose properties and uses it had experimentally ascertained. For instance, an aircraft might be guided to a specified destination using a minimum amount of fuel. This task would be accomplished through the application of appropriate control signals to the object. From an observer's point of view, the machine would now be directing the execution of control tasks rather than information-gathering tasks, and its 'goals' would be goals of control rather than goals of information. Bernstein (1967), Bruner (1973a), and others have applied control-system concepts to behaviour, but the corresponding identification-system model has not been utilized to the same extent, although it has been discussed by Arbib (1972).

Identification procedures have frequently been devised by engineers (Astrom and Eykhoff, 1971; Graupe, 1972; Sage and Melsa, 1971). The playful behaviour of one such procedure (Mehra, 1972, 1973, to be discussed below) suggests that play should be viewed as optimal generic learning by experimentation in a relaxed field (where the term 'relaxed field' [Bally, 1945] refers to the absence of goals of control). The following evidence indicates that animal play behaviour and the behaviour of Mehra's identification are structurally (formally) similar.

1. Inefficiency. In general, good (informative) test signals are poor (inefficient) control signals, and vice versa (Fel'dbaum, 1966). Biologically, this result suggests that motor sequences used for information-gathering in building a model of an act or of an object would be useless in performing the act itself in a serious context, or in carrying out a control task with the object. In Mehra's identification procedure, for example, the experiments which the computer performs with the system studied (an aeroplane) involve sequences of test signals which would be inefficient in performing an instrumental task such as flying the aircraft to a given destination using minimum fuel or in minimum time. In these experiments, the aircraft is put through 'unusual' and 'exaggerated' manoeuvres which do not bring it to any destination or satisfy any goal other than the goal of maximum informativeness. These manoeuvres serve to highlight the dynamic properties of the aircraft and of the communication and control linkages joining computer and aircraft. While such experiments require fuel and time expenditures, they also yield benefits: increased pilot safety, more efficient quality control, design improvement, and engineering insight.

2. Persistent excitation. Unlike investigation (Hutt, 1966, 1970), which can also be performed by computer-controlled systems (Tse and Bar-Shalom, 1973; Tse, Bar-Shalom and Meier, 1973) and which is of brief duration and often passive, optimal generic learning by experimentation must be active and temporally prolonged in order to be at all effective

(Astrom and Bohlin, 1966). This mathematical result parallels the biological fact that investigation is generally a brief process, while play tends to be a prolonged one (Bruner, 1973a; Hutt, 1966, 1970).

3. *De-stabilization* (or disequilibrium). Under goals of control, computer-generated signals are designed to stabilize the controlled object and to drive it to a specified destination despite variations in external factors affecting its behaviour and despite uncertainties about its true properties. Under information goals, the signal design philosophy is fundamentally different. Optimal signals for learning must make the system studied maximally sensitive to unknown quantities and to variations, for only in this way can informative experiments be performed. Sutton-Smith (1971) has characterized animal play as 'disequilibrial', a term which necessarily describes the behaviour of procedures for optimal generic learning by experimentation.

4. *Occurs in a relaxed field.* Bally (1945) uses the expression 'relaxed field' to describe a situation in which immediate needs are satisfied and no threat to the organism's well-being is present. To restate Bally's point in the language of control and identification, play can take place, i.e. goals of information can be achieved, only when goals of control are absent. Adaptive control procedures (Tse and Bar-Shalom, 1973; Tse, Bar-Shalom and Meier, 1973) must carry out both identification and control, since they are required to control objects whose properties and responses are initially unknown. In this situation, goals of information and goals of control are in direct conflict. The programmes designed by Tse *et al.* in order to solve this problem do not 'play', since play would interfere with the control task. They learn, but only about those aspects and uses of the object which are directly relevant to the specific task which must be performed, and the behaviour of the control system resembles investigation rather than play. The test signals used by these programmes are suboptimal for identification purposes. They are of short duration and contain limited energy (one might even characterize them as 'restrained') and do not interfere with the overall goal of guiding the controlled object to a specified destination. In the presence of goals of control, play is absent. Only in a relaxed field can play occur in these model learning systems.

5. *Thoroughness.* It is informative to compare the kinds of learning that occur in the programmes of Tse *et al.* and in Mehra's programme. In the former case a goal of control is present, and experimentation only occurs with those aspects of the situation which can contribute directly to the success of the specific instrumental act which is being performed with the unknonwn object. Certain dynamic modes of the object and certain dimensions of the computer-object interaction remain completely unexplored. Sworder (1966) has discussed this problem of incomplete

learning in the presence of goals of control, remarking that 'the controller need only identify that part of the system dynamics which affects the performance measure [affects the goal of control]'. The variational nature and changing goal structure of animal play appear to be consistent with the mathematical principle that performance of a specific task using an object or motor pattern should produce only partial learning of the properties and uses of that object or motor pattern. For in animal play, as in the play of Mehra's identification procedure, a description of many modes and uses of the object or process under study can be obtained; typically in play 'a new object is fitted into as many routines as available', or 'a newly mastered act is addressed to as many different objects as available' (Bruner, 1973b).

6. *Learning 'what I can do'*. The mathematical description of the kind of system with which Mehra's procedure experiments and which the programmes of Tse *et al.* must control under uncertainty is a vector differential equation,

$$\mathbf{x}(t) = \mathbf{A}(t)\mathbf{x}(t) + \mathbf{B}(t)\mathbf{u}(t) + \boldsymbol{\epsilon}(t).$$

In this equation, $\mathbf{x}(t)$ represents the state of the system (for example, the six-dimensional position-velocity vector of an aircraft), $\mathbf{u}(t)$ represents the control or test signal generated by the computer, and $\boldsymbol{\epsilon}(t)$ represents noise which perturbs the system. In an identification problem, the matrix $\mathbf{A}(t)$, which models what the aircraft does, and the matrix $\mathbf{B}(t)$, which models what the computer can do with the aircraft, are both initially unknown and must be determined experimentally in an information-optimal manner. (But in a standard control problem, $\mathbf{A}(t)$ and $\mathbf{B}(t)$ are given quantities.) A recent study (Gupta, Mehra and Hall, 1974) indicates that an excellent test signal for identification of the dynamics of a certain aircraft contains two components, a high-frequency component which serves to identify $\mathbf{A}(t)$ and a low-frequency component which serves to identify $\mathbf{B}(t)$. In this aircraft study, the computer experimenter, like the human children in Hutt's (1966, 1970) laboratory, first learned what the object did, then learned what it could do with the object. Hutt (1966, 1970) relates play to the latter type of learning.

Mehra's programme for optimal identification by experimentation, which is playful in the six important respects cited above, furnishes the best currently available answer to the question 'How does play work', since it solves a learning problem optimally and exhibits playful behaviour in doing so. Future identification programmes may prove even more ingenious and more playful. For instance, a truly playful learner might be required to extract rules rather than merely to modify or to complete them. Might the optimal experimental learning strategy for this more difficult, more abstract problem be even more playful than that employed by present-day identification algorithms? This sort of general model-building, which might require programmes to modify themselves or to perform some type of inductive generalization from experimental results, is a current research topic in computer science, particularly in the field of artificial intelligence (Arbib, 1972; Michie, 1973; Minsky and Papert, 1972; Sussman, 1973). Such research may serve to develop programmes which can build and modify predictive descriptions and learn generically and autonomously by 'fooling around' – that is, by playing (Sussman, 1973).

To summarize, the function of play in model learning systems is best characterized as (and can be demonstrated mathematically to solve some versions of the problem of) optimal generic learning by experimentation in a relaxed field. While the strongest evidence for the existence of such experiments has been obtained from the play of human children (Bruner, 1973a; Hutt, 1966, 1970; Sylva, Bruner and Genova, this volume), playful experimentation also appears to occur in other species (Eibl-Eibesfeldt, 1967, 1970; Jones and Kamil, 1973; Leyhausen, 1973a, 1973b; Menzel, 1972, Norton-Griffiths, 1969). Conversely, certain historians of science (Butterfield, 1962; Kuhn, 1962) have discussed scientific research during a period of paradigm change almost as if it were a type of animal play. Play behaviour might even be described as extraordinary scientific research performed by animals.

Modelling the evolution of innovative play

Innovative play, like innovative research, can produce behavioural and technological novelty. Several recent studies (Dansky and Silverman, 1973; Feitelson and Ross, 1973; Hutt and Bhavnani, 1972; Sylva, Bruner and Genova, this volume) suggest a relationship between play and in-novative potential. Furthermore, it is well known that novel behaviours of unknown origin can be spread through a group of animals and perpetuated by tradition (Eibl-Eibesfeldt, 1970; Gwinner, 1966; Jones and Kamil, 1973; Kawai, 1965; Kummer, 1971; Menzel, 1972). Yet there is a problem with the hypothesis that play has evolved because it generates novel, occasionally adaptive behaviour patterns. Play may be costly, both because it requires limiting resources such as time and energy and because it can expose the organism to physical and social danger. The benefits of discovery must outweigh the cost of play if innovative play is to evolve. In animals capable of learning by observation, there is an additional problem. Observational learning can dramatically increase the selective value of genetically based predispositions towards innovative ability by permitting the propagation of new, adaptive behaviours from the innovator to his or her offspring. Yet this augmentation can be counteracted by the prompt 'theft' of these novel behaviours by individuals of other genotypes. I have developed formal mathematical models of the evolution of innovative play, both in the absence of and in the presence of observational learning, in order to investigate these problems. These models, which will be described and discussed below, show that innovative play can in fact evolve, though it will not always do so, as the discussion of results will serve to indicate.

Description of models of innovative play

In a large, randomly mating population of diploid animals, consider an autosomal locus (D,d) such that dd animals, and these alone, are capable of discovering novel behaviour patterns through play. Since innovative potential may only rarely result in discovery, I will suppose that a fraction $f, 0 \leq f \leq 1$, of the potential innovators (i.e. of the dd animals) make useful discoveries each generation as a result of their play, and that non-innovators (DD and Dd animals) can neither make discoveries nor, in the absence of observational learning, profit from others' discoveries. Each generation is assumed to consist of three phases: mating, discovery and selection according to the fitness tableau of Table 1, in which discovery produces fit-

Table 1 Population description and fitness tableau when observational learning absent

Genotype	Performance status	Fitness
DD	Non-performer	1
Dd	Non-performer	1
dd	Performer	$1+\sigma-\tau$
dd	Non-performer	$1-\tau$

Parameter σ is defined to be > 0;
parameter τ is defined to lie between 0 and 1.

ness increment σ while play causes fitness decrement τ. It follows from these assumptions that in the absence of observational learning the d allele will be fixed (play will evolve) if and only if $f\sigma > \tau$; otherwise, the play allele will be lost (Appendix). This condition may be interpreted biologically as follows.

Since $f\sigma$ must be greater than τ for play to evolve, innovative play leading to rare discoveries causing small increments in fitness will be found, in the absence of observational learning, only in the most benign environments. In such environments it may be particularly difficult for human observers to demonstrate that play has adaptive value for the organisms performing it, since f might be so low that only one animal in hundreds or thousands would ever discover anything worth-while. But f has another interpretation. Discoveries may be rare not because of their intrinsic difficulty but because play itself is inefficient; this argument shows that inefficient play behaviour will not necessarily be counter-selected.

The properties of this model become more complicated if observational learning is assumed to occur. In this more complex model (Fagen, 1974), each generation is assumed to consist of four phases: discovery, intra-generational observational learning, random mating and learning from parents, and selection. Observational learning affords each animal the opportunity to become a performer through contact with other animals. The population consists of six types of individuals, with fitness assigned according to genotype and performance status (Table 2). As in the previous

Table 2 Population description and fitness tableau when observational learning present

Genotype	Performance status	Fitness
DD	Performer	$1+\sigma$
DD	Non-performer	1
Dd	Performer	$1+\sigma$
Dd	Non-performer	1
dd	Performer	$1+\sigma-\tau$
dd	Non-performer	$1-\tau$

Parameters σ and τ have values as defined above.

model, a constant fraction of the playful non-performers discovers a novel behaviour pattern every generation; after discovery, the animals observe the behaviour of one another, and a certain fraction of the non-performers learns to perform the novel act; the value of this fraction is not constant but depends on the number of performers already present.

For simplicity, it is assumed that only one type of novel behaviour pattern is current in any given generation; but it would be unrealistic not to allow more than one type of discovery over a long period of time. I am merely assuming that different types of discoveries cannot overlap in time. Since overlap would favour the play allele by allowing discoveries to occur more rapidly, this assumption is a conservative one. In the model, whenever playful animals begin to make a new type of discovery, this new discovery type remains current during a g-generation period, and until this period ends no other types of discoveries are made.

When this model is translated into equations and its properties studied, the following results are obtained. The frequency of the play allele increases at the beginning of each cycle of discovery when this allele is rare, since then most performers also possess play alleles (Figure 1). Later in the same cycle, when the discovery begins to 'leak out' into the population at large, the *dd* animals are still penalized because of their playfulness but no longer enjoy exclusive possession of the new act. The frequency of the *d*

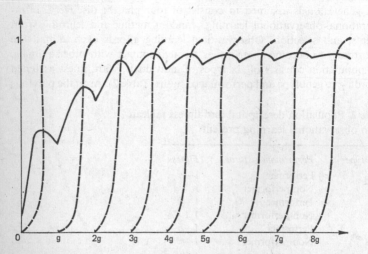

Fig. 1. Frequency of *d* allele (solid curve) and frequency of performers (dashed curve) as a function of time in population of animals capable of observational learning.

allele therefore begins to decrease. This decrease is halted only at the beginning of the next cycle, when a new type of discovery becomes current. But now the frequency of the *d* allele is higher, producing more performers to act as models, and now this faster spread of the new behaviour through the population results in decline in the frequency of the *d* allele earlier in the cycle. (When the play allele is very common, however, its frequency may begin to decrease at the very beginning of the cycle because so many performers are already present.) After a large number of generations, the frequency of the play allele reaches a unique, stable, small-amplitude equilibrium cycle having a period of *g* generations. During each cycle of discovery a new behaviour spreads through the population; by the end of that cycle, most animals have become performers.

The model of the evolution of innovative play in a population of observational learners has four parameters: *f*, the fraction of playful nonperformers discovering the new behaviour per generation; *g*, the number of generations per cycle of discovery; *σ*, the fitness increment resulting from performance; and τ, the fitness decrement resulting from playfulness. The effect on the equilibrium frequency of the play allele of changes in the numerical values of these parameters (where this equilibrium frequency is defined as the play allele frequency at the beginning of the equilibrium cycle) can be studied by means of numerical experiments in which certain

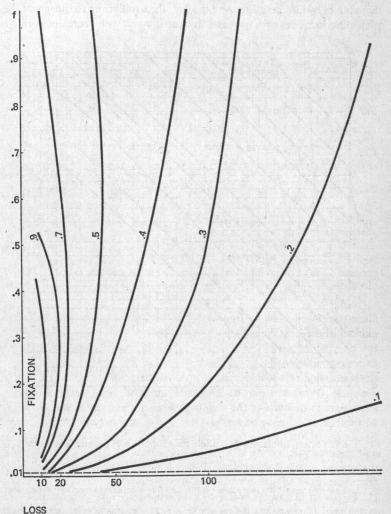

Fig. 2. Equilibrium frequency of *d* allele as a function of parameters *f* and *g* for $\sigma = 1 \cdot 0$, $\tau = 0 \cdot 01$.

parameters are held fixed while others are varied. Parameter values producing the highest equilibrium frequencies for the play allele correspond to conditions which might be considered optimal for the evolution of play. Figures 2 and 3 present the results of the two series of numerical experiments reported in Tables 3 and 4; data for the figures was obtained from these tables by interpolation. As expected, the equilibrium frequency of the play allele increases with increases in benefit σ and with decreases in risk τ

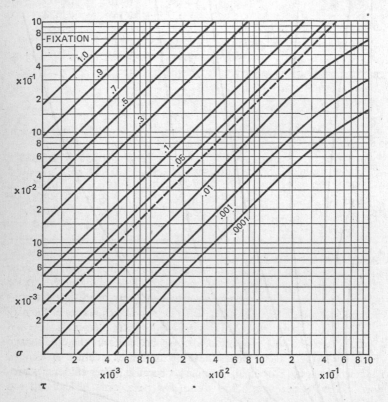

Fig. 3. Equilibrium frequency of d allele as a function of parameters σ and τ for $f = 0.5$, $g = 10$.

(1) 'Fixation' and 'loss' refer to d allele equilibrium frequencies less than 10^{-4} and greater than $1 - 10^{-4}$, respectively.

(2) The dashed line indicates the contour $f\sigma = \tau$. This contour is of interest because it forms the boundary between regions in which the play allele would be fixed in the absence of observational learning and regions in which the play allele would be lost in the absence of observational learning.

Table 3 β_{eq} as a function of f and g for $\sigma=1$, $\tau=0.01$

	$g = 10$	20	50	100	200
$f = 0.001$	0.0636	0.0304	0.00889	0.00303	0.00156
0.005	0.282	0.132	0.0440	0.0167	0.00693
0.01	0.466	0.230	0.0791	0.0323	0.0128
0.05	0.970	0.562	0.235	0.110	0.0479
0.1	$1-10^{-4}$	0.694	0.323	0.165	0.0772
0.5	0.925	0.771	0.487	0.296	0.165
0.8	0.796	0.694	0.501	0.323	0.190
1.0	0.735	0.651	0.495	0.335	0.200

Table 4 β_{eq} as a function of σ and τ for $f=0.5$, $g=10$

	$\sigma = 0.001$	0.01	0.1	0.2	0.05	1.0
$\tau = 0.001$	0.0108	0.267	0.913	$\geq 1-10^{-4}$	$\geq 1-10^{-4}$	$\geq 1-10^{-4}$
0.005	$\geq 10^{-4}$	0.0421	0.450	0.675	0.921	$\geq 1-10^{-4}$
0.01	$\geq 10^{-4}$	0.0108	0.267	0.454	0.755	0.925
0.05	$\geq 10^{-4}$	$\geq 10^{-4}$	0.0421	0.108	0.276	0.478
0.1	$\geq 10^{-4}$	$\geq 10^{-4}$	0.0108	0.421	0.142	0.284
0.5	$\geq 10^{-4}$	$\geq 10^{-4}$	$\geq 10^{-4}$	0.000832	0.0128	0.040

and cycle length g (Figures 2, 3). Intuitively, one might suppose that higher discovery probabilities would always increase the equilibrium frequency of the play gene, but although this is usually the case, there do exist combinations of parameter values such that the highest frequencies of the play gene occur for f values less than 1. Figure 2 indicates that when f is large and g small, increases in f can actually cause decreases in the equilibrium frequency of the d allele. Under these circumstances a certain amount of inefficiency in play is optimal, presumably because higher efficiencies produce too many performers and cause new behaviours to leak out too rapidly.

Since play will evolve in the presence of observational learning even when $f\sigma > \tau$, observational learning may be said to provide a mechanism for the evolution of inefficient (low f) play behaviour leading to discoveries with small (low σ) payoffs in high-risk (high τ) environments. But in a benign environment with play efficient and discoveries valuable, play may disappear when observational learning abilities are present in a population. How is this prediction to be reconciled with the fact that extremely playful animals such as primates, corvids, and domestic cats can learn observationally at rates which would cause new behaviours to become fixed in a population within a single generation?

The model's failure in this case is an informative one, since it suggests that additional biological factors must be operating to produce play in the animal groups cited. For example, increased generic learning ability and a more variable environment would tend to decrease the time interval separating new types of discoveries and would therefore tend to favour play. Playful animals might even seek out novelty in their environment in order to increase environmental variability. The existence of multiple types of discoveries within a single generation could produce high play gene frequencies even in a population of animals capable of observational learning, and it is often the case that multiple discoveries within a single generation are observed in animal populations (Gwinner, 1966; Kawai, 1965). Formation of playgroups including only *dd* animals would favour the evolution of play. Intentional secrecy, misinformation regarding discoveries made in play (advertisement and display of useless discoveries, concealment of useful ones), and free exchange of discoveries among littermates along with restricted interactions with less closely related conspecifics would favour playful animals. Also possible are negotiations with non-playful animals during which information about new discoveries could be traded for protection (where protection refers to a decrease in the value of τ as a consequence of non-playful animals' behaviour). As Boorman and Levitt (1973) and Trivers (1971) have shown, such negotiations need not be direct; they could occur in evolutionary time, through the selection of alternative alleles.

The models discussed here assume that play only functions to produce innovative potential. We might call this the 'pure research' aspect of play. But play might also be required in development if an individual is to become a functioning adult (Bruner, 1973a). An infant's 'discovery' of flexible patterns of cup use (Bruner, 1973a) or of language skill (Weir, 1962) may not constitute invention, but it is nevertheless important in individual ontogeny. This 'applied research' aspect of play may permit the evolution of play behaviour even during epochs when 'pure research' is not supported by the environment.

Conclusions

Behaviour formally resembling animal play can be shown mathematically to be optimal for generic learning by experimentation in a relaxed field, while innovative play can evolve even in a population of animals capable of observational learning. In both cases, studies of model systems justify use of the term 'play' by behavioural biologists.

**Appendix: A model of the evolution of innovative behaviour
in the absence of observational learning**

This appendix is intended to serve two purposes: to illustrate what is meant
by a model of behavioural evolution and to derive a condition for the evolution of innovative behaviour in the absence of observational learning
using this model. Readers unfamiliar with the elementary concepts of
population genetics on which the model is based might consult Wilson and
Bossert (1971), a non-specialized introduction to these and other concepts
in population biology.

Let (D,d) be two alleles at one locus in a diploid organism belonging to a
large, randomly mating population. Assume that the dd genotype, and only
this genotype, confers upon its bearers a tendency towards discovery of
novel acts through play. Assume further that a constant fraction f,
$0 \leq f \leq 1$, of all dd animals discovers a novel act each generation. Any
generation consists of three phases: random mating, discovery of new acts
by the offspring of these matings, and natural selection acting on these offspring according to the fitness tableau of Table 1. An animal which has discovered a novel act will be called a performer, and an animal which has not
discovered a novel act will be called a non-performer. In this model, it is
assumed that no animal is capable of observational learning. In particular,
DD and Dd animals are unable to learn observationally, and since they can
neither discover new acts nor learn to perform such acts through observation, these animals will always be non-performers.

The mathematical model embodying these assumptions will now be
stated.

Define

$P(n) =$ frequency of DD animals in the population after mating in
generation $(n-1)$ and before discovery in generation n

$2Q(n) =$ frequency of Dd animals during this phase

$R_1(n) =$ frequency of dd performers during this phase

$R_2(n) =$ frequency of dd non-performers during this phase

Singly primed quantities $(P'(n), Q'(n), R_1'(n), R_2'(n))$ are valid after discovery and before selection in generation n, and otherwise defined as above.
Doubly primed quantities $(P''(n), Q''(n), R_1''(n), R_2''(n))$ are valid after
selection and before mating in generation n, and otherwise defined as above.

The frequency of the d allele in any given phase is defined as the proportion of alleles in the population which are of type d. For example, after
selection and before mating in generation n, the frequency $\beta''(n)$ of d
allele is defined by $\beta''(n) = Q''(n) + R_1''(n) + R_2''(n)$.

Models of mating, discovery, and selection are given by the following
sets of equations.

Mating:

$$P(n) = [P''(n-1) + Q''(n-1)]^2$$
$$Q(n) = [P''(n-1) + Q''(n-1)][Q''(n-1) + R_1''(n-1) + R_2''(n-1)]$$
$$R_1(n) = 0$$
$$R_2(n) = [Q''(n-1) + R_1''(n-1) + R_2''(n-1)]^2 \tag{1}$$

The equations above embody the random mating assumption and correspond to the Hardy-Weinberg formula (Wilson and Bossert 1971).

Discovery:

$$P'(n) = P(n)$$
$$Q'(n) = Q(n)$$
$$R_1'(n) = fR_2(n)$$
$$R_2'(n) = (1-f)R_2(n) \tag{2}$$

Equations (2) reflect the assumption that *DD* and *Dd* offspring are unable to make discoveries: the frequencies of these two genotypes in the population are not changed by the process of discovery. But a fraction f of the *dd* offspring of the previous generation discovers a novel act, and the frequencies of *dd* performers and *dd* non-performers in the population change as a result.

Selection:

$$P''(n) = \frac{P'(n)}{1 + \sigma R_1'(n) - \tau[R_1'(n) + R_2'(n)]}$$

$$2Q''(n) = \frac{Q'(n)}{1 + \sigma R_1'(n) - \tau[R_1'(n) + R_2'(n)]}$$

$$R_1''(n) = \frac{R_1'(n)(1 + \sigma - \tau)}{1 + \sigma R_1'(n) - \tau[R_1'(n) + R_2'(n)]}$$

$$R_2''(n) = \frac{R_2'(n)(1 - \tau)}{1 + \sigma R_1'(n) - \tau[R_1'(n) + R_2'(n)]} \tag{3}$$

The quantity in the denominator of Equations (3) is a normalization factor, required so that the sum of the frequencies $P''(n)$, $2Q''(n)$, $R_1''(n)$, $R_2''(n)$ will be equal to (1) following selection.

Equations (1), (2), and (3) define a mathematical model of the evolution of innovative tendencies in a population of animals which do not learn observationally. What evolutionary fate does the model predict for innovative animals (i.e. for the *d* allele)? Will the frequency of this allele increase or decrease in time, or remain fairly constant? We can answer these questions by analyzing the equations of the model. In particular, it will prove useful in the sequel to derive an equation which specifies $\beta''(n)$, the frequency of the d allele after selection and before mating in generation n, in terms of $\beta''(n-1)$ and the three model parameters f, σ, and τ. This derivation amounts to substitution for $P'(n)$, $20'(n)$, $R_1'(n)$, and $R_2'(n)$ in Equations (3) using Equations (1) and (2) and the definition of $\beta''(n)$ to obtain an expression for $\beta''(n)$ which contains only the quantities $\beta''(n-1)$, f, σ, and τ. The equation resulting from this derivation is

$$\beta''(n) = \frac{\beta''(n-1)[1+(f\sigma-\tau)\beta''(n-1)]}{[1+(f\sigma-\tau)\beta''^2(n-1)]} \tag{4}$$

Equation (4) may be recognized as the standard recursion for selection of a recessive allele with selection coefficient $s = \tau - f\sigma$ (Wilson and Bossert, 1971). Since the frequency of the recessive allele as determined by this recursion will eventually increase to 1 if $s < 0$ but will eventually decrease to 0 if $s > 0$, we can conclude that a condition for the evolution of innovative tendencies, under the assumptions of the above model, is given by $f\sigma - \tau > 0$.

References

ARBIB, M. (1972), *The Metaphorical Brain*, Wiley, New York, pp. xii, 243.

ASTROM, K.-J., and BOHLIN, T. (1966), 'Numerical identification of linear dynamic systems from normal operating records', in *Theory of Self-Adaptive Control Systems*, P. H. Hammond (ed.), Plenum Press, New York, pp. 96–111.

ASTROM, K.-J., and EYKHOFF, P. (1971), 'System identification – a survey', *Automatica*, No. 7, pp. 123–62.

BALLY, G. (1945), *Vom Ursprung und von den Grenzen der Freiheit, eine Deutung des Spieles bei Tier und Mensch,* Schwabe, Basle, p. 140.

BEACH, F. A. (1945), 'Current concepts of play in animals', *Am. Nat.*, No. 79, pp. 523–41.

BERNSTEIN, N. A. (1967), *The Co-ordination and Regulation of Movements*, Pergamon Press, pp. xii, 196.

BOORMAN, S. A., and LEVITT, P. R. (1973), 'A frequency-dependent natural selection model for the evolution of social cooperation networks', *Proceedings of the National Academy of Sciences*, No. 70, pp. 187–9.

BRUNER, J. S. (1973a), *Beyond the Information Given: Studies in the Psychology of Knowing*, J. M. Anglin (ed.), W. W. Norton, New York, pp. xxiv, 502.

BRUNER, J. S. (1973b), 'Organization of early skilled action', *Child Development*, No. 44, pp. 1–11.

BUTTERFIELD, H. (1962), *The Origins of Modern Science*, Collier Books, New York, p. 225. [Cited by Kuhn, 1962.]

DANSKY, J. L., and SILVERMAN, I. W. (1973), 'Effects of play on associative fluency in pre-school-aged children', *Dev. Psych.*, No. 9, pp. 38–43.

EIBL-EIBESFELDT, I. (1967), 'Concepts of ethology and their significance in the study of human behavior', in *Early Behavior: Comparative and Developmental Approaches*, H. W. Stevenson, E. H. Hess, and Harriet L. Rheingold (eds), Wiley, New York, pp. 127–46.

EIBL-EIBESFELDT, I. (1970), *Ethology: the Biology of Behavior*, Holt, Rinehart & Winston, New York, p. 530.

EWER, R. F. (1968), *Ethology of Mammals*, Plenum Press, New York, p. 418.

FAGEN, R. (1974), 'Theoretical bases for the evolution of play in animals', Harvard University Division of Engineering and Applied Physics doctoral dissertation.

FEITELSON, D., and ROSS, G. S. (1973), 'The neglected factor – play', *Human Development*, No. 16, pp. 202–23.

FEL'DBAUM, A. A. (1966), *Optimal Control Systems*, Academic Press, New York.

GRAUPE, D. (1972), *Identification of Systems*, Van Nostrand Reinhold, New York, pp. xi, 276.

GREGORY, R. L. (1969), 'On how so little information controls so much behavior', in *Towards a Theoretical Biology*, C. H. Waddington (ed.), Edinburgh University Press, pp. 236–47.

GUPTA, N. K., MEHRA R. K., and HALL, W. E. (1974), 'Frequency domain synthesis of optimal inputs for aircraft parameter identification', Paper presented at meeting of A.S.M.E., New York, November 1974.

GWINNER, E. (1966), 'Uber einige Bewegungsspiele des Kolkraben, (*Corvus corax* L.)', *Z. Tierpsych.*, No. 23, pp. 28–36.

HUTT, C. (1966), 'Exploration and play in children', *Symp. Zool. Soc. Lond.*, No. 18, pp. 23–44.

HUTT, C. (1970), 'Specific and diversive exploration', *Adv. Child Dev. Behav.*, No. 5, pp. 119–80.

HUTT, C., and BHAVNANI, R. (1972), 'Predictions from play', *Nature*, No. 237, pp. 171–2.

JONES, T. B., and KAMIL, A. C. (1973), 'Tool-making and tool-using in the Northern blue jay', *Science*, No. 180, pp. 1076–7.

KAWAI, M. (1965), 'Newly acquired pre-cultural behavior of the natural troop of Japanese monkeys on Koshima Islet', *Primates*, No. 6, pp. 1–30.

KUHN, T. S. (1962), *The Structure of Scientific Revolutions*, University of Chicago Press, pp. xv, 172.

KUMMER, H. (1971), *Primate Societies*, p. 160, Aldine, Chicago.

LEYHAUSEN, P. (1973), 'On the function of the relative hierarchy of moods (as exemplified by the phylogenetic and ontogenetic development of prey-catching in carnivores)', in *Motivation of Human and Animal Behavior*, K. Lorenz and P. Leyhausen, Van Nostrand Reinhold, New York, pp. 144–247.

LEYHAUSEN, P. (1973), 'Verhaltensstudien an Katzen', *Z. Tierpsych. Beiheft 2*, (3rd ed.), Paul Parey, Berlin and Hamburg, p. 232.

LOIZOS, C. (1966), 'Play in mammals', *Symp. Zool. Soc. Lond.*, No. 18, pp. 1–9.

LOIZOS, C. (1967), 'Play behavior in higher primates: a review', in *Primate Ethology*, D. Morris (ed.), Weidenfeld & Nicolson, pp. 176–218.

MEHRA, R. K. (1972), 'Optimal inputs for linear system identification', paper 28–5, *Preprints*, Joint Automatic Control Conference, Stanford, California.

MEHRA, R. K. (1973), 'Frequency-domain synthesis of optimal inputs for linear system parameter estimation', *Technical Report*, No. 645, Harvard University Division of Engineering and Applied Physics, U.S.A.

MENZEL, E. W., JR. (1972), 'Spontaneous invention of ladders in a group of young chimpanzees', *Folia Primat.*, No. 17, pp. 87–106.

MICHIE, D. (1973), 'Machines and the theory of intelligence', *Nature*, No. 241, pp. 507–12.

MINSKY, M., and PAPERT, S. (1972), 'Research at the Laboratory in vision, language, and other problems of intelligence', *Artificial Intelligence Memo*, No. 252, Artificial Intelligence Laboratory, M.I.T.

MULLER-SCHWARZE, D. (1971), 'Ludic behavior in young mammals', in *Brain Development and Behavior*, M. B. Sterman, D. J. McGinty, and A. M. Adinolfi (eds), Academic Press, New York.

NICE, M. M. (1943), 'Studies in the life history of the song sparrow', *Trans. Linnaean Soc.*, New York, No. 6, pp. 1–238.

NORTON-GRIFFITHS, M. (1969), 'The organization, control and development of parental feeding in the oyster-catcher (*Haematopus ostralegus*)', *Behaviour*, No. 34, pp. 55–114.

SAGE, A. P., and MELSA, J. L. (1971), *System Identification*, Academic Press, New York, pp. xi, 221.

SUSSMAN, G. J. (1973), 'A computational model of skill acquisition', *Technical Report*, No. 297, Artificial Intelligence Laboratory, M.I.T.

SUTTON-SMITH, B. (1971), 'Conclusion', in *Child's Play*, R. Herron and B. Sutton-Smith (eds), Wiley, New York.

SWORDER, D. (1966), *Optimal Adaptive Control Systems*, Academic Press, pp. xi, 187.

SYLVA, K., BRUNER, J. S., and GENOVA, P. 'The role of play in the problem-solving of children 3–5 years old'. (See this volume, p. 244.)

SYMONS, D. (1973), 'Aggressive play and communication in rhesus monkeys (*Macaca mulatta*)', paper presented at meeting of A.A.A.S., December 1973.

TRIVERS, R. L. (1971), 'The evolution of reciprocal altriusm', *Quart. Rev. Biol.*, No. 46, pp. 35–57.

TSE, E., and BAR-SHALOM, Y. (1973), 'An actively adaptive control for linear systems with random parameters via the dual control approach', *I.E.E.E. Trans. Automatic Control*, AC–18, pp. 109–17.

TSE, E., BAR-SHALOM, Y., and MEIER, L. (1973), 'Wide-sense adaptive dual control for nonlinear stochastic systems', *I.E.E.E. Trans. Automatic Control*, AC–18, pp. 98–108.

WEIR, R. (1962), *Language in the crib*, Mouton, The Hague. (And see this volume, p. 609.)

WILSON, E. O., and BOSSERT, W. H. (1971), *A Primer of Population Biology*, Sinauer Association, Stanford, Connecticut, p. 192.

B Play Signals and Meta-Communication

There is a universal need in many species to signal that the activity that follows is a special non-consequential one, play. Play faces are excellent signals of this kind, but in man there are many other ways of signalling 'this is not for real': intonation, syntactic markers, and lexis to name a few linguistic examples, as well as such other characteristic human devices as smiling, antic postures, mock irony. Instinctively inherited patterns seem no more effective than these, though we use them, too. We may even use sports uniforms to show that the aim of the act is not to murder the opponent but only to score a goal. And in sexual activity we use forms of flirtation only remotely related to instinctual activity. Here, as in play, we signal that it is a special kind of behaviour that follows. In all these examples the signal, no matter how abstract, is a *meta-communication*. It is a statement *about* the statement that follows and provides a context for interpreting it.

But there is an ambiguity that results when play forms are transferred to the realm of the serious. In Part Four we consider the difficulty in distinguishing between what is play and what is real. We read the newspaper, for example, with its highly selected version of reality and pay for it with pieces of metal. Many such forms of social convention contain 'pretend' features. But it is quite striking that when someone plays with social convention, the typical response is moral indignation. 'You're playing around with that woman' or 'You're playing around with that rule' or even 'You're not serious about what you're doing'. From the point of view of the society that sanctions the convention, no play signal is possible. Meta-communication fails in that ambiguous border between social reality and play. And, when it does, the consequences are severe.

Yet the great mediator, the astute diplomat, has a light touch in the control of human affairs. He allows transgressions as if they were performed without evil intent. The player is treated as though he were trying out the flexibility of the system. One of the gifts of leadership is to make light of things which ordinarily cause heaviness, moral indignation. Meta-communication here is not just 'I'm playing' but 'Let's be a bit flexible about the way we look at things'. John F. Kennedy used the phrase 'grace under pressure' for characterizing the gift. It is an ancient story in politics. But players beware! It is also a crime to exceed the limits of grace. The opposition benches in the Commons may chant, 'Charm, Charm'.

A Theory of Play and Fantasy

This research was planned and started with a hypothesis to guide our investigations, the task of the investigators being to collect relevant observational data and, in the process, to amplify and modify the hypothesis.

The hypothesis will here be described as it has grown in our thinking.

Earlier fundamental work of Whitehead, Russell (1910–13), Wittgenstein (1922), Carnap (1937), Whorf (1940), etc., as well as my own attempt (1951) to use this earlier thinking as an epistemological base for psychiatric theory, led to a series of generalizations:

1. That human verbal communication can operate and always does operate at many contrasting levels of abstraction. These range in two directions from the seemingly simple denotative level ('The cat is on the mat'). One range or set of these more abstract levels includes those explicit or implicit messages where the subject of discourse is the language. We will call these meta-linguistic (for example, 'The verbal sound "cat" stands for any member of such and such class of objects', or 'The word, "cat", has no fur and cannot scratch'). The other set of levels of abstraction we will call meta-communicative (e.g., 'My telling you where to find the cat was friendly', or 'This is play'). In these, the subject of discourse is the relationship between the speakers.

It will be noted that the vast majority of both meta-linguistic and meta-communicative messages remain implicit; and also that, especially in the psychiatric interview, there occurs a further class of implicit messages about how meta-communicative messages of friendship and hostility are to be interpreted.

2. If we speculate about the evolution of communication, it is evident that a very important stage in this evolution occurs when the organism gradually ceases to respond quite 'automatically' to the mood-signs of another and becomes able to recognize the sign as a signal: that is, to recognize that the other individual's and its own signals are only signals which can be trusted, distrusted, falsified, denied, amplified, corrected and so forth.

Clearly this realization that signals are signals is by no means complete even among the human species. We all too often respond automatically to newspaper headlines as though these stimuli were direct object-indications of events in our environment instead of signals concocted and transmitted by creatures motivated in such complex ways as ourselves. The non-human mammal is automatically excited by the sexual odour of another; and rightly so, inasmuch as the secretion of that sign is an 'involuntary' mood-sign; i.e., an outwardly perceptible event which is a part of the physiological process which we have called a mood. In the human species a more complex state of affairs begins to be the rule. Deodorants mask the involuntary olfactory signs, and in their place the cosmetic industry provides the individual with perfumes which are not involuntary signs but voluntary signals, recognizable as such. Many a man has been thrown off balance by a whiff of perfume, and if we are to believe the advertisers, it seems that these signals, voluntarily worn, have sometimes an automatic and auto-suggestive effect even upon the voluntary wearer.

Be that as it may, this brief digression will serve to illustrate a stage of evolution – the drama precipitated when organisms, having eaten of the fruit of the Tree of Knowledge, discover that their signals are signals. Not only the characteristically human invention of language can then follow, but also all the complexities of empathy, identification, projection and so on. And with these comes the possibility of communicating at the multiplicity of levels of abstraction mentioned above.

3. The first definite step in the formulation of the hypothesis guiding this research occurred in January 1952, when I went to the Fleishhacker Zoo in San Francisco to look for behavioural criteria which would indicate whether any given organism is or is not able to recognize that the signs emitted by itself and other members of the species are signals. In theory, I had thought out what such criteria might look like – that the occurrence of meta-communicative signs (or signals) in the stream of interaction between the animals would indicate that the animals have at least some awareness (conscious or unconscious) that the signs about which they meta-communicate are signals.

I knew, of course, that there was no likelihood of finding denotative messages among non-human mammals, but I was still not aware that the animal data would require an almost total revision of my thinking. What I encountered at the zoo was a phenomenon well known to everybody: I saw two young monkeys *playing*, i.e. engaged in an interactive sequence of which the unit actions or signals were similar to but not the same as those of combat. It was evident, even to the human observer, that the sequence as a whole was not combat, and evident to the human observer that to the participant monkeys this was 'not combat'.

Now, this phenomenon, play, could only occur if the participant organisms were capable of some degree of meta-communication, i.e. of exchanging signals which would carry the message 'this is play'.

4. The next step was the examination of the message 'this is play', and the realization that this message contains those elements which necessarily generate a paradox of the Russellian or Epimenides type – a negative statement containing an implicit negative meta-statement. Expanded, the statement 'this is play' looks something like this: 'These actions in which we now engage do not denote what those actions *for which they stand* would denote.'

We now ask about the italicized words, '*for which they stand*'. We say the word 'cat' stands for any member of a certain class. That is, the phrase 'stands for' is a near synonym of 'denotes'. If we now substitute 'which they denote' for the words 'for which they stand' in the expanded definition of play, the result is: 'These actions, in which we now engage, do not denote what would be denoted by those actions which these actions denote.' The playful nip denotes the bite, but it does not denote what would be denoted by the bite.

According to the Theory of Logical Types such a message is of course inadmissible, because the word 'denote' is being used in two degrees of abstraction, and these two uses are treated as synonymous. But all that we learn from such a criticism is that it would be bad natural history to expect the mental processes and communicative habits of mammals to conform to the logician's ideal. Indeed, if human thought and communication always conformed to the ideal, Russell would not – in fact could not – have formulated the ideal.

5. A related problem in the evolution of communication concerns the origin of what Korzybski (1941) has called the map-territory relation: the fact that a message, of whatever kind, does not consist of those objects which it denotes ('the word "cat" cannot scratch us'). Rather, language bears to the objects which it denotes a relationship comparable to that which a map bears to a territory. Denotative communication as it occurs at the human level is only possible *after* the evolution of a complex set of meta-linguistic (but not verbalized)* rules which govern how words and sentences shall be related to objects and events. It is therefore appropriate to look for the evolution of such meta-linguistic and/or meta-communicative rules at a pre-human and pre-verbal level.

It appears from what is said above that play is a phenomenon in which the actions of 'play' are related to, or denote, other actions of 'not play'. We therefore meet in play with an instance of signals standing for other events, and it appears, therefore, that the evolution of play may have been an important step in the evolution of communication.

6. *Threat* is another phenomenon which resembles play in that actions

* The verbalization of these meta-linguistic rules is a much later achievement which can only occur after the evolution of a non-verbalized meta-meta-linguistics.

denote, but are different from, other actions. The clenched fist of threat is different from the punch, but it refers to a possible future (but at present non-existent) punch. And threat also is commonly recognizable among non-human mammals. Indeed it has lately been argued that a great part of what appears to be combat among members of a single species is rather to be regarded as threat (Tinbergen, 1953, Lorenz, 1952).

7. Histrionic behaviour and deceit are other examples of the primitive occurrence of map-territory differentiation. And there is evidence that dramatization occurs among birds: A jackdaw may imitate her own mood-signs (Lorenz, 1952), and deceit has been observed among howler monkeys (Carpenter, 1934).

8. We might expect threat, play, and histrionics to be three independent phenomena all contributing to the evolution of the discrimination between map and territory. But it seems that this would be wrong, at least so far as mammalian communication is concerned. Very brief analysis of childhood behaviour shows that such combinations as histrionic play, bluff, playful threat, teasing play in response to threat, histrionic threat, and so on form together a single total complex of phenomena. And such adult phenomena as gambling and playing with risk have their roots in the combination of threat and play. It is evident also that not only threat but the reciprocal of threat – the behaviour of the threatened individual – are a part of this complex. It is probable that not only histrionics but also spectatorship should be included within this field. It is also appropriate to mention self-pity.

9. A further extension of this thinking leads us to include ritual within this general field in which the discrimination is drawn, but not completely, between denotative action and that which is to be denoted. Anthropological studies of peace-making ceremonies, to cite only one example, support this conclusion.

In the Andaman Islands, peace is concluded after each side has been given ceremonial freedom to strike the other. This example, however, also illustrates the labile nature of the frame 'this is play', or 'this is ritual'. The discrimination between map and territory is always liable to break down, and the ritual blows of peace-making are always liable to be mistaken for the 'real' blows of combat. In this event, the peace-making ceremony becomes a battle (Radcliffe-Brown, 1922).

10. But this leads us to recognition of a more complex form of play; the game which is constructed not upon the premise 'this is play' but rather around the question 'is this play?' And this type of interaction also has its ritual forms, e.g., in the ragging of initiation.

11. Paradox is doubly present in the signals which are exchanged within the context of play, fantasy, threat, etc. Not only does the playful nip not denote what would be denoted by the bite for which it stands but, in ad-

dition, the bite itself is fictional. Not only do the playing animals not quite mean what they are saying but, also, they are usually communicating about something which does not exist. At the human level, this leads to a vast variety of complications and inversions in the fields of play, fantasy and art. Conjurers and painters of the *trompe l'oeil* school concentrate upon acquiring a virtuosity whose only reward is reached after the viewer detects that he has been deceived and is forced to smile or marvel at the skill of the deceiver. Hollywood film makers spend millions of dollars to increase the realism of a shadow. Other artists, perhaps more realistically, insist that art be non-representational; and poker players achieve a strange addictive realism by equating the chips for which they play with dollars. They still insist, however, that the loser accept his loss as part of the game.

Finally, in the dim region where art, magic and religion meet and overlap, human beings have evolved the 'metaphor that is meant', the flag which men will die to save, and the sacrament that is felt to be more than 'an outward and visible sign, given unto us'. Here we can recognize an attempt to deny the difference between map and territory, and to get back to the absolute innocence of communication by means of pure mood-signs.

12. We face then two peculiarities of play: (a) that the messages or signals exchanged in play are in a certain sense untrue or not meant; and (b) that that which is denoted by these signals is non-existent. These two peculiarities sometimes combine strangely to a reverse conclusion reached above. It was stated (4) that the playful nip denotes the bite, but does not denote that which would be denoted by the bite. But there are other instances where an opposite phenomenon occurs. A man experiences the full intensity of subjective terror when a spear is flung at him out of the 3D screen or when he falls headlong from some peak created in his own mind in the intensity of nightmare. At the moment of terror there was no questioning of 'reality', but still there was no spear in the movie house and no cliff in the bedroom. The images did not denote that which they seemed to denote, but these same images did really evoke that terror which would have been evoked by a real spear or a real precipice. By a similar trick of self-contradiction the film makers of Hollywood are free to offer to a puritanical public a vast range of pseudo-sexual fantasy which otherwise would not be tolerated. In *David and Bathsheba*, Bathsheba can be a Troilistic link between David and Uriah. And in *Hans Christian Andersen*, the hero starts out accompanied by a boy. He tries to get a woman, but when he is defeated in this attempt, he returns to the boy. In all of this there is, of course, no homosexuality, but the choice of these symbolisms is associated in these fantasies with certain characteristic ideas, e.g. about the hopelessness of the heterosexual masculine position when faced with certain sorts of women or with certain sorts of male authority. In sum, the pseudo-

homosexuality of the fantasy does not stand for any real homosexuality, but does stand for and express attitudes which might accompany a real homosexuality or feed its etiological roots. The symbols do not denote homosexuality, but do denote ideas for which homosexuality is an appropriate symbol. Evidently it is necessary to re-examine the precise semantic validity of the interpretations which the psychiatrist offers to a patient and, as preliminary to this analysis, it will be necessary to examine the nature of the frame in which these interpretations are offered.

13. What has previously been said about play can be used as an introductory example for the discussion of frames and contexts. In sum, it is our hypothesis that the message 'this is play' establishes a paradoxical frame comparable to Epimenides' paradox. This frame may be diagrammed thus:

> All statements within this
> frame are untrue.
> I love you.
> I hate you.

The first statement within this frame is a self-contradictory proposition about itself. If this first statement is true, then it must be false. If it be false, then it must be true. But this first statement carries with it all the other statements in the frame. So, if the first statement be true, then all the others must be false; and *vice versa*, if the first statement be untrue then all the others must be true.

14. The logically minded will notice a *non sequitur*. It could be urged that even if the first statement is false, there remains a logical possibility that some of the other statements in the frame are untrue. It is, however, a characteristic of unconscious or 'primary process' thinking that the thinker is unable to discriminate between 'some' and 'all', and unable to discriminate between 'not all' and 'none'. It seems that the achievement of these discriminations is performed by higher or more conscious mental processes which serve in the non-psychotic individual to correct the black-and-white thinking of the lower levels. We assume, and this seems to be an orthodox assumption, that primary process is continually operating, and that the psychological validity of the paradoxical play frame depends upon this part of the mind.

15. But, conversely, while it is necessary to invoke the primary process as an explanatory principle in order to delete the notion of 'some' from between 'all' and 'none', this does not mean that play is simply a primary process phenomenon. The discrimination between 'play' and 'non-play',

like the discrimination between fantasy and non-fantasy, is certainly a function of secondary process, or 'ego'. Within the dream the dreamer is usually unaware that he is dreaming, and within 'play' he must often be reminded that 'this is play'.

Similarly, within dream or fantasy the dreamer does not operate with the concept 'untrue'. He operates with all sorts of statements but with a curious inability to achieve meta-statements. He cannot, unless close to waking, dream a statement referring to (i.e. framing) his dream.

It therefore follows that the play frame as here used as an explanatory principle implies a special combination of primary and secondary processes. This, however, is related to what was said earlier, when it was argued that play marks a step forward in the evolution of communication – the crucial step in the discovery of map-territory relations. In primary process, map and territory are equated; in secondary process, they can be discriminated. In play, they are both equated and discriminated.

16. Another logical anomaly in this system must be mentioned: that the relationship between two propositions which is commonly described by the word 'premise' has become intransitive. In general, all asymmetrical relationships are transitive. The relationship 'greater than' is typical in this respect; it is conventional to argue that if A is greater than B, and B is greater than C, then A is greater than C. But in psychological processes the transitiveness of asymmetrical relations is not observed. The proposition P may be a premise for Q; Q may be a premise for R; and R may be a premise for P. Specifically, in the system which we are considering, the circle is still more contracted. The message 'All statements within this frame are untrue' is itself to be taken as a premise in evaluating its own truth or untruth. (Cf. The intransitiveness of psychological preference discussed by McCulloch, 1945, and paradigm for all paradoxes of this general type, Russell's 'class of classes which are not members of themselves'. Here Russell demonstrates that paradox is generated by treating the relationship, 'is a member of', as an intransitive.) With this caveat, that the 'premise' relation in psychology is likely to be intransitive, we shall use the word 'premise' to denote a dependency of one idea or message upon another comparable to the dependency of one proposition upon another which is referred to in logic by saying that the proposition P is a premise for Q.

17. All this, however, leaves unclear what is meant by 'frame' and the related notion of 'context'. To clarify these, it is necessary to insist first that these are psychological concepts. We use two sorts of analogy to discuss these notions: the physical analogy of the picture frame and the more abstract, but still not psychological, analogy of the mathematical set. In set theory the mathematicians have developed axioms and theorems to discuss

with rigour the logical implications of membership in overlapping categories or 'sets'. The relationship between sets are commonly illustrated by diagrams in which the items or members of a larger universe are represented by dots, and the smaller sets are delimited by imaginary lines enclosing the members of each set. Such diagrams then illustrate a topological approach to the logic of classification. The first step in defining a psychological frame might be to say that it is (or delimits) a class or set of messages (or meaningful actions). The play of two individuals on a certain occasion would then be defined as the set of all messages exchanged by them within a limited period of time and modified by the paradoxical premise system which we have described. In a set-theoretical diagram these messages might be represented by dots, and the 'set' enclosed by a line which would separate these from other dots representing non-play messages. The mathematical analogy breaks down, however, because the psychological frame is not satisfactorily represented by an imaginary line. We assume that the psychological frame has some degree of real existence. In many instances, the frame is consciously recognized and even represented in vocabulary ('play', 'movie', 'interview', 'job', 'language', etc.). In other cases, there may be no explicit verbal reference to the frame, and the subject may have no consciousness of it. The analyst, however, finds that his own thinking is simplified if he uses the notion of an unconscious frame as an explanatory principle; usually he goes further than this and infers its existence in the subject's unconscious.

But while the analogy of the mathematical set is perhaps over-abstract, the analogy of the picture frame is excessively concrete. The psychological concept which we are trying to define is neither physical nor logical. Rather, the actual physical frame is, we believe, added by human beings to physical pictures because these human beings operate more easily in a universe in which some of their psychological characteristics are externalized. It is these characteristics which we are trying to discuss, using the externalization as an illustrative device.

18. The common functions and uses of psychological frames may now be listed and illustrated by reference to the analogies whose limitations have been indicated in the previous paragraph:

a. Psychological frames are exclusive, i.e., by including certain messages (or meaningful actions) within a frame, certain other messages are excluded.

b. Psychological frames are inclusive, i.e. by excluding certain messages, certain others are included. From the point of view of set theory these two functions are synonymous, but from the point of view of psychology it is necessary to list them separately. The frame around a picture, if we consider this frame as a message intended to order or organize the perception of the viewer, says 'Attend to what is within and do not attend to what is outside.' Figure and ground, as these terms are used by Gestalt psychologists, are not symmetrically related as are the set and non-set of set theory. Perception of the ground must be positively inhibited and perception of the figure (in this case the picture) must be positively enhanced.

c. Psychological frames are related to what we have called 'premises'. The picture frame tells the viewer that he is not to use the same sort of thinking in interpreting the picture that he might use in interpreting the wallpaper outside the frame. Or, in terms of the analogy from set theory, the messages enclosed within the imaginary line are defined as members of a class by virtue of their sharing common premises or mutual relevance. The frame itself thus becomes a part of the premise system. Either, as in the case of the play frame, the frame is involved in the evaluation of the messages which it contains, or the frame merely assists the mind in understanding the contained messages by reminding the thinker that these messages are mutually relevant and the messages outside the frame may be ignored.

d. In the sense of the previous paragraph, a frame is meta-communicative. Any message, which either explicitly or implicitly defines a frame, *ipso facto* gives the receiver instructions or aid in his attempt to understand the messages included within the frame.

e. The converse of (d) is also true. Every meta-communicative or meta-linguistic message defines, either explicitly or implicitly, the set of messages about which it communicates, i.e. every meta-communicative message is or defines a psychological frame. This, for example, is very evident in regard to such small meta-communicative signals as punctuation marks in a printed message, but applies equally to such complex meta-communicative messages as the psychiatrist's definition of his own curative role in terms of which his contributions to the whole mass of messages in psychotherapy are to be understood.

f. The relation between psychological frame and perceptual gestalt needs to be considered, and here the analogy of the picture frame is useful. In a painting by Roualt or Blake, the human figures and other objects represented are outlined. 'Wise men see outlines and therefore they draw them.' But outside these lines, which delimit the perceptual gestalt or 'figure', there is a background or 'ground' which in turn is limited by the picture frame. Similarly, in set theoretical diagrams, the larger universe within which the smaller sets are drawn is itself enclosed in a frame. This double framing is, we believe, not merely a matter of 'frames within frames' but an indication that mental processes resemble logic in *needing* an outer frame to delimit the ground against which the figures are to be perceived. This need is often unsatisfied, as when we see a piece of sculpture in a junk shop window, but this is uncomfortable. We suggest that the need for this outer limit to the ground is related to a preference for avoiding the paradoxes of abstraction. When a logical class or set of items is defined – for example, the class of matchboxes – it is necessary to delimit the set of items which are to be excluded, in this case, all those things which are not matchboxes. But the items to be included in the background set must be of the same degree of abstraction, i.e., of the same 'logical type' as those within the set itself. Specifically, if paradox is to be avoided, the 'class of matchboxes' and the 'class of non-matchboxes' (even though both these items are clearly not match boxes) must not be regarded as members of the class of non-match-boxes. No class can be a member of itself. The picture frame then, because it delimits a background, is here regarded as an external representation of a very special and important type of psychological frame – namely a frame whose function is to delimit a logical type. This, in fact, is what was in-dicated above when it was said that the picture frame is an instruction to the viewer that he should not extend the premises which obtain between the figures within the picture to the wallpaper behind it.

But it is precisely this sort of frame that precipitates paradox. The rule for avoiding paradoxes insists that the items outside any enclosing line be of the same logical type as those within, but the picture frame, as analysed above, is a line dividing items of one logical type from those of another. In passing, it is interesting to note that Russell's rule cannot be stated with-out breaking the rule. Russell insists that all items of inappropriate logical type be excluded (i.e., by an imaginary line) from the background of any class, i.e., he insists upon the drawing of an imaginary line of precisely the sort which he prohibits.

19. This whole matter of frames and paradoxes may be illustrated in terms of animal behaviour, where three types of message may be recognized or deduced: (a) Messages of the sort which we here call mood-signs; (b) messages which simulate mood-signs (in play, threat, histrionics, etc.); and (c) messages which enable the receiver to discriminate between mood-signs and those other signs which resemble them. The message 'This is play' is of this third type. It tells the receiver that certain nips and other meaningful actions are not messages of the first type.

The message 'This is play' thus sets a frame of the sort which is likely to precipitate paradox: it is an attempt to discriminate between, or to draw a line between, categories of different logical types.

(From *Psychiatric Research Reports*, No. 2, 1955, pp. 39–51.)

References

CARNAP, R. (1937), *The Logical Syntax of Language*, Harcourt Brace, New York.

CARPENTER, C. R. (1934), 'A field study of the behavior and social relations of howling monkeys', *Comp. Psychol. Monog.*, No. 10, pp. 1–168.

KORZYBSKI, A. (1941), *Science and Sanity*, Science Press, New York.

LORENZ, K. S. (1952), *King Solomon's Ring*, Metheun.

MCCULLOCH, W. S. (1945), 'A heterarchy of values, etc.', *Bull. of Math. Biophys.*, No. 7, pp. 89–93.

RADCLIFFE-BROWN, A. R. (1922), *The Andaman Islanders*, Cambridge University Press.

RUESCH, J., and BATESON, G. (1951), *Communication: the Social Matrix of Psychiatry*, Norton, New York.

TINBERGEN, N. (1953), *Social Behaviour in Animals with Special Reference to Vertebrates*, Methuen.

WHITEHEAD, A. N., and RUSSELL, B. (1910–13), *Principia Mathematica* (2nd ed.), Cambridge University Press.

WHORF, B. L. (1940), 'Science and linguistics', *Technology Review*, No. 44, pp. 229–48.

WITTGENSTEIN, L. (1922), *Tractatus Logico-Philosophicus*, Routledge & Kegan Paul.

A Comparative Approach to the Phylogeny of Laughter and Smiling

Possible primate homologues of laughter and smiling

A comparative study of the facial displays of the higher primates (van Hooff, 1967) put forward the hypothesis that laughter and smiling could be conceived as displays with a different phylogenetic origin, that have converged to a considerable extent in *Homo*. The material that has become available since then with a few exceptions, still mostly of a qualitative nature, supports this hypothesis.

When searching for possible homologues or phylogenetic precursors of the expressive movements of smiling and laughter it is important first of all to see whether one can detect in the phyletic range of the primates morphologically similar movements that resemble our expressive movements more strongly, the closer in that range the species are to our own. Similarity with respect to the causal context and the functional aspects are also important criteria, but less easy to use since motivational shifts appear to take place much more readily during phylogenetic development than changes in the motor patterns (Baerends, 1959).

With respect to the present issue two primate displays come to our attention immediately. The first is the '*grin*'-*face* (van Hooff, 1962; Andrew, 1963) or *silent bared-teeth* display (van Hooff, 1967). The second is the *play-face* (van Hooff, 1962; Andrew, 1963; Bolwig, 1964) or *relaxed open-mouth* display (van Hooff, 1967).

1. The silent bared-teeth display

This display is characterized by: fully retracted mouth-corners and lips so that an appreciable part of the gums is bared; closed or only slightly opened mouth; absence of vocalization; inhibited body movements and eyes that are widely or normally open and can be directed straight or obliquely towards an interacting partner (Fig. 1).

The *silent bared-teeth* display strongly resembles a class of *vocalized bared-teeth* displays, with which it shares the marked horizontal and vertical lip retraction. The vocalizations are mostly high-pitched and often loud. Depending on other (for instance temporal) characteristics these can best be denoted as screams, squeals, barks, geckers.

The *vocalized bared-teeth* display occurs not only in probably all pri-

Fig. 1. *Silent bared-teeth* display by a 'submissive' crab-eating monkey (*Macaca irus*).

mates (van Hooff, 1967), but also in most other mammals. It is phylogenetically one of the oldest facial expressions. In primitive mammals like marsupials (cf. Gewalt, 1966; Ewer, 1968), insectivores (cf. Herter, 1957), rodents (cf. Eibl-Eibesfeldt, 1957; Allin and Banks, 1968), primitive carnivores (cf. Hoesch, 1964; Pohl, 1967) and primitive primates (cf. Kaufmann, 1965; Epple, 1967) it is often the only facial expression. In primitive mammals the expiration is not always vocalized, but there may be a forceful 'spitting' or 'hissing' instead. Moreover, the lip retraction may not be very obvious, if the lips are not very prominent (cf. Ewer, 1968).

These animals characteristically show this intense vocalized display when they are subject to some threat or strong aversive stimulation. It is shown, for instance, in a situation of defence. Usually the actor manifests a strong or moderate tendency to flee (cf. Fig. 2). The display occurs especially when this tendency is thwarted, for instance when the actor simply cannot flee because it is cornered, or when other factors (e.g. the tendency to stay with youngsters or near some favoured possession) inhibit flight. In infants it may be a signal of discomfort.

With respect to the derivation of the display, i.e. to the original function of the different display elements that compose it, several possibilities exist that do not necessarily exclude each other. Strong expiration, lip retraction and other elements like tongue protrusion and horizontal headshaking are protective responses evoked by strong, aversive stimulation of the face and especially the oesophagus (Andrew, 1963). In the defensive posture the widely opened mouth and the baring of the teeth, which are usually accompanied by shrill barks or hisses, may be regarded as a preparedness to bite, should the attacker suddenly advance (cf. van Hooff, 1962). Given the strong vocalization, the baring of the teeth may also be seen as a secondary effect of the vocalization reflex, the muscles of mouth and throat region being tensed during strong vocalization in order to protect the vibrating tissue (Andrew, 1963). The signal effect that the pattern elements undoubtedly also had may have led, during the course of evolution, to a generalization of causes and a differential facilitation and ritualization of the elements.

The *silent bared-teeth* display is a submissive gesture in most higher primates (for a review see also Spivak, 1968). A few species are now known in which the display can also be given by a dominant animal towards a

Fig. 2. *Silent bared-teeth* display during greeting by a 'confident' Celebes ape (*Cynopithecus niger*).

subordinate (see Fig. 2) *Macaca maurus, Cynopithecus, Pan* (van Hooff, 1967); *Mandrillus, Theropithecus* (van Hooff, 1967; Spivak, 1968). The context in which it then occurs suggests that it may function also as a reassuring signal or even as a sign of attachment in these species.

2. *The relaxed open-mouth display*

Beside the *silent bared-teeth* display another display, the *play-face* (van Hooff, 1962; Andrew, 1963; Bolwig, 1964) or *relaxed open-mouth* display (van Hooff, 1967), is of interest. In the majority of primates it has much in

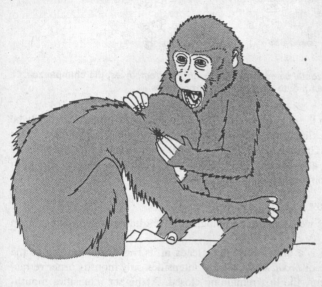

Fig. 3. 'Gnaw-wrestling' (social play) by crab-eating monkeys (*Macaca irus*); the animal on the right shows the *relaxed open-mouth* display as an intention movement to gnaw.

common with the aggressive *staring open-mouth* display. It is likewise characterized by a rather widely opened mouth, and lips that remain covering all or the greater part of the teeth. It differs from the *staring open-mouth* display by the free and easy nature of the eye and body movements and by the fact that the mouth-corners are not pulled forward (Fig. 4). It is often accompanied by quick and shallow rather staccato breathing. In some species, the breathing may be vocalized (e.g. the chimpanzee). The vocalizations then sound like 'ahh ahh ahh'.

In all the primates in which it occurs the *relaxed open-mouth* display typically accompanies the boisterous mock-fighting and chasing involved in social play (Loizos, 1967). It can be regarded as a ritualized intention movement of the *gnawing* which is a characteristic part of the play of many mammals (see, for instance, Eibl-Eibesfeldt, 1957), and may function as a meta-communicative signal that the ongoing behaviour is not meant seriously, but is to be interpreted instead as 'mock-fighting' (Bateson, 1955)

(a)   (b)

Fig. 4. (a) *Horizontal bared-teeth* display in *Pan troglodytes*, the chimpanzee. (b) *Relaxed open-mouth* display in *Pan troglodytes*.

(cf. Fig. 5). In the chimpanzee the *relaxed open-mouth* display can easily be elicited by tickling, and many authors (e.g. Darwin, 1872; Foley, 1935; Kohts, 1937; Grzimek, 1941; Yerkes, 1943) were struck by its resemblance both in form and context with our laughter. The data suggest that both displays are phylogenetically closely related.

Human displays

In humans, as well, smiling and laughter have qualitatively different form and function.

First, there is a dimension which leads in its most intense form to the 'cheese' smile or *broad smile*. At low intensities only mouth-corner retraction may occur, the lips remaining closed. At higher intensities mouth-corner retraction becomes very marked; the mouth may open slightly and vertical retraction of the lips occurs leading to baring of the upper teeth and part of the upper gums and occasionally also of the lower teeth. (For a description of various types of smiles see also Grant, 1969.) The *broad smile* may be seen, for instance, in greeting and has been recorded in this context by Eibl-Eibesfeldt (1968). It may then be accompanied by an eyebrow-lift and head-nod. It would seem that this type of smile, with active baring of the teeth, is associated particularly with the emphatic manifestation of a non-hostile, friendly attitude (e.g. during greeting, from adults towards children, when apologizing, etc.). (See photo inset.)

At the extreme of the other dimension is the full-hearted *wide-mouth laugh* with relatively widely-opened mouth, mild to moderate baring of the upper teeth, mild retraction of the mouth-corners, characteristic 'ha ha' vocalizations, throwing backwards of head and a decreased tendency to maintain visual contact (Fig. 5). At milder intensities it may appear in a diminutive form: the mouth is only slightly opened, and there is only slight retraction of the mouth-corners, and hardly any vertical retraction of the lips. The vocalizations also appear in a reduced form: they may

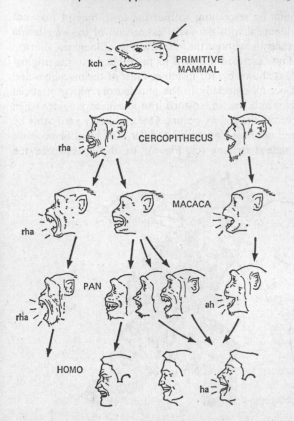

Fig. 5. The phylogentic development of laughter and smiling as suggested by homologues in existing members of the phyletic scale leading to *Homo*. On the left is the speciation of the *silent bared-teeth* display and the *bared-teeth scream* display. The *sbt*-display, initially a submissive, later also a friendly response, seems to converge with the *relaxed open-mouth* display (on the right).

consist of a series of chuckles or, at the lowest intensities, even of a little staccato unvocalized expiration, given through the nose if the lips are closed. Such casual chuckles and snorts occur frequently during normal relaxed social contact. So, in the intensity range leading to the full-hearted *wide-mouth laugh* the silent *broad smile* does not necessarily occur.

The *wide-mouth laugh* is very characteristic of children's play. There it alternates with a typical expression that in its intense form is rare in adults. It is characterized by a wide open mouth, and only slight to moderate vertical and horizontal lip retraction, so that the teeth may or may not show. It is almost identical with the facial expression of the *wide-mouth laugh* but it is given silently without the vocalizations of laughter. Blurton Jones (1967), who first described it, noted its resemblance to the original primate 'play-face', as shown by, for instance, most of the macaques and the chimpanzee. It occurs especially in the anticipatory phase of social play both in the actor and reactor, to turn into vocalized laughter when the expected unexpected, the *pointe*, occurs. One can easily verify this by playing hide-and-seek or chase-play with a toddler. The resemblance with the chimpanzee is indeed striking (cf. Fig. 6). In the chimpanzee the

Fig. 6. Inter-specific social play. Chimpanzee, in active role, shows *relaxed open-mouth* display, regularly accompanied by 'ah ah'-vocalizations. Boy, mainly in passive or reactive role, shows *wide-mouth laugh*.

staccato 'ahah' that may accompany the *relaxed open-mouth* display reaches its maximum also when some sudden move occurs or the grip is suddenly tightened during play. One can observe this best by playing with and tickling a tame chimpanzee.

Ontogeny of human laughter and smiling

Many studies have been made of the early development of smiling and laughter in human infants (for a review see Laroche and Tcheng, 1963). Only a few authors have paid attention to the actual form of the expressions and specified what they understood by 'smile' and 'laugh'. Washburn (1929), who has given detailed descriptions, noted that the first expression to be generally interpreted as a social smile has an unusual shape. The mouth is widely opened, the lips are not much retracted, and the mouth has a round aperture. Though mouth-corner retraction occurs soon after birth, the 'croissant' type of smile appears in social settings only at an age of 4 to 5 months. In the 'croissant' smile the mouth is not opened widely, but instead the mouth-corners are pulled back and slightly upwards. In true laughter and in the human 'play-face' the open-mouth posture remains. At about the time the *croissant-smile* appears, the human infant starts to differentiate between familiar and strange faces and smiling becomes selective (see e.g. Laroche and Tcheng, 1963; Gewirtz, 1965). One wonders whether the morphological differentiation corresponds with a motivational differentiation that is in agreement with the distinctions between laughter and smiling proposed above. Is the early *round-mouth smile* comparable to the *relaxed open-mouth face*, and is the manifestation of a relaxed attitude when vital needs are fulfilled in which 'playful' interaction is appreciated? Does the *croissant smile* bear more an affinity to the *silent bared-teeth* display, and is it perhaps more a greeting display, in which the infant greets with relief the recognized familiar?

The present essay has certainly not provided definitive answers, but the comparative perspective in which the phenomena of laughter and smiling have been placed, and the questions that have come to mind as a result, may contribute to further clarification of the role of these displays in human non-verbal communication.

(From Hinde, R. A. (ed.), *Non-verbal Communication*, Cambridge University Press, 1972, pp. 209–37.)

References

ALLIN, J. T., and BANKS, E. M. (1968), 'Behavioural biology of the collared lemming (*Dicrostonyx groenlandicus* Traill)', I. 'Agonistic behaviour', *Animal Behaviour*, Vol. 16, pp. 245–62.

ANDREW, R. J. (1963), 'The origin and evolution of the calls and facial expressions of primates', *Behaviour*, No. 20, pp. 1–109.

BAERENDS, G. P. (1959), 'Comparative methods and the concept of homology in the study of behaviour', *Arch. Neerl. Zool. Suppl.*, Vol. 1, No. 13, pp. 401–17.

BATESON, G. (1955), 'A theory of play and phantasy', *Psychiat. Res. Rept. A*, No. 2, pp. 39–51. (And see this volume, p. 119.)

BLURTON JONES, N. G. (1967), 'An ethological study of some aspects of social behaviour of children in nursery schools', in D. Morris (ed.), *Primate Ethology*, Weidenfeld & Nicolson. (And see this volume, p. 352.)

BOLWIG, N. (1964), 'Facial expression in primates with remarks on a parallel development in certain carnivores (a preliminary report on work in progress)', *Behaviour*, No. 22, pp. 167–93.

DARWIN, C. (1872), *The Expression of the Emotions in Man and Animals*, John Murray.

EIBL-EIBESFELDT, I. (1957), 'Ausdrucksformen der Säugetiere', *Handb. Zool. Berl.* 8 (8) 10, 6, pp. 1–26.

EIBL-EIBESFELDT, I. (1968), 'Zur ethologie der menschlichen Grussverhaltens. I. Beobachtungen an Balinesen, Papuas und Samoanern nebst vergleichende Bemerkungen', *Z. Tierpsychol.*, 25, pp. 727–44.

EPPLE, G. (1967), 'Vergleichende Untersuchungen über Sexual – und Sozialverhalten der Krallenaffen (Hapalidae)', *Folia primat.*, No. 7, pp. 37–65.

EWER, R. F. (1968), 'A preliminary survey of the behaviour in captivity of the dasyurid marsupial *Sminthopsis crassicaudata* (Gould)', *Z. Tierpsychol.*, No. 25, pp. 319–65.

FOLEY, J. P. (1935), 'Judgement of facial expression of emotion in the chimpanzee', *J. Soc. Psychol.* No. 6, pp. 31–67.

GEWALT, W. (1966), 'Kleine Beobachtungen an seltenen Beuteltieren im Berliner Zoo. III. Tüpfelbeutelmarder (*Satanellus hallucatus albopunctatus* Schlegel 1880)', *D. zool. Garten*, No. 32, pp. 99–107.

GEWIRTZ, J. L. (1965), 'The course of infant smiling in four child-rearing environments in Israel', *Determinants of Infant Behavior*, Vol. III, B. M. Foss (ed.), Wiley, New York.

GRANT, E. C. (1969), 'Human facial expression', *Man*, No. 4 (n.s.), pp. 525–36.

GRZIMEK, B. (1941), 'Beobachtungen an einem Schimpansenmädchen', *Z. Tierpsychol*, No. 4, pp. 295–306.

HERTER, K. (1957), 'Das Verhalten de Insectivoren', *Handb. Zool. Berlin*, 8, 10 (10), pp. 1–50.

HOESCH, W. (1964), 'Beobachtungen an einem zahmen Honigdachs (*Mellivora capensis*)', *D. zool. Garten*, No. 28, pp. 182–8.

HOOFF, J. A. R. A. M. VAN (1962), 'Facial expressions in higher primates', *Symp. Zool. Soc. Lond.*, No. 8, pp. 97–125.

HOOFF, J. A. R. A. M. VAN (1967), 'The facial displays of the catarrhine monkeys and apes', in *Primate Ethology*, D. Morris (ed.), Weidenfeld & Nicolson, pp. 7–68.

KAUFMANN, J. H. (1965), 'Studies on the behavior of captive tree shrews (*Tupaia glis*)', *Folia primat.*, No. 3, pp. 50–74.

KOHTS, N. (1937), 'La conduite du petit chimpanzé et de l'enfant de l'homme', *J. Psychol. Norm. Pathol.*, No. 34, pp. 494–531.

LAROCHE, J. G., and TCHENG F. (1963), 'La sourire du nourisson. (La voix comme facteur declenchant)', *Publication Université de Louvain*.

LOIZOS, C. (1967), 'Play behavior in higher primates: a review', in *Primate Ethology*, D. Morris (ed.), Weidenfeld & Nicolson. pp. 176–218.

POHL, A. (1967), 'Beitrage zur Ethologie un Biologie des Sonnendachses (*Helictis personata* Gray 1831) in Gefangenschaft', *D. zool. Garten*, No. 33, pp. 225–47.

SPIVAK, H. (1968), 'Ausdrucksformen und soziale Beziehungen in einer Dschelada-Gruppe (*Theropithecus gelada*) im Zoo', Juris-Verlag, Zurich.

WASHBURN, R. W. (1929), 'A study of the smiling and laughing of infants in the first year of life', *Genet. Psychol. Monogr.* 6, pp. 397–535.
YERKES, R. M. (1943), *Chimpanzees, a Laboratory Colony*, Yale University Press.

Ontogenesis of the Play Face among Stumptail Monkeys

This paper is based on a filmed 500-hour observational study of a laboratory social group of stumptailed macaques. It demonstrates the visual and tactile communicative repertoire of the species and shows how the adult communication system develops in infants.

Anthropologists are concerned with the communication systems of non-human primates because of their implications for the evolution of human communication. The study on which the following discussion is based attempted to discover how individual stumptailed macaques (*Macaca arctoides*) become communicating members of a social group. The study defined communication as 'the process by which the behaviour in one individual regularly affects the behaviour in another' (Chevalier-Skolnikoff, 1971).

Methods

The development of communication patterns in the stumptailed macaques was filmed during 500 hours of observation of a laboratory colony of macaques at the Primate Laboratory of the Department of Psychiatry, Stanford University School of Medicine (Chevalier-Skolnikoff, 1971). Three infants were studied in a social group consisting of one adult male, four adult females (three of them mothers), one sub-adult male, and one sub-adult female.

The animals were housed in an indoor enclosure 12 feet wide by 18 feet long by 7 feet high. The developing infants were observed and filmed as they intereacted with their mothers, with peers, and with other members of their social group. A detailed analysis of behaviour was achieved through frame-by-frame and stop-motion examination of motion picture film, and analysis of audio tapes, as well as through direct observation. The film analysis systematically focused on the different body-parts of the animals as they interacted socially. In this way, the 'expressive elements', i.e., the anatomical features that assume particular positions (van Hooff, 1962) for particular behaviours could be examined and compared.

Description of the film

Part I. Introduces the visual communicative repertoire of adult stump-tailed macaques. Adults of this species as well as the adults of other macaque species communicate with each other by means of a combination of facial expressions, gestures, and body postures; tactile behaviours; vocalizations; and olfactory stimuli. Visual behaviour is probably the most important means of communication in macaques, although tactile communication is also of great importance for stump-tailed macaques.

Part II. Demonstrates the behaviour of the newborn stumptailed macaque. The neonate is relatively helpless but is capable of making several reflexive movements, he can grasp and cling and root and suck. The newborn communicates by means of these reflexes. This reflexive communication is exclusively tactile and is very different from the primarily visual adult, communicative repertoire. Nevertheless, many of the visual communication patterns of the adult communication system appear to develop from these infantile reflexes.

Part III. Illustrates the ontogenetic development of some adult communicative patterns.

The lip-smacking, puckered-lips, and mutual mouth nibble (or 'kissing') complex

For the first ten days, the infant's behaviour is primarily reflexive and occurs in response to tactile and kinesthetic stimuli. However, from birth infants occasionally visually fixate on other monkeys. When this occurs they often make *puckered-lips* expressions accompanied by sucking mouth movements. These puckered-lips expressions are the same expressions that infants have when they are on their mother's nipple (Fig. 1). The lips are extended and

Fig. 1. The facial expression of the infant when nursing on its mother's nipple. Note that the tongue protrudes slightly and encircles the underside of the nipple. (All figures, which are based on the film, are drawn from the same angle to facilitate comparison.)

contracted both horizontally and vertically, thereby forming a pucker, with horizontal lines running along the muzzle. The mouth movements that accompany this expression are the same as the sucking movements that occur during nursing. The tongue is protruded slightly as it is during nursing (when it partially encircles the nipple, thereby forming a vacuum for sucking); and air appears to be sucked into the mouth. As the infants mature, these behaviours develop gradually into the friendly adult *puckered-lips* (Fig. 2) and *lip-smacking* expressions. The adult puckered-lips ex-

Fig. 2. The adult puckered-lips expression, a friendly expression. (*This figure is used by permission of the copyright owner, Academic Press, Inc.*)

pression is essentially the same as the infantile puckered-lips expression, except that the adult's ears are consistently drawn back. The lip-smacking expression consists of rapidly repeated movements of the jaws, lips, and tongue from a closed-mouthed, puckered-lips position to a position with jaws and lips slightly opened (and lips still puckered) and with the tongue slightly protruded, as the infant's tongue is when the infant has the nipple in its mouth. The mouth movements of adult lip smacking are more rapid and consist of longer series of smacks than do the sucking movements of small infants as they make puckered-lips expressions. By two weeks of age, infants make the puckered-lips and lip-smacking expressions regularly in friendly social contexts; and air is no longer sucked into the mouth although the ear position is still variable. By three weeks of age, the expressions have achieved their adult form: and the ears are regularly retracted, as they are in the adult.

Puckered-lips expressions and sucking also occur in small infants in response to oral contacts with wet body parts, such as the eyes and mouths, of other monkeys. As infants mature, they frequently appear, as do adults, to seek out such oral contacts. These mutual mouth contacts, or *mutual mouth nibbles*, occur during friendly social interactions and in form and context resemble the human kiss.

Thus, lip smacking, the puckered-lips expression, and mutual mouth nibble (or 'kiss') of the adult appear to develop ontogenetically from the infantile sucking reflex. This development involves changes in both the forms and the functions of the behaviours. The formal changes have just been described. Functionally the reflex behaviours of the neonate serve the vital functions of nursing and of maintaining body contact with the mother while the adult behaviours serve social communicative functions.

The open-mouthed, eyelids-down play expression and the open-mouthed stare threat expression

At approximately one or two weeks of age, the infant begins to explore his environment, first his own body and his mother's and then inanimate objects and other monkeys. Like the six-month-old human infant, the infant monkey initially explores everything with his mouth. This mouthing appears to be a continuation of infantile rooting for the nipple and, in fact, the two are at first indistinguishable. The indiscriminate mouthing becomes more and more exclusively directed towards other monkeys, rather than towards the mother. As the infant matures, mouthing and open-mouthed approaches appear more and more frequently as initiations of social interactions with other monkeys. At first, the nature of these interactions appears to be ambiguous; it is hard to tell whether they are playful or aggressive. But as the infant becomes older, the two patterns diverge. By the time an infant is one to two months old, the open-mouthed play face and the open-mouthed threat have become distinguishable, the former

Fig. 3. The open-mouthed, eyelids-down play expression. (*This figure is used by permission of the copyright owner, Academic Press, Inc.*)

being characterized by an open mouth with ears back, lowered eyelids, and eye contact avoidance (Fig. 3) and the latter by an open mouth with ears forward, eyes wide, and eye contact (Fig. 4). These developmental sequences indicate that the *open-mouthed, eyelids-down* play expression and the *open-*

Fig. 4. The open-mouthed stare, a threat expression. (*This figure is used by permission of the copyright owner, Academic Press, Inc.*)

mouthed stare threat expression develop ontogenetically from the infantile rooting reflex, first through a stage of indiscriminate mouthing, and then through a period of open-mouthed social approaches.

Embracing and huddling behaviours

Adults frequently embrace and huddle together as greetings or as friendly gestures. These adult tactile patterns appear to derive from the reflex grasping and clinging seen in the newborn. Indeed, embracing is indistinguishable from infantile clinging except for the contexts in which it occurs and for the facial expression of intense emotion (*teeth-chattering* expression) which accompanies the adult pattern. Adult huddling includes grasping and kneading of the partner's fur, the same kind of grasping that occurs during infantile clinging. Although all the motor behaviours involved in embracing and huddling have been performed by the time the infant is two or three weeks old, embracing does not occur until the infant is around three months old; and huddling does not occur until the infant is around six months old.

Grooming behaviour

Rudimentary grooming movements are first seen in three to five-week-old infants. These early behaviours are fragmentary and barely recognizable as incipient grooming. They consist of horizontal *sliding* movements of the two hands across mushy or furry substances. The other motor components of the adult grooming behaviour complex are incorporated into grooming as the infant becomes older. By the seventh week, *picking* movements usually are incorporated into the behaviour. By the tenth week, infants were observed *pulling* the hair apart along the parts they had made in the hair by means of sliding movements, and *licking* the skin. By ten weeks of age, infants generally were using all the motor patterns that have been observed during adult grooming (i.e., sliding, picking, pulling, and licking).

Part IV. Presents a partial species repertoire of the adult visual and tactile communicative behaviour of *Macaca arctoides* and demonstrates the interaction of these two modes of behaviour in the communication of stumptailed monkeys.

(From 'Visual and tactile communication in *Macaca arctoides* and its ontogenetic development', *American Journal of Physical Anthropology*, Vol. 38, 1973, pp. 515–18.)

References

CHEVALIER-SKOLNIKOFF, S. (1971), 'The ontogeny of communication in *Macaca speciosa*', Doctoral dissertation, University of California, Berkeley.

HOOFF, J. A. R. A. M. VAN (1962), 'Facial expressions in higher primates', *Symp. Zool. Soc. Lond.*, No. 8, pp. 97–125.

An Ethogram for Rhesus Monkeys: Antithetical Contrasts in Posture and Movement

This report is based on observations of free-ranging rhesus monkeys on Cayo Santiago, Puerto Rico.

Darwin (1872) showed that moods which contrast markedly are accompanied by expressive behaviours which emphasize opposite or strongly contrasting characteristics. Behaviourists have since found that the principle of antithesis applies to a wide variety of animal taxa. Antithesis of displays reduces confusion between communicative signals, particularly between signals implying threat on the one hand, and subordinance or appeasement on the other. Most users of the principle of antithesis have contrasted pairs of communicative acts.

A consideration of the expressive postures and movements of the rhesus monkey, insofar as they contrast in the direction and orientation of movement within the anatomical planes, indicates that at least five moods may be distinguished by the antithetical characteristics of their outward expression.

The anatomical planes

The mid-sagittal plane divides a monkey along its axis of bilateral symmetry. The frontal or coronal plane lies perpendicular to the mid-sagittal plane and parallel to the longitudinal axis of the body or the vertebral column. The transverse plane is perpendicular to both the frontal and sagittal planes and transects the longitudinal axis of the body.

The mid-sagittal plane undoubtedly represents a very real and important axis of self-reference for the animal in his orientations to his physical, biotic and social surroundings (Von Uexküll, 1921). The frontal and transverse planes are convenient, geometrically defined, reference loci for the anatomist in describing the relations of anatomical parts or positions, but they do not correspond to anatomically defined natural divisions of the body. Figure 1G shows the relations of the anatomical planes superimposed upon a rhesus monkey in a neutral attitude.

Concept of the neutral mood

The neuro-musculo-skeletal system carries out the primary functions of balance and locomotion. Evolution has made use of this primary system by superimposing upon it a repertoire of movements and poses which serve the function of indicating the mood of the animal and communicating it in the visual channel to conspecifics. Usually the functions of balance and locomotion will be manifest and take precedence over the expressive functions. The independence of the expressive functions in the organization of the animal's behaviour is indicated by occasions when a highly aroused individual performs a communicative display with such intensity on an inappropriate substrate, such as a narrow tree limb, that he loses his balance and falls to the ground.

The neuro-musculo-skeletal system also provides the mechanisms by which an individual orients towards events, objects or other individuals in the environment. Orientation may involve a modification in posture whether or not a mood which normally is accompanied by expressive behaviour is also active at the moment.

Expressive movements may be altered by the requirements of simultaneously activated locomotor or orienting movements. Unusual or bizarre postures may result when the display is directed towards a partially concealed individual, or towards one who is vertically removed from the displaying monkey. Conversely, if the modifications of posture and locomotion due to the activation of a particular mood are minimal or absent, the animal's posture and movement may be considered neutral in respect of expressive behaviour and the animal may be said to be in a neutral mood.

The descriptions which follow apply to cases in which the masking effects of the primary locomotor requirements of balance and orientation are minimally present. The sketches do not contain information about the temporal patterning of the shifts in posture. The sketches only indicate the kinds of contrasts which are more easily observed in life or on film, where the temporal patterning of the changes in pose are also observable.

General arousal

The transformation of a relaxed individual into an aroused and alert one has often been observed. The alert state has correlates in facial expression which have been described by Van Hooff (1967), and in postures which have been described by Hinde and Rowell (1962). General arousal or alertness can be distinguished from the activation of the particular moods to be discussed below.

Movements of attack

An attack by a confident animal may begin with a bobbing of the head accompanied by an open mouth directed towards the victim, grade into a lunging of the shoulders towards the victim, and finally become a charge ending when the dominant individual bites the victim. These are some of the best known of the expressive movements of the rhesus monkey and are recognized by all the above cited authors who have studied this species. Careful analysis of the behaviour of the attacker show that movements from a high to a low position in the mid-sagittal plane are emphasized (Fig. 1A, B). If a mildly aroused attacker is not facing his opponent at the beginning of a fight, he may begin by merely turning and bobbing his head towards the victim. In the same episode, however, if the victim does not respond satisfactorily, the attacker will usually adjust his posture so that the longitudinal axis of his body is oriented directly towards the victim and the bobbing movements now involve head, shoulders and thorax. The point here is that as the attacker becomes increasingly aroused the high to low movements in the mid-sagittal plane become exaggerated.

Movements of submission

The postures and movements of the victim contrast strongly to those of the attacker in that they emphasize lateral flexion of the vertebral column and other movements within the frontal plane. As is well known, the victim may attempt to present both his hind quarters and his grimacing face towards the attacker simultaneously, so that the animal's body is displayed laterally to the attacker. If the victim flees, the tendency for lateral flexion disappears, undoubtedly overridden by the requirements of rapid and directed locomotion. Nevertheless a slight lateral flexion in the frontal plane is almost always given by a subordinate threatened by a dominant, if only for a fleeting second, and has given rise to such appellations as cringing or cowering (Fig. 1C, D).

Amicable, non-hostile, non-fearful approach behaviour

Fig. 1E, F shows a display which contrasts strongly with both the movements of the threatening or attacking animal and also with the movements of a frightened subordinate. It consists of a monkey in a neutral pose rapidly extending (dorsiflexing) its head and sometimes torso upwards in the mid-sagittal plane. This movement may be repeated in a series of jerks in which the upward movement is strongly emphasized in contrast to the return downward movement. At the extreme high position the head cannot be further extended (or dorsiflexed). At this point, as if the mood were frustrated by the limitations of the cervical articulations, some rotatory

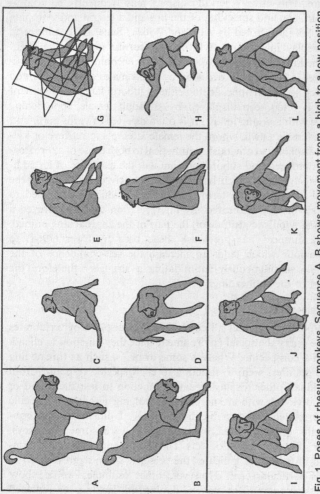

Fig. 1. Poses of rhesus monkeys. Sequence A, B shows movement from a high to a low position in the mid-sagittal plane indicating threat. Pose C shows the lateral flexion in the frontal plane characteristic of a subordinate animal. Pose D shows another animal displaying subordinance. Sequence E, F shows an animal giving an upward jerk in the mid-sagittal plane. Pose G is a monkey in a neutral sitting posture upon whom the anatomical planes have been superimposed. Pose H shows one member of a wrestling pair rotating head and torso in the transverse plane. Sequence I, J, K, L shows the oblique bobbing movements of a querying animal.

movements (not illustrated) take place as the upward pointed chin strives to remove itself even further from its horizontally directed position in the neutral posture. This upward jerking display may frequently be accompanied by protrusion and smacking of the lips and a lateral and whipping motion of the tail (also noted by Altmann, 1962a; Sade, 1971; Lindberg, 1971). This display in its mildest form may consist merely of a slight elevating of the muzzle in the mid-sagittal plane accompanied by protrusion of the lips. It is given on occasion by adult males and females and juveniles of each sex when approaching either a subordinate or a dominant individual. It is often seen displayed by an adult female approaching another female with a young infant. It is often directed towards an infant, other than the female's own, whom the female attempts to retrieve or kidnap. Since the display is so obviously antithetical to both those of a threatening and of a frightened and subordinate animal, the existence of an additional mood is suggested which has not been clearly pointed out in the primatological literature. The term 'reassurance', which I first used to characterize this display, indicated my interpretation that it conveyed a friendly and non-agonistic attitude on the part of the approaching animal. However, 'reassurance' has previously been used by Ewer (1968) to designate behaviour which tends to increase the self-confidence of the performer while simultaneously intimidating a stranger: therefore the circumlocution of the subheading.

Querying movements

Count (1969) pointed out that all communicative displays of vertebrates are attempts to query the social environment since they function to elicit a response from a conspecific. Whereas some displays, such as threatening or submissive gestures, seem to function to elicit specific responses from another individual, other displays seem to function to test the mood of the second individual without necessarily bringing about any specific response. The sequence shown by fig. 1I, J, K, L illustrates the bobbing movements often directed by monkeys towards other monkeys, humans, other species, or novel objects. The open-mouth face of the monkey illustrated in fig. 1I, K indicates the presence of an aggressive component in this particular case. However, other examples would show that the aggressive component may be diminished, lacking, or replaced by some other mood. The aspect of this display which is antithetical to the previously discussed displays is the rapid alternation of downward and upward movements and especially the emphasis on oblique movements of the head, which crosses the mid-sagittal plane as it is lowered and raised. An animal who alternates rapidly between attack and flight shows movements which have little in common with the oblique bobbing display. An animal so motivated switches rapidly from the mid-sagittal attacking movements to the laterally flexed cowering movements of submission. A subordinate animal attacking a dominant likewise displays postures and facial expressions which are clearly resultants of the simultaneous activation of attack and flight tendencies (defensive threat) and which bear little similarity to the oblique movements discussed here. The antithesis of these oblique and erratic bobbing movements to the other displays discussed above suggests that a different mood is active, which I call the 'querying mood'.

Play

Any normal movement may be exaggerated during episodes of play among monkeys and play behaviour is often interpreted as representing an incomplete or distorted form of behaviour characteristic of some other mood (Meyer-Holzapfel, 1956). However, observation of play episodes among rhesus monkeys indicates that a postural component is often present which seems to be unique to play behaviour, namely rotation of the head or torso in the transverse plane (Fig. 1H). An animal running towards a play episode or in the chases which commonly occur between bouts of wrestling usually is recognized by its peculiarly bouncing or gambolling locomotion. Careful observation indicates that this type of locomotion differs from a neutral, aggressive, or subordinate type in part by the tendency of the playfully running animal to rotate its head and even shoulders and to abduct its limbs during the non-contact phases of the gait. This produces the impression of movement around the longitudinal axis of the body, or movement in the transverse plane. It may be that this tendency for movement in the transverse plane is the 'metacommunicative' message which Altmann (1962b) postulated as being necessary for play to be distinguished from activities with more serious consequences. Another interpretation could be that because the movements of play are clearly antithetical to those of the other moods discussed above, play should be considered a mood in its own right and not simply derived from other aspects of behaviour.

Comparative

Limitations of space preclude detailed comparison between this study and other reports. However, examination of photographs of *Papio hamadryas* (Kummer, 1968), *Theropithecus gelada* (Spivak, 1968), *Miopithecus talapoin* (Gautier-Hion, 1971) and unpublished personal observation on *Cercopithecus aethiops* indicate that these postural characteristics may be widespread in the Cercopithecidae.

(From the *American Journal of Physical Anthropology*, Vol. 38, 1973, pp. 537–42.)

References

ALTMANN, S. A. (1962a), 'A field study of the sociobiology of rhesus monkeys, *Macaca mulatta*', *Annals of the New York Academy of Science*, No. 102, pp. 338–435.

ALTMANN, S. A. (1962), 'Social behavior of anthropoid primates: Analysis of recent concepts', in *Roots of Behavior*, E. L. Bliss (ed.), Harper, New York, pp. 277–85.

ALTMANN, S. A. (1965), 'Sociobiology of rhesus monkeys. II. Stochastics of social communication', *J. Theoret. Biol.*, No. 8, pp. 490–522.

ALTMANN, S. A. (1968), 'Primates', in *Animal Communication*, T. A. Sebeck, (ed.), Indiana University Press, pp. 466–522.

COUNT, E. W. (1969), 'Animal communication in man-science: An essay in perspective', in *Approaches to Animal Communication*, T. A. Sebeck and A. Ramsay (eds.), Mouton, The Hague, pp. 71–130.

DARWIN, C. (1872), *The Expression of the Emotions in Man and Animals*, John Murray, pp. 1–366.

EWER, R. F. (1968), *Ethology of Mammals*, Plenum Press, New York.

GAUTIER-HION, A. (1971), 'Répertoire comportemental du Talapoin (*Miopithecus talapoin*)', *Ext. Rev. Biol. Gabon*, No. 7, pp. 293–391.

HINDE, R. A., and ROWELL, T. E. (1962), 'Communication by postures and facial expressions in the rhesus monkey (*Macaca mulatta*)', *Proceedings of the Zoological Society of London*, No. 138, pp. 1–21.

HOOFF, J. A. R. A. M. VAN (1967), 'The facial displays of the Catarrhine monkeys and apes', in *Primate Ethology*, D. Morris (ed.), Weidenfeld & Nicolson, pp. 7–68. (And see this volume, p. 130.)

KUMMER, H. (1968), *Social Organization of Hamadryas Baboons. A Field Study*, University of Chicago Press.

LINDBERG, D. G. (1971), 'The rhesus monkey in North India. An ecological and behavioral study', in *Primate Behavior*, Vol. II, L. A. Rosenblum (ed.), Academic Press, New York, pp. 1–106.

MEYER-HOLZAPFEL, M. (1956), 'Das Spiel bei Säugetieren', *Handb. d. Zool.*, No. 8, pp. 1–36.

SADE, D. S. (1967), 'Determinants of dominance in a group of free-ranging rhesus monkeys', in *Social Communication Among Primates*, S. A. Altmann (ed.), University of Chicago Press, pp. 99–114.

SADE, D. S. (1971), 'Communication by tail positions in rhesus monkeys (*Macaca mulatta*)'. *American Journal of Physical Anthropology*, No. 35, p. 294.

SPIVAK, H. (1968), 'Ausdrucksformen und soziale Beziehungen in einer Dschelada-Gruppe (*Theropithecus gelada*) im Zoo', Juris Verlag, Zürich.

UEXKÜLL, J. VON (1921), *Umwelt und Innenwelt der Tiere* (2nd ed.), Springer, Berlin.

Part Two

Play and the World of Objects and Tools

This section deals with an ancient topic in the study of play. The maxim is that play provides practice to ready the young for performing the acts necessary to adult survival. But surely this could not be the case. Consider play fighting among savannah baboons. When one young animal fails to see the play signals of another, he takes the play attack for real. He responds not awkwardly but with fighting that is both efficient and smooth. Why do they play at aggression if they already know how to do it?

We suggest that in play the animal learns to combine certain behavioural routines and sub-routines. Freed from both internal and external pressures, the player combines constituent acts in a fashion that leads to a flexibility extending the range of his activity. The difference between play and work is that in the latter the objective is held invariant and the means are varied for achieving it. In play, an animal varies both means and objectives, gaining a better conception of the possibilities of connections and consequences that can be stored as generative knowledge for the future.

The thrust of the evidence in this book is that the major benefit of play is the combinatorial flexibility it bestows on behaviour. Yet mastery of constituent routines is important in its own right. Jane van Lawick-Goodall describes the rich locomotor play of chimpanzees: walking, running, climbing, and finally leaping. In the somewhat older chimpanzee she notes the importance of these practised sub-routines in more complex skills like termite fishing, a skill he will lack in adulthood if its constituents are not developed in earlier play. Jean Piaget reminds us, too, of the importance of early mastery play in human infants, play that is necessary if the child is to construct internal representations of the world he inhabits and acts upon.

It is the young of any species who are fascinated by novelty, as papers by Emil Menzel and M. Bertrand show. Studies of semi-domesticated Japanese macaques illustrate the route towards cultural innovation through the play of the young (Kawai, 1965). The inventions of the young, such as wheat winnowing and sweet potato washing, were transmitted from generation to generation, often 'up' to the mothers and then 'down' to subsequent offspring. This surely earns the name 'cultural innovation' for it is distinct from idiosyncratic or isolated invention that is lost at the death of the animal who produced it. Cultural innovation appears, then, to require the penchant of youth for novelty plus some rage for developing skills in new combination. The same taste for novelty and exploration among our own species is examined by Corrine Hutt and Alison Uttley in Part Two, and again by Erik Erikson in Part Four.

It is puzzling why the capacity for play should decline with age. Is it that culture and species adaptation depend on the acceptance of conventional rule structures and that these cannot tolerate the variation that would result if play extended into adulthood? Without some degree of playfulness, even in adults, there would be no inventiveness. But there seem to be upper and lower bounds on the amount of variation permissible – perhaps to ensure swift responses to crises.

References

KAWAI, M. (1965), 'Newly-acquired pre-cultural behaviour of the natural troop of Japanese monkeys on Koshima Islet', *Primates*, Vol. 6, No. 1.

A   Mastery Play

Chimpanzee Locomotor Play

It is no accident that many sections in this book begin with descriptions of the behaviour of chimpanzees at the Gombe Stream Reserve. Jane van Lawick-Goodall's accounts have a directness and naturalism that make them compelling. It is nowhere more evident than in her descriptions of mothers and their infants at play. Her Goblins, Merlins and Flos, each studied longitudinally and individually, make clear the later consequences of early play in a manner that no cross-sectional study can match.

By the time the chimpanzee infant is one year old, it is able to walk in a normal adult fashion, although (as we shall see below) it seldom proceeds in this manner until it is about 18 months old. During its second year the infant frequently moves along with an occasional 'crutching' step, even when on completely level ground.

Chimpanzee infants apparently make efforts to climb at about the same time as they begin to walk. Goblin, when first I saw him climb, moved up four hand- and footholds without difficulty: at that point his mother lifted him down again. Flint, however, was not so successful. I watched him as he clung to an upright stem, pulled himself into a bipedal position and made repeated efforts to grip to the stem with first one and then the other foot. Finally he fell back onto the ground and was quickly gathered up by his mother. A month later Flint was able to climb easily a few feet up a thin sapling; he then dangled down for ten minutes at a time. When he wanted to re-establish contact with his mother he usually reached towards her rather than try to climb down, until he was 8 months old. When he did try, however, I never saw him proceeding down a branch head first, in the manner described for some captive rhesus monkeys (Hinde, Rowell and Spencer-Booth, 1964).

About two weeks after they were first observed to climb, infants were able to clamber clumsily from one thin branch to another. Brachiation, with up to four hand movements, was observed in one infant at 36 weeks and another at 41 weeks of age.

Flint, when he was 28 weeks old, began to try to walk bipedally. At first he was only able to remain upright for a split second, but gradually he improved and by the time he was 39 weeks old he was able to take five or six steps. Usually he stood swaying for a second and then ran towards some object which he could grab (Fig. 1d). For a four-month period he invariably tried to walk bipedally rather than quadrupedally. Other chimpanzee infants were also observed walking bipedally between 9 and 11 months of age. Rhesus monkey infants between 7 and 25 weeks of age also move about frequently in an upright position (Hinde, Rowell and Spencer-Booth, 1964).

Throughout the first two years of its life the infant usually moves with care in the branches, making sure of each new hand- and foothold before relinquishing the last, and it usually moves along horizontal branches in the 'sloth' position (Fig. 1a) which presumably enables it to cling on more securely.

Locomotor play. Behaviour was called locomotor play, which involved the performance of locomotor patterns in a context which suggested that the only goal was the actual performance of the pattern itself. Thus Flint when he was 19 weeks old repeatedly climbed through his mother's groin, up her back, and then dived down head first over her other shoulder into her lap. Infants of between 8 and 12 months of age frequently dangled from a branch first from one hand and then the other whilst kicking about with their free limbs or grabbing at their own toes. Sometimes they did this for fifteen minutes on end. One infant of 9 months spent ten minutes climbing laboriously some four or five feet up a thick sloping branch and then sliding down backwards again. Flint began to turn somersaults when he was 45 weeks old. Most other infants, two juveniles, two adolescents and one old female were also observed turning somersaults (Fig. 1e).

Once the infant has become reasonably stable on its feet, it normally progresses with either a type of galloping locomotion, similar to that of the adult (Fig. 1b) or a series of leaps in which the feet are stamped heavily on the ground one after the other.

Some patterns may be 'invented' by a particular infant. One (Gilka) frequently pirouetted, spinning round and round as she moved forward (Fig. 1f). (Subsequently a second infant began to pirouette – this may have been imitation.) Gilka also, for several weeks on end, frequently moved along in the 'crutching' gait with one foot (either one) tucked firmly into the opposite groin. Another infant, as he ran, kicked one foot backwards.

Play in the trees becomes more active as the infant grows older. It swings and leaps from branch to branch, twirls and spins from side to side as it dangles, hangs down by its feet and may let go of its branch and plunge, head first, into the foliage below.

In many instances, locomotor play patterns are repeated time and time again. When the pattern involves a complicated series of swings and leaps from branch to branch the infant is sometimes markedly more proficient during the final round than it was during the first. This is a pointer which

Fig. 1. Showing various locomotor patterns of infants. (a) The 'sloth' position, (b) 1½-year-old 'galloping', (c) 7-month-old walking; note 'heel' of hand resting on ground, (d) 40-week-old infant (Flint) approaching rock in bipedal position, (e) 3-year-old somersaulting, (f) sequence of 3-year-old (Gilka) 'pirouetting'.

suggests that locomotor play may function, at least in part, as an aid in the development of muscular co-ordination as well as being beneficial to the development of the muscles themselves.

Some infants fell when they were playing in the trees. One dropped some eight feet to the ground when a brittle branch on which she was swinging broke off. Subsequently I saw her on three occasions holding firmly to a thick branch of the same type of tree whilst she tested a smaller branch, pulling downwards, and only gradually entrusting it with her whole weight. Thus, during locomotor play the infant also becomes increasingly familiar with its environment and learns which branches are safe and which it must avoid when it is jumping high above the ground.

Loizos (1967) has argued that 'it is simply not necessary to play in order to learn about the environment', and that, while play may be helpful in this context, such learning may equally be acquired through exploration and normal day-to-day activity. This is undoubtedly true in many cases. Once for example I saw a two-year-old start to climb a palm tree trunk using the dead ends of the previous year's fronds; he fell from a height of some ten feet when one of these broke. Normally, however, a young chimpanzee, as we have seen, moves through the trees with extreme caution during the course of feeding, following its mother, etc. When it moves in this way along dead or brittle branches these seldom break under its small weight. However, if the same infant leaps wildly onto the same branch during locomotor play (either alone or with other youngsters) there is a likelihood that it will break. Infants have been seen falling or nearly falling for this reason on a number of occasions.

Adolescent and mature individuals were observed to take wild leaps through the trees for a variety of reasons, such as during aggressive encounters, during social excitement when two groups met, when a sexually attractive female was first encountered or when they were suddenly frightened by the approach of a human, etc. Infants, however, were normally carried by their mothers during such situations, and almost the only occasion when they were seen to take risks – jumping wildly from branch to branch or down to the ground – occurred during locomotor play. This type of play, then, may be vital in order that the chimpanzee can learn certain types of information about its environment at a time when its bones are supple and it is still light in weight and less likely to hurt itself by falling than an older individual.

(From *The Behaviour of Chimpanzees: Animal Behaviour Monographs*, Vol. 1, Part 3, Baillière, Tindall & Cassell, 1968.)

References

HINDE, R. A., ROWELL, T. E., and SPENCER-BOOTH, Y. (1964), 'Behaviour of socially living rhesus monkeys in their first six months', *Proceedings of the Royal Society of London*, No. 143, pp. 609–49.

LAWICK-GOODALL, J. VAN (1967), 'Mother–offspring relationships in chimpanzees', in *Primate Ethology*, D. Morris (ed.), Weidenfeld & Nicolson.

LOIZOS, C. (1967), 'Play behaviour in higher primates: a review', in D. Morris, op. cit.

Object-Play in Cats

Kittens provide an illustration of the adaptive nature of play. Their play with objects appears to be closely related to actual predatory behaviour. Not only is it elicited by similar stimulus factors, but it is also stimulated in a similar manner by competition from litter-mates. This supports the view that while play is not a pastime exclusive to primates, it may be more closely linked to recognizably adaptive behaviour in sub-primate mammals.

My research indicates that object-play in cats is not a category of behaviour distinct from true predation. It uses the same motor-patterns as prey-catching, it occurs in response to stimuli found in prey, and it also seems to be influenced by some of the same causal factors as predation. Moreover, experiments show that as a play object incorporates more prey-like characteristics (e.g. small size, fur, 'animal' smell, movement) the range and relative proportions of the motor-patterns used by young cats became more like those found in play with a dead mouse, which in turn resembles play with live prey. Since play with live prey is a part of predatory behaviour, it can be argued that play with inanimate, inedible objects is only removed from predation by a matter of degree, and that those factors which are largely responsible for the differences between behaviour directed towards live prey and that directed towards inanimate objects are the stimulus characteristics, which limit the possible response.

Sequences of patterns seem to develop in response to feedback from the object, and it could be argued that if the object were live prey these would be part of the functional chain leading to killing and eating: consummatory acts do not occur because of the limitations of the stimulus objects.

Typically an object is first sniffed and/or patted; the stimulation received determines whether or not it is bitten (fur is the stimulus most effective in eliciting biting). If it is bitten it might then be picked up in the mouth, then shaken or thrown (with live prey this would serve to stun it) or carried (with prey to a corner perhaps, where it might eventually be eaten). Alternatively, the initial patting might cause the object to roll, in which case it might elicit crouching and pouncing (movement being the stimulus for these patterns) which, as with prey, would serve to immobilize it. A fur-less object is seldom bitten, carried, shaken or thrown; playing with it therefore entails the repetition of other than mouth patterns. Similarly, since with objects there can be no progression to the consummatory acts of killing and eating, it is logical to expect that if the cat sustains any interest in them sequences will be repeated. Repetition is a common phenomenon in play, and this sort of argument might help to explain it. However, it leaves unexplained the fact that cats play with live prey, which possess all the stimuli necessary for eliciting killing and eating. Even if we prove that there is a continuum between inanimate objects and live prey in the type of behaviour cats exhibit towards them, we still have to explain this hiatus in predatory behaviour between playing and killing. Obviously other factors have to be examined.

It has in fact been found (Baerends, personal communication) that an early training period with live prey (particularly between four and eight weeks) is important in making cats quick and efficient predators in that they catch, kill and eat their prey in a rapid sequence without playing. In other words, the build-up of excitement which Leyhausen considers was usually necessary for killing to occur (1965) is not necessary if a cat has had the opportunity to develop its predatory behaviour from an early age. Further, Baerends found that a minor disturbance could make cats which normally caught and killed quickly play for long periods instead. These observations indicate that there are causal factors involved in killing which are not necessary for play to occur, and vice versa. An argument which tries to prove that play is only divided from predation by a matter of degree must obviously take these into account.

Food-deprivation

Under experimental conditions food-deprivation was found not to affect the type or amount of play with objects, although the general response seemed to be less lively and less relaxed. As food-shortage is known to depress play in many species, and play is generally considered to occur only when all an animal's immediate needs have been satisfied, object-play in cats would be expected to be depressed by food-deprivation if it were causally distinct from predatory behaviour. Since play was hardly affected by hunger it might be inferred that this is not the case. Moreover, food-shortage tends to depress most forms of activity other than food-seeking (e.g. Loy, 1970) which supports the possible conclusion that object-play is causally related to or even classifiable with, feeding behaviour in the cat.

This brings us back to the problem of why cats play with their prey. We noted that trained cats often do not, and Leyhausen (1956) found that starved laboratory cats, unlike satiated ones, played with only the first one or two mice when presented with many in quick succession. (Catching and killing were apparently not affected by hunger, although eating was.) It seems then that the occurrence or omission of play during predation depends on both training and motivation. We might then argue that in playing with prey or objects cats are responding in a species-specific manner to specific stimulus properties. We can explain play with live prey if we postulate that play is an interim activity between catching and killing. The rapid succession of acts in the full predatory sequence depends on early training and on motivation. Play with prey can be seen as an expression of the tendency to respond to prey-stimuli when, and although, the necessary early training or motivation to kill is lacking. (The factors which dictate if, or at what point, play leads on to killing have not as yet been adequately researched.) Play with objects is an expression of the same tendency even though consummatory stimuli are lacking.

In other words, cats respond to certain stimuli by engaging in a range of predatory patterns appropriate to the properties of the object. If the cat is an experienced predator, it is likely that it will respond to live prey by immediately catching and killing it and, if hungry, by eating it.* If it lacks appropriate experience it may play before killing, even if hungry, or play without ever killing if well fed.

Social factors

We have seen that both prey and prey-like objects elicit similar behaviour in cats, and it has been suggested that object-play might belong in the category of feeding behaviour. When cats were tested with play objects under different social conditions it was found that the effect of social companions on play was closely comparable to the effect they have been found to exert on predation. Furthermore, it was possible to show how this would have adaptive significance for a cat in aiding the development of successful predatory behaviour.

The presence of other kittens appears to stimulate object-play, but active competition in group tests results in one cat at a time possessing an object and defending it from the others. These then appear to respect this possession, and avoid the possessor. By comparing the relative effects of five different social conditions on play, it can be argued that although companions might give a kitten confidence, the effect they exert on play is mainly one of rivalry (i.e. the presence of the onlooking kittens offers a threat of competition which intensifies or creates the desire to be in control of the object).

This can be compared with social behaviour during prey-catching. Some kittens are bolder in their approach to prey than others (Baerends, op. cit.; Leyhausen, 1956). These are initially quicker to 'possess' prey than

* Experienced farm-cats commonly kill rodents without eating them (Elton, 1953).

their siblings, thus establishing a precedent whereby they are the first to take prey in a prey-catching situation. (Both authors allude to the possibility of a dominance hierarchy influencing this behaviour, but there are good arguments against it.) A precise analogy is found in group tests with objects. The kitten who initially possesses the object (usually by biting it) is then avoided by its siblings. Only when the object is abandoned is it taken by another kitten, who in turn is avoided by the others. However, a kitten who is the last to possess an object is no less carefully avoided than the one who had it first, and the one who habitually takes an object first does not necessarily take precedence in other situations. These observations indicate that kittens in a litter learn how to interact with each other in each situation. In a predatory one the rivalry between siblings encourages a prompt approach to a prey-like object or real prey.

Both Baerends and Leyhausen (1956) say that if a mouse is not seized quickly it may become aggressive, and this intimidates the kitten. A rat or mouse must be caught before it turns to attack if a kitten is to gain confidence in the predatory situation. Rivalry between kittens would ensure that the prey would be seized quickly by one of the litter. The absence of a dominance hierarchy ensures that all members of the litter are able to gain experience with prey. Since cats are solitary hunters this is of obvious adaptive significance for the species.

Rosenblatt and Schneirla (1962) state that the kitten was normally introduced to the killing of small mammals first through the eating of killed prey brought to the nest by the mother and later through accompanying the female on her hunting trips. Baerends found that a mother's behaviour with prey had a marked effect on kittens: those who had watched their mother behave in a 'quiet' fashion with a mouse gradually approached and killed mice, while those whose mothers reacted overvigorously to a mouse would not approach one. (The latter, however, after watching a quiet mother with a mouse, approached and patted mice but would not bite them.)

Experiments with objects and observations such as these suggest that the mother and siblings have complementary roles in the development of prey-catching. While the mother introduces the kitten to prey and demonstrates certain skills, the siblings, through competition, stimulate the kitten to take the prey quickly, which is an important first step in the integration of all the responses to prey into successful predatory behaviour.

Moreover, it has been argued from experiments with objects that cats like to be watched playing. It seems that cats also like to be seen with prey: Baerends says that house-cats signal vocally to their kittens when they come in with prey. House-cats without kittens frequently call loudly before bringing prey into the presence of the owner, where they play with it, kill, and perhaps eat it. If the rivalry between siblings involves seeking to be watched when in the possession of prey, a female cat with a litter may transfer this relationship to her kittens. If she then brings prey to the nest and plays with it (or kills it) in front of her kittens, they have the opportunity to be introduced to prey-catching at an age when experience is vital and several weeks before they can follow her far on hunting trips.

The evidence indicates, then, that the family unit of mother and kittens is an important learning unit, where knowledge of local prey and expertise in dealing with it are transmitted from one generation to the next, thus aiding the survival of the species. The effect of social companions on play with objects, and on reactions to live prey, complements the powerful effect of the stimulus properties of a prey object in eliciting predatory behaviour in a young cat.

Conclusion

It may not be meaningful to make a rigid distinction between play behaviour and the serious performance of the same types of response. Object-play may function in cats as direct training for solitary hunting – not so much in the acquisition of motor skills, but in the ability to deal with certain important aspects of the situation that prey-catching presents.

References

ELTON, C. S. (1953), 'The use of cats in farm rat control', *British Journal of Animal Behaviour*, No. 1, pp. 151–5.

LEYHAUSEN, P. (1956), 'Verhaltensstudien bei Katzen', *Z. Tierpsychol.*, Beiheft 2.

LEYHAUSEN, P. (1965), 'Über die Funktion der Relativen Stimmungshierarchie', *Z. Tierpsychol.*, No. 22, pp. 412–94.

LOY, J. (1970), 'Behavioral responses of free-ranging rhesus to food shortage', *American Journal of Physical Anthropology*, No. 33, pp. 263–71.

ROSENBLATT, J. S., and SCHNEIRLA, T. C. (1962), 'The behaviour of cats', in *The Behaviour of Domestic Animals*, Hafez (ed.), Ballière, Tindal, and Cox.

Mastery Play

Jean Piaget is the foremost student of child development in the world today. In his view, intelligence develops from an internalization of adaptive action upon the environment. Mastery play is of particular importance for him since in such play the child adapts his behaviour through the crucial processes of assimilation and accommodation – by modifying the world to his own notions and by changing his actions to suit the world's demands. This excerpt on mastery play is based on close observations of his own children and includes Stages I through IV of the period of sensory-motor intelligence. Stages V and VI appear on pp. 555–69.

An attempt to interpret play through the structure of the child's thought

A baby sucks his thumb sometimes as early as the second month, grasps objects at about four or five months, shakes them, swings them, rubs them, and finally learns to throw them and retrieve them. Such behaviours involve two poles: a pole of accommodation, since there must be adjustment of movements and perceptions to the objects, but also a pole of assimilation of things to the child's own activity, since he has no interest in the things as such, but only insofar as he finds them useful for a behaviour learnt earlier or for one he is in process of acquiring. This assimilation of reality to sensory-motor schemata has two complementary aspects. On the one hand it is active repetition and consolidation, and in this sense it is essentially functional or reproductive assimilation, i.e. growth through functioning. On the other hand, it is mental digestion, i.e. perception or conception of the object insofar as it is incorporated into real or possible action. Each object is assimilated as something 'to be sucked', 'to be grasped', 'to be shaken', etc., and is at first that and nothing more (and if it is 'to be looked at' it is still being assimilated to the various focusings and movements of the eyes and acquires the 'shapes' which perceptive assimilation gives it). It is obvious that in the actual activity these two functions of assimilation become one, for it is by repeating his behaviours through reproductive assimilation that the child assimilates objects to actions and that these thus become schemata. These schemata constitute the functional equivalent of concepts and of the logical relationships of later development. At all stages of the development of intelligence we find both accommodation and assimilation, but they are increasingly differentiated, and consequently more and more complementary in their increasing equilibrium. In scientific thinking, for instance, accommodation to reality is nothing but experiment, while assimilation is deduction, or incorporation of objects into logical or mathematical schemata. But there are two important differences between this rational assimilation and the initial sensory-motor assimilation. In the first place, rational assimilation is not centred in the individual, the mental activity in this case being only an assimilation of things one to another,* while the initial assimilation is centred in the individual, and is therefore non-operational, i.e. it is egocentric or distorting. In the second place, and this second difference explains the first, rational assimilation is complementary to accommodation to things, and therefore in almost permanent equilibrium with experience, while sensory-motor assimilation is as yet undifferentiated from accommodation and gives rise to a fresh 'displacement of equilibrium' with every new differentiation. Phenomenism and egocentrism are the two undissociated aspects of elementary consciousness as distinct from experimental objectivity and rational deduction.

This being so, children's play is merely the expression of one of the phases of this progressive differentiation: it occurs when assimilation is dissociated from accommodation but is not yet reintegrated in the forms of permanent equilibrium in which, at the level of operational and rational thought, the two will be complementary. In this sense, play constitutes the extreme pole of assimilation of reality to the ego, while at the same time it has something of the creative imagination which will be the motor of all future thought and even of reason.

Play begins, then, with the first dissociation between assimilation and accommodation. After learning to grasp, swing, throw, etc., which involve both an effort of accommodation to new situations, and an effort of repetition, reproduction and generalization, which are the elements of assimilation, the child sooner or later (often even during the learning period) grasps for the pleasure of grasping, swings for the sake of swinging, etc. In a word, he repeats his behaviour not in any further effort to learn or to investigate, but for the mere joy of mastering it and of showing off to himself his own power of subduing reality. Assimilation is dissociated from accommodation by subordinating it and tending to function by itself, and from then on practice play occurs. Since it requires neither thought nor social life, practice play can be explained as the direct result of the primacy of assimilation. The 'functional pleasure' and pleasure of being the cause, which accompany this type of play, raise no particular problem, since the first comes from the *sui generis* character of this assimilation for the sake of assimilation,

---

* It is, of course, real activity, and the assimilation of things one to another therefore amounts to assimilating them to 'operations', i.e., to active schemata constructed by the mind.

with no need for new accommodation, and the second from the fact that when the child has overcome the difficulties inherent in the corresponding 'serious' action, the assimilation is more concentrated on his own activity.

The beginnings of play

When does play begin? The question arises at the *first stage*, that of purely reflex adaptations. For an interpretation of play like that of K. Groos, for whom play is pre-exercise of essential instincts, the origin of play must be found in this initial stage since sucking gives rise to exercises in the void, apart from meals. But it seems very difficult to consider reflex exercises as real games when they merely continue the pleasure of feeding-time and consolidate the functioning of the hereditary set-up, thus being evidence of real adaptation.

During the *second stage*, on the other hand, play already seems to assume part of the adaptive behaviours, but the continuity between it and them is such that it would be difficult to say where it begins, and this question of boundary raises a problem which concerns the whole interpretation of later play. 'Games' with the voice at the time of the first lallations, movements of the head and hands accompanied by smiles and pleasure, are these already part of play, or do they belong to a different order? Are 'primary circular reactions' generally speaking ludic, adaptive, or both? If we merely apply the classical criteria, from the 'pre-exercise' of Groos to the 'disinterested' or the 'autotelic' character of play, we should have to say that everything during the first months of life, except feeding and emotions like fear and anger, is play. Indeed, when the child looks for the sake of looking, handles for the sake of handling, moves his arms and hands (and in the next stage shakes hanging objects and his toys) he is doing actions which are an end in themselves, as are all practice games, and which do not form part of any series of actions imposed by someone else or from outside. They no more have an external aim than the later motor exercises such as throwing stones into a pond, making water spurt from a tap, jumping, and so on, which are always considered to be games. But all autotelic activities are certainly not games. Science has this characteristic, and particularly pure mathematics, whose object is immanent in thought itself, but if it is compared to a 'superior' game, it is clear that it differs from a mere game by its forced adaptation to an internal or external reality. In a general way, all adaptation is autotelic, but a distinction must be made between assimilation with actual accommodation and pure assimilation or assimilation which subordinates to itself earlier accommodations and assimilates the real to the activity itself without effort or limitation. Only the latter seems to be characteristic of play; otherwise the attempt to identify play with 'pre-exercise' in general would involve the inclusion in it of practically all the child's activity.

But although the circular reactions have not in themselves this lucid character, it can be said that most of them are continued as games. We find, indeed, though naturally without being able to trace any definite boundary, that the child, after showing by his seriousness that he is making a real effort at accommodation, later reproduces these behaviours merely for pleasure, accompanied by smiles and even laughter, and without the expectation of results characteristic of the circular reactions through which the child learns. It can be maintained that at this stage the reaction ceases to be an act of complete adaptation and merely gives rise to the pleasure of pure assimilation, assimilation which is simply functional: the *Funktionslust* of K. Bühler. Of course, the schemas due to circular reaction do not only result in games. Once acquired, they may equally well become parts of more complete adaptations. In other words, a schema is never essentially ludic or non-ludic, and its character as play depends on its context and on its actual functioning. But all schemas are capable of giving rise to pure assimilation, whose extreme form is play. The phenomenon is clear in the case of schemas such as those of phonation, prehension (watching moving fingers, etc.), and certain visual schemas (looking at things upside down, etc.).

It will be remembered that T., at 0; 2, adopted the habit of throwing his head back to look at familiar things from this new position. He seemed to repeat this movement with ever-increasing enjoyment and ever-decreasing interest in the external result: he brought his head back to the upright position and then threw it back again time after time, laughing loudly. In other words, the circular reaction ceased to be 'serious' or instructive, if such expressions can be applied to a baby of less than three months, and became a game.

At 0; 3 T. played with his voice, not only through interest in the sound, but for 'functional pleasure', laughing at his own power.

At 0; 2 he smiled at his hands and at objects that he shook with his hand, while at other times he gazed at them with deep seriousness.

In short, during this second stage, play only appears as yet as a slight differentiation from adaptive assimilation. It is only in virtue of its later development that we can speak of two distinct facts. But the later evolution of play enables us to note the duality even at this stage, just as the evolution of imitation compels us to see the birth of imitation in the self-imitation of the circular reaction.

During the *third stage*, that of secondary circular reactions, the process remains the same, but the differentiation between play and intellectual assimilation is rather more advanced. Indeed, as soon as the circular reactions no longer involve only the child's own body or the perceptive canvas of elementary sensorial activity, but also objects manipulated with increasing deliberation, the 'pleasure of being the cause' emphasized by K. Groos is added to the mere 'functional pleasure' of K. Bühler. The action on things, which begins with each new secondary reaction, in a context of objective interest and intentional accommodation, often even of anxiety (as when the child sways new hanging objects or shakes new toys which produce sound) will thus unfailingly become a game as soon as the new phenomenon is grasped by the child and offers no further scope for investigation properly so called.

There are many examples of the transition from assimilation proper to secondary reactions, to the pure assimilation which characterizes play properly so called. For example, in obs. 94, L. discovered the possibility of making objects hanging from the top of her cot swing. At first she studied the phenomenon without smiling, or smiling only a little, but with an appearance of intense interest, as though she was studying it. Subsequently, however, from about 0; 4, she never indulged in this activity, which lasted up to about 0; 8 and even beyond, without a show of great joy and power. In other words assimilation was no longer accompanied by accommodation and therefore was no longer an effort at comprehension: there was merely assimilation to the activity itself, i.e., use of the phenomenon for the pleasure of the activity, and that is play.

These observations might be repeated in the case of each of the secondary reactions. But it is more curious to note that even the 'procedures for prolonging an interesting spectacle', i.e., the behaviours resulting from a generalization of the secondary schemas, give rise to an activity which is real play. Movements such as drawing oneself up so as not to lose a visual picture or a sound, carried out at first with great seriousness and almost with anxiety as to the result, are subsequently used on all occasions and almost 'for fun'. When the procedure is successful, the child uses it with the same 'pleasure of being the cause' as in simple circular reactions, and moreover, even when the child himself sees it to be unsuccessful, he ends by repeating the movement without expecting anything from it, merely for amusement. This action must not be confused with the sensory-motor gestures of recognition, of which we spoke earlier: the attitude of the child shows whether he is playing or striving to recognize the object.

During the *fourth stage*, that of co-ordination of the secondary schemas, two new elements related to play make their appearance. Firstly, the behaviours most characteristic of this period, or 'the application of known schemas to new situations' are capable, like the earlier ones, of being continued in ludic manifestations insofar as they are carried out for mere assimilation, i.e., for the pleasure of the activity and without any effort at adaptation to achieve a definite end.

At 0; 7, after learning to remove an obstacle to gain his objective, T. began to enjoy this kind of exercise. When several times in succession I put my hand or a piece of cardboard between him and the toy he desired, he reached the stage of momentarily forgetting the toy and pushed aside the obstacle, bursting into laughter. What had been intelligent adaptation had thus become play, through transfer of interest to the action itself, regardless of its aim.

Secondly, the mobility of the schemas allows of the formation of real ludic combinations, the child going from one schema to another, no longer to try them out successively but merely to master them, without any effort at adaptation.

At 0; 9 J. was sitting in her cot and I hung her celluloid duck above her. She pulled a string hanging from the top of the cot and in this way shook the duck for a moment, laughing. Her involuntary movements left an impression on her eiderdown: she then forgot the duck, pulled the eiderdown towards her and moved the whole of it with her feet and arms. As the top of the cot was also being shaken, she looked at it, stretched up then fell back heavily, shaking the whole cot. After doing this some ten times, J. again noticed her duck: she then grasped a doll also hanging from the top of the cot and went on shaking it, which made the duck swing. Then noticing the movement of her hands she let everything go, so as to clasp and shake them (continuing the preceding movement). Then she pulled her pillow from under her head, and having shaken it, struck it hard and struck the sides of the cot and the doll with it. As she was holding the pillow, she noticed the fringe, which she began to suck. This action, which reminded her of what she did every day before going to sleep, caused her to lie down on her side, in the position for sleep, holding a corner of the fringe and sucking her thumb. This, however, did not last for half a minute and J. resumed her earlier activity.

This sequence of behaviours makes plain the difference between play and strictly intelligent activity. In the case of the schemas successively tried out with new objects J. merely sought to assimilate the objects, and, as it were, to 'define them by use'. Since there was adaptation of the schemas to an external reality which constituted a problem, there was intelligence properly so called. In the present case, on the contrary, although the process is the same, the schemas follow one after the other without any external aim. The objects to which they are applied are no longer a problem, but merely serve as an opportunity for activity. This activity is no longer an effort to learn, it is only a happy display of known actions.

(From *Play, Dreams and Imitation in Childhood*, Routledge & Kegan Paul, 1951.)

B Play, Exploration and Novelty

Responsiveness to Objects in Free-Ranging Japanese Monkeys

Introduction

The purpose of this study was to describe and test the reactions of free-ranging *Macaca fuscata* to inanimate objects, and to explore the following questions: What do subjects (Ss) in the field do with objects that are not food or social beings? How are their reactions organized across time and distance? How does behaviour vary with the age and sex of S and with the characteristics of the object? What relationships exist between social behaviour and responses to inanimate objects? For the most part, I wished to extend previous laboratory work with chimpanzees and rhesus, and to see what additional factors must be taken into account in natural situations.

General method

The data were collected in Japan between October 1963 and July 1964. During this time, periodic visits were made to Kambanotaki, Katsuyama, Okayama prefecture, where a troop of about 150 monkeys live. Also, two weeks in April 1964 were spent at Takasakiyama, Oita Prefecture, where there are three troops totalling about 880 individuals. A few supplementary observations were made at Minooyama. (For locations and general descriptions of the Japanese field stations see Frisch, 1959, and Kotera and Suzuki, 1961.) In all three areas Ss live on steep mountain sides and come with varying regularity to parksites which are provisioned with food. The basic data reported stemmed from observations made in or within 400 metres of the feeding sites. Every attempt was made to conduct observations in quiet areas, or to minimize distractions during actual test time.

Normative observations

In addition to numerous periods of intermittent observation approximately fifty hours, spaced across the entire year, were allocated solely to watching for overt signs of responsiveness to already-available inanimate objects. Responses to foods and behaviours directly associated with food gathering (e.g., pushing aside small stones) were excluded from consideration. Tree-shaking was also not recorded. I concentrated most upon activities involving prehension and upon objects that could be moved or carried, e.g., stones, rocks, straws, sticks and litter. Some non-manipulative signs of responsiveness (e.g., smelling an object) were occasionally seen during these hours but strong overt emotional reactions to inanimate objects were rare. A major outstanding exception was when a visitor at Takasakiyama released a small helium-filled balloon. This produced a panic almost as great as that produced by several low-flying aeroplanes and more than that produced by a hawk that once swooped within a few feet of the monkeys at Kambanotaki. It is also worth noting that an aggressive monkey could be got rid of very effectively by pointing an umbrella at him and opening it suddenly. This was in fact a more effective deterrent than swiping at the S with a stick or a closed umbrella. Other investigators have noted strong reactions to an opening umbrella in other species (Melzack, 1954), and it seems likely that avoidance of other sudden expansions of a visual stimulus (Tinbergen's 'hawk shape', 1951; Schiff, Caviness and Gibson, 1962) are related phenomena. Subsequent informal tests on caged chimpanzees, orang-utans and various species of Old-World monkeys of the Yerkes colony in Orange Park, Florida, suggested the umbrella is effective for at least 80 per cent of these Ss too.

Forms of reaction could be described easily in terms of categories derived from work with laboratory chimpanzees (Menzel, 1964a; Schiller, 1952). Not surprisingly, however, many of the common chimpanzee responses were seen rarely or not at all. For example, I saw less than five instances each of supine play (lying on the back while manipulating the object overhead), draping an object around the neck or over the head, and vigorous wrestling. In contrast to the more than fifteen ways in which laboratory chimpanzees carry objects, the present Ss grasped objects principally in hand and mouth, relatively seldom in a foot, and rarely or not at all in the groin, under an arm, etc. In carrying an infant, of course, there might be greater variety than with inanimate objects. I never saw an object being systematically related to other features of the environment or used for poking or striking. Nor were Ss ever observed handling two objects other than food concurrently. If S was alone, object manipulations were usually performed in the seated position, although occasionally an infant climbed and hung from a limb by his feet while grasping the object in play. Climbing and quadrupedal running with the object were frequent if S was approached by another individual, and foot-carrying usually occurred at such times also.

Of 111 instances of manipulation on which I took specific notes, 81 involved Ss one year of age or younger, 24 were by the 2-year-old group, 3 were by 3-to 4-year-olds, and 3 were by adults. It is estimated that the infants and juveniles accounted for only about thirty to forty per cent of the total monkeys in the group but these Ss accounted for ninety-five per cent of these recorded responses. I would rate the $1\frac{1}{2}$- to 2-year-olds first in variety of forms of manipulation, albeit the low frequency of observations in other groups makes this a hazardous rating. It was surprising to note that Ss as young as six weeks of age showed more frequent contact activities than the 2-year-olds. For the most part their responses consisted of simple mouthing and grasping of objects, which occurred when they wandered a metre or two from their mothers at times when the mother was resting or grooming.

One further instance of manipulation in adults is in a special category. At Kambanotaki a female carried with her constantly a withered and almost unrecognizable body, presumably that of her dead infant. (Another female at Minooyama was observed doing the same thing.) This type of situation is the only one of which I am aware where a macaque will transport and retain an inanimate object for extended periods of time, and even here I was told by caretakers at the feeding stations that the dead infants must have been born alive (cf. Jay, 1962).

The recorded manipulation level of scarcely more than two cases per group per observation hour is not a precise representation of a general manipulation level. It has little meaning apart from the particular circumstances and criteria of observation. (Observations of juvenile groups at times when the group was resting after midday feeding in good weather would, for example, give a higher rate.) However, it could be several hundred per cent higher and still form a striking contrast to the statements of some workers that all normal apes and monkeys are inveterate explorers and are given to poking, prodding, mauling, manipulating and generally squeezing every possible drop of entertainment out of any object that crosses their path. I was impressed by the seeming indifference of these field macaques to inanimate objects other than foods. The higher levels of manipulation reported in laboratories are probably related to various factors associated with caged life, such as the decreased necessity of vigilance, fewer social possibilities and lack of objects. This notion was fortified by informal observation of five juveniles that were trapped from the Kambanotaki area and transported to the Osaka University Laboratory. These Ss seemed to become much more attentive to objects and certainly manipulated more readily than did other members of the same troop and of the same ages in the field. Kawamura (1959) has reported similar contrasts in the responses of caged and feral monkeys to novel foods.

Social manipulations of all sorts were at a high level during these observation hours in all age groups. The fact that Ss spend much of their day attending to other monkeys is certainly one factor that limits their reactions to inanimate objects. It is important to note further that the most prolonged and intense object manipulation occurred as part of social interactions, usually play. Unless another monkey came over to the manipulator, the handling of everyday objects most often consisted of brief grasping and mouthing without any other gross activity, and the average estimated duration of contact was considerably less then thirty seconds. With another interested monkey present, however, the object assumed more importance. Chasing, wrestling and scrambling around on trees or rocks over an object were common, especially if the object was a branch or stick. Sometimes the object was abandoned after a few minutes but social wrestling continued. On over a dozen occasions if the other monkey stopped pursuing the one with the object, the latter returned to his pursuer. If no further chase or wrestling resulted, the object was soon discarded. Why a solitary monkey picks up an object in the first place is certainly a question of some importance, but it is different from asking why a second monkey then comes over. An object which is being held by one monkey or which has just been released, evokes greater attention than the identical object simply lying on the ground.

Spontaneous reactions to novel objects

During the course of the year, I frequently placed novel objects, usually small plastic toys of various shapes and bright colours, in the woods, along paths, or on rocks. Manipulation was by no means always seen, but if it was seen it was usually more prolonged than reactions to naturally occurring objects. Moreover, in most cases of prolonged manipulation of novel objects the manipulator seemed to try much more seriously to keep the object to himself. If pursued, he occasionally ran bipedally, as with a large piece of food, to get away faster (cf. Hewes, 1964). Sometimes the pursuers were bitten seriously enough to screech and run off, or the manipulator climbed to the top of a tree and remained there as long as he had the object. On three occasions an infant with an object eluded an older pursuer by running to its mother.

Interestingly, in these cases the mothers glanced once at the object and then turned their backs to it. One mother slapped her infant when she was accidentally touched by the object. Studied indifference was in fact the typical adult reaction to most novel objects. On more than six occasions, females with infants showed clearly that some caution underlies their indifference when they pulled their offspring away from an approach to an object. Cases like the following are also relevant: an old adult female and her baby were walking independently, with the mother first. The mother paused nine feet away from the novel object, oriented towards it for about three seconds and then immediately turned and looked at the baby. At this the baby ran to her and hopped upon her back. Carrying the baby, the mother circled sharply around the object. After they got about 10 metres past the object the baby hopped off the mother's back, ran back to the object, stopped about one metre away, stared for about five seconds, and then raced back to the mother. They walked off again, this time walking independently.

At Takasakiyama I placed objects on a large rock about fifty metres uphill from the feeding area. Sizeable numbers of monkeys had previously been observed to stop to rest or groom on this rock after feeding. As long as at least four or five monkeys were in the area, testing was to be conducted. On alternate half hours of observation a set of nine innocuous toys was placed on the crown of the rock (the position usually assumed by the most dominant monkey present). In control observations, the monkeys were watched with no objects present. The questions were, first, whether the objects would affect resting and grooming activity; and, second, what the monkeys would do with the objects. The test had to be abandoned after four days because the monkeys stopped coming almost entirely. It is most likely that they had come actively to avoid the area because of the objects. Several days later when I was testing in a new and different location the monkeys started to return to the rock.

Insofar as it was possible to judge from the data (a total of five formal sessions with objects and six with no objects were all that could be conducted under the above circumstances), the objects did seem to affect general activity. Thus social or auto-grooming was observed in only 10 per cent of the one-minute intervals in which Ss came onto the rock when objects were present; whereas if Ss came onto the rock when no objects were present, the comparable figure is sixty-two per cent.

It was often difficult to determine whether or not S was responding to the objects. If detectable reactions were seen, however, they were tentative or cautious. Thus of thirty-two individuals that definitely oriented toward the objects, only one, a young adult male, made physical contact. All the others moved away. Three adult females who oriented also immediately retrieved an infant. No S ever 'dethroned' the objects from their place on the crown of the rock or shared this position by sitting among the objects.

The conditions under which an object was presented seemed to be crucial for avoidance. Thus, for example, a rope that was stretched out along a path in the woods was avoided, but the same object would be picked up and carried off if it was bunched up, or if another monkey was handling it. The following episode is also pertinent. During the period when observations were being made at the rock at Takasakiyama, I left a collection of about twenty novel objects in the woods overnight, under a crate. Among the objects were those being avoided on the rock. On returning the next morning the monkeys were in the area, the box had been overturned and all of the objects with the exception of two rubber snakes and some scraps of paper were gone. The same procedure was repeated twice more with fewer objects. Results were the same, except that on the third time one of the rubber snakes had been torn in two. Several plastic ropes were found high in the trees tangled around limbs, and various other objects were strewn through the woods, some of them a full fifty metres from the site of the theft. Periodically throughout the morning following the thefts an infant would be observed carrying one of the objects. Thus, as in young laboratory chimpanzees and rhesus (Menzel, 1962, 1964a, 1964b), avoidance of an object gives way to approach if the conditions of presentation are varied only slightly. The object as such is only one factor affecting response. Taking these objects from the overturned box is not attributable to simple habituation. On repeated tests at the rock, similar objects were avoided.

A more systematic account of the relative frequency of various responses to novel objects, and of age and sex differences, was obtained with a single standardized object, a two-metre rope of yellow plastic tied to the end of a small red toy. The object was stretched across various regular routes of travel at Takasakiyama and Kambanotaki. (Previous observations had indicated that such an elongated object was better for test than smaller items, including rubber snakes, which were too easily bypassed.) A written note was made on each S (excluding infants that were being carried) that came within one metre of the rope or showed any detectable change from his previous behaviour at a greater distance. A total of 399 observations was collected, excluding a few cases in which a group of Ss passed too rapidly for a record to be scored on each.

The first finding to emerge was the great importance of S's ongoing behaviour as he approached the object. Signs of responsiveness were almost never recorded if S was already running; there were only two cases of returning to smell the rope and one case of coming to a sudden stop half a metre in front of the rope in fifty-six cases of running. In the 343 cases in which S had been walking 188 (fifty-five per cent) showed some detectable sign of reaction.

It is apparent that age is an important variable and that sex differences probably appear at about adolescence (three to four years). The predominant reaction for adults and for the adolescent males was simply 'no detectable change' from the baseline of walking along. That is, the reactions of these Ss were usually impossible for an observer to distinguish from responses to everyday objects.

No doubt there is a human factor involved here too. Adult responsiveness is harder for the observer to judge. Adult monkeys seemed to actually inhibit signs of emotional reaction. A clear example of this was shown by a male who was looking back over his shoulder until he was within half a metre of the object. Suddenly confronted with the object, he glanced down for a fraction of a second, stepped very slowly across, and then sat down with his rump almost on the rope. After about ten seconds of simply sitting, he got up and started off, casting another very brief glance back over his shoulder. On several other occasions females acted as if they might be sexually presenting to the rope, but on only one of these occasions did S so much as glance towards the object.

If any detectable reactions were seen in adults, they were apt to consist of a very slight angling off from the line of travel instead of a sharp circling around the rope, or they consisted of a mere glance instead of a definite pause with prolonged orientation, staring, or smelling without touching. Adults did not step across the rope any more frequently than did younger Ss, even though the latter were much more apt to show a definite reaction to the rope. The most frequent of all responses in children and in adolescent females was pausing and orienting, and sharp circling of the rope was more frequent than a slight angling off. Occasionally an S would stand bipedally to stare or would approach to smell the rope, or possibly physical contact would be made. However, vigorous exploitation or play reactions were certainly infrequent in all groups. Initial contacts were cautious and usually made by touching with the lips or tapping with the fingers. (In tapping, all Ss held the fingers together and the palm down. Contact was made with the first joints of the fingers, and tapping motions were away from S.) Grasping occurred in only twenty-eight cases and the object was carried off one metre or more a total of three times.

It should be noted that strong emotional reactions were never seen.

Conclusions
Complex manipulative behaviours

While some forms of instrumental activities with objects no doubt do occur in feral Japanese monkeys (e.g., Miyadi, 1964), they are rare. The present data suggest why this is so. Tool using and instrumentation are properly viewed as an outgrowth and specialization of manipulative tendencies in general (Schiller, 1952; Menzel, 1964a), and as we have seen, manipulative reactions other than simple mouthing and grasping would account for only a fraction of responses to inanimate objects, and an even smaller portion of the daily routine of activity. Thus, over and above any possible limitations in genetically-determined capacity for instrumentation, free-ranging *M. fuscata* even as a juvenile, seems to have little motivation to practise and elaborate upon the component patterns of instrumentation (see Schaller, 1963, for a similar statement regarding gorilla). And in adults the dominant mode of reaction to most inanimate objects is either avoidance or indifference. The repertoire of these Ss is effectively lacking, at least by comparison with some other species. Behaviour in all age groups is centred about social objects, food objects, and general vigilance activities. It is interesting that spontaneous reactions to everyday objects begin to decrease sharply right at those ages (3-4 years) when Ss, particularly males, become subjected to the strongest pressures of social behaviour.

Mechanisms of group changes in behaviour

Taken together, the data also suggest why it is usually juveniles, rather than adults, who are the originators of group adaptation processes and 'proto-cultural' changes in relatively complex behaviours such as coming into a newly established feeding area, acquiring new food habits, or adopting new methods of collecting foods (Itani, 1958; Kawamura, 1959; Miyadi, 1964). Innovations in adaptive behaviour often require more in the way of reaction skills than very young infants seem capable of, but they also require tendencies which the adults rarely express. A new food, for example, cannot be treated as a food until S picks it up and mouths it, or approaches and wrestles another S for the object, and adults simply do not do this with unidentified objects unless they see another S actually eating the object. (Behaviour associated with eating evokes a marked interest, and an observer can often get monkeys to 'beg' simply by taking his hand from his pocket, putting it to his mouth, and making chewing movements.) By responding to signs in the young, the process of individual adaptation to new objects is short-circuited.

The role of various age groups in bringing the troop into a newly-established feeding area is probably more complicated than the above suggests. Such large-scale adaptations would certainly merit further special study because in them time is measured in months, distance is measured in hundreds of metres, and movements in space concern an entire troop instead of individuals or small sub-groups. A high degree of temporal and spatial integration and social organization are thus required. As has been noted, the young are the first to enter a new area and to take food. But who controls the troop movements which bring the young from some distance day after day? If it is the usual adult leader males – who are also the slowest of all to habituate – it would seem that these individuals might actually be relying upon the juveniles to test out the situation.

On the other hand, a much simpler possibility should also be considered. By using the present situations and laboratory conflict experiments as small scale models, some aspects of the process of group adaptation might be derived from a knowledge of approach and avoidance gradients. In responses to a situation containing novel or noxious elements, the avoidance gradient is much steeper than the approach gradient, i.e., Ss do not avoid the situation entirely; they often approach from a distance, but then circle or stop short. Thus at the distance of hundreds of metres, the avoidance tendency is weak, and approach occurs. The adults head from their sleeping area toward the newly-discovered location which contains food. The young follow. The troop stops a hundred metres or so away from the area, and adults go no farther. The juveniles, however, are not so timid. Their avoidance gradient is much steeper. They go in even closer before stopping, or even proceed all of the way to the food. The process of close range, small scale, habituation then eventually spreads upward through the troop and to the adult males. Part of the adults' habituation would probably take place anyway, with sufficient time; but of course the signs of other animals feeding greatly facilitate the process.

Age-sex differences

Whether one age-sex group or another is judged to be most responsive would vary somewhat with the class of objects, the criterion of response, and the circumstances of testing. Under most conditions studied here, overt signs or displays were seen more often in females than in males, and more often in young than in old Ss. By this criterion, the sex difference is what one would expect from laboratory studies of the closely related *M. mulatta*, but the age differences in emotional displays toward complex objects are the opposite (Mason, 1964; Mason, Green and Posepanko, 1960).

It seems likely, however, that the greater impassiveness of adults vs juveniles in the field resides in the more pronounced tendency of adults to simply stay out of situations that would otherwise cause them to become upset or show displays (Hebb and Thompson, 1954). Even in the laboratory, adult rhesus and chimpanzees seem to show such a tendency if given enough space. In the present study, adults rarely ran into an object 'by accident', as infants did, and if they circumvented an object they started to do so at a greater distance than younger Ss. Age differences in displays or apparent responsiveness are thus in part a function of probable differences in the spatial and temporal scope of attention, in the ability to classify an object at a distance, and in the tendency to react in all-or-none fashion on the basis of such classifications.

(From *Behaviour*, No. 26, 1965, pp. 130–50.)

References

FRISCH, J. E. (1959), 'Research on primate behaviour in Japan', *American Anthropologist*, No. 61, pp. 584–96.

HEBB, D. O., and THOMPSON, W. R. (1954), 'The social significance of animal studies', *Handbook of Social Psychology*, G. Lindzey (ed.), pp. 532–61, Addison-Wesley Press.

HEWES, G. (1964), 'Hominid bipedalism. Independent evidence for the food carrying theory', *Science*, No. 146, pp. 416–18.

ITANI, J. (1958), 'On the acquisition and propagation of a new food habit in the natural group of the Japanese monkey at Takasakiyama', *Primates*, No. 1, pp. 84–98.

JAY, P. C. (1962), 'Aspects of maternal behavior among langurs. The relatives of man: Modern studies of the relation of the evolution of nonhuman primates to human evolution', J. Buettner-Janusch (ed.), *Annals of the New York Academy of Science*, No. 102, pp. 468–76.

KAWAMURA, S. (1959), 'The process of sub-culture propagation among Japanese macaques', *Primates*, No. 2, pp. 43–60.

KOTERA, S., and SUZUKI, K. (1961), 'On supply of Japanese monkeys for research at Japan Monkey Centre', *Primates*, No. 3, pp. 47–58.

MASON, W. A. (1964), 'Sociability and social organization in monkeys and apes', *Advances in Experimental Social Psychology*, Academic Press, pp. 277–305.

MASON, W. A., GREEN, P. C., and POSEPANKO, C. J. (1960), 'Sex differences in affective-social responses of rhesus monkeys', *Behaviour*, No. 16, pp. 74–83.

MELZACK, R. (1954), 'The genesis of emotional behavior: An experimental study of the dog', *J. Comp. Physiol. Psychol.*, No. 47, pp. 166–8.

MENZEL, E. W. JR (1962), 'The effects of stimulus size and proximity upon avoidance of complex objects in rhesus monkeys', *J. Comp. Physiol. Psychol.*, No. 55, p. 1044–6.

MENZEL, E. W. JR (1964), 'Patterns of responsiveness in chimpanzees reared through infancy under conditions of environmental restriction', *Psychol. Forsch.*, No. 27, pp. 337–65.

MENZEL, E. W. JR (1964), 'Responsiveness to object-movement in young chimpanzees', *Behaviour*, No. 24, pp. 147–60.

MIYADI, D. (1964), 'Social life of Japanese monkeys', *Science*, No. 143, pp. 783–6.

SCHALLER, G. (1963), *The Mountain Gorilla: Ecology and Behavior*, University of Chicago Press.

SCHIFF, W., CAVINESS, J. A., and GIBSON, J. J. (1962), 'Persistent fear responses in rhesus monkeys to the optical stimulus of "looming"', *Science*, No. 136, pp. 982–3.

SCHILLER, P. H. (1952), 'Innate constituents of complex responses in primates', *Psych. Rev.*, No. 59, pp. 177–91.

TINBERGEN, N. (1951), *The Study of Instinct*, Oxford University Press.

The Reactions of Stumptail Monkeys to Animals and Novel Objects

The method used to test the reactions of captive individuals to various stimuli differed from the method generally used by investigators in laboratories. Instead of being presented for one or a few minutes to a single monkey restrained in a small cage, the stimulus was left for an amount of time varying from thirty minutes to a few days in the large enclosure where the monkeys lived. It was also displayed outside the enclosure for twenty minutes before introduction. Whenever possible, the same stimulus, or similar one, was offered to different groups, and to other species of monkeys. If the stimulus was an animal, it was free to move. In the case of the six monkeys brought to my country home, both the monkeys and the test animals were free to go anywhere in the garden and the adjacent fields.

The assumptions underlying this method were the following: the reactions of an animal to a given stimulus evolve with time, and depend, in the case of a social animal, on the reactions of the other group members. They also depend upon the degree of freedom which the subject has to initiate or avoid contact with the stimulus.

Potential prey species: birds, insects, toads

These are animals which the monkeys may eat, if they are not afraid of them or repelled by them.

In the wild, birds eating in the same *Ficus* trees as stumptails left the trees when the monkeys arrived. In Calcutta, a crow *Corvus splendens* and two mynah birds *Acridotheres tristis* were released within the enclosures containing two groups. The mynah birds were caught within two and four minutes by a juvenile female and a sub-adult male. The adult killed the bird immediately, probably by choking it, but the juvenile began to chew and tear it when it was still alive. Eleven monkeys were seen eating or chewing the birds. Part of the feathers were plucked out with hands and mouth, and the remaining ones spat out.

Shaped objects

Trying to elucidate which factors are responsible for the avoidance or attraction to objects, I presented all the stumptail groups in Calcutta with objects varying in shape, texture, size and colour. This was done in a limited time and without the necessary material to make true dummies. The conclusions of these limited experiments are therefore only tentative, and need further systematic checking.

The initial experiment which started this series of trials was the discovery that a 30-centimetre-high brown teddy bear was a frightening stimulus for stumptails of both sexes and all age categories, in spite of the fact that it was smaller than any stumptail except for young infants. When I first placed it in front of the open door of one pet's cage, the pet recoiled in a corner, with threats and temper tantrums, and would not come out. When the bear was introduced in the various groups, it elicited threats and fear reactions such as teeth-chattering, grinning, running away or feigned indifference. It was touched only once, by an infant, and the monkeys avoided coming near it, even when the bear was reintroduced several times in the same group. I had to put it on the food basket to force the monkeys to approach it, and in two groups one juvenile started on the second trial to rock the basket in order to make the bear fall off without touching it, a technique which was immediately adopted by several other juveniles and infants.

A plastic teddy bear of the same size and colour was almost immediately touched and removed manually. A bear identical to the brown furry one, but pink, elicited as much avoidance, which led me to conclude that the furry texture was more important than the colour. A tiny 9-centimetre-high, white, furry bear was immediately removed from the food basket, as were the body and the head of the decapitated pink bear. Hence a minimal size and a certain shape seemed necessary to elicit avoidance behaviour.

Similar reactions were observed with liontail, Japanese and Barbary macaques. In Beaverton (Oregon Regional Primate Research Center), the best way to prevent the monkeys to pile up on the hood of the observation jeep was to tie a 25-centimetre-high white furry bear on it. The bear was left in the corral for three weeks after my departure, and, according to the Beaverton staff, was not manipulated during that period.

I tried a number of other objects which all had in common a smooth, hard or polished texture, i.e., the opposite of fur. Furthermore, they did not look like a macaque or one of the macaques' potential predators. They were china dolls, wooden storks, balloons with rough animal shapes, a plastic human skull, etc. They elicited either manipulation or indifference, but not fear.

Factors influencing investigative behaviour

Each time a new animal or object was introduced, I recorded the order in which group members came to investigate it, and, whenever possible, the amount of time spent by each individual in investigation. Depending on whether it elicited approach, avoidance or a mixture of both, a stimulus would be classified as attractive, frightening or ambivalent. The main factors influencing investigation were the social rank, age and personality of each monkey, and the conditions of captivity.

1. Social Rank

When the stimulus was attractive, it was investigated according to rank order, which often resulted in preventing the lower ranking animals from investigating it at all. When the stimulus was frightening or ambivalent, the personality of the dominants also interfered. In more than thirty experiments, two alpha animals, the male 'Leader' and the female 'Kate', were always the first to approach the stimulus, even when it was frightening. Two other alpha animals – the juvenile male Machiavel and the adult female f-3 – let the second dominant investigate the stimulus when it was frightening (for instance the snake or the stuffed langur), except when the stimulus was a conspecific. Rhesus also tended to investigate according to rank order. This was less pronounced in liontails, at least among infants and juveniles: the boldest animals were often the highest ranking ones, but they did not prevent other group members from investigating.

2. Age

As in many other primate species, young stumptails were generally more curious than older animals, and often did not show fear when these did. For instance, the infants and juveniles of the first group approached the teddy bear quicker and closer than the adults and sub-adults of group II. In some cases, when the dominants did not come into physical contact with a stimulus, an infant did. The same was true of rhesus, liontail, Barbary, and Japanese macaques.

In the Beaverton group, no adult ventured to climb on the observation jeep, except to rescue young animals who were uttering fear or threat vocalizations.

3. Personality

Between animals of close social ranks and of the same age, there were great differences in degrees of investigation. One pet, for instance, was far more adventurous than the other. The female 'Neutral' never showed a great interest in objects or unknown animals, and this peculiarity has kept up over three years.

4. Captivity

The level of investigation was greater in captivity than in the wild, and in a 'poor' than in a 'rich' environment. In Kao Tao stumptails were never seen to manipulate objects, in spite of the fact that they had been introduced recently in an habitat deeply modified by human activities. The same individuals who were spending so much time in the Paris zoo investigating everything thrown to them by the public, spent much less time with strange objects when let free in the garden of my home. They would only bother to investigate strange objects when these were placed directly in the 'core areas', and only for a brief period. When the objects were removed and placed outside the core areas, they were ignored. Individuals kept in small cages spent more time investigating new objects than those kept in social groups in the enclosure. Menzel [see next essay] has also noted that wild Japanese macaques investigate much less than captive ones.

(From 'The Behavioural Repertoire of the Stumptail Macaque', *Bibliotheca Primatologica*, Vol. II, S. Karger, Basle, 1969.)

Proto-Cultural Aspects of Chimpanzees' Responsiveness to Novel Objects

Introduction

By the terms 'social tradition' and 'group custom' one usually means only that a given behaviour is acquired through social experience and is transmitted across several groups or social generations. On this definition, it is strange that so much non-human behaviour is still viewed as cultureless. It is well known that early experience with conspecifics is extremely important for many aspects of normal mammalian behavioural development (Newton and Levine, 1968), that many species are capable of observational learning, imitation, social facilitation, etc. (Hall, 1963; Yerkes, 1943), and that in some cases there are substantial variations among different groups of the same species in, for example, feeding habits, travel paths, home ranges, general boldness and timidity, and patterns of communication (Frisch, 1968; Miyadi, 1964). Taken together, these findings suggest that even seemingly 'simple' and 'instinctive' behaviours are influenced by culture-like processes.

The major operational step from a test of dyadic social learning to a test of cultural transmission is the use of a temporal series or chain of social groupings, rather than independent pairs of interacting individuals. Thus, if animal A 'teaches' animal B this might satisfy the criterion for social learning, but cultural processes or tradition can be invoked only if B also 'teaches' C what he had learned from A, and C in turn 'teaches' this to D, and so on. The present experiment used a serial-grouping paradigm to study habituation to novel objects in chimpanzees. It shows that a given response to a novel object can be passed along several 'social generations', even after the original instigators of the change in response are no longer present. The data are of special interest because most of the individuals involved had been reared with extremely limited social and object experience, and by comparison with wild-born controls were grossly retarded in social behaviour and learning performance. Thus, some forms of tradition and culture might not require even normal chimpanzee intelligence.

Material and method
Subjects

The subjects were nineteen 3-year-old chimpanzees, here arbitrarily identified by letters A–S, according to their age and the sequence in which they were tested. Individuals A, B, E, F, G, H, I, J, M, Q, R, and S had been separated from the mother at birth and raised in total social isolation to about two years in small enclosed cubicles with very limited exposure to objects. Individuals C, D, N and O had been raised in the same types of restricted environments, except that two cages were abutted, so that a pair of animals could interact through a set of bars. Individuals K, L and P were wild-born controls, obtained through importers when less than 1 year of age raised together as a group. Further details on these rearing conditions may be found elsewhere (Menzel *et al.*, 1963; Davenport and Rogers, 1970). None of the animals had seen the test objects before the time of test. Only the wild-borns had lived in any sort of group setting; and the restriction-reared animals had only a limited opportunity for social experience, most of it through the bars of their cages.

Apparatus

The chimpanzees were housed together, three at a time, in a standard indoor-outdoor cage at the former Orange Park facilities of the Yerkes Laboratories. They were tested in the indoor section of the cage, which measured approximately 3×1.8 metres and was 2 metres high, and had walls and ceiling of large wire mesh.

Two test objects were used: (1) A swing constructed of two 1·2 metre strands of 1·25 centimetre metal chain, and a 40-centimetre horizontal cross bar of metal pipe. This object was selected because of its possibilities for various forms of vigorous play. However, since the object was a highly complex one for these subjects, some initial caution was anticipated. (2) A plastic ball about 15 centimetres in diameter with a battery-operated motor inside which caused the ball to move around the cage floor in irregular patterns, and to make loud 'beeping' noises (toy 'satellite'). This was selected as an object which would maintain an avoidance reaction on the part of the animals.

Results

Figure 1 shows the reaction of each 'group as a whole' to the objects; i.e. it shows the number of 30-second intervals in which *any* member of a given trio grasped the objects. The first several trios avoided the objects or approached them with extreme hesitancy, subsequently there was a steady rise in contact activity across the various groupings of animals, until asymptotic responsiveness was achieved and the dominant activity became play. Pooling the data from both objects, there is a Spearman rank-order correlation of 0·62 between the amount of grasping and the ordinal number of the trio ($N = 17$ trios; $p < 0.01$). Although there was a decrease in

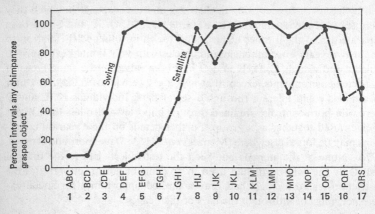

Fig. 1. Changes from one 'generation' to the next in group reactions to the test objects.

responsiveness in the last trios, the animals did not re-institute a pattern of total object avoidance; instead, they simply played less vigorously and persistently than their predecessors. In this connection it might also be noted that the same one toy 'satellite' lasted through the first several trios; but once group asymptotic performance was achieved, each trio managed to smash a new object on almost every session.

It is important that the acquisition of a 'play tradition' proceeded at somewhat different rates for the two objects. Thus one cannot account for all the data on the basis of a single bold individual or even a single trio. There were two trios (No. 1, 2) that avoided both objects, other trios (No. 4–6) that were bold towards one object and cautious toward the other, and still other trios (No. 7–17) that were bold towards both objects. The two individuals who led the process of habituation (individual E for one object, individual F for the other) had, in previous tests of manipulatory responsiveness (Menzel *et al.*, 1963) been relatively bold towards new objects. Nevertheless, there was no significant correlation overall between a given trio's score in the present test and the frequency with which the constituent individuals contacted strange objects or a test person when alone (Spearman's *rho* = 0·33 and −0·02, respectively).

Each individual's performance is in some respects less consistent than the group data of Fig. 1. Thus there was no clear tendency for individuals to manipulate more with repeated exposures to these objects – even though this was true of the 'cage culture as a whole'. This superficially surprising finding reflects several facts. First, an animal's manipulation score depended not only upon his boldness toward the object, but also upon his status within the group and the responsiveness of other individuals. Over all groupings, there was no significant relationship between dominance status (as measured by competition for food) and manipulation, or between earlier manipulation tests conducted on individual animals, and the present manipulation scores in a group setting. Secondly, ordinarily only one animal at a time contacted a given object. The typical group reaction was for each individual to take his turn; and the order in which various individuals took their turns was often different for the two objects. One of the most striking phenomena here was that many 'timid' animals hid in a corner and whimpered while the 'bold' animal in that trio played vigorously with the object and caused it to move unpredictably about the cage; and yet, in the next grouping, the timid animal became the bold one and someone else cowered in the corner. Some reverse cases also occurred. For example, F in the fifth trio instituted the first few vigorous interactions with the 'satellite' object; but when he started to grasp the object again in the first sessions of the sixth trio, a new animal followed his example and then displaced him and took control. It would seem that in general individual behaviour could be predicted better from what other individuals or even groups had done, than from what the individual himself had previously done. In this sense, the concept of social 'roles' seems appropriate (Bernstein and Sharpe, 1966; Crook, 1970).

The performance of the three wild-born animals (individuals K, L and P) should be distinguished from that of the others. The wild-borns yielded the three highest individual total scores in the whole experiment. This is consistent with our previous data on the wild-borns vs. restricted comparison (Menzel *et al.*, 1963). Except when displaced by a more dominant animal, wild-borns manipulated readily from the start. They also displayed a unique behaviour with the swing, namely standing on the crossbar and swinging as a child might. Several restricted animals seemed to copy this behaviour on a few occasions after observing a wild-born animal; but they did so erratically. 'Swinging behaviour' never became a tradition.

Discussion

If it can be assumed that, apart from the experimental treatment that was imposed on them, the restricted chimpanzees were selected without *a priori* bias and were relatively interchangeable with respect to behaviour on the present task – and all our other observations on the same individuals suggest that this is a valid assumption – then it seems reasonable to conclude that a culture-like process was at work in the data. Further support for this conclusion can be obtained by asking simply: why did the curves of performance start off at near-zero level? The answer lies in the rearing history and previous experience of most of the subjects (Menzel *et al.*, 1961, 1963; Welker, 1956). Juvenile chimpanzees that have been raised in 'normal' fashion for the first year or so of life – i.e. mother-reared and wild chimpanzees – never do show the strong and pervasive fear of novelty (at least in laboratory settings) that is characteristic of 'cultureless' mother-deprived and restriction-raised infants. Thus wild-borns in one way or another acquire a general boldness (or, conversely, do not develop patterns of generalized timidity) as a direct result of events that occurred before they were brought to the laboratory. The extent to which their boldness can be attributed to social factors *per se*, as opposed to individual experience with inanimate objects, is at present not known with certainty, but we strongly suspect that simply being provided with the emotional security of the mother is the most important single variable. Thus, for example, Yerkes and Yerkes (1936) found that mother-reared laboratory infant chimpanzees are bolder towards many types of novel objects than are mother-reared and wild-born adults.

If anything, the normal infant chimpanzee starts out over-bold; it has to acquire many of its fears of specific classes of objects, such as snakes, strangers and predatory species. It seems reasonable to assume that these fears can be transmitted in the same fashion that the present animals transmitted a play tradition; and not every individual must be personally shot or bitten to acquire a fear.

What in fact did the present chimpanzees acquire from each other? Whether the actual process that is involved in our experiment is non-specific emotional responsiveness, stimulus enhancement, copying, matched-dependent imitation, observational learning, operant conditioning, or some other such traditional category of psychological process is an extremely important question, but is, at the same time, secondary to our original problem. As stated in the first paragraph of this paper, our problem is quite crude: do chimpanzees show behaviour that is 'cultural' in the sense that it is: (1) influenced by social experience; (2) characteristic of groups rather than being idiosyncratic, and (3) transmissible across 'several generations' (successive groupings)? This problem is, we believe, settled. We must leave it for future research to settle *how* a given result comes about. In the meantime, as Hall (1963) put it, one's predilection for particular theories of how habits are diffused socially should not be permitted to obscure the phenomena of diffusion as such.

(From *Folia Primat.*, No. 17, 1972, pp. 161–70.)

References

BERNSTEIN, I. S., and SHARPE, L. G. (1966), 'Social roles in a rhesus monkey group', *Behaviour*, No. 26, pp. 91–104.

CROOK, J. H. (1970), 'Social organization and the environment. Aspects of contemporary social ethology', *Animal Behaviour*, No. 18, pp. 197–209.

DAVENPORT, R. K., and ROGERS, C. M. (1970), 'Differential rearing of the chimpanzee: A project survey', in Bourne, *The Chimpanzee*, Vol. 3, Karger, Basle, pp. 337–60.

FRISCH, J. E. (1968), 'Individual behavior and intertroop variability in Japanese macaques', in Jay (ed.), *Primates. Studies in Adaptation and Variability*, Holt, Rinehart & Winston, New York, pp. 243–52.

HALL, K. R. L. (1963), 'Observational learning in monkeys and apes', *Brit. J. Psychol.*, No. 54, pp. 201–26.

MENZEL, E. W., DAVENPORT, R. K., and ROGERS, C. M. (1961), 'Some aspects of behavior toward novelty in young chimpanzees', *J. Comp. Physiol. Psychol.*, No. 54, pp. 16–19.

MENZEL, E. W., DAVENPORT, R. K., and ROGERS, C. M. (1963), 'The effects of environmental restriction upon the chimpanzee's responsiveness to objects', *J. Comp. Physiol. Psychol.*, No. 56, pp. 78–85.

MIYADI, D. (1964), 'Social life of Japanese monkeys', *Science*, No. 143, pp. 783–6.

NEWTON, G., and LEVINE, S. (1968), *Early Experience and Behavior*, Thomas, Springfield, Illinois.

WELKER, W. I. (1956), 'Effects of age and experience on play and exploration of young chimpanzees', *J. Comp. Physiol. Psychol.*, No. 49, pp. 223–6.

YERKES, R. M. (1943), *Chimpanzees. A Laboratory Colony*, Yale University Press.

YERKES, R. M., and YERKES, A. W. (1936), 'Nature and conditions of avoidance (fear) response in chimpanzee', *J. Comp. Physiol. Psychol.*, No. 21, pp. 53–66.

Taboo or Toy?

The transmission from generation to generation of what was originally an individually acquired pattern of food acquisition or food preparation has been suggested to demonstrate proto-cultural development in Japanese macaques (Kawai, 1965; Kawamura, 1959; Miyadi, 1959). Considering the effectiveness of avoidance training in psychology laboratories, a study was designed to study the possible transmission of avoidance-learning responses in six captive groups of Old-World monkeys, including four macaque representatives.

In each of six outdoor compounds, a network of lumber and pipe structures were constructed including six vertical poles, four to five metres tall. One pole was later fitted with an electric grid, approximately one metre wide, just short of the top of the pole. Baseline data were collected on each group to measure spontaneous use of the pre-selected and five control poles. Training sessions began with the installation of the charged grids and data collection continued for twelve hours a day indicating the identity of all animals climbing part of the way up and to the top of each pole, sitting at the base of the 'taboo' pole and receiving shocks. During the twelve hours beginning at sunset, the groups were locked into their indoor quarters. After three successive days with no animal receiving a shock, the power was disconnected and animals were given free access to the outdoor compounds, but a time sampling procedure was begun to monitor individual usage of all poles, and to record social interactions which appeared related to the 'taboo' pole.

Theoretically, some animals would learn to avoid the grid by direct experience with the shock, others by observation, and, later on, animals born into the group after the training period would likewise learn to avoid the grid, thus demonstrating a 'taboo'. A few theoretical modifications to the theory were required.

First, during the baseline phase, the geladas (*Theropithecus gelada*) displayed an amazing appetite for redwood and reduced the lumber portions of our structure to ground level stubs by systematically including mouthfuls of redwood in their daily menu, beginning, logically, with the poles closest to their food boxes. Further efforts with this group were therefore suspended while we turned out attention to a problem with the second non-macaque group, the sooty mangabeys (*Cercocebus atys.*)

The mangabeys were very active on their elevated structures, but demonstrated a preference for running and jumping rather than climbing. As seen in Table 1, vertical poles leading to nowhere had little appeal to the twenty-eight mangabeys in the group. Compounding these initial difficulties was the natural caution of this group such that no animal approached the newly introduced grid during training, thus producing perfect avoidance learning in zero trials. The strength of this learning was apparent when two months of testing revealed perfect retention of grid avoidance. Two years later we were still waiting to shock our first mangabey. Perhaps we should have been forewarned by our first experiences with winter bedding materials. Whereas our macaques jumped and rolled and scattered straw everywhere in wild play sessions initiated within thirty seconds of release, and whereas the geladas had promptly proceeded to eat their bedding straw, the mangabeys waited more than two hours before contacting the bales and most of the bales were intact several days later.

Considering this performance, it was no surprise that the macaque groups made immediate contact with the grids upon installation and release. In every group, several animals were shocked repeatedly before showing any avoidance of the grids. But others never needed to experience the shock personally to avoid the grid. Young males were among the first animals to be shocked, as might have been predicted (Bernstein, 1966), and especially dramatic responses were seen by two of the alpha males. The pigtail (*Macaca nemestrina*) alpha was the sixth animal up the pole and attempted to cross the grid without responding to the shocks. He gave up after taking three or four pulses and never climbed the pole again, although other animals persisted. The stumptail (*Macaca arctoides*) alpha in contrast threatened the pole after being shocked and, with the aid of the second adult male, chased the entire group into the indoor quarters. For the rest of the morning the stumptails remained indoors with the alpha male hanging out the doorway, threatening and watching the grid. Even when the group came outside that afternoon, the two males periodically threatened the grid.

After a variable number of shocks, all four macaque groups achieved 'learning' criterion of three successive days without being shocked. The use of the poles during training, as revealed in Table I, clearly presages the ultimate failure of the experiment. Despite individual variation, baseline data revealed no particular discrimination for or against climbing the preselected taboo pole. During the shock phase, use of the other poles remained unchanged whereas there was a dramatic *increase* in proximities to and use of the taboo pole with animals exploring the base of the pole and the grid.

Table 1 Scores during baseline, training and test phases showing animals on or adjacent to 'taboo' pole and average scores for other poles combined.

Group (members in 1970)	Baseline			Training			Test			
	Adjacent	Taboo pole	Other poles	Adjacent	Taboo pole	Other poles	Shocks	Adjacent	Taboo pole	Other poles
Pigtails (31)	158	11	20·2	1187	1991	25·2	114	225	22	21·7
Crabeaters (37)	296	18	27·0	987	300	45·0	43	1451	19	19·2
Black Apes (15)	117	13	5·0	107	113	3·8	12	8	4	0·4
Stumptails (13)	578	20	7·8	7	41	—	7	133	3	2·0
Mangabey (28)	16	—	1·0	36	—	—	—	110	1	14·8
Combined	1165	62	61	2324	2445	74	176	1927	49	58·1

Notes: Group to group comparisons are not strictly possible due to differences in training and test sessions to first failures and differential group sizes.

After power had been disconnected, interest in the taboo pole declined to baseline levels.

In every group, however, the taboo pole was destroyed, or the grid and connecting wires dismantled, within a few months. Each time, training was re-instituted with sturdier poles and grids and more severe shocks such that final training sessions used ordinary straight house current (with amazingly little effect). An examination of individual identities and age-sex membership of animals returning to the grid was most revealing. In the pigtail group, which destroyed the pole twice and broke the wires nine times, the six fully adult females were never shocked and had the fewest scores on or near the taboo pole. The two old males received only one shock (the alpha) during training and never climbed the pole again. The immature animals received 111 shocks during initial training. The ten juvenile males consistently outscored the twelve juvenile females in all subsequent phases. The single sub-adult male escaped the compound by climbing out on the wires after destroying the grid, but was killed when he attacked the main power lines just outside the laboratory. The same pattern of excessive interest in the grids on the part of immature animals, and young males in particular, pertained in the other groups, as did also the pattern of grid and pole destruction. In the crabeater (*M. fascicularis*) group and in the black ape (*M. nigra*) groups, grid wires had been pulled loose while electrically hot. In the first case five juvenile males, and in the second case two juvenile males and a juvenile female, were found playing with the hot wires when the damage was discovered. In both cases play with the sparking wires continued despite occasional shocks to the participants.

With the exception of two cases in which victims of aggression within the group climbed the live grid to escape their pursuers, the evidence was overwhelming that we had created an attractive toy rather than a taboo. The same animals that most frequently participated in vigorous play sessions were the most frequently associated with the taboo pole 'failures'. Individuals would try to leap over the grid, or to the top of the pole from other nearby structures. They repeatedly tested the grid by slapping at it, biting the insulation and rocking the structure. When convinced the grid had been subdued during a shock-off period, the animals then tore the apparatus apart. Even during shock periods, these animals were extraordinarily persistent (and embarassingly successful) in their efforts to thwart the system. Neither our technically very superior final models, nor our frustrated use of direct-line current ever succeeded in converting the toy into a taboo. We failed to institute a proto-cultural tradition, but learned something about the power and function of play.

References

BERNSTEIN, I. S. (1966), 'An investigation of the organization of pigtail monkey groups through the use of challenges', *Primates*, Vol. 7, No. 4, pp. 471–80.

KAWAI,.M. (1965), 'Newly-acquired pre-cultural behavior of the natural troop of Japanese monkeys on Koshima Islet', *Primates*, Vol. 6, pp. 1–30.

KAWAMURA, S. (1959), 'The process of sub-culture propagation among Japanese macaques', *Primates*, Vol. 2, pp. 43–60.

MIYADI, D. (1959), 'On some new habits and their propagation in Japanese monkeys groups', *Proceedings of the 15th International Congress of Zoology*, pp. 857–60.

Field Toys

This very well-known writer of stories for children recalls her own childhood. The country child plays in and with a natural environment of plants and trees and animals – resourceful, inventive and exploratory. The same wealth of play materials is available to any chimpanzee, and was available to evolving hominids. The uses to which it is put – the making of burr-baskets and clay five-stones – and above all the aesthetic joy in curling reed-pith or petal peep-show – are the human reaction to this enduring environment. The human child attaches symbolic significance to the objects he finds around him.

'Have you any toys? Toys! We plays with anything, with sticks, stones and flowers, and we run about and look at things and find things and sings and shouts. We don't have toys.'

The fields were our toyshops and sweetshops, our market and our storehouses. We made our toys from things we found in the pastures. We ate sweet and sour food of the wild. We hunted from hedge to hedge as in a market, to find the best provisions, and we had our wild shops in corners of fields, or among the trees.

The flowering spikes of plantain were picked for the game of 'Soldiers'. With a bunch of the green flower-heads we chose out the likely warriors and challenged another soldier flower to combat. When his head flew off a fresh one from the bunch took his place, and fought on. The conquering plantain counted his kills, thirty, forty, fifty kills a good soldier plantain would make and he was borne home with his bruised stalk-body bent, but his head intact, to rest, the happy warrior.

We picked green rushes from the little hollows by the springs. We chose them with care, the stoutest and longest of the smooth fine plants. We stripped the green covering, taking off thin slips at a time to preserve the long white pith intact. The discovery of the pith, its texture, resilient and pliable, always gave me great pleasure. A bird's egg, a ribbon of pith from rushes, and an oxlip were treasures prized for their beauty.

From the pith we made pretty devices. We curled it into roses, little baskets, a purse with a handle, a doll's stool.

We treasured these toys until the pith was yellow, and then we tossed them in the fire and watched them fade away. Light as air they seemed to be, fairy toys, and a servant boy or girl who could fashion a new pith toy was in high favour. One boy could make a bird's nest, twining the snowy pith in basket-work. Another could fashion a bridal ring with twisted coils, or a brooch. Sometimes we made little pith men, and electrified them with warmed brown paper, to see them prance and leap on the kitchen table.

The green rushes made whips, plaited for the lash and tightly bound for the handle. They made bracelets with brown flowers for clasps. They were girdles and shoelaces, and necklaces with flowers as beads. They were woven into round baskets to hold a couple of hen's eggs, into rattles for a baby, into mats and frames for tiny pictures, and many a small conceit and game. We wore a rush ring on every finger, and a necklace, and we felt like Cap-o'-rushes.

We picked the rye-grass, which we called 'Tinker, tailor grass', and we counted the little ears to find out whom we should marry. Tinker, tailor, soldier, sailor, rich man, poor man, beggar man, thief. We asked it, 'This year, next year, sometime, never.'

Blackberries and bilberries, wild strawberries and raspberries, and even gooseberries we found growing in the woods and quarries and fields. The gooseberries were little old trees belonging to a ruined cottage, where we stepped light as feathers as we fearfully plucked the hard little berries and glanced behind for shadows and dreams.

We hunted for Robin's-pincushions, and oak-galls and toadstools, each of which had its own value of magic or beauty. Puff-balls were our purses to hold imaginary money. With oak-galls we played many games. From acorn cups we sipped the water from the spring which flowed into the field troughs. It tasted better that way.

One of these water troughs provided us with a new set of toys, for there was a bed of fine clay beside it. We dug it out, and moulded it into bricks about an inch square. We baked them in the oven, and rejoiced over the result. We grew bolder in our experiments, and we made little cups and bowls and marbles and sets of 'five-stones'. They were untrue, they split and broke, but the five-stones were a triumph for many a long day's play.

Nut trees were granaries for children and squirrels. We climbed them on the way home from school and filled our pockets with clusters of hooded brown nuts. We had convenient flat stones in lanes and on walls, our nutting-stones where we hammered them and ate the kernels, and left piles of shells and curly sheathes to lie till next year when we came again.

In our wood there were some sweet chestnut trees, which supplied us with nuts in the autumn. We stripped off the prickly husks and amber skins and ate the sweetest nut we knew. Horse chestnuts were rarer, we had to go to the village for them, or swap marbles for a set. From them, with pins and coloured wool we made dolls' furniture, the correct size for the penny dolls. Every little boy played conkers, with a nut threaded on a string.

We gathered the burrs from the giant burdock and pressed them together to form baskets and nests. There were games with flowers too, when we popped the seed of the great balsam, which went off like a fairy's gun, and we listened to the broom shooting its own ammunition in the fields. We made peepshows out of the smallest prettiest flowers, or dolls from the garden poppies, or a set of glove fingers from foxgloves. Cowslip-balls and daisy-chains – there was no end to the toys we found. The peepshow was lucrative for it brought the wealth of a pin. A few brightly coloured flowers – primroses, violets, a jay's feather, a jockey-grass, a crimson leaf – were arranged in a pattern close to a slip of glass. This little picture was enclosed in an envelope, sealed, and a flap cut to make a window.

'A pin to see a peepshow' we demanded of all whom we met, and one after another came with a pin to see the sight. We carried little round pin-cushions, the size of pennies, to hold the pins, and we rejoiced over the beauty of some of the charming little scenes hidden in the peepshows. The tiny bouquets had an air of magic in the cupped hands of the little country children who made them.

We ate the leaves of field-sorrel, which we called 'Sour-dock', after its sweet-sour taste. We tasted the Trinity leaves of the delicate wood sorrel, which we called 'Wood-sour'. Hawthorn leaves in their small lovely rosettes in early spring were our bread-and-cheese, called always by that name by country folk. The 'aiges', crimson fruit of hawthorn, were our field bread. Long tender shoots of blackberry briars we stripped of their leaves under the tuition of a servant lad, and we nibbled the sweet inner core, which was the farm boy's means of staying hunger. We dug up pig-nuts from the White Field where they grew among the grasses. Certain grasses too were good and tender, sweet and succulent as if honey were stored within the stalks. Then there was clover, and we sucked the honey-stalks of the red and white flowers which grew in abundance as we strolled along the paths to see the cattle and horses. Cowslip bells were a store-house of honey for the human little bees, and so were the horns of honey-suckle. Like the bees themselves we sipped and tasted and hovered about the meadows, wild and happy and free.

Down by the river grew willows, but we never played by the wild waters of the stream, which galloped along faster than the horses on the road alongside. Death lurked there, pot-holes and currents, and crumbling falling banks. We kept to our own hillside, to the small kingdom that was our country, and there we found enough to amuse and entertain us during the long years of childhood.

(From *Country Hoard*, Faber & Faber, 1943.)

Exploration and Play in Children

Introduction

Exploration and play are often regarded as one class of behaviour. Welker (1956a,b) in describing some determinants of exploration and play in chimpanzees, as well as the variability manifested in these behaviours, treats them as indistinguishable. More recently (1961) he has acknowledged this more explicitly: 'The term play is often used in conjunction with, or in place of, the term exploration. In other instances play is used as the generic term, exploration being only one type of play.' On the grounds that a distinction between play and exploration is not always ready-made, he justifies a perfunctory attempt to define these behaviours. Hayes (1958), in studying the maintenance of play activities in children, included games with marbles as well as visual exploration of pictures. Thorpe (1963), too, implicitly assumes the equivalence of exploration and play; he states that where appetitive behaviour and consummatory behaviour are not too strictly tied, we may begin to get general exploration of the environment which often takes the form of play, and he sees learning deriving from this process of play or exploration. Berlyne (1960) has discussed the perceptual and intellectual activities which are engaged in for their own sake, and calls them comprehensively 'ludic behaviour', defining this category as 'any behaviour that does not have a biological function that we can clearly recognize'.

At the same time, it is clear that these authors are aware of this conceptual confusion and of the need for clarification and distinction. Thorpe says 'there are various possible explanations for behaviour which can be described as play, and it would be a mistake to think that at present they can all be brought together in one category'. Berlyne states 'ludic behaviour forms such a motley assortment that it is highly unlikely that all of it has just one function . . . so far it is mainly our ignorance that binds them all together'. But, in general, theories of exploration have subsumed play and theories of play have failed to take cognizance of exploratory activities.

Exploration

Most definitions of exploratory behaviour have tended to be over-inclusive: exploratory behaviour is defined as 'any behaviour which tends to incr ase the rate of change in the stimulation falling on the animal's receptors which is not impelled by homeostatic or reproductive need' (Barnett, 1963), or 'those responses that alter the stimulus field' (Berlyne, 1960). These are hardly operationally useful definitions, but attempts have been made to classify these behaviours more precisely in terms of the receptors involved, e.g. orienting, locomotor, and investigatory responses (Berlyne, 1960; Hayes, 1960; Welker, 1961). Whatever the measure of behaviour used it is generally accepted that novel situations and objects elicit exploratory behaviour (Berlyne, 1950; Montgomery, 1953; Carr and Brown, 1959a), and that this responsiveness shows a decrement with continued exposure (Adlerstein and Fehrer, 1955; Inhelder, 1955; Welker, 1956b; Glanzer, 1961), and a recovery after a period of non-exposure (Montgomery, 1951; Berlyne, 1955).

On the other hand, workers from the Wisconsin Laboratory have shown that visual exploration persists in the monkey over a long period of time (Butler and Harlow, 1954) and shows a non-decremental steady pattern from day to day (Butler and Alexander, 1955). Similar results were reported for manipulatory investigation by Harlow *et al* (1956), and Carr and Brown (1959b). At first sight, these two sets of results appear contradictory, and Harlow's (1956) conclusion that 'manipulatory behaviour is self-sustaining', adds little to the description of the behaviour. If, however, one examines the conditions under which the animal is reported as showing a maintenance or increase in exploratory activity with time, these are in general those we would describe as sensorily depriving or at least unstimulating; typically, small bare cages were used. The animal was therefore deprived of the opportunity of alternative activities other than those directed towards himself or to the predetermined stimulus objects. Under these conditions, the animal strives to vary sensory input: rats press a lever for no other 'reward' than microswitch clicks and relay noises (Kish and Antonitis, 1956); monkeys bar press for a change in brightness (Moon and Lodahl, 1956), or show increasing manipulation and chewing of a door which is the only variable object in its restricted environment (Symmes, 1959); children in an empty room engage in bodily manipulations and gestural patterns (Hutt *et al.*, 1965); adults in sensory deprivation experiments talk and whistle to themselves (Bexton *et al.*, 1954).

Play

The term 'play' covers a heterogeneous assortment of activities from the darts and gambols of young birds and mammals to the extremely ritualized games of adult humans. In his review, Beach (1945) lists five characteristics of play, only three of which are relevant to its definition. These are: (1) that it carries an emotional element of pleasure; (2) that it is characteristic of the immature animal rather than the adult; (3) that it differs from non-playful responses in having no relatively immediate biological result.

The first characteristic has clearly impressed many authors: Bally (1945) refers to play as appetitive activity in a 'relaxed field' (*im entspannten Feld*), Bertalanffy (1960) as activities which are accompanied by 'functional pleasure', Meyer-Holzapfel (1956) as activities which are characterized by the 'disinterested' atmosphere concerning the consummatory act, and Lorenz (1956) comments that 'the usual opposition between play and being serious has a very real background'.

Experiment

The main aim of the experiment was the study of curiosity or exploratory behaviour elicited in young children by the presentation of a novel object, and the habituation of this behaviour with time. Since we were concerned with the attraction of novelty to the child, rather than a forced responsiveness, it was decided to allow it alternative choices. These consisted of five familiar toys.

Subjects

The subjects were all nursery school children between the ages of 3 and 5 years. They were seen in a small room in the school which was relatively familiar to them. The furniture was stacked against one wall, leaving most of the floor area free for the child to move around in. Altogether thirty nursery school children were studied under the conditions to be described.

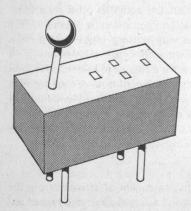

Fig. 1. The novel object: a red metal box on four brass 'legs' and a lever ending in a blue wooden ball. The directional manipulations of the lever are registered on four counters which could be left open as here, or covered up.

Apparatus

The novel object was designed to allow for the assessment of both novelty and complexity variables, although the latter was not parametrically varied. The object consisted of a red metal rectangular box on four brass legs (Fig. 1). On top was mounted a lever at the end of which was a blue wooden ball. The four directional movements of the lever were registered by four Post Office counters which could be made visible to the child. It was also possible to allow the child differential auditory feedback contingent upon specific manipulatory movements (a bell in one of the horizontal directions and a buzzer in one of the vertical). Four conditions of relatively increasing complexity were thus available:

(i) No sound or vision: the bell and buzzer switched off and the counters covered up.
(ii) Vision only: noises off, but counters visible.
(iii) Sound only: bell and buzzer on, but counters covered.
(iv) Sound and vision: noises on and counters visible.

Procedure

The six experimental sessions were preceded by two pre-exposure sessions which additionally served to familiarize the children with the room and the five toys. These pre-exposure sessions were procedurally identical to the experimental sessions, except for the presence of the novel object. All sessions were of ten minutes duration. An experimental design was used that ensured that the week-ends were equally distributed over the experimental sessions under each condition. The experimental sessions were otherwise forty-eight hours apart. In the nursery school observations were entered in check-lists, an entry being made every ten seconds by the observer who sat in a corner of the room. The child was asked if he would like to play for a few minutes while the observer finished off some work. Further details were recorded at the end of each session. The counters on the object were read at the end of each session.

Results

In general, when the children entered the room they looked at the novel object immediately, or approached it, often asking the observer what it was. They would then examine the object manually or inspect it visually while holding the lever, and finally engage in active manipulation of the lever.

The amounts of time spent exploring the object under conditions (i) and (ii) are shown in Fig. 2. There is a progressive decrement of exploratory

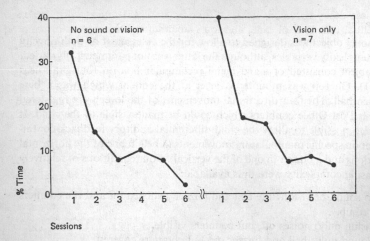

Fig. 2. Proportions of time spent exploring the novel object on successive trials under (i) no sound or vision, and (ii) vision only, conditions (n = number of subjects).

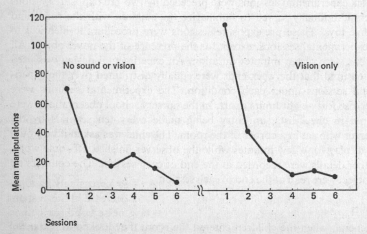

Fig. 3. Mean amounts of manipulatory exploration under (i) no sound or vision, and (ii) vision only, conditions.

activity with repeated exposure. If the counter readings are used as a measure of investigatory manipulation, a similar trend is seen under both these conditions (Fig. 3).

These decay curves, whether of time or manipulatory activity, are exponential functions of time, and if a Napierian logarithm transformation of the number of manipulations is used to plot manipulations against trials, the two lines of best fit are seen to have different slopes (Fig. 4). The regressions of manipulations on trials are significant under both conditions (i) (variance ratio 11·5, d.f. = 4, $P < 0.05$); and (ii) (variance ratio = 27·56, d.f. = 4, $P < 0.01$). Thus, addition of the visual feedback slightly decreased the rate of habituation to the novel object. The initial amount of exploration was greater with the visual incentive than with no such incentive.

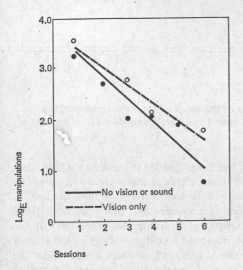

Fig. 4. Linear regressions of manipulations on trials under (i) no sound or vision, and (ii) vision only, conditions, when a Naperian logarithmic transformation of manipulations is used.

Under both conditions (iii) and (iv) the object was increasingly manipulated, and only after the fifth exposure was there a decrease in this responsiveness (Fig. 5). It appeared that simply making noise contingent upon certain manipulatory responses completely altered the temporal pattern of activity towards the object. Addition of the visual to the auditory feedback only served to enhance this pattern.

Analysis of activities

It was clear that under conditions (iii) and (iv) the nature of activities engaged in changed markedly over the six sessions. Investigative responses

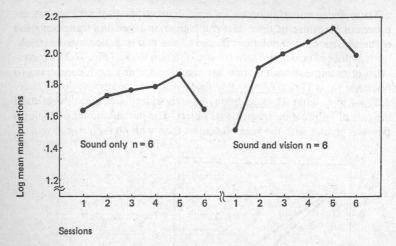

Fig. 5. Manipulatory exploration of the novel object on successive trials under (iii) sound only, and (iv) sound and vision, conditions (n = number of subjects).

gave way to other behaviours, and it was decided to separate the time spent investigating the object from other activities involving it. Investigative responses were those responses that involved visual inspection, and feeling, touching or other manipulations accompanied by visual inspection. These had in common the characteristic of 'learning the properties' of the object. Whereas under the two no-sound conditions nearly all the activity directed towards the object was of this kind, this was not so under the sound conditions. The time spent in investigatory responses decreased progressively from session one to six under both conditions (iii) and (iv) (Fig. 6); Grant's analysis of variance (1956) involving the use of orthogonal polynomials indicates that the linear components of these trends are significant ($F = 557 \cdot 5/31 \cdot 24$, d.f. = 1 and 30, $P < 0 \cdot 001$; $F = 1457/94 \cdot 5$, d.f. = 1 and 30, $P < 0 \cdot 001$ respectively).

As investigation of the object decreased other activities involving it increased. When analysed these consisted of repetitive motor movements, manipulations of long duration accompanied by visual inspection of other objects, and a sequence of activities incorporating both the novel object and other toys – in other words a 'game'. Examples of these were respectively: patting the lever repeatedly, leaning on the lever making the bell ring continuously while looking around the room, and running round with the truck ringing the bell each time the object was passed. There is another group of responses which can be termed 'transposition-of-function' –

those responses which resulted in the object explicitly fulfilling another function, e.g. something to climb, a bridge, or a seat. All these activities (i.e. repetitive movements, 'games' and 'transposition-of-function'

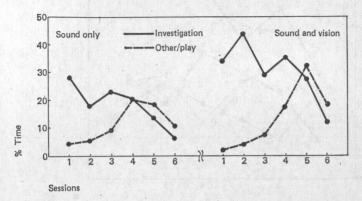

Fig. 6. Proportions of time spent in (a) investigating and (b) other activities involving the novel object under conditions (iii) and (iv).

responses) are those which an observer would recognize and label as *play*. They occurred hardly at all under the no-sound conditions, and when they did they were entirely of the 'transposition-of-function' kind. By the sixth session, however, even 'play activities' directed towards the object decreased and it seems likely that these responses are a quadratic function of time, though more results are required to demonstrate this.

In all children, once active investigation had commenced, it generally proceeded vigorously, all aspects of the object being explored. It was only once the child had apparently learned all there was to know about the object that it was incorporated in play activities, and any further learning was purely incidental. In fact one boy who started a 'game' after a relatively brief period of investigation failed to find the buzzer. However, if during play a new property or aspect of the object was chanced upon, a further spell of investigation would follow.

The transition from investigative exploration to playful activities was marked by certain features: during investigation all receptors were oriented towards the object, the general expression being one of 'concentration' (see photo inset): at a later stage (intermediate between investigation and play), manipulation might occur with simultaneous visual exploration of other stimuli, and the intent facial expression changed to a more relaxed one. Finally in play for much of the time, the receptors were

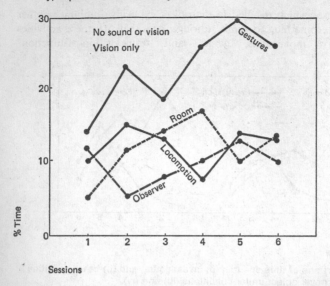

Fig. 7. Proportions of time spent gesturing, exploring the room, looking at the observer, and in locomotion, from session to session under conditions (i) and (ii).

desynchronized (i.e. vision and manipulation were no longer simultaneously directed towards the object) and the behaviour towards the object might almost be described as 'nonchalant' (see photo inset).

The relative amounts of time spent on other activities from session to session are shown in Figs. 7 and 8. Under the no-sound conditions gestures increased with continued exposure to the same situation; this was probably a reflection of the child's boredom, particularly as yawning and stretching figured prominently in the latter sessions. That the situation had become less attractive under these conditions was indicated by two children who showed some reluctance to being exposed to it for the fifth or sixth time. Under the sound conditions, however, locomotion progressively increased over the sessions; presumably once the children had started moving about as they did when playing a game, they continued to do so, even when they had tired of the object. On the whole, orienting responses towards the adult were most frequent in the first and last experimental sessions, i.e. at the initial presentation of the novel object, and when the child had become more or less tired of the situation. In the first case the adult provided assurance, in the second the possibility of further stimulation when other objects had lost their attraction.

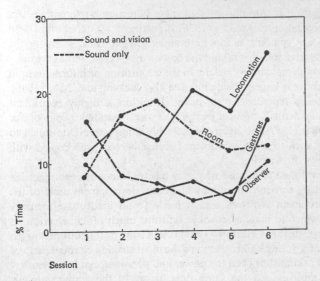

Fig. 8. Proportions of time spent gesturing, exploring the room, looking at the observer, and in locomotion, from session to session under conditions (iii) and (iv).

Discussion

Consideration has primarily been given to specific exploration of a novel object and its habituation as well as those responses which might be termed play. By restricting myself to these responses directed towards the same stimulus object, I have tried to draw some distinction between exploration and play. These behaviours can be differentiated on a number of grounds. Investigative, inquisitive or specific exploration is directional, i.e. it is elicited by or oriented towards certain environmental changes. Its decay is a monotonic function of time, and any overall response measure would mask this. The goal is 'getting to know the properties', and the particular responses of investigation are determined by the nature of the object.

Play, on the other hand, only occurs in a known environment, and when the animal or child feels he knows the properties of the object in that environment; this is apparent in the gradual relaxation of mood, evidenced not only by changes in facial expression, but in a greater diversity and variability of activities. In play the emphasis changes from the question of 'what does this *object* do?' to 'what can *I* do with this object?'.

While investigation is stimulus-referent, play is response-referent. In this respect an observation of Mead's (1956) is pertinent: 'You will find with children who are spinning a top or bouncing a ball that stopping the action is the deprivation, not taking the ball away.' Again, while investigative exploration demonstrably results in the acquisition of information, in play such learning is largely incidental (see also Jackson and Todd, 1946). Indeed, by being repetitive, play is by definition a highly redundant activity, and can actually prevent learning as was illustrated by one of our subjects. Schiller (1957) too describes how his chimpanzee Don failed to learn to use a stick to solve a problem because he was preoccupied with the play activity of 'weaving'.

It is of interest then to inquire why play has traditionally been regarded as an exploratory activity. In infancy and early development most of the animal's environment is novel, and it has also an inadequate memory store against which to match new objects; thus, much of its behaviour is likely to be investigatory. Harlow (1953) is less equivocal about this in his observations of a young child: 'Perhaps the most striking characteristic of this particular primate has been the power and persistence of her curiosity-investigatory motives.' At the same time, many of the young animal's responses are of a repetitive nature – a pattern which commonly characterizes play (see, for example, primary, secondary and tertiary circular reactions described by Piaget, 1953). Thus, in infancy it is perhaps difficult to distinguish between investigatory responses and play responses. During ontogeny, however, these two activities diverge, and become more easily separable, until in the adult there is a sharp distinction between investigatory activities on the one hand, and play activities on the other, which are often of an extremely ritualized kind. There may indeed be many instances where both features of exploration and play are present, but these should not prevent us from attempting to make the distinction. It may be that many of the young animal's responses are investigatory rather than playful. Certainly, so-called play activities in the developing organism may be a preparation for future skills in the sense that any motor activity is, e.g. walking. Lorenz (1956) points out that such activities in any animals cannot be regarded simply as a rehearsal of instinctive or innate behaviour patterns, since 'play is most prominent in species which combine a minimum of equipment of instinctive movements with a maximum of exploratory learning'. They may also utilize much energy, but to consider this as 'surplus' is to regard the organism as a closed system (Bertalanffy, 1960). It does seem, however, that play is relatively low in the motivational hierarchy, i.e. it can be inhibited by fear, hunger, curiosity or almost any other drive. Morris (1956) makes a similar point more neatly: he suggests that in play 'the mechanisms of mutual inhibition and sequential ordering', evident in other drive states, are not operational and hence there is less control over the nature and sequence of motor patterns.

In the human species there are many kinds of play that are not engaged in by other mammals. Certain forms of imitative play and dramatic play are associated with a greater degree of conceptual sophistication in the human, and it may be that for a better understanding of these activities, which have their analogies more on the stage than in the cot, we need an analysis of their linguistic content as well. My concern up to the present has been with less symbolic forms of play.

A difference between the determinants of exploration in children and in lower mammals, chiefly rodents, may be noted *en passant*. Rodents will explore a new environment but not a new object in a familiar setting (Chitty and Southern, 1954; Shillito, 1963). Children, on the other hand, will not readily explore a new environment on their own, but will explore a new object if placed in a relatively familiar environment. This difference may represent a shift in biological emphasis from prey to predator.

Conclusions

Studies of exploration have been concerned with *at least* two different kinds of behaviour having somewhat contrary functions. In psychophysiological terms *diversive* exploration has been seen by Hebb (1955) as an attempt to avoid states of monotony or low arousal; by Fiske and Maddi (1961) as an attempt to vary stimulation in order to sustain a certain level of activation; and by Berlyne (1960) as an effort to increase sensory input so as to avoid a state of boredom or high arousal. Investigative or *specific* exploration, on the other hand, seeks to reduce uncertainty and hence arousal or activation produced by the novel or complex stimulation. Play in its morphology, determinants and functions often appears to be more similar to diversive exploration than specific exploration.

(From *Symposia of the Zoological Society of London*, No. 18, 1966, pp. 61–81.)

References

ADLERSTEIN, A., and FEHRER, E. (1955), 'The effect of food deprivation on exploratory behaviour in a complex maze', *J. Comp. Physiol. Psychol.*, No. 48, pp. 250–53.

BALLY, G. (1945), *Vom Ursprung und den Grenzen der Freiheit*, Schwabe, Basle.

BARNETT, S. A. (1963), *A study in behaviour*, Methuen.

BEACH, F. A. (1945), 'Current concepts of play in animals', *Am. Nat.*, No. 79, pp. 523–41.

BERLYNE, D. E. (1950), 'Novelty and curiosity as determiners of exploratory behaviour', *Br. J. Med. Psychol.*, No. 41, pp. 68–80.

BERLYNE, D. E. (1955), 'The arousal and satiation of perceptual curiosity in the rat', *J. Comp. Physiol. Psychol.*, No. 48, pp. 238–46.

BERLYNE, D. E. (1960), *Conflict, Arousal and Curiosity*, McGraw-Hill, New York.

BERTALANFFY, L. VON (1960), in *Discussions on Child Development*, J. M. Tanner and B. Inhelder (eds), Tavistock Publications, p. 73.

BEXTON, W. A., HERON, W., and SCOTT, T. H. (1954), 'Effects of decreased variation in the sensory environment', *Can. J. Psychol.*, No. 8, pp. 70–76.

BUTLER, R. A., and ALEXANDER, H. M. (1955), 'Daily patterns of visual exploratory behaviour in the monkey', *J. Comp. Physiol. Psychol.*, No. 48, pp. 247–9.

BUTLER, R. A., and HARLOW, H. F. (1954), 'Persistence of visual exploration in monkeys', *J. Comp. Physiol. Psychol.*, No. 47, pp. 258–63.

CARR, R. M., and BROWN, W. L. (1959a), 'The effect of the introduction of novel stimuli upon manipulation in rhesus monkeys', *J. Genet. Psychol.*, No. 94, pp. 107–11.

CARR, R. M., and BROWN, W. L. (1959b), 'Manipulation of visually homogeneous stimulus objects', *J. Genet. Psychol.*, No. 95, pp. 245–9.

CHITTY, D., and SOUTHERN, H. N. (1954), *Control of Rats and Mice*, Vols. 1 and 2, Clarendon Press, Oxford.

FISKE, D. W., and MADDI, S. R. (1961), 'A conceptual framework', in *Functions of Varied Experience*, D. W. Fiske and S. R. Maddi (eds), Dorsey Press, Homewood, Illinois, U.S.A.

GLANZER, M. (1961), 'Changes and interrelations in exploratory behaviour', *J. Comp. Physiol. Psychol.*, No. 54, pp. 433–8.

HARLOW, H. F. (1953), 'Mice, men, monkeys and motives', *Psych. Rev.*, No. 60, pp. 23–32.

HAYES, J. R. (1958), 'The maintenance of play in young children', *J. Comp. Physiol. Psychol*, No. 51, pp. 788–9.

HAYES, K. J. (1960), 'Exploration and fear', *Psychol. Rep.*, No. 6, pp. 91–3.

HEBB, D. O. (1955), 'Drives and the C.N.S. (conceptual nervous system)', *Psych. Rev.*, No. 62, pp. 243–54.

HUTT, C., HUTT, S. J., and OUNSTED, C. (1965), 'The behaviour of children with and without upper C.N.S. lesions', *Behaviour*, No. 24, pp. 246–8.

INHELDER, E. (1955), 'Zur Psychologie einiger Verhaltensweisen – besonders des Spiels – von Zootieren', *Z. Tierpsychol.*, No. 12, pp. 88–144.

JACKSON, L., and TODD, K. M. (1946), *Child Treatment and the Therapy of Play*, Methuen.

KISH, G. B., and ANTONITIS, J. J. (1956), 'Unconditioned operant behaviour in two homozygous strains of mice', *J. Genet. Psychol.*, No. 88, pp. 121–9.

LORENZ, K. (1956), 'Plays and vacuum activities', in *L'Instinct dans le Comportement des Animaux et de l'Homme,* Masson, Paris.

MEAD, M. (1956), in *Discussion on Child Development*, J. H. Tanner and B. Inhelder (eds), Tavistock Publications, p. 139.

MEYER-HOLZAPFEL, M. M. (1956), 'Über die Bereitschaft zu Spiel und Instinkthandlunge', *Z. Tierpsychol.*, No. 13, pp. 442–62.

MONTGOMERY, K. C. (1951), 'Spontaneous alternation as a function of time between trials and amount of work', *J. Exp. Psychol.*, No. 42, pp. 82–93.

MONTGOMERY, K. C. (1953), 'Exploratory behaviour as a function of "similarity" of stimulus situations', *J. Comp. Physiol. Psychol.*, No. 46, pp. 129–33.

MOON, L. E., and LODAHL, T. M. (1956), 'The reinforcing effect of changes in illumination on lever-pressing in the monkey', *Am. J. Psychol.*, No. 64, pp. 288–90.

MORRIS, D. J. (1956), 'Discussion on plays and vacuum activities', in *L'Instinct dans le Comportement des Animaux et de l'Homme*, Masson, Paris.

PIAGET, J. (1953), *The Origin of Intelligence in the Child*, Routledge and Kegan Paul.

SCHILLER, P. H. (1957), 'Innate motor action as a basis of learning: manipulative patterns in the chimpanzee', in *Instinctive Behaviour*, C. H. Schiller (ed.), Methuen. (And see this volume, p. 232.)

SHILLITO, E. E. (1963), 'Exploratory behaviour in the short-tailed vole, *Microtus agrestis*', *Behaviour*, No. 21, pp. 145–54.

SYMMES, D. (1959), 'Anxiety reduction and novelty as goals of visual exploration by monkeys', *J. Genet. Psychol.*, No. 94, pp. 181–98.

THORPE, W. H. (1963), *Learning and Instinct in Animals*, Methuen.

WELKER, W. I. (1956), 'Some determinants of play and exploration in chimpanzees', *J. Comp. Physiol. Psychol.*, No. 49, pp. 84–9.

WELKER, W. I. (1956), 'Variability of play and exploratory behaviour in chimpanzees', *J. Comp. Physiol. Psychol.*, No. 49, pp. 181–5.

WELKER, W. I. (1961), 'An analysis of exploratory and play behaviour in animals', in *Functions of Varied Experience*, D. W. Fiske and S. R. Maddi (eds), Dorsey Press, Homewood, Illinois, U.S.A.

Predictions from Play

In a series of studies of curiosity and exploration in young children (Hutt, 1966; 1967a; 1967b; 1970a; 1970b), it was found that 3- to 5-year-olds could be placed in one of three categories, according to their responses to a new toy. Usually, when a child is confronted with a new toy, he first inspects and investigates it; then, when he is familiar with it, he 'plays' with it. These two categories of behaviour have been more formally characterized as 'specific' and 'diversive exploration' respectively, and their distinctive behavioural features have been described. Essentially, in specific exploration or investigation the implicit query seems to be 'What can this object do?'; in diversive exploration or play it is 'What can I do with this object?'.

The three mutually exclusive categories into which nursery school children fell were as follows: non-explorers (N.E.) who looked at the new toy and even approached it but did not inspect or investigate it; explorers (E) who actively investigated the toy but thereafter did very little else with it; inventive explorers (I.E.) who, after investigating the toy, used it in many imaginative ways. Girls were over-represented in the first category, and boys in the third.

But, more specifically, we wished to know if these early individual differences observed in patterns of exploration and play were characteristic and enduring ones, or whether they were simply a function of the experimental situation. In other words, were these behavioural differences predictive of any subsequent tendencies and abilities? The failure to explore, for instance, could be due to a lack of curiosity generally, or in that particular toy, or it could be due to a personality trait such as inhibition, shyness, etc. Again, the differences in inventive play could be due to more active and vigorous play, or they might be the precursors of differences in convergent and divergent thinking, usually referred to as creativity.

It has been possible to re-examine forty-eight children (twenty-three boys, twenty-five girls) of the original sample of almost 100. These children are now at primary school and aged between 7 and 10 years. They were administered the Wallach and Kogan (1965) battery of creative tests which have been shown to be reliable and valid (Cropley and Maslany, 1969).

Two measures can be obtained from these tests: fluency, the total number of responses given to the items; and originality, the number of unique responses given by an individual. Although there is some correlation between the two measures, the performances of boys and girls were not found to be comparable on both measures, hence only the originality scores, duly weighted (Cropley, 1967), are considered here. The children also answered a personality questionnaire especially designed for this age group (Porter and Cattell, 1959), and were rated by teachers and parents on a number of personality traits and behavioural characteristics.

The numbers in the three categories in the earlier study and in the present study are shown in Table 1. Should there be an association be-

Table 1

	Numbers		
Original study	N.E.	E	I.E.
Boys	5	20	25
Girls	15	27	6
Present study			
Boys	3	10	10
Girls	6	14	5

	Mean originality scores and standard deviations		
Boys	24·5 (11·3)	44·9 (21·7)	76·3 (29·6)
Girls	36·2 (15·8)	39·8 (16·3)	61·5 (20·2)

	Significance of differences		
Boys versus girls	$t = 2·42$	$t = 1·02$	$t = 3·87$
	$P < 0·05$	n.s.	$P < 0·01$
Boys	N.E. vs E	E vs I.E.	
	$t = 2·78$	$t = 4·51$	
	$P < 0·02$	$P < 0·001$	
Girls	N.E. vs E	E vs I.E.	
	$t = 0·53$	$t = 2·45$	
	n.s.	$P < 0·05$	

tween inventiveness in play and creativity in ideas, children in the I.E. group would be expected to score higher on the Wallach–Kogan tests than those in the E. or N.E. groups. The means and standard deviations (in parentheses) are given in Table 1 as well as the significance of the differences between the means. These results indicated that failure to explore novelty was not necessarily associated with convergent thinking in girls, and that inventive play was positively associated with the propensity for divergent and creative thinking, but particularly so in boys. This is shown conclusively by the rank-order correlations.

To obtain adequate sample sizes, groups E and I.E. were combined and the boys and girls ranked separately according to the amount of creative play they had shown (by C. H.), and according to their originality scores (by R. B.). The Spearman rank-order correlation was 0.516 ($P < 0.05$) for boys and 0.368 (not significant) for girls.

On the personality questionnaire, the non-exploring girls rated themselves as apprehensive, tense, reserved and conforming; the boys in this category saw themselves as unadventurous and inactive. The creative girls rated themselves as assertive and independent, mostly outgoing and more often placid than apprehensive. The boys, on the other hand, did not conform to a recognizable pattern: some saw themselves as tough-minded, others as tender-minded, some as phlegmatic, others as excitable; but most rated themselves as fairly independent and venturesome.

The parents' ratings were rather more difficult to evaluate, mainly because they tended to cluster around the middle or 'neutral' point of the 5-point scale; when the extremes of the scale were used they were invariably the socially 'acceptable' values. In this way, discrepancies arose between the ratings of the parents and those of the teachers, but only in two or three instances were they on opposite sides of the scale.

All three boys who were non-explorers were described as 'non curious' by both teachers and parents. The girls in this category were said to be sensitive and easily discouraged, preferring sedentary to physical activities; they had difficulty mixing with their peers, and the concentration of three of them was said to be very poor. The I.E. girls were described as curious and independent; they mixed easily and concentrated well, but teachers found the classroom behaviour of two of them 'undesirable'. The boys in this category were most often described as very curious – they also mixed well and preferred physical to sedentary activities. The teachers, however, found them to be disruptive influences in the classroom, and parents tended to rate them on the negative end of the 'calm and stable' scale.

In summary, the failure to explore in early childhood seemed to be related to lack of curiosity and adventure in boys and to difficulties in personality and social adjustment in girls. This interpretation is strengthened by the scores on the creativity tests: the N.E. boys scored considerably lower than the E boys, but there was no difference between the performances of the N.E. and E girls. Perhaps more important, a child's inventiveness and creativity in play were associated with his subsequent facility in divergent thinking. This association was greater and more direct in boys than in girls: that is, the more inventive the boy was in early childhood, the more divergent he was likely to be later on. This difference is not surprising since, even by the age of 4 years, girls are linguistically and socially more competent than boys (Moore, 1967; Hutt, 1972); their creativity therefore may be symbolic and covert, even involving sophisticated role-play which might not be very obvious to an observer. Boys, on the other hand, are actively exploratory for a much longer period of their life, and their activity is more explicit. In other words, though a divergent cognitive style is likely to be expressed in the play of boys, it may not necessarily be so in that of girls.

Nevertheless, the inventive boys turned out to be highly divergent thinkers, more so than the girls; they were also socially less well adjusted than the inventive girls. Whether this is the stuff of which the creative artist or scientist is made remains to be seen.

(From *Nature*, No. 237, May 1972.)

References

BERLYNE, D. E. (1960), *Conflict, Arousal and Curiosity*, McGraw-Hill, New York.

CROPLEY, A. J. (1967), *Creativity*, Longman.

CROPLEY, A. J., and MASLANY, G. W. (1969), *Brit. J. Psychol.*, No. 60.

HUTT, C. (1966), *Symp. Zool. Soc. Lond.*, No. 18, p. 61.

HUTT, C. (1967a), *Brit. J. Psychol.*, No. 58, p. 365.

HUTT, C. (1967b), *J. Child Psychol. Psychiat.*, No. 8, p. 241.

HUTT, C. (1970), in *Advances in Child Development and Behaviour*, H. W. Reese and L. P. Lipsitt (eds), Academic Press, New York.

HUTT, C. (1970), *Science Journal*, No. 6, p. 68.

MEAD, M. (1970), *Males and Females*, Penguin Books.

MOORE, T. (1967), *Human Development*, No. 10, p. 88.

PORTER, R. B., and CATTELL, R. B. (1959), *IPAT Children's Personality Questionnaire*, Institute for Personality and Ability Testing, Illinois, U.S.A.

WALLACH, M. A., and KOGAN, N. (1965), *Modes of Thinking in Young Children*, Holt, Rinehart & Winston, New York.

C Play, Problem-Solving and Tool Use

Early Tool Using in Wild Chimpanzees

Adult chimpanzees in the Gombe Stream Reserve fish for termites. They insert sticks or grass-blades into the passages which termites make to the surface of their rock-hard hills, ready for the nuptial flight of the season's queens and males. Termites bite on to the intruding tools; the chimpanzees carefully withdraw the sticks and lick off the termites, with tongue and rubbery lower lip. Termite-fishing is a learned tradition which appears only in some, not all, chimpanzee populations. Young chimpanzees begin to fish with behaviours which range from play to 'serious study'. Thus, chimpanzee play appears to be one of the behaviours giving rise to adult tool use.

I saw chimpanzees using natural objects as tools for a variety of purposes.

Stalks, stems and small twigs were used when the chimpanzees fed on termites. The material used was generally between six and twelve inches in length. Some animals inspected several clumps of grass, etc., before selecting their tools: sometimes they picked several to carry back to the termite heap and then used them one at a time. Other individuals used more or less anything within reach, including tools left by others. Sometimes tools were carefully prepared: leaves were stripped from stems or twigs with the hand or lips, and long strips were sometimes pulled from a piece of grass that was too wide. Occasionally the leaf blades were stripped from the mid-vein of a palm frond leaflet and on two occasions I saw chimpanzees pull off strips of bark fibre from which they detached thin lengths for use as tools. When the end of a tool became bent the chimpanzee usually bit off the bent part, or turned it round and used the other end, or else selected a new one.

Infants under 2 years of age were not observed to poke grasses etc., into holes in termite heaps; although I frequently saw them playing with discarded tools whilst their mothers fed there. In addition, from about 9 months of age they sometimes watched their mothers or other individuals closely and picked up and ate an occasional termite. Slightly older infants between 1 and 2 years of age often 'prepare' grasses etc., stripping them lengthwise or biting pieces from the ends, apparently as a form of play. One infant of 1 year and 7 months once picked up a small length of vine and, holding it with the 'power grip' (Napier, 1961) jabbed it twice at the surface of the termite mound (there was no sign of a hole) and then dropped it.

The youngest chimpanzee of known age that I watched using a tool in a termite hole was 2 years old. From this age to about 3 years old, the tool-using behaviour of an infant at a termite heap was characterized by the selection of inappropriate materials and clumsy technique. In addition, no infant under 3 years was seen to persist at a tool-using bout for longer than five minutes – as compared with fifteen minutes during the fourth year and several hours during maturity.

On six occasions three different infants between 2 and $2\frac{1}{2}$ years were observed using, or attempting to use, objects as tools in the termite feeding context, i.e. Goblin aged 2·2 years (twice), Flint aged 2·5 years (twice) and Gilka aged approximately 2 years (twice).

The types of material selected were normally the same as those used by adults, but the infants generally tried to use tools that were far too short to be effective. Thus of the thirty tools which I saw being used by this age group twenty were less than 2 inches. Usually these tiny tools were bitten or broken by hand from a tool discarded by an adult, although sometimes an infant picked its own material. Thus one infant broke off a $1\frac{1}{2}$ inch long bit of stick: it was of similar diameter to the hole into which he pushed it and where it became firmly stuck. Of the other ten tools, three were too thin and flexible, two were bent and broken at the end and two were too thick: thus only three were suitable for the purpose. However, that selection occurs in some cases is suggested by the fact that Flint, at 2·5 years, picked up and discarded, *before* trying to use, three tiny bits of green grass and one dead stick about twice as thick in diameter as a normal hole.

The infants held their tools in more or less the same way as an adult (i.e., between thumb and side of index finger) but their techniques were clumsy. Thus typically, after prodding a tool into a hole (often one just vacated by another chimpanzee) the infant pulled it out immediately with a quick jerking movement (unlike the slow careful withdrawal made by an adult). Only once was one of these infants seen to push more than about an inch of its tool into a hole. This was when Flint, aged 2·5 years, pushed a 4 inch straw in with one hand and then used his other hand to push it in further. On this occasion he did withdraw it slowly, but the attempt was unsuccessful. Only on two occasions were infants of this age group observed to 'catch' a termite from a total of twenty-two bouts, ranging from a few seconds to five minutes.

Three infants were observed using tools for termite fishing between the ages of $2\frac{1}{2}$ and 3 years old: Flint at 2·7 years (twice); Goblin at 2·10 years (once) and Merlin at about $2\frac{1}{2}$ years (eleven times). They showed only slight improvement in their selective and manipulative ability. Thus whilst they normally used longer tools these were frequently too flexible – and one was about twice the diameter of the hole into which the infant tried twice to push it. Also the infants usually held the tools so that only 1 or 2 inches projected beyond their fingers, and only this end was usually pushed into the hole. However, each of the infants occasionally inserted his tool in more or less the adult manner, pushing it in with one hand and then sliding that hand back up the tool and pushing it again. Usually this age group pulled out the tool slowly, although one of them several times did this in such a way that the grass bent as it was withdrawn: any termites that had bitten on would undoubtedly have been scraped off. He used both hands on these occasions.

One infant (Flint), when he was 2·8 years old, was twice observed using grass tools out of context. Both instances occurred during the termite-fishing season: once he pushed a grass carefully through the hair on his own leg, touched the end of the tool to his lips, repeated the movement and then cast the grass aside. On the other occasion he pushed a dry stem carefully into his elder sibling's groin three times in succession. Schiller (1952), working with captive chimpanzees, found that once a complex manipulative pattern had been mastered, an individual frequently performed the action when it was not necessary, as a form of play. It seems likely that Flint's behaviour was of a similar nature. The same may be true of the repeated picking up or making of new tools by infants.

Four-year-olds, with the exception of one individual, showed an adult technique although they did not normally persist for more than fifteen minutes at a stretch. The exception was the infant Merlin, who, during his third year, lost his mother. During the termite season immediately following her death his tool-using behaviour was not observed. The year after, however, when he was about 4½ years old, his tool-using behaviour showed no improvement at all from that which I had watched when he was about 2 years younger – if anything it had regressed. Thus nine tools of the total of nineteen used during two sessions were under 2 inches long, one was bent and the others were always held within an inch or so of their ends. He used the same fast insertion and jerky withdrawal shown by the 2- to 2½-year-olds, and he only caught two termites during the total forty minutes. (Four others working at the same time were getting plenty of insects.) Only in one respect had he advanced: he persisted, during one of the sessions, for three minutes without interruption.

A juvenile female, estimated at being about 5 years of age, fished for termites for consecutive periods of up to an hour and a half, and her technique was exactly comparable to that of an adult. (See photo inset.)

(From *Animal Behaviour Monographs*, Vol. 1, Part 3, Baillière, Tyndall and Cassell, 1968.)

References

NAPIER, J. R. (1961), 'Prehensility and opposability in the hands of primates', *Symp. Zool. Soc. Lond.*, No. 5, pp. 115–32.

SCHILLER, P. H. (1952), 'Innate constituents of complex responses in primates', *Psych. Rev.*, No. 59, pp. 177–91.

Spontaneous Invention of Ladders in a Group of Young Chimpanzees

Introduction

These long-term observations on a group of young wild-born captive chimpanzees, who suddenly and quite spontaneously appeared to invent the use of sticks and poles as ladders, provide a qualitative case history which might be of interest to students of tool using. The observations are of special note as the reliable use of poles as ladders has not, to my knowledge, been reported either in wild chimpanzees or in untrained captive animals. Further, the full development of the behaviour almost certainly involved some proto-cultural aspects, similar to those which have been hypothesized for wild populations (Kortlandt, 1967; van Lawick-Goodall, 1968; Miyadi, 1964).

Results

The development of the use of sticks and poles as climbing instruments appeared to be divided into four stages.

In the first several months of their captive existence we saw no instance in which the infants deliberately stood a stick or pole vertically and then climbed up it. Any object would certainly be climbed if it were already positioned in such a way that climbing was possible; but if it then fell down it was not stood up or propped up again. One day, however, a caretaker noted that one of the infants in the 5×30 metres outdoor shed (a male, Shadow) was standing a large food-tray vertically and jumping from its top into the air. We gave Shadow and his three companions a 1-metre-tall broom for 15 minutes a day. At first they only chewed the broom or wrestled with it; but within two or three days they were all standing the broom at a 90° angle on its bristles, and then rapidly climbing up this 'pole' and jumping from its top to the ceiling rafters (a height of about $2\frac{1}{2}$ metres) before the 'pole' lost its balance. The same behaviour soon transferred to shovels, rakes, sticks, and almost any elongated object that the chimpanzees could get their hands on.

Even several years later, at the age of 6–7 years, vaulting and standing-up-and-climbing of poles was still a daily occurrence. All that was required to produce a half-hour spate of activity was to provide the chimpanzees with a new branch, stick, or pole. Eventually poles up to 3 metres in length were handled very efficiently and poles as long as 4 metres were used on occasion by the larger animals. In the field cage, this activity was most often performed underneath an overhead structure (e.g. a shelter), or near a large vertical structure (most often the cage wire). Nevertheless, the chimpanzees were never observed to deliberately prop the pole against another structure. Poles frequently fell against the cage wire, and the chimpanzees climbed on them there; but if the poles were removed from this position, they were not propped up in a new location, but instead they were positioned vertically for another vault or a 'climb-then-jump' to the cage wire.

Another difference between this behaviour and the later use of poles as ladders is that the apparent goal of the activity was never a third object (in addition to the pole and the overhead or the vertical towards which jumping might be directed). It is quite plausible that the chimpanzees would have vaulted in order to secure food or other objects if we had placed such objects out of their reach; but in fact the only 'inaccessible objects' they jumped for under their everyday circumstances were rafters or cage wires – which could have been reached just as easily by other means.

Extrinsically motivated pole climbing

The borderline between this and the previous stage is obviously vague. To isolate experimentally the precise basis of reinforcement would require special analyses, of a type that we did not perform. However, an unmistakable transition occurred in early May 1970, abour four-and-a-half years after vaulting was first seen. The chimpanzees always had been strongly attracted to an observation house which juts out into the field cage. Indeed, they were so persistent in their attempts to climb the corners of the house to peer into the windows when strange humans were present that we had to install an electric shocking system on the window ledges. Even this did not entirely cure the chimpanzees. The oldest animal, Rock, was the most persistent window-peeper; and he was the one who eventually hit on the use of poles to facilitate his activities.

Rock's behaviour here was a simple extension of the 'pole sitting' seen in play. An old tree branch about 3 metres long that was stripped of all its twigs was carried about 10 metres to the observation shed and stood vertically; then Rock climbed up the pole, perched on top of it with one foot while keeping the pole in balance with the other foot against the wall, and slapped at the window and threatened the observers. If chased from one window, he moved immediately to another and repeated the performance. Once it became obvious that Rock had developed a real skill here, and had not simply performed an isolated chance response, the pole was confiscated. For at least a week, Rock made no attempt to transport new poles to the scene, although at least fifteen poles were available in other parts of the compound.

Poles as ladders

On 14 May 1970, about one week after the previous incident, the chimpanzees broke into the observation shed by pulling apart a 0·65-centimetre-thick plexiglass section in a window. (One such section was installed on a sliding track in each of four windows for purposes of photography, and had been available to the animals for more than two years.) Apparently all of the chimpanzees had slept in the observation house overnight, as their hutch boxes showed no signs of having been used. There was several hundred dollars worth of damage to the contents of the observation house. Work clothes, medicine bottles, test stimuli and tools had been carried to all parts of the field cage. From the alacrity with which the chimpanzees defended their newly acquired property, it is reasonable to assume that the whole event was highly reinforcing.

The actual process of breaking-in was not seen by human observers and it is, therefore, not certain that poles were used here. However, we know of no other means by which the chimpanzees could have averted the electric shock wires and achieved full access to and adequate bodily leverage on the plexiglass windows. Furthermore, when the break-in was first detected, and two technicians were trying to drive the chimpanzees out of the observation house, at least five of the eight animals reappeared through a different window as soon as they were chased out of the first. Several old tree branches, which had been obtained from a distance of 10–30 metres, were carried from window to window wherever there was an opening.

Once the use of poles as ladders appeared in the group's repertoire (and this was literally an overnight affair), it remained and persisted as a daily occurrence. As a consequence we had to board up the observation house windows and watch the animals only from the roof tower.

Combining pole-ladders with other vertical extensions

Invention phase. In the first fifteen months after the electric shock wires were installed on the trees, the chimpanzees had managed to get into the trees on only two or three occasions, during power failures. However, on 1 June 1970, two weeks after breaking into the observation shed all eight chimpanzees were discovered up in the live trees. There was no discoverable defect in the electric shock system. We were at a loss for any explanation for this event until that evening, when we found a 2·75-metre pole standing up on top of the runway, and braced against a tree at an angle of about 70°, with its tip well above the highest shock wire. (It had not, of course, been observed in that position earlier; but in the morning it had lain at the base of the tree.) Rock – the chimpanzee who was the most skilled at setting up poles as ladders – sat less than 1 metre from the pole. When he saw us he got up and shook the runway, and the pole fell down. He descended to the ground, grasped the pole in his foot, climbed up onto the runway using his hands, hauled the pole up onto the runway, placed its base carefully on the 15-centimetre-wide runway, and then oriented up and positioned its tip against the tree (which was no thicker than 30 centimetres in diameter at that point). He let it stand thus for a few seconds, and then knocked it to the ground and walked off.

Figures show these performances. The pictures suggest that Köhler (1925) probably underestimated the ability of chimpanzees to utilize the principles of mechanical statics. No doubt other chimpanzees could, with some effort, be 'shaped' by an experimenter to perform in comparable fashion; but in our judgement it is very improbable that Rock 'shaped himself' by successive approximations to these particular sequences of muscular contractions. Rather, he transferred from the observation house situation a ladder-making performance which involved the co-ordination of (1) base of pole to substratum (ground or runway) and (2) tip of pole to vertical support (tree or wall). The 'ladder' as such was also placed in such a way as to circumvent a noxious object (shock wire) and attain a positive goal (green branches, etc.). Obviously no single motor response pattern was crucial, for the same end effect was achieved regardless of which trees was selected, and regardless of whether two animals or one worked at setting up the ladder. (See photo inset.)

Diffusion phase. By October 1970 each of the chimpanzees save one (a female, Belle) had been observed to set up ladders into the trees. Rock's two closest companions, Bandit and Gigi, were the first to acquire the skill. However, Shadow became the most skilled of any animal, and on one occasion we timed him while he performed the entire sequence (getting the pole, vaulting from ground to the runway, positioning the pole on the runway and against the tree, and getting up into the tree) in less than 15 seconds. Eventually, all the accessible trees had been completely killed and denuded by the chimpanzees. Finally, all trees had to be cut down.

Thus, it was clear that Rock's skill had passed into the general repertoire of the group as a whole, and could be used for a 'new purpose'; and this is perhaps the final reason for using the term invention without any apologetic quotation marks around it.

Discussion
Chimpanzees as experimenters

Most primatologists have on occasion had the disquieting feeling that the animal rather than the primatologist is the experimenter. In the present case, this impression was based on fact. Not only did the chimpanzees try to observe, manipulate and control their environment and their captors, but also the findings of each of their sub-experiments were cumulative and became public knowledge and tradition of the whole group; and the subtlety and degree of the group's control increased as time went on. The wisest scientific course for the author was to interfere only as much as was necessary and simply report what Dr Hofer (personal communication) calls 'the experiments of the primates themselves'.

The nature of the response

This sort of observation fails to support the contentions of Schiller (1957) and Hall (1963) that primate tool using can be reduced to certain 'innate movement patterns' and that seemingly intelligent performance is the chance occurrence of one of these movement patterns in a situation where it is likely to be reinforced. Ladder using cannot even be described and distinguished from infantile general manipulation, let alone explained, without taking into account the *stick*'s behaviour (Köhler, 1925; Menzel *et al.*, 1970). In other words, the crucial 'behavioural elements' of ladder using involve attention to and perceptual differentiation of specific consequences of the stick's contrasts with other objects. Just as the neonate learns to take his hand for granted and use it as a functional extension of the body for grasping a stick that captures his attention (Held and Bauer, 1967), so also the normal juvenile chimpanzee learns to treat the stick as a 'functional extension of the arm' (Birch, 1945), and the present animals went still farther, using the stick as a portable extension of the environment, and focusing their attention not on hand *per se*, or stick *per se*, or the hand-stick connection, or even the stick-tree connection, but on the higher-order relation between the animal himself, the stick, the ground and the tree.

It is noteworthy that even from the age of one year, and on, the animals had on innumerable occasions knocked a stick or pole over against a wall, and climbed on it with every indication that the whole event was reinforcing. Yet, the transition from one stage or level of performance to the next seemed in most cases to transpire almost overnight, as a consequence of one or two of these accidents. Why is one accident 'lucky' when all previous ones were not? Any learning theory must explain this puzzle before it dismisses the role of visual attention and the intellectual ability to profit from accidents. How the chimpanzee bridges the gap between motor action and tool using performance is no more obvious and elementary than how he gets from knowing what to do to doing it.

(From *Folia Primat.*, No. 17, 1972.)

References

BIRCH, H. G. (1945), 'The relation of previous experience to insightful problem solving', *J. Comp. Psychol.*, No. 38, pp. 367–83.

HALL, K. R. L. (1963), 'Tool-using performances as indicators of behavioral adaptability', *Curr. Anthrop.*, No. 4, pp. 479–94.

HELD, R. and BAUER, T. (1967), 'Visually guided reaching in infant monkeys after restricted rearing', *Science*, No. 155, pp. 718–20.

KÖHLER, W. (1925), *The Mentality of Apes*, Routledge & Kegan Paul.

KORTLANDT, A. (1967), 'Experimentation with chimpanzees in the wild', in *Progress in Primatology*, Starck, Schneider, and Kuhn (eds), Fischer, Stuttgart, pp. 208–24.

LAWICK-GOODALL, J. VAN (1968), 'The behaviour of free-living chimpanzees in the Gombe Stream Reserve', *Anim. Behav. Monog.*, No. 1, pp. 161–311. (And see this volume, p. 222.)

MENZEL, E. W. JR, DAVENPORT, R. K., and ROGERS, C. M. (1970), 'The development of tool using in wild-born and restriction-reared chimpanzees', *Folia Primat.*, No. 12, pp. 273–83.

MIYADI, D. (1964), 'Social life of Japanese monkeys', *Science*, No. 143, pp. 783–6.

SCHILLER, P. H. (1957), 'Innate motor action as a basis of learning', in *Instinctive Behavior*, Schiller (ed.), Methuen. (And see this volume, p. 232.)

Innate Motor Action as a Basis of Learning: Manipulative Problems in the Chimpanzee

This classic study was the first, and remains the most detailed, description of object play by captive apes. With the hindsight offered by Jane Goodall's wild chimpanzees, we know that Schiller was right in connecting stick-shaking with threat, weaving with nest building, and that many of the stripping and poking motions are used by wild chimpanzees in termite-fishing. The play which Schiller describes is the raw material which is channelled into useful adaptations in the wild. In the strange conditions of captivity, some parts of these patterns appear in play which seem 'serious' in the wild.

The apparently immediate adaptation to problem-solving situations in the gorilla and chimpanzee (Köhler, 1921; Yerkes, 1925) suggested that there is a special higher type of learning by ideation or insight in apes. Attempts to reduce these performances of apes to conventional learning doctrines have not yet been successful. It is quite possible, however, that the wide range of behaviour adjustment in apes may have a basis in innate organization. Instrumental behaviour, for example, seems not to be based on an understanding of its usefulness but on the activation of a generalized play activity (Schiller, 1952).

The learning of useful manipulations in primates might be traced back to some of its native constituents. With this idea in view, I have studied the problem-solving manipulation of sticks, and compared it with the spontaneous manipulation of various objects, in fifty chimpanzees of the colony founded by R. M. Yerkes of Yale University.

Free play

The importance of a maturational factor that can be facilitated but certainly not replaced by general experience and specific training suggested a study of spontaneous behaviour of the manipulative patterns with implements which are used in giving problem situations to primates. Therefore, practically all chimpanzees of the Yerkes colony were tested in situations with no incentive whatever, in that natural handling of objects. Some observations on the play of apes have been reported earlier, but as curiosities rather than as a subject of systematic study. Köhler has described how some chimpanzees would throw away the stick if frustrated in getting in the food, how they would poke at chickens, explore ant-hills or pools of water with sticks, place covers (garlands, cloths) over their shoulders or tramp in a circle around a pole.

These careful descriptions, however, did not induce his followers to check upon the contribution these playful patterns made towards problem-solving. My original plan was to provide the chimpanzees with facilities for play and see whether they would derive any benefit from their acquaintance with tools in subsequent problem situations. This would have been, if positive, a demonstration of latent learning of instrumentation. Learning, without any specific motivation, how to handle a stick would, as I hoped, enable them to use the stick for some purpose, as a tool. This plan had to be abandoned, for I have found just an opposite relationship. With no incentive the chimpanzees have displayed a higher variety of handling objects than under the pressure of a lure which they attempt to obtain.

Let me start with the end. Fifty-two chimpanzees were given the double stick, in two parts, to play with (in the cage, the animal alone, about one hour after feeding). Of the twenty adults thus tested, nineteen performed the insertion of the peg into the hole, a complete connection of the two sticks, within a fifteen-minute test period, the majority of them right at the beginning.

Of the younger animals, between 5 and 8 years of age, only about half performed the joining of the sticks; of the infants and children up to 4 years of age, not one. This fact points obviously to a correlation with the ability of the chimpanzee to handle several objects at a time. It is clear that a maturational component is present in the spontaneous play activity of connecting sticks that can be fitted together. There is some suggestion of a correlation with sexual factors, inasmuch as males are faster in performing the connection, and females less inclined to do so in their sexually inactive periods.

The act itself shows some primitive appearances in the poking and exploring activities of the younger animals: if they do not place the peg into the hole, they explore the latter, pushing a finger as deeply as can be into the hole, pressing their lips and tongue into it, and so forth. They also use the peg as something to explore with, in holes in the ground, in the fence, in cracks, and the like; but not so readily in the other stick, which they have to hold in one hand while the other hand is performing the activity of poking. This co-ordination of the two hands needs to be developed before the active connection or joining can take place. In the adult act this poking and exploring is most obviously the basic pattern that results in a connection. In this sense, inasmuch as it does not require any external reinforcement, it is not a product of specific learning, but of maturation facilitated by general functional experience of the capacities of the effectors. It is in this sense that I have chosen to use the adjective 'innate' or 'pre-functional'.

The same animals who performed the stick-connecting in play were not all able to solve a pulling-in problem by connecting the same sticks. The youngest animal who connected the sticks in play was 6 years old, the youngest one who did it in the work situation was 8. Those who used the stick connection for work took much more time to develop this habit than to join the sticks in play: in repeated trials, of five minutes each, it took them eight to ten trials or many times the maximum time in which they carried out insertion when there was no problem to solve with its aid. The problem of joining sticks was never solved, of course, by animals who had not performed the connection previously in play: chimpanzees under 5 or 6 years of age, and monkeys (five spider and five rhesus were tested) never do it and are helpless in the problem situation requiring the joining of two sticks. Those who were slow in performing connection in play were more retarded in utilizing it for work than the ready players. It is obvious, then, that presence of the play-performance is a prerequisite for the solution of the stick-joining problem. The pattern must be readily available before it can be utilized, and it is not the pressure of a need that makes it emerge, but, on the contrary, such a pressure represses it, if it is not highly available.

This rather unexpected state of affairs led me to search for pre-problem patterns in less complex tool-using situations. An analysis of the very first attempts to use the stick when a lure is offered along with the stick has shown the following. The stick is accepted as a secondary or as an equivalent lure by practically all chimpanzees. Many of them are more interested in the stick than in the food. This is invariably the case with the youngest ones, especially after a few frustrating experiences or when they have obtained enough food for the work involved. They will not work any more, though they eat readily when food is offered. The stick is then taken immediately, without any attempt before or after to bring it into relationship with the food. The stick is only used to play with.

I had one male adult, a castrate, who was so fond of playing with the sticks that he snatched one away as soon as it was presented and fled to a far corner, ignoring the 'bait'. Several hours of fasting did not improve the situation, until he was conditioned to expect food; whenever he touched the stick a piece of food was thrown to him. By this technique he was brought to look around for food after he had touched the stick and the food could then be placed in such a way that a straight pull on the stick would bring it in to him. Even then he kept the stick for play after consuming the food and would not part with it. When bait was placed in front of the grille, he, Don, soon tried to put the stick in front of it, but became involved in placing the stick across the bars. This activity fascinated him so much that as soon as half of the stick was outside, he grabbed the outer part with his free hand and pulled the stick back. This alternate pushing out and pulling back in another gap is a characteristic pattern that can be observed outside problem situations as well: I call it the *weaving* pattern. Don performs it in play by preference on the top mesh of the cage, and if he has the stick thoroughly entangled, he swings on the free end, with the frequent result of breaking it. Now, in the problem situation, he is attracted to the grille-window by the bait and the experimenter and, sitting in front of it, displays his favourite games there. He cannot resist 'weaving', though it obviously does not bring him closer to his 'goal', which he certainly devours eagerly, if he by chance gets it.

A few repetitions of the 'weaving' pattern seem to exhaust his reservoir of this specific pattern, and he suddenly shifts over to another form of activity. This is the *pointing and shaking* pattern. The stick is thrust through the grille and pointed towards the food, or equally frequently, toward the experimenter (the camera, if present, is a favourite 'goal' too). With outstretched hand the stick is pointed in the air, often lowered to the ground or lifted as high as it will go.

By placing the food carefully, the pointing and shaking can be utilized to develop it into sweeping or angling. The latter is a pattern of hitting the fruit closer with the stick hanging in the air and leaning from above with its point on the ground; it was well described by Guillaume and Meyerson (1934). Yet this attempt at a reinforcement has to overcome another natural tendency of the younger chimpanzees (and of Don). As soon as the shaking hits the fruit so that the latter moves, this distant effect of an action fascinates the animal and he repeats it with the most likely results that the food is pushed aside and often out of reach. For this reason, students of stick-using behaviour in primates build side-frames on their platforms. This precaution pays because the angling pattern has better chances to become correlated with moving the food, if both the food and the point of the stick are prevented from skidding away and are forced to move along the straight line of an edge. This way only two alternatives remain: to pull the food in or to push it away.

To be sure, these two alternatives are originally equally frequent. In a few monkeys and chimpanzees I have tried to develop the push-away rather than the pull-in pattern, and the result was easy learning of a very well-adjusted and generalized pattern; even two sticks could be used to produce a very intricate double push (if food was dropped from elsewhere after performance). There is no indication that the congruent activity is preferred to the incongruent one of pushing food beyond any possible reach or even sight (cf. Schiller, 1950, 1952). The struggle with stick and food frequently results in throwing the stick away, mostly towards the food or other frustrating objects, like the experimenter or the camera. Sometimes it is thrown in the air, sometimes scooted along the ground.

This pattern has been observed by Köhler, and interpreted as a 'good error', expressing the general direction of a desirable activity but not attaining its end. I am inclined to believe that this type of activity contains no intention of obtaining the food by a pseudo logical act, but is simply the emotional outburst of a pattern which otherwise has a higher threshold. The stick is sometimes just placed quietly out in front of the grille, somewhere between food and experimenter, and the animal gives up work and play, resorts to rocking himself like a baby and making grooming sounds. He is giving up and turns his back to the scene of frustration. Later, he turns back and then he suddenly picks up the stick again and points or shakes it toward the 'goal'. If there is no effect on the goal, the stick is scooted or thrown away.

Comparing this sequence to the free play with sticks, it is clear that the throwing is an end-member of a series of activities which seem to induce one another. The exploratory activity, *poking and sounding* in holes and meshes with the stick, easily develops into waving and shaking if there is open space behind the crack or hole. This waving goes over into 'weaving' if there is nothing on the other side, but it turns into a distant poking if there is something to bring the stick into relation with. This poking and hitting is likely to be directed toward a social partner, if there is one. The hitting of the food and subsequent pulling-in is a modified, usefully adapted form of the social challenge of exploring companions behind a partition.

This interpretation is derived from the fact that the shaking of the stick toward a partner is directed as a *challenge*: as soon as the other chimpanzee or man attempts to seize the offered stick, it is violently withdrawn and the free hand of the challenger grabs at the accepting hand of the naïve victim. Such an instinctive pattern seems to be at the basis of placing a stick out across a network of bars, shaking it there and pulling it back or throwing it away: the elements of problem-solving. Whichever components are reinforced by the responses of the outside world, those will be produced in the proper sequence, omitting repetitions, and develop into a unified pattern that the human observer calls a problem solution.

The fact, described by Köhler, that chimpanzees try to perform changes in the sticks as if they would construct implements (Klüver found similar attempts in a Cebus monkey) is also due to native patterns of handling movable objects. That a chimpanzee breaks off a branch if excited has nothing to do with his desire to get at the food. Once he has the stick in his hands, he will use it sooner or later. Such a sequence can easily be re-inforced in a couple of trials and then it appears to be a coherent, continuous pattern. All problem-solving patterns look like this but they are really composites of originally independent reactions, just like the detour performances of lower vertebrates.

The same pertains to breaking off branches from fork-shaped sticks that are not easily placed across bars. If frustrated, the animal resorts to a different activity from the one in which he was actually engaged and displays aggression, bites or breaks the stick. Once he has it this way, he again returns to his previous activity, and now gets the stick smoothly through the grille and sweeps in his food. It was anger that made him a good craftsman, not an intention, ideation, or insight.

The same happens if the sticks that are to be joined do not fit exactly. Köhler describes how his Sultan pulled out a peg and then chewed the peg smaller 'in order to' achieve better fitting. This is benevolent interpretation. Chimpanzees only too often chew at sticks, and more at their ends than in the middle. The stick is turned end for end almost always with the help of the mouth, which is also utilized in getting it through the bars and the like. If the animal has a set developed to join sticks, everything impeding him in doing so makes him angry. Take away one of the sticks, and the chimpanzee will furiously bite the other one, making it less rather than more fit to be used. If there is difficulty in connecting them, the chimpanzee will chew the ends of the sticks, the socket as well as the pin; if there is a stopper, it will be removed; if there is a too thick peg, by splitting off a splinter it now stands a better chance to be fitted. This is accident, but once the sticks fit, the chimpanzee uses the double stick when he sees the food. It happens, though, that after fitting, the stick is pulled apart and refitted, and this goes on in series. The first observation of this kind (Köhler's) points out that the joining was made in play, but then was immediately utilized for work. My chimpanzees learned it rapidly after a few trials, but they played a lot with the double stick before incorporating it into the problem solution and in the latter situation frequently disconnected the sticks while grasping with an empty hand, meanwhile, for the food. Play and work for food were separate spheres of activity, that became correlated with repeated experience. The complex stick-handling is a pattern that develops independently of its external utilization. Learning connects this pattern with certain external situations (not S with R), like perceiving food beyond reach, and then it gradually develops into a skill that is applied with a large range of generalization, once the association is established, and the action sequence can become elicited by a perception associated with the commencing act of the chain (stick pointed to the experimenter). Repetition condenses the chain, to a unified skill pattern.

An analysis of the competition of learning with the unlearned display of spontaneous play forms is a further subject amenable to experimental study. In this paper it is only attempted to draw attention to the fact that even the highest vertebrates, primates, have certain peculiar manipulative forms of activity available, without specific training to develop them. They are present uniformly in all individuals of the same age group, and are invariably displayed if the general condition of the animal favours them. They bear all the criteria of instinctive activities, and can be correlated to known patterns of functional cycles such as nesting, mating, social activities, and so forth. These internally co-ordinated manipulative patterns are not derived from experience but, on the contrary, the adaptive learned performances seem to be derived from them, by a mechanism of association with external and internal cues in consequence of repeated and consistent occurrences.

(From *Instinctive Behaviour*, C. H. Schiller (ed.), Methuen, 1957.)

References

GUILLAUME, P., and MEYERSON, I. (1934), 'Recherches sur l'usage de l'instrument chez les singes', *J. de Psycho.*, No. 31, pp. 497–554.

KÖHLER, W. (1921), *Intelligenzprüfungen an Menschenaffen*, Springer, Berlin.

NISSEN, H. W. (1931), 'A field study of the chimpanzee', *Comp. Psychol. Monog.*, No. 8, pp. 1–105.

SCHILLER, P. H. (1937), 'Purposeless manipulations', *XI Congr. Internat. Psychol.*, Paris.

SCHILLER, P. H. (1949), 'Analysis of detour behavior (fish)', *J. Comp. Physiol. Psychol.*, No. 42, pp. 463–75.

SCHILLER, P. H. (1950), 'Analysis of detour behavior (cats)', *J. Exper. Psychol.*, No. 40, pp. 217–27.

SCHILLER, P. H. (1951), 'Figural preferences in the drawings of a chimpanzee', *J. Comp. Physiol. Psychol.*, No. 44, pp. 101–11.

SCHILLER, P. H. (1952), 'Innate constituents of complex responses in primates', *Psych. Rev.*, No. 59, pp. 177–91.

YERKES, R. M. (1925), *Chimpanzee Intelligence*, Williams & Wilkins, Baltimore.

Play and Imitation in Dolphins

These intelligent creatures, with no 'hands', nevertheless exhibit a 'tool-using' programme, and a marked propensity for play and imitation. The observations described
here were made at the Port Elizabeth Oceanarium.

The lack of experimentation on problem solving in delphinids leaves, for
the present, the question of the relative cognitive abilities of dolphins and
non-human primates an open-ended one and possibly explains the fact that
delphinids have not figured prominently in comparative assessments of
animal intelligence in the literature. Further, non-human primates, which
have received proportionately more attention have possibly been considered
to be more important because of theories concerning the evolutionary
development of man. Although the question of the use of tools by animals
is also a highly controversial one (Hall, 1963), it is generally agreed that the
predisposition to manipulate, explore and exhibit advanced object-play is a
fundamental prerequisite for the emergence of the skilful use of tools (Jay,
1968), for which the primate, both anatomically and neurologically, has
been admirably selected by evolutionary pressure.

It is therefore remarkable that the virtually limbless dolphin, specialized
for high-speed locomotion in a three-dimensional aquatic environment, all
but barren of inanimate objects, can readily demonstrate in captivity unconditioned and spontaneous behavioural sequences, including the elementary
use of tools, on a level comparable to that displayed by non-human primates when similarly placed in captive surroundings.

The captive bottlenose dolphins showed a marked propensity to play;
this was true particularly of younger animals, but playing was prominent in
the daily activity cycle of the mature dolphins as well. Dolly was much
occupied with the investigation and exploration of such objects as cleaning
nets, penguins, water inlets and drains. The dolphins developed games with
the other species in the tank as focal points of activity. They took it in turns
to chase a penguin and to prevent its exit from the water. A single dolphin
swam close to the penguin at speed while the others followed behind it;
after a few minutes a second dolphin took over the active role. Some play
activities were clearly social in nature, such as when dolphins chased each

other, but they frequently played on their own, tossing and retrieving a variety of objects such as fish skins, bits of seaweed, stone or balls. Stones were treated as balls, pushed down through the water and bounced on the bottom of the tank. Elaborate manoeuvres were carried out while swimming, balancing an inanimate object, such as paper or a feather, allowing it to slide down the length of the body only to be caught and held by flippers or flukes. Dolly, the youngest animal, exhibited the most marked play and exploratory activity whereas Lady Dimple, the oldest dolphin, was the least exploratory of the group, although she played extensively with her calf Dolly.

Play groups, rarely seen in free-ranging dolphins, generally consisted of two to four mature animals disporting together, leaping over non-partici-pating adult animals, chasing each other, head jerking and side-swimming. Playful activity was identifiable in the wild by some of its vigorous yet non-aggressive nature – however, in adult animals it was not readily distin-guishable from sexual behaviour except when single animals played, tossing scraps of seaweed or fish skin, very much as did the dolphins in captivity. When butterflies were numerous by the coast, all age classes of dolphins, with white bellies showing and zigzagging at speed, frequently chased them when they flew out over the water.

It is interesting to speculate concerning the functional role which imi-tation may play in the social life of dolphins under normal conditions. It is noteworthy that the active and passive roles in pre-copulatory behaviour and courtship displays in captive bottlenose dolphins are continuously interchangeable between bulls and cows so that it is not possible to identify the sex of the individuals in unknown pairs on the basis of their behaviour alone (Saayman, Tayler and Bower, in press). We have obtained similar findings from the frame-by-frame analysis of ciné-films of mating trios of southern right whales (*Eubalaena australis*) in Algoa Bay (unpublished observations). Furthermore, the sequence of events in bottlenose dolphins varies constantly, and it may differ markedly in the same animal with different partners. In our current systematic studies of free-ranging dol-phins, as many as three bulls, all displaying erections, have been observed simultaneously attempting to mate with a single cow in groups of up to ten animals all engaged in courtship displays. In these courtship contexts, imitation may very well play a decisive role in the selection of mating partners. This explanation is particularly suggested when both partners engage in closely co-ordinated formation swimming, in which both simultaneously adopt identical postures, prior to mating attempts. It is proposed, therefore, that imitation of the behavioural posture of the partner may provide the stimulus for selective mating responses or, at the least, may serve to reinforce social bonds and to strengthen group cohesiveness in a highly social animal whose mode of social progression is generally characterized by closely co-ordinated formation swimming. The imitative propensity in the dolphin, therefore, may be so inherently programmed as to be inappropriately released under abnormal conditions in captivity.

As increasing amounts of data accumulate from the systematic studies of trained observers on a variety of animals in their natural habitat, the significance of encounters between different forms, such as those reported here as well as the numerous instances in which dolphins have approached human bathers (Alpers, 1963; Tayler and Saayman, 1972), may become clear. At present no explanation for the behaviour observed can be offered, but it is nevertheless noteworthy that the approaches thus far observed have been initiated by the dolphins.

Evidence of observational learning by bottlenose dolphins

Imitation of the postures and swimming behaviour of fish, turtles and penguins were frequently observed. For example, skates (*Raja sp.*), swimming in a straight line, often came into contact with the circular wall of the tank and then progressed for a distance using one wing to change direction by pushing away from the tank wall. Haig often swam behind the skate, similarly pushing herself from the wall with the outer surface of her flipper.

Haig lay flat on the bottom alongside a sleeping loggerhead turtle (*Caretta caretta*), rising to the surface together with it for air. Subsequently she began to take the turtle repeatedly down to the bottom just before it had reached the surface to breathe. A number of turtles were drowned in this way, particularly after Lady Dimple adopted a similar procedure.

The bull dolphin Daan, after repeatedly observing a diver removing algae growth from the glass underwater viewing port, was seen cleaning the window with a seagull feather while emitting sounds almost identical to that of the diver's air-demand valve and releasing a stream of bubbles from the blowhole in a manner similar to that of exhaust air escaping from the diving apparatus. Comprehensive ciné- and sound-recordings were obtained of this behaviour. Subsequently Daan used food-fish, seaslugs, stones and paper to perform similar cleaning movements at the window. He commandeered the vicinity of the viewing port for a period of fifty-four days, during which time he actively prevented divers from approaching the window by open-mouthed threats, jaw clapping and by forcibly pushing them away. The other dolphins were similarly prevented from approaching the window. At night, contrary to his normal practice of resting in the centre of the pool, he took up a resting position above the viewing port. Divers hold with one hand on the stainless steel frame of the viewing port whilst cleaning the window glass with a brush held in the other hand. In the absence of the diver, the dolphin cleaned the length and breadth of the window with similar strokes, rubbing away the *filamentus algae* which grows where the glass meets the frame, whilst maintaining contact with the window frame with his flipper. Haig displayed similar behaviour, without the aggressive overtones. She was encouraged to perform this act, using a brush, but persistently put the hard wooden handle to the glass, holding the bristles in her mouth.

At six months of age the calf Dolly spontaneously began to manipulate the apparatus which her mother, Lady Dimple, had been trained to use during public demonstrations, and, with appropriate reinforcement, soon became an integral part of the demonstrations.

Dolly sought the attention of observers scoring dolphin behaviour from the underwater viewing chamber by presenting a variety of objects, such as feathers, stones, seaweed or fish skins, which she pressed against the glass. Frequently the same objects, or a preferred stone, were used. When ignored, she made off and returned on three or four successive occasions with different objects.

At the end of an observation session, a cloud of cigarette smoke was once deliberately released against the glass as Dolly was looking in through the viewing port. The observer was astonished when the animal immediately swam off to its mother, returned and released a mouthful of milk which engulfed her head, giving much the same effect as had the cigarette smoke. Dolly subsequently used this behaviour as a regular device to attract attention.

Tool-using derived from observational learning

During tank cleaning operations, the dolphins showed a close interest in the manipulation of the steel hollow scraper attached to the suction hose which the diver pushed along the concrete bottom of the tank to remove and dispose of debris and a thick growth of seaweed (*Enteromorpha*). The dolphins hovered above and around the diver and watched his every move. After several days of use the apparatus was on one occasion left in the tank overnight. In the morning, Haig, the younger dolphin, was found manipulating the apparatus by lying flat along the hose, which she clasped with her flippers, her rostrum resting on the metal scoop. She investigated the apparatus from a variety of angles, manipulating it by pushing it in all directions and repeatedly rolling it over. Employing a rocking motion, she moved the apparatus back and forth, raising a cloud of debris from the pool bottom and dislodging seaweed which she ate. (The dolphins regularly eat considerable quantities of this seaweed. However, we have no evidence of plant eating in free-ranging dolphins, and consequently do not imply that this behaviour occurs under normal conditions.) Hours after the apparatus had been removed, Haig was seen holding a piece of broken tile, approximetely 6×8 centimetres in her mouth. She dislodged quantities of seaweed by swimming with the tile in contact with the bottom of the pool. She then dropped the tile, ate the seaweed, picked up the tile and repeated the process. After watching Haig for some time, Lady Dimple used the same piece of tile to scrape off seaweed and subsequently both dolphins were seen, each with their own piece of tile, removing seaweed together. This apparently had novelty value, since the dolphins initially removed large quantities of seaweed far in excess of their eating requirements. The frequency of this behaviour decreased with time until the pieces of tile were removed for fear that the dolphins would swallow them.

(From 'Imitative behaviour by Indian Ocean bottlenose dolphins [*Tursiops aduneus*] in captivity', *Behaviour*, No. 44, 1973, pp. 286–98.)

References

ALPERS, A. (1963), *Dolphins*, John Murray.

HALL, K. R. L. (1963), 'Tool-using performances as indicators of behavioural adaptability', *Current Anthropology*, No. 4, pp. 479–94.

JAY, P. (1968), 'Primate field studies and human evolution', in *Primates: Studies in Adaptation and Variability*, P. Jay (ed.), Holt, Rinehart & Winston, New York.

TAYLER, C. K. and SAAYMAN, G. S. (1972), 'The social organization and behaviour of dolphins and baboons: some comparisons and assessments', *Ann. Cape Prov. Mus. (Nat. Hist.)*, No. 9.

The Role of Play in the Problem-Solving of Children 3-5 Years Old

The essence of play is in the dominance of means over ends. This is not to say that play is without goals – witness the toddler building a tower of blocks – but in play the process is more important than the product. Freed from the tyranny of a tightly held goal, the player can substitute, elaborate and invent. Eibl-Eibesfeldt (1970) describes the play of animals as bits of behaviour borrowed from non-play modes, e.g., defence or reproduction, and strung together in unusual sequence. With a slightly different emphasis, Bruner (1972) describes the human infant playing with an object, say a cup, by fitting it into a variety of action programmes. He raises it to the lips, bangs it on the table, then drops it to the floor. In both the human and non-human examples, we see play as practice in assembling bits of behaviour (or means) into unusual sequences.

Because play behaviours are so often borrowed from non-play sequences, Reynolds (this volume) describes it as taking place in the 'simulative mode'. A young baboon simulates attack; a child simulates meal preparation. These acts share with other simulations, e.g., wind tunnels for aircraft and dress rehearsals for drama, the lessening or elimination of risk. The second characteristic of play, then, is its lessening the risk of failure.

A third characteristic of play is the temporary moratorium on frustration that it affords the player. Because process takes precedence over product, an obstacle that would be deplored if met while problem-solving is met in play with equanimity or even glee (Miller, 1973).

Play offers still another freedom, this one being the peculiar vulnerability of the player to the world around him. Robert White (1959) hints at this in his contrast between the busy man rushing off to an appointment and the man strolling leisurely for pleasure. One is unaware of the streets, trees and people whereas the other is alert to both detail and novelty. The person at play shares with the strolling man his openness to the surrounding world. He has 'free attention'. The fourth characteristic of play, then, is its invitation to the possibilities inherent in things and events. It's the freedom to notice seemingly irrelevant detail.

The fifth characteristic of play, and the one underlying all others, is its voluntary nature. The player is free from environmental threats and urgent needs. Play behaviour is self-initiated. The sulky child forced to 'play' a maths game by his teacher is not really at play.

The fruits of play stem from its characteristics outlined above. The person who plays with objects and actions gains practice in assembling them in unusual ways. He pays attention to their details and possibilities. Because play's 'low risk' nature allows for experiment and reduces frustration, he sustains activity over a long period of time. Throughout this volume it has been argued that the animal with a rich history of play has prepared himself to be an 'opportunist'. He is able to solve the problems he encounters in both an organized and flexible way.

The work to be described investigates the relationship between play and the solving of mechanical problems. There is a long and rich literature on the ways that humans and other creatures go about solving such problems. The chimpanzee Sultan was an early star in the field because of his clever solutions to the problems set before him by Köhler (1925). When a banana was placed beyond his reach outside his cage, Sultan grabbed a stick and used it as a rake. If the sticks in the cage were too short to reach the banana, Sultan joined together two bamboo sticks (one end telescoped into the other), thereby constructing a tool long enough to reach the goal. Köhler attributed Sultan's success at both the single and double stick problems to *sudden insight* into the functional relations inherent in the problem situation. In other words, Köhler saw no need to study the relation between problem solving and *prior* experience because of his claim that the solution derived from the perceptual present.

Others thought differently. Birch (1945) argued that insight such as Sultan's depended on the animal's prior experience with sticks. Sultan's clever acts might have been the consequence of prior manipulation of sticks and not sudden 'perceptual re-organization of the visual field'. Birch experimented with six young chimpanzees by presenting them the single-stick-as-rake problem. Unlike Sultan, detailed histories of these chimps were on hand and only one of them, Jojo, had ever been seen to manipulate sticks. When confronted with an attractive lure outside the test cage, Jojo immediately seized a nearby stick and used it effectively as a rake. Only one other chimp solved the problem, and this animal's solution occurred after he 'accidentally' touched the banana with the stick and noticed it move towards him. The remaining four chimps in Birch's experiment spent thirty minutes in frustrated efforts to get the banana. Following the initial presentation of the problem, all the chimps were provided with sticks in the home cage and they were seen to manipulate them for three days. When tested again, all six chimps solved the stick problem within twenty seconds. Thus it appears that prior experience with sticks led to problem solution whereas lack of it was most often associated with failure.

Reported next are the results of a study in which children were presented with the stick-as-rake problem. The study examines the contribution of play, as well as other forms of prior experience, to the child's subsequent approach to the stick problem.

Method

The task

The child sat at a low table in a quiet room. Directly in front of him, but out of reach, was a transparent plastic box approximately $14 \times 8 \times 6$ inches. The box opened on the side facing the child, although its door was held closed by a 'J' shaped hook. A piece of coloured chalk was placed inside the box and the child's task was to retrieve it.

In front of the child were three bright blue sticks ($15 \times 1\frac{1}{4} \times \frac{1}{4}$; $13 \times 1\frac{1}{4} \times \frac{1}{4}$; $5 \times 1\frac{1}{4} \times \frac{1}{4}$ inches) and two 'C' clamps ($4\frac{3}{4}$ inches at longest part). Figure 1

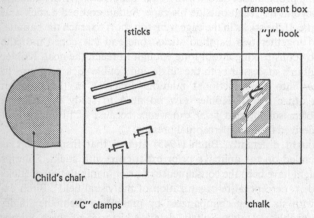

Fig. 1. Schematic view of the task.

shows the mechanical aspects of the problem. All children were given the following instructions:

See the coloured chalk? That's the prize in a game you're going to play. Your job is to figure out a way to get the chalk. If you do, you can take it home and keep it. You can take as much time as you wish to play the game and can use any object you think will help you. There's only one rule to the game. You can't get out of your chair.

The sticks and clamps were the only objects within the child's reach. The box was placed at a distance such that the longest stick would not reach it. The straightforward solution to the problem is, of course, for the child to construct an elongated tool by rigidly joining two long sticks with a clamp. He needs such a tool to open the latch and rake the chalk towards him.

The adult sat quietly at the table with a stop-watch and notepad on his lap. Each child worked at his own pace, although the adult gave hints under the following circumstances: (a) if a child got up from the chair and walked toward the door, (b) if a child ignored the problem for at least one minute, e.g., stared at hands in lap, sang a song, gazed out of the window, (c) if a child repeatedly asked to leave. Hints were standardized and given in the following sequence.

#1 Have you used everything you can think of that might help you?

#2 Can you think of a way that you can use the clamp to help you?

#3 Can you think of a way that you can use both the clamp and the sticks to help you?

#4 You could clamp the two long sticks together and make a longer stick.

#5 I will hold these two sticks together here. Can you clamp them tightly together with this clamp? (Direct physical assistance given if child unable to follow this instruction.)

Subjects

There were 180 children tested in the two experiments that follow. All participants were tested at the day-care centres they attend in towns surrounding Boston. With a very few exceptions, children were middle-class and white.

Experiment 1: treatment conditions

In this experiment, we compare three kinds of experience prior to presentation of the stick problem. There were thirty-six children in each treatment condition, six boys and six girls at 3, 4, 5 years of age. The treatments are summarized in Table 1 below.

Experiment 1: results

A. *Spontaneous solutions*. The number of children in each group who constructed the tool and used it to retrieve the chalk is shown in Table 2.* These solutions are 'spontaneous' in that the children required no hints from the adult. The various treatments led to different performances ($x^2 = 11 \cdot 73$, $df = 2$, $p < 0.01$). For example, *play* and *no treatment* are significantly different from one another ($x^2 = 9 \cdot 32$, $df = 1$, $p < 0.01$).

B. *Effective use of hints*. By comparing children in the *play* and *observe*

---

* One-way analysis of variance showed that there were no significant differences in the times it took children to solve the problem or to construct the tool. Differences among groups appear in frequencies of solvers in each group.

Table 1 Treatment conditions in Experiment 1

Name	Nature of experience prior to presentation of problem	Duration of prior experience	Manipulation of sticks and clamps?
Play	Adult demonstrates one clamp tightened onto middle of one long stick Child allowed free play with 10 blue sticks and 7 clamps	10 min.	yes
Observe Principle	Adult demonstrates one clamp tightened onto middle of one long stick Adult demonstrates construction of elongated tool by rigidly joining two long sticks with clamps	2 min	no
No Treatment	Adult demonstrates one clamp tightened onto middle of one long stick	1 min.	no

Table 2 Spontaneous solutions according to treatment condition

	Play	Observe principle	No treatment
Solve	14	15	3
No solve	22	21	33

principle groups, it is clear that those given opportunity to play make more effective use of the early hints. Each child received a score (0–5) for the number of hints required to solve the problem. The Mann-Whitney U test, corrected for ties, shows that children in the *play* group required fewer hints than those in the group that observed the principle. ($U = 4.246, p < 0.01$).

C. *Various approaches to the problem as a function of treatment.* A most suggestive finding of the study is that the various treatments prior to presentation of the problem led children to approach the task in different ways. When confronted with the chalk in the distant box, the children who

Table 3 Six means to obtain goal (chalk)

Means	Description	Object Configuration (if any)
I	Use of hands/arm to attain goal	(hand/arm) ↑
II	Use of a single object as tool to extend the arm. (This is always one stick or clamp).	(single stick) ↑
III	Use of two unco-ordinated tools. (Usually child held stick in either hand).	(two sticks) ↑
IV	Assembly and use of an elongated but disjointed tool construction. (Usually child used one stick to push the other forward).	(two sticks in line) ↑
V	Assembly and use of rigidly jointed tool but one which is not sufficiently elongated.	(stick) ↑
VI	Assembly and use of an elongated tool consisting of two long sticks, rigidly joined by clamp at point of overlap.	overlap (clamped sticks) ↑

played first were eager to begin, continuous in their efforts to solve the problem, and flexible in their hypotheses. In contrast, children who observed the principle first were prone to an 'all or nothing' approach.

Children chose a variety of means for retrieving the chalk, some more complex than others. In analysing problem-solving behaviour, we confined ourselves to the child's use of hands. If a behaviour that involved the hands seemed directed towards the goal, we called it a *means* towards the end of chalk retrieval.

Table 3 lists the most common means. Its categories encompass about 80 per cent of the children's manual responses.

Table 4 shows the total number of all responses (according to treatment condition) made by children when presented with the problem. These include goal-directed actions (here called means) as well as those that are not, e.g., toying with the clamp, stacking the sticks in a pile, or arranging the sticks to form alphabet patterns on the table.

Table 4 Total number of (a) responses and (b) goal-directed responses in each group

	Play	Observe principle	No treatment
Total number of all manual responses	68 mean = 1·89	48 mean = 1·33	51 mean = 1·42
Total number of goal-directed manual responses	62 mean = 1·72 N = 36	31 mean = 0·86 N = 36	33 mean = 0·92 N = 36

Although the children who had played first appeared slightly more active in the problem-solving situation, the differences among groups are not statistically significant (two-way analysis of variance, age × treatment: $F_{treatment} = 2·34$, $df = 2$). The groups are notably different, however, when we look at goal-directed responses. Children given a prior chance to play are significantly more goal-directed (two-way analysis of variance, age × treatment: $F_{treatment} = 7·27$, $df = 2$, $p < 0·01$) once the problem is presented.

The data of Table 4 indicate that a playful experience prior to problem-solving encourages children towards more goal-directed behaviour. It does more than that, however. The six means described in Table 3 comprise a hierarchically ordered sequence. Children whose prior experience consisted of play observation of the principle worked their way 'up' from simple to more complex means. In contrast, children in the control group chose means in an apparently random order. Both play and observation of the principle led children to approach the problem in an orderly (simple to complex) manner; play, however, produced more goal-directed behaviour than observing the principle.

It is interesting to note the number of children in each group who 'opted out' or 'opted into' solving the problem. Table 5 shows the number of

Table 5 Frequency in each group of children who demonstrate at least one means

	Play	Observe principle	No treatment
Use one or more means	28	21	23
Absence of means	8	15	13

children in each group who demonstrated at least one goal-directed behaviour. Comparing children in the *play* and *observe principle* groups, it is clear that the latter tend to 'opt out' more frequently (Fisher exact test, $p < 0.04$).

Although the *play* children characteristically attempt solution, they tend to begin their problem-solving efforts with simple means, e.g., using the arm or just one stick. Table 6 shows the number of children in each group whose first attempt at solution was Means I or II, contrasted with those whose initial means was III, IV, V, or VI. (Note that children who show no means at all have been eliminated from analyses that follow in Tables 6, 7, 8.) Comparison between the *play* and *observe principle* groups shows that

Table 6 Frequency of children in each group who begin with simple means (I–II) or complex means (III–VI)

	Play	Observe principle	No treatment
Begin simple (Means I–II)	21	9	16
Begin complex (Means III–VI)	7	12	7

the former tend to begin with simple means whereas the latter begin with complex ones that include at least two objects ($x^2 = 5.22$, $df = 1$, $p < 0.05$).

It has been shown that the *play* children engage in more goal-directed behaviour, yet they begin with simple means. How do they manage to solve the problem? They do so by using means of increasing complexity, step-by-step. We define 'learners' as those children who begin lower than Means III but eventually reach Means IV or higher. This means that they began *at best* with one stick but reached a means that includes two co-ordinated objects. 'Non-learners' are of two types: those who remain at the level of simple means or those who begin with very complex ones. Table 7 shows the number of 'learners' in each group. Again, comparing *play* and *observe principle* groups we find more 'learners' in the former (Fisher exact test, $p = 0.05$).

Table 7 Frequency of children in each group who are Learners and Non-Learners

	Play	Observe principle	No treatment
Learners	12	4	1
Non-learners	16	17	22

To complete the examination of differences between *play* and *observe principle* groups, we focused only on children who solved the problem (without hints) and then counted the number in each group whose first goal-directed action was the correct one. We called these children 'immediate solvers' and found significantly more of them in the *observe principle* group than in the *play* group ($x^2 = 4.44$, $df = 1$, $p < 0.05$). Table 8 shows again that the children who had observed are of the 'all or

Table 8 Frequency of children in each group who are Immediate and Eventual Solvers

	Play	Observe principle	No treatment
Immediate solvers	3	9	2
Eventual solvers	11	6	1

nothing' variety. They tend to opt out of the problem or go directly to the solution. On the other hand, children allowed to play reach solution more often by the step-by-step route.

Experiment 2: treatment conditions

The second experiment holds constant duration of prior experience and once again varies the nature of the experience prior to presentation of the stick problem described in Experiment 1. Table 9 describes its treatment conditions.

Table 9 Treatment conditions in Experiment 2

Name	Nature of experience prior to presentation of the problem	Duration of prior experience	Manipulation of sticks and clamps?
Observe components	Adult and child sit at table and adult creates a 'puppet show' in which sticks and clamps become characters in a drama. Mr Clamp and his brothers 'eat' members of the Stick Family by clamping their 'jaws' around the 'waists' of the Sticks.	10 min.	no
Training on components	Training consists of demonstration, specific commands (e.g., 'Turn the handle the other way') and verbal encouragement (e.g. 'You're getting it tightened; don't give up')	10 min.	yes

As in the previous experiment, there were thirty-six children in each group, six boys and six girls at ages 3, 4, 5 years. To test for the effect of configurational richness on subsequent problem-solving, children in both groups of Experiment 2 were yoked to the *play* children in Experiment 1. An example of the yoking will clarify. Subject #31 in the *play* group was a five-year-old girl named Ginny. She made five distinct configurations in her ten minutes of free play. Three of them consisted of simple clampings of a single clamp to one stick. Two of Ginny's play configurations were more complex: twice she clamped two sticks together to make a longer, double-stick object. Her yoke mates in the two conditions of Experiment 2 were five-year-old girls like Ginny. They experienced the identical configurations constructed by Ginny – except that one of the new girls observed the adult build Ginny's configurations while the other new girl was trained by the adult to construct Ginny's configurations. One might say that the child in the *observe components* condition watched Ginny whereas the child in the *training on components* condition was instructed by the adult to copy Ginny's configurations.

One of the questions asked in Experiment 2 concerned the effect of richness of configuration on subsequent problem-solving performance. If all three children in the yoked trio experienced complex configurations, would their performance be similar to one another and different from the performances of another trio who had experienced simple configurations?

Experiment 2: results

A. *Spontaneous solution.* Table 10 shows that the two groups did not differ significantly in the number of children who spontaneously solved the problem.

Table 10 Frequency of spontaneous solutions
according to treatment condition in Experiment 2

	Observe components	Training on components
Solve	6	7
No solve	30	29

Although the two treatments produced roughly equal numbers of solvers, there is a slight trend showing that children who received training made better use of hints. In general, however, the children in the two conditions of the second experiment acted similarly.

B. *Various approaches to the problem as a function of treatment.*

Another way that children in the two groups are similar is in their characteristic approach to the problem. They both tend to start with simple means, e.g., Means I or II. Although there were about the same number of 'learners', in the two groups, there were many fewer than in the *play* condition of the first experiment. Those who did discover the solution did so in the 'eventual' style rather than going 'immediately' to the correct solution.

C. *Effect of configurational richness.* Did the yoking make a difference? More precisely, were the scores of children in the two yoked conditions correlated with the scores of their yoke mates in the *play* group of Experiment 1? Each child's score for number of hints (0–5) was correlated with the score of his yoke mate in the free play condition. The correlations were all statistically significant. Spearman rank correlations between *play* and *observe components* were $rs = 0.673$, $p < 0.05$; between *play* and *training on components* $rs = 0.672$, $p < 0.05$. We conclude that the richness of the configuration to which the child is exposed affects his subsequent performance in problem-solving.

D. *Comparison between Experiments 1 and 2*. Having established that the two groups in Experiment 2 were very similar in problem-solving performance, we compare them to the *play* group of Experiment 1. Table 11

Table 11 Frequency of spontaneous solutions in Experiments 1 and 2

	Play	Observe principle	No treatment	Observe components (yoked to play)	Training on components (yoked to play)
Solve	14	15	3	6	7
No solve	22	21	33	30	29

shows the number of spontaneous solvers in both experiments. It is difficult to make direct statistical comparisons between the two groups since most tests required independence that the yoking procedure does not allow. However, one can compare the two groups in the second experiment with the earlier *play* group by assigning scores for number of hints (0–5) and then applying to them tests for matched pairs. *Play* is superior to *observe components* (Wilcoxen test for two matched samples, $T = 41 \cdot 5$, $p < 0 \cdot 05$, two-tailed and also superior to *training on components*, $T = 90 \cdot 0$, $p < 0 \cdot 05$, two-tailed).* This is an especially interesting finding because the three children in each trio experienced identical configurations. One 'invented' a configuration in free play, one observed construction of the same configuration, and one was trained to construct it by the adult. Only the behaviour of the *play* child, of course, was self-initiated.

Discussion and conclusion

Which aspects of the *play* treatment contributed to its efficacy as preparation for problem-solving? Clearly manipulation of the actual sticks and clamps will not, by itself, lead to problem solution. In the training session of Experiment 2 the children who handled the materials (but not with their own plans of operation) did not perform well when later presented with the problem. Nor was a long experience with the adult (10 minutes as in the original *play* condition) sufficient to explain the results since both groups

---

*Some caution must be exercised in proclaiming the *play* children superior to those in Experiment 2. Although children were yoked on age and sex, they were not yoked on intelligence since these data were not available. However, although it's true that a very bright child in the second experiment might have been constrained by being exposed to a barren stick-and-clamp configuration, a duller child might well have been helped by exposure to an especially rich one. Children were randomly assigned to their yoke mates.

in Experiment 2 experienced this and yet they did not perform as well on the problem.

We look for clues to the benefits of play in the characteristic approach demonstrated by the children who had played prior to testing. Although there are no differences in total number of responses made by children in the various groups, the *play* children engage in many more goal-directed ones. *Play* children, moreover, tend to begin with simple means but progress systematically towards complex ones. In other words, a failed attempt (e.g., using one stick to try to reach the box) did not frustrate them. They neither persevered nor gave up. Used to playing, they more often used the information from a failure to arrive at the next hypothesis, which was usually to combine two sticks. But play produced more than enthusiasm; the *play* children were productive and organized in their problem-solving as well.

The children with prior play experience did as well in solving the problem as those children who had been shown the principle of making a tool appropriate to the task. It is a nice question to ask why those children who had been shown the principle did not outperform the players. In a sense, their problem was easier: to apply a general principle in a specific task. The playing children had also to *discover* the principle. Obviously the experiment cannot shed direct light on this issue, for it was not designed with it in mind. All that can be said is that it might be worthwhile in future research to explore whether play with the application of general principles to specific problems is of help in problem-solving of this order. It may also be the case that observing the application of a principle creates a rather monolithic view of the procedure – with the means–end structure appearing too fixed for easy adaptation to later tasks. If this were the case, then one can understand why some of the observer children did not succeed, and why prior play may have been a real advantage to the other group.

In sum, then, those who play before attempting problem-solving seem to do better for the following reasons. (1) Solving problems required self-initiation and our playing children were the only ones in the experiments whose actions were self-initiated. (2) Tool invention (like other forms of problem-solving) requires serial ordering of the constituent acts involved. The players were the only ones who had an opportunity to explore alternative serial orders. (3) Play reduces the stress of anticipating success and failure. Our players, less stressed, were able to proceed with less frustration and fear of failure – they were more goal-directed. They could benefit from hints and could approach the solution gradually without breaking off. To reiterate the point with which we started, the effect of prior play seems to be not only in combinatorial practice, but also in shifting emphasis in a task from ends to means, from product to process.

References

BIRCH, H. G. (1945), 'The relation of previous experience to insightful problem-solving', *J. Comp. Physiol. Psychol.*, No. 38, pp. 367–83.

BRUNER, J. S. (1972), 'The nature and uses of immaturity', *Amer. Psychol.*, No. 27, pp. 1–28. (And see this volume, p. 28.)

EIBL-EIBESFELDT, I. (1970), *Ethology: the Biology of Behavior*, Holt, Rinehart & Winston, New York.

HERRON, J., and SUTTON-SMITH, B. (1971), *Child's Play*, Wiley, New York.

KOESTLER, A. (1967), *The Ghost in the Machine*, Hutchinson. (And see this volume, p. 643.)

KÖHLER, W. (1925), *The Mentality of Apes*, Routledge & Kegan Paul.

MILLER, S. (1973), 'Ends, means, and galumphing: some leitmotifs of play,' *Amer. Anthropologist*, No. 75, pp. 87–98.

REYNOLDS, P. (1972), 'Play and the evolution of language', paper delivered at Annual meetings of American Academy for Advancement of Science, December 1972. (And see this volume, p. 621.)

SYLVA, K. (1974), 'The role of play in the problem-solving of children 3–5 years old', Harvard University Dept of Psychology and Social Relations, Ph.D.Dissertation.

WHITE, R. W. (1959), 'Motivation reconsidered: the concept of competence', *Psych. Rev.*, No. 66, pp. 297–330.

Play and the Social World

In Part Three we examine the ways in which play prepares the young for their roles in the social world. Its contents are necessarily diverse. It opens with an account of how very early play ensures bonding between mother and offspring as a prerequisite to the infant's later interaction with other members of his species. There follow papers showing how later play fits the growing organism for competitive and co-operative roles, for the conventions that govern interaction between members of the society with respect to the division of labour, of wealth, and of prestige. Children of technologically complex societies play at occupational roles in fantasy; children in less technically advanced societies play at productive rules in the company of working adults.

The rules of social interaction are more loosely formed than those governing language, to be examined in Part Four. But there is an intermediate case – games. The rule-bound nature of games has fascinated workers in fields as diverse as ecology, mathematics and economics. Games presumably restrain the spontaneity of their players by an increased explicitness of rules. They are so explicit, indeed, that they can often be given mathematical formulation (von Neumann and Morgenstern, 1953). The manner in which the child learns the rules of the game provides a window through which to observe how any formal structures are learned. The great master of such analysis is Jean Piaget. His description of the rules of the game of marbles may be the finest piece of developmental anthropology ever written. In contrast, the great naturalists of children playing games are Iona and Peter Opie, justly famous for their beautiful descriptions of children's games in their natural settings. And on the practical level, James Coleman reports on the deliberate use of games for pedagogical ends. Coleman and Rivka Eifermann are both concerned with the function of games in helping the young develop skills.

We turn next to subtle issues of how play and games are used for indoctrinating the child into the conventions of his culture. Having played at competitive games, competition later in life comes as no surprise. The Tangu game described by K. L. Burridge is a lovely example of game-like preparation for co-operative activity of a sort rare in our own society. The theme of cultural indoctrination recurs throughout the book, especially in Part Four where the symbolic play of humans is explored in more detail.

Part Three closes with a look at factors disrupting play, ranging through a dismal catalogue of disasters: protein deficiency, social isolation, excessive frustration. This closing section tells the story of the cost in productivity and zest when play is disrupted in childhood.

References

NEUMANN, J. VON and MORGENSTERN, O. (1953), *A Theory of Games and Economic Behavior* (3rd Ed.), Wiley, New York.

A Early Interaction Play

Mother Chimpanzees' Play with their Infants

'Distraction' of infant

Chimpanzee mothers, when their offspring persisted in trying to attain a desired objective, reacted on many occasions by tickling or grooming their children rather than by punishing them. For example, when Fifi first tried to pull her sibling away from their mother and when Gilka approached her mother, whimpering, when she wanted to suckle. The mother, Flo, also distracted her infant, Flint, by playing with him on many occasions when he tried to suckle during her period of oestrus.

There are a number of other occasions when the playful behaviour of a mother towards her infant may also function to distract the latter. Thus a mother frequently played with her infant when it made early attempts to leave her and explore its environment. Indeed, one mother, Passion, who was seldom observed to restrict her infant's movements, was only rarely observed to play with the latter during this stage of her development.

The mother Flo was observed to behave in this way when Flint persisted in playing with some object which, for some reason, she objected to. Once this was a tiny piece of red colobus monkey skin and hair. Twice Flo hit it away from Flint. When he retrieved it for a third time she threw it forcefully away and began to play with him. Similar behaviour was seen when Flint played close to his mother with a large stick, a big piece of polythene, and a tin can. The same mother played with her infant to prevent him from approaching mature males.

Mothers were also observed to play with, as well as gently push away, infants that approached to look at or try to play with their own small babies. Subsequently, when the latter were older, the mothers permitted them to play but often joined in, tickling or dabbing at their own children's playmates when the play became boisterous.

Behaviour of this category does not appear to be widespread amongst primates, but Jay (1963) observed something similar in some langur mothers when their infants were being weaned: 'If she grooms her infant before it becomes tense and aggressive, this has a calming effect and at least postpones a weaning tantrum.'

Behaviour which probably functions to strengthen and reinforce the mother–offspring relationship

During infancy, affectionate behaviour, play and grooming are all probably helpful in establishing a strong social tie between a mother and her offspring. As the latter grows older, sessions of social grooming become increasingly longer and probably serve to reinforce this tie when the offspring returns to its mother after leaving her for longer and longer periods.

Affectionate behaviour

Mothers of small infants frequently stared down at them intently, often without touching them. On one occasion, Flo put her index finger under Flint's chin, tilted up his face and then stared at him for a full half a minute. Mothers were also observed to caress their infants, either gently stroking them with their fingers or making a few idle grooming movements whilst gazing down at their babies. All mothers kissed their infants by lightly putting their lips to some part of their bodies: Mandy and Flo both picked up their infants' hands and then kissed the palms on several occasions. Similar behaviour has been seen in rhesus monkey mothers (Hinde, Rowell and Spencer-Booth, 1964) and langurs (Jay, 1963).

Mothers of small infants often lifted up one of their feet and then moved it idly up and down so that the knee and hip joints were alternately flexed and extended. Flo sometimes did this for at least half a minute at a time during Flint's first three months.

When an infant is over 1 year old, the above types of behaviour are not normally observed. The mother of an older infant, however, may occasionally lay her hand on her child or hold its hand, seemingly for social or affectionate reasons only. Similarly an infant often leaves some game for no apparent reason except to go and sit in contact with its mother. Schaller (1963) observed similar behaviour between gorilla mothers and their infants.

Play

All chimpanzee mothers were seen to play with their infant, and one, Flo, was also seen to play with her juvenile and adolescent offspring. Figure 1 suggests that the frequency of this behaviour depends on the age of the offspring concerned and may vary between different mother-offspring pairs. This figure shows that both Flo and Melissa played most frequently with their infants when they were between 4 and 6 months old and were making attempts to pull away from their mothers: this maternal play, as we have seen, possibly functioned to distract the infants for a while.

Most mothers initiated playing during the first few months of their

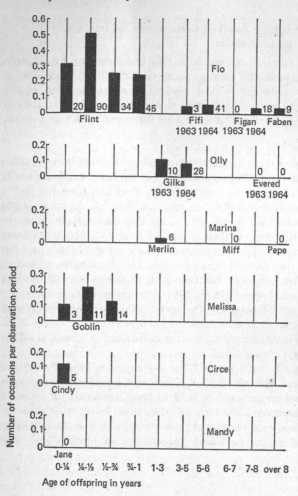

Fig. 1. Changes in frequency of maternal play with relation to the age of the offspring. (The total number of occasions when play was seen between a particular mother–offspring pair in each age group is shown at the foot of the relevant column.)

infants' lives by tickling them with their fingers, usually under the chin or in the groin. Flo frequently tickled Flint with small nibbling movements of her worn teeth. Also, on many occasions, she lay on her back, held Flint above her with one of his ankles or wrists clasped in her foot, and tickled him. Melissa was only observed to play with Goblin in this way on one occasion and the other mothers not at all.

When Flint was about 12 weeks old, Flo began to tickle or fiddle with his penis, either with her fingers or her lips, and continued to do this frequently for several months. Flo also occasionally tickled Fifi's clitoris during a game, and twice tried to tickle Figan's penis when he was an adolescent. This behaviour was very rarely observed in other mothers. Schaller observed one gorilla mother manipulate the genital area of her 3½-year-old infant until his penis became erect and she then held it several times with her lips (Schaller, 1963).

Flint was first observed to respond to tickling with a 'play face' when he was 11 weeks old; other infants were not seen with this facial expression until they were between 17 and 24 weeks old. Flint was heard 'laughing'* for the first time when he was 12 weeks old, and two other infants were also heard laughing about a week after they were seen showing play faces for the first time. Flint and Goblin made play responses at between 18 and 19 weeks of age, grabbing and patting at their mothers' hands during tickling; data on the other infants do not indicate when this behaviour was first seen. Slightly older infants frequently try to initiate play, pulling their mothers' hands towards them with play faces. Flo and Circe invariably responded to such invitations but Melissa and Passion often ignored their infants.

Play behaviour of mothers with their one-year-old infants included rolling the infants over, mock biting and tickling them, gently sparring with them or pushing them to and fro as they dangled from a branch (van Lawick-Goodall, 1967, Plate XIII). The infants responded by grabbing and biting the mothers' hands, flinging themselves onto the mothers with flailing arms or tickling them.

As infants grow older, mothers normally play with them less frequently. Marina seldom played with Merlin after he was about 2 years old unless he himself initiated the playing, pulling her hands towards his tummy for tickling. Olly played with Gilka fairly frequently until she was about 4 years old but seldom intensively unless it was to distract the child from suckling (see above).

The play behaviour of Flo seemed unusual. During 1963, before the birth of Flint, she was seen to play with Fifi on three occasions only, and was not seen to play with her two sons. In 1964, however, she played intensively with all her offspring. It seems possible that this sudden increase in playful activity in the mother was a direct result of the birth of another infant. For one thing, as we have seen, she frequently tickled Fifi in order

* During play chimpanzees frequently make a series of low panting noises 'aach-e-aach' which sounds roughly like human laughter.

to divert her attention from the infant. For another, chimpanzees sometimes develop temporary habits, fashions in their behaviour patterns. Possibly, as a result of tickling Flint and Fifi, playing became such a habit for Flo, stimulating her to playful activities with her older offspring. Figure 2 shows that Flo's frequency of play with each of her offspring did in fact follow a similar pattern during the first year in Flint's life. (The sharp decrease which occurred during Flint's ninth and tenth months was between October and January, when Flo spent a great deal of each day in feeding on termites.)

Play between Flo and her adolescent offspring frequently commenced when they grasped each other's hands or feet; this was followed by tickling or mock biting, particularly of the fingers and ears. On two occasions Flo joined her three older offspring in a game which consisted of chasing each other round and round the base of a tree. The children sometimes played this game with Flo sitting in the middle.

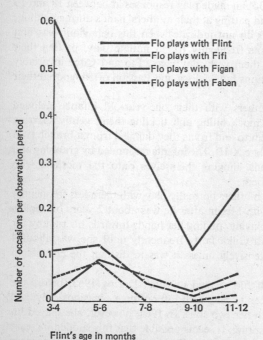

Fig. 2. Changes in frequency of the mother Flo's play with her four offspring during 9 months of her infant Flint's life. At the end of the period of these observations Fifi was about 6, Figan about 9 and Faben about 12 years old respectively.

From about the middle of 1965 Flo played less and less frequently with Figan and Faben, and during 1966 gradually stopped playing with Fifi. Thus in 1967, although she sometimes played with Flint at the same time as one of his siblings was playing with him, Flo was not seen to initiate play with her older offspring.

No mother was observed to play with youngsters other than her own offspring except when an infant or juvenile was playing with, or trying to touch, her own infant.

(From 'The Behaviour of Chimpanzees', *Animal Behaviour Monographs*, Vol. 1, Part 3, Baillière, Tindall & Cassell, 1968.)

References

JAY, P. (1963), 'Mother-infant relations in langurs', in *Maternal Behavior in Mammals*, H. L. Rheingold (ed.), Wiley, New York.

HINDE, R. A., ROWELL, T. E., and SPENCER-BOOTH, Y. (1964), 'Behaviour of socially living rhesus monkeys in their first six months', *Proceedings of the Royal Society*, No. 143, pp. 609–49.

SCHALLER, G. (1963), *The Mountain Gorilla: Ecology and Behavior*, University of Chicago Press.

LAWICK-GOODALL, J. VAN (1967), 'Mother-offspring relationships in chimpanzees', in *Primate Ethology*, D. Morris (ed.), Weidenfeld & Nicolson.

Smiling, Cooing and 'The Game'

'The game' hypothesis

The hypothesis of 'The Game' proposes that when an infant perceives the occurrence of a neutral or positive stimulus, a process termed 'contingency analysis' begins (Watson, 1966, 1967). If, across successive exposures of the stimulus, this analysis confirms the existence of a contingency between the stimulus and a response, then this contingent stimulus and eventually the stimuli which mark this contingency situation gain new meaning for the infant. The new meaning is that the stimuli become the releasing stimuli for vigorous smiling and cooing. In essence, the stimuli begin functioning as 'social stimuli'. It is assumed that this process of defining what shall be viewed as social is limited to some set of initial contingency experiences.

In most situations in which the average infant finds himself during the first two to three months, the combination of slow response recovery and short contingency memory prohibits his becoming aware of contingencies between his behaviour and its stimulus effects in the physical environment because by the time he is able to repeat an effective response, he has usually forgotten why it was selected for repetition. Then one day someone begins playing a game with the infant. They touch his nose each time he widens his eyes, or they bounce him on their knee each time he bobs his head, or they blow on his belly each time he jiggles his legs, or they make sounds after he makes a sound. These games are variants of 'The Game'. There are many other potential variants, but what makes them a special and singular class is that they share the features of presenting a clear stimulus contingent upon a response which is small or mature enough to have a relatively quick recovery time. As the specific game is played more times, the infant experiences an increasing awareness of a clear contingency, and with that, vigorous smiling and cooing begins.

Studies of response-contingent stimulation

One might ask why 'The Game' hypothesis proposes that 'The Game' initially elicits vigorous smiling and cooing, rather than proposing that initial games are taken up with and progressively reward the smiling and cooing responses themselves. This proposal arises from a set of studies which have presented the possibility of instrumental learning over a period of days in early infancy. The first research to take special note of the apparent release of vigorous smiling and cooing to response-contingent stimulation was that of Hunt and Uzgiris (1964). In that study some infants had a mobile which was fixed to their cribs so that if they jiggled, the mobile would move. Other infants had a mobile attached outside the crib, which prevented control of the mobile's movement. The authors report that a few infants, whose mobiles jiggled neither too little nor too much, were able to establish clear control of their mobiles and showed smiling and cooing when doing so. They interpreted their results as indicating the pleasure in the process of assimilating responsive stimulation. In some recent studies by my colleagues and myself many infants have been observed to blossom into vigorous smiling and cooing during our attempts to provide early beneficial learning experiences. Before our data which corroborate Hunt and Uzgiris' finding are described, however, an important difference in interpretation of the smiling and cooing reaction should be noted.

Hunt and Uzgiris' interpretation of smiling and cooing, indeed the interpretation of many of the proponents of familiarity hypotheses, is one in which the responses serve two functions, one to release the emotional energy of pleasure and the other to serve as a behavioural basis for the recognition process in a manner similar to Piaget's proposal of 'recognitive assimilation' (Piaget, 1952). While it may be true that smiling and cooing do indeed serve as aids to recognition and as avenues of emotional release, it seems unlikely that they would have survived behavioural evolution within our species as so distinct and so external a set of responses were it not for their social functions. Why should the offspring of our species be so vigorously expressive of their pleasure in recognizing their control of the environment? The young of other species seem to gain comparable control without a similar display of emotion. The recognition hypothesis appears to say we do so simply because we are what we are, while 'The Game' hypothesis proposes that we do so because in this way we are normally guaranteed to begin vigorous smiling and cooing at fellow species members.

Our data come from a series of studies aimed at stimulating the development of contingency awareness in early infancy. Encouraging the arrival of contingency awareness before its normally expected appearance in the natural environment was intended to have beneficial effects in accord with certain theoretical proposals made elsewhere (Watson, 1966a) and which need not be restated here. Special machines were constructed for these studies, the essential feature of which is a very sensitive pillow which is designed to allow very small and quick recovery responses to have discrete and clear contingent effects on a visual display hanging over the infant.

Experiment 1. The initial study was carried out by Craig Ramey and myself (Watson and Ramey, 1969). The machines were placed in the homes of eighteen infants who were exposed to them for 10 minutes a day for two weeks, starting when they were eight weeks old. For these eighteen infants a mobile hanging over them turned for one second after each time they pressed their head on the pillow. Experiment 1 also had two control groups, each composed of eleven infants. In one group the infants saw a stabile that did not move, and in the other control group the infant saw a non-contingent mobile which turned periodically and unrelated to their head movements. These infants and those of the following three experiments were children of college-educated fathers, and virtually all were caucasian. The machines accumulated the daily records of the infants, and these are shown in Figure 1. The infants of Experiment 1 who had contin-

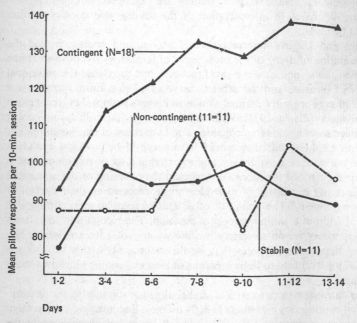

Fig. 1. Pillow responses across two weeks by the three groups in Experiment I.

gent mobiles showed a significant increase in daily activity across the two weeks (change in pillow response rate from days 1–2 to 13–14, $t = 3.72$, $p < .01$). The two control groups did not change appreciably in their activity. In short, these 8-week-old infants showed they could learn in this situation. But more dramatically for us at the time, and more importantly for this paper at this time, the mothers of the infants with contingent mobiles almost unanimously reported the appearance of vigorous smiling and cooing in their infants on approximately the third or fourth day of exposure. Considering the fact that the machines were not rewarding smiling and cooing, it seems reasonable to assume that the contingency experience was releasing these responses. The mothers of control infants reported that they saw some smiling among their infants, but at a much lower degree of vigour and duration than that observed among infants with contingent mobiles.

In our next experiment (II), fourteen infants exposed to two experimental conditions, one with a contingent stimulus and the other with a (different) non-contingent stimulus, showed no higher response level in the contingent than in the non-contingent condition. Experiment III examined the effects of different ratios of reinforcement: a mobile was turned either forty per cent or sixty per cent of the time the pillow was pressed. In neither partially-contingent group did infants show an increase in rate of pillow response or in vigorous smiling and cooing.

Experiment IV. At this point we began to doubt the findings of Experiment I. We had observed twenty-six infants in Experiments II and III for whom we had had reasonable expectancies of seeing both learning and the associated release of social responses, yet we had seen essentially none of either. We then speculated that if an infant is committed to making a clear discrimination between contingent and non-contingent situations, he may be very sensitive to situations which are ambiguous. This hypothesis seemed more probable once we realized there was a potential stimulus basis for confusion in Experiment II, where infants experienced both contingent and non-contingent sessions. In both sessions the infant was placed in the unique position of having his head on the pillow. With this in mind we conducted Experiment IV in which we presented nineteen 8-week-old infants the opportunity to experience only a clear contingency. This was thus a return to the condition experienced by the eighteen infants in the contingency group of Experiment I. Across subjects in Experiment IV we did vary the specific nature of the contingency, but for any given subject his experience was a particular contingency for ten minutes each day for two weeks. For approximately half the subjects the contingent stimulus was a lighted umbrella, and for the other half the event was a turning mobile. Half the infants controlled their contingent stimulus with head movement and half with feet movement. As Figure 2 shows, the infants of this study increased in their daily activity rates across the two weeks (change in pillow response rate from days 1–2 to 13–14, $t = 2.21$, $p < .05$) just as the contingency group of Experiment I had, and we again received almost

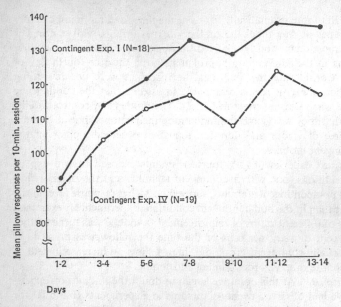

Fig. 2. Pillow responses across two weeks for contingent group of Experiment IV and contingent group of Experiment I.

unanimous reports of vigorous smiling and cooing arising after about three to five days. It is not likely to be a coincidence that the average normal infant is expected to show peak vigorous smiling to a human face at about the third or fourth month, which is also the time he is expected to show active instrumental behaviour. If the proposal made here is correct, both developments arise from an infant's initial experience of a clear contingency.

Overview of 'the game' hypothesis

Taken as a whole, then, these studies of reactions to facial orientation and response-contingent stimulation have led us to the hypothesis of 'The Game'. Let us consider the hypothesis one more time in graphic form prior to relating it to some alternative proposals in the attachment literature. Figure 3 shows the graphic form of the hypothesis. The graph indicates that as a stimulus initially becomes more familiar, it increasingly becomes a candidate for classification as contingent. At this point one of three things can occur. First, if contingency analysis through successive exposures of the stimulus indicates that the stimulus is indeed a clearly contingent one,

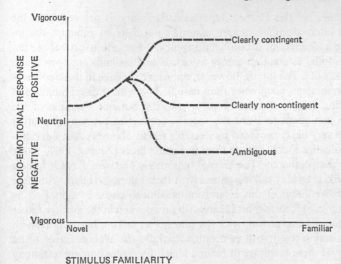

Fig. 3. Theoretical relationship between stimulus familiarity and socio-emotional response for three types of stimulation.

then the smiling and cooing and attention of the infant is expected to increase sharply to an asymptote of vigorous responding. Secondly, if the continuing contingency analysis indicates that the stimulus is clearly non-contingent, then the modest level of smiling and cooing is expected to decline back to the base rate elicited by completely novel stimuli. Thirdly, if, through continuing exposure, the contingency analysis of the stimulus is continuously indeterminate due either to ambiguous aspects of the contingency itself or to confusing situational characteristics, then the response to the stimulus is expected to become progressively less positive and eventually to begin eliciting negative emotional responses.*

*If one now adds a proposal that familiarity of a previously exposed stimulus may be diminished through distortion of the stimulus, then a number of additional predictions can be made. For instance, if a stimulus has a history which has established it as clearly non-contingent (or a marker of a situation which is clearly non-contingent), then it would be responded to with a minimal level of smiling and cooing. However, if the stimulus were distorted and therewith reduced in its familiar characteristics, then a backward movement on the graph would be called for; and a concomitant rise in smiling and cooing would be predicted for certain moderate distortions. By contrast, if a stimulus which had been established as clearly contingent (or as a marker of a contingency situation) were to be distorted, then a backward movement on the graph would lead one to predict a decline in smiling and cooing for the stimulus. Finally, if a stimulus were presented to an infant which was similar to both a previously established

That, then, is 'The Game' hypothesis. Its name is derived from the game-like interactions which are assumed normally to generate the infant's first awareness of a clear contingency. Most adults probably view these occasional interaction games as casual and insignificant episodes in their infant's life. The infant, however, appears to engage in these episodes with a commitment far greater than casual. The refined discrimination of facial orientation by 3-month-olds is possibly but one example of the infant's commitment to learn the specific context of his game. Another example is very likely provided by Zelazo's recent discovery that 3-month-old girls vocalize more to male than to female faces (Zelazo, 1967, 1969). From the perspective of 'The Game' hypothesis one would ask if fathers are more likely to play talking games with their infant girls than with their boys. The likelihood of this interesting sex-linked game is supported by recent findings of Rebelsky and Hanks (in press) wherein the average father of an infant girl engaged in twice the number of talking interactions with his infant during the first three months than did the average father of an infant boy. If these examples of refined facial discrimination are testimony to the infants' attentional commitment to 'The Game', then there seems little doubt that infants take their initial games most seriously.

Some competing hypotheses

Before closing it should be acknowledged that there are some hypotheses about the origin of social responsiveness which are quite similar to 'The Game' hypothesis proposed here. Notable are the recent proposals of Rheingold (1961), Ainsworth and Wittig (1969), and Bowlby (1969). Also relevant are some writings by Shaffer and Emerson (1964), Walters and Parke (1965), and Bettelheim (1967). These theorists have emphasized to a greater or lesser extent that a significant aspect of the infant's caretaker, which makes him an arousing stimulus and a candidate for attachment, is his responsiveness to the social behaviour initiated by the infant. Clearly, then, these theorists have noted the infant's need to sense a contingency between his behaviour and resulting stimulus events. In this regard 'The Game' hypothesis adds nothing especially new. However, it is my belief that all of these proposals have centred their attention on the social nature of the infant's behaviour or on the social nature of the contingent stimulation from the caretaker. That is, these previous hypotheses appear to have implicitly, and at times explicitly, assigned special significance to the type of responses an infant normally makes when interacting with a care-

---

clearly contingent stimulus and a previously established non-contingent stimulus, the infant's response would be predicted by the line indexing negative responsiveness toward an ambiguous stimulus.

taker, and likewise special significance to the type of stimulation normally provided by caretakers when interacting with infants. If these previous proposals are correct, then one could state in summary that 'The Game' is important to the infant because people play it.

On the other hand, if 'The Game' hypothesis does add something new to the speculations of early social responsiveness, it does so in denying special significance for one type of stimulation as opposed to another or one type of response as opposed to another. The hypothesis states that what is important is the perception of the relationship of contingency between a specific stimulus and a specific response. With this proposal, in contrast to previous proposals, an infant can be expected to release smiling and cooing and perhaps even begin the initial stages of attachment with innumerable artificial or even mechanical situations if they should happen to be correctly arranged. Thus, if 'The Game' hypothesis adds anything, it is that it states 'The Game' is NOT important to the infant because people play it, but rather people become important to the infant because they play 'The Game'.

(From Merrill-Palmer Quarterly, No. 18, 1972.)

References

AINSWORTH, M., and WITTIG, B. (1969), 'Attachment and exploratory behavior of one-year-olds in a strange situation', in Determinants of Infant Behavior, Vol. 4, B. Foss (ed.), Methuen.

BETTELHEIM, B. (1967), 'The Empty Fortress: Infantile Autism and the Birth of the Self, Free Press, New York.

BOWLBY, J. (1969), Attachment and Loss, Vol. 1, Attachment, Hogarth Press.

HUNT, J., and UZGIRIS, I. (1964), 'Cathexis from recognitive familiarity: An exploratory study', paper presented at the 1964 Convention of the American Psychological Association, Los Angeles, California, September, 1964.

PIAGET, J. (1952), The Origins of Intelligence in Children, International Universities Press, New York.

REBELSKY, F., and HANKS, C., 'Fathers' verbal interactions with infants in the first three months of life', Child Development, in press.

RHEINGOLD, H. (1961), 'The effect of environmental stimulation upon social and exploratory behaviour in the human infant', in Determinants of Infant Behavior, B. Foss (ed.), Methuen.

SCHAFFER, A., and EMERSON, P. (1964), 'The development of social attachments in infancy', Monographs of the Society for Research in Child Development, Vol. 29.

WALTERS, R. and PARKE, R. (1965), 'The role of the distance receptors in the development of social responsiveness', in Advances in Child Development and Behavior, Vol. 2, L. Lipsitt and C. Spiker (eds), Academic Press, New York.

WATSON, J. (1966a), 'Perception of object orientation in infants', Merrill-Palmer Quarterly, Vol. 12, pp. 73–94.

WATSON, J. (1966b), 'The development and generalization of "contingency awareness" in early infancy: Some hypotheses', *Merrill-Palmer Quarterly*, Vol. 12, pp. 123–35.

WATSON, J. (1967), 'Memory and "contingency analysis" in infant learning', *Merrill-Palmer Quarterly*, Vol. 13, pp. 55–76.

WATSON, J., and RAMEY, C. (1969), 'Reactions to response-contingent stimulation in early infancy', revision of paper presented at biennial meeting of the Society for Research in Child Development, Santa Monica, California, March, 1969.

ZELAZO, P. (1967), 'Social reinforcement of vocalizations and smiling of three-month-old infants', unpublished doctoral dissertation, University of Waterloo, Belgium.

ZELAZO, P. (1969), 'Differential three-month-old infant vocalizations to sex-of-strangers', paper presented at the International Congress of Psychology, London.

Peekaboo and the Learning of Rule Structures

Peekaboo surely must rank as one of the most universal forms of play between adults and infants. It is rich indeed in the mechanisms it exhibits. For, in point of fact, the game depends upon the infant's capacity to integrate a surprisingly wide range of phenomena. For one, the very playing of the game depends upon the child having some degree of mastery of object permanence, the capacity to recognize the continued existence of an object when it is out of sight (e.g. Piaget, 1954). Charlesworth (1966) has shown, moreover, that the successful playing of the game is dependent in some measure on the child being able to keep track of the location in which a face has disappeared, the child showing more persistent effects when the reappearance of a face varied unexpectedly with respect to its prior position. Greenfield (1970) has also indicated that the initial effect of the game depends upon the presence not only of the reappearing face, but also of an accompanying vocalization by the mother, although with repetition the role of vocalization declines. She also found that the voice was increasingly important the less familiar the setting in which the game was played. It is quite plain, then, that complex expectancies are built up in the infant in the course of playing the game, and that these expectancies are characterized by considerable spatio-temporal structuring.

Another way of saying the same thing is to note that the child very soon becomes sensitive to the 'rules of the game' as he plays it. That is to say, he expects disappearance and reappearance to be in a certain place, at a certain time, accompanied by certain vocalizations, in certain general settings. The bulk of the studies reported in the literature suggest that these 'conventions', though they may rest upon certain pre-adapted readinesses to respond to disappearance and reappearance, are soon converted into rules for defining the pattern of play. If this were the case, one would expect that not only would the child have learned procedures, but would have learned them in a way that is characteristic of rule learning – i.e., in a general form, with assignable roles, with permissible substitutions of moves, etc.

The present study is concerned specifically with the conversion of peekaboo procedures into rule structures and, without intending to minimize the importance of pre-adapted patterns of response in making the game possible, we shall concentrate upon this aspect of the matter.

The study is based upon an intensive investigation of six infants over a period of ten months, from seven to seventeen months of age. The infants and their mothers were seen once a fortnight at our laboratory for an hour and among the instructions given to them was one asking them to show us the games that they and their infants most enjoyed playing. Our observations of peekaboo are all based upon behaviour spontaneously produced by the mothers in play, all but one of them including peekaboo in the play they exhibited. All sessions were videotaped and analysis was carried out on the video records. Partly for convenience of reporting and partly because each pair developed somewhat different procedures, we shall concentrate on a single mother–infant dyad over the ten-month period. The corpus of such play for this dyad consisted of twenty-two episodes of peekaboo, the first at ten months, the last at fifteen months. Peekaboo starts earlier than our initial age and goes on later, but the sample of games over the five-month period suffices to illustrate the points we wish to make. Though the other infant–mother dyads show some differences from the one we are reporting, they are in no sense different in pattern.

Observations

The first thing to be noted in the one mother-daughter (Diane) dyad on which we shall concentrate is that all instances of the game are quite notably constrained with respect to their limits. That is to say, the game always starts after the two players have made an explicit contact. This is the opening move, but it should be noted immediately that here as in other features of the game, variation prevails. In most instances, initial contact is by face-to-face mutual looking. Where this does not occur, the mother may use either vocalization to contact the child or make the hiding 'instrument' conspicuous. The following table gives the frequencies of opening moves:

Face-to-face contact	16 (of 21 episodes in which orientation could be ascertained)
Vocalization	9 (of 22)
Highlighting of instrument	3 (of 22)

Typically, vocalization and face-to-face contact go together, with seven out of nine episodes of vocalization being accompanied by face-to-face contact. Interestingly enough, the mother will sometimes use a chance event as a 'starter' as when, inadvertently, her smock hides the child's face and the mother uses this as a start for a round of peekaboo. Also, there is what might best be called the 'opportunistic start', in which the mother when drying the child's hair after a bath, 'lightens' the occasion by turning the drying with towel into an episode of peekaboo – a pattern also used by mothers to divert a fretting baby.

As Garvey (p. 570) has put it, social games can be described in terms of (a) the nature of the format, (b) the turns of each player, and (c) the round in which the turns are sequenced. In the peekaboo situation, the initial round is a mutual attention-focusing episode that seems invariant although its form, as we have seen, may vary from one instance of the peekaboo format to the next.

The second round of peekaboo is the actual act of hiding and its accompaniments. Note first that there are four alternatives possible: mother can be hidden, or child, and the act of hiding can be initiated by the mother or the infant. The four alternatives and their frequencies are as follows:

M Initiated, M hidden	8
C initiated, C hidden	2
M Initiated, C hidden	11
C initiated, M hidden	0
[Ambiguous	1]

We may note that whilst there are at most three instances of the child initiating the hiding act, and all of these came at fifteen months, they indicate that the child is by no means always a passive participant. We shall have more to say of this later in discussing role reversal. One of the striking features of what is hidden is that it is about equally distributed between the mother's face being masked and the child's – one of the forms of variation that the mother uses in order to keep uncertainty operative within the game. The child seems readily to accept this variation in the format and, indeed, seems to take a certain delight in it.

What is very notable is that there is virtually complete openness with regard to the instrument and mode used for hiding. The game when first observed was carried out exclusively with a nappy and hiding was controlled by the mother, and this occurred six times, hiding herself four times and the child twice. Thereafter, the distribution of the remaining episodes was five times nappy, five times clothing, three times a towel, two times a chair, and once with the child averting her head. In short, the nature of the hiding instrument and the masking act might almost be called optional in contrast to certain obligatory features, such as the requirement of initial contact.

During the period of hiding, and we shall discuss the limits on its length below, there is a further ancillary feature of the game – a mode of sustaining contact during hiding. This occurs both on the mother's side and on the child's. In sixteen of the twenty-two episodes, mother uses either the rising intonation pattern of the typical Wh question ('Where's Diane?' or 'Where's baby?' or 'Where's mummy?') or employs an extended 'Ahhhh' sometimes with a rising intonation pattern. In one sense, this act on the part of the mother can be thought of as helping the child sustain attention and bridging any uncertainty concerning the mother's 'conservation' behind the hiding instrument. The child's responses during hiding seem, on the other hand, to be expressions of excitement or anticipation, though they help the mother control her own output of bridging vocalizations to keep the child at an appropriate activation level. There are thirteen in nineteen episodes involving a hiding cloth where the child actively seeks to remove the hiding mask from the mother's or her own face. It is to these initiatives that the mother often responds with vocalization as if to control the child's activation. This part of the game is characteristically 'non-rule bound' and seems to be an instance, rather, of the mother providing a scaffold for the child.

We come now to a crucial round in the game: uncovering and reappearance. Note first a point already made – hiding time is very constrained. Nineteen of the twenty-two episodes range between two and seven seconds, with only one being above seven (at ten months) and two at one second. It is only at 15 months, when the child consistently controls reappearance, that there is a fairly homogeneous and rapid hiding time: five episodes in a row ranging from one to two seconds. But note that at this age the child has virtually given up 'static' peekaboo for an ambulatory version so that variation is now in format rather than in timing. The five uniformly fast episodes were all with a nappy – an old and familiar game that is much less exciting for the child than the ambulatory game we shall describe below. One of these episodes, a one-second instance, was completely controlled by the child, and was an instance where the child demanded the game vocatively after she had failed to cover her own face successfully. We believe that the constraint on time of hiding is a reflection of the appreciation of the child's limited attention span by both members of the pair – the mother reacting to signs of the child's impatience, the child responding directly to his own.

The actual act of uncovering is open to considerable variation. We find instances where it is controlled by the child, others where the mother controls uncovering. Occasionally the mother, by drawing near and vocalizing, provokes the child into removing the mask from her face, as if to stimulate more control from the infant. Indeed, one even encounters partial, 'tempting' uncovering by the mother to provoke the child into completion, where the mother exposes a corner of her eye. In terms of control of unmasking, we note that before twelve months, nine of twelve of the episodes of unmasking are controlled by the mother. From twelve on, none are, and six in ten are controlled by the child alone – a phenomenon seen only once before this age.

Following uncovering, there is again a rather standard ritual: remaking contact. In the nineteen episodes where we were able to determine it, fourteen uncoverings were accompanied by face-to-face contact immediately or shortly after. In all instances of uncovering but one, mother sought to establish such contact, though in four she failed to do so. Moreover, in sixteen of twenty-two episodes, mother vocalized upon uncovering, usually with a 'boo' or a 'hello' or a 'ahhh'. Obviously, there is considerable release of tension at this point, since laughter accompanies the above fifteen times for the child (and indeed twelve for the mother, always in accompaniment with the child).

At 15 months, the child invents and controls a new variation of the game, as already noted. It consists of her moving behind a chair, out of sight of her mother, then reappearing and saying 'boo'. She has now become the agent in the play, mother being recipient of her action. The format has been revised by the child and the prior role of agent and recipient reversed. This variation in agency has, of course, appeared before in the more static form of the game involving a hiding instrument. But it is important to note that the child has now extended the rules under her own control to a new, but formally identical, format – again involving initial face-to-face contact, hiding and reappearing by self-initiated movement, and re-establishing contact. From there on in, peekaboo is a game embedded in self-directed movement by the child that produces disappearance and reappearance. The child has not only learned to conform to the rules of the static game as initiated by mother and by child, but also to use the rules for the initiation of a variant of the old format. At this point, the range of possible games incorporating the basic rules of peekaboo become almost limitless, and what provides unity is the agreement of mother and infant to maintain a skeleton rule structure with new instruments for hiding and new settings in which to play. We can say that at this point the child is no longer performance-bound, but rather has achieved a proper 'competence' for generating new versions of an old game.

But we must turn now to the question of what brought the child to a full realization of the 'syntax' of the game of peekaboo so that he can henceforth be fully 'generative' in his disappearance-reappearance play. Before we do so, however, we must examine briefly three of the other children on whom we have sufficient data for analysis.

In the case of Lynn and her mother, the pattern is much the same as described, save for the fact that she begins to take over the active role of initiator of the game and controller of the mask as early as ten months. She too, at ten months, begins to use a stationary object, a chair, as a hiding mask behind which she moves, looking through the legs to effect reappearance. But she is still quite confused about it and when mother says 'boo' to herald her reappearance, hides again rather than remaking contact. But she is on the way towards mastering the ambulatory variant.

Where Nan is concerned, the game is rather more sophisticated in an important respect. She and her mother share control. For example, at 11 months Nan lifts her petticoat over her face and leaves it in place until her mother says 'boo' and then lowers it. This joint feature is a very consistent aspect of their games, but it must be regarded as a variant, for instances occur without joint control as well. Their turn-taking is also much more precisely segmented. For example, Nan raises her petticoat over her face, then lowers it after a few seconds, and waits for mother to say 'boo' before showing any reaction herself – then usually responding to the mother's vocalizations with laughter. There is, in this instance, a separation between unmasking and vocalization, with a further timing element between the two.

Sandy and his mother are instances of a failure to develop workable rules because of excessive variation and some misreading by the mother. But the failure is instructive. Too often, the mother starts the game without having enlisted Sandy's attention. In other instances, when Sandy is having difficulty in hiding his own face behind a cloth, the mother takes the cloth (and the initiative) away from him and tries to do the masking herself. Interestingly, the game does not develop, and in its place there emerges a game in which Sandy crawls away from mother, she in pursuit, with excitement being exhibited by both when she catches him. He never serves as agent in this game. They are an instructive failure and the disappearance of the game is reminiscent of the failures reported by Nelson (1973) that occur when mother attempts to correct the child's linguistic usage or insists upon an interpretation of the child's utterance that does not accord with his own. Under the circumstances, the lexical items in question disappear from the child's lexicon, just as peekaboo disappears from the game repertory of this pair.

Discussion

When peekaboo first appears, our mothers often report, it is an extension or variation of a looming game in which the mother approaches the child from a distance of a metre or so, looms towards him almost face-to-face contact, accompanying the close approach with a 'boo' or a rising intonation. We know from the work of Bower (1971), Ball and Tronick (1971) and White (1963) that such looming produces considerable excitement and, indeed, when the loom is directly towards the face, a real or incipient avoidance response. The play may start by substituting disappearance of the face at a close point at which excitement has already been aroused. But this is not necessary. The only point one would wish to make is that, at the start, peekaboo involves an arousal of responses that are either innate or fairly close to innate. For even without the link to the looming game, disappearance and reappearance are 'manipulations' of object permanence, which is itself either innate or maturing through very early experience along the lines indicated by Piaget (1954). At least one can say unambiguously that at the outset, peekaboo is not a game in the sense of it being governed by rules and conventions that are, in any respect, arbitrary. It is, rather, an exploitation by the mother of very strong, pre-adapted response tendencies in the infant, an exploitation that is rewarded by the child's responsiveness and pleasure.

William James (1890) comments in the *Principles* that an instinct is a response that only occurs once, thereafter being modified by experience. And surely one could say the same for the interaction involved in peekaboo. For once it has occurred, there rapidly develops a set of reciprocal anticipations in mother and child that begin to modify it and, more importantly, to conventionalize it. At the outset, this conventionalization is fostered by a quite standard or routine set of capers on the part of the mother – as we have noted, the early version involves a very limited range of hiding instruments, masking acts, vocalizations and time variations. At the outset, it is also very important for mother to keep the child's activation level at an appropriate intensity, and one is struck by the skill of mothers in knowing how to keep the child in an anticipatory mood, neither too sure of outcome nor too upset by a wide range of possibilities.

But what is most striking thereafter is precisely the systematic introduction of variations constrained by set rules. The basic rules are:

Initial contact;
Disappearance;
Reappearance;
Re-established contact.

Within this rule context, there can be variations in degree and kind of vocalization for initial contact, in kind of mask, in who controls the mask, in whose face is masked, in who uncovers, in the form of vocalization upon uncovering, in the relation between uncovering and vocalization, and in the timing of the constituent elements (though this last is strikingly constrained by a capacity variable). What the child appears to be learning is not only the basic rules of the game, but the range of variation that is possible within the rule set. It is this emphasis upon patterned variation within a constraining rule set that seems crucial to the mastery of competence and generativeness. The process appears much as in concept attainment in which the child learns the regularity of a concept by learning the variants in terms of which it expresses itself. What is different in peekaboo is that the child is not only learning such variants, but obviously getting great pleasure from the process and seeking it out.

It is hard to imagine any function for peekaboo aside from practice in the learning of rules in converting 'gut play' into play with conventions. But there may be one additional function. As Garvey has noted, one of the objectives of play in general is to give the child opportunity to explore the boundary between the 'real' and the 'make-believe'. We have never in our sample of peekaboo games seen a child exhibit the sort of separation pattern noted by Ainsworth (1964) when mother *really* leaves the scene. Mothers often report, moreover, that they frequently start their career of playing peekaboo by hiding their own faces rather than the infant's for fear of his being upset. Eight of the nine mothers asked about this point reported behaving in this way (Scaife, 1974). This suggests a sensitivity on the part of mothers to where the line may be between 'real' and 'make-believe' for the child. This function doubtless dwindles in time. Yet the game continues in its formal pattern, sustained in its attractiveness by being incorporated into new formats involving newly emergent behaviours (such as crawling or walking). An old pattern seems, then, to provide a framework for the pleasurable expression of new behaviour and allows the new behaviour to be quickly incorporated into a highly skilled, rule-governed pattern.

(The authors wish to express their thanks to Ms Cathy Caston for her assistance in analysis of data.)

References

AINSWORTH, M. D. S. (1964), 'Patterns of attachment behavior shown by the infant in interaction with his mother', *Merrill-Palmer Quarterly*, No. 10, pp. 51–8.

BALL, W., and TRONICK, E. (1971), 'Infant responses to impending collision: optical and real', *Science*, No. 171, pp. 818–20.

BOWER, T. G. R. (1971), 'The object in the world of the infant', *Sci. American*, No. 225, pp. 30–38.

CHARLESWORTH, W. R. (1966), 'Persistence of orienting and attending behavior in infants as a function of stimulus-locus uncertainty', *Child Development*, No. 37, pp. 473–91.

GARVEY, C. (1974), 'Some properties of social play', *Merrill-Palmer Quarterly*, Vol. 20, No. 3, pp. 163–80. (And see this volume, p. 570.)

GREENFIELD, P. M. (1970), 'Playing peekaboo with a four-month-old: a study of the role of speech and nonspeech sounds in the formation of a visual schema', unpublished manuscript.

JAMES, W. (1890), *The Principles of Psychology*, Henry Holt, New York.

NELSON, K. (1973), 'Structure and strategy in learning to talk', *Monographs of The Society for Research in Child Development*, No. 38, pp. 1–137.

PIAGET, J. (1954), *The Construction of Reality in the Child*, Basic Books, New York.

SCAIFE, M. (1974), personal communication, Department of Experimental Psychology, Oxford University, Oxford.

WHITE, B. L. (1963), 'Plasticity in perceptual development during the first six months of life', paper presented to the American Association for the Advancement of Science, Cleveland, Ohio.

Cognitive Development Through Verbalized Play: The Mother–Child Home Programme

This is just one of the many programmes that use play as a means of deliberate pedagogy. It is designed to help mothers enrich their linguistic play with young children, capitalizing on the reciprocal routines that mothers and babies build jointly.

A major problem is posed to society by the personal and social consequences of the cumulative educational disadvantage suffered by a very large number of low-income school children in the U.S.A. Low-income infants' cognitive growth appears to proceed normally at least until about 20 months, but the intellectual development linked to later academic success seems to be closely tied to the child's verbal development within the family occurring between 20 months and four years (Bruner, 1964; Bruner *et al.*, 1966; Deutsch, 1963; Schaefer, 1970). The Mother–Child Home Programme was devised by the Verbal Interaction Project, starting with a pilot study in 1965 and continuing with full research in 1967, to reach down to this crucial verbal-cognitive learning period of the child's life for the purpose of preventing later educational handicap through the nurture of his early cognitive growth.

This project grew out of the conviction, based on considerable research evidence, that a child's intellectual development is closely linked to his verbal growth and that his mother can influence his cognitive development by the amount and quality of her verbal interaction with him. Whether she is aware of it or not, the mother of a pre-school child is likely to be the principal environmental agent of her child's intellectual growth. In this role, which is essentially that of a cognitive socializer, she is, as in all of her socialization of the child, the representative of the family, which is the major conduit from societal culture to the individual. The school, society's formal institution for cognitive socialization of the older child, must eventually assume a major part of her role. If the family, through the mother, has not laid a cognitive foundation to prepare the child for making the most of school experience, we are likely to hear once more the familiar cry of the educator, 'Too late!'

This cry is heard less often about the child whose home has been rich in verbal interaction between child and family and in the ordered sensory materials and experiences that make up the categories available to the child and his family for that verbal interaction (Brown, 1958). Such enrichment is to be found so often in families with relatively prosperous parents that we have come to speak of the 'hidden cognitive curriculum' of such families. The investigation to be described here explores the effects of helping some low-income families to assume the same function of incidental cognitive socialization which is apparently an important result of this 'curriculum'. This attempt to install such a 'curriculum' into the homes of low-income children to prepare them for later school achievement was an outgrowth of an earlier pilot study which suggested that low-income mothers could be helped by an intrinsically attractive, relatively simple and time-honoured means to assume major responsibility for their preschool children's verbal growth (Levenstein and Sunley, 1968).

The programme consisted of visits of interveners, called Toy Demonstrators, to low-income, mother–child dyads in their homes, starting when the child was about two years old, and continuing until he or she was about four.

The main activity of the Home session was demonstration to the mother, through a structured, yet fun-oriented, 'curriculum' of verbalized play with the child, how to interact verbally with her child to foster his or her conceptual growth. This demonstration was focused around Verbal Interaction Stimulus Materials brought as gifts by the Toy Demonstrator to the child in the first visit of each week.

The toy demonstrators

The goal of the Toy Demonstrator was to involve the mother in each play session with the child and to transfer the main responsibility for promoting verbal interaction to the mother as early in each session and the programme as possible. Although the role was pioneered in the pilot study and for the first year of full research by qualified social workers, it was then transferred to an educationally and vocationally varied group of relatively unscreened non-professionals trained by the original professionals. The new Toy Demonstrators proved as effective in two years as the professionals had been in one, and children treated by them retained their I.Q. gains into kindergarten with high psycho-social ratings by both nursery and kindergarten teachers. Paid, high-school-educated interveners with no prior job skills were as effective as volunteers with college degrees, some of them with experience as teachers.

In addition to the major task of emphasizing verbal categorization, the Toy Demonstrator used eight kinds of verbal-stimulation techniques. She:

1. Gave information (labels, form, colour, size, etc.);
2. Described her own toy manipulation (building, matching, etc.);

3. Elicited responses (questions, etc.);
4. Verbalized social interaction (invited, directed, etc.);
5. Encouraged reflection (alternatives, consequences, etc.);
6. Encouraged divergence (independence, curiosity, etc.);
7. Engaged interest in books (fostering 'representational competence' [Rosenthal, 1967] by eliciting verbalization about illustrations, etc.);
8. Gave positive reinforcement (verbal support, helping, etc.).

The Toy Demonstrators were instructed thus:

Treat the mother as a colleague in a joint endeavour on behalf of the child. Share your verbal stimulation techniques with her by demonstrating them in play with her child: then draw her into the play, and take a secondary role as soon as you can while she repeats and elaborates what she has seen you do. Encourage her to play and read with the child between Home Sessions. Keep constantly in mind that the child's primary and continuing educational relationship is with his mother; do all you can to enhance that relationship without stepping into a casework role.

The verbal interaction stimulus materials

Since the design of special stimulus materials for the programme would have made replicators dependent for programme supplies on our programme resources, a restricting and perhaps precarious procedure, only commercially available supplies were used. For a description of the criteria used for selecting these materials, see Appendix I.

Before giving the results of the several replication studies which have been conducted by organizations throughout the country, it might be best to detail the first full research project which began in Freeport, New York, in 1967 (follow-up and ongoing replication are still continuing).

The initial study

Design and subjects: A 'before-after' quasi-experimental design was followed, with the subjects fifty-four children, aged 20 to 43 months, and their mothers, divided into three geographically separated groups: Experimental ($N = 33$), Comparison$_1$ ($N = 9$), and Comparison$_2$ ($N = 12$). Classification as to the 'race' of the subjects was not made, as mothers were not asked for such self-identification, and interviewers were not 'required to make clinical judgements which a trained physical anthropologist would hesitate to make' (Gottesman, 1968). Probably at least ninety per cent of the dyads could be socially classified as 'Negro', an expected reflection of the over-representation of this (socially defined) ethnic group in this country's low-income population.

The means of the three groups were found to be similar on many other background variables: children's ages, parents' ages, parents' education;

number of parents who were reared to adolescence in the South; education of grandparents; rate of fathers' unemployment; proportion of mothers employed full time and of those receiving welfare support; the amount of cognitive stimulation in the home; the differing physical 'comfort' standards of the structurally similar homes; the physical condition of the children (except for one child in the Experimental group with a motor handicap). The families were large, ranging from a mean of five for families in the Comparison$_2$ group to six in the Experimental families. The small differences in background variables which did emerge tended to favour the Comparison$_2$ group in the direction of higher socio-economic status.

Procedure: The Home Sessions are described above: the thirty-three Experimental mother–child dyads were visited for an average of 32·4 Home Sessions by the Toy Demonstrator.

To control for the Hawthorne effect on the Experimental group of a positive response to the visits, gifts, and attention to the Toy Demonstrator rather than to the stimulation of verbal interaction, the children in the Comparison$_1$ group were exposed during the intervention period to an average of twenty-four non-verbally stimulating visits by a social worker. Each week she brought 'non-Verbal Interaction Stimulus Materials' as gifts to the child and his siblings at home during visits (to equalize for the Experimental children's siblings' opportunity to play with the subjects' Verbal Interaction Stimulus Materials). Her activity was to sit in the same room with the child, kindly but deliberately avoiding verbal interchange, and occasionally playing children's records on a portable phonograph. Mothers were encouraged not to be present.

The children in the Comparison$_2$ group received no intervention beyond the tests.

The Cattell or Stanford-Binet Intelligence Scales and the Peabody Picture Vocabulary Test were used to measure the general and verbal cognitive status of all the children before and after the seven months of intervention for the Experimental and Comparison$_1$ groups. In addition, all mothers were tested (Peabody Picture Vocabulary Test) and interviewed before and after intervention, four kinds of ongoing data were compiled on the Experimental group, and two kinds on the Comparison$_2$ groups. Most of the Experimental and Comparison$_1$ group mothers filled out anonymous evaluations of their respective programmes at mid-intervention.

Since the psychologist examining the children before and after the intervention was unable to test blind, an elaborate procedure was followed to detect the presence, if any, of unconscious bias on the part of the examiner. The post-intervention test sessions were tape-recorded in randomized positions on pre-prepared tapes. The tape-recorded sessions were identified only by the date and the child's name. Four judges unfamiliar with the investigation and drawn from the fields of psychology and child development were then asked to listen to twelve (randomized) test sessions and to make a judgement from the examiner's treatment of the child as to the child's membership in the Experimental or Comparison groups.* This procedure was followed in order to identify the presence of bias in the examiner which might influence the subject's post-intervention test functioning and thus the final effect of the intervention as seen in the post-test I.Q. scores. (The procedure was suggested by Rosenthal's observation (1967) regarding the sound filming of an experimenter's instructions to subjects: that the experimenter's bias, which influenced the subjects' later performances, was apparent to judges from the sound track of the film alone.) Of the forty-eight professionally experienced judgements as to the Experimental or Comparison group membership of the child, twenty were correct and twenty-eight were incorrect, a difference no greater than chance. Further, the twenty-eight incorrect judgements were almost evenly distributed between the Experimental and Comparison groups, with fifteen incorrect judgements of the group membership of the Experimental children and thirteen incorrect judgements of the group membership of the Comparison children. Thus there appeared to be no examiner bias in favour of either the Experimental or Comparison group.

Results.† As predicted, and as shown in Table 1, the Experimental group children demonstrated a mean gain of 17 I.Q. points on the Cattell and Stanford-Binet tests, which was significantly higher (at the ·001 level) than that of one point for the Comparison$_1$ group and two points for the Comparison$_2$ group. The prediction of a rise in verbal I.Q. for the Experimental children was also confirmed, although not as markedly in comparison with the other two groups. The Experimental children's mean Peabody Picture Vocabulary Test gain of 12·2 I.Q. points was significantly higher (at the ·01 level) than the Comparison$_1$ children's loss of 4 points, though no higher than chance over the 4·7 gain of the Comparison$_2$ children.

Replication studies

Following the success of this initial Mother–Child Home Programme and its repetition in 1968 and 1969, it was decided to test the programme in a variety of organizations representing different services and geographical settings – all outside of the laboratory and its concomitant specialized

*Appreciation is expressed to the judges: Dr Eric Aronson, Mrs Renee Meer, Dr Samuel Meer, Dr Margaret Woerner.

†Analysis of other variables may be found in 'Cognitive Growth in Pre-Schoolers Through Verbal Interaction with Mothers' (Levenstein, 1970).

Table 1 Intelligence test means – Experimental (E), Comparison₁ (C₁), and Comparison₂ (C₂) groups

Test	E Group			C₁ Group			C₂ Group			Difference E and C₁ Groups		Difference E and C₂ Groups	
	N	Mean	S.D.	N	Mean	S.D.	N	Mean	S.D.	t	Significance[a]	t	Significance[a]
Pre-test													
Children – C or SB[b]	33	84.9	10.5	9	87.4	11.0	11	92.0	9.7	0.62	n.s.	1.92	n.s.
Children – PPVT[c]	29	76.8	7.4	9	82.6	8.0	10	84.1	12.9	1.93	n.s.	2.12	$p < 0.05$
Mothers – PPVT	26	82.5	16.4	9	86.0	15.2	10	87.8	13.9	0.55	n.s.	0.88	n.s.
Post-test													
Children – C or SB	33	101.9	14.7	9	88.4	9.5	11	94.0	8.8	2.55	$p < 0.05$	1.66	n.s.
Children – PPVT	29	89.0	12.6	9	78.6	12.3	10	88.8	13.0	2.13	$p < 0.05$	0.04	n.s.
Mothers – PPVT	26	84.2	13.6	9	82.8	9.3	10	87.5	14.8	0.29	n.s.	0.61	n.s.
Change													
Children – C or SB	33	+17.0	10.6	9	+1.0	9.0	11	+2.0	9.3	4.03	$p < 0.001$	4.08	$p < 0.001$
Children – PPVT	29	+12.2	12.3	9	−4.0	9.6	10	+4.7	16.3	3.51	$p < 0.01$	1.48	n.s.
Mothers – PPVT	26	+1.8	8.7	9	−3.2	11.8	10	−0.3	7.4	1.3	n.s.	0.65	n.s.

[a]Two-tailed test. [b]Cattel or Stanford-Binet. [c]Peabody Picture Vocabulary Test.

conditions. The four organizations involved in the programme between October 1970 and June 1971 were: an inner city family service agency in a medium-sized New Jersey city ($N = 10$); a family service agency in the suburbs of Boston ($N = 3$); a public school system in a small Massachusetts city ($N = 16$); and a private child welfare agency in New York City ($N = 8$). The target population ranged over four differing groups of children vulnerable to educational disadvantage (inner city black, small city black and white, suburban mixed ethnic origin, and black foster home children). The results showed a combined general I.Q. gain of 16·2 points for the 37 pre-schoolers in the four programmes. The children had begun these programmes with a mean general I.Q. of 89·8, which was increased to a mean general I.Q. of 106·0. The testing of thirty-two of the thirty-seven children yielded both a pre- and post-test verbal I.Q., which rose 10·3 points from a mean pre-test verbal I.Q. of 79·5 to a mean post-test verbal I.Q. of 89·8. Both I.Q. differences were statistically significant at the ·001 level.

Interestingly, the children in the model Mother–Child Home Programme beginning their first year in the programme in October 1970 presented a similar intellectual picture. Thirty-seven Verbal Interaction Project children gained 17·5 points in general I.Q., from a pre-test general I.Q. of 88·1 to a post-test general I.Q. of 105·6, a difference that is statistically significant at the ·005 level. Their verbal I.Q. gains were lower than those of replicator subjects, a mean of 5·0 points from a mean pre-test verbal I.Q. of 85·2 to a mean post-test verbal I.Q. of 90·2, a difference still statistically significant at the ·025 level. The data for these programmes is given in Table 2, and those for later replication studies in Table 3.

Discussion

It seems clear that not only was dramatic cognitive gain associated with the experimental intervention but that it was linked within the programme to the attempt to stimulate verbal interaction in the mother-child dyad. Of major importance is the fact that such learning can take place in the home, with major involvement of the mother, even when the mother has limited mastery of symbolic modes of representation and is harried by the problems of large families and small income. The continued co-operation and enthusiasm of almost all the mothers is an impressive demonstration of the willingness of women to extend themselves on behalf of their children's preparation for education: keeping appointments, welcoming strangers into their homes, duplicating the Toy Demonstrator's activity within the limits of their ability, supervising the care of the toys – all the adjustments which had to be made by mothers participating in the programme.

The Mother – Child Home Programme seems to capitalize on already

Table 2 Intelligence test results, mother–child home programme, replications and model programme, 1970–71

Test	Model programme			Replicated programme		
	N	Mean	SD	N	Mean	SD
Pre-test I.Q.:						
Cattell (General)	37	88·1	10·7	37	89·8	13·4
PPVT (Verbal)	37	85·2	11·2	32	79·5	13·1
Post-test I.Q. (after 1 year):						
Stanford-Binet (General)	37	105·6	14·5	37	106·0	17.0
PPVT (Verbal)	37	90·2	15·9	32	89·8	14·6
I.Q. Difference, pre-test vs. post-test:						
Cattell, Binet (General)	37	17·5†	11·7	37	16·3‡	10·7
PPVT (Verbal)	37	5·0*	13·9	32	10·3‡	15·0

*$p < 0.025$
†$p < 0.005$
‡$p < 0.001$

Table 3 Verbal interaction project (VIP)/mother–child home programme (MCHP) VIP/Mother – Child home programme replicators, 1970–72, general IQ results

Replicator	Year	Pre-test		Post-test-1		Post-test-2		Difference	
		N	I.Q.	N	I.Q.	N	I.Q.	Pre-P1	Pre-P2
1. Paterson, N. J. Family Counselling	1970–72	7	88·9	7	97·6	7	99·0	8·7	10·1
Serv.	1971–72	7	96·6	7	98·3	—	—	1·7	—
2. Newton, Massachusetts Family Counselling Serv. (Region	1970–72	5	87·8	4	106·5	5	106·6	15·3	18·8
West)	1971–72	5	107·0	5	115·8	—	—	8·8	—

Table 3 *(cont.)*

Replicator	Year	Pre-test		Post-test-1		Post-test-2		Difference	
		N	I.Q.	N	I.Q.	N	I.Q.	Pre-P1	Pre-P2
3. Pittsfield, Mass.	1970–72	16	92·2	16	116·0	16	109·9	23·7†	17·6†
Public Schools	1971–72	27	97·4	27	111·4	—	—	14·0†	—
4. New York, New York	1970–72	6	83·8	6	97·0	6	98·0	13·2‡	14·2†
Sheltering Arms Childrens Serv.	1971–72	6	91·7	6	94·2	—	—	2·5	—
5. Norristow, Penna. Family Services of Montgomery County	1971–72	8	91·2	6	107·2	—	—	15·8*	—
6. Conway Springs, Kansas Public Schools	1971–72	6	102·7	6	109·0	—	—	6·8*	—
7. Albuquerque, New Mexico Bureau of Indian Affairs (Apache and Pueblo Tribes)	1971–72	11	89·7	11	95·5	—	—	4·7	—
(Control Group, Tested only)	(1971–72)	(10	86·3)	(10	85·6)	(—	—)	(0·7	—)
8. Mineola, New York Nassau County Family Day Care	1971–72	9	97·3	NA		—	—	NA	—
Total (excluding BIA Controls)	1971–72	114	94·0	102	106·0	34	105·1	12·0‡	15·6‡

*p < 0·05
†p < 0·01
‡p < 0·001
(t-test, two-tailed)

existing positive intra-family variables in low-income families to enhance the child's cognitive growth while simultaneously strengthening family ties. The value question of whether such ties should be reinforced cannot, of course, be decided empirically. But note should be taken of the view of Hobart (1963) that the family 'remains a necessary condition of the development and expression of humanity', a protection against the proliferation of the 'Cheerful Robot' described by Mills (1959) as being an anti-democratic, typological trend of the times.

The experimental programme tested in these investigations, with its easy replication at relatively modest expense, may well make a small but important contribution to the intactness of the low-income family at a period of the pre-school child's life when he (like the young child in other income groups) is most in need of family nurture.

Appendix 1
Criteria for choice of toys

The toys selected should appeal to sensory, motor and intellectual needs. They should catch and hold the child's attention, provide repetition, and stimulate new kinds of exploration. Specifically, the toys should have strong primary and secondary colours so that the child can learn and repeat their names. They should come in a variety of sizes so that he can learn the meaning of big, little, medium-sized – and even tiny, huge, larger, smallest. There should be many shapes among them: squares, circles, triangles, oblongs. Some objects should fit into others so that Johnny can learn to distinguish (and say) which forms go together.

There should be opportunities for sorting parts by many kinds of classifications: by colour, by size, by shape, by what they can do. The toys should be explored for the kinds of sound they make – clacking or ringing, for example – and for how they feel – soft, hard, rough, smooth.

The motor possibilities for the child to put into words should include building (as with blocks), pushing (cars), pulling (wheeled toys on a string). The small owner should be able to fit parts together and separate them, both with large actions (fitting round blocks into round holes) or with small ones (putting small jigsaw puzzle pieces together). The actions required should not be too easy, so that he has the satisfaction of seeing his motor skills grow.

Learning the language for the characteristics of the toys will develop his conceptual ability – in other words, his ability to build larger ideas from smaller ones while refining his baby-vague notions about the world. For instance, he will learn that red, brown, green, and blue are all colours and that not every four-legged creature is a dog or a cow.

Toys should stretch his imagination by inviting fantasy and make-believe play. They should also offer possibilities for inventing novel uses. In short, they should develop creativity. A child's attempts to devise unconventional ways of playing with a particular toy should be encouraged and, like his other play activities, be put into words for him by the person playing with him.

A most important feature for conceptual growth is the toy's challenge to problem-solving. The problem should be just enough beyond the child's developmental level to present an interesting difference between what is familiar and known and what is not. The door on the little car, for example, should have a special way of being opened instead of just being pulled. The jointed legs on little animals should have to be angled just so for the animal to stand up.

When the difficulty of the problem is well matched to the child's stage of comprehension, the toy is automatically interesting to him – 'amusing', as the dictionary puts it. The triple result is that his wish to learn is greatly heightened; with the help of language, he does indeed learn from his experience; and his sense of competence is once again confirmed so he is eager to take on another challenge.

Like toys, the content of the toddler's picture books should be geared to his age and interests, yet should widen his experience and lead easily into discussions of illustrations or events in the story. The books should be of high literary quality, even though the language must be simple and even repetitious. There should be an illustration on almost every page, and the pictures should be clear, colourful and detailed.

Not only are pictures a good source of labelling and classifying words, but they can lead to what one psychologist calls representational competence – the ability to recognize three-dimensional objects presented in flat two-dimensional form, an important skill for schoolwork.

It is an old saying that play is the work of the young child. The truth of the statement is apparent when we think of a child's work as learning to learn. The main tool for this task of toddlers is language; toys provide the material with which they work.

References

BROWN, R. (1958), *Words and Things*, Free Press, Glencoe, Illinois.

BRUNER, J. (1964), 'The course of cognitive growth', *Amer. Psychol.*, No. 19, pp. 1–15.

BRUNER, J., et al. (1966), *Studies in Cognitive Growth*, Wiley, New York.

DEUTSCH, M. (1963), 'The disadvantaged child and the learning process', in *Education in Depressed Areas*, A. H. Passow (ed.), Teachers College, New York.

GOTTESMAN, I. (1968), 'Biogenetics of race and class', in *Social Class, Race, and Psychological Development*, N. Deutsch, I. Katz, and A. R. Jensen (eds), Holt, Rinehart & Winston, New York.

HOBART, C. (1963), 'Commitment, value conflict and the future of the American family', *Mar. & Fam. Living*, No. 25, pp. 405–14.

LEVENSTEIN, P. (1970), 'Cognitive growth in preschoolers through verbal interaction with mothers', *American Journal of Orthopsychiatry*, No. 40, pp. 426–32.

LEVENSTEIN, P. (1971a), 'Are toys passé?', *The P.T.A. Magazine*, November, 1971.

LEVENSTEIN, P. (1971b), 'Learning through (and from) mothers', *Childhood Education*, December 1971, pp. 130–34.

LEVENSTEIN, P. (1972), 'But does it work away from home?', *Theory into Practice*, No. 11, pp. 157–62.

LEVENSTEIN, P. (1973), 'Research in the real world: recent data on the Mother-Child Home Program', paper presented at a Colloquium, Department of Psychology, Yale University on 31 October 1973.

LEVENSTEIN, P., KOCHMAN, A., and ROTH, H. A. (1973), 'From laboratory to real world: Service delivery of the Mother-Child Home Program', *American Journal of Orthopsychiatry*, Vol. 43, No. 1, pp. 72–8.

LEVENSTEIN, P., and LEVENSTEIN, S. (1971), 'Fostering learning potential in preschoolers', *Social Casework*, No. 52, pp. 74–8.

LEVENSTEIN, P., and SUNLEY, R. (1968), 'Stimulation of verbal interaction between disadvantaged mothers and children', *American Journal of Orthopsychiatry*, No. 38, pp. 116–21.

MILLS, C. W. (1959), *The Sociological Imagination*, Oxford University Press.

ROSENTHAL, R. (1967), 'Unintended communication of interpersonal expectations', *Amer. Behav. Scien.*, pp. 24–6.

SCHAEFER, E. S. (1970), 'The need for early and continuing education', in *Education of the Infant and Young Child*, Vol. 2, Denenberg (ed.), Academic Press, New York.

B Co-operation and Competition

Sibling Relationships and Play among Wild Chimpanzees

Sibling relationships

To date we have only been able to study the relationships between comparatively few known siblings. The following will serve merely as a general outline of the type of interactions which may occur between offspring of different ages of the same female. I hope to publish a fuller report, with quantitative details, in the future.

Touching, grooming and playing amongst siblings

Touching during the early months. The efforts of the juvenile Fifi to touch, groom and play with her sibling Flint at this time have been described. When Flint was 3 months old he was seen, for the first time, touching and being touched by his elder siblings, Figan and Faben (adolescent males about 8 to 11 years of age respectively). These early contacts usually took place when the mother was socially grooming with the son concerned.

The first time Flint was seen to touch Figan the latter stared with slightly open mouth and then turned away. The following day Flint again touched Figan, and after a few moments Figan stroked Flint's hand with his foot. After this Figan, for several days in succession, reached towards Flint and cupped the infant's hand with his own, or gently held his arm. Gradually playful patting, kicking or tickling movements took the place of these early touchings. On three occasions when Flint (during his fourth and fifth months) reached towards Figan and gripped hold of his hair the elder sibling responded by leaning slightly away, raising his hands with the fingers turned in and away from Flint and giving a 'hoo' whimper with a pout face. Flint, in each instance, was with his juvenile sibling Fifi and Figan kept darting quick looks in the direction of their mother Flo who was several yards away. Once Flint also gave a 'hoo' whimper and when Flo hurried up to rescue the infant Figan raised his arms even higher and his pout became more pronounced. It seems likely that Figan's gestures were made with relation to the mother, but the motivation was unclear.

When Flint reached towards his eldest sibling Faben, the latter normally responded by gently patting or briefly grooming the infant. Sometimes he appeared to ignore him, however, and once when Flint whimpered and appeared to try and cling ventrally, Faben also raised his hands and whimpered softly as the mother approached to retrieve her infant.

Two other siblings, Little Bee and Honey Bee, were observed only at very infrequent intervals during the first year of Honey Bee's life. When their interactions were recorded, however, the juvenile female, Little Bee, in marked contrast to Fifi, paid little attention to the new sibling. Indeed, even when the infant reached out to touch her, Little Bee often ignored her sibling completely.

The relationship between the juvenile female Gilka and her infant sibling Grosvenor was not comparable to the above sibling relationship since Grosvenor became ill and died of a paralytic disease during his second month. Prior to this illness I saw Gilka on two occasions cautiously touch his hand whilst grooming her mother. The day before the infant's death, when he was obviously ill and whimpering frequently, Gilka touched and groomed him on and off for about twenty minutes during social grooming with her mother. The latter did not attempt to interfere with this be-haviour. After the infant was dead Gilka constantly reached out to touch the body, both when it was being carried by the mother and when it was lying on the ground. She also groomed the corpse and tried to initiate play, pulling the hand of the dead infant to her and, as she made poking move-ments with it, showing the play face and 'laughing'.

Play between siblings. When Flint was able to totter about on his own feet (from 5 months onwards) his three siblings all played with him frequently, particularly Fifi, who was with him almost constantly during the second half of his first year. Throughout Flint's second year of life playful interactions between him and his three siblings continued to be frequent; they became more boisterous and lasted for longer periods of time. During his third year he still played constantly with Fifi, but slightly less often, though still vigorously, with his elder brothers.

In all cases but one, infants of less than 3 years of age frequently played and were played with by elder siblings. Thus Merlin, when he was between 2 and 3 years of age, played with both Miff and Pepe; Gilka, until she was about 3 years old, played often with her brother Evered; and Fifi, Figan and Faben all played together on many occasions until 1965 after which they gradually did so less and less. Playful interactions between Little Bee and Honey Bee, however, were relatively infrequent. Thus on the irregular occasions that this family was observed when Honey Bee was between 8 and 17 months, she was seen playing on forty-seven occasions. Of these, eight sessions involved the two siblings only – six of them were initiated by Honey Bee, and only two by the elder sister. Twelve of the sessions were already in progress between Little Bee and another youngster when Honey Bee joined in. And the remainder did not involve the elder sibling at all. In addition Honey Bee was seen to try to initiate play with Little Bee on six occasions when she was ignored. Subsequent interactions have not yet been extracted from the notes, but if the two siblings did play more frequently, it was only slightly.

Grooming. As we have seen, small infants were often groomed briefly by their elder siblings, and the former, particularly when they were over 2 years old, occasionally groomed their elder siblings during grooming sessions involving the family as a whole. Fifi, Gilka and Miff, as juveniles, all groomed their adolescent brothers occasionally, although the latter rarely reciprocated, and Fifi (rarely) and Miff (more often) groomed their elder brothers when the former became adolescents. Figan and Faben were never observed to groom each other as juveniles or adolescents, but began to do so when both were socially mature.

Social play and social grooming

These two activities bring chimpanzees into close physical contact for long periods of time. It can be said in general that chimpanzees groom more and play less frequently as they grow older. It is probably also true that the decrease in play is approximately proportionate to the increase in the intensity and length of grooming sessions, but confirmation of this must await more complete analysis of the data. In captive individuals, the behaviour of young pairs of chimpanzees as compared with that of adult pairs showed that the former made more than sixteen times as many social contacts as the adults, most of them during social play; but that the older animals surpassed the young ones in social grooming (Mason, 1965).

(a) *Social play*

Play has been the subject of argument and controversy (as to definition, causation and function) for a long time. However, despite the difficulties involved in making a concise definition, Mason (1965a) has pointed out that observers show considerable agreement in judging whether behaviour is playful: he describes playful responses as being part of the 'heightened responsiveness of youth'.

Nearly all field studies on primates have reported frequent play amongst young animals (e.g. Jay, 1963; DeVore, 1963) and the literature contains many references to the playful behaviour of infant and juvenile chimpanzees both in the wild (Nissen, 1931; Reynolds and Reynolds, 1965) and in captivity (e.g. Yerkes, 1943; Hayes, 1952).

Infant chimpanzees in the wild, once they have attained locomotor independence, spend much of the day in playful activity, either on their own or with conspecifics, when they are not sleeping or feeding. The bouts are short, about five minutes, at 9 months but often last thirty to forty minutes in the third and fourth year. Juveniles also play frequently, although they spend more time in feeding and other social activities such as grooming. From puberty onwards the frequency of play decreases and bouts seldom last more than ten minutes. Nevertheless adolescents of both sexes played on many occasions, as did mature males and mothers of infants. Mature females without infants have been seen playing only on rare occasions, with the recent exception of one female (Gigi).

Play sessions may involve two or more individuals of the same or different age groups.

When a group of adults is resting or grooming, the youngsters (if any are present) usually form such a play group near by. Play sessions vary from a few seconds to over an hour: those involving 3- to 6-year-olds were usually the longest.

Play behaviour. Typically play was initially non-aggressive although amongst juveniles and adolescents and even older infants play sessions sometimes became aggressive. Behaviour classified as social play consisted of chasing, wrestling, sparring (when one individual hits towards another who fends him off, and vice versa), play biting, thumping and kicking (when the playmate is hit hard with the palm or knuckle of one or both hands or the heel or sole of the foot), butting with the head and a variety of 'tickling' and poking movements. Tickling was done either with the mouth, when the animal made a series of nibbling nuzzling movements with the lips pulled inwards over the teeth or with the hands when the chimpanzee made prodding flexing movements of the fingers in the same way as does a human when tickling. A variant on this was 'finger wrestling' when an individual (usually mature male) reached to the hand or foot of another and made gentle tickling, pulling and squeezing movements. During play sessions, chimpanzees made use of a wide variety of the objects of their environment: they climbed, jumped, swung and dangled from branches of trees, chased round tree trunks, broke off and waved or carried branches, leaves, or fruit clusters, grappled with each other for an assortment of small objects, dragged and hit each other with branches, and so on.

Two patterns and one call which were only observed in the play context were the 'play walk', and the 'play face' (the 'relaxed open-mouth face' of van Hooff, 1967) and 'laughing'. The play walk occurred during initiation of play and during play sessions: the chimpanzee walks with rounded back, head slightly bent down and pulled back between shoulders, and takes small almost 'stilted' steps. Often there is a side-to-side movement as he moves forward, rather like a seaman's roll.

It has been stated that an important aspect of social play in mammals is that social inhibitions are normally maintained, even when the play is violent (Lorenz, cited in Thorpe, 1956). Play between two or more adolescent male chimpanzees, however, often ended with one of the group being hurt and running off screaming, and on a number of occasions play ended in fighting. Adolescent males sometimes also became rough when they played with juveniles, causing the latter to run off screaming. I only saw adolescents become slightly boisterous with infants on four occasions, and juveniles were normally gentle with younger animals as well. Play between infants sometimes ended with one screaming and hitting at the other, which then often hit back: this type of situation either resulted in one of the mothers threatening her own offspring's playmate or, occasionally, in the higher-ranking of the two mothers attacking the other.

Initiation of play session. The method used to initiate play varied with the age of the individual in relation to its chosen play partner. Thus a 2-year-old infant usually walked slowly to a younger one and gently reached out to pat or tickle it, whereas when initiating play with a peer or older animal it often ran up with a boisterous play walk or gambol and flung itself onto the other, hitting, mock-biting, flailing or kicking. Infants often bounced after mature or adolescent males grabbing hold of their feet or ankles as they walked; often the male concerned kicked backwards, sometimes quite hard, but, apparently, playfully. Sometimes infants approached a chosen playmate with a play walk whilst holding some 'toy' and, if the other reached to grab this, the initiator ran off looking back over its shoulder. This often started a play session.

Juveniles normally initiated play, either with peers or infants, by simply approaching and reaching out to thump or tickle the chosen playmate. Sometimes they approached with a play walk. Adolescent females and young adolescent males initiated play with peers or younger individuals in a similar manner.

Older adolescent males and adult males, on most occasions when they initiated play with younger animals, showed the play walk and, as mentioned above, one usually showed a play face. The male then either reached to tickle or thump the chosen partner, or walked past the other, often kicking back one foot and sometimes starting to move round a tree, often the youngster followed and a session began. Mature males initiated play with other adults either by 'finger wrestling' (often when both individuals were lying resting close to each other) or, occasionally, with patting, tickling movements under the chin of the chosen partner, particularly when the latter was an adult female.

There were, of course, occasions when playful approaches of the above-mentioned kind were ignored: the individual who had been approached either made no move at all, or moved away, or, rarely, mildly threatened the other (if the latter was subordinate). Some juveniles, adolescents and females often seemed afraid when mature males tried to play with them.

One adolescent for instance, when a male four times approached him with a play walk and tickled him, only 'grinned', presented and tried to creep away.

Frequency. Figure 1 shows the frequency of play in the different age and

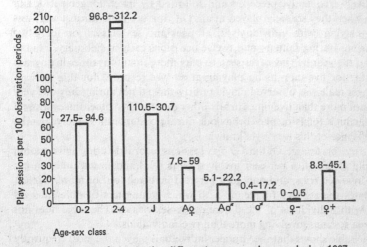

Fig. 1. Frequency of play in the different age-sex classes during 1967. Figures above columns represent the range of play per 100 observation periods for each class.

sex classes during one year. It demonstrates clearly the marked increase of frequency in play behaviour during the second half of infancy, and the gradual decline as the chimpanzee grows older. The comparatively high frequency of play behaviour in mothers with infants has been discussed elsewhere* – it represents mainly play behaviour directed towards their own infants together with some play with their infants' playmates. Only once was a mature female (a mother) seen playing with another mature female (also a mother): the two tickled and wrestled as they lay on the ground. Mature females without infants were observed to play only on two or three occasions during 1967 but one is frequently doing so in 1968.

The fact that mature males play as often as they do is of interest since this class of animal has only been observed playing in a few other primate species to date. Adult male bonnet macaques and rhesus monkeys have been recorded playing quite frequently (Simonds, 1965; Kaufmann, 1967). I have seen mature males (and females) in a troop of red colobus monkeys joining in chasing games on a number of occasions and twice seen adult male baboons playing with slightly younger adult male baboons at the

* See this volume p. 262.

Gombe Stream Reserve. This has not yet been reported in baboons from other areas.

Examination of data collected on male chimpanzees playing during 1967 revealed that some individuals had 'playful phases' when they played relatively frequently, preceded and followed by much longer periods of time when they scarcely played at all. One mature male for instance, was seen playing (with individuals of all ages and sex classes) on forty-two occasions during January and twelve occasions early in February. For the rest of the year he was never seen to play more than four times in any one month; for five months no playing at all was recorded for this male. A younger male was observed playing thirty-three times during July one year and not more than five times in any other month. Two other males showed similar high totals of play behaviour during one month of the year. The significance of this is not yet known.

Partner preference. Of the 539 play sessions recorded during a two-month sample seventy-five per cent involved pairs of chimpanzees, nineteen per cent involved trios, and only four per cent involved four or more. Table 1 indicates the relative frequency with which youngsters of different ages play with individuals of the different age–sex classes. The table does not include sessions involving more than two individuals.

The table shows that the younger individuals played the most frequently with other infants; older individuals spent increasingly more time in playing with juveniles and older animals. The three youngest infants played more frequently with adult females – in all cases these were the mothers of their playmates – and the interactions occurred when the play sessions were taking place close to the mothers of the youngsters concerned.

The percentage of occasions when infants played with their mothers reflects, for the most part, differences in individuality of the mothers concerned. The table shows that the youngest infant played frequently with her sibling (Sniff) and he frequently interrupted grooming sessions with his mother to play with the infant. Infants younger than five to six months seldom play outside the family circle since attempts made by other infants to play with them are normally repulsed by the mother. This means that small infants without siblings seldom play socially except with their mothers. Flint did not play during the months represented in Table 1 with either of his elder brothers (although during some other months he played fairly frequently with his mature male brother). Gilka did not play with her mature male sibling, nor was she seen to at any time since 1965.

Table 2 shows the frequency with which the two mature male classes and the mature females (all mothers with infants) played with the other age–sex classes as a percentage of the number of times that each was seen to play during 1967.

Table 1 Percentage of relative frequency with which individual youngsters of different ages played with the different age–sex classes during two months

| Age in years | Infants | | | | | | | Juveniles | |
	1·1 Sorema	1·9 Mustard	2·2 Pom	2·8 Cindy	3·1 Goblin	3·6 Flint	Gilka	6 to 7 Sniff	Sherry
Infants	57	88	79	69	62	32	20	66	59
Juveniles		3	3	12	20	20	80	14	25
Mothers	9	6	15	17	7	19			
Siblings	28*					15†	‡	13§	
Adolescent females					4	2		5	9
Adolescent males				1	4	4			3
Mature Males				1	3	6		2	4
Mature Females	6	3	3			2			
Total number of sessions	35	72	63	97	144	254	18	78	44

* Juvenile male (Sniff)
† Adolescent female (Fifi)
‡ Young mature male (Evered). Gilka had no sibling
§ Infant (Sorema)

The play sessions between class 1 males and adult females were all initiated by the males concerned. In most cases the females' infants then joined in the play. Often the latter got hurt by the slightly rough play of the male and whimpered or screamed. On these occasions either the infant leapt ventral to the mother or she reached out to embrace it: in either case this appeared to stimulate aggression in the male who sometimes attacked the female.

One point which may be mentioned here is that one female (Fifi) when she was a juvenile, played frequently with class 1 males. That this was a result of Fifi's individuality is suggested by the fact that even during that year other juveniles were not seen playing with class 1 males.

Conditions which may inhibit play behaviour. Mason (1965b) measured

Table 2 Percentage of relative frequency with which mature chimpanzees played with the different age–sex classes during one year

	Class 1	Class 2	Mature female
Class 1 males	4	12	4
Class 2 males	10	0	0
Mature Females	17	0	<1
Adolescent females	<1	13	0
Adolescent males	2	0	0
Juveniles	0	4	0
Infants	66	70	3
Own infants	0	0	93
Total no. sessions	134	81	455

the frequency of the play response over clinging and grooming in pairs of young captive chimpanzees and found that play was always commonest unless the animals were frightened or in unfamiliar surroundings. Other conditions which may prohibit play are extremes of environmental pressures such as heat, cold, wet and the presence of predators, or adverse physiological pressures such as the need for food, drink, sleep or a sexual partner (Lorenz, 1956; Bally, 1945 – both cited in Loizos, 1967).

Conditions of the above type normally appeared to inhibit play amongst wild chimpanzees. Sometimes during heavy rain, however, youngsters, after sitting huddled for a while, began to play vigorously, either on their own or with a partner*. Once they had become really wet and cold, however, they were not observed to play. There were also instances when adolescent or young mature males who were frustrated in feeding situations at the feeding area, directed a type of aggressive play towards other individuals. One adolescent male under such circumstances often approached his sibling with a play walk and buffeted her violently. The latter sometimes responded playfully but more often showed avoidance, in which case she was several times mildly attacked.

Recent evidence from laboratories has stressed not only the importance of the mother but also of play between peers for the normal development of social behaviour in rhesus monkeys (e.g. Harlow and Harlow, 1962). Thus infants raised on artificial, cloth mothers but allowed to play with a peer group for twenty minutes daily became socially normal adults despite

*It is interesting to consider in this context, the branch-waving displays of older chimpanzees which occurred at the start of, or during, heavy rain. Possibly the motivation is similar for both infant and adult.

the lack of normal mothering. On the other hand, infants raised in isolation with their mothers for eight months before their first introduction to others of their age also quickly learned complex social play patterns although certain fearful and hostile characteristics were still evident during their third year of life (and would probably persist) (Harlow and Harlow, 1966).

In the wild the relative value of interactions with mother or play with peers must, of necessity, be influenced by the fact that the animals are constantly interacting with all other members of the social unit. Nevertheless there is one type of situation which has occurred amongst the Gombe Stream chimpanzees which is of interest in this context. An infant chimpanzee (Merlin) who lost his mother when he was approximately 3 years old, gradually became emaciated, listless and socially abnormal. He developed a number of stereotyped behaviours of the sort normally associated with varying degrees of social deprivation in laboratory-reared chimpanzees. These included rocking, hair pulling, and hanging upside down from his feet for several minutes with scarcely any movement. In addition, although his social interactions for the first three or four months after his mother's death seemed normal for an infant of his age, he subsequently showed a gradual decline in playful behaviour with a corresponding increase in grooming behaviour (both of himself and others). He displayed a high frequency of submissive behaviour and, on occasions, was unusually aggressive for his age. About one and a half years after his mother's death he fell victim to a paralytic disease and died.

A second infant (Beattle) who was orphaned between the age of 3 and 4 years, also showed a low frequency of play, but in other respects her behaviour was more normal. Both of these infants were adopted by their elder female siblings, both were fully integrated into the community, and both had ample opportunity for play with peers. The main difference in the social situation of these two orphans lay in the fact that Merlin was allowed to ride on his sister's back only a few times whilst Beattle did so constantly. It is tempting to speculate that the added social security derived by the female orphan in this way may have helped her social development.

Unfortunately we do not know whether it was deprivation of maternal milk (causing some nutritional deficiency), some other illness, or merely psychological disturbance that was responsible for Merlin's emaciation and lethargy – a condition which in itself might well have accounted for some of his abnormal behaviour. One factor, however, suggests that his poor physical condition alone did not account for all his peculiarities: during a period of some four to five months before his death, when he looked, if possible, even more emaciated, his play behaviour became slightly more frequent, and his social interactions in other ways showed signs of becoming more normal. Shortly after his mother's death, for instance, he stopped both interfering during copulations and mounting receptive females himself. This behaviour reappeared on occasions during the last four or five months of his life. The play behaviour of the orphan Beattle had returned to normal frequency about two to three years after her mother's death.

This rather inconclusive evidence suggests that the death of the mother, even during the fourth year of an infant's life, may cause profound psychological disturbance. It also suggests that, in some cases at least, constant opportunity to interact with other chimpanzees (including play with youngsters), and in particular with the sibling foster-mother, may eventually offset (completely or partly) the loss of the mother.

Another situation observed at the Gombe Stream suggests that when a youngster is temporarily deprived of *frequent* opportunities for play, this may have a slight effect, for a while, on its behaviour. Thus during 1964 when the infant Gilka was about 3½ years old there was a period of about seven months when she had less opportunities for social play than in previous years. During this time she developed some stereotyped patterns such as hanging by her arms with one foot tucked into the opposite groin for minutes on end, or methodically plucking off small pieces of twig and dropping them to the ground whilst her mother fed. However, since this occurred at a time when the child was undergoing weaning it is hard to tell whether this factor or the lack of play contributed most to her temporary abnormal behaviour. (See photo inset.)

(From 'The Behaviour of Chimpanzees', *Animal Behaviour Monographs*, Vol. 1, Part 3, Baillière, Tindall & Cassell, 1968.)

References

DEVORE, I. (1963), 'Mother-infant relations in free-ranging baboons', in *Maternal Behavior in Mammals*, H. L. Rheingold (ed.), Wiley, New York.

HARLOW, H. F., and HARLOW, M. K. (1962), 'Social deprivation in monkeys', *Sci. American*, No. 207, pp. 137–46.

HARLOW, M. K., and HARLOW, H. F. (1966), 'Affection in primates', *Discovery*, No. 27, pp. 11–17.

HAYES, C. (1952), *The Ape in Our House*, Gollancz.

HOOFF, J. A. R. A. M. VAN (1967), 'The facial displays of the catarrhine monkeys and apes', in *Primate Ethology*, D. Morris (ed.), Weidenfeld & Nicolson.

JAY, P. (1963), 'Mother-infant relations in langurs', in *Maternal Behavior in Mammals*. H. L. Rheingold (ed.), Wiley, New York.

KAUFMANN, J. H. (1967), 'Social relations of adult males in a free-ranging band of rhesus monkeys', in *Social Communication among Primates*, S. A. Altmann (ed.), University of Chicago Press.

LOIZOS, C. (1967), 'Play behavior in higher primates: a review', in *Primate Ethology*, D. Morris (ed.), Weidenfeld & Nicolson.

MASON, W. A. (1965a), 'The social development of monkeys and apes', in *Primate Behavior*, I. DeVore (ed.), Holt, Rinehart & Winston, New York.

MASON, W. A. (1965b), 'Determinants of social behavior in young chimpanzees', in *Behavior of Nonhuman Primates*, C. A. M. Schrier, H. F. Harlow, and F. Stollnitz (eds), Academic Press, New York.

NISSEN, H. W. (1931), 'A field study of the chimpanzee', *Comp. Psychol. Monog.*, No. 8, pp. 1–22.

REYNOLDS, V., and REYNOLDS, F. (1965), 'Chimpanzees of the Budongo Forest', in *Primate Behavior*, I. DeVore (ed.), Holt, Rinehart & Winston, New York.

SIMONDS, P. E. (1965), 'The bonnet macaque in South India', in *Primate Behavior*, I. DeVore (ed.), Holt, Rinehart & Winston, New York.

THORPE, W. H. (1956), *Learning and Instinct in Animals*, Methuen.

YERKES, R. M. (1943), *Chimpanzees, A Laboratory Colony*, Yale University Press.

At Play in the Fields

If the hours a young monkey spends each day in play are any indication, then play must be a major category of primate behaviour. This conclusion is underscored by the complexity of play and by the amount of energy a young monkey devotes to it.

Play is probably important in the development of all mammals, but it appears to be particularly important for the slow-maturing monkeys and apes. Juvenile monkeys play for years, investing thousands of hours of activity, energy and emotion. Such an expenditure of biological resources must serve important biological functions. The theory of natural selection compels us to look for the adaptive reasons for this behaviour.

Perhaps in part because of the values of our culture, play has not been considered a major research problem. Field studies have relegated play to one of a long list of kinds of behaviour. To appreciate the subtleties of its performance and to attempt to understand the nuances of its functions, play must be evaluated in the natural setting of the species, rather than in a laboratory.

For most primates the context of normal life is a social group – in all its complexity and stability. This group is a small world with few intrusive events. A majority of monkeys live their entire life in the group of their birth; hence they know it and its location well. This is the setting of play: a rich blend of social relationships and ecological pressures, dangers, times of plenty and scarcity, and seasonal changes in both environment and group. Play behaviour is characteristic primarily of large infants and juvenile monkeys, although adults may play on rare occasions. This fits in with the notion that play is preparation for adult life, that it is of major importance in the learning process. In contrast to adult activities, play is its own reward. Play does not lead to the attainment of some other goal, such as food. The playing juvenile uses the same kinds of behaviours as the adult, but often in odd sequences or combinations. Play fighting may be aggressive, but it still includes actions that would be suicidal in a serious encounter. Little monkeys make great efforts to play: they go to other juveniles, in-itiate games, and stimulate each other. In this sense, play comes from within, it can be pleasurable, and its actions are repeated over and over again, year after year.

Superficially, play may seem simple. There is chasing, wrestling and boxing. But closer inspection shows that the actions are not simple. If it is an important part of the education of a species and if many adult behaviours are practised in games, then we should expect to find great variety behind the apparent simplicity of play. This is, in fact, the case.

When a large number of monkeys play, there are rapid alternations of participants, actions, and individual moods, which all produce variations of activity. Some motor patterns appear regularly. A group of playing rhesus monkeys may, in a few minutes, push, pull (hair, fingers, limbs, ears, tails), spin, squint, drag feet, rub with hands, scratch with nails, run, jump, chase, fall down, charge, swing by the feet, lean, mouth and shove. The list usually also contains gestures of threat and submission. When threats appear, tension may develop, turning play into aggression.

The intensity of play can be measured only imprecisely. The human observer cannot use the frequency of cries as an index of pain; cries may reflect the mother's closeness and willingness to back up her infant more than it reflects how much the infant is hurt. Social context can affect play in ways that are not obvious. An animal may ignore pain in play if the intentions of the inflicter are non-aggressive, whereas in other interactions a bite or slap of the same intensity will produce a severe reaction. The sound of heads banging on tree limbs or on hard ground in play makes the human observer wince, but often appears not to deter the monkey whose head was banged. Instead, he sits for a moment, then jumps back into the fray.

Subtle glances, tensing of muscles, pressure of grasp, severity of nipping are but a few of the many cues that are not available to the human observer, who is aware of only a small portion of what the players experience.

Consider the following examples of play, which I have observed among wild primates:

1. In a village in northern India, a group of four large and two small juvenile langurs were playing on top of an abandoned irrigation well. The two largest sat face to face boxing each other's shoulders. Next to and touching them was another pair of juveniles, wrestling in a ball. All four were bumped by the smaller juveniles who ran around and over the well in a wild game of chase and reverse chase. From time to time individuals would pause, look around them, and flop to the wall or ground for a few seconds, as though gathering strength for another onslaught of wrestling or boxing. Occasionally, partners changed; and even the smallest langur eventually sparred with the largest, although for a much briefer time than a

pair equally matched. Most of the action took place in pairs, and the participation of each langur appeared to be completely voluntary.

2. In the Singapore botanical gardens, two crab-eating juvenile male macaques were sitting close to one another on a limb. The larger was looking at the smaller, who was quietly regarding his navel. The larger got up, glanced again at the smaller, reached out and poked him with a finger, then quickly sat down in the same spot. The smaller jerked his body away from the larger and looked in the opposite direction. After a second's hesitation the smaller looked toward the larger, who immediately slapped him again. The small monkey jumped four feet back along the branch and the larger immediately followed and grabbed the retreating animal's tail. There was a momentary tug-of-war, which ended with the younger falling from the branch and the larger holding him by the tail in mid-air. When his tail was released, the smaller fell to the ground. The larger macaque then jumped down and chased the smaller one out of sight. Depending upon how this was recorded, it could be tallied as play or aggression.

3. A small juvenile rhesus monkey was rough-housing with an infant on a forest pathway in northern India. The infant was fairly passive and the juvenile turned him over and over quite roughly, mouthing him all the while. The infant began to make faint 'uh-uh-uh' sounds, and the juvenile immediately paused in his handling, glanced around to see which animals were near by, and then resumed mauling the infant. The infant used the vocalization repeatedly whenever the juvenile appeared to be rougher than the infant could tolerate. Always the response of the juvenile was to cease, look and check the reactions of all nearby adults, and when there were none, to continue.

At one point the juvenile pushed the infant forcefully against a limb and the thud of the impact could be heard for twenty feet. The infant squealed sharply and the juvenile stopped. An adult female sitting near by moved towards the pair and the juvenile ran off. In this instance the infant was using the vocalization very skilfully to force the juvenile to modulate his play activity. The infant was, in fact, controlling the 'play' situation. Whether the activity was in any way pleasurable for the small monkey is questionable; that it was for the larger seemed apparent.

4. Two small rhesus monkeys were sitting side by side on a rooftop in Lucknow, India, and one reached out and leaned on the other. The leaned-on one moved three feet away and sat down. The first again leaned towards him, this time reaching out and cuffing him lightly on the knee. After the slap the first rhesus bent back to a normal sitting position and looked solemnly at the little monkey he had just slapped. The latter sat quietly and gazed directly ahead, away from the other monkey. The first rhesus repeated the slap, this time with a little more force; still no response, then

another slap – each time he leaned forward and then quickly bent back. Finally, he reached out, grabbed a handful of fur, and tugged at it hard enough to pull the skin away in a fold. The solicited monkey grimaced at him and bent as far away from him as he could without standing and moving. The rhesus that had been trying to gain the other's attention then sat quietly and after a minute moved away.

In another, similar, instance, where the two monkeys were juveniles, the one who was slapped responded after several approaches with a threat and attempted to bite the slapper. This started a fight that was broken up by a dominant adult male. In a third example, one young monkey tried to solicit play in a similar manner, but in this instance the response of the slapped monkey was to join the first in boisterous wrestling and chasing play for some time.

A special gesture called a 'play face' is described for many species and signals the non-aggressive intent of the monkey or ape that wants to play. This is an over-simplification, since a monkey soliciting a play partner signals in many ways. It may roll its head from side to side, close its eyes, move in an un-coordinated, jerky manner, bow or bob up and down, or approach backward. The face is only one element of a complex set of movements that carry the message of intent to interact in a manner we call playful. An invitation to play might be a slap and quick retreat; it might even be a bite or a shove, repeated in different ways. There are many ways to start an interaction, to determine the mood of the desired partner, and to communicate the intention of the solicitor.

Field workers who have observed monkey infants grow to maturity can suggest many benefits that derive from social play, including the practice of a number of social gestures and motor skills. Patterns appear in fragments, hardly recognizable as the stereotyped social signals they will become if they are to be effective signals among group members. These patterns are practised over and over, in myriad contexts and among all the young of the troop. There is a slow but certain increase in the motor skills of each young monkey, from the time it first leaves its mother, stumbling off a few inches to investigate bits of its environment, to the time when it will leave her to play for hours. Although it is unlikely that we would call the very early sensory or motor experimentation play, there is no question about much of the later activity of the older infant.

Motor and social skills are practised in play, but it has not been demonstrated that play is the context in which these skills are originally stimulated or learned. This distinction must be made if the benefits of playful activity are to be understood. If play is considered a context for consolidating skills, for adding small increments of ability and mastery over motor, manipulatory and social tasks, then the vast repetition of play patterns makes a great deal of sense. Play is not for solving problems from scratch, unless perhaps they are problems with objects, but it may help once the process of solution has been started.

Repetition is a key descriptive word for play – and repetition is essentially practice. Elements of sexual behaviour and dominance gestures appear early in social play, but they appear as fragments and often in no apparent relationship to reproductive or actual dominance contexts until the monkey is much older. Playing animals are involved in a great deal of physical contact and continuous social interaction. The ability to control one's own behaviour and the actions of other monkeys becomes very important.

Given the amount of direct interaction – especially physical contact – in play, each monkey soon learns differences in the size, strength, reaction time and tolerance of each player. Rules of dominance are essentially based on strength and ability to use social signals, and if learning which animals are stronger involves some pain, the young monkey may learn the rules rapidly. For young juveniles, especially males, the opportunity to play dominant, as well as subordinate, roles may be a part of the attractiveness of play. From a broader view, the total experience of play makes ranking possible and seemingly inevitable.

Social cues and complex communication patterns are developed in the relative safety of play. It does not do any good to be the strongest and largest in the group if at the same time most other adults can bluff their way past to a desired object. A monkey must know not only the form and context of each social gesture, it must also be able to execute each with style and finesse. Timing must be perfect, and since most fights are avoided by complex gestures of threat and submission, the monkey that bluffs best probably goes furthest in the long run.

Play is often considered by humans to be pleasurable. Among free-ranging monkeys some play appears to be pleasurable and fun, but much does not. The tensions aroused during play often appear to result in the dissolution of the play group. It is possible that a degree of what we think of as pleasure is obtained from increased competence of movement and skill in the use of signals. We can only guess the motivations of a non-human primate; it cannot tell us anything from introspection.

A juvenile male wrestling in the arms of an adult male may appear tense and inhibited in his movements. He may finally utter a squeal of fear and succeed in breaking free from the adult. The latter may have been making a play face towards the younger male the entire time they were in contact, but the gesture did not avert the juvenile's breaking away. What may surprise the observer is the juvenile's immediate return to the adult male; this pattern may be repeated again and again, with the juvenile fleeing each time, only to return for more rough play. The juvenile's ambivalence is apparent; his actions continually shift from approach to withdrawal. Such conflict situations, with their tensions and anxieties, are present in the behaviour of monkeys and apes. It remains to be demonstrated whether or not any of them are resolved in play.

An ape may pound on a tree when it cannot pound on another ape that annoyed or frightened it. Whether a young ape destroys a twig in play because it would like to do the same to a new sibling is a matter of human conjecture. The play group may be a location for working out aggression that the animal might otherwise wish to direct towards larger and stronger individuals. Helplessness for the younger infant monkey relates most clearly to locomotion and anxiety about leaving its mother. As it grows, it will also experience anxiety related to relationships with others.

Much play appears to be testing of one kind or another. Players constantly push to the limits of tolerance of aggressive behaviour, especially older male juveniles that are large and strong and able to inflict injury. An aggressive invitation can be followed by avoidance, play or fighting – depending upon the mood of the solicited, the actions of the solicitor, their past experience, nearby animals, and probably a long list of other factors that are not apparent to the human observer. No wonder the human reports that rough play borders on serious aggression and that it is difficult to know whether to fit these episodes into aggression or play. The apparently ambiguous actions of large immature monkeys doubtless reflect their ambivalent feelings as to whether they will fight, mildly test relative rankings, or tussle and chase in a frankly playful manner.

The immature monkey constantly tests its strength and social skills, its bluffs, evasive abilities, and allies in playful activity. It also tests its environment, but not, at first, in play. Strange surroundings or unusual events appear to inhibit playful activity. New corners of the environment are first investigated; then and only then, played in. The initial response to strange objects or events is one of great caution.

As a way of testing and gaining small increments of skill or mastery, play is tremendously important for the individual. Play has been described as uneconomical, but this is a judgement that ignores its long-term benefits. In terms of immediate goals, playful activity is expensive in energy and time, but if the eventual behaviours of the adult are considered, it is a good investment of both.

Play is one of the most important factors in the establishment of social relationships that last a lifetime. The non-human primate is born into the highly structured social context of the group and the specific relationships its mother has with the group. Her personality directly and indirectly affects the infant's contacts with other group members – the effect may be restricting or it may be encouraging of wide contact. If the mother is very subordinate and constantly tense when she is near other adults, she may stay away from most of the adults and deliberately restrict the movements of her infant so that it will not be able to play. If, on the other hand, she is a confident, dominant, and socially active female, her infant may be in the centre of action and have a lot of contact with other monkeys. A mother that is quick to threaten young that solicit her infant to play reduces the total amount of time her infant spends in play. Her presence, regardless of her temperament, certainly facilitates early exploration and play. Young of dominant females can afford to take liberties against other monkeys when the mother will back them up against reprisals.

Various types of play characterize different stages of development, each with its attendant problems and challenges. Play and other activities must have been designed through evolution to help meet the demands of each level of maturation. While we can observe social and motor tasks being worked out by infants and juveniles, the human can only guess at the psychological tasks. We cannot determine what, if any, utilitarian internal functions play has for the monkey.

Playful behaviour gradually drops out of the repertoire of the monkey as it matures. Most adult male monkeys rarely, if ever, play, and the situation is similar for adult females although they may interact playfully with their infants. In any event, play is not a notable feature of adult life. Why does it drop out along the way and why don't adults play?

There is no satisfactory or final answer to these questions, but it does seem that the following factors are relevant. The adult may find it too difficult to indicate playful intentions. The signals of playfulness, including the so-called play face, may not be sufficient to counteract the strength and potential ability to damage that other members of the group have learned to associate with that adult. Most play involves a lot of physical contact and sudden movements – two qualities of interaction generally avoided by adult males unless the situation is clearly one of relaxed grooming or similar activity. The rough and tumble of play may be potentially too dangerous for adults and also incompatible with their important roles of leadership and dominance. Intentions that are ambiguous or misread only once could mean the difference between safe play and a serious wound or fatality.

The adult monkey, and especially the adult male, is generally very sensitive to which other adult comes close to him. A sudden invasion of the adult's personal space or the area around him that he considers his private domain might be disastrous. The normal tensions of dominance relationships are seldom evident; in part they are hidden because the actors in the structure carefully avoid getting into situations where positions must be challenged. One of the best ways to avoid a fight is to avoid physical proximity. Play is contra-indicated.

Aside from these considerations – of animals getting too close, invading each other's personal space, or misreading the signals of intention – there is another, more basic suggestion as to why it is not worth the risk for adults to play. The learning activities of play, so important for the infant and juvenile, are no longer necessary for the adult. Presumably, by the time the individual has matured, it has mastered the skills it will need, learned the land it occupies, established its social relationships, and become co-ordinated motorically. Major forms of adult behaviour are established and relatively immutable.

Mammals are so constituted that learning takes incredible repetition. Mastery comes slowly, and the years of immaturity are the time of life when they can afford the most mistakes. Increments of skill can only be seen over time and are based on the repetition and practice of activities like play.

Laboratory studies have demonstrated the importance of peer contact for the young monkey, but only field studies have indicated the full complexities of social life and the environment and their importance to the developing primate. The dangers and challenges of life in nature and the rewards to the individual of successful social life are only apparent in the field. The multiple functions of play may be obscure, indeed, when viewed for only a short time in an artificial context, and are not even obvious from watching only the young. The juvenile patas monkey jumping up and down in the tall grass may seem to be enjoying a nice sport, but the full importance of these motor patterns is not obvious until you see an adult male patas jumping to divert the attention of a lion from the rest of the group. Then the significance of this life-saving skill will reach the observer.

The healthy young monkey plays. It does so for a substantial portion of its immature years, and to a significant degree the success of its adult life may depend upon the intensity and variety of its play experience. Play in monkeys is more complex than the word signifies to most humans. There may be no fun in play, and it might be tension and anxiety producing for the playing monkey. Whatever the differences in form that play takes among the many different species of non-human primates, it is a major category of adaptive behaviour that must be analysed if we are to understand primate behaviour.

(From a Special Supplement of the *Natural History Magazine*, December 1971.)

Rough-and-tumble Play in Stumptails

Rough-and-tumble play

Among stumptails certain elements of agonistic behaviour are used in play, and vice-versa (Table I). Rank order is generally ignored, and a subordinate can perform many behaviour patterns which would not be tolerated by a dominant outside the play situation. Self-handicapping is practised: the stronger animal does not use its full strength and often wrestles on the back; throwing oneself on the back is both a locomotor play and a play invitation. The faster animal lets itself be caught in a chase. Contrary to agonistic encounters, play fighting and play chases are silent, and the predominant facial expression is the play face. The games often start and stop suddenly, with the participants engaging in completely different activities.

Rough-and-tumble play can become agonistic in play bullying, or when mock wrestling degenerated into true fighting or punishment.

In captivity sub-adult males would sometimes play wrestle between themselves or with younger animals, and this was also the case of the two zoo reared females. None of the wild trapped sub-adult or adult females did it.

A. Play chases: tag, ring around the bush

Contrary to what happens in real chase, the pursued animal often solicits chasing, and when not pursued any more, it may wait for or come back towards the pursuer. Roles are often reversed, this being a general rule for all rough-and-tumble games. The chase is frequently followed by or interspersed with mock wrestling.

In 'tag', one monkey approaches another often with play leaps or the play face, hits it and runs away in order to be chased. The 'hit' may be a simple touch, a slap, a pull, a shove, or only a direct look. In 'ring around the bush' two or more monkeys chase one another around an obstacle which may be a tree trunk as well as a group of sitting monkeys. The obstacle partly hides the chaser from the chased, allowing one or the other to suddenly reverse its direction. Several obstacles may be involved, and the players chase one another again and again over a complex and definite circuit.

Table I Comparison of patterns used in agonistic behaviour and rough-and-tumble play in *Macaca speciosa*

Patterns	Agonistic	Rough-and-tumble play
Eye expressions		
Stare	+	direct look
Apprehensive looking	+	0
Eye contact avoidance	+	0
Feigned indifference	+	0
Ignore	+	+
Feigned interest	+	0
Facial expressions		
Bite	+	play bite
Attack face	+	0
Open mouth threat face	+	play face, laughing face
Bared teeth threat face	+	0
Pant threat face	+	0
Grin face	+	0
Teeth chattering face	+	0
Lipsmacking face	+	rare
Pout face	+	+
Gestures, postures and motions		
Pat, slap, cuff	+	+, also sparring
Pull, pinch, grab	+	+
Fur plucking	+	0
Dragging	+	0
Push, kick	+ kick?	+
Lunge	+	+
Threat sequence	+	0
Branch shaking	+	+
Chase	+	play chase,* tag, ring around the bush
Physical contact	+	play wrestling,* king of the castle, tug of war
Turning back on, profile sitting	+	0
Withdrawing and displacing	+	Mock withdrawal
Crouch	+	+
Freezing, staying put, passivity	+	self-handicapping
Grooming solicitations	+	0
Grooming, being groomed	+	0

Table 1 *(cont.)*

Patterns	Agonistic	Rough-and-tumble play
Perineal investigation	+	+
Hip touch	+	+
Lifting the hindquarters forcibly	+	+
Dismount signals:		
Looking at mounter	+	+
Touching mounter's side	+	+
Sitting, crouching, walking away	+	+
Harassing	+	?
Perineal presenting	+	+
Genitalia rubbing	+	+
Mounting	+	+
Genital manipulation	+	rare
Autostimulation while being mounted	+	0
Autonomic responses		
Face reddening	+	?
Pilo-erection	+	?
Urination and defecation	+	0
Penis erection	+	+
Tension yawn, threat yawn	+	0
Sounds		
Varied	+	only staccato panting
Complex patterns		
Bullying	+	0†
Enlisting	+	0
Re-directed aggression	+	0

*Play chases and wrestling are often accompanied by locomotor play, such as: playful leaps and playful canter, hanging upside down, inverted walk, waving and dangling limbs, etc.

†As soon as bullying appeared, play was considered to degenerate into agonistic behaviour.

B. Mock wrestling, sparring, king of the castle

In mock wrestling, some elaborate sequences are involved, such as pinning down the partner, or making it fall by throwing oneself on the back while holding it between arms and legs. More primitive mammalian patterns subsist, such as a prolonged mouthing of a part of the partner's body. A wrestling bout might last as long as 10 or 15 minutes, and be repeated over short intervals for more than one hour and a half.

Two other types of fighting did not seem to be practised outside the play situation. In 'sparring', both partners are sitting or squatting, and fence with open or partly open hands, slapping and cuffing at each other. This often precedes wrestling. In 'king of the castle', one animal occupies an elevated support and prevents one or several partners coming from below to displace or join him by slapping, pushing, play biting, and wrestling. In a 'serious' situation, a dominant stumptail who wants to prevent another from joining needs only to stare.

C. Tug of war

In captivity, tugs of war developed naturally when young stumptails were given sticks or ropes. One would grab the object and run away, chased by others; sometimes more than two animals might tug at each end. This game too has no parallel in a non-play situation (see also Struhsaker, 1967).

D. Comparisons

Table II shows the patterns of rough-and-tumble play practised by some primates species which have been observed in the wild or in semi-normal captive conditions. Prosimians seem to have the smallest number of games, and chimpanzees the largest, although it is difficult to know, when a pattern is absent, whether it does not exist or has not been pointed out by the observer. Two points are worth noting: (i) infra-human primates, like certain other mammals, are practising games which involve a rule, (ii) these games are still practised by humans. The most elementary rule is self-handicapping, which all studied primates practise, except for the night monkeys who do not seem to engage in play wrestling at all, 'presumably as another consequence of their slight degree of gregariousness' (Moynihan, 1964, p. 12). Another rule, in 'ring around the bush' or 'follow the leader', is to repeat the same motions over a definite circuit (see Carpenter, for instance 1934, p. 80). Ripley (1967, p. 162), points out that:

In chases among juveniles on the ground, a jump to a low branch seems to be the langur equivalent to 'home', a position of sanctuary from which he would not be chased farther.

The rules of 'king of the castle' and 'hide and seek' are obvious.

A monkey can play social games by itself. For instance Carpenter (1940, p. 148), observed a young gibbon 'running and jumping repeatedly over a circuitous route' by himself, before doing so in play chase with another juvenile. I observed an infant mona monkey play with several partners the

Table II Patterns of rough-and-tumble play in some primate species

Species and references	Chase — Simple or unspecified	Tag	Ring around the bush or follow the Leader	Hide and seek
Prosimians				
Galago senegalensis[1]	✕		✕ (ball jumping with play catching)	
Propithecus verreauxi[2]	?			
Lemur catta[2]	?			
New World monkeys				
Aotus trivirgatus[3]	probably none			
Callicebus moloch[4]	✕			
Spider monkey[5,6]	✕	✕	✕	
Howler monkey[7]	✕	?	✕	
Old World monkeys				
Stumptail macaque[8]	✕	✕	✕	
Japanese macaque[8]	✕	✕	✕	
Barbary macaque[8]	✕	✕	?	
Liontail macaque[8]	✕	✕	✕	
Rhesus macaque[8,9,10]	✕	✕	✕ and 'peekaboo'	
Olive baboon[8,11]	✕	✕	✕	
Hanuman Langur[12]	✕	✕	✕	
Mona monkey[8]	✕	✕	✕	
Putty-nosed monkey[8]	✕	✕	✕	
Vervet[13]	✕			✕
Patas[14]	✕	✕ (inviting play)	?	✕
Apes				
Lar gibbon[15]	✕		✕	
Gorilla[16,17,18]	✕	✕	✕	
Chimpanzee[19,20,21,22]	✕	✕	✕	✕

[1] Sauer and Sauer, 1963; [2] Jolly, 1966; [3] Moynihan, 1964; [4] Moynihan, 1966; [5] Carpenter, 1935; [6] Eisenberg and Kuehn, 1966; [7] Carpenter, 1934, p. 79; [8] personal observations; [9] Hines, 1942, p. 199; [10] Altmann, 1962, p. 380; [11] DeVore and Washburn,

Table II *(cont.)*

Wrestling			
Simple	*King of the castle*	*Tug of war*	*Tickling*
⊠			
⊠ also sparring and bicycling			
⊠ also sparring			
probably none			
⊠			
⊠			
⊠	⊠		
⊠ also sparring	⊠	⊠	
× also sparring	×	×	
× also sparring	×	×	
× also sparring	×	×	
		×	
⊠	×	×	
×	×		
× also sparring	×	×	
× also sparring	⊠	×	
× also sparring		×	
⊠ also sparring			
	?		
	?		
⊠ also sparring and boxing	?	× and 'Keep away' game	×

1960; [12] Ripley, 1967; [13] Struhsaker, 1967; [14] Hall, 1965; [15] Carpenter, 1940; [16] Carpenter, 1937; [17] Lang, 1962; [18] Schaller, 1963; [19] Yerkes and Yerkes, 1929, p. 254; [20] Reynolds and Reynolds. 1965; [21] Van Lawick-Goodall, 1967.

arboreal version of 'king of the castle', which consists in forcing the partner down and off a limb. Then he went on climbing on the same branch and jumping off from it for about six minutes by himself. Two infant stumptails, each caged from birth with its mother and two 'aunts', started to try and play tag when about 2·5 months old. Yet none of the adult females was willing to play with them or had done so previously. Thus the appearance of certain social games may be a matter of maturation rather than of social learning. (See photo inset.)

(From M. Bertrand, 'The Behaviour Repertoire of the Stumptail Macaque', *Bibliotheca Primatologica II*, S.Karger, Basle, 1969.)

References

ALTMANN, S. A. (1962), 'A field-study of the sociobiology of Rhesus monkeys, *Macaca mulatta*', *Ann. N.Y. Acad. Sci.*, No. 102, pp. 338–435.

CARPENTER, C. R. (1934), 'A field study of the behavior and social relations of Howling monkeys', *Comp. Psychol. Monog.*, No. 10, pp. 1–168.

CARPENTER, C. R. (1935), 'Behavior of red spider monkeys in Panama', *J. Mammal*, No. 16, pp. 171–80.

CARPENTER, C. R. (1940), 'A field-study in Siam of the behavior and social relations of the gibbon, *Hylobates lar*,'. *Comp. psychol. Monog.*, No. 16, pp. 1–212.

DEVORE, I., and WASHBURN, S. L. (1906), 'Baboon behavior' (16 mm sound color film), University Extension, Berkeley, California.

EISENBERG, J. F., and KUEHN, R. E. (1966), 'The behavior of *Ateles geoffroyi* and related species', *Smithson Misc. Coll.*, No. 151, pp. 1–63.

HALL, K. R. L. (1965), 'Behavior and ecology of the wild Patas monkey, *Erythrocebus patas*, in Uganda', *J. Zool.*, No. 148, pp. 15–87.

HINES, M. (1942), 'The development and regression of reflexes, postures and progression in the young macaque', *Carneg. Found. Contrib. Embryol.*, No. 196, pp. 155–209.

JOLLY, A. (1966), *Lemur Behavior, a Madagascar Field Study*, University of Chicago Press.

LANG, E. M. (1962), *The Baby Gorilla*, Gollancz.

LAWICK-GOODALL, J. VAN (1967), *My Friends, the Wild Chimpanzees*, National Geographic Society, Washington.

MOYNIHAN, M. (1964), 'Some behavior patterns of Platyrrhine monkeys. I. The night monkey (*Aotus trivirgatus*)', *Smithson Misc. Coll.*, No. 146, pp. 1–84.

MOYNIHAN, M. (1966), 'Communication in the Titi monkey, *Callicebus*', *J. Zool.*, No. 150, pp. 77–127.

REYNOLDS, V., and REYNOLDS, F. (1965), 'Chimpanzees of the Budongo forest', in *Primate Behavior*, I. DeVore (ed.), Holt, Rinehart & Winston, New York, pp. 360–424.

RIPLEY, S. (1967), 'The leaping of langurs: a problem in the study of locomotor adaptation', *Amer. J. Physiol. Anthrop.*, No. 26, pp. 149–70.

SAUER, E. G. F., and SAUER, E. M. (1963), 'The South West African bushbaby of the *Galago senegalensis* group', *Journal of the South-West Africa Society*, No. 16, pp. 5–36.

SCHALLER, G. B. (1963), *The Mountain Gorilla: Ecology and Behavior*, University of Chicago Press.

STRUHSAKER, T. T. (1967), 'Behavior of vervet monkeys (*Cercopithecus aethiops*)', *Univ. Calif. Publ. Zool.*, No. 82.

YERKES, R. M., and YERKES, A. W. (1929), *The Great Apes*, Yale University Press.

Social Play: the Choice of Playmates Observed in the Young of the Crab-Eating Macaque

Primates and carnivores are the orders of mammals which play the most and longest (Loizos, 1966, 1967), but it has been shown that considerable interspecific differences occur as to the time spent in play: there is every degree of variation from the chimpanzee, the most playful of primates (Washburn and Hamburg, 1965), to the gorilla, which plays very little, especially 'when the clouds hang low in the saddle and the vegetation is wet' (Schaller,1963). However, during their infancy and especially during their youth, most primates spend a large amount of time in play: seventy per cent for the chimpanzee (Mason, 1965a), eighty per cent for the young of *Alouatta palliata* (Carpenter, 1965), and four to five hours per day for young of the *Presbytis entellus* (Jay, 1963).

Young chimpanzees have sixteen times more social contacts than adults, mainly because of social play; the indices of movement and of contact with the physical environment are distinctly higher than for adults, the latter being superior only in handling and in removal of vermin (Mason, 1965a). Thus most of the social interactions between young primates take place during play.

The object of the present work was to see whether in these interactions the young monkeys showed any preference for particular playmates.

A. Method
1. Subjects

The troop of *Macaca irus* monkeys in the municipal zoological and botanical garden at Mulhouse comprises eighteen adults (two males, sixteen females), one juvenile female, thirteen young monkeys from 3 months to 3–4 years and five infants of less than 3 months. The study of play relates essentially to the thirteen young monkeys, which had first been clearly identified in order to be able to recognize them with certainty at a glance. The social rank of the mothers had been established by previous observations. The infants below 3 months were excluded from this study: they are highly dependent on their mother, who systematically obstructs their attempts to leave her and closely supervises all their social interactions (Hinde and Spencer-Booth, 1967).

2. Methods

Each morning, about an hour after the daily distribution of food, the play interactions among the young monkeys were carefully noted for 150 minutes. The types of social play recorded all belonged to the three categories of Rosenblum (1961): rough-and-tumble play (somersaults, scuffles, tussles, etc.), approach-withdrawal play (chasing, hide-and-seek behind the concrete posts in the pit, reverse chasing, etc.), and mixed play in which these two types are intermingled.

B. Results

The results are shown in Table 1. The unequal distribution of play among participants is evident: the value of x^2 is above the one per cent probability level for all the animals studied. Thus the young monkeys do not play equally with all partners, but have individual preferences for certain others.

1. Influence of age

The age of the young monkeys is not known exactly, since the records of the zoological garden give no precise identification of them or assessment of their age. However, they can be divided into two classes: those from 3 to 18 months (stage I) and those from 18 months to 3–4 years (stage II). The latter group have a general tendency to play less than the younger ones, but this is not significant, because there are too few members of the older group; see (1) in Table 2.

The animals in stage II have, on average, a slight tendency to play with younger animals, but this is again not significant; see (2) in Table 2. On the other hand, the 3–18-month-old animals on average play much more often with one another than with older monkeys, this result being highly significant at the five per cent level; see (3) in Table 2.

2. Influence of social rank

The stage I animals (3–18 months) with mothers of high social rank (Nos. 5, 6 and 8) play more often among themselves than with others whose mothers have a very low rank (Nos. 14, 17 and 18); moreover, these animals with high-rank mothers tend to play with one another more often than those with low-rank mothers do.

The ones with mothers of very low rank play with one another, on average, to the same extent as with others that have high-rank mothers (Nos. 5, 6 and 8). Thus the young monkeys with high-rank mothers prefer to seek their playmates from the same class, while those with low-rank mothers look for partners among the young of both high- and low-ranking mothers.

Table 1 The chosen partners are indicated by the columns and the animals, whose play was observed, by the rows. In each line the figures show the numbers of play interactions. The names in capitals are those of the stage II animals (18 months to 3–4 years); those in small letters are stage I animals. The mother's social rank is shown below that of each young animal.

	BARET	BING	DELU	LULU	LUPA	Fino	Mini	Mohica	Nion	Omo	Puncta	Rasa	Totals
Hierarchy	?	12'	4'	13'	10'	17'	6'	10'	8'	14'	5'	18'	
BARET	×	7	4	6	13	8	14	5	12	1	12	3	85
BING	1	×	0	4	3	5	11	4	10	7	4	1	50
LUPA	11	1	28	11	×	10	44	2	12	15	20	16	170
Fino	8	4	8	46	18	×	29	4	48	78	75	54	372
Mini	9	13	4	9	14	40	×	2	32	13	52	14	202
Mohica	7	4	10	6	29	8	20	×	10	15	4	13	126
Nion	10	13	0	26	14	35	45	4	×	11	126	12	296
Omo	5	15	1	8	11	15	4	9	6	×	17	4	95
Puncta	6	12	3	20	17	25	20	3	67	9	×	13	195
Rasa	2	2	1	13	18	17	35	44	14	6	35	×	187

Table 2 Variance analyses.

Cause of variation	Sum of Squares	Degrees of freedom	Mean square	F. exp.	F. th. 5%
[1] Group differences	24841	1	24841	F = 24841/7794	
Error	62354	8	7794	3,18	5,32
[2] Group differences	12,90	1	12,90	F = 12,90/31,46	
Error	125,87	4	31,46	= 0,41	7,71
[3] Group differences	768,1	1	768,1	F = 768,1/101,0	
Error	1212,0	12	101,0	= 7,6	4,75

3. Size of play group

More than three quarters of the games involve two young monkeys and last for not more than ten seconds. Groups of three are found fairly often; foursomes are very rare, and we have never observed games with more than

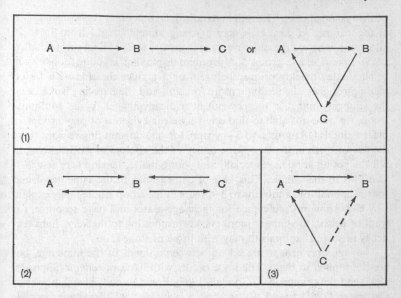

Fig. 1. Types of game. (1) A plays with B, who plays with C; C may either refuse the invitation to play, or play with A (chasing, hide-and-seek round a concrete post, and some types of tussle). (2) A and C attack B, who defends against one with teeth and forepaws and against the other with hindpaws. (3) A and B play together; C joins in the game by playing with either A or B.

four participants. There are three types of games for three monkeys, two types predominating – (2) and (3) in Fig. 1.

C. Discussion

Age is one of the factors involved in the choice of playmates. Young monkeys of 3–18 months make a very clear choice of others of the same age. This social play with the same age group has often been reported: by Itani (1954) for *Macaca fuscata*, Altmann (1962), Southwick, Beg and Siddiqi (1965) for *Macaca mulatta*, Simonds (1965) for *Macaca radiata*, Jay (1965) for *Presbytis entellus*, Carpenter (1965) for *Alouatta palliata*, and Goodall (1965) for the chimpanzee. This is normal, since young monkeys of greatly differing age have quite different weights and physical strengths, and only with partners of more or less equal weight and strength does each have an equal chance of controlling the play interaction. Thus, in games with older animals, the latter have to adapt and withhold their physical strength in order to be able to take part in a permanent, mutual and repeated play, mainly in games of contact (Rosenblum, 1961) with the weaker younger ones. The weight handicap is sometimes very considerable, as for instance in gorillas, where a young animal weighs from 15 to 20 kilograms, whereas the older ones are from 200 to 250 kilograms (Schaller, 1965). Likewise, in a group of older animals playing, a young monkey will be eliminated quickly or even before the start, since the chasing is faster, tussling rougher, the scuffling more forceful, and the harrying fiercer, and the younger animal is thereby put at a disadvantage. In the Mulhouse troop, we were not able to find any very clear evidence of play groups of older animals (18 months to 3–4 years), for one outstanding reason: there are few of them in the troop, the policy of the zoological garden being to sell the young animals, especially the young males, leaving very few 2–4-year-olds in the sample. This lack of companions in the same age group for the animals of 18 months to 3–4 years in the troop studied may explain why they show no preference for their age-mates and have recourse, for want of better, to younger monkeys, corresponding to the very slight tendency of stage II animals to play with those of stage I.

Thus the play groups are set up between animals of the same age, but are not limited to these. The same occurs with *Macaca radiata* (Simonds, 1965) and the chimpanzee (Goodall, 1965). For *Alouatta palliata*, however, Carpenter (1965) found no age-linked play groups: the young animals played together regardless of age from 6 months to 4–5 years.

Another factor that influences the choice of playmates is the social rank of the young animal's mother. Young monkeys of 3–18 months from the higher ranks play with one another more than with those from the lower ranks; the play of the former is more vigorous and aggressive (Altmann, 1962), and they would therefore have to reduce the force of their play to accommodate it to that of lower-rank partners (Altmann calls this 'self-handicapping'). This should lead the high-rank young monkeys to prefer play with others of similar rank, where no such precautions are necessary. The 3–18-month-old monkeys with low-rank mothers show no preference for partners of either high or low rank, since they can play with each kind without having to modify their vigour. It might be thought that these low-rank animals have a preference for play among themselves but that this is partly neutralized or masked by the socially 'advantageous' search for high-rank partners. Some observations of human play show that children of high social class prefer to play with one another rather than with working-class children, whereas those from lower in the scale have no preference as between rich and poor playmates. Should we than assume that similar effects exist in troops of monkeys?

The sex of the playmate(s) must certainly have an effect, but we were unable to investigate it, because of the smallness of the troop. Mason (1965b), in a study of the rhesus monkey, has shown that the males tend to prefer games of contact, and the females those of approach and withdrawal. But Hinde and Spencer-Booth (1967) were unable to find in the same species any sex-dependent difference between rough-and-tumble and approach-withdrawal games. They also report that the males are more active and the females more passive in their social games, the males more often initiating play and also taking part more often in rough-and-tumble games.

Southwick, Beg and Siddiqi (1965) say that the closest associations in vermin-removal, rest periods and play periods are found between siblings. The recent work of Koford (1965) on the rhesus has also emphasized the hitherto unsuspected links between brothers and sisters. This family factor must certainly influence the choice of playmates, but for the reason already mentioned (the sale of young monkeys by the zoological garden) we were unable to investigate it.

Some associative relations between females (Rowell, Hinde and Spencer-Booth, 1964) may very well affect the choice of playmates, with preference for those belonging to the same 'mothers' club'. This factor should definitely be taken into consideration.

Games between two or three individuals are the most frequent in many primates. For the chimpanzee, Reynolds and Reynolds (1965) noted fifty-three per cent of games between two and five per cent between three, but these figures include the few games with adults. For the mountain gorilla (Schaller, 1965), eighty-one per cent of games are between two individuals, but the size of the play group increases with age, from 2 or 3 for young animals to 4–10 for juveniles. The same is true for *Macaca mulatta* (Southwick, Beg and Siddiqi, 1965); for *Alouatta palliata*, the play groups contain 6 to 8 individuals (Carpenter, 1965).

The necessary conditions for the occurrence of play have not yet been clearly established, and it is easier to give the inhibiting than the motivating conditions (Loizos, 1967): the occurrence of play is promoted by absence of causes of conflict of motivations, absence of environmental pressures (heat, cold, humidity, predators) and of physiological pressures (hunger, thirst, weariness and sexual desire; see Lorenz, 1956 and Bally, 1945). Thus play appears to be a 'relaxation activity', and occurs mainly with young animals and those living in captivity, whose essential physical and physiological needs are satisfied by their parents, their keepers or the public.

Summary

The choice of playmate depends on several factors.

(1) *Age*. Playmates of the same age are preferred.

(2) *Social rank*. Those with high-rank mothers prefer to play with one another; those with low-rank mothers do not show any rank-dependent preference in their choice of playmates.

(3) *Sex*. Males prefer and initiate games of physical contact; females prefer less violent games without physical contact.

(4) *Family*. Brothers and sisters play more often with one another than with other young monkeys.

(5) *'Mothers' club'*. Those whose mothers belong to the same club play more often with one another.

The criteria of choice are best seen in games between two individuals.

Our observations in a zoological garden are very similar to those of other authors for closely related species in the wild or in captivity.

(From *Folia primat.*, No. 11, 1969, pp. 134–43.)

References

ALTMANN, S. A. (1962), 'Social behavior of anthropoid primates: analysis of recent concepts', in *Roots of Behavior: Genetics, Instinct and Socialization in Animal Behavior*, E. L. Bliss (ed.), Harper & Brothers, New York, pp. 277–85.

BALLY, G. (1945), *The Origin of the Limits of Freedom: An Interpretation of Animal and Human Play*, Schwabe, Basle (in German).

CARPENTER, C. R. (1965), 'The howlers of Barro Colorado island', in *Primate Behavior*, I. DeVore (ed.), Holt, Rinehart & Winston, New York, pp. 250–91.

GOODALL, J. (1965), 'Chimpanzees of the Gombe Stream Reserve', in *Primate Behavior*, I. DeVore (ed.), Holt, Rinehart & Winston, New York, pp. 425–73.

HINDE, R. A., and SPENCER-BOOTH, Y. (1967), 'The behaviour of socially living rhesus monkeys in their first two and a half years', *Anim. Behav.*, No. 5, pp. 169–96.

ITANI, J. (1954), *Monkeys of Mount Takasaki*, Kobunsha, Tokyo (in Japanese).

JAY, P. (1963), *The Ecology and Social Behavior of the Indian Langur Monkey*, unpublished doctoral dissertation, University of Chicago.

JAY, P. (1965), 'The common langur of North India', in *Primate Behavior*, I. DeVore (ed.), Holt Rinehart & Winston, New York, pp. 197–249.

KOFORD, C. B. (1965), 'Population dynamics of rhesus monkeys on Cayo Santiago', in *Primate Behavior*, I. DeVore (ed.), Holt, Rinehart & Winston, New York, pp. 160–74.

LOIZOS, C. (1966), 'Play in mammals', in *Play, Exploration and Territory in Mammals*, O. Jewell and C. Loizos (eds), Academic Press & Zoological Society of London, pp. 1–9.

LOIZOS, C. (1967), 'Play behaviour in higher primates: a review', in *Primate Ethology*, D. Morris (ed.), Weidenfeld & Nicolson, pp. 176–218.

LORENZ, K. (1956), 'Plays and vacuum activities', in *Instinct in Animal and Human Behaviour*, M. Autuori *et al.* (eds), Masson, Paris, pp. 633–45.

MASON, W. A. (1965), 'Determinants of social behavior in young chimpanzees', in *Behaviour of Non-human Primates*, A. M. Schrier, H. F. Harlow, and F. Stollnitz (eds), Vol. II, Academic Press, New York, pp. 335–64.

MASON, W. A. (1965b), 'The social development of monkeys and apes', in ·

Primate Behavior, I. DeVore (ed.), Holt, Rinehart & Winston, New York, pp. 514–43.

REYNOLDS, V., and REYNOLDS, F. (1965), 'Chimpanzees of the Budongo forest', in *Primate Behavior*, I. DeVore (ed.), Holt, Rinehart & Winston, New York, pp. 368–424.

ROSENBLUM, L. M. (1961), 'The development of social behavior in the rhesus monkey', unpublished doctoral dissertation, University of Wisconsin.

ROWELL, T. E., HINDE, R. A., and SPENCER-BOOTH, Y. (1964), ' "Aunt" – infant interaction in captive rhesus monkeys', *Anim. Behav.*, No. 12, pp. 219–26.

SCHALLER, G. B. (1963), *The Mountain Gorilla: Ecology and Behavior*, University of Chicago Press.

SCHALLER, G. B. (1965), 'The behavior of the mountain gorilla', in *Primate Behavior*, I. DeVore (ed.), Holt, Rinehart & Winston, New York, pp. 324–67.

SIMONDS, P. E. (1965), 'The bonnet macaque in South India', in *Primate Behavior*, I. DeVore (ed.), Holt, Rinehart & Winston, New York, pp. 175–96.

SOUTHWICK, C. H., BEG, M. A., and SIDDIQI, M. R. (1965), 'Rhesus monkeys in North India', in *Primate Behavior*, I. DeVore (ed.), Holt, Rinehart & Winston, New York, pp. 111–59.

WASHBURN, S. L., and HAMBURG, D. A. (1965), 'The study of primate behavior', in *Primate Behavior*, I. DeVore (ed.), Holt, Rinehart & Winston, New York, pp. 1–13.

Exploration and Social Play in Squirrel Monkeys

This intriguing study indicates that squirrel monkeys can survive, reproduce and maintain cohesive troops in the absence of social play. It forces us to consider alternate developmental routes to adult behaviour. If other activities can serve in place of play, then we must determine their structure and find which components can substitute for play.

Introduction

Socially living groups of squirrel monkeys (*Saimiri*) have been studied in an interesting variety of different environments. Several of these studies have dealt with exploration and play, and taken together, they show that the development of play varies among different environments. Ploog and his colleagues at the Max Planck Institute for Psychiatry in Munich have been conducting diversified laboratory research for over a decade (Ploog *et al.*, 1963, 1967). Rosenblum (1968) has conducted laboratory research on infant development and mother–infant relationships. Thorington (1967, 1968) conducted the first field-study on squirrel monkeys in 1965 on the llanos of Colombia. Our research has included studies on a semi-free-ranging troop in Florida, a field-study in Panama, a survey of forty-three troops in Panama, Colombia, Brazil and Peru, and a laboratory study at the Max Planck Institute (Baldwin, 1969; Baldwin and Baldwin, 1971, 1972). Klein and Klein (personal communication) made observations on social play in squirrel monkeys during a 19-month field study on spider monkeys (*Ateles belzebuth*) in the La Macarena area of Colombia. Recently, Bailey has been conducting observations on free-ranging troops on Santa Sophia Island in the Amazon River in Colombia. Although play has been only one target of research interest in these studies, all of the studies have provided valuable data on the relationship between play and the environment.

It is already clear that there is considerable variation in the play of squirrel monkeys. For example, in some environments, young squirrel monkeys have been reported to play for three hours per day, but in one natural environment not a single bout of social play was observed during a ten-week, intensive study. Numerous intermediate levels of play activity have been observed. The differences in play patterns covary with numerous complex ecological and social factors, such as forest size, troop size, food abundance, adult sociability, etc. The large number of interacting conditions that vary among environments demonstrates the complexity of factors that influence and are influenced by play. In spite of the complexity, however, certain patterns do emerge.

Ploog *et al.* (1967), identified several types of peer play. The two main forms were (i) contact play, with wrestling and scuffling, and (ii) distance play, with chasing. During contact play one animal holds and sham-bites the second while the second struggles to get away. The two players of a dyad often exchange roles frequently and quickly. They roll around on the floor until one animal pulls away, and a pause occurs in play until they jump on each other again to resume contact. During distance play, the animals chase each other through the cage, often switching between the roles of chasing and fleeing. They keep eye contact, but they stay out of each other's reach. Several times a day, young animals were observed to engage in periods of social play that lasted up to an hour each. Young animals could spend as much as several hours a day in active social play.

Llanos of Colombia

In 1965 Thorington (1967, 1968) conducted the first systematic field study on squirrel monkeys in a fifteen-hectare forest on the llanos of Colombia. At the beginning of the study the troop of eighteen animals consisted of three adult males, five adult females, and ten young, and during the ten-week study four infants were born. The troop tended to fragment into subgroups of five to eight animals during foraging periods in which the animals looked for dispersed fruits and insect foods. There was usually a one- to two-hour midday rest period in the heat of the day, and most activities subsided as the animals descended to low, dense thickets. It was during these periods when the adults were resting and the troop remained in one place that play among the juveniles was most common. Play behaviour 'principally involved hanging by the hind legs and wrestling, or mock biting and chasing' (Thorington, 1968, p. 79). 'All the play observed took place in trees. Since the troop was surprised very near the ground on only one occasion, it is doubtful that any play took place on the ground . . .' 'No vocalizations were observed to be given by the juveniles as they played . . .' After the midday rest period, the troop again fragmented into several subgroups for afternoon foraging. From Thorington's report and from personal observations on twelve troops on the llanos of Colombia, we would estimate that a young monkey in these troops plays between five and thirty minutes per day.

Semi-natural environment

Our research on squirrel monkeys began with a 1966–7 study in the semi-natural forest established by DuMond in Florida. In most ways our observations on play agree with DuMond's (1968), but having had the opportunity to spend many more hours making observations on social behaviour, we were able to trace the ontogeny of play in greater detail (Baldwin, 1969).

During the first three months of play, infants sometimes spent one or two hours per day in social play; however, they often travelled together or came near each other without engaging in play activities. In this respect they had weaker play habits than the older infants and juveniles.

Play between the early infants and the juveniles that were one year older was not common. Infants often attempted to initiate such play if juveniles came near them in play periods, but the juveniles showed little interest in playing with early infants.

During the second half of infancy (fifth through eleventh month), peer group activities increased steadily as mother–infant separation became more complete. By the end of infancy, the young animals travelled with their peer group nearly all day – engaging in foraging, resting or play – although the young often tried to be near their mothers at night. Infant play had developed to include most of the juvenile patterns: chasing, hopping, presenting, sparring, mild threatening, and rougher tumbling and wrestling. As the late infants developed greater competence in the play patterns typical of juveniles, they began to play more frequently with the juveniles that were one year older than they.

The young animals were classified as juvenile between the ages of eleven and thirty months. Play activities reached a peak for the females during the early juvenile period, and they peaked for the males in the mid-juvenile period. Sex differences in play activity had begun to appear in late infancy, but they became much more important in the juvenile period. For the females, play was the roughest at the early juvenile stage, then became progressively milder such that by the late juvenile stage the females engaged only in quiet play interactions. By the late juvenile age, the females spent much time travelling near, or huddling with the adult females, and they had become almost as passive as the adult females. The juvenile males, on the other hand, played progressively more roughly and more aggressively throughout the juvenile age period, although they played less frequently after the mid-juvenile period. Quiet play did occur among the juvenile males, but it was prone to escalate into rough activity. With increasing roughness, the animals showed an increasing tendency to avoid physical contact. Juvenile play often consisted of standing back from or hopping around just beyond reach of each other, as if somewhat hesitant to engage in contact; and more threats were given during play, as if to keep others from making contacts.

By the mid-juvenile age, both males and females began to show brief organized patterns of copulatory behaviour.

Panama, Colombia, Brazil, and Peru

In 1968 and 1969 we surveyed thirty-one separate troops of squirrel monkeys in Panama, Colombia, Brazil, and Peru. The purpose of the studies was to locate possible sites for extended field work on squirrel monkeys and to note possible variations in ecology and behaviour. Troops were observed in the following locations: eight troops in small forests in Panama, twelve troops in the small to moderate-size forests on the llanos of Colombia, four troops in natural areas of the rain forests of Amazonia, and seven troops in areas of Amazonia that had been altered by human activities.

In the small forests of Panama and the llanos of Colombia, troop size varied between ten and thirty-five animals, but in the natural forests of Amazonia, troop size varied from 120 to 300 or more individuals. In altered Amazonia, troop size appeared to range from twenty to eighty animals, though good estimates were difficult to obtain.

The frequency of social play varied considerably among the troops in the different locations. In the small troops of Panama and the llanos of Colombia, play was not nearly so common as in the large troops of natural Amazonia. It is difficult to make estimates of the time that individuals spent in play, because of the limited contact that we had with each troop. However, our observations in conjunction with Thorington's (1968) data suggests that the young animals in the small troops of Panama and the llanos may play between five and thirty minutes per day. Our subjective impression from spending 59 hours with the large troops in natural Amazonia was that they played about half as much as the semi-natural troop in Florida: this would imply about one to two hours per day of play per individual.

An interesting correlation with the frequency of play was the fact that the adults of the large troops maintained closer individual distances and interacted more frequently than the adults of the small troops. The comparative data from the thirty-one study sites suggested the following hypothesis (Baldwin and Baldwin, 1971): young animals in small troops have fewer potential play partners and hence less opportunity to play than animals in large troops; this restricted experience with play gives them less opportunity to learn strong habits for social activity, and thus animals maturing in small troops tend to be less social as adults than animals that grow up in large troops with ample opportunity to play. In other words, the young monkeys in small troops have few age mates with whom to play, and this apparently creates a low probability that there will be two or more animals ready to play at any point in time. In large troops with many infants and juveniles, there is usually a sub-set of young animals ready to play during many hours of the day. The higher frequency of play in large troops provides the maturing monkeys with many and varied social experiences in conjunction with the positive reinforcers that are intrinsic in social play. Thus, the monkeys in large troops are reinforced for maintaining close individual distances during social play, they develop larger repertoires of social interaction patterns and they emit these social behaviours at higher frequencies as long as the behaviours remain reinforcing.

The data from the thirty-one study sites in South America consistently supported the hypothesis that increases in social play experience lead to decreases in the average individual distances maintained by animals during the infant, juvenile and adult years. In other words, the peer group that plays together stays together. Play increases the reinforcers for maintaining close proximity and strengthens the habits of interacting socially.

Barqueta, south-western Panama

Between 19 December 1970 and 25 February 1971, we observed two troops of squirrel monkeys consisting of twenty-three and twenty-seven animals in a natural forest in Hacienda Barqueta in south-western Panama. The squirrel monkeys habituated to our presence within two weeks and could be observed from distances of 3 to 15 metres for long periods of time. In a total of 261 hours of observation on the squirrel monkeys during all hours of their working day, not one instance of social play was observed among any of the animals in either troop.

Presumably, the lack of play at the Barqueta study site was due to the dearth of foods preferred by the squirrel monkeys. The monkeys spent ninty-five per cent of each hour of their 14-hour working day engaged in foraging and in travelling between foraging areas. This pattern of daily activity left little time for any social interactions, including the two social activities that are most common for squirrel monkeys in other environments, resting together and playing. During the five per cent of the time when the animals were not foraging or travelling, however, the young animals came into many situations that would have led to play in the other environments studied, but not once did the animals play. In spite of the lack of play, the Barqueta troops were very cohesive and the animals maintained very close individual distances. The earlier hypothesis that playing together was a necessary pre-condition for staying together in close, integrated troops was clearly inadequate.

The following evidence shows a great difference between the non-playing squirrel monkeys at Hacienda Barqueta and the playful squirrel monkeys at other study sites. The fact that the two Barqueta troops consisted of only twenty-three and twenty-seven members respectively places them near the small end of squirrel monkey troop size (which varies from ten to 300 or more animals). In general, the young monkeys in small troops tend to have few play partners and to engage in less play than monkeys in larger troops (Baldwin and Baldwin, 1971). However, animals in small troops do play. At Barqueta there were also opportunities for play. There were five infants and seven juveniles in the main study troop of twenty-three animals. These young animals were frequently within 5 metres of one or more age-mates. The two main food sources at Barqueta often attracted the whole troop into an area of 180 square metres. The fruits of the palm *Scheelea* and the cactus-like plant *Achmea* both grew in tight clusters that forced the monkeys to come into very close contact as they spent fifteen to 120 seconds locating and picking suitable fruits. The animals regularly came into physical contact, often crawling over each other's bodies, without a single playful interaction. Playful infant and juvenile squirrel monkeys in other environments often began bouts of social play when they came equally close.

At Barqueta during the periods between bouts of foraging when the monkeys did rest, they occasionally rested within arm's reach of each other. Yet, on only six occasions did one animal reach out and touch another. All of these touches were very brief; none led to a bout of social play, and one evoked a mild threat from the touched animal. Playful infants and juveniles in other environments very often became drawn into play under such circumstances. In short, the opportunities for play (i.e., the stimuli of the environmental setting and social cues) were present at Barqueta, but the animals never showed playful responses. If the monkeys were playful in other seasons of the year, one might expect that their play habits would appear with at least some moderate frequency under these favourable social circumstances.

Loy (1970) studied rhesus monkeys on Cayo Santiago Island before, during, and after a twenty-two-day period when very little food was available. The starvation period was so severe that six of the sixty-nine animals died. The frequencies of all behaviours except foraging dropped significantly during the twenty-two-day period. The frequency of social play decreased from 2·54 to 0·15 bouts per hour. The fact that play did not decrease to zero under these severe starvation contingencies suggests that more factors beside temporary food deprivation must be operating to explain the total absence of play at Barqueta. If food were abundant in other seasons at Barqueta, and the monkeys played then, we doubt that a temporary deprivation period would reduce play to zero bouts in 261 hours of observation.

Exploration behaviour at Barqueta was somewhat less frequent than in other environments we have studied, but it is difficult to quantify the amount of time spent in exploration. Infants and juveniles at Barqueta showed exploration tendencies at various times during their daily travelling. Most of this exploration was directed to investigating things in the environment, like tree holes, abandoned squirrel nests, wasp nests, sources of food, broken branches, birds, insects, etc.

The young squirrel monkeys often travelled near each other in the troop. The infants still nursed from their mothers and they spent less time foraging for fruits and insects than did the adults. This gave them more time to explore and/or interact, but no investigatory or play behaviour was directed towards another monkey. Nor did the young rest together, cuddle together, or show other friendly interactions.

Despite the absence of play and a reduced amount of exploratory behaviour, the troops at Barqueta appeared to be cohesive and stable. The troops seldom fragmented and animals often travelled at close individual distances without signs of uneasiness or tension. Agonistic interactions were somewhat less frequent than in other environments: chases and displays occurred forty to forty-five times a day, and no fights were ever observed. Copulations were observed, though they consisted of very brief and simple episodes of mounting and thrusting, without any of the consort activities seen in other environments. The fact that eighty-five per cent of the adult females were accompanied by infants indicates that the reproductive success rate was normal for the species. When comparing the behaviour of the adults at Barqueta to adults in other environments, the most outstanding features are that their social behaviours were very simple and infrequent. However, a simple, basic repertoire can be adequate to allow survival.

The Barqueta data suggests that squirrel monkeys can survive, reproduce and maintain cohesive troops even in the absence of social play. There are other developmental routes to 'normal' adult behaviour besides the socializing experiences of social play; several of these are described and discussed elsewhere (Baldwin and Baldwin, 1973). Hopf (1972, personal communication) also presents data that indicate that social play experience is not crucial to social development. Infants raised in all-adult laboratory groups, without peers to play with, had minimal play experience but showed no marked differences from animals raised with peers and with social play experience. Hopf points out that there are numerous socializing factors that all make overlapping contributions to social development. These factors combine so differently for each maturing individual that each animal develops its own unique personality and role in the group structure. Presumably, the individuals raised without social play are exposed to enough other socializing factors that they can develop within the limits of what is perceived as 'normal'.

(From *American Zoology*, No. 14, 1974, pp. 303–15.)

References

BALDWIN, J. D. (1968), 'The social behavior of adult male squirrel monkeys (*Saimiri sciureus*) in a seminatural environment', *Folia Primat.*, No. 8, pp. 281–314.

BALDWIN, J. D. (1969), 'The ontogeny of social behavior of squirrel monkeys (*Saimiri sciureus*) in a seminatural environment', *Folia Primat.*, No. 11, pp. 35–79.

BALDWIN, J. D., and BALDWIN, J. I. (1971), 'Squirrel monkeys (*Saimiri*) in natural habitats in Panama, Colombia, Brazil and Peru', *Primates*, No. 12, pp. 45–61.

BALDWIN, J. D., and BALDWIN, J. I. (1972), 'The ecology and behavior of squirrel monkeys (*Saimiri oerstedi*) in a Natural Forest in Western Panama , *Folia Primat.*, No. 18, pp. 161–84.

BALDWIN, J. D., and BALDWIN, J. I. (1973), 'The role of play in social organization: comparative observations of squirrel monkeys (*Saimiri*)', *Primates*, No. 14.

BALDWIN, J. D., and BALDWIN, J. I. (1975), in *Primate Socialization*, F. E. Poirier and S. Chevalier-Skolnikoff (eds), Aldine Press, Chicago.

DUMOND, F. V. (1968), 'The squirrel monkey in a seminatural environment', in *The Squirrel Monkey*, L. A. Rosenblum and R. W. Cooper (eds), Academic Press, New York.

HOPF, S. (1972), 'Sozialpsychologische Untersuchungen zur Verhaltensentwicklung des Totenkopfaffens', Ph.D. Thesis, Phillipps-Universität, Marburg/Lahn, pp. 1–137.

LOY, J. (1970), 'Behavioral responses of free-ranging rhesus monkeys to food shortage', *Amer. J. Phys. Anthrop.*, No. 33, pp. 263–72.

PLOOG, D. W., BLITZ, J., and PLOOG, F. (1963), 'Studies on social and sexual behavior of the squirrel monkey (*Saimiri sciureus*)', *Folia Primat.*, No. 1, pp. 29–66.

PLOOG, D., HOPF, S., and WINTER, P. (1967), 'Ontogenese des Verhaltens von Totenkopfaffen (*Saimiri sciureus*)', *Psychol. Forsch.*, No. 31, pp. 1–41.

ROSENBLUM, L. A. (1968), 'Mother–infant relations and early behavioral development in the squirrel monkey', in *The Squirrel Monkey*, L. A. Rosenblum and R. W. Cooper (eds), Academic Press, New York, pp. 207–33.

THORINGTON, R. W., JR (1967), 'Feeding and activity, of Cebus and Saimiri in a Colombian Forest', in *Neue Ergebnisse der Primatologie*, D. Starck, R. Schneider and H. J. Kuhn (eds), Gustav Fischer Verlag, Stuttgart, pp. 180–84.

THORINGTON, R. W., JR (1968), 'Observations of squirrel monkeys in a Colombian Forest', in *The Squirrel Monkey*, L. A. Rosenblum, and R. W. Cooper (eds), Academic Press, New York, pp. 69–85.

An Ethological Study of
Chimpanzee Play

Observers agree that social play and agonistic behaviour in the captive chimpanzee closely resemble each other. This paper attempts to provide both a behavioural basis for distinguishing between them and a discussion of the relationship between their underlying motivational states.

Subjects

The subjects were a small group of adult chimpanzees established at the London Zoo five years ago. They were housed in a circular building fifty feet in diameter, half indoors and half outdoors. The group consisted of one male and five females, two of whom produced infants during the year. None of the animals was handled by keepers or by the observer and only half the cage was open to public viewing.

Methods

The group was observed for an hour a day during the year. Sequences of behaviour that involved interaction between two or more animals were recorded. A sequence was considered to be a succession of behaviour patterns that occurred between two divisions termed breaks. Briefly, a break was recorded when one animal left the scene, when both animals stopped interacting, or when activity changed after a pause. At the end of a sequence either 'dispersal' or 'non-dispersal' was scored, according to whether or not the participating animals were further away from each other at the end of the sequence than they had been at the beginning.

A fairly consistent dominance hierarchy existed within the group. This had been established on the basis of feeding order before beginning the year's recorded observations. When two animals sitting together were offered food, the first or the only one to take it was termed the dominant. Thus when one animal is described as dominant to another in a given interaction it is on the basis of feeding priority. Occasionally an animal dominant in a feeding situation would act as subordinate in another situation, although in general dominance expressed in this way remained constant for all situations.

Table 1 shows the behaviour patterns most frequently occurring in

Table 1 List of behaviour patterns used in analysis of dispersal and non-dispersal sequences

1. Gross	2. Limb	3. Facial	4. Vocalization
Rock	Grab	Bite	Pant
Pull	Hit	Pout	Scream
Push	Drum	Grinface	Whimper
Wrestle	Kick	Playface	Hoot
Chase	Footslap	Mouth open	Bark
Flee	Touch	Tongue out	
Shake		Look at	
Swing			
Crouch			
Jump up and down			

sequences either containing, or associated with, patterns generally agreed to be agonistic, such as biting, kicking, hitting and so forth. These patterns occurred both in sequences ending in dispersal and in sequences ending in non-dispersal.

The data presented in this paper consists of extracts from the main body of data collected over the year. The sequences extracted were the following: the first fifty sequences containing two or more of the patterns listed in Table 1 which ended in dispersal, and the first fifty sequences containing two or more of these patterns which ended in non-dispersal. The patterns within these 100 sequences were then analysed for their correlation with dispersal and non-dispersal.

They were initially divided into two types, action and signal patterns. Action patterns were those considered to be equally available to an animal for use in either a dispersal or a non-dispersal context. It was anticipated that signal patterns on the other hand would correlate closely with either dispersal or non-dispersal, and would therefore fall into two distinct groups.

Results

Tables 2 and 3 give the frequencies with which both action and signal patterns are correlated with dispersal and non-dispersal. Figure 1 presents these results schematically. It can be seen that if the action patterns are preceded or accompanied by the group of signal patterns labelled A, they will then be countered by similar behaviour on the part of the recipient and the interaction will not end in dispersal. If they are preceded or accom-

Table 2 Numbers of behaviour patterns in sequences ending in dispersal and non-dispersal

1. Action patterns

Behaviour pattern	Dispersal	Non-dispersal	p
Bite	5	19	< 0.001
No bite	45	31	$(X^2 = 12.34)$
Pull	4	27	< 0.001
No pull	46	23	$(X^2 = 26.93)$
Grab	5	30	< 0.001
No grab	45	20	$(X^2 = 29.71)$
Hit	3	6	> 0.1
No hit	47	44	$(X^2 = 1.95)$
Kick	4	8	> 0.1
No kick	46	42	$(X^2 = 2.37)$
Chase	31	29	> 0.95
No chase	19	21	$(X^2 = 0.04)$
Flee	34	27	> 0.2
No flee	16	23	$(X^2 = 1.51)$
Wrestle	1	23	< 0.001
No wrestle	49	27	$(X^2 = 29.0)$

panied by the group of signals labelled B they are succeeded by another set of patterns altogether and the interaction ends in dispersal.

Two of the action patterns that occur equally frequently in both dispersal and non-dispersal contexts were then looked at in more detail. Table 4 shows where in both a dispersal and a non-dispersal context chasing precedes fleeing, or fleeing precedes chasing; and secondly, in any given pair, whether the dominant or the subordinate animal was the initiator of the interaction. Unless stated otherwise, the probabilities given are two-tailed, using the binomial test of significance. The results show that in a dispersal context, chasing precedes fleeing more than fleeing precedes chasing ($32/13$; $p = 0.01$). In the non-dispersal situation, however, fleeing precedes chasing more than chasing precedes fleeing ($13/31$; $p = 0.01$).

Table 3 Numbers of behaviour patterns in sequences ending in dispersal and non-dispersal

II. Signal Patterns

Behaviour pattern	Dispersal	Non-dispersal	p
Playface	1	42	<0·001
No playface	49	8	($X^2 = 71·97$)
Pant	1	6	<0·02
No pant	49	44	($X^2 = 5.53$)
Rock	8	0	<0·05
No rock	42	50	($X^2 = 5·15$)
Hair erection	25	1	<0·001
No hair erection	25	49	($X^2 = 27·49$)
Grinface	4	0	>0·2
No grinface	46	50	($X^2 = 1·13$)
Whimper	3	0	>0·5
No whimper	47	50	($X^2 = 0·39$)
Scream	21	0	<0·001
No scream	29	50	($X^2 = 22·73$)
Bark	16	0	<0·001
No bark	34	50	($X^2 = 15·26$)
Hoot	32	0	<0·001
No hoot	18	50	($X^2 = 48·96$)

In a dispersal situation the dominant animal is initiating the chasing in a chase-before-flee situation significantly often (32/0; $p = 0·0001$), and the subordinate animal is initiating the fleeing in a flee-before-chase situation (3/10; $p = 0·046$, 1-tailed). However, in a non-dispersal situation, the dominant animal is doing significantly more of the initiating in both a chase-before-flee situation (10/3; $p = 0·046$, 1-tailed) and a flee-before-chase situation (21/10, $p = 0·037$, 1-tailed).

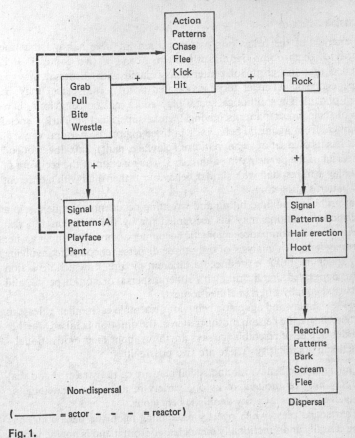

Fig. 1.

Table 4 Number of occasions in dispersal and non-dispersal sequences in which chasing and fleeing were initiated by dominant or subordinate animals

| | Chase precedes flee | | Flee precedes chase | | |
	Dominant initiates	Subordinate initiates	Dominant initiates	Subordinate initiates	Total
Dispersal	32	0	3	10	45
Non-dispersal	10	3	21	10	44

Discussion

This analysis of the behaviour patterns listed in Table 1 shows that the majority of them occur significantly often in one of two contexts. It is suggested that the group of patterns associated with dispersal may be termed agonistic whereas those associated with non-dispersal may be termed playful. Thus although social play and agonistic behaviour share some of their motor patterns, giving them a superficial similarity, social play differs from agonistic behaviour in three major behavioural ways:

1. It has its own set of signal patterns (playface, pant). 2. It does not end in dispersal of the participating animals. 3. The reaction of the recipient of social play is to respond with similar behaviour rather than with a different set of patterns altogether.

That grabbing, pulling, biting and wrestling occur most frequently in a non-dispersal situation may be accounted for by the fact that the vast majority of adult chimpanzee agonistic encounters consist of threat alone; they rarely fight. An analysis of only those dispersal encounters involving actual attack might have produced a different picture, in which no action patterns correlated significantly with either dispersal or non-dispersal, and all occurred equally often in either context.

Since social play and agonistic behaviour resemble each other at least to the extent of sharing certain motor patterns, the question is raised whether or not this degree of resemblance says anything about their motivational – or functional – similarity. There are two possibilities:

1. That agonistic behaviour and social play are causally related and that social play may be thought of as one variety of agonistic behaviour, or possibly even as low intensity agonistic behaviour.

2. That social play, while overtly resembling agonistic behaviour, has become causally and functionally emancipated from it and is now separately organized; as for example some writers believe to be the case in the use of sexual patterns in dominance behaviour in the rhesus macaque.

The results of the analysis of the chase-flee interactions suggest a possible argument in favour of the fundamental motivational similarity of the aggression-play complex of behaviours. In the vast majority of cases in a non-dispersal situation, the fleeing comes before the chasing, and in the majority of these cases it is the dominant animal which is initiating this fleeing. In other words, in order for the play interaction to continue and be reacted to with similar behaviour on the part of the recipient, the dominant animal has to behave like a subordinate when it comes to a chase-flee interaction: he has to be the one who is chased. He is still the initiator but what he initiates is fleeing. It is suggested that the level of threat implicit in a situation where a subordinate animal is being chased by one more dominant is being reduced – or eliminated – by this simple mechanism of role reversal. If social play had no aggressive content at all, role reversal would be unnecessary. If there was no aggression there would be no threat, and the dominant animal could afford to chase as often as he was chased without running the risk of abruptly terminating the interaction.

More analysis of this kind may show that there are many other ways of reducing the potential threat conveyed by patterns and sequences of behaviour traditionally associated with attack. It is hoped that this paper indicates one way in which it is possible to tackle the problems of disentangling play from the other forms of behaviour it closely resembles.

(From *Proc. 2nd Int. Congr. Primat.*, Vol. 1, Karger, New York, 1969, pp. 87–93.)

Rough-and-tumble Play among Nursery School Children

Introduction

One of the research programmes in the Department of Growth and Development at the Institute of Child Health, University of London, is an attempt to apply ethological methods of observation and interpretation to the behaviour of normal children. Our aim is to extend this into a longitudinal study of development, after doing the groundwork on suitable age cross-sections.

Between November 1963 and May 1964 I carried out a pilot study on four- to five-year-old children in a London nursery school. Previously I had observed three- to five-year-old children in a variety of nursery schools in two other cities.

It became obvious that one can study human behaviour in just the same way as Tinbergen (1953 and 1959), and Moynihan (1955) and others have studied gulls, and van Hooff (1962), Andrew (1963, who also gives comparative data from a child), and others have studied non-human primates.

This paper describes the crude preliminary observations which gave rise to this conclusion. It is a provisional, descriptive account, much like a report on the first season's ethological field work on any new species. It is subject to similar criticisms.

The observation situation

My observations have all been made on nursery school children, aged three to five, in a variety of schools but chiefly at one school in London during 1963–4. The aspects of behaviour I deal with in this paper vary little from school to school, despite differences in social background. Many aspects of behaviour do vary but I saw all the fixed action patterns described here in all the schools that I visited.

I used no special observation techniques, but simply visited the school repeatedly, and sat on a chair in a corner with a notebook. The children gradually reacted less and less to me, as I tried to be as unresponsive as possible without antagonizing them. Of course I can never say that my presence does not affect their behaviour but their initial responses to me do certainly disappear. They always have at least one teacher there and visitors and students are common. Nursery school teachers seem to have a policy of non-interference broken only by giving limited guidance and encouragement when asked, or direly needed. This makes nursery school an ideal situation for studying the unrestrained behaviour of three- to five-year olds.

Agonistic behaviour

Among three- to five-year-old children in nursery school, fights occur over property and little else. One child pulls at another's toy and the owner pulls back, then one of them kicks, pushes, bites or pulls the hair of the other. The beating movement is the commonest and is rather consistent in form. It is an overarm blow with the palm side of the lightly clenched fist. The arm is sharply bent at the elbow and raised to a vertical position then brought down with great force on the opponent, hitting any part of him that gets in the way. Biting seems to be more commonly done by girls than by boys. These attacks are often preceded and accompanied by fixating the opponent and by what looks like a frown with lowering of the eyebrows and rather little vertical furrowing of the brow ('low frown') and no conspicuous modification of the mouth expression. Often the child shouts 'no' or 'let go', with a characteristic tone, low pitch and hard explosive quality being evident. Andrew (1963) published a spectrograph of this sound. Usually in these property fights little locomotion is involved, they end quickly with one child gaining possession of the object and one or the other walking a short way off. The beating movement, and the preparatory position with bent arm held high and clenched fist, is confined to property fights; it occurs with low frowns and fixation and in situations where the opponents end up separated.

When there are signs, such as stepping back from the opponent, that something is inhibiting the attack, the mouth expression changes and the child shows a 'fierce' expression with lower teeth bared and the corner of the mouth drawn down. I haven't seen this often but it has an interesting place in 'folklore'. It is the expression illustrated by Netter (1958) for rage in man (whatever rage may be), but Netter adds an eye component, with brows up and eyelids wide open, which is characteristic of a child fleeing from an unusually violent opponent!

Occasionally a robbed child would scream long and loud, a lowish-pitched scream or roar, and, red in the face, beat at, with closed fist, but not hit, and not approach its opponent. This performance sometimes looks rather like what has been called a temper tantrum and the child gives the appearance (because of his beating movements and orientation towards the opponent) of being highly stimulated to attack but for some reason not actually doing so and in addition showing features (scream and red face) of a defeated child.

The child who gets hit, or whose property is grabbed, often gives a brief high-pitched scream. This is rarely repeated, subsequent behaviour being either a verbal call for help, or retaliation, or letting go often followed by weeping. Weeping is associated with, and usually preceded by, puckering the brows (see also Darwin, 1872) and reddening of the face. Often the child then stays immobile for a minute or more, frequently sitting down, and may suck its thumb, hold on to a lock of its own hair, and even rock back and forward. The last two are not common but occur mostly after crying. Sucking often also occurs when the children are sitting listening to a story, and so sometimes do hair-holding and rocking. Thumb-sucking is also common as a child goes to sleep, so that perhaps it is most closely associated with 'inactivity' or low arousal rather than with 'distress', or is going to sleep a lonely, distressing situation? (Do children who do not suck never complain about going to bed, and go to sleep quicker than those who do, or does a child suck more on those occasions when he complains about going to bed?) Weeping and the associated patterns seem to be most commonly elicited by social factors, although of course a child does often cry after it falls over. But a child pushed over by another in rough-and-tumble play rarely cries, whereas one pushed over in a fight frequently does so. Also it seems that crying, puckered brow, red face, inactivity, differentiate sharply from actual escape or fleeing behaviour. If a child runs away from another it doesn't cry or go red or pucker its brows, it screams in briefly interrupted bursts and has raised eyebrows and wide-open eyelids. The raised eyebrows can precede actual fleeing, as when a child suddenly meets another who commonly attacks and pursues others (there was one such rare individual in my study group).

One other conspicuous but rare response of a child in fights is to raise the arm over or in front of the head, with forearm horizontal providing a protection against the opponent's beating. Sometimes the eyebrows are raised as well. This seems to be an alternative to fleeing, happening when the child is cornered, and once I saw it made by a child being beaten by one it spent a lot of time with and from which it would be unlikely to go away.

The more precise description of attacking, and threatening and tantrums and weeping and fleeing, should clarify the relationship between them and between ill-defined categories such as frustration, distress, fear and aggression. I would speculate that a temper tantrum is the behaviour shown when attack is stimulated but the opponent is overwhelmingly powerful and/or a friend (e.g. a parent; in my observations it has been a child opponent, but a playmate and one who usually wins his fights). It must somehow relate to weeping and the inactivity of the robbed or beaten child, but this again is quite separate from fleeing and the components accompanying fleeing.

To judge from the child behaviour, popular ideas of human threat gestures seem to be quite erroneous. Mostly they refer to more intimidating displays. The cold direct stare is the real danger sign (and the one people react to most readily). It is interesting that punching, wrestling, use of weapons or of more sophisticated methods of attack are not in the child's battle repertoire at this age. Wrestling occurs, not with any of the behaviours described above but with alternating chases and laughing and falling over, between children who stay together for a long time and neither of whom is holding a toy. It falls into a group almost identical with 'rough-and-tumble play' in the Harlow laboratory's monkey studies.

Rough-and-tumble play

Harlow's and his colleagues' (Harlow and Harlow, 1962; Hansen, 1962; Rosenblum, 1961) recent experiments have emphasized the importance of playmates in the development of social and sexual behaviour in rhesus monkeys, and stressed the part occupied by the chasing and fighting play between individuals. It is therefore interesting, though obvious, that almost identical patterns of play occur, and are clearly definable, in human children. It is important to define this kind of play firstly because it surely must not be confused with all the other things which we call 'play' just because they are done by children, and secondly because in investigating its distinctiveness from other behaviour we may get some idea how it differs from other behaviour in its effects and function and in its causal organization.

The human 'rough-and-tumble play', as I shall call it (Harlow *et al.*, use this term for one out of three or more kinds of social play) consists of seven movement patterns which tend to occur at the same time as each other and not to occur with other movements. These are running, chasing and fleeing; wrestling; jumping up and down with both feet together ('jumps'); beating at each other with an open hand without actually hitting ('open beat'); beating at each other with an object but not hitting; laughing. In addition, falling seems to be a regular part of this behaviour, and if there is anything soft to land on children spend much time throwing themselves and each other on to it.

There seems to be a common facial expression in this play besides the smile-like expression involved in laughing. This is seen when a child is about to be chased by another and stands slightly crouched, side-on to the chaser and looking at it with this 'mischievous' expression, an open-mouthed smile with the teeth covered, which morphologically resembles the 'play-face' of *Macaca* and *Pan* (van Hooff, 1962).

Rough-and-tumble play subsequently seems to develop rather sharply into formalized games like 'tag' and 'cowboys and Indians'. There are the same motor patterns but rules and verbal explanations have been added.

Most of the rough-and-tumble play consists of behaviour which on the surface looks very hostile: violent pursuit, assault and fast evasive retreat. However, the roles of the participants rapidly alternate and the behaviour does not lead to spacing out or capture of objects; the participants stay together even after the chasing ends. Also the movements involved are quite different from those involved in fights over property. The facial expressions and vocalizations, and the motor patterns involved separate out into two quite different clusters. Thus beating with clenched fist occurs with fixating, frowning, shouting, and not with laughing and jumping. Wrestling and open-handed beats occur with jumping and laughing and not with frown, fixate and closed beat. So although rough and tumble looks like hostile behaviour it is quite separate from behaviour which I call hostile because of its effects, i.e. involving property ownership and separation of individuals.

Not only does rough and tumble include patterns like wrestling or beating sticks at each other (or 'shooting' at each other) which adults might think and often do think are aggressive; in some circumstances children react to them as dangerous and conceivably aggressive. Children new to school do not join in these games straight away. Those I have seen have watched the games and followed them around but always ran to the teacher or some refuge (a wall or corner or seat) if the players happened to move towards them. If they got caught up in a game they were more likely to cry than established children.

Some children seem permanently unable to join in and take the rough and tumble 'in fun'. What are these individuals like as adults? They are not all 'only children', but is there a critical period for developing the ability to rough and tumble, or are these children unusual in some way other than deprivation of the chance to play at the right age? Since the rough-and-tumble motor patterns and expressions appear quite as early as eighteen months old and maybe even younger, the nursery school starting age of three years could be too late for those who had no playmates of the right age in or near home.

Sometimes the fleeing involved seems to 'turn real'. A child fleeing for a long time without chasing back, going faster and faster, may raise its eyebrows and stop smiling and its laugh changes and becomes a more continuous vocalization, a tremulous scream. I have heard the same noise in response to an insect running about on the ground, the child stamping rapidly with alternate feet and looking at it and running away, returning, running away again, etc.

In this age group the attack-like behaviour involved in rough and tumble does not seem to turn into real attacks, but in older rhesus, to judge from Hansen (1962), (and in rats too) it gets more difficult to distinguish play-fighting from real fighting; there is for instance more actual biting. Possibly human children follow the same development; I have not observed older children enough to say.

Rough-and-tumble play relates to real hostile behaviour in that:

1. It looks like it to adults, and quite often one sees adults responding as if a play pattern (e.g. open-handed beat plus play-face) were really hostile.

2. Some children respond as if it were hostile, e.g. they flee from play attack movements.

3. Sometimes play fleeing becomes real fleeing.

4. Some motor patterns are similar, e.g. orientation of locomotion (though there is little locomotion in property fights), and a possible similarity in form between laughing and screaming with intermediates between them, and the arm position and movement of beating, in both rough and tumble and hostile behaviour.

Most of the time, despite these similarities, the players neither respond as if their playmates were hostile nor show any indication of their own motivation being hostile (i.e. of the causes of rough and tumble being at all related to the causes of fighting). Short-term effects of this play are eventual exhaustion, continuing to stay with the playmates, seeking them out another time to play with. If anything, its short-term effect is to gain friends rather than to lose them.

Atypically, some children initiate rough-and-tumble play with newly arrived strange adults. Some do this by running up and beating at the adult, or jumping and making beating movements with an object. These are the children who get called 'cheeky'. They evoke hostility in adults and can only be persuaded to stop this behaviour, and subsequent wrestling, by the adult genuinely giving way to his hostile feelings. Making a fixating-threat face with no trace of a smile is the least one can get away with. Other children use a less objectionable approach, inviting the adult to chase them both verbally and by adopting the posture and play-face that elicits chasing and precedes their play fleeing with other children. These two per-formances, in a greeting situation, are not typical of the situations in which rough-and-tumble play occurs (mostly with friends and not decreasing with familiarity), but they are suggestive of some remote connection between rough and tumble and more aggregative and hostile behaviour.

No doubt some would argue that the laughing and jumping up and down which are characteristic of rough-and-tumble play are just signs that the children are 'excited' or 'enjoying themselves'. It is hard to tell what this would mean in terms of observables. Perhaps it would mean that laughing and jumping occur in any situation where the child was in a state of high general arousal (and this still does not mean anything in terms of observable behaviour) and was in sight of positive reinforcement. In any case it would suggest a rather wide occurrence of the behaviour, in many situations and accompanying a variety of other behaviours. But the evidence at present is that laughing has mainly to do with chasing and wrestling and is not linked to a wider range of active behaviour. A child running to greet its mother is presumably aroused, but I have never seen them laugh or jump up and down. A child painting is surely enjoying it (they keep doing this!) and must have an aroused E.E.G. but the child does not laugh and jump. I think that laughing and jumping are both very specific signals (in causation and function) indicating the friendly meaning of the hostile-looking behaviour involved in rough-and-tumble play.

Discussion: evaluation

I have shown above how one can treat the behaviour of three- to five-year-old human beings exactly as ethologists have treated the behaviour of many different animals in field studies. The next question is whether this is a good way to investigate the behaviour of any animal. Such ethological soul-searching mainly belongs elsewhere than in this paper, except to say that I think one cannot do an ethological study of human behaviour without becoming even more concerned about methodology. Secondly, one must ask whether this is a useful way to study *human* behaviour, and what the differences are between ethology and various branches of psychology.

Correlations and other statistical investigations of fixed action patterns may give rise to a more objective and accurate picture of the organization of behaviour than the arbitrary categories of motivation in use in everyday life and in the more armchair branches of psychology. But perhaps the ethologist is merely pushing the arbitrariness one step further down. Thus, just as factor analysis studies of motivation or personality ultimately depend on the selection of questionnaire items, so an ethological study relies on the identification of fixed action patterns. In the present paper some of my items of behaviour are not even all at the same level of description, e.g. 'beating' and 'painting'. Obviously one has ideally to examine the fixed action patterns carefully to show just how constant they are, and just how one differs from another, right down to description of the particular combinations and sequences of components or even the muscle contractions and skeletal movements involved. This, it seems to me, is something that any further ethological study of human behaviour should go into quite deeply.

In addition there is the probability that this approach stems from much too simple a view of the mechanisms of behaviour. This shows up most when one tries to think about the creative activities of the children and about some of their more complex, verbally organized games. However, I believe that the approach illustrated in this paper (at its most primitive and preliminary level) can provide a lot of new and useful information on social and emotional behaviour, even quite complex aspects of it, and may eventually go further than one can at present see in analysing verbal and intellectual behaviour. I also feel that to criticize direct observation as a method on the grounds that it is incapable of elucidating some of the more complex (and obscure) aspects of motivation is wrong in two ways. One is that it may reflect a simple lack of talent and experience as an observer; the other is that the concepts about motivation may themselves be at fault.

Many of these obscure and highly verbalized ideas about motivation or organization of behaviour are attempts to describe very complex and barely understood relationships between environment and behaviour. One should aim to make these relationships explicit and phrase them in terms of observables, thereby making them available for scientific study. Sometimes the ideas will turn out to be meaningless but sometimes not. But in addition, studies based on observation of normal uncontrolled behaviour show up previously neglected important aspects of behaviour. The extremely obvious rough-and-tumble play has always been regarded as unimportant by psychologists. Although its importance was shown up by Harlow's experimental studies, it is such conspicuous behaviour and so interesting in its relationship to hostile behaviour that one could not have long disregarded it and its effects in an ethological study of children.

A more specific common criticism of the ethological approach is one that is made by laymen of psychology, and, surprisingly, by psychologists of ethology. This is that the wide range of individual differences makes such a study nearly impossible. I do not think it does. There seems to be less individual difference in the measures I used than in many, because I concentrate on movements that I find to occur in most individuals. While the frequency of occurrence of the movements may vary greatly the association between movements usually persists, i.e. if one scores individuals separately the correlations I report here would be found in most individuals. For example, although some may rarely chase others they also more rarely laugh and jump up and down (Fig. 1). The behaviour of one child in my 1963–4 study group cut across some of the correlations, and I would think this provided a useful characterization of his behaviour, which was conspicuously abnormal to me, the teachers, and the children (each in our different terms!). Even at this age there are individual mannerisms and even occasional complex individual stereotypes. In such a case one could still usefully analyse the place of that individual fixed action-pattern in the behaviour of that individual. I think its occurrence would be very predictable.

In using the term 'action pattern' I have intended to stress the relative constancy of some observable, complex motor activities, and not necessarily to imply species specificity or universality, nor imply anything about the ontogeny of the behaviour. Development is a topic to investigate rather than to classify out of existence with terms like 'innate' and 'learned'. But there is an interesting possibility concerning rough-and-tumble play. There appears (as in Fig. 1) to be a sex difference in the amount of rough-and-tumble play by children, males playing more often than females. The same difference is well established in rhesus monkeys. Young, Goy and Phoenix (1964) report nearly male frequencies of rough-and-tumble play in a young female rhesus whose mother was injected with testosterone during pregnancy. It looks as if this may be one sex difference in human behaviour which is not culturally determined, although it could result from differences in physique rather than direct C.N.S. effects of hormones.

Discussion: comparative aspects

An advantage of this kind of study for comparative primatology is that it allows comparisons of the same kind of data about man and other primates, rather than comparisons of our everyday inside knowledge of man with a more empirical knowledge of other species. Thus we could compare counts of occurrence of smiles before, after or with attacks, avoidances, approaches and other behaviour, from both man and other species. Although it is premature to attempt extensive comparison, one or two points are worth mentioning here.

In the children smiling indeed comes out as closely related to approaching and embracing or staying with, as opposed to the closer relationship to avoiding which occurs in macaques and chimpanzees. But one sometimes feels that human smiles are also partly 'fear' motivated. These 'frightened smiles' may look different only because they are often momentarily interrupted if there is a strong tendency to flee, although they still result from a simultaneous strong stimulus to approach and stay with the other person. Also, the flickering timid smiles often occur with respiration reminiscent of laughing and I wonder if one might not find they resembled

Rough-and-tumble play is as common in the human young . . .

. . . as it is in the young of other species. Chimpanzees, 6 to 8 years old, playing on the ground of the rain forest in Gabon

The human 'wide-mouthed smile' at its most joyful (*see* van Hooff, p. 134)

Stumptail macaque play-face (the monkey is being tickled by a human) (*see* Bertrand, pp. 320–26)

Stumptail macaque fear-grin (*see* Bertrand, pp. 320–26)

Efforts to use one's hands in play . . .

. . . lead to practised skills in more complex play (*see* Bruner, p. 37)

. . or to more serious behaviour, possibly essential for survival, as in termite 'fishing'. Goblin, an adolescent male chimpanzee, just beginning to master termiting after a long period of playing at it (*see* van Lawick-Goodall, pp. 222–4)

Children eagerly investigate the real properties of things when they explore . . .

. . . and take off into the realm of the imagined when they start to play with what they have explored (*see* Hutt, pp. 209, 210)

Useful inventions may be the by-products of play – as with this group of young
chimpanzees filmed in the act of breaking and entering (*see* Menzel, p. 229)

Early interaction play between infant and adult: Assumbo, a baby gorilla born at the Jersey Zoo, playing with Quentin Bloxam, Curator of Mammals

Barbary macaques: in play, the head male encourages an infant to walk
(*see* Burton, p. 383)

Social play among the Gombe Stream chimpanzees. Prof, on left, tries to join in
play between Goblin and Pom (both Prof and Goblin have play faces)
(*see* van Lawick-Goodall, pp. 302–10)

'I am a giant'

'I am an Indian'

'We're space-men'
(*see* Vygotsky,
pp. 546–54, on
material used as
'play pivots')

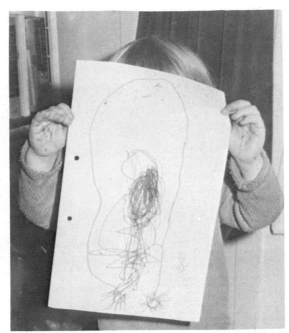

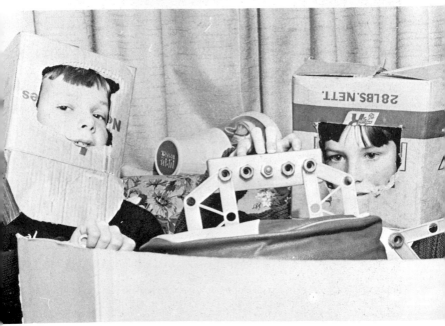

Games of chance and skill can give opportunities for creative variations – though sometimes severely constrained by rules (*see* Piaget, pp. 413–41)

And one of the most powerful and creative sets of rules is language itself, even in making up fanciful sentences from word bricks (*see* Auden, pp. 584–5; Cazden, pp. 603–7)

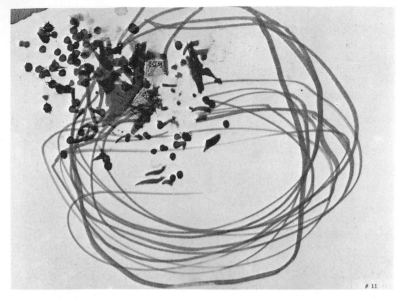

1. Douglas's earliest 'combat art', done at the age of 3. This incorporates stamp fragments (*see* Feinburg, pp. 589–93)

2. At the age of 5, Douglas draws recognizable symbols of ships, men and equipment (*see* Feinburg, pp. 589–93)

3. A mixed-media drawing of a land encounter, where men are equipped with hats and machine-guns. (Drawn at the age of 8) (*see* Feinburg, pp. 589–93)

4. Schematic figures drawn at the age of 9, when Douglas was capable of far more detail, show his preference for creating a playful environment to making a finished artistic product (*see* Feinburg, pp. 589–93)

A cock-fight in Bali: in 'deep play', what you may lose is incommensurably greater than what you stand to win (*see* Geertz, pp. 656–74)

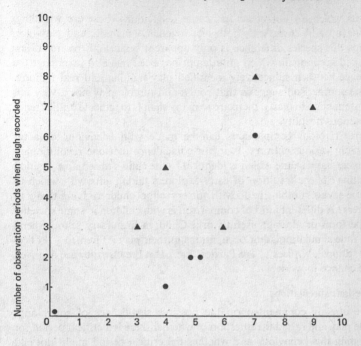

Fig. 1. Graph showing for each individual the number of observation periods in which laughing occurred against the number in which running occurred. It appears that individuals who run little also laugh little, and that girls do less of both these rough and tumble play patterns than do boys. Triangles represent boys, solid circles represent girls.

laughing more closely than smiles. I have already mentioned that laughter and screams during fleeing can intergrade in form. Andrew (1963) uses his concept of 'stimulus contrast' to relate these various expressions and vocalizations in a more uni-dimensional scheme.

While fixation in attack, with relatively inconspicuous facial changes (lowering brows), raised eyebrows in fleeing, and the play face are described in other species, I have not identified in the children any equivalent of grooming or lip-smacking, or the appeasement presenting.

In the age group studied, rough-and-tumble play seems to be more clearly differentiated from hostile behaviour than it is in any other species. Besides showing frequent alternation of chaser and chased, lack of threat postures, persistence, and lack of spacing effect and lack of injury, as in most animals, rough-and-tumble has at least four characteristic motor patterns which do not occur in hostile behaviour. These are wrestling, jumping up and down with both feet together, laughing, and play-face. Perhaps this species difference is only apparent because there are so few published accounts in which an attempt has been made to document the difference between subjectively identified play fighting and real fighting. But the comparison suggests that rough-and-tumble play has a very important function in man if there are so many signals to indicate its difference from serious hostility.

More frivolous comparisons can be made with behaviour of adult humans in various cultures. Is it just coincidence that one revolutionary movement has a salute which is identical to the child's raised arm position in beating? Is the tradition of early explorers taking gifts with which to greet the savages nothing to do with nursery school children giving things to strangers? A different kind of comparison is with children in some societies who perform or attempt useful work. Children in nursery school spend much time simulating adult occupations in their play ('Firemen', 'Policemen', 'Shops', 'Offices', 'Tea Parties', etc.). Is it because they are deprived of the chance to work?

Discussion: speculations

I have already commented on the possible significance of rough-and-tumble play and raised the question of whether there is a critical period for developing this behaviour and whether the critical period might not end before three years old. This would have obvious educational implications where an only or oldest child is concerned. One could only produce answers to these suggestions by longitudinal study of a rather large number of children, but they would be good answers. More indirect evidence can be gathered in short-term studies, for instance on the differences in the other social behaviour of children who do or do not do rough-and-tumble play. Are those who do not play usually extreme in their aggression or fearfulness?

Only two of the children in my study group spent much time looking at books. These two spent little time making things or painting. They were also often alone, seldom moving about alone or with others, almost never joining in rough-and-tumble play. They talked a lot and very well, to themselves, to the teachers, one of them to me, and to any passing child. The other children spend a lot of time making things or painting, move about a lot, don't talk to me or to teachers much, do not hold long monologues, do join in rough-and-tumble play now and again. Is this the beginning of the 'two cultures', or just a chance occurrence? If a division of 'doers' and 'verbalists' is a general division at this age, it corresponds remarkably closely with Bibby's (1964) modified delineation of the 'Two Cultures' (which themselves need proper documentation) to which Tanner (1964) drew my attention after I commented on these 'verbalist' children. The division is surprising in the way it goes so widely through other aspects of the child's behaviour. Is one of the clues to the cause of a child's taking to one 'culture' or another to be found in these other aspects of the behaviour, for instance its early sociability?

These are speculations but speculation is justified when one can so easily see what further evidence to gather. I felt it worth indicating some of those implications of ethological study of human behaviour which potentially ethology can investigate rather thoroughly.

(From 'An ethological study of some aspects of social behaviour of children in nursery schools', *Primate Ethology*, Desmond Morris (ed.), Weidenfeld & Nicolson, 1967.)

References

ANDREW, R. J. (1963), 'The origin and evolution of the calls and facial expressions of the primates', *Behaviour*, No. 20, 5, p. 1–109.

BIBBY, C. (1964), 'Science as an instrument of culture', *Nature*, No 202, pp. 331–3.

DARWIN, C. R. (1872), *The Expression of Emotions in Man and Animals*, John Murray.

HANSEN, E. W. (1962), 'The development of maternal and infant behavior in the rhesus monkey', unpublished thesis, Wisconsin.

HARLOW, H. F. (1962), 'The Heterosexual affection system in monkeys', *Amer. Psychol.*, No. 17, pp. 1–9.

HARLOW, H. F., and HARLOW, M. K. (1962), 'Social deprivation in monkeys', *Sci. American*, No. 207 (5), p. 136.

HOOFF, J. A. R.A.M. VAN (1962), 'Facial expressions in higher primates', *Evolutionary Aspects of Animal Communication, Symp. Zool. Soc. Lond.*, No. 8, pp. 97–125.

MOYNIHAN, M. (1955), 'Some aspects of reproductive behaviour in the Black-headed Gull (*Larus ridibundus L.*) and related species', *Behaviour Supplement*, No. 4.

NETTER, F. H. (1958), 'Nervous System', *Ciba Collection of Medical Illustrations*, Vol. 1, Ciba.

ROSENBLUM, L. A. (1961), 'The development of social behavior in the rhesus monkey', unpublished thesis, Wisconsin.

TANNER, J. M. (1964), 'Human biology in general university education', *Teaching and Research in Human Biology*, No. 7, pp. 23–37.

TINBERGEN, N. (1953), *The Herring Gull's World*, Methuen.

TINBERGEN, N. (1959), 'Comparative studies of the behaviour of gulls (*Laridal*): a progress report', *Behaviour* No. 15, pp. 1–70.

YOUNG, W. C., GOY, R. W., and PHOENIX, C. H. (1964), 'Hormones and sexual behaviour', *Science*, No. 143, pp. 212–18.

A Tangu Game

Among the Tangu people of New Guinea, co-operative play (the *taketak* game) has a formal rule structure that is strikingly like the co-operative pattern of the adult society.

One of the ideas dominating Tangu relationships and activities is equivalence: a notion of moral equality between persons which receives primary expression in the attempt to exchange equivalent amounts of foodstuffs – a task entailing almost insuperable practical difficulties and rarely explicitly attained except by mutual consent and agreement. The same idea of equivalence is expressed in a game, popular with Tangu, which is played mostly by children but which is also a pastime of adults and youths.

The game, known as *taketak*, takes its name from the word for the hard spines of coconut palm fronds. Before play the spines are stripped and stuck in the ground about six inches apart so that they form two lots of massed spines standing rather less than three feet in height. Each lot would contain about thirty spines, and is separated from the other by approximately five yards. Care is taken to plant the *taketak* so that there are no empty spaces and so that the *taketak* do not form parallel or diagonal lines. Tops – hollow hemispheres about two inches in diameter, made from a dried rind, the half of a wild jungle fruit, with a stick forced through the apex of the hemisphere – are also made.

The two teams that form up are usually roughly equal as regards numbers of persons, but what is important is that the number of tops used by each team should be the same. A player spins a top in the palms of his hands, and, in one movement throws it into one lot of spines with the object of striking as many as possible – either during the flight of the top or when it is spinning on the ground. Those *taketak* which have been hit by the top are pulled out and laid aside. When the first team have completed their play into one lot of *taketak*, the second take up their tops and play into the other. Supposing the first team to have struck three *taketak*, and the second two, two *taketak* are replaced in the lot into which the first team is spinning. If, with their second turn, the first team hit one *taketak*, it is removed – leaving both teams with two *taketak* out of each lot. Both teams are now equivalent as to the number of *taketak* removed but the second team owe their series of spins: their object is to throw their tops into the *taketak* without hitting one. Should they succeed in *not* hitting any *taketak* – and the top has to be thrown fully into the middle of the lot – the game is over and both teams are equivalent. If, on the other hand, the second team should strike one *taketak*, two are replaced. The game goes on in this wise until either the players tire of the game – when equivalence is reached by mutual consent – or until all the *taketak* are replaced in both lots.

Another and significantly different version of the game came into vogue in a particular settlement which, incidentally, had had most to do with Tangu Cargo cult activities. In this version the two teams spin their tops in the lots of *taketak* without any replacements. The game continues until one team has struck and extracted all the *taketak* belonging to the other. The first round is then over and the winning team are described as *gtangi* – strong, obdurate, not susceptible to persuasion. Another round follows. Should the losers of the first round win the second, the teams are regarded as equivalent and only rarely is a third and decisive round embarked upon. If the winners of the first round also win the second they are described as emphatically *gtangi*, and no third round is initiated.

In the second version the Pidgin term 'gol', derived from our own 'goal' in its context in Association Football, is used to acclaim the striking of a *taketak*. Much simpler to play than the original game, the later version – both in its form and in the spirit in which it is played – is biased towards selecting a 'stronger' or winning team. Yet no team that loses is content to leave it at that. A return match is arranged in which every effort is made by *both* sides to come out equivalent in the series. To remain *gtangi* at the expense of others in the community may, today, give a pinch of self-satisfaction to the winners – but they also feel anxious about the ill-feeling it generates. The older version of the game, which may be taken to be relatively unaffected by European contacts, has much the same competitive spirit during play as the other and it is also more subtle. It does not require perfecting a single skill in order to strike down more *taketak* more rapidly: it requires the ability to hit *taketak* when necessary, and to miss them if it is expedient. Finishing the game by consent and agreement is not only in itself a mutual recognition of parity, but it is also an acknowledgement that the game can end in no other way.

Food exchanges and the rivalries that go with them can also be ended by mutual consent. Theoretically at least, though not often in practice, the game can be completed.* But there is no third factor to pronounce on equivalence in food exchanges: failing the mutual consent they go on until death or retirement.

(From *Man*, June 1957, pp. 88–9.)

*But I have never seen a game ended other than by mutual consent. 'Missing' requires an almost impossible combination of skill and fortune.

C Playing Sex Roles

Play-mothering: the Relations between Juvenile Females and Young Infants among Free-ranging Vervet Monkeys

Introduction

Until the studies of the past decade on primate social behaviour became available, it seemed to many that the major behaviour patterns of a species, such as mating or maternal behaviour, were largely instinctive. It was assumed by most scientists that vital activities like reproduction could not be left to the chances of a learning process and that such patterns were probably relatively fixed genetically. Recent field and laboratory workers have shown that in many species of mammals, and especially in monkeys and apes, learning and experience play vital roles in the development of the behaviour patterns used in mating and maternal care. For example, Harlow and Harlow (1965) have shown that monkeys who have been raised in cages with only their mothers and deprived of chances to play with their peers are very ineffective in mating. Their motor patterns are poorly coordinated and directed, and their motivation is very low. As adults these monkeys can be given a kind of encounter group therapy that helps improve their mating performance, but it is still unlikely that they will develop into really effective adult animals. There is also an indication that there is an optimal period for learning behaviour patterns such as copulation. This optimal period occurs before puberty. During the pre-adolescent period young animals spend much of their time in play groups in which they perform many of the patterns of mating and aggression that they will use in their adult lives.

These findings have encouraged a new focus for research on the juvenile period of development as a critical time for the establishment of patterns to be used in adulthood. The play of juveniles not only gives them opportunities to practice their motor skills but also contributes to the establishment of emotional attitudes that are essential to fulfilling their adult roles. This new point of view helps us to look at learning and experience from a biological perspective. It is clear that for many species besides man experience is important in the development of the major classes of behaviour that are needed for survival and reproduction. This learning must occur for the individual to be a normal adult, and much of this learning and experience occurs in the context of juvenile play. Since it is clear that juvenile monkeys gain experience in mating, self-defence, and aggression through play, it is logical to wonder whether juvenile females gain experience in maternal behaviour patterns before they become mothers themselves. Monkey and ape females have relatively few offspring during their lifetimes. Most do not mate until their third year of life or even later, and the long gestation combined with annual breeding patterns and single births make the loss of an infant through neglect or inexperience very costly.

Relations between infants and other group members in monkeys and apes

A number of field workers have reported that in many species of monkey and ape the small infant acts as a social magnet for other group members. The mother with her new infant forms the centre of a cluster of interested group members, and she and her infant are especially attractive to the other females of the group. In some species, such as the baboon (DeVore, 1963) and the Japanese macaque (Sugiyama, 1965), this orientation towards a new infant may be limited to peering at or trying to touch the infant. In other species the mother may permit group members to hold and carry her infant, as in the langur (Jay, 1962; Poirier, 1968; Sugiyama, 1965), the vervet monkey (Gartlan, 1969; Struhsaker, 1967b), and the chimpanzee (van Lawick-Goodall, 1968). In a recent summary, Hamburg (1969) has emphasized that the handling of infants by juvenile and adolescent females is common in monkeys and apes; a pre-adult female that is truly naïve with respect to maternal behaviour is probably very rare in the wild.

A similar interest in infants has been reported in laboratory studies of a rhesus monkey colony (Hinde and Spencer-Booth, 1967; Rowell *et al.*, 1964; Spencer-Booth, 1968). Hinde and his associates found that in all their social groups some females played maternal roles towards infants of other females. This greatly affects the social experience of the young infant as it matures.

Non-human primate males may also display protective and affectionate responses towards young infants but this behaviour seems to be much more variable in both pattern and extent (DeVore, 1963; Chalmers, 1968; Lahiri and Southwick, 1966; Mitchell, 1969). For example, Itani (1959) reports a type of annual adoption of yearlings by dominant males at the time when the females are giving birth to new infants. This behaviour occurs in high frequencies in some groups of Japanese macaques, whereas in others it is rare or absent. Mitchell (1969) has recently summarized the evidence for parental behaviour displayed by non-human primate males. This care is rarely directed to the very small infant before the coat changes to the adult coat colour. When a nurturing or protective role is played by a male, he is likely to be a sub-adult or a fully adult male and sometimes a fairly high-ranking one. Such roles have not been reported for young, low-dominant males except in the special situation where a young male is protective of his younger sibling (Kaufmann, 1967; Koford, 1963; van Lawick-Goodall, 1968; Sade, 1965, 1967).

This article is particularly concerned with maternal, or protective and nurturing, behaviour displayed by juvenile females towards infants. This behaviour is of particular interest because it first occurs long before puberty has been reached and thus must reflect some very early sex differences in orientation towards the playing of a maternal role. Only a few field studies specifically discuss the attraction of infants for juvenile females as opposed to sub-adult and adult females, but this behaviour is mentioned briefly by DeVore (1963) and Anthoney (1968), for baboons; by Jay (1962) for langurs; by Struhsaker (1967b) for vervets; and by Altmann (1965) and Kaufmann (1966) for rhesus macaques. Such behaviour can be inhibited very easily by tension in the group or even by the mild anxiety raised by the presence of an observer. At Cayo Santiago, for example, Altmann (1965) noted that juvenile female rhesus showed strong interest in infants, but since adult females were so highly protective of their infants, the juvenile females were rarely permitted to hold or even touch them. Altmann's observations were originally made when the colony was rapidly expanding in numbers and tension was high. But only a few years later, at Cayo Santiago, Kaufmann (1966) often saw juvenile females holding and carrying infant siblings in the birth season. Wilson reports that this behaviour is now common there but that it is usually seen in the evening after most of the workers and technicians have left the island for the night. It is reasonable to expect that a mildly anxious mother monkey would tend to be more restrictive of her infant than a relaxed mother would be. She would be less likely to hand it over to a juvenile female who is inexperienced and clumsy with infants. Even though other kinds of behaviour such as play or copulation may not be inhibited by very low levels of anxiety or tension, it is possible that the mothers' permissiveness towards the handling of infants by juveniles would be. This may be a kind of behaviour that is often suppressed by the mere presence of an unfamiliar observer. As more field studies are done on animals that are highly habituated to an observer, caring for infants by juvenile females may emerge as a very common behaviour pattern in non-human primates.

Play-mothering

Among vervet monkeys living near the Zambezi River in Central Africa, juvenile females are often seen carrying, holding, or grooming infants.

This behaviour is seasonal because vervets in this area give birth to infants only during a four-month period each year. The first infants are born in late October, just before the beginning of the rainy season, and more are born in November, December and January. With vervets it is the small black infant that gets the most attention. During the first three months of life the black infant's social contacts are restricted. It spends its time in close proximity with its mother, its older siblings, and juvenile and adolescent females from other genealogies. By the time the infant is three months old, its coat changes from the natal black to the light grey adult colour. At about the same time the mother begins to refuse to carry the infant unless there is some immediate difficulty or danger. At this same age infants also begin to enter the juvenile play group and to form social bonds with other young animals and with adult males.

The onset of the birth season marks an abrupt change in the behaviour of juvenile females. Before the infants are born each year, juvenile females spend most of their time either in the company of their mothers and siblings or in play groups with other juveniles. However, during the months when there are young black infants in the group, the juvenile females have a new focus for their interest that draws them away from their family groups and from play with each other and with young males. The small black infant acts as a magnet for a juvenile female regardless of her age or social position. It is common to see each new mother acquire an entourage of juvenile females, who follow her about during the day waiting for a chance to touch the infant. Even infant females who are only 9 months old and not yet weaned themselves show great interest in newborns. Young females will spend as much time with an infant as they possibly can, and it is the mother's attitude that usually determines how long the juvenile females will be able to handle an infant.

This great attraction of the young infant for juvenile and adolescent females has been observed in vervet populations in two other localities. Gartlan (1969) working on Lolui Island in Lake Victoria observed maternal responses to infants displayed by juvenile and sub-adult females during the early period before the infants' colour change. He also emphasized that adult and sub-adult males were never observed to show interest in small infants (Gartlan and Brain, 1968). Struhsaker (1967b), who worked in Amboseli Reserve, Kenya, reports similar behaviour in his monograph, and his films contain a number of sequences showing sub-adult or large juvenile females carrying or holding infants.

Vervet mothers are normally relaxed about their infants. Vervets do not go to the extreme of passing infants around among all the adult females of the group as do langurs (Jay, 1963; Poirier, 1968; Sugiyama, 1965). Nevertheless, a vervet mother will often let another female come and sit nearby and touch or hold the infant as long as she remains near the mother. Juvenile female vervets show far greater interest in infants than do the adult females. A total of 347 observations of affectionate contacts between females and infants not their own was made between 12 October 1968 and 28 February 1969, during a total of 464 observation hours. Only fifty-two of these contacts were made by adult females, that is, females who were 3 years old or older and who had had infants either in previous years or during the birth season of 1968–9. There were 295 contacts between infants and nulliparous females aged 1, 2, and 3 years old. Excluding infants, the nine nulliparous females, only two of which were adolescent, composed thirty-eight per cent of the females, yet they accounted for eighty-five per cent of the contacts with infants. (Data from a nulliparous 3-year-old female have been discarded because she had a severely broken leg at the beginning of the birth season and was barely able to keep up with the group.) Furthermore, contacts with infants by juvenile females tend to be more sustained than do those of adult females. Typically an adult female will stride over to a mother with a new infant and greet the infant by briefly nuzzling or sniffing its head. She may then reach down and pull the infant up by its tail or hindquarters and nuzzle its genitals. Because the infant maintains contact with its mother by clinging with its hands and mouth, it is raised up hingelike from its mother's body. After nuzzling the genitals, the adult female will abruptly let the infant go and then will direct her attention to grooming the mother, showing no more interest in the infant itself. Virtually identical behaviour has been reported by Gartlan (1969) and by Struhsaker (1967b) for vervet monkeys living in East Africa.

During the first few weeks after the infant is born, the mother tends to restrict the infant's movements and to keep it close to her body. Juvenile females will follow the mothers of new infants and sit beside them and peer at or try to touch the infant. Often the juvenile female will begin by grooming the mother, only gradually, but very obviously to the observer, working her way over towards the infant. If the mother moves or seems disturbed by this attention to the infant, the juvenile female will hurriedly begin to groom the mother again. Similar behaviour to this has been described by Hinde, Rowell, and Spencer-Booth (1964) for their rhesus colony, by Kaufmann (1966) for rhesus on Cayo Santiago, and by Gartlan (1969) for vervet monkeys in Uganda. This pattern contrasts with the behaviour of adult females, who seem to groom the mother for the sake of grooming her and not to be near the infant, which is only briefly greeted by nuzzling or sniffing. During the early weeks of the infant's life the juvenile female will try to pull it away from its mother, or she will quickly scoop it up if the mother sets it down for a few moments. Usually the mother will take the infant back again fairly quickly, but the juvenile female will have a chance to hold the infant and briefly groom it or hug it to her chest. The youngest infant observed being held by a juvenile female was eight days old. By the time the infant is three weeks old, the mother is usually much more relaxed in her attitude towards it, and juvenile females will often be permitted to hug and carry it for quite some time.

When the very young juvenile females get their first chance to hold an infant or carry it, they often have difficulty in orienting its body properly or in instilling enough confidence in the infant to make it cling when the female tries to walk with it. Infants will cling readily to experienced

Table 1 Mode of return of infant to its mother after being held by a juvenile or adolescent female

Mother takes infant back	23
Mother presents for grooming	19
Mother grooms female	13
Mother threatens female	12
Infant returns by itself	19
Total	86

females who are not their mothers, but often they will struggle when a young juvenile has them. Because the infant refuses to cling properly, it is common to see a juvenile female carrying an infant by walking along on three legs while clutching the infant to her chest with one hand. Sometimes a juvenile female will even hold an infant with both arms and run bipedally to try to get it out of its mother's view. Juvenile females soon learn how to carry infants properly, and they also learn that if they can keep the infant quiet and content the mother will probably not try to retrieve it. One of the best ways to pacify any monkey is by grooming it, and this works just as well with infants as with adults. A juvenile female is often seen pinning down an infant with her leg or arm and then intensely grooming it until it relaxes. In fact, this is such a common pattern that almost all an infant's grooming experience is with juvenile females rather than with its own mother, who usually only grooms it when it is obviously dirty or has something sticking to its skin or fur. The infant does not receive strictly social grooming from its mother but rather from the juvenile females.

The juvenile female usually plays a maternal or protective role towards the infant. Play is not observed between the infant and juvenile when the infant is very young. The earliest instance of such play was seen when an infant was thirty-six days old. As the weeks go by, social play in the form of chasing and wrestling gradually increases in frequency until it seems to replace the mothering behaviour. By the time an infant is four months old and has finished its colour change, it no longer seems to arouse maternal responses in juvenile females; instead it is seen as a social partner for play. During July, August, September and most of October, no maternal behaviour by juvenile females directed towards infants was observed, although play sequences were common. By the time observations were ended on the study group in March, mothering behaviour had already begun to decline in frequency, although there were still some small infants in the group.

By the time an infant is six or seven weeks old, it is actually spending a good proportion of its waking hours in the company of juvenile females. Mother vervets often take advantage of this and go off on their own to feed. Often when a mother vervet wants to feed out in the open or in a fruit tree with a number of other monkeys who may be excited and aggressive, she may leave her infant behind with some juvenile females. An infant may be left for as long as a half-hour or even an hour while its mother is feeding perhaps one-tenth of a mile away. Mothers will sometimes leave their infants with juvenile baby-sitters under other circumstances when bringing it along might be dangerous. For example, in one situation when a snake alarm call went up after the group had come across a python lying in the grass, a primiparous female stopped, pulled her infant from her chest, and set it down beside a juvenile female. She then ran over to the snake and joined the others in chattering at it while her infant remained about twenty feet behind with the juvenile.

No male of any age was seen to direct any maternal behaviour such as hugging, carrying or grooming towards a new-born infant. Fully adult males were tolerant of infants and the infants were attracted to them, but this occurred only after the infant was three months old or older. Juvenile males were never seen to show protective or maternal behaviour to new-born infants, although older male siblings were seen to investigate their new siblings by touching or nuzzling them. However, only three infants were known to have juvenile male siblings, and two of these were born late in the field study, so that this type of behaviour was rarely observed. Older male siblings oriented their behaviour more often towards their mother than towards her infant during the early months. It was only when the infant became socially playful that juvenile males showed much interest in it.

Pre-puberty sex differences in behaviour

One of the most interesting questions raised by this data is whether there is a strong sex difference before puberty in the development of maternal behaviour patterns. It has already been established in laboratory studies that sex differences in the behaviour of rhesus monkey infants are readily apparent in such patterns as mounting and presenting, branch-shaking, and the roughness and duration of play bouts (Harlow and Harlow, 1965; Hinde and Spencer-Booth, 1967). Furthermore, clear differences have been found between male and female juvenile rhesus in the behaviour they direct towards infants (Spencer-Booth, 1968). A special study of this problem was done by Chamove *et al.* (1967) in which they tested a series of fifteen pre-adolescent male–female pairs which had been raised under a variety of social conditions. Each monkey was put alone in a cage with a one-month-old infant. They found that the males showed ten times more hostility towards the infant than the females, whereas the females directed four times as much positive social behaviour towards the infant. The juvenile females typically showed maternal, affiliative patterns such as hugging or grooming the infant, whereas the males were either indifferent or actively hostile (one male bit off an infant's finger). These sex differences were apparent in juveniles that had been raised with only a mother or with only a peer; however, they were absent in monkeys that had been reared in social isolation. These sex differences were the most marked in monkeys who experienced real monkey mothering.

Hamburg and Lunde (1966) have summarized some of the latest research in the development of sex differences in mammals. As an example of such research see the work of Goy (1969) and his associates on the rhesus monkey. Hamburg and Lunde note the high levels of hormones circulating in the blood of new-borns. They suggest that during foetal or neo-natal life hormones act in an inductive way on the undifferentiated brain to organize certain circuits into male and female patterns. Early exposure to these hormones may then affect the ease of learning and expression of the appropriate behaviour patterns later in life, even though the level of sex hormones is very low during the period between infancy and adolescence. Hamburg and Lunde summarize a number of ways in which the hormones may act to produce the behaviour patterns. For example, hormones at a critical period may affect later sensitivity to certain stimulus patterns. This may account for the differential behaviour of young male and female vervets towards infants; it was mentioned earlier in this article that a number of field and laboratory studies have noted that males are usually indifferent to the infant in its black natal coat, whereas females are particularly attracted to an infant at that early stage of development.

Hormones may act also by making the brain react in such a way that certain patterns of action are perceived as more rewarding than others. For example, the hugging of an infant to the chest may be very pleasurable to a female, whereas the large muscle movements and fast actions used in play-fighting and aggressive behaviour may be felt as more pleasurable to a male.

Sex differences in behaviour sometimes may be developed partly by the dynamics of social interaction within the group. As suggested by the laboratory studies of Chamove et al. (1967), animals with no social experience do not show marked sex differences in behaviour. In another study, on pigtail macaques, Jensen et al. (1968) found clear sex differences in the development of independence from the mother. Almost identical sex differences were found in the development of infant rhesus monkeys by Mitchell (1968). These studies noted that both the mother and the infant showed differences in behaviour that depended upon the sex of the infant. The mothers of males were more punishing and rejecting than the mothers of females, who tended to be restrictive and protective of their daughters. From the beginning of life male and female infants were treated differently by their mothers. The authors suspected that male infants behaved differently from females and that their mothers were in fact responding to this difference. Unfortunately the measures used in the study were too gross to pinpoint exactly what these primary differences were. It may be worth noting here that many field-workers have observed that group members pay close attention to the genitals of new-born monkeys and apes. This behaviour which includes peering at, touching, and sniffing or mouthing the genitals may represent a classifying of new group members as either male or female. As Benedict (1969) has suggested, even in animal societies social roles are not strictly inheritable, and it is through the interaction of individuals that social organization is produced. The way the individual learns roles, even male and female sex roles, may be just as heavily influenced by the environment of the moment as by the genetics of the individual.

The question remains whether juvenile female monkeys actually learn and benefit from experience in handling and caring for infants before they reach puberty. Although some of the basic patterns of maternal behaviour may be relatively inborn, it is very likely that learning plays an important part in the development of skill in performing those patterns. It is clear from a number of field studies that young juvenile females are very inept in handling infants, but by the time a female reaches sub-adulthood, she carries and handles an infant with ease and expertise. Several field-workers have reported their impression that they could see some development of skill in individual females as their experience with infants increased (Jay,

1962; Lancaster, this article; Struhsaker, 1967b). The dynamics of this learning process occur under the eyes of the real mothers. Instances of carelessness, clumsiness or real abuse will, in effect, be punished. Normally, if anything should make an infant cry out, its mother will immediately come and retrieve it. If the infant is being abused, she may even bite the juvenile female. In this way through a simple kind of conditioning, juvenile females learn appropriate behaviour patterns with their reward being the continued presence of the infant.

Two laboratory studies tend to support the idea that this early experience may in fact be practice for adult maternal behaviour patterns. Seay (1966) found that he could not distinguish between primiparous and multiparous rhesus mothers that had been raised in the wild in respect to the mechanical aspects of skilful handling and caring for infants such as cradling, restraining, retrieving, embracing, and ventral and nipple contact. He found that primiparous mothers tended to be more anxious and sometimes more restrictive towards their new infants, but this in no way made them less effective mothers. In contrast experienced mothers were often more rejecting and punishing. In field studies done by Gartlan (1969) on vervets and by Kaufmann (1966) on rhesus no significant differences were noted between primiparous and multiparous females in their effectiveness as mothers. This does not mean that maternal behaviour patterns are completely inborn. We know that a total lack of social experience does lead to the development of very infantile and aggressive mothers. Harlow *et al.* (1966) found that motherless mothers raised in semi-isolation without mothers or peer relationships responded to their first infants with active rejection and hostility. However, they also found that social experience with an infant, however minimal and late in life, still affected maternal behaviour. The same females who rejected their first infants often accepted their second ones. Although these females would probably not have made good mothers in the wild because of their lack of experience and skill in handling infants, their attitude towards infants clearly changed and they were able to take a nurturing and protective role towards their subsequent offspring.

It is clear that the opportunities to handle and care for infants before reaching puberty may play an important role in the development of maternal behaviour patterns in the adult female. There are no data that suggest that primiparous females are less effective mothers than are multiparous ones, and it seems reasonable to assume that playing a mothering role as a juvenile may contribute to the success of the primiparous mother. Further laboratory studies will help to define some of the contributing factors and perhaps settle such problems as the effects of deprivation on the development of maternal behaviour or the possibility of a critical period for learning maternal behaviour patterns. However, the true test of adequate mothering can only come from studies on free-ranging animals. Adequate mothering in the laboratory may involve no more than passive acceptance of the offspring, whereas adequate mothering in a natural setting concerns a far wider range of problems including predation, safe locomotion over dangerous areas, and relations with other group members. It involves not only the skilled performance of maternal behaviour patterns but also the motivation to play a maternal role and the ability to feel anxiety over the well-being of the infant.

Play has always presented a problem when a comprehensive definition is needed. In a recent review Loizos (1967) has tried to bring together the published accounts of play in the higher primates. Most often play is described in terms of patterns relating to aggression and sexual behaviour or, more rarely, to predator defence. Aside from man there seems to be no published account of play in mammals that involves maternal behaviour patterns. This is somewhat surprising, since play is often mentioned as possibly serving the function of providing practice for behaviour patterns important in adult life (Beach, 1945; Loizos, 1967; Welker, 1961). When we see a juvenile female of the human species display similar maternal behaviour patterns towards a doll, we do not hesitate to call it play.

It is interesting that during the season when the juvenile and adolescent vervet females are preoccupied with small infants, they are conspicuously absent from the juvenile play groups. After the first bout of feeding every morning the group normally settles down for a rest. For adults this usually includes dozing or grooming either alone or with others, and for juvenile and sub-adult males this is a period of play-fighting and chasing. For juvenile females this is the best time to handle and groom infants. It is only after the infants have had their colour change and have joined the play groups themselves that the juvenile females reappear with the male juveniles. Even then their primary orientation is first in romping with the infants and not with the juvenile males.

This behaviour, in which juvenile females spend much more time caring for infants than play-fighting with their peers, may correlate with the dominance relations that seem to characterize the adult members of the group. Adult vervet females appear to be ranked in a linear hierarchy with offspring taking their dominance rank directly under their mothers. From the field data it is clear that a juvenile female vervet can dominate any adult female that her mother can dominate even if her mother is absent at the time (Lancaster, this article). Dominance hierarchies described by Struhsaker (1967b) suggest that this is also true for vervets in Kenya. This same phenomenon has been reported for rhesus monkeys (Sade, 1965, 1967) and for Japanese macaques (Kawai, 1958; Kawamura,

1958). In these species on which long-term studies have been made and biological relationships are known, it is clear that a rank dependent on that of the mother carries over into adult life, at least for females. In contrast to females, male rhesus and Japanese macaques originally take their rank from their mothers, but at puberty a son can achieve rank above his mother through successful fights and threats, or by forming a coalition with another male. It is quite likely that the vervets follow a pattern similar to that of the macaques, although only long-term field studies can demonstrate whether this similarity is genuine or only superficial. If in fact female vervets do take their rank from their mothers even as adults, then it would be unimportant to a vervet female whether she is bigger, stronger, or a more skilled fighter compared with the other females in her group. Her dominance rank does not appear to relate to these qualities at all. Accordingly, play-fighting is far less important in her life, since she does not need to practise highly the motor patterns and to develop skill in fighting, nor does she need to test herself against the other females. As adaptive preparation for adult behaviour patterns it is appropriate that the young male vervet should spend his time play-fighting, while the young female spends much of hers playing with infants.

Loizos (1967) has suggested that play-fighting in primates may serve a function similar to that of imprinting in birds. It marks a period in which a young animal learns about the physical qualities of its conspecies and learns 'which species it belongs to' (Loizos, 1967, p. 211). It may well be that juvenile female vervets also go through a period of 'imprinting' on vervet infants while they are playing with them. The early appearance of maternal behaviour patterns may serve two separate functions in the development of a juvenile female: first to help her to develop skill in caring for infants, and second to help her learn to accept the role of mother towards an infant. Both of these functions are equally crucial to the survival of the infant, and it is not surprising that some practice in them should occur before the first infant is actually born.

This kind of data also raises questions about the development of maternal behaviour patterns in humans. There is no doubt that if a human female is to be a truly effective mother, she must derive some kind of satisfaction from body contact with her baby. Nursing, cradling, and carrying must be positively motivated from within if the infant is to develop normally with a feeling of security. A mother who rejects her infant may go through the motions of caretaking, but the infant may respond to the way she does these patterns and react to the rejection. Perhaps more attention should be paid to what young girls are learning when they are playing with infant siblings or with their dolls, activities that seem to be universal. How important is this play in the development of maternal behaviour patterns? Is it possible that there may be a kind of optimal period before puberty in which the emotional attitudes towards infants are first established? The ontogeny of maternal behaviour patterns has been very poorly described or understood in our own species. We know something about cultural differences in ways that children are socialized in various societies but we know almost nothing about what important biological forces underlie the development of maternal behaviour patterns in all human societies.

(From *Folia Primat.* No. 15, 1971, pp. 161–82, and F. E. Poirier (ed.), *Primate Socialization*, Random House, New York, 1972.)

References

ALTMANN, S. A. (1965), 'Sociobiology of rhesus monkeys. 4. Testing Mason's hypothesis of sex differences in affective behavior', *Behavior*, No. 32, pp. 49–68.

ANTHONEY, T. R. (1969), 'The ontogeny of greeting, grooming and sexual motor patterns in captive baboons (superspecies *Papio Cynocephalus*)', *Behavior*, No. 31, pp. 358–72.

BEACH, F. A. (1945), 'Current concepts of play in animals', *Am. Nat.*, No. 79, pp. 532–41.

BENEDICT, B. (1969), 'Role analysis in animals and man', *Man*, No. 4, pp. 203–14.

CHALMERS, N. R. (1968), 'The Social Behavior of Free-living Mangabeys in Uganda', *Folia Primat.*, No. 8, pp. 263–81.

CHAMOVE, A., HARLOW, H. F., and MITCHELL, C. D. (1967), 'Sex differences in the Infant-directed behavior of preadolescent rhesus monkeys', *Child Development*, No. 38, pp. 329–35.

DEVORE, I. (1963), 'Mother-infant relations in free-ranging baboons', in *Maternal Behavior in Mammals*, H. L. Rheingold (ed.), Wiley, New York, pp. 305–35.

GARTLAN, J. S. (1969), 'Sexual and maternal behavior of the vervet monkey, *Cercopithecus aethiops*', *Journal of Reproductive Fertility*, Supplement 6, pp. 137–50.

GARTLAN, J. S., and BRAIN, C. K. (1968), 'Ecology and Social variability in *Cercopithecus aethiops* and *C. mitis*', in *Primates: Studies in Adaptation and Variability*, P. Jay (ed.), Holt, Rinehart & Winston, New York, pp. 253–92.

GOY, R. W. (1969), 'Organizing effects of androgen on the behavior of rhesus monkeys', in *Endocrinology and Human Behaviour*, R. P. Michael (ed.), Oxford University Press, pp. 12–31.

HAMBURG, D. A. (1969), 'Observations of mother-infant interactions in primate field studies', in *Determinants of Infant Behaviour*, B. M. Foss (ed.), Vol. IV, Methuen, pp. 3–14.

HAMBURG, D. A., and LUNDE, D. T. (1966), 'Sex hormones in the development of sex differences in human behavior', in *The Development of Sex Differences*, R. Maccoby (ed.), Stanford University, Press, pp. 1–24.

HARLOW, H. F., and HARLOW, M. K. (1965), 'The Affectional Systems', in *Behavior of Nonhuman Primates*, A. M. Schrier, H. F. Harlow, and F. Stollnitz (eds), Vol. II, Academic Press, New York, pp. 287–334.

HARLOW, H. F., HARLOW, M. K., *et al.* (1966), 'Maternal behavior of rhesus monkeys deprived of mothering and peer associations in infancy', *Proceedings of the American Philosophical Society*, No. 110, pp. 58–66.

HINDE, R. A., ROWELL, T. E., and SPENCER-BOOTH, Y. (1964), 'Behavior of socially living rhesus monkeys in their first six months', *Proceedings of the Zoological Society of London*, No. 143, pp. 609–49.

HINDE, R. A., and SPENCER-BOOTH, Y. (1967), 'The effect of social companions on mother-infant relations in rhesus monkeys', in *Primate Ethology*, D. Morris (ed.), Weidenfeld & Nicolson.

ITANI, J. (1959), 'Paternal care in the wild Japanese monkey, *Macaca fuscata fuscata*', *Primates*, No. 2, pp. 61–93.

JAY, P. (1962), 'Aspects of maternal behavior among langurs', *Ann. N.Y. Ad. Sci.* No. 102, pp. 468–76.

JAY, P. (1963), 'Mother-infant relations in langurs', in *Maternal Behavior in Mammals*, H. L. Rheingold (ed.), Wiley, New York, pp. 282–304.

JENSEN, G. D., BOBBITT, R. A., and GORDON, B. N. (1968), 'Sex differences in the development of independence of infant monkeys', *Behavior*, No. 30, pp. 1–14.

KAUFMANN, J. H. (1966), 'Behavior of infant rhesus monkeys and their mothers in a free-ranging band', *Zoologica*, No. 51, pp. 17–29.

KAUFMANN, J. H. (1967), 'Social relations of adult males in a free-ranging band of rhesus monkeys', *Social Communication among Primates*, S. A. Altmann (ed.), University of Chicago Press, pp. 73–98.

KAWAI, M. (1958), 'On the rank system in a natural group of Japanese monkeys', *Primates*, No. 1, pp. 111–48.

KAWAMURA, S. (1958), 'Matriarchal social ranks in the Minoo-B troop: A study of the rank system of Japanese monkeys', *Primates*, No. 1, pp. 149–56.

KOFORD, C. B. (1963), 'Rank of mothers and sons in bands of rhesus monkeys', *Science*, No. 141, pp. 356–7.

LAHIRI, R. K., and SOUTHWICK, C. H. (1966), 'Parental care in *Macaca sylvana*', *Folia Primat.*, No. 4, pp. 257–64.

LAWICK-GOODALL, J. VAN (1968), 'The behavior of free-living chimpanzees in the Gombe Stream Reserve', *Anim. Behav. Mono. Series* 1, pp. 161–311.

LOIZOS, C. (1967), 'Play behavior in higher primates: A review', in *Primate Ethology*, D. Morris (ed.), Weidenfeld & Nicolson.

MITCHELL, G. D. (1968), 'Attachment differences in male and female infant monkeys', *Child Development*, No. 39, pp. 611–20.

MITCHELL, G. D. (1969), 'Paternalistic behavior in primates', *Psychology Bulletin*, No. 71, pp. 399–417.

MITCHELL, G. D., *et al.* (1966), 'Long-term effects of multiparous and primiparous monkey mother rearing', *Child Development*, No. 37, pp. 781–91.

POIRIER, F. E. (1968), 'The Nilgiri langur (*Presbytis johnii*): Mother-infant dyad', *Primates*, No. 9, pp. 45–68.

ROWELL, T. E., HINDE, R. A., and SPENCER-BOOTH, Y. (1964), ' "Aunt"-infant interaction in captive rhesus monkeys', *Animal Behavior*, No. 12, pp. 219–26.

SADE, D. S. (1965), 'Some aspects of parent-offspring and sibling relations in a group of rhesus monkeys, with a discussion of grooming', *American Journal of Physical Anthropology*, No. 23, pp. 1–17.

SADE, D. S. (1967), 'Determinants of dominance in a group of free-ranging rhesus', in *Social Communication Among Primates*, S. A. Altmann (ed.), University of Chicago Press, pp. 99–114.

SEAY, B. (1966), 'Maternal behavior in primiparous and multiparous rhesus monkeys', *Folia Primat.*, No. 4, pp. 146–69.

SPENCER-BOOTH, Y. (1968), 'The behavior of group companions towards rhesus monkey infants', *Animal Behavior*, No. 16, pp. 541–57.

STRUHSAKER, T. T. (1967a), 'Auditory communication among vervet monkeys (*Cercopithecus aethiops*)', in *Social Communication Among Primates*, S. A. Altmann (ed.), University of Chicago Press, pp. 281–325.

STRUHSAKER, T. T. (1967b), 'Behavior of vervet monkeys, *Cercopithecus aethiops*', *Univ. of Calif. Publ. Zool.*, No. 82, pp. 1–74.

SUGIYAMA, Y. (1965), 'Behavioral development and social structure in two troops of Hanuman langurs (*Presbytis entellus*)', *Primates*, No. 6, pp. 313–48.

WELKER, W. I. (1961), 'An analysis of exploratory and play behavior in animals', in *Functions of Varied Experience*, D. W. Fiske and S. R. Maddi (eds), Dorsey Press, Illinois, pp. 175–226.

Male Barbary Macaques 'Help with the Babies'

In Barbary macaques the adult males play the principal part in socializing the young. The males use infants as pawns in a status game, but often they are seen caring for the young as well. A male takes an infant, lip-smacks its bottom, and then presents it to a more dominant male. The infant is then ignored while the two males groom each other. There seems no end to the variability in the primate series. In this case, dominance behaviour and infant care behaviour have found joint expression. In Dr Burton's account, females continue to play a role in the care of the young, but more as mediators than as care-givers.

The adult female is the first environment for the neonate, and thus the context for the most important biological maturation. The infant first sees and makes its first oriented movements with her arms. However, since the leader male takes the neonate from as early as the first day of life, it is the leader male who is the pre-eminent influence in socialization of the infant until it is approximately two weeks of age. The leader male encourages biological maturation by reinforcing the infant's mouth sucking movements until they become the social chatter gesture, and by encouraging the infant in locomotor skills and to take the dorsal transport position. These basic body movements are of prime importance for all future social contact. The leader male reorients the infant away from its mother, himself, and other adults, by permitting sub-adult males to first snatch the infant, and later to take it away for greater and greater distances. (See photo inset.) It is while the infant is under the care of the sub-adult male that it increasingly contacts juveniles and later age-mates. From contact with sub-adult males and juveniles, as well as from this social context, the infant learns, as he develops motor skills, all the necessary information to become a functioning member of the troop. The information ranges from what to eat to available routes from one area to another. Sub-adult females play a very small role in socialization of the infants, as this age group is largely isolated from other troop members, and as they are rebuffed by all adults and sub-adult males when they make overtures. The adult females are more important in socializing juveniles and sub-adults than in socializing infants. Their relationship to the infants is primarily as feeder, and later groomer, that is, a relationship of comfort and support. Although they do defend and protect the infants, this is more the task of sub-adult males.

Females influence the older animals primarily by rebuffing them as they approach infants, play with juveniles too roughly, or come for food the female herself is approaching. But what they learn from these females seems more to be how to respond to the personalities and temperaments of the individual animals.

(From 'The integration of biology and behaviour in the socialization of *Macaca sylvana* of Gibraltar', in F. E. Poirier (ed.), *Primate Socialization*, Random House, New York, 1972.)

Sex Role Playing in Pre-School Children

Differential role requirements for males and females are universal, and sex differences provide the basis for the division of labour in all societies. To emphasize briefly the importance of sex roles, one might note that achievement expectations, appropriate affective responses, societal tasks, and role opportunities all differ for men and women. Because of the pervasiveness of sex role distinctions within a society, an understanding of sex role acquisition and development in children is essential for a theory of socialization.

Most of the research on sex-related differences in children's social activity has focused on particular behaviour characteristics and activity preferences of boys and girls. Boys have been found to be more aggressive than girls in experimental, observational and rating studies (e.g. Bandura, Ross, and Ross, 1963; Feshbach, 1969; Jersild and Markey, 1935). Also, boys tend to engage in more physical activity than girls (cf. Dawe, 1934). These studies highlight specific differences between sexes rather than actual sex role patterns.

A more specific approach is to assess children's sex preferences. A variety of techniques have been used for this purpose. One popular device is Brown's *It Scale for Children* (Brown, 1956). This test was designed to investigate children's preferences for sex-related objects and activities. Other popular devices include toy preference inventories and doll play measures. Since all of these methods deal with children individually, they provide no information about children's interactive play. Further, as Lynn (1959) has noted, one should distinguish between sex role preferences and sex role adoption: the former concerns a child's preferences for his own or the opposite sex role, while the latter concerns the child's actual behaviour. Although a little girl may express preferences for male activities, her actual behaviour may accord with female norms. Consequently these methods are inappropriate for determining which sex roles children actually adopt.

In response to Lynn's distinction between adoption and preference, Ward (1969) conducted a study to determine children's patterns of sex role adoption. His procedure assessed the degree to which children imitated the responses of either a man or woman in a game situation. Another study by Fling and Manosevitz (1972) measured sex role adoption by gathering information on children's toy usage. While both studies found that children adopt sex-appropriate roles, neither concerns the sex roles adopted by children in spontaneous play.

Several other studies have focused on children's knowledge of role-appropriate objects and activities (e.g. Heise and Roberts, 1970). Vener and Snyder (1966) demonstrated that children as young as $2\frac{1}{2}$ are able to associate objects such as screwdriver and dustpan with Father and Mother. However, whether or not children use this knowledge during play has not been carefully examined.

To determine simultaneously if children use their role knowledge and if they adopt sex-appropriate roles, direct observations of children at play are appropriate. A variety of questions can be asked concerning the use of sex roles in children. Specifically, when children are left alone, do they actually adopt sex roles spontaneously, without any adult encouragement? If so, what is the frequency of role adoption? Further, do children routinely play sex-appropriate roles, or do they adopt male and female roles equally often? Finally, are roles used in an interactive context, and if so, what effect do peers have on sex role playing?

The present study was designed to answer some of these questions. The observational approach was used to examine sex role playing in pre-school children in a free play situation. Videotapes of children at play were analysed to determine the frequency of role playing, and the relationship between specific roles played and the sex of the child. If children actively use their role knowledge during play, then role playing should occur spontaneously. Further, if socialization of children into appropriate sex roles begins early, then nursery school children should already be playing sex-appropriate roles. To answer these questions, pre-school children were observed under controlled conditions.

Procedure

The sample consisted of twenty-four nursery school children from white, middle-class, professional families. Twelve of the children ranged in age from $3\frac{1}{2}$–$4\frac{1}{2}$; the other twelve ranged from $4\frac{1}{2}$–$5\frac{1}{2}$. There were six girls and six boys in the younger group, and seven girls and five boys in the older group.

Three children of the same age from the same nursery school class came to the psychology building where a playroom was available. All groups contained children of both sexes. When they arrived, the children were greeted by an adult who explained that they would be playing some games.

Since children went to the playroom in pairs, they drew straws to determine which two would go to the playroom first. The first two were then taken to the playroom which was comfortably furnished like a living room and contained a variety of toys, including toy telephones, stuffed animals, and a wooden car large enough to seat two. Children were told that they could play with anything they liked, and were left alone in the room for approximately fifteen minutes. After the session, one child left the playroom and the third child was brought in. This procedure was repeated once more so that all possible pairs were made. Thus, each child participated in two play sessions, with a different playmate each time.

All sessions were videotaped through a one-way mirror. Also, audio tapes were made to facilitate transcriptions of the children's speech. After speech from the tapes was transcribed, the transcripts were divided into utterances, defined as stretches of one person's speech separated by pauses greater than one second or by another person's speech (cf. Garvey and Hogan, 1973).

Since there are no available methods for assessing sex role playing from observational data, specific criteria were devised to identify role playing episodes. Because children also engaged in much pretend play, five categories were necessary to code each child's activity. These were: role play, role preparation, pretend play, pretend preparation, and other activity.

Role play refers to any activity in which the child assumes a distinct identity different from his own. Sometimes this role is clearly stated, as in the example of the boy who declared, 'I'm Tarzan.' At other times, one can infer a child's role from a combination of his speech and behaviour. For example, one four-and-a-half year old girl interrupted her house cleaning activities to say to her male playmate, 'Don't forget to take your lunch, husband.' If the role which a child assumed was associated primarily with one sex, the role was classified as a sex role (e.g. fireman, bride).

Role preparation concerns a child's structuring a situation for role play. Sometimes the children planned what roles they would play; at other times one child announced his role to his playmate. Examples of this category include such statements as, 'Let's pretend you're my brother,' and 'I'll be the mother and you be the father, O.K.?'

Behaviour which was clearly make-believe, in that the child was required to pretend something but did not assume a distinct identity, was classified as pretend play. This does not imply that role play is unrelated to pretend play. Rather, role play is a special case of the more general category of pretend play. Examples of pretend include statements such as, 'I'm driving to the store,' said while sitting on a wooden car. One pair of children prepared a meal, and while eating their non-existent food the girl exclaimed, 'This ice-cream is yummy!' Behaviour which seemed like role play but which had no clear role referent was classified as pretend play.

Pretend preparation, the fourth category, was analogous to role preparation. Behaviour concerned with planning make-believe play was classified as pretend preparation. For example, one child told his playmate, 'Pretend this snake is real.'

The final category, other activity, was used to classify behaviours not included in the other four categories. These episodes included discussions of the playroom; exchanges about T.V. shows, especially cartoons; and play which involved no pretending (e.g. pushing a toy truck around the room). Children also revealed their thoughts to each other. For instance, statements such as 'I don't like to be alone,' and 'I wonder where teacher is' were classified as other activity.

The activity of each child was classified into the five specified categories, using utterances to denote changes from one category to another. Two observers independently coded thirty-three per cent of the sequences into these categories. Interscorer agreement averaged eighty-three per cent.

Results

All results are based on the proportion of speech falling into each of the five categories. Across both age groups, an average of forty-four per cent of the children's utterances were related to imaginative activity, of which thirteen per cent were related to sex roles, and twenty-four per cent concerned pretend play. An additional seven per cent of all speech involved structuring future interactions for pretend or role play. It seems, then, that pre-school children devote a considerable amount of their play time to imaginative activity.

Examination of these results by age groups reveals an interesting trend. The average amount of sex role play was five per cent for younger children, but increased to twenty-two per cent in the older children. Concomitantly, the amount of pretend play decreased, from twenty-nine per cent in younger children to eighteen per cent in older children. It is interesting to note that within age groups, there were no sex differences in activity distributions. Thus, the amount of speech related to each of the categories was the same for boys and girls, indicating that boys and girls participated in the same amount of imaginative play.

The absence of sex differences in *frequency* of activities does not imply that there were no differences in the *content* of activities. Since it appeared that girls and boys were adopting different sex roles, a descriptive analysis of specific activities was made to determine if some types of play were more common to one sex than to the other.

The descriptive analysis revealed noticeable differences in the types of sex roles which children played. The most popular roles were those of mother and father, and in almost all cases girls played the mother and boys played the father. Also, among boys the role of son was popular. Traditional female roles such as daughter and wife were played exclusively by females. Conversely, in addition to father, roles of son and husband were played by males. Further, only females played the roles of baby and bride, and mostly males played the role of fireman. Thus children not only played roles spontaneously, but they also adopt sex-appropriate roles at a very early age.

Discussion

Results revealed several interesting findings concerning the free play activity of pairs of pre-school children. First, sex role playing appears spontaneously when children are in a free play situation. The occurrence of sex role playing indicates that children not only possess the requisite knowledge and skills for role play, but are able and eager to use them. Second, in most instances of role playing, children adopted sex-appropriate roles, regardless of the sex of their playmates. This suggests that not only are sex role patterns acquired at an early age, but they are actually being practised by pre-school children. Finally, children engaged in a considerable amount of imaginative activity, including both sex role play and pretend play.

Older children displayed significantly more sex role play than younger children. Around age four-and-a-half the amount of sex role play increases sharply. Concurrently, the amount of pretend play decreases, indicating that role play and pretend play are related activities. Although younger children frequently engage in pretend activities, such as going to the store, driving a car, and eating a meal, they do not integrate any of these pretend sequences into specific sex roles. On the other hand, older children fit a variety of pretend activities into sex role patterns. For example, whereas younger children would simply 'cook' some food and then 'eat' it, among older children the little girl might 'cook' supper for her 'husband' while playing the role of 'wife'.

A striking observation was the large amount of play time children spend interacting. Most instances of sex role playing involved both playmates. Sex role play among children is clearly a social activity. That younger children engage in little role play does not imply that they are asocial and egocentric. Rather, if children are considered to be innately sociocentric, the small amount of noticeable interaction among younger children may reflect a lack of interaction *skills* rather than a lack of motivation. Thus, these preliminary findings provide additional support for a view that children are naturally sociocentric rather than egocentric.

That children play sex-appropriate roles does not mean that they are unaware of complementary roles. In fact, there were several indications that children knew quite well the behaviour appropriate to the opposite sex role. For instance, after deciding to play mother and father, a five-year-old 'mother' was rummaging through a bag of clothes and found items for father. First, she gave him a man's hat, then a tie. In another case, a little 'daddy' asked 'mummy' to cook supper for him.

The pattern of exceptions to sex-appropriate role playing is interesting to examine. Most role reversals involved little girls who wanted to play male roles. In one case, an aggressive five-year-old girl persisted in labelling her male playmate 'mother'. He was quite upset, and kept protesting that he wasn't mother, but was father. His playmate reluctantly relinquished the role of father only when he threatened to tell on her if she continued calling him mother! Although these observations are based on a small sample size, the pattern of exceptions seems to indicate that the male role was more desirable, a finding in keeping with the general view that male roles have more status (cf. Lynn, 1966).

Summary

This paper has reviewed findings from an observational study of sex role playing in pre-school children. It was reported that pairs of children in a free play setting spontaneously engage in role play including the use of sex roles, with sex role playing more common among children aged $4\frac{1}{2}$–$5\frac{1}{2}$ than among children $3\frac{1}{2}$–$4\frac{1}{2}$. Further, children regularly adopt sex-appropriate roles. Finally, this study questions the view that children are egocentric. Since most sex role playing took place in an interactive context, it seems that children actively seek social contact, and role play serves to initiate and facilitate this contact.

Although these findings are based on a small, homogeneous group of children, this paper has provided a foundation for future work in this area. Specifically, shifts in the frequency and types of sex roles used, and the effects of peers and adults on children's sex role performances, need to be examined. Through careful observation of actual sex role activity we can further elucidate the development of sex roles in children.

References

BANDURA, A., ROSS, D., and ROSS, S. A. (1963), 'Imitation of film-mediated aggressive models', *Journal of Abnormal and Social Psychology*, No. 66, pp. 3–11.

BROWN, D. G. (1956), 'Sex role preference in young children', *Psych. Monog.*, No. 70.

DAWE, H. C. (1934), 'An analysis of 200 quarrels of preschool children', *Child Development*, No. 5, pp. 139–56.

Sex Role Playing in Pre-School Children **391**

FESHBACH, N. D. (1969), 'Sex differences in children's modes of aggressive responses towards outsiders', *Merrill-Palmer Quarterly*, No. 15, pp. 249–58.

FLING, S., and MANOSEVITZ, M. (1972), 'Sex typing in nursery school children's play interests', *Dev. Psych.*, No. 7, pp. 146–52.

GARVEY, C., and HOGAN, R. (1973), 'Social speech and social interaction: egocentrism revisited', *Child Development*, No. 44, pp. 562–8.

HEISE, D. R., and ROBERTS, E. P. (1970), 'The development of role knowledge', *Genet. Psycho. Monog.*, No. 82, pp. 83–115.

JERSILD, A. T., and MARKEY, F. V. (1935), 'Conflicts between pre-school children', *Child Development Monographs*, No. 21.

LYNN, D. B. (1959), 'A note on sex differences in the development of masculine and feminine identification', *Psych. Rev.*, No. 66, pp. 126–35.

LYNN, D. (1966), 'The process of learning parental and sex-role identification', *Journal of Marriage and the Family*, No. 28, pp. 466–70.

VENER, A. M., and SNYDER, C. A. (1966), 'The preschool child's awareness and anticipation of adult sex-roles', *Sociometry*, No. 29, pp. 159–68.

WARD, W. D. (1969), 'Process of sex-role development', *Dev. Psych.*, No. 1, pp. 163–8.

D   The Special Case of Games

Street Games: Counting-Out and Chasing

'And the streets of the city shall be full of boys and girls playing in the streets thereof.'
Zechariah, viii. 5

When children play in the street they not only avail themselves of one of the oldest play-places in the world, they engage in some of the oldest and most interesting of games, for they are games tested and confirmed by centuries of children, who have played them and passed them on, as children continue to do, without reference to print, parliament, or adult propriety. Indeed these street games are probably the most played, least recorded, most natural games that there are. Certainly they are the most spontaneous, for the little group of boys under the lamp-post may not know, until a minute before, whether they are to play 'Bish Bash' or 'Poison' or 'Cockarusha', or even know that they are going to play.

A true game is one that frees the spirit. It allows of no cares but those fictitious ones engendered by the game itself. When the players commit themselves to the rhythm and incident of 'Underground Tig' or 'Witches in the Gluepots' they opt out of the ordinary world, the boundary of their existence becomes the two pavements this side of a pillar-box, their only reality the excitement of avoiding the chaser's touch.

The appeal of the games

Play is unrestricted, games have rules. Play may merely be the enactment of a dream, but in each game there is a contest. Yet it will be noticed that when children play a game in the street they are often extraordinarily naïve or, according to viewpoint, highly civilized. They seldom need an umpire, they rarely trouble to keep scores, little significance is attached to who wins or loses, they do not require the stimulus of prizes, it does not seem to worry them if a game is not finished. Indeed children like games in which there is a sizeable element of luck, so that individual abilities cannot be directly compared. They like games which restart almost automatically, so that everybody is given a new chance. They like games which move in stages, in which each stage, the choosing of leaders, the picking-up of sides, the determining of which side shall start, is almost a game in itself. In fact children's games often seem laborious to adults who, if invited to join in, may find themselves becoming impatient, and wanting to speed them up. Adults do not always see, when subjected to lengthy preliminaries, that many of the games, particularly those of young children, are more akin to ceremonies than competitions. In these games children gain the reassurance that comes with repetition, and the feeling of fellowship that comes from doing the same as everyone else. Children may choose a particular game merely because of some petty dialogue which precedes the chase:

'Sheep, sheep, come home.'
'We're afraid.'
'What of?'
'The wolf.'
'Wolf has gone to Devonshire
Won't be here for seven years,
Sheep, sheep, come home.'

As Spencer remarked, it is not only the amount of physical exercise that is taken that gives recreation, 'an agreeable mental excitement has a highly invigorating influence'. Thus children's 'interest' in a game may well be the incident in it that least appeals to the adult: the opportunity it affords to thump a player on the back, as in 'Strokey Back', to behave stupidly and be applauded for the stupidity, as in 'Johnny Green', to say aloud the colour of someone's panties, as in 'Farmer, Farmer, may we cross your Golden River?' And in a number of games, for instance 'Chinese Puzzle', there may be little purpose other than the ridiculousness of the experiment itself.

'Someone, as to be on. The one who is on, as to turn round while the others hold hands and make a round circul. Then you get in a muddle, one persun could clime over your arms or under your legs or anything ales that you could make a muddle, then when they have finished they say "Chinese Puzzle we are all in a muddle", then the persun turns round and goes up to them and gets them out of the muddle without breaking their hands, and then the persun who was on choose someone ales, and then it goes on like that. It is fun to play Chinese Puzzle.'

Here, indeed, is a British game where little attempt is made to establish the superiority of one player over another. In fact the function of such a game is largely social. Just as the shy man reveals himself by his formalities, so does the child disclose his unsureness of his place in the world by welcoming games with set procedures, in which his relationships with his fellows are clearly established. In games a child can exert himself without having to explain himself, he can be a good player without having to think whether he is a popular person, he can find himself being a useful partner to someone of whom he is ordinarily afraid. He can be confident, too, in particular games, that it is his place to issue commands, to inflict pain, to steal people's possessions, to pretend to be dead, to hurl a ball actually at someone, to pounce on someone, or to kiss someone he has caught. In ordinary life either he never knows these experiences or, by attempting them, makes himself an outcast.

It appears to us that when a child plays a game he creates a situation which is under his control, and yet it is one of which he does not know the outcome. In the confines of a game there can be all the excitement and uncertainty of an adventure, yet the young player can comprehend the whole, can recognize his place in the scheme, and, in contrast to the confusion of real life, can tell what is right action. He can, too, extend his environment, or feel that he is doing so, and gain knowledge of sensations beyond ordinary experience. When children are small, writes Bertrand Russell, 'it is biologically natural that they should, in imagination, live through the life of remote savage ancestors'. As long as the action of the game is of a child's own making he is ready, even anxious, to sample the perils of which this world has such plentiful supply. In the security of a game he makes acquaintance with insecurity, he is able to rationalize absurdities, reconcile himself to not getting his own way, 'assimilate reality' (Piaget), act heroically without being in danger. The thrill of a chase is accentuated by viewing the chaser not as a boy in short trousers, but as a bull. It is not a classmate's back he rides upon but a knight's fine charger. It is not a party of other boys his side skirmishes with but Indians, Robbers, 'Men from Mars'. And, always provided that the environment is of his own choosing, he – or she – is even prepared to meet the 'things that happen in the dark', playing games that would seem strange amusement if it was thought they were being taken literally: 'Murder in the Dark', 'Ghosties in the Garret', 'Moonlight, Starlight, Bogey won't come out Tonight'. And yet, within the context of the game, these alarms *are* taken literally.

The age of the players

When generalizing about children's play it is easy to forget that each child's attitude to each game, and his way of playing it, is constantly changing as he himself matures; his preferences moving from the fanciful to the ritualistic, from the ritualistic to the romantic (i.e. the free-ranging games, 'Hide and Seek', 'Cowboys and Indians'), and from the romantic to the severely competitive. The infants, 5–7 years old, may play some of the same games in their playground that the juniors do across the way, but in a more personal, less formalized style. Their chasing game, in which they clutch the railings to be safe, is called, perhaps, 'Naughty Boys'. 'We're playing naughty boys, we've run away from home.' ('Touch Iron' or 'Touch Green' is only emerging from make-believe.) The boys who are moving on hands and feet, stomachs upwards, in another part of the playground, say they are being Creatures, 'horrible creatures in the woods'. The juniors, in the next playground, would not play like this, not move about publicly on hands and feet, unless, that is, it was part of a 'proper' game, one in which they were *chasing* each other.

When I was five I played at Beddies. At seven I learned to play E.I.O. At nine I played 'Alla Baba who's got the ball-a'. Now I am fourteen I play tennis and netball, not the games I used to play when I was smaller.

The age of the games

These games that 'children find out for themselves when they meet', as Plato put it, seem to them as new and surprising when they learn them as the jokes in this week's comic. Parties of schoolchildren, at the entrance to the British Museum, secretly playing 'Fivestones' behind one of the columns as they wait to go in, little think that their pursuits may be as great antiquities as the exhibits they have been brought to see. Yet, in their everyday games, when they draw straws to see who shall take a disliked role, they show how Chaucer's Canterbury pilgrims determined which of them should tell the first tale. When they strike at each other's plantains, trying to decapitate them, they play the game a medieval chronicler says King Stephen played with his boy-prisoner William Marshal to humour him. When they jump on a player's back, and make him guess which finger they hold up ('Husky-bum, Finger or Thumb?') they perpetuate an amusement of ancient Rome. When they hit a player from behind, in the game 'Stroke the Baby', and challenge him to name who did it, they unwittingly illuminate a passage in the life of Our Lord. And when they enter the British Museum they can see Eros, clearly depicted on a vase of 400 B.C., playing the game they have just been told to abandon.

Even more revealing, perhaps, than the age of the games, is the persistence of certain practices during the games. The custom of turning round a blindfold player *three times* before allowing him to begin chasing seems already to have been standard practice in the seventeenth century. The quaint notion that a player becomes 'warm' when nearing the object he is seeking was doubtless old when Silas Wegg adopted it (*Our Mutual Friend*). The stratagem of making players choose one of two objects, such as an 'orange' or a 'lemon', to decide which side they shall take in a pulling match, was almost certainly employed by the Elizabethans. The rule that a special word and finger-sign shall give a player respite in a game appears to be a legacy of the age of chivalry. The convention that the player who does worst in a game shall be punished, rather than that he who does best shall be rewarded, has an almost continuous history stretching from classical antiquity. And the ritual confirmation that a player has been caught, by crowning him or by tapping him three times, prevalent today even in such sophisticated places as Ilford and Enfield, was mentioned by Cromek in his *Remains of Nithsdale and Galloway Song* in 1810 ('If the intruder be caught on the hostile ground he is *taend*, that is, clapped three times on the head, which makes him a prisoner'), and is also the rule – as are other of these conventions – amongst children in France, Germany, Austria, Italy and the United States.

Where children play: playing in the street

Where children are is where they play. They are impatient to be started, the street is no further than their front door, and they are within call when tea is ready. Indeed the street in front of their home is seemingly theirs, more theirs sometimes than the family living-room; and of more significance to them, very often, than any amenity provided by the local council. When a young coloured boy from Notting Hill was being given a week's holiday in a Wiltshire village, and was asked how he liked the country, he promptly replied, 'I like it – but you can't play in the road as you can in London.' . . .

Play in restricted environment

It is a pleasant sight to see the young play with those of their own age at tick, puss in the corner, hop-scotch, ring-taw, and hot beans ready buttered: and in these boyish amusements much self-denial and good nature may be practised. This, however, is not always the case . . .

The Boy's Week-Day Book, 1834

The places specially made for children's play are also the places where children can most easily be watched playing: the asphalt expanses of school playgrounds, the cage-like enclosures filled with junk by a local authority, the corners of recreation grounds stocked with swings and slides. In a playground children are, or are not, allowed to make chalk diagrams on the ground for hopscotch, to bounce balls against a wall, to bring marbles or skipping ropes, to play 'Conkers', 'Split the Kipper', 'Hi Jimmy Knacker'. Children of different ages may or may not be kept apart; boys may or may not be separated from girls. And according to the closeness of the supervision they organize gangs, carry out vendettas, place people in Coventry, gamble, bribe, blackmail, squabble, bully and fight. The real nature of young boys has long been apparent to us, or so it has seemed. We have only to travel in a crowded school bus to be conscious of their belligerency, the extraordinary way they have of assailing each other, verbally and physically, each child feeling – perhaps with reason – that it is necessary to keep his end up against the rest. . .

Recent extensive studies of apes and monkeys have shown, perhaps not unexpectedly, that animal behaviour in captivity is not the same as in the wild. . .

Our observations of children lead us to believe that much the same is true of our own species. We have noticed that when children are herded together in the playground, which is where the educationalists and the psychologists and the social scientists gather to observe them, their play is markedly more aggressive than when they are in the street or in the wild places. At school they play 'Ball He', 'Dodge Ball', 'Chain Swing', and 'Bull in the Ring'. They indulge in duels such as 'Slappies', 'Knuckles,' and 'Stinging', in which the pleasure, if not the purpose, of the game is to dominate another player and inflict pain. In a playground it is impracticable to play the free-ranging games like 'Hide and Seek' and 'Relievo' and 'Kick the Can', that are, as Stevenson said, the 'well-spring of romance', and are natural to children in the wastelands.

Often, when we have asked children what games they played in the playground we have been told 'We just go round aggravating people'. Nine-year-old boys make-believe they are Black Riders and in a mob charge on the girls. They play 'Coshes' with knotted handkerchiefs, they snatch the girls' ties or hair ribbons and call it 'Strip Tease', they join hands in a line and rush round the playground shouting 'Anyone who gets in our way will get knocked over'. . .

Starting a game

'Zig zag zooligar
Zim zam bum.'
   A Manchester 'dip'

Such is the capacity of the young for turning whatever they do into a sport, that collecting players for a game can be a game in itself. Two or three children, arms round each other's shoulders, reel across the play-ground chanting in the way they have heard other children chant before them: 'Who wants a game of *Sticky Toffee*? Who wants a game of *Sticky Toffee*?' Those who want to play attach themselves to the line, the line becomes unwieldy, the chant becomes a roar, there are more than enough players for the game, yet nobody now seems in the least inclined to break the line and begin playing. 'Sticky Toffee', or whatever the game pro-posed, has been forgotten in the very success of their summons to play it, a summons which varies according to local prescription, for instance: 'All join-ee join-ee up', or 'Arly-arly-in, who's a playing?', or 'All in, all in – hands in the dip'. In Pontypool:

All in, all in, a bottle of gin,
All out, all out, a bottle of stout.

In Brighouse:

All here who's laiking [playing],
Mary Ann's baking.

And in Whalsay, Shetland, when a game of 'Aggie Waggie' is proposed:

'Whã's cŏmĭn ĭ wĭr fun ăggie wăggie?'

('They seem able to fit any name into the rhythm', commented their teacher.)

Sometimes, however, playground recruitment is less voluntary. Two or three youngsters form a ring round a solitary child and threaten: 'Have a smack or join in the ring', or 'Pinch, punch, or join the bunch', or

Pinch, punch, join in the ring,
Pinch, punch, no girls in.

Avoidance of disliked role

On occasion a game starts in a flash, the players themselves hardly knowing how it began. More often children feel a game is not a proper one if such matters have not first been settled as who is to be allowed to play, what the boundaries are to be, and whether dropping-out is to be permitted. Yet the chief impediment to a swift start is the fact that in most games one player has to take a part that is different from the rest; and all children have, or affect to have, an insurmountable objection to being the first one to take this part. Tradition, if not inclination, demands that they do whatever they can to avoid being the chaser, or the seeker, or the one who, as they express it, is 'on', 'on it', 'he', or 'it'. Thus it is recognized throughout Britain (by everyone except the slowcoach) that the last person to exempt himself shall be the first to be 'on'; and this rule is so embedded in children's minds that their immediate response to the proposal of a game is to cry out 'Bags no on', 'I bags not on it', 'Me fains first', 'Foggy not on', or whatever is the locally accepted term of exemption. (In Banbury it is 'Baggy laggy', in Bishop Auckland 'Nanny on', in Forfar 'Chap no out', in Wigan 'Brit'.) On occasion, even the person suggesting the game may feel he must safeguard himself by saying in one gulp, 'Let's-play-Tig-fains-I-be-on-it'.

Yet, in some places, words are not enough to give exemption. In Norfolk the person who becomes the chaser is the one who last bobs down to the ground saying 'Vains'. In Putney it is he or she who last touches the ground, turns around, and says 'Bags I'm not on it'. In Swansea it is the child who last says and acts upon the words 'Not on this tippits', touching his shoe-cap; or 'Tippits, touch the ground, turn around, no back answers, one, two, three'. In Ruthin one child holds out his arms in a circle in front of him, shouting 'Hands in the bucket', and the last person to put his hands in the circle is 'out'.

Such methods of settling who shall be 'on' appear eminently fair to the alert; and they will try any device to make someone other than themselves be he. They say, 'A, B, C, D, F, G, H. What have I missed out?' and when some half-awake replies 'E', he is told 'That's right, you are!' They say 'Whose shoes are the shiniest?' and when a player claims the distinction he is promptly given the important role. They shout 'Cannon' or 'Quick Fire', and the player who is dolt enough to inquire what this means will have talked himself into a job. In parts of Lincolnshire (e.g. Cleethorpes and Market Rasen) the children who are to play a game silently form a circle, giving each other instructions by signs, and even pushing each other into place without saying anything, for 'the first person to speak is *it*'. In some places, indeed, a player may require fortitude if he is to avoid the obnoxious role. In Sale, after the boys have formed a circle, one of them walks round pretending to kick each lad on the shins, and 'the one who flinches is on'. At Chapeltown, near Sheffield, the boys made a circle, putting one foot forward into the ring, and a player takes round a brick which he pretends to drop on their foot to make one of them move. And at Lydney, says a 13-year-old boy, there is no pretending about it: 'When you want to start a game you pick a stone and throw it at the people's feet. The first to jump back or say anything is on it.'

He-names

Children's dislike of being the player with a certain power in a game, of being the one, that is, from whom the others flee or hide, has led some folklorists to suppose that this player originally represented a being who was evil or supernatural. They observe that in France and Germany such a player is sometimes termed a wolf, that in Spain he is 'El Dimoni', and in Japan, likewise, 'Oni'. In some games in Britain, too, the chaser is 'Old Mr Wolf', 'Old Mother Witch', or 'the Devil'; yet in the majority of instances there seems little reason to think these roles have, or ever had, much significance. When awe of the Evil One is genuine, people fear even to pronounce his name. They refer to him obliquely as 'Old Harry', 'Old Nick', 'Old Splitfoot', 'Old Scratch', 'the old one', 'the gentleman downstairs', or use even more indirect terms. Parish, for instance, in his *Sussex*

Dialect, 1875, noted that the devil was always spoken of as 'he', with a special emphasis. ('In the Downs there's a golden calf buried.' 'Then why döant they dig it up?' 'Oh, it is not allowed; *he* would not let them.')

It is, of course, true that in London and southern England the player is usually called 'he' (often spelt 'hee', although pronounced 'ee', and sometimes actually believed to be 'E'); and that in the south-west, the midlands, and north, the ordinary term is 'it'. (The player who is 'it' is then said to be either 'on' or 'on it'. Thus a child may say 'Who's going to be it?' Everyone cries 'No it!' and the last person to say 'no it' is 'on it'.) But although these expressions have a regional bias, it is difficult to learn much about their age. They have, it seems, always been exclusive to children, and consequently their appearances in literature are rare.

Selection made by chance

When players exert themselves to avoid being 'on' the procedure is simple, the execution quick, but it is not always decisive, and not invariably the saving in time and temper that it ought to be. 'We all shout "no on", and we keep shouting "no on", and we go on and on until it is near the end of playtime and we don't start the game at all, like', confessed one lad. In consequence most children prefer the allotment of the disliked role to be a matter of chance. They feel that if the choice has been made by providence there is no possibility of argument, especially if the choice has fallen on someone other than themselves. Thus one boy will stand in the middle of a circle, shut his eyes, hold out his arm, and turn round and round until he has no idea which way he is facing. The player he is pointing at when he stops is 'on'. Likewise a player turns round and round with his eyes shut and throws a ball, and whoever he happens to hit is 'on'. Or a player bounces a ball in the middle of a circle, each player having his legs wide apart, and the one through whose legs the ball rolls is 'on' (see further under 'Kingy', p. 409). Or a boy puts his hand behind his back, holds up a certain number of fingers, and the child who is unlucky enough to say the correct number is 'on'. Or one player goes out of hearing, the rest pick colours, including a colour for the person who is away, and when the person comes back and names a colour, the player who has chosen that colour is declared 'on'.

Such methods of determining who is to take the unpopular role are obvious enough, and might occur to anyone. Yet children also indulge in practices that are not likely to come to the minds of any but the initiated, and which, indeed, have something in common with old forms of divination now supposedly forgotten. Thus girls in South Elmsall, aged nine and ten, sometimes use mud to decide who is to be the chaser. 'We dip our fingers in the mud and the people playing choose a finger each first, and if the finger they have chosen come out with the most mud that person is "on".'

Odd man out

Another way a player can condemn himself to the unwanted role is by the process known as 'Chinging up' or 'Odd Man Out'. For this operation, much resorted to in Greater London, the players stand in a circle facing inwards, with their hands behind their backs, and chant in unison certain words, which vary from district to district, but are in Walworth, for example:

'Allee in the middle, and the odd man's out!'

On the word *out* they whip their hands from behind their backs, holding them in front for all to see, either with their fists clenched, or with their fingers stretched out palms downwards, or with their hands clenched but first two fingers spread out. They then look round to see if one player is 'odd', that is to say, holding his hands in one of the three positions but different from everyone else, in which case that player becomes 'ee'. If no one is odd they try again; and sometimes increase the likelihood of one player being odd by introducing a fourth finger position, known as 'grab' or 'crane', in which the fingers point downwards . . .

Dipping

Fanciful as it would seem to somebody who had never been a child, the normal way the young decide who is to have the unpopular part in a game is to form the players up in a line or circle, and count along the line the number of counts prescribed by the accented syllables of some little rhyme, such as the following which has fifteen counts:

Err′ie, orr′ie, round′ the ta′ble,
Eat′ as much′ as you′ are a′ble;
If′ you're a′ble eat′ the ta′ble,
Err′ie, orr′e, *out*!

One child gabbles the words at speed, pointing briefly at each player in turn as he does so, and if there are less than fifteen players, he continues round the circle or along the line a second time, counting himself in first. The player the last count falls on is then either made the chaser, and the game begins; or, more often, he is counted 'out' and stands aside while the rhyme is repeated and a second player eliminated, and so on, until only one player remains – on whom the count has never fallen – and that player is the unlucky one. Virtually every child in England now calls this procedure 'dipping', a term that seems to have become general only in the early 1940s. It has not been known to our older correspondents; it does not appear in the accounts of games we possess written by children in the 1920s and 1930s; and it is not current in Scotland, Canada, or the United States. In the 1930s, however, children often used to touch the ground or point at the ground when they began counting, saying 'Dip' as they did so: 'Dip – Eeny, meeny, miney, mo', 'Dip – Each, peach, pear, plum'; and it is possible that this gave rise to the term, 'dipping' being easier to say than 'counting-out'. . .

Dips

'There are so many dips that I've lost count.'
Girl, 9, West Ham

To the outsider it appears that any wretched doggerel will do for a dipping rhyme. A 'dip', it seems, can be of almost any length, cast in almost any mould, be either sense or nonsense (usually the latter), and need not even be a rhyme. On occasion the dipper may merely count to twenty-one, and whoever the number twenty-one falls on becomes the catcher. He may recite the alphabet to the twenty-first letter, 'A, B, C, D, E, F, G, H, I, J, K, L, M, N, O, P, Q, R, S, T, *You*', or just repeat the vowels, 'A, E, I, O, *You*', or say 'One, two, sky blue, all out but you', or 'Red, white, and blue, all out but you', or occasionally 'A, B, C, D, E, F, G, H, I, J, K, L, M, N, O, P, Q, R, S, T, U – are – He'; or in areas where the chaser is known as 'it' – 'A, B, C, D, E, F, G, H, I for It' (Pendeen), or 'I – T spells it, thou art it' (Blackburn), or 'Tom Tit you are it' (Cleethorpes).

More often, as we have already said, the process of dipping is more anxious and time-taking: the dip has to be repeated as many times, less one, as there are players, since the player the dip ends on is not selected but eliminated:

Ip, dip, sky blue,
Who's it? Not you
God's words are true,
It must not be *you*.
East Dulwich

The person pointed to stands aside, and the rest face the ordeal of being counted again. Thus certain phrases are thought appropriate simply because they end with the word *out*, as 'Pig's snout, walk out', and 'Boy Scout walk out' which sometimes gets extended to:

Boy Scout walk out,
Girl Guide step aside.

Or, Boy Scout walk out
With your breeches inside out.

... Any deceit that may still be supposed possible, is finally frustrated if the question asked in the dipping rhyme is one to which a player can give only one answer, and which yet varies with the player asked, for instance his birth date.

Eachie, peachie, pear, plum
When does your birthday come?
– *Fourteenth of December*.
1, 2, 3, 4, 5, 6, 7, 8, 9, 10, 11, 12, 13, 14,
D-E-C-E-M-B-E-R. You are out.

The most ardent disciplinarian should be satisfied with a dip such as this, even if he finds after carrying it out that no time remains for playing the game to which it was intended to be a preliminary. But this, he will find, troubles only the serious-minded. It is evident that even participation dips are repeated as much for fun as for fairness. The two participation dips that follow are almost the most popular of all, yet the responses they elicit have no effect on the count whatever.

There's a party on the hill, will you come?
Bring your own cup and saucer and a bun.
   Dipper aside: What's your sweetheart's name?
   Player: Mary.
Mary will be there with a ribbon in her hair,
Will you come to the party will you come?
> *Versions current throughout Britain. Based
> on a nineteenth-century song 'Will you come
> to my wedding, will you come?'*

As I climbed up the apple tree
All the apples fell on me.
Bake an apple, bake a pie,
Have you ever told a lie?
– No.
Yes you did, you know you did,
You broke your mother's teapot-lid.
What colour was it?
– Blue.
No it wasn't, it was gold,
That's another lie you've told.
> *Well known in England, Scotland, Wales, and
> the United States, since nineteenth century*

To the majority of young players dipping is not so much a means of getting a game started as part of the game itself. When children describe a game they may spend as much time giving details of how they decide who is to be on as they do in describing the game; and these details they will very properly repeat with renewed earnestness when they describe further games. Preliminaries such as we have given here precede most games in which one player has a part different from the rest. It will however be appreciated that in the descriptions of games that follow we have – with the impatience of juvenile affairs which is a well-known adult characteristic – not felt it necessary to recount these preliminaries each time.

Chasing games

'The rules are very simple, if you are ticked on any part of the body, you are man. But that's when the trouble starts. Some players deny that they were took, and a fight starts.'

Boy, 13, Liverpool

In chasing games a touch with the tip of the finger is enough to transform a player's part in the game. It is as if the chaser was evil, or magic, or diseased, and his touch was contagious. His touch can immobilize a player, or make him clutch his body as if hurt, or put him out of the game. Simultaneously it can free the chaser of his task, and enable him to be an ordinary player again. It is not even necessary that the touch be given fairly for it to be effective ('Sometimes when I can't catch anyone I pretend to be giving up in a huff,' said an 8-year-old, 'then I turn round quickly'). Nor is it necessary that a player be aware who is the chaser (in one game, 'Tig No Tell', this is deliberately kept obscure). Rather the touch seems to have power in itself; and chasing games could well be termed 'contaminating games' were it not that the children themselves do not, on the whole, think of the chaser's touch as being strange or contagious. Their pleasure in chasing games seems to lie simply in the exercise and excitement of chasing and being chased; and the contagious element, which possibly had significance in the past, is today uppermost in their minds only in some unpleasant aberrations, which are here relegated to a subsection.

Touch

The basic game, in which one person chases the rest, can start almost spontaneously, be played virtually anywhere, and once started, is self-perpetuating. 'It is an endless game', as one child observed. No sooner has the chaser succeeded in touching someone (and perhaps said 'it' or 'tick' to emphasize the touch) than that person becomes the new chaser. Sometimes, the unceasingness of the game is stressed by a name such as 'No Barlies Tick' (Welshpool), making it clear that players are not permitted to drop out or claim respite, even after using the truce word 'Barley'. Indeed girls sometimes complain that the game goes on until they are puffed out: 'The only thing you can do if you want to stop is run into the toilets.' The game is usually played within a defined area. The only other restrictions are that the chaser must not keep after the same person all the time; and that when a person is touched or 'tigged' he cannot 'tig back', or, as they express it in many places 'You can't tig your butcher', or, at Hemsworth, 'No sharps'. The player must first chase someone else.

If, however, the chaser is slow, or seems uncertain whom to follow, the game is liable to be enlivened by some confident fellow flaunting himself in front of the chaser, or by the introduction of vocal stimuli. The chaser is goaded with little rhymes that are no less traditional for being witless, the usual couplet (recited in places as far apart as Swansea and Golspie) being:

Ha, ha, ha, hee, hee, hee,
Can't catch me for a bumble bee.

The language of the chase

In juvenile speech the word for the significant touch that affects another player is not synonymous with either of the standard English words *touch* or *catch*. Children in the north country, for instance, 'tig' each other, but they do not say they 'tig' wood, even when they touch it significantly for protection in 'Tiggy Tiggy Touchwood'. Again, 'tig' cannot be equated to *catch* when, in a game such as 'Tig and Releivo', a person has to be 'tigged' to be released. The word 'tig', which is now used only by the young, subsists throughout the greater part of northern Britain, the past tense very often being 'tug' or 'tugged' or even, in New Cumnock, 'tuggen'. However, in the far north of Scotland (Golspie, Inverness, Stornoway), and in parts of Wales, (e.g. Fishguard and Ruthin), they 'tip' a person. In the west Midlands they 'tick' him, and he is then said to have been 'took', 'tuck', or sometimes 'tucked'. In Monmouthshire, Gloucestershire, and Oxfordshire, they speak of 'tagging' each other, and the person who 'tags' may be called 'tag' or 'the tagger', as he also is in the United States, not only in chasing games but in baseball when a runner is put out by being 'tagged' with the ball. In Nottingham children 'dob' each other, in Romsey they 'dab', in the Forest of Dean they 'dap', at Hereford and Crickhowell they always 'tap', and in Jersey they 'take' ('First of all you dip to find out who takes'). In London, and fairly generally in the south-eastern counties, the 'He' or 'Ee' who chases strives to 'have' someone, a term which gives rise to such verbal infelicities as:

He has to 'have' another boy, if he 'has' one the boy he 'has' has to hold the place where he was 'had'.

Boy, 13, Croydon, describing 'French He'

And:

We played He and I was had, so I had to be he.

Occasionally the past tense 'had' itself becomes the verb and the English language is placed under considerable strain:

If she hads a person when she is he the person she hads becomes he.

Girl, 11, West Ham, on 'Ball He'

... Further confusion may arise, at least in the adult mind, in Devon, Lincolnshire, and parts of Scotland where, no matter how lightly a person is touched, he is said to be 'hit'. 'When you get 'it on the shoulder you hold the place where you got 'it' (Girl, 9, Plympton St Mary, describing 'Fleabite Its'). 'If the man does hit him he must stand with his legs parted' (Girl, 13, Whalsay, where the chaser – whether boy or girl – is always 'man'). And confusion may turn to alarm in Orkney, where the word for tigging is 'stoning', if a child is overheard saying, 'When somebody stones you, you have got to go and stone somebody else.'

Players restricted to particular way of moving

In some chasing games the ordinary rules of Touch are maintained, but all players, including the chaser, are restricted in the way they may move. They play 'Walking He' in which no player may run, 'Hopping He' in which no player may put both feet on the ground at once, and 'Bob He' in which the players squat, and progress is made by bunny jumps ('it is quite a hot game'). At Timberscombe in Somerset the game of the moment when we paid a visit in 1964 was 'Spider Touch', the players progressing on all fours, but with their fronts facing the sky. In Lincolnshire, where a popular game is 'Crab Tiggy', the players attain the 'crab' position by doing a handstand and dropping backwards on to their feet, so that their bodies are *arched* inside out. (A headmaster commented: 'If we tried to *make* them do this, parents would write to their M.P.s'.) In Camberwell, where one of the games is 'Butterfly He', they run in pairs holding hands, but with one player back to front. And another form of Touch in which the players move in pairs is 'Piggyback He' (otherwise known as 'Donkey Touch' or 'Horsie Tig'), in which the important rule is that the chaser must be properly mounted, or his touch does not count. The same rule applies in 'Bike He' (in Wigan known as 'Ticky on Bikes'), but in this game the chaser's art is to steer his bike across the front of the person he is chasing, thus forcing the rider to put a foot on the ground, which makes him the chaser as effectively as if he had been touched. Each of these games is best played in a small area (even 'Bike He'), and with plenty of players, although there must not be too many players in 'Bike He', or the result is hair-raising, or, more precisely, knee-grazing.

French Touch

The fancy that a chaser's touch is contagious or even wounding is here given logical expression. The game starts as ordinary 'Touch', but when the chaser succeeds in touching someone, the new chaser has to keep one hand covering the spot where he was touched until he, in his turn, manages to touch someone else. The sport, therefore, is for the chaser not merely to touch another player, but to touch him on a part of his anatomy that will be an embarrassment to him to keep a hand on while he is chasing, for instance, the top of his head, his nose, backside, a shoulder-blade, elbow, knee, or foot. 'It looks so funny when someone is tuck on the foot and one sees him hopping about', remarks a 12-year-old. In fact one of the joys of the game seems to be envisaging the awkward places where a person might be touched. 'He might be tug on the eyes then he won't be able to see. Then he can't tig us at all,' suggested a Birmingham 8-year-old. It is, of course, a strict rule of the game that the chaser has no power of touch unless one of his hands is covering the affected spot.

Names: The majority are evocative of the game, for instance: 'Hospital Touch', 'Poison Touch', 'Poisonous Tiggy', 'Body Tick', 'Flea-Bite Its', 'Ticky Wounded', 'Wounded Tiggy', 'Doctor Touch', 'Lame Tig', 'Ticky Lame Horse', 'Sticky Touch', 'Sticky Glue Touch', and, in Kirkwall, 'Funny Picko'. The name 'French Touch' probably reflects the feeling that a touch which is so pernicious must be an importation. This is also implicit in the names 'London Touch' (in Bristol) and 'Chinese Touch' (in London). And it is consistent that children in Berlin think of it as foreign too. They call it 'Englisch Zeck' or 'Englisch Einkriege' (Reinhard Peesch, *Das Berliner Kinderspiel der Gegenwart*, 1957, p. 34).

Kingy

This fast-moving game has all the qualifications for being considered the national game of British schoolboys: it is indigenous, it is sporting, it has fully evolved rules, it is immensely popular (almost every boy in England, Scotland, and Wales plays it), and no native of Britain appears to have troubled to record it.

'Kingy' is a ball game in which those who are not He have the ball hurled at them, without means of retaliation, and against ever-increasing odds, an element that obviously appeals to the national character. Anyone who is hit by the ball straightway joins the He in trying to hit the rest of the players. Those who are throwing may not run with the ball in their hands, but pursue their quarry by passing the ball to each other. Those being thrown at may run and dodge as they like, and may also punch the ball away from them with their fists. For this purpose players sometimes wrap a handkerchief round their hand, as 'fisting' the ball can be painful. The game continues until all but one have been hit and are 'out', and this player is declared 'King'. When the contestants are skilled (and boys of fifteen and sixteen readily play the game), the ball gets thrown with considerable force: it shoots back and forth across the street or playground, and the game can be as exciting to watch as a tennis match.

As befits a sport in which so much energy is expended, the preliminaries are sometimes wonderfully ritualistic. At Bishop Auckland, for instance, one person shouts 'King' to start the proceedings, and two others follow up by crying 'Sidey'. The players then form a circle round the King, with the two who shouted 'Sidey' standing on either side of him like heirs-apparent. The players making the circle stand with legs apart, each foot touching the foot of their neighbour on either side. The King picks up the ball and bounces it – or, as they say in Bishop Auckland, 'stounces' it – three times in the ring, and then lets it roll. Everyone watches to see whose legs it will go through. If it does not roll through anybody's legs the King picks it up and bounces it again, and if his second turn fails he has a third try. If the ball still has not passed between anyone's legs, he hands it to the first sidey (the 'foggy-sidey') who, as necessary, repeats the performance – for the moment the ball does pass between someone's legs that person is 'on', and everyone runs. At the end of the game whoever becomes King takes the place in the centre of the ring to start the next game, and the first two people to shout 'Sidey' stand beside him.

In Grimsby, where they also start with the circle, they select the person who is first to bounce the ball in the centre by counting round the players with the words:

Double circle's not complete
Till it goes through someone's feet.

The person pointed to at 'feet' goes into the centre. In some places, however, it is the person who provides the ball who first goes in the centre.

In Scarborough, especially among younger children, the circle-start to the game becomes virtually a game in itself. If the ball is about to roll between a person's legs he can shout 'Knick-knock', which entitles him to use his knees to prevent the ball going through; or he can shout 'Kicks' which means he may kick the ball away, provided others have not already shouted 'No knick-knocks' or 'No kicks'. Likewise, should the ball touch someone else's foot before passing through his legs the player can shout 'Rebounds', and the ball has to be picked up and dropped in the centre anew. Or again, should somebody say 'Tricks' before anyone has declared 'No tricks', the one in the middle may aim the ball through whose legs he chooses, and that person straightway becomes 'it'.

This selection of the chaser by the fortuitous rolling of the ball is customary throughout England and Wales, and much care is taken to see that the ground is flat, so that nobody will be at a disadvantage. In some places, particularly in Wales, there is the difference that the players stand in a tight circle, sometimes having their arms round each other's shoulders, and each puts his right foot forward. It is enough then that the ball touches someone's foot for that person to be 'it'. In Aberystwyth if the ball is dropped in the ring three times and does not touch anybody's right foot, the player who has been dropping the ball becomes the chaser. In Welshpool, however, he hands the ball to the person called 'Second King', who was second last out in the previous game, and he himself 'goes for a walk', which ensures that he will not be touched by the ball and become the new chaser.

In the Walworth district of London the boys sit on the kerb with their feet apart. One boy rolls the ball towards them from across the road, and the one whose legs it goes between is He. In Wandsworth, in much the same way, the players line up facing a wall with their legs apart. And in Cleethorpes, Lincolnshire, they stand in a row but with their heels together and toes apart. The ball is rolled towards them and the person whose feet the ball touches is 'it'.

Throughout most of Scotland, although not in Edinburgh, the players form a circle and hold out their clenched fists in front of them. The player in the middle throws the ball to somebody and he catches it between his fists and throws it to someone else in the circle, who throws it to someone else, all with closed fists. When somebody drops the ball that person is 'hit' or 'het'. Sometimes the person throwing the ball is allowed to pretend to throw it to one person and in fact throw it to another. In Forfar this is known as 'jinkies', and can be prevented by the cry 'No jinkies'.

The Rules. Although the ways of choosing the chaser are numerous, the game itself is played with little variation. Reports from more than fifty places have been so similar, it is as if a mimeographed sheet of rules was carried in every grubby trouser pocket. Such a set of rules would read as follows:

1. The number of players shall be not less than six or more than twenty: the best number is about twelve.

2. The boundaries of the game shall be agreed on before the game begins. A flat area of 20×20 yards, or a length of street of about 20–30 yards, depending on the number of players, is ample.

3. One person shall be chosen chaser, and the game shall start immediately he is chosen. The chaser shall, however, bounce the ball ten times before he throws it at anyone, to give the players time to scatter.

4. The chaser may not run with the ball; but while he is the sole chaser he may bounce the ball on the ground as he runs.

5. A player shall be 'out' when the ball hits him on the body between his neck and knees (or, as may be agreed, between his waist and ankles). It shall be determined beforehand whether a hit shall count if the ball has first bounced on the ground or ricocheted off a wall; or whether only a direct hit shall count.

6. As soon as a player is 'out' he shall assist the chaser in getting the other players out.

7. When there are two or more chasers they may not run with the ball, but may manoeuvre as they wish by passing it to each other.

8. Players being chased may take what action they like to avoid being hit by the ball, including 'fisting' it, i.e. punching it away with their fist. They may also pick up the ball between their fists and chuck it away.

9. Should a chaser catch the ball when it has been 'fisted', or touch a player while he is holding the ball in his fists, the player shall be 'out'.

10. Should a player kick the ball, or handle it other than with his fists, he shall be 'out'.

11. Should a player run out of bounds when trying to avoid being hit by the ball he shall be 'out'.

12. The last player left in shall be 'King', and shall officiate at the selection of the next chaser.

(From *Children's Games in Street and Playground*, Clarendon Press, 1969.)

The Rules of the Game of Marbles

The rules of the game

Children's games constitute the most admirable social institutions. The game of marbles, for instance, as played by boys, contains an extremely complex system of rules, that is to say, a code of laws, a jurisprudence of its own. Only the psychologist, whose profession obliges him to become familiar with this instance of common law, and to get at the implicit morality underlying it, is in a position to estimate the extraordinary wealth of these rules by the difficulty he experiences in mastering their details.

If we wish to gain any understanding of child morality, it is obviously with the analysis of such facts as these that we must begin. All morality consists in a system of rules, and the essence of all morality is to be sought for in the respect which the individual acquires for these rules.

Now, most of the moral rules which the child learns to respect he receives from adults, which means that he receives them after they have been fully elaborated, and often elaborated, not in relation to him and as they are needed, but once and for all and through an uninterrupted succession of earlier adult generations.

In the case of the very simplest social games, on the contrary, we are in the presence of rules which have been elaborated by the children alone. It is of no moment whether these games strike us as 'moral' or not in their contents. As psychologists we must ourselves adopt the point of view, not of the adult conscience, but of child morality. Now, the rules of the game of marbles are handed down, just like so-called moral realities, from one generation to another, and are preserved solely by the respect that is felt for them by individuals. The sole difference is that the relations in this case are only those that exist between children.

Before playing with his equals, the child is influenced by his parents. He is subjected from his cradle to a multiplicity of regulations, and even before language he becomes conscious of certain obligations. These circumstances even exercise, as we shall see, an undeniable influence upon the way in which the rules of games are elaborated. But in the case of play institutions, adult intervention is at any rate reduced to the minimum. We are therefore in the presence here of realities which, if not amongst the mentary, should be classed nevertheless amongst the most spontaneous and the most instructive.

With regard to game rules there are two phenomena which it is particularly easy to study: first, the *practice* of rules, i.e. the way in which children of different ages effectively apply rules; second, the *consciousness* of rules, i.e. the idea which children of different ages form of the character of these game rules, whether of something obligatory and sacred or of something subject to their own choice, whether of heteronomy or autonomy.

It is the comparison of these two groups of data which constitutes the real aim of this chapter. For the relations which exist between the practice and the consciousness of rules are those which will best enable us to define the psychological nature of moral realities.

We shall therefore confine ourselves to a short analysis of the content of the game as it is played in Geneva and Neuchâtel, in the districts where we conducted our work.

The rules of the game of marbles

Three essential facts must be noted if we wish to analyse simultaneously the practice and the consciousness of rules.

The first is that among children of a given generation and in a given locality, however small, there is never one single way of playing marbles, there are quantities of ways. There is the 'square game' with which we shall occupy ourselves more especially. A square is drawn on the ground and a number of marbles placed within it; the game consists in aiming at these from a distance and driving them out of the enclosure. There is the game of 'courate' where two players aim at each other's marble in indefinite pursuit. There is the game of 'troyat' from 'trou' (= hole) or 'creux' (= hollow), where the marbles are piled into a hole and have to be dislodged by means of a heavier marble, and so on. Every child is familiar with several games, a fact that may help according to his age to reinforce or to weaken his belief in the sacred character of rules.

In the second place, one and the same game, such as the Square game, admits of fairly important variations according to when and where it is played. As we had occasion to verify, the rules of the Square game are not the same in four of the communes of Neuchâtel situated at two to three kilometres from each other. They are not the same in Geneva and in Neuchâtel. They differ, on certain points, from one district to another, from one school to another in the same town. In addition to this, as through our collaborators' kindness we were able to establish, variations occur from one generation to another. A student of twenty assured us that in his village the game is no longer played as it was 'in his days'. These variations according to time and place are important, because children are often aware of their existence.

Finally, and clearly as a result of the convergence of these local or historical currents, it will happen that one and the same game (like the Square game) played in the playground of one and the same school admits on certain points of several different rules. Children of 11 to 13 are familiar with these variants, and they generally agree before or during the game to choose a given usage to the exclusion of others. These facts must therefore be borne in mind, for they undoubtedly condition the judgement which the child will make on the value of rules.

Having mentioned these points, we shall give a brief exposition of the rules of the Square game, which will serve as a prototype, and we shall begin by fixing the child's language so as to be able to understand the reports of the conversations which will be quoted later on. Besides, as is so often the case in child psychology, some aspects of this language are in themselves highly instructive.

Then comes a set of terms of ritual *consecration*, that is, of expressions which the player uses in order to announce that he is going to perform such-and-such an operation and which thus consecrate it ritually as an accomplished fact. For, once these words have been uttered, the opponent is powerless against his partner's decision; whereas if he takes the initiative by means of the terms of ritual *interdiction*, which we shall examine in a moment, he will in this way prevent the operation which he fears. For example, in order to play first in circumstances when it is possible to do so, the child will say (at Neuchâtel) 'prems' – obviously a corruption of the word 'premier' (first). If he wants to go back to the line that all the players start from at their first turn and which is called the 'coche', he simply says 'coche'.

As soon as these terms have been uttered in circumstances which of course are carefully regulated by a whole juridical system, the opponent has to submit. But if the opponent wishes to anticipate these operations, it is sufficient for him to pronounce the terms of ritual *interdiction*, which at Neuchâtel are simply the same terms but preceded by the prefix 'fan', from 'défendu' (forbidden), for example, 'fan-coche'.

In the same way, the word 'glaine' legitimizes piracy in certain well-defined conditions. When one of the players has succeeded, either by luck or by skill, in winning all his partners' marbles, it is a point of honour similar to that which sociologists designate with the term 'potlatch' that he should offer to play a fresh set and should himself place in the square the necessary marbles, so as to give his less fortunate playmates the chance of recovering a portion of their possessions. If he refuses, of course no law can force him to do this; he has won and there is the end of it. If, however, one of the players pronounces the word 'glaine' then the whole gang falls upon the miser, throws him down, empties his pockets and shares the booty. This act of piracy which in normal times is profoundly contrary to morality (since the marbles collected by the winner constitute his lawfully acquired possession) is thus changed into a legitimate act and even into an act of retributive justice approved by the general conscience when the word 'glaine' has been pronounced.

This word 'glaine' really has a wider sense. According to several children it entitles whoever pronounces it simply to pick up all the marbles that are on the ground when a discussion arises about them, or if a player forgets to take possession of what is his due.

Our reason for emphasizing these linguistic peculiarities is only to show from the first the juridical complexity of game rules. Let us therefore return to what is the essential point so far as we are concerned, namely, the rules themselves.

The Square game thus consists, in a word, in putting a few marbles in a square, and in taking possession of them by dislodging them with a special marble, bigger than the rest. But when it comes to details this simple schema contains an indefinite series of complications. Let us take them in order, so as to get some idea of their richness.

First of all, there is the 'pose' or outlay. One of the players draws a square and then each places his 'pose'. If there are two players, each one puts down two, three, or four marbles. If there are three players, each put down two marbles. If there are four or more players, it is customary to put down only one marble each. The main thing is equality: each one puts down what the others do.

Then the game begins. A certain distance is agreed upon where the 'coche' is drawn; this is the line from which the players start. It is drawn parallel to and generally one or two metres away from one of the sides of the square, and from it each player will fire his first shot. (To 'fire' is to throw one's shooter – 'agathe' or 'cornaline' – into the square.)

All, therefore, start from the coche. In some games you return to the coche at each fresh turn, but it is more usual after the first shot to play from the place that your marble has rolled to. Sometimes this rule is limited by saying that the marble must not be further removed from the square than the coche. Thus if your marble has rolled two metres away from the square in any direction whatsoever, you bring it back to a distance of 1m. 50 if this is the distance at which the coche itself stands.

But before the game begins you must settle who is to play first. For the first player has the advantage of 'firing' into a square full of marbles, whereas those who follow are faced only with what is left after the gains of the preceding players. In order to know who is to begin, a series of well-known rites are put in action. Two children walk towards each other stepping heel to toe, and whichever steps on the other's toe has the right to begin. Or else rhymed formulae or even syllables devoid of any meaning are recited in sacramental order. Each syllable corresponds to a player, and he on whom the last syllable falls is the lucky one. In addition to these customary usages there is a method of procedure peculiar to the game of marbles. Each boy throws his 'shooter' in the direction of the coche or of a line specially traced for the purpose. Whoever comes nearest to the line begins. The others follow in order of their nearness to the line. The last to play is the boy who has gone beyond the coche, and if several have gone beyond it, the last to play will be the boy whose marble has gone furthest.

The order of the players having been settled in this way, the game begins. Each player in turn stands behind the coche and 'fires' into the square. There are three ways of throwing one's marble: 'Piquette' (English, 'shooting') which consists in projecting the marble by a jerk of the thumb, the marble being placed against the thumb-nail and kept in place by the first finger; 'Roulette' (English, 'bowling') which consists simply in rolling your marble along the ground; and 'Poussette' (English, 'hunching') which consists in addition in carrying your hand along with it over a sufficient distance to correct the initial direction. Poussette is always banned and may in this connection be compared to the push stroke of a bad billiard player.

The players are therefore throwing in the manner that has been agreed upon. Suppose one of the marbles included in the square has been hit. If it has gone outside the square it becomes the property of the boy who has dislodged it. If it remains inside the enclosure it cannot be taken. If, finally, it remains on the line the case is judged by the partners: a marble which is half outside is regarded as out, not otherwise. Here, naturally, a whole lot of subsidiary rules will establish the procedure in disputed cases. There remains the case of the marble with which one shoots (the shooter, or taw, etc.) remaining in the square or failing to lie beyond one of the lines of the square by at least half of its diameter: its owner is 'cuit' (dished), i.e. he cannot play any more. If this marble is projected outside the square by that of another player, it becomes, like the others, the latter's property, except in the case of special conventions generally agreed upon at the beginning of the game. Finally, there are the possible complications arising from cases of rebounding marbles. A marble that bounces out of the square off another is sometimes not held to be won, and *a fortiori* in the case of a marble of value. In other cases, everything that goes outside the enclosure belongs to the player who has expelled it. The particular cases that arise in this way are settled in conformity with principles that are established either before or during the game by mutual agreement between all the participants.

Then comes the question of the number of 'shots' to be allowed to each. The player who has succeeded in winning one or more marbles has the right to play again, and so on, for as long as he wins. But sometimes the following reservation is made: for the first round in each game every player plays once in turn, independently of gains or losses. Here again, therefore, it is a matter of previous arrangement.

In addition – and this is an essential rule – everyone has the right not only to 'fire' at the marbles in the square, but also to 'tanner' (hit) his neighbour's shooter, even outside the enclosure and indeed wherever it may happen to be in the course of the game. And of course the great difficulty is to shoot at the square without placing yourself within reach of your partners. This is why, when a shot would involve too many risks, you are allowed to say 'coup-passé' and to remain where you are, provided, of course, that no one has foreseen this decision and said 'fan-coup-passé'. And this, really, is why you are allowed to change your position provided you place yourself at the same distance from the square as before, and provided you first say 'du mien' (mine), unless, once again, your opponent has anticipated your move by saying 'du-tien' (yours).

The game, regulated in this way by an indefinite number of rules, is carried on until the square is empty. The boy who has pocketed the largest number of marbles has won.

We simply asked ourselves (1) how the individuals adapt themselves to these rules, i.e. how they observe rules at each age and level of mental development; (2) how far they become conscious of rules, in other words, what types of obligation result (always according to the children's ages) from the increasing ascendancy exercised by rules.

The interrogatory is therefore easy to carry out. During the first part, it is sufficient to ask the children (we questioned about twenty boys ranging from 4 to 12–13) how one plays marbles. The experimenter speaks more or less as follows. 'Here are some marbles.' (The marbles are placed on a large baize-covered table beside a piece of chalk.) 'You must show me how to play. When I was little I used to play a lot, but now I've quite forgotten how to. I'd like to play again. Let's play together. You'll teach me the rules and I'll play with you.' The child then draws a square, takes half the marbles, puts down his 'pose,' and the game begins. It is important to bear in mind all possible contingencies of the game and to ask the child about each. This means that you must avoid making any sort of suggestions. All you need do is to appear completely ignorant, and even to make intentional mistakes so that the child may each time point out clearly what the rule is. Naturally, you must take the whole thing very seriously, all through the game. Then you ask who has won and why, and if everything is not quite clear, you begin a new set.

It is of paramount importance during this first half of the interrogatory to play your part in a simple spirit and to let the child feel a certain superiority at the game (while not omitting to show by an occasional good shot that you are not a complete duffer). In this way the child is put at ease, and the information he gives as to how he plays is all the more conclusive. Many of our children became absorbed in the game to the extent of treating me completely as one of them. 'You are dished!' cries Ben (10 years) when my marble stops inside the square.

In the case of the little ones, who find difficulty in formulating the rules which they observe in practice, the best way is to make them play in pairs. You begin by playing with one of them in the manner described above, and ask him to tell you all the rules he knows. Then you make the same request of the second boy (the first being no longer present), and finally you bring the two together and ask them to a have game. This control experiment is not needed for older children, except in doubtful cases.

Then comes the second part of the interrogatory, that, namely, which bears upon the consciousness of rules. You begin by asking the child if he could invent a new rule. He generally does this easily enough, but it is advisable to make sure that it really is a new rule and not one of the many existing variants of which this particular child may already have knowledge. 'I want a rule that is only by you, a rule that you've made up yourself and that no one else knows – the rule of N—— (the child's name).' Once the new rule has been formulated, you ask the child whether it could give rise to a new game: 'Would it be all right to play like that with your pals? Would they want to play that way? etc.' The child either agrees to the suggestion or disputes it. If he agrees, you immediately ask him whether the new rule is a 'fair' rule, a 'real' rule, one 'like the others', and try to get at the various motives that enter into the answers. If, on the other hand, the child disagrees with all this, you ask him whether the new rule could not by being generalized become a real rule.

When you are a big boy, suppose you tell your new rule to a lot of children, then perhaps they'll all play that way and everyone will forget the old rules. Then which rule will be fairest – yours that everyone knows, or the old one that everyone has forgotten?

The formula can naturally be altered in accordance with the turn which the conversation is taking, but the main point is to find out whether one may legitimately alter rules and whether a rule is fair or just because it conforms to general usage (even newly introduced), or because it is endowed with an intrinsic and eternal value.

Having cleared up this point it will be easy enough to ask the two following questions. (1) Have people always played as they do to-day: 'Did your daddy play this way when he was little, and your grand-dad, and children in the time of William Tell, Noah, and Adam and Eve, etc., did they all play the way you showed me, or differently?' (2) What is the origin of rules: Are they invented by children or laid down by parents and grown-ups in general?

It goes without saying that the main thing is simply to grasp the child's mental orientation. Does he believe in the mystical virtue of rules or in their finality? Does he subscribe to a heteronomy of divine law, or is he conscious of his own autonomy? This is the only question that interests us. The child has naturally got no ready-made beliefs on the origin and endurance of the rules of his games; the ideas which he invents then and there are only indices of his fundamental attitude, and this must be steadily borne in mind throughout the whole of the interrogatory.

The results which we obtained from this double interrogatory and which we shall examine in greater detail later on, are roughly the following.

From the point of view of the practice or application of rules four successive stages can be distinguished.

A first stage of a purely *motor* and *individual* character, during which the child handles the marbles at the dictation of his desires and motor habits. This leads to the formation of more or less ritualized schemas, but since play is still purely individual, one can only talk of motor rules and not of truly collective rules.

The second may be called *egocentric* for the following reasons. This stage begins at the moment when the child receives from outside the example of codified rules, that is to say, some time between the ages of two and five. But though the child imitates this example, he continues to play either by himself without bothering to find play-fellows, or with others, but without trying to win, and therefore without attempting to unify the different ways of playing. In other words, children of this stage, even when they are playing together, play each one 'on his own' (everyone can win at once) and without regard for any codification of rules. This dual character, combining imitation of others with a purely individual use of the examples received, we have designated by the term 'Egocentrism'.

A third stage appears between 7 and 8, which we shall call the stage of incipient *co-operation*. Each player now tries to win, and all, therefore, begin to concern themselves with the question of mutual control and of unification of the rules. But while a certain agreement may be reached in the course of one game, ideas about the rules in general are still rather vague. In other words, children of 7–8, who belong to the same class at school and are therefore constantly playing with each other, give, when they are questioned separately, disparate and often entirely contradictory accounts of the rules observed in playing marbles.

Finally, between the years of 11 and 12, appears a fourth stage, which is that of the *codification of rules*. Not only is every detail of procedure in the game fixed, but the actual code of rules to be observed is known to the whole society. There is remarkable concordance in the information given by children of 10–12 belonging to the same class at school, when they are questioned on the rules of the game and their possible variations.

These stages must of course be taken only for what they are worth. It is convenient for the purposes of exposition to divide the children up in age-classes or stages, but the facts present themselves as a continuum which cannot be cut up into sections. This continuum, moreover, is not linear in character, and its general direction can only be observed by schematizing the material and ignoring the minor oscillations which render it infinitely complicated in detail. So that ten children chosen at random will perhaps not give the impression of a steady advance which gradually emerges from the interrogatory put to the hundred odd subjects examined by us at Geneva and Neuchâtel.

If, now, we turn to the consciousness of rules we shall find a progression that is even more elusive in detail, but no less clearly marked if taken on a big scale. We may express this by saying that the progression runs through three stages, of which the second begins during the egocentric stage and ends towards the middle of the stage of co-operation (9–10), and of which the third covers the remainder of this co-operating stage and the whole of the stage marked by the codification of rules.

During the first stage rules are not yet coercive in character, either because they are purely motor, or else (at the beginning of the egocentric stage) because they are received, as it were, unconsciously, and as interesting examples rather than as obligatory realities.

During the second stage (apogee of egocentric and first half of co-operating stage) rules are regarded as sacred and untouchable, emanating from adults and lasting forever. Every suggested alteration strikes the child as a transgression.

Finally, during the third stage, a rule is looked upon as a law due to mutual consent, which you must respect if you want to be loyal but which it is permissible to alter on the condition of enlisting general opinion on your side.

The correlation between the three stages in the development of the consciousness of rules and the four stages relating to their practical observance is of course only a statistical correlation and therefore very crude. But broadly speaking the relation seems to us indisputable. The collective rule is at first something external to the individual and consequently sacred to him; then, as he gradually makes it his own, it comes to that extent to be felt as the free product of mutual agreement and an autonomous conscience. And with regard to practical use, it is only natural that a mystical respect for laws should be accompanied by a rudimentary knowledge and application of their contents, while a rational and well-founded respect is accompanied by an effective application of each rule in detail.

There would therefore seem to be two types of respect for rules corresponding to two types of social behaviour. This conclusion deserves to be closely examined, for if it holds good, it should be of the greatest value to the analysis of child morality. One can see at once all that it suggests in regard to the relation between child and adult. Take the insubordination of the child towards its parents and teachers, joined to its sincere respect for the commands it receives and its extraordinary mental docility. Could not this be due to that complex of attitudes which we can observe during the egocentric stage and which combines so paradoxically an unstable practice of the law with a mystical attitude towards it? And will not co-operation between adult and child, insofar as it can be realized and insofar as it is facilitated by co-operation between children themselves, supply the key to the interiorization of commands and to the autonomy of the moral consciousness? Let us therefore not be afraid of devoting a certain amount of time to the patient analysis of the rules of a game.

The practice of rules. I. The first two stages

We need not dwell at any length upon the first stage, as it is not directly connected with our subject. At the same time, it is important that we should know whether the rules which come into being previous to any collaboration between children are of the same type as collective rules.

Three points should be noted . . . In the first place, the lack of continuity and direction in the sequence of behaviour. The child is undoubtedly trying first and foremost to understand the nature of marbles and to adapt its motor schemas to this novel reality. This is why it tries one experiment after another: throwing them, heaping them into pyramids or nests, letting them drop, making them bounce, etc. But once it has got over the first moments of astonishment, the game still remains incoherent, or rather still subject to the whim of the moment.

The second thing to note is that there are certain regularities of detail, for it is remarkable how quickly certain particular acts in the child's behaviour become schematized and even ritualized. The act of collecting the marbles in the hollow of an arm-chair is at first simply an experiment, but it immediately becomes a motor schema bound up with the perception of the marbles. After a few days it is merely a rite, still performed with interest, but without any fresh effort of adaptation.

In the third place, it is important to note the symbolism* that immediately becomes grafted upon the child's motor schemas. These symbols are undoubtedly enacted in play rather than thought out, but they imply a certain amount of imagination: the marbles are food to be cooked, eggs in a nest, etc.

We shall conclude this analysis of the first stage by repeating that before games are played in common, no rules in the proper sense can come into existence. Regularities and ritualized schemas are already there, but these rites, being the work of the individual, cannot call forth that submission to something superior to the self which characterizes the appearance of any rule.

The second stage is the sage of *egocentrism*. In studying the practice of rules we shall make use of a notion which has served on earlier occasions in the descriptions we have given of the child's intellectual behaviour; and, in both cases, indeed, the phenomenon is of exactly the same order. Egocentrism appears to us as a form of behaviour intermediate between purely individual and socialized behaviour. Through imitation and language, as also through the whole content of adult thought which exercises pressure on the child's mind as soon as verbal intercourse has become possible, the child begins, in a sense, to be socialized from the end of its first year. But the very nature of the relations which the child sustains with the adults around him prevent this socialization for the moment from reaching that state of equilibrium which is propitious to the development of reason. We mean, of course, the state of co-operation, in which the individuals, regarding each other as equals, can exercise a mutual control and thus attain to objectivity. In other words, the very nature of the relation between child and adult places the child apart, so that his thought is isolated, and while he believes himself to be sharing the point of view of the world at large he is really still shut up in his own point of view.

To confine ourselves to the game of marbles, the child of 3 to 5 years old will discover, according to what other children he may happen to come across, that in order to play this game one must trace a square, put the marbles inside it, try to expel the marbles from the square by hitting them with another marble, start from a line that has been drawn before-

---

* We use the term 'symbol' in the sense given to it in the linguistic school of Saussure, as the contrary of sign. A sign is arbitrary, a symbol is motivated. It is in this sense, too, that Freud speaks of symbolic thought.

hand, and so on. But though he imitates what he observes, and believes in perfect good faith that he is playing like the others, the child thinks of nothing at first but of utilizing these new acquisitions for himself. He plays in an individualistic manner with material that is social. Such is egocentrism.

Let us analyse the facts of the case.

Mar (6)* seizes hold of the marbles we offer him, and without bothering to make a square he heaps them up together and begins to hit the pile. He removes the marbles he has displaced and puts them aside or replaces them immediately without any method. 'Do you always play like that? – *In the street you make a square.* – Well, you do the same as they do in the street. – *I'm making a square, I am.*' (He draws the square, places the marbles inside it and begins to play again.) I play with him, imitating each of his movements. 'Who has won? – *We've both won.* – But who has won most? . . .' – (Mar does not understand.)

Baum (6½) begins by making a square and puts down three marbles, adding: '*Sometimes you put four, or three, or two.* – Or five? – *No, not five, but sometimes six or eight.* – Who begins when you play with the boys? – *Sometimes me, sometimes the other one.* – Isn't there a dodge for knowing who is to begin? – *No.* – Do you know what a coche is? – *Rather!*' But the sequel shows that he knows nothing about the coche and thinks of this word as designating another game. 'And which of us will begin? – *You.* – Why? – *I want to see how you do it.*' We play for a while and I ask who has won: '*The one who has hit a mib,*† well, *he has won.* – Well! who has won? – *I have, and then you.*' I then arrange things so as to take four while he takes two: 'Who has won? – *I have, and then you.*' We begin again. He takes two, I none. 'Who has won? – *I have.* – And I? – *You've lost.*'

Not only do [egocentric stage children] tell us of totally different rules (this still occurs throughout the third stage), but when they play together they do not watch each other and do not unify their respective rules even for the duration of one game. The fact of the matter is that neither is trying to get the better of the other: each is merely having a game on his own, trying to hit the marbles in the square, i.e. trying to 'win' from his point of view.

This shows the characteristics of the stage. The child plays for himself. His interest does not in any way consist in competing with his companions and in binding himself by common rules so as to see who will get the better of the others. His aims are different. They are indeed dual, and it is this

---

*The numbers in brackets give the child's age. The words of the child are in italics, those of the examiner in Roman lettering. Quotation marks indicate the beginning and end of a conversation reported *verbatim*.

†English equivalent for 'marbre'. [Trans.]

mixed behaviour that really defines egocentrism. On the one hand, the child feels very strongly the desire to play like the other boys, and especially like those older than himself; he longs, that is to say, to feel himself a member of the very honourable fraternity of those who know how to play marbles correctly. But quickly persuading himself, on the other hand, that his playing is 'right' (he can convince himself as easily on this point as in all his attempts to imitate adult behaviour) the child thinks only of utilizing these acquisitions for himself: his pleasure still consists in the mere development of skill, in carrying out the strokes he sets himself to play. It is, as in the previous stage, essentially a motor pleasure, not a social one. The true 'socius' of the player who has reached this stage is not the flesh and blood partner but the ideal and abstract elder whom one inwardly strives to imitate and who sums up all the examples one has ever received.

It little matters, therefore, what one's companion is doing, since one is not trying to contend against him. It little matters what the details of the rules may be, since there is no real contact between the players. This is why the child, as soon as he can schematically copy the big boys' game, believes himself to be in possession of the whole truth. Each for himself, and all in communion with the 'Elder': such might be the formula of egocentric play.

The practice of rules. II. Third and fourth stages

Towards the age of 7–8 appears the desire for mutual understanding in the sphere of play (as also, indeed, in the conversations between children). This felt need for understanding is what defines the third stage. As a criterion of the appearance of this stage we shall take the moment when by 'winning' the child refers to the fact of getting the better of the others, therefore of gaining more marbles than the others, and when he no longer says he has won when he has done no more than to knock a marble out of the square, regardless of what his partners have done.

Mere competition is therefore not what constitutes the affective motive-power of the game. In seeking to win the child is trying above all to contend with his partners *while observing common rules*. The specific pleasure of the game thus ceases to be muscular and egocentric, and becomes social.

As to the difference between the third and fourth stages, it is only one of degree. The children of about 7 to 10 (third stage) do not yet know the rules in detail. They try to learn them owing to their increasing interest in the game played in common, but when different children of the same class at school are questioned on the subject the discrepancies are still considerable in the information obtained. It is only when they are at play that these same children succeed in understanding each other, either by copying the boy who seems to know most about it, or, more frequently, by omitting any usage that might be disputed. In this way they play a sort of simplified game. Children of the fourth stage, on the contrary, have thoroughly mastered their code and even take pleasure in juridical discussions, whether of principle or merely of procedure, which may at times arise out of the points in dispute.

Let us examine some examples of the third stage, and, in order to point more clearly to the differentiating characters of this stage, let us begin by setting side by side the answers of two boys attending the same class at school and accustomed to playing together. (The children were naturally questioned separately in order to avoid any suggestion between them, but we afterwards compared their answers with one another.)

Ben (10) and Nus (11, backward, one year below the school standard) are both in the fourth year of the lower school and both play marbles a great deal. They agree in regarding the square as necessary. Nus declares that you always place four marbles in the square, either at the corners or else three in the centre with one on top (in a pyramid). Ben, however, tells us that you place two to ten marbles in the enclosure (not less than two, not more than ten.).

To know who is to begin you draw, according to Nus, a line called the 'coche' and everyone tries to get near it: whoever gets nearest plays first, and whoever goes beyond it plays last. Ben, however, knows nothing about the coche: you begin '*as you like*. – Isn't there a dodge for knowing who is to play first? – *No*. – Don't you try with the coche? – *Yes, sometimes*. – What is the coche? – . . . (he cannot explain).' On the other hand, Ben affirms that you 'fire' the first shot at a distance of two to three steps from the square. A single step is not enough, and '*four isn't any good either*'. Nus is ignorant of this law and considers the distance to be a matter of convention.

With regard to the manner of 'firing', Nus is equally tolerant. According to him you can play 'piquette' or 'roulette', but '*when you play piquette everyone must play the same. When one boy says that you must play roulette, everyone plays that way*'. Nus prefers roulette because '*that is the best way*': piquette is more difficult. Ben, however, regards piquette as obligatory in all cases. He is ignorant, moreover, of the term 'roulette' and when we show him what it is he says: '*That is bowled piquette!* [Fr., Piquette roulée] *That's cheating!*'

According to Nus everyone must play from the coche, and all through the game. When, after having shot at the square you land anywhere, you must therefore come back to the coche to 'fire' the next shot. Ben, on the contrary, who on this point represents the more general usage, is of the opinion that only the first shot should be fired from the coche: after that '*you must play from where you are*'.

Nus and Ben thus agree in stating that the marbles that have gone out of the square remain in the possession of the boy who dislodged them. This is the only point, this and the actual drawing of the square, on which the children give us results that are in agreement.

When we begin to play, I arrange to stay in the square (to leave my shooter inside the enclosure). '*You are dished* (Fr. cuit),' cries Ben, delighted, '*you can't play again until I get you out!*' Nus knows nothing of this rule. Again, when I play carelessly and let the shooter drop out of my hand, Ben exclaims '*Fan-coup*' to prevent me from saying 'couppassé' and having another shot. Nus is ignorant of this rule.

At one point Ben succeeds in hitting my shooter. He concludes from this that he can have another shot, just as though he had hit one of the marbles placed in the square. Nus, in the same circumstances, does not draw the same conclusions (each must play in turn according to him) but deduces that he will be able to play the first shot in the next game.

In the same way, Ben thinks that everyone plays from the place the last shot has led him to and knows the rule that authorizes the player to change places, saying '*du mien*' or '*un empan*', whereas Nus, who has certainly heard those words, does not know what they mean.

These two cases, chosen at random out of a class of 10-year-old pupils, show straight away what are the two differential features of the second stage. (1) There is a general will to discover the rules that are fixed and common to all players (cf. the way Nus explains to us that if one of the partners plays piquette '*everyone must play the same*'). (2) In spite of this there is considerable discrepancy in the children's information.

Such then is the third stage. The child's chief interest is no longer psycho-motor, it is social. In other words, to dislodge a marble from a square by manual dexterity is no longer an aim in itself. The thing now is not only to fight the other boys but also and primarily to regulate the game with a whole set of systematic rules which will ensure the most complete reciprocity in the methods used. The game has therefore become social. We say 'become' because it is only after this stage that any real co-operation exists between the players. Before this, each played for himself.

As yet, however, this co-operation exists to a great extent only in intention. Being an honest man is not enough to make one know the law. It is not even enough to enable us to solve all the problems that may arise in our concrete 'moral experience'. The child fares in the same way during the present stage, and succeeds, at best, in creating for himself a 'provisional morality', putting off till a later date the task of setting up a code of laws and a system of jurisprudence. Nor do boys of 7 to 10 ever succeed in agreeing amongst themselves for longer than the duration of one and the same game; they are still incapable of legislating on all possible cases that may arise, for each still has a purely personal opinion about the rules of the game.

A child who, with regard to the rules of games, has reached the third stage, will achieve momentary co-ordinations of a collective order (a well ordered game may be compared on this point to a good discussion), but feels no interest as yet in the actual legislation of the game, in the discussions of principle which alone will give him complete mastery of the game in all its strictness. (From this point of view the juridico-moral discussions of the fourth stage may be compared to formal reasoning in general.)

It is, on an average, towards the age of 11 or 12 that these interests develop. In order to understand what is the practice of rules among children of this fourth stage let us question separately several children from the same class at school, and we shall see how subtle are their answers, and how well they agree with one another.

Rit (12), Gros (13) and Vua (13) often play marbles. We questioned them each separately and took steps to prevent them from communicating to each other during our absence the contents of our interrogatory.

With regard to the square, the 'pose', the manner of throwing, and generally speaking all the rules we have already examined, these three children are naturally in full agreement with each other. To know who is to play first, Rit, who has lived in two neighbouring villages before coming to town, tells us that various customs are in usage. You draw a line, the coche, and whoever gets nearest to it plays first. If you go beyond the line, either, according to some, it does not matter, or else '*there is another game: when you go beyond the line, you play last*'. Gros and Vua know only of this custom, the only one that is really put into practice by the boys of the neighbourhood.

But there are complications about which the younger boys left us in the dark. '*Whoever,*' according to Gros, '*says "queue" plays second. It's easier because he doesn't get "hit"* [if a player's shooter lands near the square, it is exposed to hits from the other players].' In the same way, Vua tells us that '*whoever says "queue de deux" plays last*'. And he adds the following rule, also recognized by Gros: '*When you are all at the same distance from the coche whoever cries "egaux-queue" plays second*' (the problem is therefore to play sufficiently soon still to find marbles in the square, but not first, for fear of being hit).

On the other hand, Gros tells us: '*Whoever takes out two* [two of the marbles placed inside the square, i.e., the equivalent of the player's 'pose'] *can say "queue-de-pose". In that way he can play second from the coche in the next game.'* And Vua: '*When there are two outside* [when two marbles have been knocked out of the square] *you can dare to say "queue-de-pose", and you can play second from the coche again in the second game.'* Rit gives us the same information.

This is not all. According to Rit, '*if you say "deux-coups-de-coche" you can have two shots from the line. If you say "deux-coups-d'empan" you play the second shot from where you are. You can only say that when the other* [the opponent] *has made up his pose* [has won back as many marbles as he had originally deposited in the square].' This rule is observed in the same way by the other two children.

In addition, there is a whole set of rules, unknown to the younger boys, which bear upon the position of the marbles in the square. According to Gros '*the first boy who says "place-pour-moi"* (Eng., place-for-me) *does not have to place himself at one of the corners of the square*', and '*the one who has said "places-des-marbres"* (Engl., place for the marbles) *can put them down as he likes, in a "troyat"* (all in a heap) *or at the four corners'.* Vua is of the same opinion and adds: '*If you say "place-pour-toi-pour-tout-le-jeu"* (Engl., your-place-for-the-whole-game) *the other chap* [the opponent] *must stay at the same place.'* Rit, who knows both these rules, adds the further detail that '*you can't say "place-pour-moi" if you have already said "place-pour-toi".'* This gives some idea of the complications of procedure!

Our three legal experts also point the measures of clemency in use for the protection of the weak. According to Vua '*if you knock out three at one shot and there's only one left* [one marble in the square] *the other chap* [the opponent] *has the right to play from half-way* [half-way between the coche and the square] *because the first boy has made more than his "pose".'* Also: '*the boy who has been beaten is allowed to begin'.* According to Gros, '*if there is one marble left at the end, the boy who has won, instead of taking it, can give it to the other chap'.* And again, '*When there's one boy who has won too much, the others say "coujac", and he is bound to play another game.'*

These answers show what the fourth stage is. Interest seems to have shifted its ground since the last stage. Not only do these children seek to co-operate, to 'fix things up', as Vua puts it, rather than to play for themselves alone, but also – and this undoubtedly is something new – they seem to take a peculiar pleasure in anticipating all possible cases and in codifying them. Considering that the square game is only one of the five or ten varieties of the game of marbles, it is almost alarming in face of the complexity of rules and procedure in the square game, to think of what a child of twelve has to store away in his memory. These rules, with their overlapping and their exceptions, are at least as complex as the current rules of spelling. It is somewhat humiliating, in this connection, to see how heavily traditional education sets about the task of making spelling enter into brains that assimilate with such ease the mnemonic contents of the game of marbles. But then, memory is dependent upon activity, and a real activity presupposes interest.

In conclusion, the acquisition and practice of the rules of a game follow very simple and very natural laws, the stages of which may be defined as follows: (1) Simple individual regularity. (2) Imitation of seniors with egocentrism. (3) Co-operation. (4) Interest in rules for their own sake. Let us now see whether the consciousness of rules describes in its evolution an equally uncomplicated curve.

Consciousness of rules. I. The first two stages

As all our results have shown, consciousness of rules cannot be isolated from the moral life of the child as a whole. We might, at the most, study the practical applications of rules without bothering about obedience in general, i.e., about the child's whole social and moral behaviour. But as soon as we try, as in the present case, to analyse a child's feelings and thoughts about rules, we shall find that he assimilates them unconsciously along with the commands to which he is subjected taken as a whole. This comes out particularly clearly in the case of the little ones, for whom the constraint exercised by older children evokes adult authority itself in an attenuated form.

Thus the great difficulty here, even more than with the practice of rules, is to establish the exact significance of the primitive facts. Do the simple individual regularities that precede the rules imposed by a group of players give rise to the consciousness of rules, or do they not? And if they do, is this consciousness directly influenced by the commands of adults?

With regard to consciousness of rules, we shall designate as the first stage that which corresponds to the purely individualistic stage studied above. During this stage the child, as we noted, plays at marbles in its own way, seeking merely to satisfy its motor interests or its symbolic fantasy. Only, it very soon contracts habits which constitute individual rules of a sort. This phenomenon, far from being unique, is the counterpart of that sort of ritualization of behaviour which can be observed in any baby before it can speak or have experienced any specifically moral adult pressure. Not only does every act of adaptation extend beyond its content of intellectual effort into a ritual kept up for its own sake, but the baby will often invent such rituals for its own pleasure; hence the primitive reactions of very young children in the presence of marbles.

But in order to know to what consciousness of rules these individual schemas correspond it should be remembered that from its tenderest years everything conspires to impress upon the baby the notion of regularity. Certain physical events (alternation of day and night, sameness of scenery during walks, etc.) are repeated with sufficient accuracy to produce an awareness of 'law', or at any rate to favour the appearance of motor schemas of prevision. The parents, moreover, impose upon the baby a certain number of moral obligations, the source of further regularities (meals, bed-time, cleanliness, etc.) which are completely (and to the child indissociably) connected with the external regularities. From its earliest months the child is therefore bathed in an atmosphere of rules.

What then does consciousness of rules amount to during our first stage? Insofar as the child has never seen anyone else play, we can allow that it is engaged here upon purely personal and individual ritual acts. The child, enjoying as it does any form of repetition, gives itself schemas of action, but there is nothing in this that implies an obligatory rule. At the same time, and this is where the analysis becomes so difficult, it is obvious that by the time a child can speak, even if it has never seen marbles before, it is already permeated with rules and regulations due to the environment, and this in the most varied spheres. It knows that some things are allowed and others forbidden. Even in the most modern form of training one cannot avoid imposing certain obligations with regard to sleeping, eating, and even in connection with certain details of no apparent importance (not to touch a pile of plates, daddy's desk, etc., etc.). It is therefore quite possible that when the child comes across marbles for the first time, it is already convinced that certain rules apply to these new objects. And this is why the origins of consciousness of rules, even in so restricted a field as that of the game of marbles, are conditioned by the child's moral life as a whole.

This becomes clear in the second stage, the most interesting of our thesis. This second stage sets in from the moment when the child, either through imitation or as the result of verbal exchange, begins to want to play in conformity with certain rules received from outside. What idea does he form of these rules? This is the point that we must now try to establish.

We made use of three groups of questions for the purpose of analysing the consciousness of rules in this second stage. Can rules be changed? Have rules always been the same as they are today? How did rules begin? Obviously the first of these questions is the best. It is the least verbal of the three. Instead of making the child think about a problem that has never occurred to him (as do the other two), it confronts the subject with a new fact, a rule invented by himself, and it is relatively easy to note the child's resulting reactions, however clumsy he may be in formulating them. The other two questions, on the contrary, incur all the objections that can be made against questioning pure and simple – the possibility of suggestion, of perseverance, etc. We are of opinion, nevertheless, that these questions have their use, if only as indices of the respect felt for rules and as complementary to the first.

Now, as soon as the second stage begins, i.e., from the moment that the child begins to imitate the rules of others, no matter how egocentric in practice his play may be, he regards the rules of the game as sacred and untouchable; he refuses to alter these rules and claims that any modification, even if accepted by general opinion, would be wrong.

Actually, it is not until about the age of 6 that this attitude appears quite clearly and explicitly. Children of 4–5 seem, therefore, to form an exception and to take rules rather casually, a feature which, if judged purely externally, recalls the liberalism of older children. In reality, we believe that this analogy is superficial, and that little children, even when they seem not to be so, are always conservative in the matter of rules. If they accept innovations that are proposed to them, it is because they do not realize that there was any innovation.

Let us begin by one of the more difficult cases, the difficulty being all the greater because the child is very young and consequently very much inclined to romance.

Fal (5) is at the second stage with regard to the practice of rules. 'Long ago when people were beginning to build the town of Neuchâtel, did little children play at marbles the way you showed me? – *Yes.* – Always that way? – *Yes.* – How did you get to know the rules? – *When I was quite little my brother showed me. My Daddy showed my brother.* – And how did your daddy know? – *My Daddy just knew. No one told him.* – How did he know? – *No one showed him!*' – 'Am I older than your Daddy? – *No, you're young. My Daddy had been born when we came to Neuchâtel. My Daddy was born before me.* – Tell me some people older than your Daddy. – *My grand-dad.* – Did he play marbles? – *Yes.* – Then he played before your Daddy? – *Yes, but not with rules!* [said with great conviction] – What do you mean by rules? – ... (Fal does not know this word, which he has just heard from our lips for the first time. But he realizes that it means an essential property of the game of marbles; that is why he asserts so emphatically that his grand-dad did not play with rules so as to show how superior his daddy is to everyone else in the world.) – Was it a long time ago when people played for the first time? – *Oh, yes.* – How did they find out how to play? – *Well, they took some marbles, and then they made a square, and then they put the marbles inside it* ... etc. (he enumerates the rules that he knows). – Was it little children who found out or grown-up gentlemen? – *Grown-up gentlemen.* – Tell me who was born first, your Daddy or your grand-dad? – *My Daddy was born before my grand-dad.* – Who invented the games of marbles? – *My Daddy did.* – Who is the oldest person in Neuchâtel? – *I dunno.* – Who do you think? – *God.*

We then arrange the marbles in the shape of a T, we put them on a matchbox, etc. Fal says he has never seen this done before, but that it is all quite fair and that you can change things as much as you like. Only his daddy knows all this!

Fal is typical of the cases we were discussing above. He is ready to change all the established rules. A circle, a T, anything will do just as well as the square. It looks, at first, as though Fal were not near those older children who, as we shall see, no longer believe in the sacred character of rules and adopt any convention so long as it is received by all. But in reality this is not the case. However great a romancer Fal may be, the text of which we have quoted the greater part seems to show that he has a great respect for rules. He attributes them to his father, which amounts to saying that he regards them as endowed with divine right. Fal's curious ideas about his father's age are worth noting in this connection; his daddy was born before his grand-dad, and is older than God!

To the child who attaches no precise meaning to the terms 'before' and 'after' and who measures time in terms of his immediate or deeper feelings, to invent means almost the same thing as to discover an eternal and pre-existing reality in oneself. Or to put it more simply, the child cannot differentiate as we do between the activity which consists in inventing something new and that which consists in remembering the past. (Hence the mixture of romancing and exact reproduction which characterizes his stories or his memory.) For the child, as for Plato, intellectual creation merges into reminiscence. What, then, is the meaning of Fal's tolerance with regard to the new laws we suggested to him? Simply this, that confident of the unlimited wealth of rules in the game of marbles, he imagines, as soon as he is in possession of a new rule, that he has merely re-discovered a rule that was already in existence.

In order to understand the attitude of the children of the early part of the second stage – they all answer more or less like Fal – we must remember that up till the age of 6–7 the child has great difficulty in knowing what comes from himself and what from others in his own fund of knowledge. This comes primarily from his difficulty in retrospection, and secondly from the lack of organization in memory itself.

The child very often feels that what he makes up, even on the spur of the moment, expresses, in some way, an eternal truth. This being so, one cannot say that very young children have no respect for rules because they allow these to be changed; innovations are not real innovations to them.

Added to this there is a curious attitude which appears throughout the whole of the egocentric stage, and which may be compared to the mental states characteristic of inspiration. The child more or less pleases himself in his application of the rules. At the same time, Fal and others like him will allow any sort of change in the established usage. And yet they one and all insist upon the point that rules have always been the same as they are at present, and that they are due to adult authority, particularly the authority of the father. Is this contradictory? It is so only in appearance. If we call to mind the peculiar mentality of children of this age, for whom society is not so much a successful co-operation between equals as a feeling of continuous communion between the ego and the Word of the Elder or Adult, then the contradiction ceases. Just as the mystic can no longer dissociate his own wishes from the will of his God, so the little child cannot differentiate between the impulses of his personal fancy and the rules imposed on him from above.

Pha (5½): 'Do people always play like that? – *Yes, always like that.* – Why? – *'Cos you couldn't play any other way.* – Couldn't you play like this (we arrange the marbles in a circle, then in a triangle)? – *Yes, but the others wouldn't want to.* – Why? – *'Cos squares is better.* – Why better? – . . .' We are less successful, however, with regard to the origins of the game: 'Did your daddy play at marbles before you were born? – *No, never, because I wasn't there yet!* – But he was a child like you before you were born. – *I was there already when he was like me. He was bigger.*' 'When did people begin to play marbles? – *When the others began, I began too.*' It would be impossible to outdo Pha in placing oneself at the centre of the universe, in time as well as in space! And yet Pha feels very strongly that rules stand above him: they cannot be changed.

Stor (7) tells us that children played at marbles before Noah's ark: 'How did they play? – *Like we played.* – How did it begin? – *They bought some marbles.* – But how did they learn? – *His daddy taught them.*' Stor invents a new game in the shape of a triangle. He admits that his friends would be glad to play at it, '*but not all of them. Not the big ones. the quite big ones.* – Why? – *Because it isn't a game for the big ones* – Is it as fair a game as the one you showed me? – *No.* – Why? – *Because it isn't a square.* – And if everyone played that way, even the big ones, would it be fair? – *No.* – Why not? – *Because it isn't a square.*'

With regard to the practical application of rules all these children therefore belong to the stage of egocentrism. The result is clearly paradoxical. Here are children playing more or less as they choose; they are influenced, it is true, by a few examples that have been set before them and observe roughly the general schema of the game; but they do so without troubling to obey in detail the rules they know or could know with a little attention, and without attributing the least importance to the most serious infringements of which they may be guilty. Besides all this, each child plays for himself, he pays no attention to his neighbour, does not seek to control him and is not controlled by him, does not even try to beat him – 'to win' simply means to succeed in hitting the marbles one has aimed at. And yet these same children harbour an almost mystical respect for rules: rules are eternal, due to the authority of parents, of the Gentlemen of the Commune, and even of an almighty God. It is forbidden to change them, and even if the whole of general opinion supported such a change, general opinion would be in the wrong: the unanimous consent of all the children would be powerless against the truth of Tradition.

As far as the game of marbles is concerned, there is therefore no contradiction between the egocentric practice of games and the mystical respect entertained for rules. This respect is the mark of a mentality fashioned, not by free co-operation between equals, but by adult constraint. When the child imitates the rules practised by his older companions he feels that he is submitting to an unalterable law, due, therefore, to his parents themselves. Thus the pressure exercised by older on younger children is assimilated here, as so often, to adult pressure. This action of the older children is still constraint, for co-operation can only arise between equals. Nor does the submission of the younger children to the rules of the older ones lead to any sort of co-operation in action; it simply produces a sort of mysticism, a diffused feeling of collective participation, which, as in the case of many mystics, fits in perfectly well with egocentrism. For we shall see eventually that co-operation between equals not only brings about a gradual change in the child's practical attitude, but that it also does away with the mystical feeling towards authority.

In the meantime let us examine the subjects of the final period of the present stage. We found only three stages with regard to consciousness of rules, whereas there seemed to be four with regard to the practice of the game. In other words, the co-operation that sets in from the age of 7–8 is not sufficient at first to repress the mystical attitude to authority, and the last part of the present stage (in the consciousness of rules) really coincides with the first half of the co-operative stage (in the practice of the game).

Ben (10), whose answers we have given with regard to the practice of rules (third stage) is still at the second stage from the point of view that is occupying us just now: 'Can one invent new rules? – *Some boys do, so as to win more marbles, but it doesn't always come off. One chap* (quite recently, in his class) *thought of saying "Deux Empans"* (two spans) *so as to get nearer* (actually this is a rule already known to the older boys). *It didn't come off.* – And with the little ones? – *Yes, it came off all right with them.* – Invent a rule. – *I couldn't invent one straight away like that.* – Yes you could. I can see that you are cleverer than you make yourself out to be. – *Well, let's say that you're not caught when you are in the square.* – Good. Would that come off with the others? – *Oh, yes, they'd like to do that.* – Then people could play that way? – *Oh, no, because it would be cheating.* – But all your pals would like to, wouldn't they? – *Yes, they all would.* – Then why would it be cheating? – *Because I invented it: it isn't a rule! It's a wrong rule because it's outside of the rules. A fair rule is one that is in the game.* – How does one know if it is fair? – *The good players know it.* – And suppose the good players wanted to play with your rule? – *It wouldn't work. Besides they would say it was cheating.* – And if they all said that the rule was right, would it work? – *Oh, yes, it would . . . But it's a wrong rule!'*

Later on, however, Ben admits that his father and grandfather played differently from him, and that rules can therefore be changed by children. But this does not prevent him from sticking to the view that rules contain an intrinsic truth which is independent of usage.

Borderline cases like these are particularly interesting. Ben stands midway between the second and third stages. On the one hand, he has already learned, thanks to co-operation, the existence of possible variations in the use of rules, and he knows, therefore, that the actual rules are recent and have been made by children. But on the other hand, he believes in the absolute and intrinsic truth of rules. Does co-operation, then, impose upon this child a mystical attitude to law similar to the respect felt by little children for the commands given them by adults? Or is Ben's respect for the rules of the game inherited from the constraint that has not yet been eliminated by co-operation? The sequel will show that the latter interpretation is the right one. Older children cease to believe in the intrinsic value of rules, and they do so in the exact measure that they learn to put them into practice. Ben's attitude should therefore be regarded as a survival of the features due to constraint.

Generally speaking, it is a perfectly normal thing that in its beginnings co-operation – on the plane of action – should not immediately abolish the mental states created – on the plane of thought – by the complexus: egocentricity and constraint. Thought always lags behind action and co-operation has to be practised for a very long time before its consequences can be brought fully to light by reflective thought.

Consciousness of rules. II. Third stage

After the age of 10 on the average, i.e. from the second half of the co-operative stage and during the whole of the stage when the rules are codified, consciousness of rules undergoes a complete transformation. Autonomy follows upon heteronomy: the rule of a game appears to the child no longer as an external law, sacred insofar as it has been laid down by adults; but as the outcome of a free decision and worthy of respect in the measure that it has enlisted mutual consent.

This change can be seen by three concordant symptoms. In the first place, the child allows a change in the rules so long as it enlists the votes of all. Anything is possible, so long as and to the extent that you undertake to respect the new decisions. Thus democracy follows on therocracy and gerontocracy: there are no more crimes of opinion, but only breaches in procedure. All opinions are tolerated so long as their protagonists urge their acceptance by legal methods. Of course some opinions are more reasonable than others. Among the new rules that may be proposed, there are innovations worthy of acceptance because they will add to the interest of the game (pleasure in risks, art for art's sake, etc.). And there are new rules that are worthless because they give precedence to easy winning as against work and skill. But the child counts on the agreement among the players to eliminate these immoral innovations. He no longer relies, as do the littles ones, upon an all-wise tradition. He no longer thinks that everything has been arranged for the best in the past and that the only way of avoiding trouble is by religiously respecting the established order. He believes in the value of experiment insofar as it is sanctioned by collective opinion.

In the second place, the child ceases *ipso facto* to look upon rules as eternal and as having been handed down unchanged from one generation to another. Thirdly and finally, his ideas on the origin of the rules and of the game do not differ from ours: originally, marbles must simply have been rounded pebbles which children threw about to amuse themselves, and rules, far from having been imposed as such by adults, must have become gradually fixed on the initiative of the children themselves.

Here are examples:

Ross (11) belongs to the third stage in regard to the practice of rules. He claims that he often invents new rules with his playmates: '*We make them* [up] *sometimes. We go up to 200. We play about and then hit each other, and then he says to me:* "*If you go up to 100 I'll give you a marble.*" – Is this new rule fair like the old ones, or not? – *Perhaps it isn't quite fair, because it isn't very hard to take four marbles that way!* – If everyone does it, will it be a real rule, or not? – *If they do it often, it will become a real rule.* – Did your father play the way you showed me, or differently? – *Oh, I don't know. It may have been a different game. It changes. It still changes quite often.* – Have people been playing for long? – *At least fifty years.* – Did people play marbles in the days of the "Old Swiss"? – *Oh, I don't think so.* – How did it begin? – *Some boys took some motor balls* (ball bearings) *and then played. And after that there were marbles in shops.* – Why are there rules in the game of marbles? – *So as not to be always quarrelling you must have rules, and then play properly.* – How did these rules begin? – *Some boys came to an agreement amongst themselves and made them.* – Could you invent a new rule? – *Perhaps . . .* [he thinks] *you put three marbles together and you drop another from above on to the middle one.* – Could one play that way? – *Oh, yes.* – Is that a fair rule like the others? – *The chaps might say it wasn't very fair because it's luck. To be a good rule, it has to be skill.* – But if everyone played that way, would it be a fair rule or not? – *Oh, yes, you could play just as well with that rule as with the others.*'

Vua (13), whose answers about the practice of rules we have already examined (fourth stage) tells us that his father and his grandfather played differently from him. 'In the days of the "Three Swiss" did boys play at marbles? – *No. They had to work at home. They played other games.* – Did they play marbles in the days of the battle of Morat? – *Perhaps, after the war.* – Who invented this game? – *Some kids. They saw their parents playing at bowls, and they thought they might do the same thing.* – Could other rules be invented? – *Yes* (he shows us one he has invented and which he calls "the line" because the marbles are arranged in a row and not in a square). – Which is the real game, yours or the square? – *The square, because it is the one that is always used.* – Which do you like best, an easy game or a difficult one? – *The more difficult, because it is more interesting. The "Troyat"* (a game that consists in heaping the balls into piles) *is not quite the real game. Some boys invented it. They wanted to win all the marbles.*' On this point Vua seems to be answering like a child of the preceding stage who will invoke the 'real game' that conforms to tradition as against contemporary innovations. But Vua seems to us rather to be contrasting a demagogic procedure (the 'Troyat', which by allowing too great a part to chance gives rise to illicit and immoral gains) with practices that are in keeping with the spirit of the game, whether they are ancient, like the square, or recent like his own game. The proof of this would seem to lie in the following remarks relating to his own playing: 'Is the game you invented as fair as the square, or less fair? – *It is just as fair because the marbles are far apart* (therefore the game is difficult). – If in a few years' time everyone played your line game and only one or two boys played the square game, which would be the fairest, the line or the square? – *The line would be fairest.*'

The psychological and educational interest of all this stands out very clearly. We are now definitely in the presence of a social reality that has rational and moral organization and is yet peculiar to childhood. Also we can actually put our finger upon the conjunction of co-operation and autonomy, which follows upon the conjunction of egocentrism and constraint.

Up to the present, rules have been imposed upon the younger children by the older ones. As such they had been assimilated by the former to the commands given by adults. They therefore appeared to the child as sacred

and untouchable, the guarantee of their truth being precisely this im-
mutability. Actually this conformity, like all conformity, remained external
to the individual. In appearance docile, in his own eyes submissive and
constantly imbued as it were with the spirit of the Elders or the Gods, the
child could in actual fact achieve little more than a simulation of sociality,
to say nothing of morality. External constraint does not destroy egocentrism. It covers and conceals when it does not actually strengthen it.

But from henceforward a rule is conceived as the free pronouncement of
the actual individual minds themselves. It is no longer external and coercive: it can be modified and adapted to the tendencies of the group. It
constitutes no revealed truth whose sacred character derives from its
divine origin and historical permanence; it is something that is built up
progressively and autonomously. But does this not make it cease to be a
real rule? Is it perhaps not a mark of decadence rather than of progress in
relation to the earlier stage? That is the problem. The facts, however,
seem definitely to authorize the opposite conclusion: it is from the moment
that it replaces the rule of constraint that the rule of co-operation becomes
an effective moral law.

In the first place, one is struck by the synchronism between the appearance of this new type of consciousness of rules and a genuine observation
of the rules. This third stage of rule consciousness appears towards the
age of 10–11. And it is at this same age that the simple co-operation
characteristic of the third stage in the practice of rules begins to be complicated by a desire for codification and complete application of the law.
The two phenomena are therefore related to each other. But is it the consciousness of autonomy that leads to the practical respect for the law, or
does this respect for the law lead to the feeling of autonomy? These are
simply two aspects of the same reality: when a rule ceases to be external to
children and depends only on their free collective will, it becomes incorporated in the mind of each, and individual obedience is henceforth purely
spontaneous. True, the difficulty reappears each time that the child, while
still remaining faithful to a rule that favours him, is tempted to slur over
some article of the law or some point of procedure that favours his opponent.
But the peculiar function of co-operation is to lead the child to the practice
of reciprocity, hence of moral universality and generosity in his relations
with his playmates.

This last point introduces us to yet another sign of the bond between
autonomy and true respect for the law. By modifying rules, i.e. by becoming a sovereign and legislator in the democracy which towards the age of
10–11 follows upon the earlier gerontocracy, the child takes cognizance of
the *raison d'être* of laws. A rule becomes the necessary condition for agreement. '*So as not to be always quarrelling,*' says Ross, '*you must have rules*

and then play properly [= stick to them].' The fairest rule, Gros maintains, is that which unites the opinion of the players, '*because* [then] *they can't cheat*'.

Thirdly, what shows most clearly that the autonomy achieved during this stage leads more surely to respect for rules than the heteronomy of the preceding stage is the truly political and democratic way in which children of 12–13 distinguish lawless whims from constitutional innovation. Everything is allowed, every individual proposition is, by rights, worthy of attention. There are no more breaches of opinion, in the sense that to desire to change the laws is no longer to sin against them. Only – and each of our subjects was perfectly clear on this point – no one has the right to introduce an innovation except by legal channels, i.e. by previously persuading the other players and by submitting in advance to the verdict of the majority. There may therefore be breaches but they are of procedure only: procedure alone is obligatory, opinions can always be subjected to discussion. Thus Gros tells us that if a change is proposed '*some want to and some don't. If boys play that way* [allow an alteration] *you have to play like they do.*' As Vua said in connection with the practice of rules '*sometimes people play differently. Then you ask each other what you want to do . . . We scrap for a bit and then we fix things up.*'

In short, law now emanates from the sovereign people and no longer from the tradition laid down by the Elders. And correlatively with this change, the respective values attaching to custom and the rights of reason come to be practically reversed.

This is why, when innovations are proposed to the child, he regards them as fair or unfair not only according as they are likely or not to rally the majority of players in their favour, but also according as they are in keeping with that spirit of the game itself, which is nothing more or less than the spirit of reciprocity. Ross tells us, for instance, concerning his own proposition, '*Perhaps it isn't quite fair, because it isn't very hard to take four marbles that way,*' and again, '*The chaps might say it wasn't very fair because it's luck. To be a good rule, it has to be skill.*'

Only someone completely ignorant of the character of childish beliefs could imagine that a change in the child's ideas about the origin of rules could be of a nature to exercise so profound an influence on his social conduct. On the contrary, here as in so many cases, belief merely reflects behaviour. There can be no doubt that children very rarely reflect upon the original institution of the game of marbles. There are even strong reasons for assuming that as far as the children we examined are concerned such a problem never even entered their heads until the day when a psychologist had the ridiculous idea of asking them how marbles were played in the days of the Old Swiss and of the Old Testament. Even if the question of the origin of rules did pass through the minds of some of these children during the spontaneous interrogatories that so often deal with rules in general the answer which the child would give himself would probably be found without very much reflection. In most cases the questions we asked were entirely new to the subject, and the answers were dictated by the feelings which the game had aroused in them in varying intensity. Thus, when the little ones tell us that rules have an adult origin and have never changed, one should beware of taking this as the expression of a systematic belief; all they mean is that the laws of the game must be left alone. And when, conversely, the older ones tell us that rules have varied and were invented by children, this belief is perhaps more thought out since it is held by more developed subjects, but it is still only valuable as an indication: the child simply means that he is free to make the law.

The discussion of the game of marbles seems to have led us into rather deep waters. But in the eyes of children the history of the game of marbles has quite as much importance as the history of religion or of forms of government. It is a history, moreover, that is magnificently spontaneous; and it was therefore perhaps not entirely useless to seek to throw light on the child's judgement of moral value by a preliminary study of the social behaviour of children amongst themselves. (See photo inset.)

(From *The Moral Judgment of the Child*, The Free Press, New York, 1965, pp. 13–76.)

It's Child's Play

The enthusiasm and devotion with which children freely plunge into playing is rarely matched in their adult-controlled activities. Even so, their play interests are highly selective, and the amount of time and energy they willingly devote to their various games are by no means evenly distributed. Naturally, boys will not often readily participate in 'soft', 'girlish' games and neither boys nor girls will happily join 'childish' games. Even the popularity of games freely acknowledged by children as theirs varies considerably; many of these games are played only very sporadically, others are rather steady in the playfield, still others may acquire the dimensions of fully-fledged, recurring 'crazes'.

What are the dynamics underlying these 'natural' processes of selection amongst games? What causes some games to be short-lived but recurrent, others steady, still others just sporadic, or even only a one-shot affair? What social, intellectual or physical factors determine the processes of selection of games by age and sex? In an attempt to answer some of these questions, I began, some six years ago, a large-scale research study on children's games in freely formed groups. This presentation is by way of a preliminary review of some of the problems explored. The major aims of our research were:

(a) The establishment of a conceptual framework adequate for
  (1) exhaustive description of children's games,
  (2) treatment of their commonalities in different cultures and subcultures,
  (3) understanding their diversities due to the variations in socialization processes;
(b) the invention of games that children would readily accept and which would increase the individual and social benefits to be drawn from them without reducing the pleasure inherent in playing them.

Neither the fact that children's games are played at every street corner, nor even the fun inherent in their study have, strangely enough, proven forces sufficiently powerful to turn this study into a popular field of research. Even the recent surge of interest in educational and simulation games has not led researchers to examine systematically the nature of natural games, with the result that the invention of games has been rather a hit-or-miss affair. Perhaps it is true, as some have argued, that children's games have not been intensively and extensively studied because they were not considered as serious activities but rather as peripheral, external to the serious business of living, neither affecting it, nor affected by it. The almost overwhelming richness of children's play activities were undoubtedly another powerful deterrent factor: because of the enormous variety in the material involved, only a very large-scale study could possibly do it justice. Moreover, while it is true that children at play are not far to seek, a valid and reliable method for observing them at play has not been readily available.

Field observations

One aim, then, was to fill in this gap to some extent. In this review, I shall try to describe how we, a group of some 150 observers, spread in various parts of Israel, went about it, and to delineate some of the tentative conclusions arrived at by our smaller research group at the psychology department of the Hebrew University of Jerusalem.

Our observations were conducted in a rather large sample of grade schools (fourteen in a preparatory study and an additional fourteen during the main stage of the research, comprising each some 7,000 pupils). In addition, supplementary observations were conducted in the streets and playgrounds of the neighbourhood of one school, after school hours. The records of play participants over the extensive observation period amounted to a cumulative total of over one hundred thousand units.

The team of observers in each school consisted of an average of nine observers, and in addition, the top enthusiast, both able and willing to serve as local co-ordinator. (After school, some fifteen observers were engaged.) They were psychology students and local teachers who underwent a period of training in their research task. Furthermore, supervising contact-men from our centre in Jerusalem went every week, by foot, bicycle, bus or plane, to each of the schools so as to be always present during observation, keep up the morale and interest and report back in detail. Though considerable cost and effort were involved, this live contact proved invaluable.

The method of observation stipulated that the area observed be subdivided so that each observer covered, on the average, five play groups. The variables recorded with reference to each group are shown in Diagram 1 representing a section of the record sheet which contains (a) general information for a day of observation, and (b) the information on one play group. The observers positioned themselves in the assigned sections at

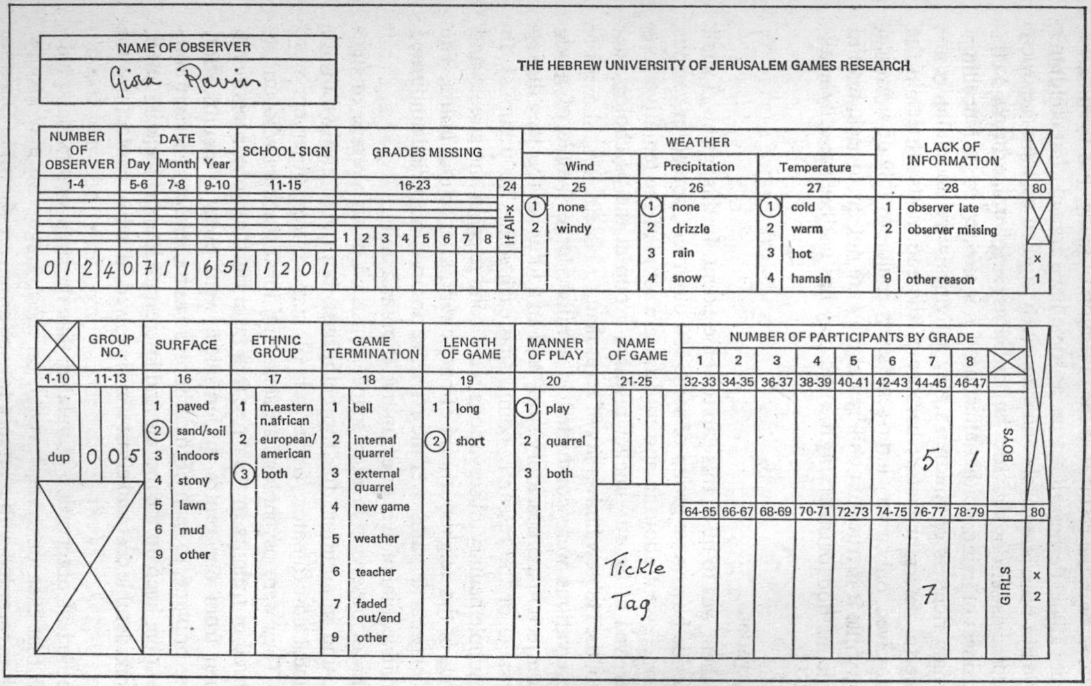

NAME OF OBSERVER Gisa Ravin

THE HEBREW UNIVERSITY OF JERUSALEM GAMES RESEARCH

Upper frame:

NUMBER OF OBSERVER 1-4	DATE Day 5-6	Month 7-8	Year 9-10	SCHOOL SIGN 11-15	GRADES MISSING 16-23	if All × 24
0 1 2 4	0 7	1 1	6 5	1 1 2 0 1	1 2 3 4 5 6 7 8	×

WEATHER

Wind 25	Precipitation 26	Temperature 27	LACK OF INFORMATION 28	80
(1) none 2 windy	(1) none 2 drizzle 3 rain 4 snow	(1) cold 2 warm 3 hot 4 hamsin	1 observer late 2 observer missing 9 other reason	× 1

Lower frame:

GROUP NO. 11-13	4-10 dup	SURFACE 16	ETHNIC GROUP 17	GAME TERMINATION 18	LENGTH OF GAME 19	MANNER OF PLAY 20	NAME OF GAME 21-25
0 0 5		1 paved (2) sand/soil 3 indoors 4 stony 5 lawn 6 mud 9 other	1 m.eastern/n.african 2 european/american (3) both	1 bell 2 internal quarrel 3 external quarrel 4 new game 5 weather 6 teacher 7 faded out/end 9 other	1 long (2) short	(1) play 2 quarrel 3 both	Tickle Tag

NUMBER OF PARTICIPANTS BY GRADE

	1	2	3	4	5	6	7	8	80
col.	32-33	34-35	36-37	38-39	40-41	42-43	44-45	46-47	
BOYS							5	1	× 2
col.	64-65	66-67	68-69	70-71	72-73	74-75	76-77	78-79	
GIRLS							7		

Diagram 1. On each day of observation general information for that day was recorded (upper frame). Specific information on each play group was recorded as illustrated (lower frame). There was one frame for each play group.

the beginning of the observation period so that, as nearly as possible, all incidents of formation, relevant fluctuations, changes in and termination of play activities would come to their attention. Of course, the children did not always respect our imaginary borders between sections (particularly when playing tag) and it was the task of both co-ordinators and contact-men to track down such groups and prevent their multiple recordings, which turned out to be surprisingly easy. In addition, the co-ordinators and contact-men were also trained to deal with 'emergencies', such as a quick re-division of sections during sudden crowding (as a result of a spectacular fight, for example). In the few cases in which such emergencies could not be properly coped with, the recordings of those data were excluded from our analysis.

My major worry before embarking on the field work centred around the feasibility of carrying out valid observations of the natural play scene with so many observers around who, moreover, were required to ask the children what grade they were in and what game they were up to. Indeed, at the beginning of the observation (overlapping with our training period) children were distracted from their normal activities. They would ask questions, become secretive and 'perform' for our benefit. Instructions to all observers at the time were that children should be freely shown the record-sheet, with the explanation that 'we want to write a book about all their games'.

To my surprise and relief, the observers did not retain their novelty value for long and curiosity subsided rather quickly. After as few as four observations, the children were once again fully involved in their games and would volunteer the information required by the recorders 'so as not to be disturbed'. In restrospect, I think that it would indeed be amazing if children gave up *any* of their games for any length of time because of these ghosts around them.

Besides the numerical information presented in the record-sheet, there was a rubric for recording the 'name of the game'. The information contained in this item was obviously insufficient for purposes of identification, since some play-activities which went by the same name were in fact completely different, whereas differently named games sometimes turned out to be identical. Nameless, *unstructured* play-activities were labelled by the observers and briefly described by them immediately following the observations. Here are the titles of a few of these descriptions, which give a flavour of the content of the activities:

'Staging a demonstration' (town),

'Jump-rope – without a rope' (town),

'Made-up lady' (town),

'Selling flowers' (town),

'Building a house for snails' (village),
'Cows' (village),
'Night watch in children's quarters' (kibbutz),
'Feeding sheep' (kibbutz),
'The camel' (Arab village),
'The pyramids' (Arab village),
'Catching flies' (immigrant town),
'A wedding' (immigrant town).

Descriptions of the *structured*, formal games were independently obtained, in special interviews and demonstrations, conducted by the coordinator and contact-man. Thus, for each school, separate descriptions were obtained for every variant of each game that appeared in the playscene (e.g. 'chocolate hopscotch', 'puppet hopscotch', 'hospital tag', 'tickle tag', 'colours tag' or 'redeemer's tag').

Classification of games

When comparing games of different age groups, there is one obvious independent variable in terms of which these games can be profitably treated, viz. the age of the players. This is no longer true with respect to their *life span* (most so-called 'seasonal games' played by children are not really seasonal at all, as will be shown below).

I have found it particularly useful to introduce the following classification of games with respect to their life span; the characterization given here applies as such only to pure (or ideal) types.

(1) *Steady Games*, which are played more or less constantly at all times, with little variation in intensity;
(2) *Recurrent Games*, which are played only intermittently but reach great intensity during each 'wave';
(3) *Sporadic Games*, which are played only intermittently, in short waves, and never reach great intensity;
(4) *One-Shot Games*, which have only one uninterrupted period of existence, and reach great intensity during that period.

Four typical curves for percentage of play activity over a time span of, say, five years would then look as depicted in Figure 1.

This classification, while mutually exclusive, is not meant to be exhaustive. Real games, will, of course, in general, turn out to be various mixtures and attenuations of these ideal types. Some games will be played only intermittently and reach great intensity on some of their waves, but only small intensity on other waves. Other games will have a steady look in one playground, but have a sporadic look in another playground, at one and the same time.

A close study of this differential behaviour should be revealing. Such a

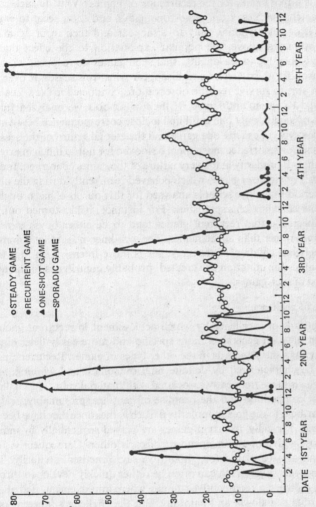

Fig. 1. Typical curves for four game categories, over a five-year span: a steady game, a recurrent game, a sporadic game, and a one-shot game.

study is still in progress. Here I can only present some preliminary findings.

What is it that makes for the recurrence of games? Why do such games as hopscotch, marbles, kites, jump-rope, jacks, and tops, seem to emerge and catch on, like wildfire, only to disappear and then recur again? As shortly intimated above, the popular explanation to the effect that recurrence is just due to seasonality, that such games do reappear when the right season for them arrives and disappear when this season is over, has not been able to survive real-life observations conducted in New Zealand, the United Kingdom and Israel. Of the five schools we analysed for recurrence of games, only one exhibited a close correspondence between the recurrence cycle of exactly one game and the eternal return of the seasons. The reason for recurrence must, then, be looked for not so much in external conditions but primarily in the very nature of the games concerned. Indeed, an analysis of eighteen games which behaved recurrently during the observation period in the five schools analysed for this purpose, has brought to light some revealing characteristics. For instance, it has turned out, not quite expectedly, that recurrent games tend to be either boys' games or girl's games rather than mixed games. The well-known fact that communication between children of the same sex is more intensive, so that more opportunities for imitation are created, probably contributes to the quick spreading of such games.

The role of challenge

The standards of excellence by which achievement in recurrent games is evaluated have, in general, a more specific and more easily determinable character than the standards in the other types of games. Recurrent games tend to be characterized by definite final outcomes, and winning, when applicable, is more frequently associated with material gain. The challenge of all-out competition and the promise of gain are, presumably, features that contribute to the great popularity of such games once they have been reintroduced. Typically, recurrent games are played sequentially by individuals whose activities are independent of each other. Consequently, these games can also be played (or, should we say, practised) solitarily. They acquire specific skills which can often be rather quickly developed through practice, unlike, e.g., competitive running where improvement, if at all, can only be obtained slowly and painfully. But the challenges inherent in recurrent games last only for a while. Many of the very same features that make for diffusion and attractiveness at first are also causes of the games' decline: after a period of training and repeated competition between individuals, a hierarchy of players is stabilized which, naturally, will tend to reduce the challenge of playing with many of the original potential competitors, either because they are 'lousy' or because they are 'too good'. Moreover, in the relevant cases, many of the poorer players will now avoid playing with their obvious superiors, for fear of material loss. Thus, the game loses its potency. It may recur only after a period long enough for the hierarchy to lose its stability and for raising new hopes in further self-improvement.

The typical form of the curve depicting a recurrent game will then be a series of waves, with lines of no activity between them, with different amplitudes in different schools, and even in the same schools. As a glance at Figures 2 and 3 will show, a new wave will begin to rise and gain strength only when some other recurrent game is beyond its apex on its contemporaneous wave. A recurrent game has a still greater chance of being re-accepted when re-introduced during a period of general slackness in play.

Other relevant conditions for the appearance of a new wave, of a more secondary character, might be the personalities of the agents who intend to re-introduce the game (a 'leader'), the networks of communication between children (geographic proximity or similarity in socio-economic level), and even seasonal weather (warming-up games in winter), and seasonal availability of implements (apricot-pits during the apricot season). The impact of the last two factors seems to have been overestimated in the past, a misevaluation which was responsible for the very term 'seasonal game'. The primary factor in the recurrence should be rather looked for in the (season-independent) specific character of the challenge.

Now, look at the profile of simple tag (Figure 4), in comparison with that of such a typically recurrent game as jump-rope reproduced here for the convenience of the reader (Figure 5). What, then, in the inherent nature of these games makes for the obvious difference? Though in tag, too, the hierarchy of physical abilities and skills (running and evading) will be rather quickly established, the game will not thereby lose its challenge, since in tag, in contradistinction to jump-rope, there enters a further factor over which the players have almost complete control. The 'it' has considerable freedom in determining the intensity of his engagement and the extent of his immediate risk of being unsuccessful in catching his target, by selecting either an easy or a tough 'catch', while the other players can vary the initial distance from the 'it', by either staying safely away from him, or getting provocatively close to him, and even teasing him otherwise. Mastery over the extent of the challenge one is ready to take upon himself in a given situation is, then, an important factor that makes for steadiness, though it need not be decisive and can be overpowered by other factors working in the opposite direction.

The situation is still different with regard to group games. Why is it that *ma hanayim*, a kind of game, I believe, similar to ghost ball, is typically

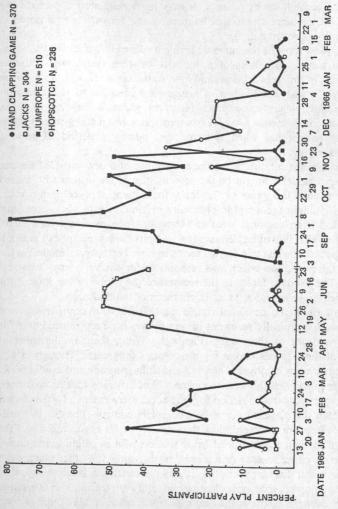

Fig. 2. The percentage of girl players of four recurrent games (out of all girl players of 'structured' games), on successive days of observation.

● HAND CLAPPING GAME N = 370
□ JACKS N = 304
■ JUMPROPE N = 510
○ HOPSCOTCH N = 236

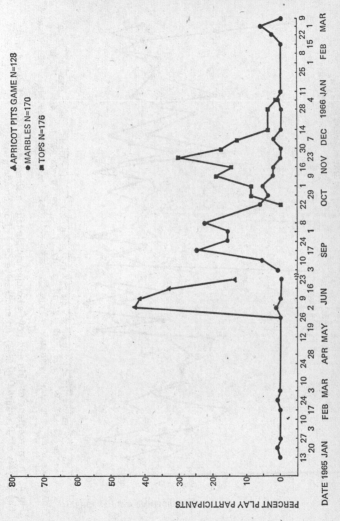

Fig. 3. The percentage of boy players of three recurrent games (out of all boy players of 'structured' games), on successive days of observation.

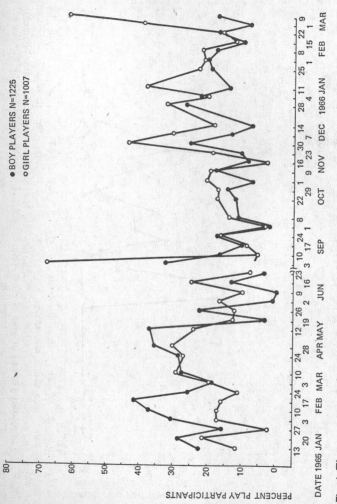

● BOY PLAYERS N=1225
○ GIRL PLAYERS N=1007

Fig. 4. The percentage of girls and boys who play simple tag – a *steady game* – (out of all girl and boy players of 'structured' games), on successive days of observation.

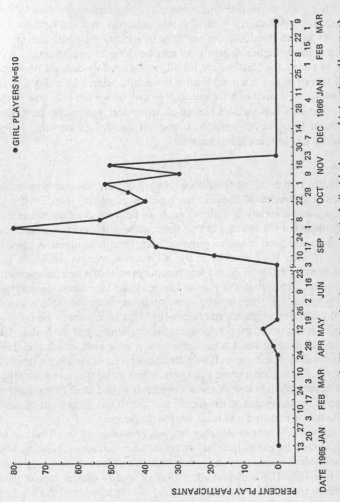

Fig. 5. The percentage of girls who play jump-rope (out of all girl players of 'structured' games), on successive days of observation.

recurrent and the only group game of this kind observed in the five schools, while soccer (which, when played by professionals, has its definite 'season') is a clearly steady game, not only when played by school children during recess but also after school hours? Again, it seems that the decisive difference lies in the possibility of making, in soccer, the challenge fit the player to a much higher degree than can be done in *ma hanayim*. True enough, in soccer the 'fatties' are usually assigned only defence positions and will therefore not often experience the exhilaration of kicking a goal. Nevertheless, their performance may still be crucial for the outcome of the game so that they will retain a feeling of active and responsible participation without being called upon to over-exert themselves beyond ability. This is much less the case in *ma hanayim*.

Theories

According to our tentative 'challenge' theory of play, the explanation of the different character of the various types of games is, then, briefly as follows: a game is steady if it allows each participant to adjust the extent of the challenge to his abilities at that time, while still leaving the outcome of an individual round of such a game sufficiently undetermined. A game is recurrent, if, after the hierarchy of the players has become stabilized, the outcome of any particular round has become predictable and independent of the extent of challenge the players are ready to take upon themselves. A game is sporadic if there is little variation in the extent of the challenge. One-shot games (of which the only clear-cut instance known to me is hula-hoop) are games with considerable initial challenge, but such that the mastery obtainable in them after some time is of a kind which the child has no hope of increasing even if he were to take it up again after a lapse of a year or two. That such a game will not be taken up by the next generation that has never played it before and for which it would have formed a live challenge, is probably due to the simple fact that it has gotten out of sight before the new generation was ready for the challenge.

The 'cathartic' theories of play lay heavy stress on its function in reducing anxiety by giving the child an opportunity to reduce, symbolically and on a lowered scale, conflicts which he is not able to successfully cope with in real life. The constant attraction of steady games would then exactly lie in the fact that in them the child is able to control the level of conflict so that it both remains a meaningful substitute and retains its resolvability. The fading away of recurrent games, on the other hand, would then be due to the fact that, after the hierarchy has been established, the outcome of the substitute conflict is predetermined to such a degree as to leave insufficient leeway for the catharsis of the real conflict troubling the child.

Such theories, so it seems, are not in a position to explain the occurrence of typically sporadic games. Such games would, however, fit rather well into Piaget's theory of playing as an exercise, for pleasure, of skills already mastered. These games, typically, provide little opportunity for improvement and little choice in determining the level of the challenge. The subjective challenge in these games is low altogether, so that their appearances will be few and brief. But Piaget's theory is, in its present form, not able to explain steady and recurrent games; as a matter of fact, it was meant to be a theory of unstructured play only, and its extension to the explanation of sporadic games is a perhaps rather unexpected bonus.

(From *Games in Education and Development*, E. Bower and L. M. Shears, eds, Charles C. Thomas, Springfield, Ill., 1972).

References

EIFERMANN, R. K. (1968), *School Children's Games*, Mimeographed Report, U.S. Department of Health, Education and Welfare, Office of Education, Bureau of Research.

PIAGET, J. (1962), *Play, Dreams and Imitation in Childhood*, Heinemann. (And see this volume, pp. 166 and 555.)

Country Games in the 1880s

Flora Thompson was born in 1876 in a hamlet on the Oxfordshire–Northamptonshire border which she calls Lark Rise. Her books show the vanished world of only 100 years ago: vividly and unsentimentally she describes the life of the farm-workers and their families in the days when walking was the normal means of transport and ready-made entertainment was non-existent.

Country playtime

'Shall we dance to-night or shall we have a game?'

Then, beneath the long summer sunsets, the girls would gather on one of the green open spaces between the houses and bow and curtsey and sweep to and fro in their ankle-length frocks as they went through the same movements and sang the same rhymes as their mothers and grandmothers had done before them.

How long the games had been played and how they originated no one knew, for they had been handed down for a time long before living memory and accepted by each succeeding generation as a natural part of its childhood. No one inquired the meaning of the words of the game rhymes; many of the girls, indeed, barely mastered them, but went through the movements to the accompaniment of an indistinct babbling. But the rhymes had been preserved; breaking down into doggerel in places; but still sufficiently intact to have spoken to the discerning, had any such been present, of an older, sweeter country civilization than had survived, excepting in a few such fragments.

Of all the generations that had played the games, that of the eighties was to be the last. Already those children had one foot in the national school and one on the village green. Their children and grandchildren would have left the village green behind them; new and as yet undreamed-of pleasures and excitements would be theirs. In ten years' time the games would be neglected, and in twenty forgotten. But all through the eighties the games went on and seemed to the children themselves and to onlookers part of a life that always had been and always would be.

The Lark Rise children had a large repertoire, including the well-known games still met with at children's parties, such as 'Oranges and Lemons', 'London Bridge', and 'Here We Go Round the Mulberry Bush'; but also including others which appear to have been peculiar to that part of the country. Some of these were played by forming a ring, others by taking sides, and all had distinctive rhymes, which were chanted rather than sung.

The boys of the hamlet did not join in them, for the amusement was too formal and restrained for their taste, and even some of the rougher girls when playing would spoil a game, for the movements were stately and all was done by rule. Only at the end of some of the games, where the verse had deteriorated into doggerel, did the play break down into a romp. Most of the girls when playing revealed graces unsuspected in them at other times; their movements became dignified and their voices softer and sweeter than ordinarily, and when hauteur was demanded by the part, they became, as they would have said, 'regular duchesses'. It is probable that carriage and voice inflexion had been handed down with the words.

One old favourite was 'Here Come Three Tinkers'. For this all but two of the players, a big girl and a little one, joined hands in a row, and the bigger girl out took up her stand about a dozen paces in front of the row with the smaller one lying on the turf behind her feigning sleep. Then three of the line of players detached themselves and, hand in hand, tripped forward, singing:

Here come three tinkers, three by three,
To court your daughter, fair ladye,
Oh, can we have a lodging here, here, here?
Oh, can we have a lodging here?

Upon which the fair lady (pronounced 'far-la-dee') admonished her sleeping daughter:

Sleep, sleep, my daughter. Do not wake.
Here come three tinkers you can't take.

Then, severely, to the tinkers:

You cannot have a lodging here, here, here.
You cannot have a lodging here.

And the tinkers returned to the line, and three others came forward, calling themselves tailors, soldiers, sailors, gardeners, bricklayers, or policemen, according to fancy, the rhymes being sung for each three, until it was time for the climax, and, putting fresh spirit into their tones, the conquering candidates came forward, singing:

Here come three princes, three by three,
To court your daughter, fair ladye,
Oh, can we have a lodging here, here, here?
Oh, can we have a lodging here?

At the mere mention of the rank of the princes the scene changed. The fair lady became all becks and nods and smiles, and, lifting up her supposedly sleeping daughter, sang:

Oh, wake, my daughter, wake, wake, wake.
Here come three princes you can take.

And, turning to the princes:

Oh, you can have a lodging here, here, here.
Oh, you can have a lodging here.

Then, finally, leading forward and presenting her daughter, she said:

Here is my daughter, safe and sound,
And in her pocket five thousand pound,
And on her finger a gay gold ring,
And I'm sure she's fit to walk with a king.

For 'Isabella' a ring was formed with one of the players standing alone in the centre. Then circling slowly, the girls sang:

Isabella, Isabella, Isabella, farewell.
  Last night when we parted
  I left you broken-hearted,
And on the green gravel there stands a young man.

Isabella, Isabella, Isabella, farewell.
Take your choice, love, take your choice, love,
Take your choice, love. Farewell.

The girl in the middle of the ring then chose another who took up her position inside with her, while the singers continued:

Put the banns up, put the banns up,
Put the banns up. Farewell.
Come to church, love, come to church, love. Farewell.

Put the ring on, put the ring on,
Put the ring on. Farewell.

Come to supper, love, come to supper love,
Come to supper, love. Farewell.

Now to bed, love, now to bed, love,
Now to bed, love. Farewell.

With other instructions, all of which were carried out in dumb show by the couple in the middle of the ring. Having got the pair wedded and bedded, the spirit of the piece changed. The stately game became a romp. Jumping up and down, still with joined hands, round the two in the middle, the girls shouted:

Now they're married we wish them joy,
First a girl and then a boy,
Sixpence married sevenpence's daughter,
Kiss the couple over and over.

(From *Lark Rise to Candleford*, Oxford University Press, 1968.)

Learning Through Games

Playing games is a very old and widespread form of learning. The child first comes to understand the meaning of a rule – that a rule must be obeyed by all – in a game with others where, if the rules are broken, the game does not function.

Recently, educators have begun devising games for high school and pre-high school students that simulate complex activities in a society. One of the ways that simulation and games were first combined was in war games. Many of the oldest parlour games (chess and checkers, for example) were developed as war simulations long ago, and today armies use war games to develop logistic and strategic skills.

From war games developed the idea of management games, a simulation of management decision-making which is used in many business schools and firms to train future executives by putting them in situations they will confront in their jobs.

The games that I and my associates at Johns Hopkins have developed simulate some aspect of society. There is a Life Career Game, a Family Game, a Representative Democracy Game, a Community Response Game (in which a community responds to some kind of disaster), a High School Game (which is really for pre-high school students), and a Consumer Game (in which the players are consumers and department store credit managers).

A description of one of the games developed at Johns Hopkins, a legislative game designed to teach the basic structure of representative government, gives some idea of what and how the games are designed to teach. Six to eleven players sit around a table or circle of desks. The chairman deals a set of fifty-two cards, each representing a segment of a constituency and giving the positions of constituents on one of eight issues. The cards a player holds represent the positions of his constituents on some or all of the eight issues: civil rights, aid to education, medical care, defence appropriation, national seashore park in Constituency A, offshore oil, federal dam in Constituency B, and retaining a military base in Constituency C.

The player, as legislator, is attempting to gain re-election, and he can do so only through satisfying the wishes, as indicated on his cards, of a majority of his constituents. For example, if he has eighty constituents in favour of an aid to education bill and twenty against it, he has a net gain of sixty votes toward re-election if the bill passes or a net loss of sixty if it fails.

After a player brings an issue to the floor, a two-minute negotiation session ensues. The negotiation consists largely of an exchange of support among the players. A legislator will offer his support for or against issues his constituents have no interest in, in return for support on legislation in which they are interested. A vote of legislators, with each player-legislator having one vote, is then taken and the session proceeds to an issue raised by the next player. When all bills have been acted on, each legislator calculates his re-election or defeat by adding up votes of satisfied and dissatisfied constituents. The overall winner is the legislator who is re-elected by the largest majority. This is the first 'level' of the game, which altogether consists of eight levels, each introducing more of the complexity of legislative functioning.

I developed an interest in simulation games several years ago while I was making a study of high school adolescents in Illinois. The study suggested that high schools either did not reward academic activity or rewarded it in wrong ways. In my opinion, the organization of academic work in school acts to keep down the amount of effort and attention a student gives to academic pursuits as compared to extracurricular activities.

The structuring of athletic activity, for example, is very different from the structuring of academic activity. A student making a touchdown for the football team or winning the half-mile at track achieves for both the school and himself, something he can seldom do academically.

It seemed, for this and other reasons, that making use of the simulation techniques of war and management games might be particularly appropriate for schools. First of all, it would make possible a reward structure which would focus on achievement for the school as well as on individual academic achievement. Last spring in Fort Lauderdale, Florida, for example, a number of schools from eight states participated in the 'Nova Academic Olympics', playing an equations game, a logic game, and a legislative game in the kind of interscholastic tournament often reserved for athletics.

A more important asset of simulation games is that they constitute an approach to learning that starts from fundamentally different premises than does the usual approach to learning schools. The first premise is that persons do not learn by being taught; they learn by experiencing the consequences of their actions. Games which simulate some aspects of reality are one way a young person can begin to see such consequences before he faces the real actions and the real consequences as an adult.

A second premise underlying the development of these games is that schools find it difficult to teach about the complexity that characterizes modern society, with the result that students have had little or no experience to prepare them for facing a multitude of decisions and problems in adult life. The games we and others have created present the student with an approximation of certain facets of modern society that he will have to face later.

Learning through games has a number of intrinsic virtues. One of these is its attention-focusing quality. Games tend to focus attention more effectively than most other teaching devices, partly because they involve the student actively rather than passively. The depth of involvement in a game, whether it is basketball, Life Career, or bridge, is often so great that the players are totally absorbed in this artificial world.

Another virtue of academic games as a learning device is that using them diminishes the teacher's role as judge and jury. Such a role often elicits students' fear, resentment, or anger and gives rise to discipline problems. It may also generate equally unpleasant servility and apple-polishing. Games enable the student to see the consequences of his actions in his winning or losing. He cannot blame the teacher for his grades; instead he is able to understand the way in which his own activity is related to the outcome. The teacher's role reverts to a more natural one of helper and coach.

In developing an appropriate sense of consequences contingent upon action, the amount of chance in a game is quite important. If a game has the appropriate mixture of chance and skill, persons of somewhat different abilities can play together, and success will depend in part, but not entirely, upon their relative skill.

A special value of academic simulation games appears to be the capacity to develop in the player a sense that he can affect his own future. A massive study conducted by the U.S. Office of Education shows that one attribute strongly related to performance on standard achievement tests is a child's belief that his future depends on his own efforts rather than on a capricious environment. Many disadvantaged pupils appear to lack this belief.

Seeing the consequences of one's actions in a game develops the sense of predictable and controllable environment. When a game simulates aspects of a student's present or future life, the student begins to see how his future depends very directly upon present actions, and thus gives meaning to these actions.

Still another virtue of academic games is the range of skills a game can encompass. A teacher's class presentation has a fairly narrow range. Some students fail to understand unless it is very simple; others are bored when it is that simple. Games, however, can encompass a much larger range of skills. One example indicating the wide range of simulation games is the successful use of the Representative Democracy Game with high school classes of slow learners and, in identical form, with a group of faculty and graduate students in political science and sociology.

Games of this sort hold the attention of bright students in part because they continue to think of new variations in strategy and in the rules. When the rules are not merely accepted but examined and perhaps modified, possibilities for creativity are opened up that the classroom situation often inhibits. The same game may be played successfully – usually at a less sophisticated level, but not always – by children who perform poorly in school. Several groups in a classroom may be playing the same game at different levels of skill.

When a game is designed to illustrate a general principle, some students understand the principle, while others will not do so without guided discussion after play. Thus games are clearly not a self-sufficient panacea for education, although they are more than simply another educational device.

They can be used in many ways ranging from merely inserting them into an existing curriculum to transforming the curriculum by using games and tournaments to replace quizzes and tests.

In the broadest sense, the development of academic simulation games is a response to two challenges: that posed by a complex, difficult-to-understand society and that posed by children uninterested in or unprepared for abstract intellectual learning. These challenges may be blessings in disguise if they force the development of approaches to learning in school that more nearly approximate the natural processes through which learning occurs outside school.

(From *National Education Association Journal*, Jan. 1967, pp. 69, 70: and *The Study of Games*, ed. Elliot M. Avedon and Brian Sutton-Smith, Wiley, New York, 1971.)

E Cultural Indoctrination through Play

At Play in African Villages

What we call children's play is in great part the consciously patterned ways in which children relate to, and experiment with, their social and physical environment and their own abilities. Therefore, theorists of progressive education have continually stressed that free and 'playful' manipulation of their environment is important for children's learning.

In pre-industrial society, as children grew to adulthood, play merged with work, and formal instruction supplemented what children were already learning through direct observation and experimentation. However, industrialization separated productive work from the flow of family and community life. 'Play' became sharply differentiated from 'work', and an ever increasing period of formal schooling preceded participation in adult occupations. Only under such harsh conditions as child labour in factories did children still learn by observing and doing.

The role of play in learning is of special relevance for the nations of Africa, which, following political independence, have made major commitments to achieving free public education for all children. African leaders are caught between the goal of striving for a life-style established by affluent European colonialists and the goal of independently resolving as Africans the problems of urban industrial society. On the one hand, they are building educational institutions in keeping with conservative Western models, while on the other, they are strongly committed to Africanizing their curricula and to finding more effective ways of preparing all children for meaningful participation in African society. In this context I shall consider children's play in Zambia and its potential for curriculum planning.

Zambia lies north of the Zambezi River in the high interior region of southern Africa. Zambians are among the many Bantu-speaking peoples of eastern and southern Africa who traditionally lived by a combination of cattle-raising and agriculture. Urban trading and political centres have risen and fallen over the centuries in eastern Africa. However, the people of Zambia have always been overwhelmingly rural, living in villages or networks of dispersed family compounds. This is still true despite the rapid growth of the cities on the Copperbelt and of the capital city, Lusaka. In spite of the great changes that followed European incursions into Africa, many qualities of a pre-industrial, self-sufficient agricultural and cattle-raising economy have persisted.

As in pre-industrial societies around the world, imitative play was basic in the training of African children. It has been described by many scholars, including Jomo Kenyatta, who writes that in their play, the Gikuyu children of Kenya

do most things in imitation of their elders and illustrate in a striking way the theory that play is anticipatory of adult life. Their games are, in fact, nothing more or less than a rehearsal prior to the performance of the activities which are the serious business of all members of the Gikuyu tribe.

'Playing house' is a rehearsal for adult roles by children around the world. In African societies it entails technical as well as social practice, for boys and girls build and thatch small houses and make and use various tools and utensils according to local practice. The boys make axes, knob-kerries, spears, shields, slings, and bows and arrows, and may also build miniature cattle kraals. Girls make pottery for cooking real or imaginary food, clay or reed dolls, and perhaps mats or baskets of plaited grass.

Play is smoothly and informally transformed into work. May Edel writes of the Chiga of Uganda:

A little girl accompanying her mother to the fields practises swinging a hoe and learns to pull weeds or pick greens while playing about. She learns the work rhythms, the cycle of the seasons, which crops must be planted in 'hard' fields, and how to tell whether a field is 'soft' and useful for certain crops or ready to lie fallow. A boy tagging after his father watches him milk the cows or thatch the house, whittle a hoe handle or roast a bit of meat on a stick. Playing with a small gourd, a child learns to balance it on his head, and is applauded when he goes to the watering-place with the other children and brings it back with a little water in it. As he learns, he carries an increasing load, and gradually the play activity turns into a general contribution to the household water supply.

Kenyatta writes that as Gikuyu boys help in the fields, their fathers teach them the names and uses of various plants. From his own childhood experience, he recounts how the Gikuyu boy roams the countryside and 'learns to distinguish a great variety of birds, animals, insects, trees, grasses, fruits and flowers. His interests bring him in contact with these things, since they constitute the furnishings of his play activities.'

Riddles and puzzles are asked of young children in the evenings, either by their mothers or by older children. Kenyatta speaks of these as 'mental exercises'. In addition to learning about manners and mores through direct instruction, young people learn about their people's history and society through lullabies and stories. As soon as they are old enough to remain quiet, they are able to listen to the adjudications that take place in the outdoor courts, and to the lengthy discussions of community affairs by the elders. Through these means, too, children are introduced to the highly valued rhetorical arts. Margaret Read recounts that in Malawi,

a perennial amusement among Ngoni boys of five to seven was playing at law courts. They sat around in traditional style with a 'chief' and his elders facing the court, the plaintiffs and defendants presenting their case, and the counsellors conducting proceedings and cross-examining witnesses. In their high, squeaky voices the little boys imitated their fathers whom they had seen in the courts, and they gave judgments, imposing heavy penalties, and keeping order in the court with ferocious severity.

As children assume adult roles in the course of play, they are praised and applauded, but they set their own pace and determine their own special interests. When they want to learn something, they set about learning by observation. There is considerable individual variation, therefore, as to when children learn things and what they choose to learn. Specialists – smiths, woodcarvers, beekeepers, tanners, shield-makers, barkcloth-makers – teach their sons their crafts, but even here there is wide latitude for individual interests.

The time comes when the freedom and casualness of play and exploration are replaced by expectations of mature performance. The older herdboys are held responsible for keeping the cattle healthy and well fed. Kenyatta describes how young herdboys are tested to see that they know each individual of as many as a hundred cattle, sheep, and goats. The boys must sort out herds that have been mixed. The ceremonial initiation into adult status that takes place at about the time of puberty is marked by formal teaching and testing about religious and social matters and adult codes for behaviour. Demands for competence, however, are based on many years of free and experimental participation and experience.

By contrast, mission schools introduced a type of education that minimized direct observation and experimentation. Learning was by rote; the question raising and problem solving that were part of informal participation and play were absent. So, too, was the direct experience of the apprentice. Kenyatta writes:

Whereas European schools in Africa provide training in nature study, woodwork, animal husbandry, etc., much of which is taught by general class instruction, the tribal method is to teach the names of particular plants, the use of different trees, or the management of a particular herd of sheep and goats or cattle. After this the child is left free to develop his own initiative by experiments and through trial and error to acquire proficiency.

The authoritarian character of mission education (like that of colonial or semi-colonial areas around the world) persists in independent Africa. When observing primary schools in Zambia, I was impressed by the strong motivation of the children and their parents, and by the ability and dedication of teachers who were working without the benefit of much training. Yet the atmosphere was restricted by an overall emphasis on education as acquiring the ability to speak, read, and write English, to handle figures, and to remember a set body of factual information that was to be imparted by rote from the teacher to the children.

While the importance of manipulation, experimentation, problem solving and question raising – based on children's direct experiences – is being accorded widespread recognition in the West, African education is still obstructed by outmoded authoritarian European patterns. As the first step out of this situation, there has been an attempt to overhaul the curriculum thoroughly; to introduce African history and institutions, names, foods, climate, and countryside into the readers and texts. In Zambia, the country with which I am most familiar, the next step in curriculum planning for the primary school has been to promote more teacher–student interchange and to introduce problem-solving devices such as dot-cards in mathematics.

A further step, then, would be to work out more fully how the children's education can be more directly built on their day-to-day experiences as they organize themselves for a variety of games and activities: count scores; handle volume, area, and linear measurement in myriad ways; engage in adult role playing; work with language, story and song; apply practical knowledge and technical skill in the making and use of varied toys and instruments; go to the local store for their families; or help about the house and kitchen garden.

It was easy to observe children's activities from the house where I lived in Matero, a large working-class suburb of Lusaka. Its yard was a local playground, and an empty field lay between it and one of the neighbourhood primary schools. Their activities were also reported on by the many children interviewed and described in detail by my research assistants.

Most commonly observed was the popular boy's sport soccer. Boys may form themselves into teams, raise funds for a ball and team shirts by doing odd jobs or soliciting money from relatives, elect a captain and administrative committee, and set up rules. In one case members were to be fined twenty ngwee (twenty-eight cents) for being absent from practice without excuse. Endless variations on other ball games were also observed, as well as local variants of worldwide children's amusements: hide-and-seek, tag, hopscotch, tug-of-war, jump-rope.

Boys and girls characteristically have their own games and play separately. A common girl's game involves throwing a ball back and forth between two lines of players, trying to hit a girl in the centre before she can fill a bottle with dirt.

From the age of six on, children play the 'husband and wife game', for which they build and thatch playhouses and make clay utensils. A girl of nine told of staying away all day and cooking real beans and *nsima*, the staple food of stiffly boiled cornmeal. Usually the girls play separately, but a boy spoke of making sun-dried bricks, using a wooden mould, for building a playhouse. Both sexes make clay cattle and other objects: the girls, often dolls and utensils; and boys, cars.

They also rummage in garbage bins for tin cans. A boy described how he and his friends stacked them up as high as they could before they fell. Little girls play filling them and pouring water and dirt back and forth. Watching their concentration, one is reminded of statements such as the following from a manual of the Nuffield Mathematics Project, so influential in the current changes in the British 'infant schools':

From the point of view of mathematical concepts water play is important in establishing a basis of experience which will lead to the eventual and true understanding of volume and capacity. The children will be filling three-dimensional space and discovering relationships between containers.

Old hunting games are not completely gone. Children set fire to dry grass in the fields to catch rats; make slings for shooting birds; and trap them with *ulibo*, a plant gum, which they collect, heat with oil, and knead. The city of Lusaka is spread out, and there is some open space for gardening. Children may help clear and work the ground. Some boys help their fathers with carpentry or brick making. Girls often report enjoying helping their mothers cook, sometimes giving recipes. And again, the Nuffield teaching manual points out:

Experience of volume, capacity, weighing, estimation, measurement of time; the appreciation of the approximate nature of measurement; and the need for standard units – all these may be derived from cooking activities.

Boys scrounge for the materials to make musical instruments – oil tins, pieces of rubber or plastic, light wires. They make banjos and guitars, drums, and bass fiddles consisting of a single heavy string attached to a drum. They often write their own songs and organize bands, hoping to collect a little money performing at informal gatherings. One day a local band led a 'parade' into the yard and around to the back of the house. More than fifty smaller children followed, showing the casually self-imposed orderliness that characterizes such situations.

Girls love *chitelele*, the traditional women's dance in which women step out of a singing clapping circle to take turns dancing individually in the centre. Girls know a great many *chitelele* songs; in fact, both sexes know an endless number of songs, both old and new, and love *mashasha*, or dancing as couples to jazz. They also know folktales, which the older tell the younger; while living in a village for a period, I collected some of these from children nine to fifteen years old.

The mélange of languages spoken in Lusaka (as in African cities generally) is great, and the children are adept at hearing, interpreting, and compensating for dialectic differences in closely related languages. Indeed, their linguistic facility and interest is so great that it suggests an area for curriculum development to enrich the cognitive content of English teaching. This verbal sophistication is illustrated by a game called *kapenta* (a fish, dried for shipment), as described to me by a twelve-year-old girl:

In this game, people sell *kapenta*. One person in the game is Nsenga and the other Bemba [two of the many national groups in Zambia]. The Bemba sells the *kapenta*, saying, 'I am selling *kapenta*.' The Nsenga asks the Bemba what he is selling in Nsenga. The Bemba misunderstands, and a fight starts due to the mis-understanding of the languages. Someone who knows both languages comes to intervene in a fight between the two and explains what each one has said to the other.

Boys are ingenious at finding and making do with available materials. Seesaws are improvised; poles found for stilts and pole-vaulting. To make a wagon, one boy says he gets planks from a brewery, finds floor-polish tins, cuts poles from trees, and makes wooden wheels. Another boy of ten re-counts difficulties making wagons:

It is difficult to obtain the wheels, because sometimes it is risky. I went to a con-struction site to look for wheelbarrows to take the wheels out. After I collected the wheels, I got a wide plank and two iron bars, to which I fixed the four wheels. I tied the axles to the plank with wires, and made a steering wheel. Friends pushed me, and one day we went to Lilanda where the traffic policeman caught us and took the car away from us.

The most characteristic of African toys is the wire car. These are models of cars and trucks that most boys start making at eight or nine. They are from one to two feet long, and made of heavy wires bent into shape and bound together with finer ones. Discarded wire is found without too much difficulty or if pilfered, becomes anonymous when reshaped. Sometimes the models are covered with pieces of packing-case cardboard. An eleven-year-old says:

I collect the wires from the rubbish pit at Mtonyo Township whenever the municipal vehicles go to dump some rubbish. After I have collected the wires, I take some of the biggest and make the chassis of a bus. Then I build up the body.

When the body is done, I take some cardboard and attach it to the bus to make it look more like the usual buses we board.

An unusual style is made by another eleven-year-old, who attaches a clothed wire person to a Honda, actually a tricycle. 'When I start driving,' he says, 'it begins dancing,' describing one which wobbled from side to side when pushed. He sells them, he says, at twenty-four ngwee each (thirty-four cents). A nine-year-old says:

The cars I like very much to design are Fiats and Land Rovers. I ask my friends who live near the municipal rubbish pit to collect wires for me, which I buy at twenty ngwee. When I make the cars, I drive them in the road, but when I am fed up with one, I sell it for 40n to a friend who doesn't know how to make them.

(The price quoted was perhaps high; it had been bruited about that I was in the market for wire cars!)

Most models are uncovered trucks, which can be loaded with miniature logs. A 12-year-old says that when he makes a car he gets together with his friends. 'We make small roads and put up road signs and signals, and one of us becomes the traffic inspector. Anyone who commits a traffic offence is charged and is liable to a fine of four buttons.'

Boys are most commonly seen running up and down with their cars, pushing them along from a standing position. A long heavy wire, bent into a circle at the driving end, is attached at the other end to the front axle of the car in such a fashion that the boy steers the car by turning the wheel in his hands. One of several steering mechanisms may be employed. After a boy decides which type of car or truck to build, he straightens and cuts lengths of heavy and light wire. The chassis is built first, and from this the proportions of the sides assessed. The model may be purely exterior or finishing touches – a front seat, driver and steering wheel – may be added. No tools are used; none but hammerstones are available. Stove- or shoe-polish tins are usually used for wheels, enclosing wire circles stemming from the axles.

Discussions I had with educators David Simmons and Delpha Keys defined the many ways in which the management of proportions, spatial relationships, symmetry, and measurement involved in the building of these cars can afford a basis for exploratory classroom discussion. Not that individual cars lend themselves to effective use; they are too complex. However, wire models of just chassis and wheels, familiar and often of interest to girls as well as boys could be used to raise such questions as: How much wire would be needed for a chassis of the same proportions, but twice as long? How much more material would be needed to cover it? Children could make wire cubes and find out how much wire is needed for a cube twice as big; how much cardboard to cover it; how much gravel to fill it. Or the children could explore the relationship between wheel size and the number of rotations a wheel makes in a metre. Or, a problem suggested by the Honda-maker, who uses a split back axle on his tricycle: What happens to each back wheel when a car with a solid back axle is turned? With a split back axle? Why?

Other games played by Matero children are variations on marbles and jacks, played with stones. Board games of various sorts are known; checkers is a favourite. Most interesting, however, is a characteristically African game, *nsoro*. A West African version is played on a thick board with carved-out hollows into which counters are placed. In Zambia, long rows of holes are simply scooped out on the ground, and pebbles are collected for playing. In certain neighbourhoods, groups of men can almost always be found standing over a game of *nsoro*.

A simplified children's version of *nsoro* is played using four parallel rows of twelve holes each. There are two players; each has two rows to move in. The game starts with two stones, or counters, placed in each hole of the two outer rows. Counters are moved to the right in the outer rows; to the left along the inner rows. When a player lands in an inner hole adjacent to an opponent's inner hole containing counters, both these and any in the corresponding hole on the outside row are 'eaten', or knocked out of the game. The winner is the first to eat all his opponent's counters. A move consists of picking up all the stones in a hole of one's choosing, reserving one of these, and placing the others one by one in successive holes. If the next hole is empty after they are played, the reserved stone is placed in it and the move is finished. If not, all stones in that hole must be picked up and played as part of the same move, which cannot end until an empty hole is reached for the reserved counter. As a player moves into the inner strip, close to his opponent's counters, he must be careful not to leave himself open to being eaten without at least being in a position to eat more of his opponent's counters in return.

In playing *nsoro*, then, children learn to weigh alternatives that involve a series of additions and subtractions of small numbers. The entire strategy of a play is complicated, but elements of the game – an enjoyable activity in which younger children watch older ones, and older children watch the more complex adult version – could be utilized for presenting concepts of number, and addition and subtraction. To quote again from the Nuffield teaching manuals.

Many teachers have realized through their own experience that *more* learning and indeed more enjoyable learning can be gained by working through the interests of children and many of these interests do, in fact, arise during play.

(From *Play – A Natural History Magazine Special Supplement*, December, 1971.)

Social and Psychological Aspects of Education in Taleland

An excerpt from an ethnographic study of the Tallensi people who live on the African Gold Coast, these observations were made several decades before those of Eleanor Leacock (*At Play in African Villages*, p. 466). The psychological processes underlying socialization remain unchanged.

The Sociological approach

We can commence from two axioms which must be regarded as firmly established both in sociological and in educational theory. It is agreed that education in the widest sense is the process by which the cultural heritage is transmitted from generation to generation, and that schooling is therefore only a part of it. It is agreed, correlatively, that the 'moulding of individuals to the social norm is the function of education such as we find it among these simpler peoples', and, it may be added, among ourselves.

Starting from these axioms, anthropologists have explored the conditions and the social framework of education in pre-literate societies. It has been shown that the training of the young is seldom regularized or systematized, but occurs as a 'by-product' of the cultural routine; that the kinsfolk, and particularly the family, are mainly responsible for it; that it is conducted in a practical way in relation to the 'actual situations of daily life'. It has been observed that manners and ethical and moral attitudes are first inculcated within the family circle in association with food and eating and with the control of bodily functions. A good deal of discussion has been devoted, also, to what appears to be overtly educational institutions, such as initiation schools and ceremonies, age grades, or secret societies. It has been proved that direct instruction in tribal history, sexual knowledge, and ritual esoterica is promoted by these institutions.

In this way a good deal of information has been accumulated about *what* is transmitted from one generation to the next in pre-literate societies, about the circumstances of this transmission, and the institutional and structural framework within which it occurs. Of the process of education – *how* one generation is 'moulded' by the superior generation, *how* it assimilates and perpetuates its cultural heritage – much less is known.

The problem has, indeed, never been precisely formulated, with the result that alleged discussions of primitive education not infrequently prove to be merely descriptions of social structure slightly disguised.

Education, from this point of view, is an active process of learning and teaching by which individuals gradually acquire the full outfit of culturally defined and adapted behaviour. In this paper I shall try to delineate briefly how it occurs in one African society, that of the Tallensi of the Northern Territories of the Gold Coast. As it will be impossible to encompass the whole process of social maturation within the limits of this paper, some of the more conspicuous changes and activities only will be examined.

Fundamental learning processes

In the course of the preceding discussion I have given several indications of how Tale children are taught and learn. But our investigation would be incomplete without a special consideration of the three fundamental processes utilized by the child in its learning – mimesis, identification, and co-operation. These are not the only learning techniques observable among the Tallensi, but they are the most important; and they usually appear not in isolation but in association with one another. They are most intimately interwoven in play, the paramount educational exercise of Tale children.

Play in relation to social development

The concept of play (*ba deemrɔme* 'they are playing') is well defined and clearly recognized by the Tallensi. The play of Tale children, it has been pointed out, emerges partly as a side-issue of their practical activities. It is also an end in itself, and has a noteworthy role in their social development. In his play the child rehearses his interests, skills, and obligations, and makes experiments in social living without having to pay the penalty for mistakes. Hence there is always a phase of play in the evolution of any schema preceding its full emergence into practical life. Play, therefore, is mimetic in content, and expresses the child's identifications. But the Tale child's play mimesis is never simple and mechanical reproduction; it is always imaginative construction based on the themes of adult life and of the life of slightly older children. He or she adapts natural objects and other materials, often with great ingenuity, which never occur in the adult activities copied, and rearranges adult functions to fit the specific logical affective configuration of play.

A typical play situation

How vividly these motifs appear in the play of Tale children will be evident to the reader if I describe shortly an actual play situation as I observed and recorded it. I shall describe a typical play episode among children at the transition from infantile egocentricity and dependence to social play and participation in peripheral economic activities. It will be noted how recreational and imaginative play are interwoven with practical activities and how infantile habits still persist. The children's interests fluctuate from moment to moment, egocentric attitudes alternate with co-operative play, and the economic task receives only sporadic attention. Later on we shall consider these factors in relation to the phases of development of children's play.

On a morning in June I found Gɔmna, aged about 7, his half-sister Zɔŋ, aged about 6, and his friend Zoo of about the same age out scaring birds on the home farm. They sat astride the trailing branch of a baobab tree on the boundary of Gɔmna's father's farm and Zoo's father's farm. They slid down to talk to me, and a bigger lad, Tɔŋ, aged about 10, joined us. Gɔmna had wandered off a few yards and now came running up with three locusts. He called to his sister and Zoo. Eagerly they squatted round the locusts. 'These are our cows,' said Gɔmna, 'let's build a yard for them.' Zoo and the little girl foraged around and produced a few pieces of de-cayed bark. The children, Gɔmna dominant, giving orders and keeping up a running commentary, set about building a 'cattle-yard' of the pieces of bark. Tɔŋ, the older boy, also squatted down to help. He and Gɔmna constructed an irregular rectangle with one side open of the pieces of bark. Zoo fetched some more pieces of bark which Tɔŋ used to roof the yard. The little girl stood looking on. Gɔmna carefully pushed the locusts in, one by one, and declared, 'We must make a gateway.' Rummaging about, the boys found two pebbles which they set up as gate-posts, with much argument as to how they ought to stand. Suddenly the whole structure collapsed and Tɔŋ started putting it up again. The little girl meanwhile had found a pair of stones and a potsherd and was on her knees, 'grinding grain'. Suddenly the two small boys dashed off into the growing grain, shouting to scare the birds. In a minute or two they returned to squat by the collapsed 'cattle-yard'. They appeared to have forgotten all about the 'cows', for they were engrossed in conversation about 'wrestling'. Some one called Tɔŋ, who departed. Zɔŋ, finishing her 'grinding', came up to the boys with the 'flour' on a potsherd and said, 'Let's sacrifice to our shrine.' Gɔmna said indifferently, 'Let Zoo do it.' Zoo declared that Gɔmna was senior to him, and an argument ensued as to who was senior. Eventually Gɔmna asserted, 'I'm the senior.' Zɔŋ meanwhile had put down her 'flour' which was quite forgotten; for Zoo challenged Gɔmna's assertion. Gɔmna retorted that he was undoubtedly senior since he could throw Zoo in wrestling. Zoo denied this, and in a few minutes they were grappling each other. Gɔmna managed to throw Zoo and rolled over him; but they stood up in perfectly good temper, panting and proud. Suddenly with a shout Gɔmna began to scramble up the baobab branch, followed by Zoo, calling out, 'Let's swing.' For a minute or two they rocked back and forth on the branch and then descended. Now Gɔmna remembered his cows. Vehemently he accused his sister of having taken them, and when she denied this challenged her to 'swear'. 'All right,' she said placidly. Gɔmna took a pinch of sand in his left hand and put his right thumb on it. Zɔŋ licked her thumb and pressed down with it on Gɔmna's thumb-nail. He stood still a moment, then suddenly withdrew his thumb. (This is a children's play ordeal.) Gɔmna examined his sister's thumb and found sand adhering. 'There you are,' he said, rapping her on the head with a crooked finger. The 'cows' were completely forgotten though, for now they turned their attention to me, asking me various questions. After a while Gɔmna, who had been observing my shoes, said, 'Let's make shoes,' and took a couple of pieces of the decayed bark previously used to build the cattle-yard to make shoes. He and Zɔŋ found some grass and old string lying about and tried to tie the pieces of bark to the soles of their feet. Gɔmna now noticed his 'cows' and picked them up, but he was still trying to make 'shoes'. The 'shoes' refused to hold together so he abandoned them and squatted over his 'cows' for a moment, moving them hither and thither. 'I'm going to let them copulate,' he burst out with a grin, and tried to put one locust on top of another. Looking up, he noticed a flutter of birds' wings. 'Zɔŋ,' he cried, jumping to his feet, 'scare the birds!' and he raced to pick up handfuls of gravel to fling at the birds. For the next five minutes they were engrossed in bird-scaring. The entire episode lasted over half an hour.

The developmental phases of play. Infant play

Up to the age of 6 or 7 a good deal of play, especially that of boys, consists in sheer motor exuberance. Small boys run about, leap and prance for the pleasure of it, frequently in a totally unorganized way. But even 3-year-old boys often introduce mimetic themes, spontaneously or in response to suggestions from older children. They 'ride horses', using a long stick as a horse, with a wisp of grass attached as bridle. In the Festival season they love 'playing drums'. Cylindrical tins discarded by our cook and useless as receptacles were in great demand for this purpose. A remnant of goatskin tied over one end with a strip of bark or grass makes a satisfactory diaphragm, and a hooked twig serves as a drumstick. Often an older boy of 8 or 9 manufactures a toy drum for himself or an infant brother. A small discarded calabash is covered with a piece of skin – a remnant of goatskin or the skin of a rat caught by the boy himself and prepared by himself. The skin is cleverly attached to the calabash with strong thorns. Small boys delight in walking round, tapping out a rhythm on a toy drum, sometimes executing a few dance steps. Another instrument they like to copy is the *kolog*, a single-string fiddle. I once saw a boy of about 6 singing to a 'fiddle' which consisted of a large bow made of a green stick and a thread of grass – the 'fiddle' – and a smaller bow of the same materials – the 'bow'. A bow of the very same sort with a short piece of thick reed as arrow is the 4- to 6-year-old's introduction to the handling of bow and arrow. They very soon develop an accurate aim at a dozen yards or so. Play of this kind is generally very egocentric. I have watched groups of children playing side by side – a boy with a 'drum' absorbed in his banging, another lying on his back absorbed in fantasy, a couple of little girls playing at housekeeping – all indifferent to one another's activities.

The little girl of 3 to 6 plays in much the same way at times; but she is already being drawn into the family play of slightly older children, and, like the small boy with the toy bow, she tends to mimic simpler features of older girls' play when she is playing alone. Hence one often sees a little girl of this age sitting and playing at 'grinding millet' – one stone as metate, a smaller stone as muller, and a handful of sand or a potsherd as the grain.

Play in early childhood

Between the ages of about 6 and 10 the play of both sexes becomes more social and more complex. This is the period when the child is beginning to co-operate in real economic activities, subject to real responsibility, and is acquiring a knowledge of his social space. His or her play reflects these experiences and reflects also the interests and activities characteristic of the stage of maturity just ahead of it. There is, in all Tale children's play, this feature of looking ahead, as it were, experimenting tentatively with what lies just beyond the present psychological horizon.

During this period the younger children, both boys and girls, have charge of the goats, scare the birds from the newly planted fields and the crops, run errands, nurse the infants, and so forth. The boys help in sacrifices to domestic shrines; the girls assist in household tasks such as sweeping and carrying water. Towards the end of this period boys whose fathers own cattle go out with the cattle-herds and girls are beginning to help in the preparation of food. A 10-year-old girl can prepare the majority of usual dishes. At the age of 6 or 7 brothers and sisters often play together; at 9 or 10 the sexual dichotomy has become firmly established.*

At this stage the play of infancy develops in three directions. The sporadic

---

*Nevertheless, this sexual dichotomy is not so absolute as to prohibit a girl or a woman from stepping into a breach if there is no male available for a man's task, and men often undertake women's work in an emergency.

motor exuberance is transformed into recreational play – organized group games and dances; the rudimentary mimetic play becomes elaborate and protracted imaginative and constructive play; and the rude toy-making of infancy grows into children's arts and crafts.

Tale children have a great many organized games, passed on from one generation of children to the next by drawing younger ones into the games played by those who already know them. The games are traditional, and often built round themes derived from the cultural idiom – farming, hunting, marriage, chiefs, etc. But their value is predominantly recreational. Children play them for the pleasure of collective singing, rhythmical physical activity, and sensory and bodily stimulation. The ordinary dances of moonlight nights in which both adults and children participate are regarded as 'play' of this kind.

At this stage, and till pubescence, boys spend a great deal of their leisure improving their dexterity with the bow and arrow. They now have bows like a man's but smaller, and real arrows with unbarbed heads. They go about in small groups practising marksmanship – shooting at a guinea corn-stalk or a chunk of wood. Sometimes they challenge one another and shoot according to certain rules. The loser forfeits an arrow to the winner. All this is recreational play; but it has a very practical aspect, recognized by adults and children. In Taleland the bow is the symbol of manhood; and every man must know how to wield it. The long years of practice necessary to become an accomplished shot begins with the small boy's first toy bow and extend through the play of childhood and pubescence. Part of this play-practice is the hunting of small field animals and birds. To the boy it is a real hunt, demanding knowledge and alertness and yielding a favourite titbit. Yet it is play as well, being neither obligatory nor dangerous, and being mimetically derived from an adult activity. This has great educational importance. The boy in his play identifies himself with the men, accepts their practical valuation of the bow and arrow, and tries out, as it were, what it feels like to be a man in this respect. Boys often hunt thus in groups, especially when they are out herding cattle, and share the spoil, thus training themselves in co-operation and fair dealing. By the age of 11–12, boys begin to accompany their fathers or elder brothers to real hunts, though they remain onlookers for the most part, whose principal task is to help carrying home anything killed. Not till adolescence will they be allowed to use barbed and poisoned arrows; but quasi-playful hunting thus shades over into the real activity for which it is a preparation.

Imaginative play is rich and frequent during this period, though its themes appear to be few. Family life, the principal economic activities, and domestic ritual supply the mimetic content. Sometimes children are entirely preoccupied with such play for hours at a time; often it is interwoven with practical activities or appears as a resonance of practical activities in which the children co-operate.

On any day in the dry season or the first half of the rainy season one can find a group of girls playing at housekeeping. Most commonly they consist of a group of sisters and ortho-cousins – two to four active participants with, perhaps, a couple of infants attached. Often one or two small boys of about 5 or 6 are in their company, sharing in their play or absorbed in their own separate play. In play, as in the simple economic duties, there is as yet no marked sex dichotomy at this age; and small boys are not ridiculed for 'grinding grain' and 'cooking porridge', or small girls for 'building houses' in play. The girls generally constitute a mixed age group, varying from 6 to 10–11 years, for even those who are already capable of real cooking enjoy playing at it. When they are of about equal maturity their play tends to be loosely organized. Each cooks for herself, but they help one another, lending one another 'utensils', 'grain', 'firewood', and exchanging 'dishes of porridge' like co-wives. When one girl is older than the others she tends to take the lead, and the smaller girls assist her on the pattern of daughter helping mother in real cooking. Infants are 'our children'; and reliable informants have told me that small boys are said to be the 'husbands' – but I have never observed boys being addressed thus, though I have watched housekeeping play very frequently. According to my observation, it is merely implied in the manner of distributing the 'cooked porridge', which follows the pattern of family feeding. Older girls sometimes introduce dolls as the 'children' – clay figures of people made by themselves or, more usually, for them by their brothers.

The essentials of the play consist in 'grinding flour', 'cooking sauce' and 'porridge', and 'sharing out' the 'food'. Every feature of the real processes is mimicked, but with the most ingenious imaginative adaptations. A pair of flattish stones or a boulder and a large pebble serve as 'grindstones'. For pots, dishes, calabashes, and ladles various things are used – old sherds chipped into roughly circular pieces the size of a half-crown or crown, fragments of old calabashes, the husks, whole or bisected, of mɔlǝmɔk or kalǝmpoo, spherical fruits of common trees varying in size from that of a large marble to that of a cricket ball, and even old tins or bits of tins, while some girls make little pots of clay. Pebbles make a fire-place, a thin piece of millet-stalk is the stirring-stick, some dried grass the firewood. Sometimes a real fire is lit, but usually it is merely imagined. Real grain is never used in such play – it is too valuable to waste thus, as the children themselves would be the first to insist. A piece of potsherd pounded up or a handful of sand serves as grain; but a much more realistic effect is sometimes achieved by using dry baobab stamens. These can be 'winnowed' and the 'grain' ground. Green weeds and leaves are vegetables.

The children play with great zest and earnestness, yet never forget that it is but play. As they grind they hum in a low voice a grinding song they have heard from mother or elder sister. They examine the 'flour' to see that it is fine enough, try to get the right proportion of water, stir the 'porridge' thoroughly, 'dish' it out with scrupulous fairness. There is a constant interchange of conversation and commands to the smaller children: 'Bring me that dish', 'Lend me your broom', 'That's my firewood', 'Don't stir so fast', 'Come and fetch your porridge', and so on. As a rule they play together most amicably. I have observed arguments in such groups about who should do some task or another, but never quarrels. There is real co-operation, based on a distribution of tasks in play.

At the next stage, too, domestic ritual begins to be reflected in the play of boys. A boy's or girl's schema of ritual and religious ideology at the age of 9 or 10 includes the main structural principles of the system. As his knowledge has been acquired by attending at sacrifices, he knows most about the ritual acts and conventional formulas connected with sacrifice and least about the beliefs and theories. He is familiar with all the concepts of Tale religion and magic but cannot assign them accurately to their relevant context. He knows that ancestor spirits and medicines are different, and can even describe some of the latter by their functions, but cannot elucidate these differences. He knows also and believes that health, prosperity and success depend on mystical agencies, that sickness, death, and misfortune are caused by them, and that sacrifices must be made to placate them or to expiate offences. He has heard talk of all this and seen consultations of diviners. As an infant, perhaps, he has been called by his mother to get off a partition wall 'lest the spirits push you off', or has seen food put out 'for the spirits' during the ritual festivals. He knows what different types of shrines look like and what are their appurtenances. But it is surface knowledge, confused in details and full of gaps.

Ritual is men's business, though women are well versed in it. Hence it emerges mostly in the play of boys and not of girls. Significantly, it is permitted till pubescence, that is, as long as a boy is not likely to take a responsible part in real ritual. After that he is liable to have to accept an ancestor spirit demanding real sacrifices and may no longer play at it. At 13 or 14 years of age, when a boy's ritual schemas approximate those of an adult, he fully understands and acquiesces in this prohibition. It suggests however, that playing at ritual has a different value for children than actual ritual has for adults. Children share the adults' interest in ritual and accept its prescriptions, but not the adults' emotional relationship to ritual. In their play they express this interest and their identifications, rehearse their knowledge, and integrate it with the rest of their educational achievements.

Small boys build shrines a few inches high for themselves in a corner of the cattle-yard. They take great pains to achieve verisimilitude and neatness, and their inventiveness is remarkable. *Kaləmpoo* husks are turned into medicine-pots; fragments of calabash or potsherd represent the hoe-blade which is essential to many ancestor shrines; a pronged twig is a shrine's 'tree'; the tail of a stillborn kid or lamb, tied with string and feathers in the same way as adults do, is a shrine's 'tail', another object commonly dedicated to real shrines. There are 'roots' – of grass – as in adult medicine-pots, and other appurtenances. Whenever they build miniature houses, during the building season, 'shrines' are added and, as in real life, each has his own.

Play with these shrines is woven into other play activities and it revolves around sacrifice. When a small boy goes out hunting for fieldmice or birds, if he happens to have a 'shrine' he will 'give it water', i.e pour a libation to it. Ashes represent flour, which is stirred up in water as in a real sacrifice. He invokes the shrine, 'My father,' (but never mentioning names as in real sacrifice since his own father is probably still alive) 'accept this water and grant that I have successful hunting. If I kill an animal, I will give you a dog.' Some time later he may catch a live mouse, and when he has played with it to satiety he 'sacrifices' it on his shrine – this is the promised 'dog'. A nestling bird found alive is 'sacrificed' as a 'fowl' or 'guinea-fowl'. If he finds a live mouse or bird by chance it will always be taken home and 'sacrificed' thus before it is cut up and eaten. Taboos like those of adults are invented for his shrines. Fetishes, like those of adults, accept only red and black 'fowls'; other shrines only white ones. Siikaɔni, a small boy of about 7 or 8, built himself a *loo* fetish, which can be dispatched to 'tie up' any one who might interfere with one's enterprises. Siikaɔni pretended to use his *loo* to keep the parents of his 'sweetheart' out of the way when he went to see her – a frequent use of a real *loo* by young men.

Play from pubescence to adolescence

The last stage of childhood coincides with the rapid absorption of the child into the economic system and his or her gradual acquisition of a responsible status in the social structure. By the age of 14 or 15 most girls are already married or being courted in marriage. They take their household duties more lightly perhaps than older women with children, but their childhood education is complete. Their education in the duties and responsibilities of wifehood and motherhood lies outside the scope of this paper. 'To play' now means to join in the dance or to dress up and go to market, there to gossip and flirt. These are recreations merely, like conversation in the evening after a good meal, when the whole family sits or sprawls about in one of the inner courts or in front of the gateway. Such 'play' is educative in quite a different sense to that of childhood.

Boys, too, between the ages of 12 or 13 and 16 to 18 are at the stage of transition from childhood to young manhood. The imaginative play still prominent at the beginning of this period is given up by degrees and usually altogether abandoned when puberty is established. Like the adolescent girl, the boy of 16 or so finds his principal recreation in the dance at certain seasons. He, too, begins to frequent markets when time permits, for he is greatly preoccupied with the opposite sex, with courtship and flirtations and even transient love affairs, and there is no place like the market for pretty girls. An adolescent youth is already applying the deftness and skill acquired in juvenile play or in the arts and crafts of his boyhood to practical ends. A 16-year-old takes an active part in building and thatching and in the manufacture of bows and arrows, or in the practice of crafts like leatherwork or the forging of tools and implements.

The transition from boyhood to manhood can readily be observed in the development of farming interests and skill during this period. The boy of 10 to 12 is extremely keen to plant, hoe and weed. Helping his father, he sows ground-nuts for himself amongst his father's early millet. Frequently he has a small plot of cereals, a few yards square, in a useless corner of one of his father's fields. He hoes and plants and weeds his plot with great energy and zest, though somewhat crudely, borrowing one of his father's discarded hoes for this purpose. He assists his mother to farm her ground-nuts and beans. But his efforts make no difference to the family commissariat or to the care and sustenance given him by his parents. He is still experimenting without responsibility, though with great earnestness. Two or three years later the play element has vanished. If he cultivates a personal plot he makes an effort to beg land which is agriculturally good, and works with the avowed purpose of obtaining a crop which, though minute compared with the needs of the family, suffices to buy himself a cap or a loincloth. The time he can now devote to his own plot or to his own ground-nuts must be adjusted in accordance with his responsibilities as a contributor to the family economy.

With boys, therefore, as with girls, the completion of their childhood education marks the end of childhood play. Mimetic and imaginative experimentation becomes redundant when the individual attains social responsibility and maturity. The play of Tale children changes, as we have seen, *pari passu* with their advancing maturity, contributing at each stage to the elaboration and integration of those interests, skills, and observances the mastery and acceptance of which is the final result of their education.

(From Supplement to *Africa 2*, No. 4, 1938. Also in Memorandum XVII of the *International Institute of African Languages and Cultures*, Oxford University Press.)

The Americanization of Rock-Climbing

Most writers justifiably stress the ways in which children's games co-opt them into the conventions of their culture. In this paper the shoe is on the other foot: instead of the game shaping the player, here the player's characteristics shape the nature of the game itself.

Those leisure-time activities which we label variously as 'play,' 'sports,' or 'games' have in common certain interesting and important characteristics. Besides being totally voluntary, these activities are all rewarding in themselves – they need not be done to secure a secondary goal. Significantly, their structure is such that it allows participants, within clearly established limits, to match themselves against some aspect of environment, other people, or some element within themselves,

The so-called dangerous sports – car racing, sky-diving, rock-climbing, and so forth – would seem to present special difficulties in fitting into the analytical scheme presented thus far. A layman observing a climbing team scaling a sheer rock face may be heard to mutter: 'They shouldn't be allowed to do that' or 'What are they trying to prove?' It is widely felt that voluntary pursuit of such dangerous activities is odd, anti-social, even perverted. Yet these sports are exactly like other games in their formal characteristics. They are voluntary, satisfying in and of themselves, and offer the player a highly structured setting in which to control external forces. They differ from other forms of play in that a failure in control may quickly result in the loss of the player's life – in other words, the feedback *must* be positive. I would like to review rock-climbing in more detail, particularly in regard to the changes in its practice in the past ten years or so. The survey will try to show how some general cultural value trends affect the norms of a fairly institutionalized form of play and, as a consequence, affect the behaviour and personality of the players.

The origins of rock-climbing

Rock-climbing is an autonomous sport which developed out of the more general activity of mountaineering. The separation began roughly three to four decades ago, when in the middle of the 1920s some climbers in the Alps and Dolomites perfected the use of equipment and techniques enabling them to make *direttissime* (most direct rather than roundabout) ascents on mountain faces previously thought to be unassailable. The two sports still overlap; but there is now a clearly established group of 'technical climbers' interested not in reaching summits but in climbing the sheerest faces, as opposed to traditional climbers.

Although rock-climbing was born in Europe, rock-climbers are a typically American phenomenon. They have developed exceptionally sophisticated techniques to negotiate the most formidable rock faces but in the process have become disinterested in almost every other aspect of mountaineering. As far as they are concerned, the rock face might just as well be underground as on a mountainside; in fact, spelunking is a favourite side activity of rock-climbers. By comparison with the new breed of American technical climbers, all but a few European climbers would define themselves as traditionals – that is as experts in rock techniques, but only within the larger context of mountain climbing, generally for the reason of reaching a summit. For the traditionals, expertise on rock is meaningful only because the rock is part of the mountain. For the rock-climber there is nothing else.

Serious climbing was introduced in America quite recently, mostly by Swiss, German, British, or French immigrants. The first major ascent in the Grand Tetons was made in 1893, but continuous climbing in the area dates only since 1925. While mountaineering continues to grow only modestly, rock-climbing has flourished in many sections of the country as a semi-independent speciality, pursued for the most part by young mathematicians and theoretical physicists. Although there are no data available, it is a curious fact well known in climbing circles – not only in the U.S. but in Korea, Japan, and Europe as well – that these two disciplines are hugely over-represented among rock-climbers. Indeed, it is difficult to find a committed rock-climber who went through higher education and is not a physicist or a mathematician.

Typically, they are college students and teachers. Among the new group of technical climbers, a growing minority consists of dropouts from academic and professional life. They work in the winter as dishwashers or carhops or, with luck, as ski-instructors; with their savings they take the whole summer off to climb. There is almost no formal communication, very little organization, and no formal rating or recognition among them. Yet there is widespread knowledge of what fellow climbers do, and news of an ascent spreads quickly. Through word of mouth, climbers learn to recognize the names of colleagues they have never met and to evaluate their accomplishments. As a result, there is an informal hierarchy, ranked according to the difficulty of their latest climbs. Although this ranking is constantly revised, it is surprising how widely it is accepted considering that it is never written down or formally recognized by a panel of experts. The leading figures are true cases of *primus inter pares* – that is, recognized and esteemed by their peers through performances.

The effects of specialization

To the traditional mountaineer, the unit of perception for a climb is the whole mountain. He thinks in terms of the approach, a snowfield or glacier to cross, which face or ridge to choose, the traverses or chimneys he has to negotiate before reaching the summit. During this process he is aware of the mountain as a whole, its faces, its relationship to neighbouring peaks. He usually is aware of the history of the mountain, and the memory of previous exploits on it makes his present climb a richer experience, part of an ongoing pattern. He is acutely mindful of the weather, both for practical and aesthetic reasons. When he reaches the summit he relaxes and feels bound to savour the mixed experience of pride and humility that the conquest of the peak entails. For the traditional mountaineer, the ascent is a gestalt including aesthetic, religious, historical, personal, and physical sensations.

In contrast, the technical climber's unit of perception is not the mountain but the particular route of ascent he has chosen. The mountain is reduced to the important pitches and holds. The summit is irrelevant, since the climax of the climb is the most difficult move rather than the highest point. I have seen rock-climbers reach an important summit, sit down to check their gear, eat a bite and be off without a glance at the view. The rock-climber becomes embarrassed if the conversation drifts to a subject out-side the strictly technical. Even if he is highly educated, as most are, he would sooner fall off a cliff than comment on natural beauty or his feelings.

In fact, the new breed of rock-climbers suspect the traditional climbers of hypocrisy and phoniness. Their attitude could be summarized in the following statement, which I have heard in one form or other from many sources:

Climbing consists in overcoming the problems posed by a more or less vertical slab of stone. The entire purpose of climbing is to do this as well as possible. Everything that is not essential to this pursuit is in fact detrimental to it, since maximum performance can be achieved only through maximum concentration. The climber who looks at the clouds or thinks in iambic pentameters is a fake. Any tourist on a ski-lift can get the same experience.

The drive towards quantification

The difficulty of a climb has been measured since the 1930s by a system devised in Europe which assigns each pitch a number from 1 to 5, in increasing order of difficulty. The numbering is subjective, based on the opinion of the most expert climber or the first to climb the pitch. There is also a '6th degree', which denotes a pitch that cannot be climbed except by employing artificial aids such as rope ladders, stirrups, prussic knots or any device which gives a climber support other than rock.

In the United States, the Yosemite climbers have introduced a decimal system which further breaks down the information: a 5·7 pitch, for example, is harder than a 5·3. In 1962 another form of grading, the National Climbing Classification System, was introduced: individual pitches are graded from F1 to F10 if they can be climbed free, A1 to A5 if they require artificial aid. In addition, a separate numbering system from I to IV was also adopted for grading the whole route.

Traditional climbers tend to be appalled by what they consider to be a pointless numbers game. The technical climber scoffs at the objection, pointing out that 'information is power' and that if one can measure something he should do so.

The emphasis on equipment

Great breakthroughs in rock-climbing have been, to a certain extent, a consequence of improvements in equipment. The crucial items in climbing are shoes, clothing, food (which has been 'improved' in the sense of being lightened and compressed), ropes and hardware. It is especially in the field of hardware – the climber's term for pitons, expansion bolts, carabiners, crack-jacks, etc. – that American rock-climbers have made the most noteworthy advances.

The traditional climber usually grows into an intimate relationship with his equipment. His shoes, his packsack, his pitons and ice-axe are used with care and pleasure, and he does not part with them unless they are absolutely worn out. Through this personal relationship with his own gear, the mountaineer adds one more dimension to the gestalt of the whole experience.

The rock-climber, although he tends to be obsessed with his gear, usually considers it simply as a means to an end. He may spend hours selecting items from a catalogue and, before each climb, more hours laying out, checking, packing, and re-packing all his equipment. But he does not hesitate to exchange any of it for more efficient gear as soon as it appears on the market.

Implications of the change

The attitudinal change we are witnessing in mountaineering reflects in a nutshell many changes taking place in the rest of society. A game activity which until a generation ago was performed leisurely, within a complex logico-meaningful framework of experiences, is now becoming a calculated, precise, expert enterprise within a much narrower framework of experiences.

The sad aspect of this case of cultural change is that there seems to be no way of reversing it. There is no point in trying to broaden the new climber's approach to the game. Even if one could convince him to try, he would surely feel that he had been right all along, that the traditional climber is indeed a phony. Where in our culture could he find justification of the traditional conception of climbing? Certainly not in the economic sphere, where efficiency rules; not in the scientific sphere, where meaning is meaningless; not in scholarship, where specialization is so valued.

We see then how a specific institutionalized activity such as rock-climbing reacts to changes in the sociocultural matrix of which it is a part. The value-system of the culture modifies the rules of the game.

(From *The University of Chicago Magazine*, Vol. 61, No. 6, 1964.)

F Factors Disrupting Play

Monkeys Without Play

In any zoo in the world, people almost always crowd around the facilities that house the monkeys. One reason primates are so popular may be that they look like furry little men with tails; another is that they are so entertaining. Young monkeys love to play, and their frolicking chases, wrestling matches, bar swinging, and ledge jumping bring awe to the face of a child, and to an adult, the wistful longing to be as agile and carefree. Our language is filled with references to monkey play – monkey business, monkeyshines, monkeying around, and monkey bars – references that connote a certain spirit of mischief and less than total seriousness.

We have watched literally hundreds of monkeys growing up, and two aspects of their development have become increasingly obvious. First, a monkey mother greatly influences the development of play in her offspring. When her infant is under two months of age the mother is best described as over-protective. Her eyes are everywhere, and her arms readily retrieve the infant who begins to wander away. But the mother loses interest in her offspring as it matures. When the infant is between three and six months of age her protective nature wanes, and at times the baby's efforts to maintain maternal contact may be actively rejected. In addition, the infant is physically and psychologically shoved into the play area, and upon returning to its mother's cage, it is often vigorously punished. The infant soon spends more and more time away from its two-faced mother. We feel that in psychological terms, the mother provides her infant with an initial security before she gives it a healthy kick in the tail. A baby monkey made bold will not be afraid to play.

The second element we notice is sexual in nature. Beginning very early in life young male monkeys differ from young female monkeys in their behaviours. These differences are first and foremost evident in play. Males play more actively, physically, and aggressively than females. Few females get caught in rough-and-tumble play, and in approach-avoidance exchanges they are chased more than they pursue. A female infant rarely initiates a play bout with a male. Male monkeys, however, try to play with anybody and anything.

As infants grow older and play becomes more sophisticated, sex differences become more obvious. By six months of age males are far more active and enthusiastic in their overall play behaviour than females. Furthermore, sexual posturing and positioning become more sex-appropriate. Initially, both males and females mount and thrust, which are adult male sexual behaviours, and both exhibit the adult female sexual 'present' with equal frequency and proficiency. By seven months, however, female mounts are infrequent and are directed almost exclusively towards other females. Males may present towards other males, but seldom towards females. In addition, female monkeys groom their peers considerably more than do males. These differences emerge regardless of whether male or female adults are present. The differences persist, in modified form, through adulthood. We strongly believe that they are biologically determined.

The development of play, which we have described for laboratory monkeys reared with mothers and peers, is chronologically identical to the development of play demonstrated by feral monkeys. If all monkeys exhibited a similar development, monkey play would be of little more than casual interest. But some of our monkeys at the Wisconsin Primate Laboratory and Research Centre do not show normative play development. We have learned from the study of these primates that monkey play is of overwhelming importance.

If one raises a group of infant monkeys without mothers or fathers, they soon develop patterns of mutual clinging behaviour. For some six to eight months, mutual clinging is essentially the only behaviour these together-together infants, as we call them, show. Mother-peer reared monkeys initially cling a great deal to their mothers, but by four months of age they have been actively pushed into a socially interactive world. Together-together reared monkeys have no mothers to send them out to play, and therefore they keep clinging to each other. Eventually, usually by six to eight months, play behaviour does emerge in these animals, but it is unsophisticated and passive. Together-together rearing retards the development of play, and when it finally emerges it is of an infantile form.

One can also rear an infant with its mother while denying it the opportunity to interact with peers. When monkeys so reared for the first eight months of life are finally exposed to peers, they are hyper-aggressive. They avoid efforts by other monkeys to achieve physical contact, but initiate intense biting attacks that are more aggressive than playful in nature. Among humans, 'mama's boys' are seldom popular or effective playmates. In monkeys, mother-only reared infants are at once socially withdrawn and unusually aggressive.

The behavioural anomalies exhibited by together-together and mother-only reared infants are somewhat ameliorated as the animals mature. Both types of monkeys exhibit relatively normal sexual behaviour at adulthood, and the females become adequate mothers, but the developmental discrepancies do not entirely disappear. Adult together-together reared monkeys are timid animals, and adult mother-only reared subjects continue to be hyper-aggressive in social situations. Thus, analysis of play behaviour exhibited by these animals as infants affords a relatively accurate prognosis of their social capabilities as adults.

The above disturbances seem mild indeed when compared with the behaviours exhibited by monkeys subjected to more sterile rearing environments. If one rears infants in bare wire cages where they can see and hear, but not physically contact, other monkeys, the young animals rapidly develop obvious disturbances. Having no mother or peers to cling to, these monkeys embrace their own bodies in intense self-clasping. Having no maternal nipple to suckle, they suck and chew their own digits. Thumb and finger sucking, common among human infants, is augmented by toe sucking and, among males, penis sucking – a manifestation of the monkey's greater physical flexibility. Having no playmates to provide motor stimulation, wire-cage reared infants develop compulsive and stereotypic rocking behaviours, strikingly reminiscent of the human autistic child.

When monkeys so reared are finally exposed to peers, they do not exhibit play behaviour. Rather, they avoid social interchange and continue in their self-directed, self-satisfying behaviours. If surrounded by peers they may initiate an aggressive attack, but more often they are the victims of aggression. The difference between these social misfits and their equal-aged playful peers is striking and sobering even to the most naïve observer.

All work and no play makes for a dull child. No play makes for a very socially disturbed monkey. When wire-cage reared animals reach physiological maturity they are incompetent in virtually every aspect of monkey social activity. They prefer to sit in a corner, rather than engage in social grooming, a prerequisite of monkey etiquette. Their aggressive behaviour is both ill-advised and ill-directed. Wire-cage reared adults will viciously attack a helpless neonate or they may suicidally attack a dominant male – an act few socially sophisticated animals are stupid enough to attempt. In the absence of social agents, wire-cage reared monkeys will attack themselves, occasionally rending skin and muscle to the bone in a flurry of self-aggression.

Monkeys denied the chance to play at sex are seldom proficient at sexual play. Although their hearts may be in the right place, more important things are not. A wire-cage reared male may attempt to mount the front or side of a willing female. Equally often he will sit next to her and mastur-bate. Wire-cage reared females do little better. It is our conclusion that impregnation of these females is best achieved via artificial insemination procedures.

When such females become mothers, another adverse consequence of lack of early play interaction becomes obvious. Motherless mothers, as we call them, are not good mothers. Most females cradle their new-born infants almost continuously. These females will leave their babies lying on a mesh floor or, if provoked, will crush them into the wire surface. If further provoked they may bite off an infant's fingers or toes.

We have found that even more severe behavioural disruption can be achieved by rearing monkeys for the first six months or more of life in total social isolation, where they receive neither visual nor physical social stimulation. Surprisingly enough, such rearing has little apparent effect on the monkey's intellectual capabilities. They solve learning test problems – with the exception of extremely complex learning problems – as rapidly and with as few errors as do mother-peer reared, laboratory-born monkeys or their feral-born counterparts. A monkey does not need playmates to perform adequately in intellectual endeavour, but it sorely needs them to become a functioning member of a social unit. A similar observation regarding human behaviour might not be far from the truth. From our observations it has become clear that play is of utmost importance for the subsequent social well-being of the individual and those around him. Why should this be the case?

We think that play among monkey infants serves two general, but important, functions. First, it provides a behavioural mechanism by which activities appropriate for adult social functioning can be initiated, inte-grated, and perfected. Play repertoires of monkeys under a year of age contain rudimentary forms of virtually all behaviours that characterize adult social life. Patterns of social grooming, aggression, sex, and domin-ance are clearly evident in infant monkey play activity. When they first emerge, these patterns are not exhibited at adult levels of competence. Rather, they are clumsy and unsophisticated. It is only after months, even years, of 'practice' that the behaviours become truly adult in form. The practice comes through peer play.

It is primarily through play that young monkeys learn to interact in a social world. In the months of early play development the infant pro-gresses from a recognition that social objects differ from the rest of the environment to a state of living with and loving fellow monkeys. Presence of peers is sought, rather than avoided, as with isolate-reared monkeys. Furthermore, the infants pick up social graces, such as how to behave in the presence of a dominant, as opposed to a lower status, peer. Dominance hierarchies established among peers early in life persist, unchanged in form, throughout adulthood. In these respects, the function of play for monkeys closely parallels the role of play among human children.

The second function of play in monkey social development is to mitigate aggression when it emerges in the monkey's behavioural repertoire. Aggressive behaviour, absent in very young monkeys, seems to manifest itself spontaneously at about seven months of age, independant of rearing conditions. For this reason we believe aggression to be genetically predisposed in the rhesus monkey. All monkeys show aggressive behaviour of some form, beginning at seven months of age. However, the situations in which aggressive behaviour is exhibited are controlled, not by genetic, but rather by social, variables. Monkeys permitted to play exhibit their aggression in their play activity. Because it is part of the play repertoire, it is of relatively mild form. Through play, the control of aggression is achieved.

What happens to aggressive behaviour when infants are denied the opportunity to play with peers? In the case of mother-only reared infants, hyper-aggression characterizes otherwise normal peer interactions. These monkeys, having received adequate maternal contact, are not afraid of other monkeys, but they control their aggression poorly in their social activity. In contrast, wire-cage and isolate-reared monkeys are generally incompetent in social situations. Like all other monkeys, these subjects exhibit aggressive behaviour, but it is neither under effective control nor is its target appropriate. Such monkeys will aggress with equal ferocity against infants, dominant adult males, and their own bodies. They have had no practice in channelling their aggression through alternative forms of social behaviour.

There is definite survival value in aggression as long as it is socialized. Monkeys in the wild must protect their social groups from predators and from competitive monkey troops. Without aggression there would be little protection. However, aggression directed unsystematically towards fellow group members can destroy any society. Hence the response must be attenuated in intra-group interactions. We believe that a major function of play is the development of control over the intensity and the target of aggressive behaviour. Play very likely has a similar function for humans. One only has to watch a professional football game to be convinced.

As we examine how play develops in monkeys, and the consequences of its lack of development, it becomes obvious that play, which appears to be so spontaneous, carefree, and frivolous, is actually one of the most important aspects of social development. The next time you go to a zoo, stroll over to the monkey island and revel in the playful antics of man's evolutionary cousins. Then pity the monkeys who are not permitted to play, and pray that all children will always be allowed to play.

(From 'Play,' a *Natural History Magazine Special Supplement*, December 1971.)

49 R. R. Zimmermann, D. A. Strobel, D. Maguire, R. R. Steere,
    H. L. Hom

The Effects of Protein Deficiency on Activity, Learning, Manipulative Tasks, Curiosity, and Social Behaviour of Monkeys

This is a compilation of several papers by the authors in which they explore the be-havioural consequences of a diet deficient in protein.

It is recognized that large numbers of people in the world, predominately children of underdeveloped countries in the tropics and subtropics, suffer from the effects of protein-calorie malnutrition (Pearson, 1968). The term protein-calorie malnutrition (PCM) was designated by Jelliffe (1959) and later proposed by the Joint Food and Agriculture Organization and the World Health Organization Expert Commission on Nutrition (FAO/WHO, 1962) to describe a large range of clinical conditions. There are two syndromes which are covered by the term PCM: marasmus, which can be described as an inadequate amount of all food, and kwashiorkor, which is a deficiency of protein in a diet that may or may not be high in calories (McCance and Widdowson, 1968). The major focus of research on this problem has been directed towards the possibility that PCM experienced early in life produces permanent alteration of the phenotypic expression for the normal intellectual and social development of the child (Scrimshaw and Gordon, 1968). Cravioto and DeLicardie (1968) in their longitudinal studies of children with severe PCM reported that most profound be-havioural deficiencies occurred in children that had suffered from severe PCM before they reached 6 months of age. These investigators found significant deficits in motor skills, adaptive behaviour, language acquisi-tion, and personal-social abilities. However, Kallen (1968) has reported that the interacting effects of economic conditions, nutrition, body weight and size, family interactions, intellectual development, and socialization may all contribute to the PCM syndrome in humans. These variables must be fully considered when attempting to evaluate the relationship between PCM and its effects on behaviour and learning.

The use of non-human laboratory primates to study the effects of PCM permits (a) a controlled dietary programme, (b) an intensive investigation of both short-term and long-term effects of PCM on behavioural develop-ment, and (c) control over the extent and kind of social interactions. For example, Kerr and Waisman (1968) have successfully produced protein malnutrition in infant rhesus monkeys in the laboratory. They found significant deviations from the normal pattern in terms of weight gain, body length, head circumference, and dietary intake. Although they observed none of the more obvious clinical signs of extreme protein malnutrition (kwashiorkor), such as edema, hair dispigmentation, and dermatitis, the social behaviour of their Ss was characterized by inactivity, lack of curiosity, and retarded peer group interaction. Further research has recently been initiated into the effects of protein malnutrition on laboratory-reared monkeys. The main areas of interest have focused on: (a) general activity, (b) learning, (c) manipulative tasks, (d) curiosity, and (e) social behaviour.

Activity

The effects of protein-calorie malnutrition on the general level of activity in man and experimental animals is little understood and has been seldom investigated. Guthrie (1968) investigated activity level in rats in order to determine the extent to which differences in learning might be explained on the basis of motivational or motor factors. It was found that undernourished rats were more active than normal rats. Similarly, Collier, Squibb, and Jackson (1965a, 1965b) found that diets deficient in protein produced higher levels of activity in an activity wheel than diets providing adequate protein. The results of an investigation by Geist, Zimmermann and Strobel (1972) show that activity in rhesus monkeys when measured as general movement around a cage produces no significant differences between any of the low protein groups when compared to the high protein animals. Failure to find activity differences over an extended period and degrees of deprivation despite the clinical manifestations of protein-calorie malnutrition would suggest that malnutrition affects activity selectivity. That is, activity levels may be dependent not only upon the measures used, but also show considerable variation across species.

Learning

The natural place to look in the behaviour of animals for evaluation of mental development is learning performance. A variety of attempts have been made to study the effects of early malnutrition on the learning behaviour of rats, pigs, and monkeys. The data are highly variable. For example, male rats seem to be more affected by the variable of early malnutrition than females in learning in a water maze (Barnes, Cunnold, Zimmermann, Simmons, MacCleod and Krook, 1966). Protein malnourished rats were inferior to controls in reversal of a position habit and in learning a black–white discrimination (Barnes et al., 1966). However, other studies by Levitsky and Barnes (1970) suggest that much of the deficit in learning performance in malnourished rats might be attributed to emotional development and motivational factors have not been ruled out.

In studies with monkeys, on the other hand, Zimmermann (1969, 1970) has reported that malnourished monkeys are actually superior to normal animals in learning and remembering discrimination problems. The superiority of the malnourished monkeys appears to be a function of the heightened value of the food incentives for the malnourished monkey. Indeed in one experiment (Zimmermann, 1970) high protein animals had to be deprived before they showed any learning in the discrimination problem. And when year-old monkeys were tested on a before- and after-diet series of discrimination and reversal learning problems, no effect of diet was found (Zimmermann, 1973).

Levitsky and Barnes (1972) have reported that rats do not differ on discrimination learning or discrimination learning reversal, but they did differ on a double alternation problem. Problem difficulty may be related to the variability of the findings. Thus, malnourished rats did not differ from controls in their rate of learning an initial position habit, but they did differ on the reversal problem. The Hebb-Williams maze in which a difference between malnourished and control rats has been reported in at least three studies (Cowley and Griesel, 1959; Zimmermann and Wells, 1971; Wells, Geist and Zimmermann, 1972) is a series of different problems that do have several features of problem difficulty built into the procedure.

Discrimination problems are rather simple for the young monkey. They are learned and remembered quite efficiently before the animal has the ability to learn learning set or has a poor learning set ability (Zimmermann, 1969). Thus, we might find very little effect of diet on the learning of simple problems. Learning and reversing to a single stimulus pair is also a rather simple problem for the rhesus monkey (Warren, 1966). After ten reversals the animals average less than four errors per reversal problem. However, the development of reversal learning to different problems might present the monkey with a more complex problem sequence and might involve attention mechanisms that could be affected by the malnourishment condition.

The present experiment was designed to test the effects of early protein malnutrition on reversal learning in developing baby monkeys. This study was an early attempt to find some differences in the learning abilities of monkeys subjected to low-protein diets at different times of life. In this experiment younger monkeys were subjected to different diets at 90 days of age and tested before they were 1 year of age.

The results in terms of errors to criterion of the original learning are shown in Fig. 1 and the same measure for reversal learning is shown in Fig. 2. As can be seen, the groups are almost identical in the learning of the original problem but the groups are quite different on the reversal prob-

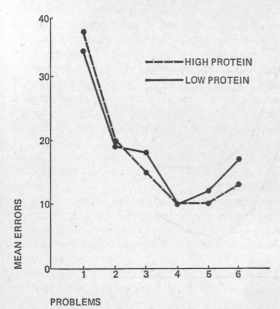

PROBLEMS

Fig. 1. Performance of 150-day-old high- and low-protein groups on discrimination learning problems.

lems. An analysis of variance of the original learning showed that the groups did not differ significantly but that differences between problems were significant beyond the 0·01 per cent level ($F = 6·227$). In the reversal condition the analysis of variance showed that the groups were significantly different at the 0·01 per cent level ($F = 25·088$) and that between problem differences are also significantly different at this level ($F = 10·64$). No interactions were significant in either analysis. The low protein Ss made significantly more errors in the reversal condition.

That the decrease in performance of low-protein animals in the experiment is related to problem difficulty rather than to all problems is evidenced by the recent findings of Strobel (1972a, b). Using planometric stimuli in which the discriminable stimuli occupied either the central or peripheral portions of the stimulus card, he found that low-protein monkeys were significantly inferior to high-protein controls when the discriminative stimulus occupied the central portion of the stimulus field and took up fifty per cent or less of the area of the field on a reversal problem. He found no differences when the discriminative stimulus occupied the peripheral or borders of the stimulus card, nor when the stimulus occupied one hundred

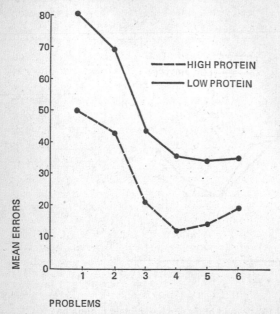

Fig. 2. Performance of 150-day-old high- and low-protein groups on discrimination reversal problems.

per cent of the stimulus area, nor were there any differences as a function of stimuli on learning the original problem.

Strobel's findings are quite consistent with the results of our experiment, but both sets of data are difficult to explain. If the low-protein diet functioned to interfere with the development of observing responses, or other attention mechanisms, we would have expected the low-protein animals to be deficient on both the original problems and on the reversal problems.

To date most of the reports of the effects of protein deficiency on learning tasks have emphasized the role of motivation and emotional variables in the decreased performance of animals raised on low-protein diets. This experiment is one of the few findings that appears to be the result of a non-motivational variable. But again, it does not seem to be tied to association factors or learning *per se*, as much as it does to attentional factors. Observations of the protein-deprived monkeys in other test situations indicates that they are highly food oriented and probably attend, as most monkeys do, to the place at which they find food, or place their fingers. Strobel (1972b) has found that protein-deprived monkeys fail to learn a discrimination requiring an observing response to a central stimulus, prior to responding to a position. Protein deprivation may only show its effects on complex problems requiring extensive observing responses, such as performance on multiple problems in the rat (Zimmermann and Wells, 1971) or on such problems as double alternation in the rat (Levitsky and Barnes, 1972) and finally in the type of problem we have presented here, a reversal or a problem that requires an observing response.

The data make it evident that the young malnourished monkey is inferior to controls on the performance of certain reversal learning tasks. What relation this has to the human condition is not clear, but it is one of the first demonstrations that complex learning is inferior as a result of malnutrition in the non-human primate. More research on the types of problems in which deficiencies might appear must be explored.

Manipulative tasks

Decreased investigative behaviour has long been considered one of the persistent features of protein-calorie malnutrition (PCM) in humans. Children suffering from this disease often appear lethargic, apathetic, withdrawn, and inert (Jelliffe and Welbourn, 1963). Similar psychomotor changes have been reported for infra-human organisms. In a study of puzzle-solving behaviour, young monkeys subjected to protein deprivation solved fewer puzzles and had lower rates of manipulation than well-fed animals (Strobel and Zimmermann, 1971b). However, in that experiment secondary infectious diseases associated with malnutrition may have contributed to these results. Similar deficits in manipulatory responsiveness have been found in year-old monkeys placed on diets deficient in protein (Zimmermann and Strobel, 1969).

In the following experiment, chain pulling was used to study the performance of protein-deprived monkeys on manipulative tasks. The chain pulling task was selected because it was a simple response which could be described as a free operant in the home cage. Harlow, Blazek, and McClearn (1956) found that normal infant monkeys reared on adequate diets will respond with immediate interest to a chain pulling manipulation task. Furthermore, the behaviour is maintained over a long period of time and increases as a function of experience with the manipulation itself as the only apparent reward (Mason, Harlow, and Rueping, 1959).

In addition to the chains, objects never experienced by the animals were introduced on the chains to test for curiosity reactions to these novel stimuli. Similar kinds of tests for passivity and apathy have been designed for malnourished children and involve the observation of the child's reactions to new brightly coloured toys (Jelliffe and Welbourn, 1963).

Monkeys of two ages (120 and 210 days) were tested and chain pulling rates for each are given in Table 1.

Table 1 Chain pulling rates for high- and low-protein monkeys receiving a sequence of chains and objects

Diet sequence (days on diet)	Before −13	After diet +6	+20	+50	+80
Test sequence	Chains	Chains	Objects	Chains	Chains
Group					
210–LP	13·99	12·06	6·38	7·30	2·66
210–HP	10·26	10·25	12·00	18·65	16·62
120–LP	—	13·16	7·08	14·10	8·08
120–HP	—	12·55	13·78	22·52	22·45

Although the experiment was not designed specifically to test for neophobic reactions, the results appear consistent with this interpretation. The monkeys had previously experienced the chains in a social setting but had never been exposed to the objects. In addition, the low-protein monkeys were observed to show distinctive fear and avoidance reactions to the new stimuli, particularly during the first day of this condition. Two monkeys in the 210-LP group refused to enter their cages after the introduction of these stimuli. Restoration of the previously experienced 'chains alone' condition resulted in partial recovery of the chain pulling response in the 120-LP group. This would suggest that for these animals the decrements in manipulation of the objects were not entirely the consequence of a general decline in responsiveness during the early phases of protein depletion.

It is also apparent that with repeated testing and with continued protein deprivation the experimental animals show a decrease in manipulatory behaviour, as measured in this experiment. This is consistent with the observation that, in general, the animals deprived of protein are less active in a variety of non-food oriented behaviours such as social behaviour, visual curiosity, and puzzle solving (Zimmermann and Strobel, 1969). In previous experiments the differences were not always reliable, and may have been influenced by the fact that the observations were taken over limited intervals and in structured situations outside of the living cage environments. A decrease in responsiveness to manipulatory stimuli and an increase in the fear or avoidance reactions to novel conditions would put a developing organism in its normal ecological environment at a considerable disadvantage. It must be evident, however, that additional experimentation is needed to determine if the reduced responsiveness to the objects by the low-protein animals in the present experiment was a neophobic avoidance reaction.

A step in this direction is the 1973 study by Aakre, Strobel, Zimmermann and Geist. Low-protein fed monkeys showed a low manipulation rate on a 12-part puzzle manipulation apparatus, as compared to high-protein animals, when the only source of reinforcement was the manipulation of the puzzles (intrinsic reward). However, when food was introduced, the low-protein fed subjects manipulated at a level equal to or greater than the high-protein fed animals. This strengthens the hypothesis that manipulation, the intrinsic reward, is a much less salient variable for protein-deprived monkeys than is extrinsic reward.

Curiosity

One of the common observations in primate laboratories is that young monkeys with adequate social and testing experience show a tendency to respond positively to new objects that are placed within their reach in familiar situations (Butler, 1965). Although there may be an initial avoidance response, within a few minutes most animals will approach, reach for, and manipulate the new object. The typical rhesus monkey has a positive, or approach, response to novelty. One might even go as far as to say that they are neophilic. In contrast to the monkey with social and testing experience, the animal raised in a restricted social or visual environment develops an aversion to new stimuli and might be described as neophobic (Mason and Green, 1962; Menzel, Davenport, and Rogers, 1961, 1963).

The present study was undertaken after several observations indicated that baby monkeys that had been maintained on a low-protein diet for 9–10 months showed abnormally strong responses to new or novel stimuli. In this instance these Ss had participated in an experiment in which the same fifty object-quality discrimination objects were presented over and over again for approximately five months. At the end of nine months they were tested on a new set of fifty objects to determine their learning set ability. Responses to the appearance of the new objects were extremely negative and many animals that were classified as excellent test Ss balked and became highly emotional. The Ss maintained on a normal protein diet did not show these negative responses.

The results confirm the qualitative observations that have been made in the authors' laboratory on the behaviour development of monkeys raised on a low-protein diet. These monkeys are very much like the socially deprived and stimulus deprived *S*s described by Mason and Green (1962).

It would appear that part of the behavioural syndrome associated with protein malnutrition in the developing baby monkey is the appearance of avoidance responses to new or novel stimulation. Indeed, the development of human mental abilities is intertwined with the primate sensitivity to curiosity and social reinforcement. With a decrease in responses to new stimulation and the development of response patterns which withdraw the infant from the environment, the stage is set for the production of a retarded organism.

Social behaviour

The following study indicates that statistically significant quantitative differences exist in the social behaviour between rhesus monkeys raised on low-protein and high-proteins diets. Ten pre-pubescent laboratory-born animals, separated from their mothers between 90 to 120 days of age and housed in individual cages, were assigned either to a low-protein dietary group or a high-protein dietary group at 210 days. These diets were isocaloric in content, but contained differing amounts of protein, either three per cent or twenty-five per cent by weight (Zimmermann and Strobel, 1969). The animals remained on these special diets throughout both phases of the experiment. Though little information is available concerning the protein content of the natural diet of rhesus monkeys, the protein content of the standard laboratory monkey chow is fifteen per cent by weight. The low-protein group (210-LP) consisted of five females and one male; the high-protein group (210-HP) included three males and one female.

In the first phase of the study five categories of behaviour were employed in an attempt to further specify apparent behavioural differences. The animals were approximately 300 days of age at the beginning of the experiment in this first phase. Social testing consisted of recording the observations of five mutually exclusive categories of behaviour: (1) approach play; (2) avoidance-submission; (3) clutching and self-stimulation; (4) grooming and sexual behaviour; and (5) non-social behaviour.

When the animals were approximately 590 days of age Phase Two of the experiment was initiated. The animals were placed in the same social room under the same conditions as Phase One. But in this part of the experiment a new recording system was used and the five mutually exclusive categories of behaviour were re-defined in an attempt to differentiate between aggressive behaviour and approach play and to further delineate the categories of nonsocial responses. The categories were:

1. *Social-aggressive interactions*: behaviours which included approach,

contact, mouthing, biting, chewing, grabbing, and pulling without reciprocity between the aggressor and aggressee. The animals aggressed against appeared motivated by fear. Also included in this category were chasing, escape and submission, and brutality which was characterized by one animal jumping on top of another animal and pulling hair out, biting, and pulling the skin.

2. *Social-tactual contact*: behaviour in which the animals mutually came into physical contact, sat quietly in a group, groomed, or mounted one another.

3. *Social-approach play*: characterized by the animals chasing, running, jumping, rough-and-tumble play with mutual participation. It did not appear motivated by fear and included active approach, mouthing, and biting with reciprocity.

4. *Object oriented* (*non-social*): consisted of chain pulling and chewing, playing in the sawdust, swinging from the poles, licking or chewing wood, bars, and other cage parts.

5. *Undirected* (*non-social*): involved sitting, standing, or pacing without visible direction, self-clutching, and self-stimulation.

The results of the first phase showed that, in general, the social behaviour of the 210-HP group appeared more normal than the 210-LP group. The 210-HP animals, for example, engaged in approach play and sexual behaviours for longer periods of time, but spent less time in clutching and non-social behaviours than the 210-LP animals. Conversely, the 210-LP animals spent longer time intervals per behaviour bout in socially abnormal behaviours such as gazing blankly, walking aimlessly around the room, or curled up in a tight ball. In addition to these quantitative differences between groups, observer reports of the animals suggested that qualitative differences between the groups remained undetected by the recording procedure outlined. For example, failure to find significant differences in the amount of aggressive behaviour suggested that a revision of the avoidance-submission category or the introduction of new categories would be necessary to further differentiate these groups of Ss.

In the second phase of the study, the high-protein monkeys, as in the first phase, continued to show more positive social responsiveness than the low-protein monkeys. For example, they engaged in approach play behaviour more frequently, for longer durations, and at higher rates, than the 210-LP group. The high-protein animals also showed significantly higher occurrence of tactual play responses than the 210-LP group. Tactual rates and percentage of duration were higher for the 210-HP group, but not statistically significant.

In comparison to the greater social responsiveness of the adequately nourished Ss, the low-protein animals engaged in non-social kinds of behaviours nearly as often as the high-protein animals. But when the 210-LP group exhibited directed or undirected non-social responses, they did so for significantly longer periods of time.

Although the malnourished monkeys showed a higher frequency and a higher rate of aggressive behaviour than did the high-protein monkeys, these differences did not reach statistical significance. However, the use of the absolute measure for analysis of aggression did not apply to the initial differences in the amount of social behaviour between the two groups. Along with approach play behaviour, aggression comprises what might be described as a composite measure of active social behaviour. If the 210-HP group were to exhibit a higher active social responsiveness, then it could increase the likelihood of more aggressive behaviour and yet at the same time constitute a small proportion of the animal's active social behaviour relative to the 210-LP group. In short, aggressive behaviour would comprise an unequal amount of behaviour between the two groups in the context of approach play behaviour. To control for this variable, an aggression ratio was derived by dividing aggression scores by the sum of aggression and approach-play scores. An analysis, utilizing the Mann-Whitney U test with 0·05 as the level of statistical significance, of the proportion of aggressive response in the total active social behaviour revealed that all three response measures were significantly higher for the 210-LP group as seen in Table 2.

Table 2 Aggression Ratio

Group	Frequency	% duration	Rates
210–LP	0·27	17	0·29
210–HP	0·13	8	0·17

Note. $p < 0.033$ in all cases.

A comparison of the behaviour of our high-protein monkeys with a description of monkeys raised in other laboratories (Sackett, 1968; Mitchell, 1970) indicated that the high protein monkeys exhibit relatively normal behavioural patterns for laboratory-reared animals, while the behavioural patterns of the low-protein monkeys are best classified as being abnormal social responses.

It appears that protein malnutrition interferes with the normal socialization processes of malnourished monkeys, but the actual mechanisms involved are not obvious. At least three hypotheses can be offered on the basis of our preliminary findings.

First, protein malnutrition could be considered to produce functional social isolates. There is a great similarity between the disrupted social behaviour of monkeys deprived of protein in this experiment and Harlow's (1965a, 1965b) monkeys deprived of early social experience. For example, Zimmermann, Strobel and Maguire (1970) and Strobel and Zimmermann (1971b) have demonstrated that the malnourished developing monkey tends to avoid new stimuli and shows neophobia in several different experimental situations. In the present experiment, low-protein monkeys consistently failed to make normal responses to social initiations, with aggression and brutality the dominant outcome of many of these social encounters. The cumulative results of these interactions might be classified as a selective punishment schedule which would further alter normal social development. Withdrawal from each new or additional social stimulus would be a self-imposed *de facto* form of stimulus deprivation. In addition, this pattern or response in the malnourished monkeys and Harlow's monkeys is not unlike that described by Fuller (1967) in puppies raised in isolation. He speculated that the major difference between normal and isolated animals is in their ability to attend and respond to appropriate stimuli in the environment. Isolated animals are stressed by a stimulus overload. Our data suggest that protein malnutrition may produce a similar set of inappropriate reactions to normal social stimulation.

A second hypothesis could be described as a channelization of drive notion. That is, the low-protein monkeys are so concerned with food-oriented behaviours that other behaviours such as normal socialization reactions are delayed or don't appear at all. Thus, the food-seeking or food-oriented behaviours would prevent the development of normal non-food-oriented acts. Evidence from a discrimination learning task (Zimmermann and Strobel, 1970), a conflict situation (Strobel and Zimmermann, 1971), and preliminary results from a manipulation task and a dominance study, all involving food reinforcement, indicated that the low-protein monkeys appear to be under a higher food motivation. Barnes, Reid, Pond and Moore (1968) also described this increased motivation for food in previously malnourished as well as in protein-restricted pigs. In the present study, the low-protein monkeys may have been preoccupied with the search for food, leaving minimal time for socialization.

Finally, protein malnutrition has produced monkeys that behave like immature animals. One of the characteristics of the behaviour of very young monkeys in the social situation is the lack of peer activity and a pre-occupation with non-social stimuli in the environment. Thus, the low protein monkeys are behaving like very young monkeys, maintaining infantile types of responses that are not compatible with normal social development. The low-protein monkeys maintain such infantile behaviours as the fear grimace and continual high-pitched screaming, while the high-protein control animals began developing adult-type threat postures and expressions as shown in Van Hooff (1969). There was an almost complete absence of sexual behaviour in the low-protein monkeys. In the high-protein group the males began to engage in grooming, presenting, and mounting with a single female in the group who began to develop sexual folds and colouring and finally menstruated at 1,935 days of age. It is interesting to note that behaviour differences attributable more to growth and maturity have been reported in protein-deprived rats. Anderson and Smith (1932) postulated that the activity and maze-learning ability of protein-deprived rats was more like that of normal animals of their own weight and size than like adequately fed rats their own age but of different weights.

The primary preliminary findings of the present paper were the drastic and widespread abnormalities in social behaviours shown by those monkeys with induced protein malnutrition. Positive social behaviours such as approach play are depressed in the low-protein monkeys, while negative social behaviours such as fear and aggression are accentuated in the malnourished monkeys. It is possible that there are a series of mutually interacting patterns of neophobia, food preoccupation, and immaturity which make some contribution to the behavioural abnormalities observed in the low-protein monkeys. Further research with more animals is needed and may throw additional light on the source of the behavioural deficits. Of particular importance is the way in which the malnourished monkeys respond to dietary rehabilitation. With the return to normal growth, normal behavioural patterns may emerge.

References

AAKRE, B., STROBEL, D. A., ZIMMERMANN, R. R., and GEIST, C. R. (1973), 'Reactions to intrinsic and extrinsic rewards in protein-malnourished monkeys', *Perceptual and Motor Skills*, No. 36, pp. 787–90.

ANDERSON, J. E., and SMITH, A. H. (1932), 'Relation of performance to age and nutritive condition in the white rat', *Journal of Comparative Psychology*, No. 6, pp. 337–59.

BARNES, R., CUNNOLD, S., ZIMMERMANN, R., SIMMONS, H., MACCLEOD, R., and KROOK, W. (1966), 'Influence of nutrition deprivations in early life on learning behavior in rats as measured by performance in a water maze', *J. Nutri.*, No. 89, pp. 399–410.

BARNES, R. H., REID, I. M., POND, W. G., and MOORE, A. U. (1968), 'The use of experimental animals in studying behavioral abnormalities following recovery from early malnutrition', in *Calorie Deficiencies and Protein Deficiencies*, R. A. McCance and E. M. Widdowson (eds), Little, Brown, Boston, U.S.A.

Butler, R. A. (1965), 'Investigative Behavior', in *Behavior of Nonhuman Primates*, A. M. Schrier, H. F. Harlow and F. Stollnitz (eds), Vol. 2, Academic Press, New York.

Collier, G., Squibb, R., Jackson, F. (1965a), 'Activity as a function of the diet: Spontaneous activity', *Psychonom. Science*, No. 3, pp. 173–4.

Collier, G., Squibb, R., Jackson, F. (1965), 'Activity as a function of the diet: Instrumental activity', *Psychonom. Science*, No. 3, pp. 175–6.

Cowley, J., and Griesel, R. (1959), 'Some effects of a low protein diet on a first filial generation of white rats', *J. Genet. Psychol.*, No. 95, pp. 187–201.

Cravioto, J. E., and DeLicardie, E. R. (1968), 'Intersensory development of school age children', in *Malnutrition, Learning and Behavior*, N. S. Scrimshaw and J. E. Gordon (eds), M.I.T. Press.

FAO/WHO (1962), *Joint FAO/WHO Expert Commission on Nutrition*, World Health Organization Report Series, Geneva.

Fuller, J. L. (1967), 'Experimental deprivation and later behavior', *Science*, No. 158, pp. 1645–52.

Geist, C. R., Zimmermann, R. R., and Strobel, D. A. (1972), 'Effect of protein-calorie malnutrition on food consumption, weight gain, serum proteins, and activity in the developing rhesus monkey (*Macaca mulatta*)', *Laboratory Animal Science*, No. 22, pp. 369–77.

Guthrie, H. (1968), 'Severe undernutrition in early infancy and behavior in rehabilitated albino rats', *Physiol. Behav.*, No. 3, pp. 619–23.

Harlow, H. F. (1965a), 'The effects of early social deprivation on primates', *Tire à Part, Symposium Bel Air II, Désafferentation Experimentale à Cliniques*, George & Company, Geneva.

Harlow, H. F. (1965b), 'Total social isolation in monkeys', *Proceedings of The National Academy of Sciences*, No. 54, pp. 90–7.

Harlow, H. F., Blazek, N. C., and McClearn, G. E. (1956), 'Manipulatory motivation in the infant rhesus monkey', *J. Comp. Physiol. Psychol.*, No. 49, pp. 444–8.

Hooff, J. A. R. A. M. van (1967), 'The facial displays of catarrhine monkeys and apes', in *Primate Ethology*, D. Morris (ed.), Weidenfeld & Nicolson.

Jelliffe, D. G. (1959), 'Protein-calorie malnutrition in tropical pre-school children', *Journal of Pediatrics*, No. 54, pp. 227.

Jelliffe, D. G., and Welbourn, H. F. (1963), 'Clinical signs of mild-moderate protein-calorie malnutrition of early childhood', in *Mild-Moderate Forms of Protein-Calorie Malnutrition*, G. Blix (ed.), Almqvist & Wiksell, Uppsala, pp. 12–31.

Kallen, D. J. (1968), 'Panel discussion on social environment, learning and behavior', in *Malnutrition, Learning and Behavior*, N. S. Scrimshaw and J. E. Gordon (eds), M.I.T. Press.

Kerr, G. R., and Waisman, H. A. (1968), 'A primate model for the quantitative study of malnutrition', in *Malnutrition, Learning and Behavior*, N. S. Scrimshaw and J. E. Gordon (eds), M.I.T. Press.

Levitsky, D., and Barnes, R. (1970), 'Effects of early protein-calorie malnutrition on animal behavior', *Nature*, No. 225, pp. 468–9.

LEVITSKY, D., and BARNES, R. (1972), 'Effects of early malnutrition on discrimination learning, reversal learning and delayed alternation in rats', annual meeting of the Eastern Psychological Association, New York, 1972.

MASON, W. A., and GREEN, P. C. (1962), 'The effects of social restriction on the behavior of rhesus monkeys: IV, Response to a novel environment and to an alien species', *J. Com. Physiol. Psychol.*, No. 55, pp. 363–8.

MASON, W. A., HARLOW, H. F., and RUEPING, R. R. (1959), 'The development of manipulatory responsiveness in the infant rhesus monkey', *J. Comp. Physiol. Psychol.*, No. 52, pp. 555–8.

MCCANCE, R. A., and WIDDOWSON, E. M. (eds), (1968), *Calorie Deficiences and Protein Deficiencies*, Little, Brown, Boston, U.S.A.

MENZEL, E. W., JR, DAVENPORT, R. K., JR, and ROGERS, C. M. (1961), 'Some aspects of behaviour toward novelty in young chimpanzees', *J. Comp. Physiol. Psychol.*, No. 54, pp. 16–19.

MENZEL, E. W., JR, DAVENPORT, R. K., JR, and ROGERS, C. M. (1963), 'The effects of environmental restriction upon the chimpanzees responsiveness to objects', *J. Comp. Physiol. Psychol.*, No. 56, pp. 78–85.

MITCHELL, G. (1970), 'Abnormal behavior in primates', in *Primate Behavior, Developments in Field and Laboratory Research*, L. S. Rosenblum (ed.), Academic Press.

PEARSON, P. B. (1968), 'Scientific and technical aims', in *Malnutrition, Learning and Behavior*, N. S. Scrimshaw and J. E. Gordon (eds), M.I.T. Press.

SACKETT, G. P. (1968), 'Abnormal behavior in laboratory reared rhesus monkeys', in *Abnormal Behavior in Animals*, M. W. Fox (ed.), W. B. Saunders.

SCRIMSHAW, N. S., and GORDON, J. E. (eds), (1968), *Malnutrition, Learning and Behavior*, M.I.T. Press.

STROBEL, D. A. (1972a), 'Cue-response relationships in protein malnourished monkeys', annual meeting of the Montana Psychological Association, Billings, Montana.

STROBEL, D. A. (1972b), 'Stimulus change and attention variables as factors in the behavioral deficiency of malnourished developing monkeys', unpublished doctoral dissertation, University of Montana.

STROBEL, D. A., and ZIMMERMANN, R. R. (1971a), 'Manipulatory responsiveness in protein malnourished monkeys', *Psychonom. Science*, No. 24, pp. 19–20.

STROBEL, D. A., and ZIMMERMANN, R. R. (1971b), 'Collaborative evidence for neophobic reactions in rhesus monkeys subjected to protein-calorie malnutrition', paper presented at the Annual Convention of the Rocky Mountain Psychological Association, Denver, Colorado, 13 May 1971.

STROBEL, D. A., and ZIMMERMANN, R. R. (1972), 'Responsiveness of protein deficient monkeys to manipulative stimuli', *Development Psychobiology*, Vol. 5, No. 4, pp. 291–6.

WARREN, J. M. (1966), 'Reversal learning and the formation of learning sets by cats and rhesus monkeys', *J. Comp. Physiol. Psychol.*, No. 61, pp. 421–8.

WELLS, A. M., GEIST, C. R. and ZIMMERMANN R. R. (1972) 'The influence of environmental and nutritional factors on problem solving in the rat', *Perceptual and Motor Skills*.

ZIMMERMANN, R. R. (1969), 'Effects of age, experience and malnourishment on object retention in learning set', *Perceptual and Motor Skills*, No. 28, pp.867–76.

ZIMMERMANN, R. R. (1970), 'Retention in learning set and latent memory as a function of malnutrition and deprivation', annual meeting of the Rocky Mountain Psychological Association, Salt Lake City, Utah.

ZIMMERMANN, R. R. (1973), 'Reversal learning in the developing malnourished rhesus monkey', *Behavioral Biology*, Vol. 8, No. 3, pp. 381–90.

ZIMMERMANN, R. R., STEERE, P. L., STROBEL, D. A., and HOM, H. L. (1972), 'Abnormal social development of protein-malnourished rhesus monkeys', *Journal of Abnormal Psychology*, Vol. 80, No. 2, pp. 125–31.

ZIMMERMANN, R. R., and STROBEL, D. A. (1969), 'Effects of protein malnutrition on visual curiosity, manipulation, and social behavior in the infant rhesus monkey', *Proceedings of the 77th Annual Convention of the American Psychological Association*, pp. 241–2.

ZIMMERMANN, R. R., STROBEL, D. A., and MAGUIRE, D. (1970), 'Neophobic reactions in protein malnourished infant monkeys', *Proceedings of the 78th Annual Convention of the American Psychological Association*, pp. 197–8.

ZIMMERMANN, R. R., and WELLS, A. M. (1971), 'Performance of malnourished rats on the Hebb-Williams closed field maze learning task', *Perceptual and Motor Skills*, No. 33, pp. 1043–50.

A Comparative Study of the Spontaneous Play Activities of Normal and Mentally Defective Children

Introduction

The numerous studies of children's play life reported in psychological literature have provided much valuable data on this important phase of child development. Most of these studies have been concerned with varied aspects of the play activities of normal children of pre-school and primary ages.

Our subjects were three groups of 25 children each: (a) a mixed group of normal children (14 boys and 11 girls); (b) a group of mentally defective girls; and (c) a group of mentally defective boys. The normal group was selected from the public Elementary School of Northville, Michigan, and the two mentally defective groups were selected from the population of the Wayne County Training School. The mental ages of these children ranged from 6 through 8 years, the average for the normal group being 7 years, 6 months, for the mentally defective girls 7 years, 5 months, and for the mentally defective boys 7 years, 6 months. The IQs for the normal group ranged from 93 to 114, with an average of 104. The IQs for the two mentally deficient groups ranged from 60 to 75, the average for the girls being 66, for the boys 68.

The play room used with the mentally defective groups was a large room which had formerly been used as a school room. On the west side of the room were the one-way screen for the hidden observer and a chair for the observer who remained in the room with the child. The sixteen play materials were arranged in a fixed order along the other three walls. Along the north wall were two tables, on the first of which were laid the sewing materials, consisting of cotton prints, needles, threads, scissors, pins, buttons, lace, and braid. Here also was the doll unit, a doll set upon the table and a bed placed beside the table. On the second table were the scrapbook materials – magazine pictures, paper, brads, paste, and scissors, and the drawing materials – paper, pencils, crayons, and scissors. In the north-east corner was a blackboard with coloured chalk. Against the wall opposite the observers was a table on which were placed a 70-piece brightly coloured children's jig-saw puzzle, jacks and ball, a deck of Flinch cards, and a pegboard. In the south-east corner were sixteen dozen building blocks of various shapes and sizes, a large brightly coloured ball, and a jump-rope. There were two tables along

Table 1 Description of subjects

Group (*Mental age range*)	*Number children*	*Average M.A.*	*Average C.A.*	*Average I.Q.*
Normal (*M.A.* 6–0 to 6–9)	8	6–4	6–3	101
Normal (*M.A.* 7–2 to 7–10)	9	7–6	7–2	105
Normal (*M.A.* 8–2 to 8–10)	8	8–7	8–3	104
Total Normal	25	7–6	7–2	104
Men. Def. Girls (6–1 to 6–11)	8	6–7	10–0	66
Men. Def. Girls (7–2 to 7–11)	9	7–6	11–5	66
Men. Def. Girls (8–0 to 8–8)	8	8–3	12–5	67
Total Men. Def. Girls	25	7–5	10–11	66
Men. Def. Boys (6–3 to 6–11)	8	6–8	9–9	68
Men. Def. Boys (7–1 to 7–11)	9	7–8	11–7	66
Men. Def. Boys (8–0 to 8–11)	8	8–4	11–9	71
Total Men. Def. Boys	25	7–6	11–0	68

the south wall. On the table farther from the observers were dishes of clay (red, green, grey, and brown) and a set of commercial moulds; pink, white, and blue wooden beads and a shoe string; and a vividly illustrated picture book. A miniature game of croquet mounted on wall board was placed on the last table. The centre of the room was clear.

It was discovered in trial runs with non-experimental mentally deficient children that it was necessary to provide concrete suggestions for the use of the various materials. Therefore, a sample scrapbook was presented with the scrapbook materials, a picture of a house was with the drawing materials, there was a house drawn on the blackboard, and a house was built with the blocks.

The experimental situation was almost identical for the normal group. For this group one end of the auditorium of the Northville Elementary School, partitioned from the rest of the room by curtains, was used. The play materials were arranged in the same order used with the mentally defective groups, and the observers were in the same relative places.

Only one child was brought into the play room at a time. He was accompanied from the cottage or school room by the observer, who told him that he was going to a room where there were a number of playthings and that he could play with anything there. The observer had previously become acquainted with the mentally defective subjects on the playground, and in each group the experiment was introduced by the preliminary observation of several children whose records were not included in the final data. When the play room was reached the child was shown around the room in a definite order, usually beginning with the doll and sewing table and continuing around. In two or three instances the children provided their own order. The observer talked about the materials, handled the different objects and urged the child to do so. This introductory period of approximately five minutes served to familiarize the child with the toys and with the experimental situation. When the child had seen all the materials he was led to the middle of the room and told to play with whatever he wished.

Both observers began to record when the child began his first activity. The time, the activity, the comments of the child, and the changes of activity were recorded. After the play period had begun the observer in the room initiated no conversation. She answered questions and praised work brought to her for inspection, but gave no material aid. The period was stopped at the end of thirty minutes. In some cases the child was allowed to finish the object on which he was working.

Analysis of data

The records were analysed quantitatively and qualitatively for each group and for each mental age within each group. In addition to a study of the popularity of the various play materials and of the length of play period, the various types of play activity were analysed and classified in the following five categories:

B, is constructive activity, that is, any activity in which the child 'makes something'. This includes making a doll dress, making a scrapbook, drawing a picture of a house without landscaping or figures, placing the pegs in any design on the peg board, building a house with the blocks, and stringing the beads in a pattern.

A, original constructive activity, is a special category of B. It describes all construction based on ideas not directly suggested by the materials themselves, if the idea is successfully followed through and the end product is of acceptable quality. It includes sewing anything other than a doll dress, drawing anything other than a house or drawing a house to which has been added landscaping and other details, building anything other than a house with blocks, moulding a figure in clay without using the commercial moulds, and placing the pegs in an original design. The first phrase of the definition of this category, all construction based on ideas not directly suggested by the materials themselves, provides a highly objective criterion which was followed with three exceptions, in which the product was of such poor quality as to exclude it from this category. These exceptions were: (1) an extremely poorly executed landscape drawing, (2) a crude drawing of a lined sheet of paper, (3) the writing of a few simple spelling words on the board.

C, defines activities with both games and toys. It includes dressing the doll and playing with her, putting the puzzle together, using the commercial moulds with the clay, playing croquet, playing jacks, playing with the cards, jumping rope, and playing with the ball.

D, is manipulative activity, that is, handling the materials when no real play activity results. It occurred as handling of sewing materials, random inspection of drawing and scrapbook materials, scribbling, and stringing the beads without pattern.

E, is called inspection and observation, and is applied only to periods ranging from thirty seconds to one minute. These are brief periods in which the child inspects the play material and then decides not to use it.

Miscellaneous includes brief play periods of less than thirty seconds, periods of going around the room inspecting several play materials, periods of merely talking to the observer about any subject other than the play materials, and any other unclassifiable periods of time.

Results

Results may be summarized under three headings: (a) choice of play materials, (b) length of play period, and (c) type of play activity. Table 2 lists all play materials in order of their popularity, from most popular to least popular for each group. Popularity of a given play material may be measured either in terms of time, that is, total number of minutes during which it is in use, or in terms of children, that is, number of different children who played with it. In this table the ordinal position is the average of the positions as determined by these two criteria.

Of greatest interest are the play materials at the beginning and at the end of the three lists. Among the five materials most popular with the normals three (blocks, drawing materials, chalk) are used entirely in constructive activity and a fourth, the clay, may be used either to construct figures or merely to mould pictures with the commerical moulds provided. Among the most popular materials for the mentally defective girls two in five (sewing materials, scrapbook materials) are used for constructive activity. No child in this group used the clay constructively. The mentally defective boys chose, among their five favourite play materials, only one which is used exclusively in 'making something', the scrapbook materials. The clay was used for construction in this group. There is some question whether the scrapbook materials are constructive in the same sense as are the blocks, drawing materials, chalk, clay, and sewing materials. They are, of course, used in making something, but it is doubtful whether pictures to be cut and pasted are raw materials in the same sense as clay, blocks,

Table 2 Play materials in order of popularity

Normal children			Ment. defective girls			Ment. defective boys		
Play object	Total min.	Number children	Play object	Total min.	Number children	Play object	Total min.	Number children
Blocks	141	13	Clay	95	16	Croquet	89	16
Drawing	109	9	Scrapbk	175	12	Scrapbk	108	11
Puzzle	98	10	Croquet	78	16	Pegboard	83	12
Chalk	75	11	Sewing	51	11	Clay	71	14
Clay	60	14	Pegboard	50	10	Puzzle	97	10
Beads	63	6	Drawing	62	6	Jacks	29	10
Scrapbk	63	4	Chalk	29	7	Ball	32	9
Sewing	53	5	Jacks	42	5	Sewing	36	6
Pegboard	33	7	Puzzle	24	6	Rope	33	7
Croquet	13	4	Cards	35	3	Beads	38	5
Ball	8	4	Doll	16	5	Drawing	33	5
Book	6	4	Beads	13	5	Book	21	8
Rope	4	3	Blocks	21	3	Doll	27	6
Doll	3	1	Rope	17	3	Cards	19	3
Jacks	1	1	Book	13	4	Blocks	3	3
Cards	$\frac{1}{2}$	1	Ball	7	4	Chalk	2	2

and chalk, with which the child must be able to visualize and carry through an idea, be it borrowed or original.

In their five most popular play materials the normal children included four which imply constructive activity, the mentally defective girls two or one as the scrapbook materials are included or excluded, and the mentally defective boys the same number as the girls. A composite list for the mentally defective boys and girls includes, in the order of their popularity, the croquet game, scrapbook materials, clay, pegboard, and puzzle.

The lists of least popular materials illustrate the complement of the greater preference of normal children for constructive play materials, that is, an almost complete lack of interest in toys which imply a more or less mechanical unimaginative, highly specific type of play activity. In these lists four of the five materials of the normals (book, rope, jacks, cards) are of this type; four of the five for the mentally defective girls (beads, rope, book, ball); and two of the five for the mentally defective boys (book, cards). Although these lists themselves exhibit several points of similarity, the actual amount of time spent and the number of children using the materials was markedly lower for the normal group. It should also be noted that they include, for the normals, no constructive play material, for the feeble-minded girls one (blocks), and for the feeble-minded boys two (blocks, chalk). The five least popular materials in the composite list for mentally defective boys and girls are book, rope, cards, chalk, blocks.

This difference in favourite kinds of play materials is strikingly illustrated in three instances. The blocks, which require highly constructive play, appear in first place on the list for normals, in thirteenth place on the mentally defective girls' list, and in fifteenth place on the mentally defective boys' list. The jacks, on the other hand, appear fifteenth for the normals, eighth for the mentally defective girls, and sixth for the mentally defective boys. The miniature croquet game was tenth in popularity among the normals, third among the mentally defective girls, and first among the mentally defective boys. These three toys appear in sixteenth, seventh, and first place respectively on the composite list.

Sex differences in the choice of play materials were minimal. The lists of five most popular choices for the mentally defective boys and girls show four identical choices (clay, scrapbook materials, croquet game, pegboard) with sewing the fifth for the girls and the puzzle for the boys. The lists of least popular articles for these two groups overlap in two instances (picture book, blocks); the other three materials are, for the girls, beads, rope, and ball, for the boys, doll, cards, and chalk. Although the number of boys, 14, and girls, 11, in the normal group is small and the data have therefore been presented as a unit, a comparison similar to the above is interesting. The most popular materials for the normal girls and boys overlap in three instances (drawing, chalk, clay) with the girls choosing beads and sewing rather than blocks and the puzzle to complete their list. The least popular choices were in four instances the same (doll, book, cards, jacks); the girls were comparatively uninterested in the croquet and the boys in the doll.

All data were analysed according to mental age groups, but since these groups were small (8 or 9 children) and no definite trends were apparent, they have been omitted from this report.

The data on length of play period show much less definite trends than the data on choice of play articles. One play period is defined as the total time spent with a given play material before a change of activity or material occurs. Brief interruptions of less than thirty seconds were not considered a change of activity, and similar brief periods of play with one material in the course of a change of activity were not considered as play periods, but were placed in the miscellaneous column.

The average length of play period for the normal children was 6·9 minutes, standard deviation 7·6 minutes, for the mentally defective girls 5·8 ± 5·6 minutes, and for the mentally defective boys 5·3 ± 6·1 minutes.

The single periods of the respective groups ranged from 30 seconds to 30 minutes, from 30 seconds to 28 minutes, 45 seconds, and from 30 seconds to 27 minutes, 9 seconds. The critical ratio of the difference between average length of play period for the normals and the mentally defective girls is 1·3, between the normals and the mentally defective boys 1·7, and between the two mentally defective groups 0·6. Although these critical ratios are not significant, several facts indicate a slight tendency of the normal children to be more stable in their play behaviour. The average play period is slightly longer, as indicated above. The normal group of 25 children had a total of 107 play periods, the feeble-minded girls 131, and the feeble-minded boys 138. Average number of play periods was, respectively, 4·3, 5·2, and 5·5. The tendency to stability is also apparent in the extreme intervals of the distribution of length of period. In the interval 30 seconds to 3 minutes fell 50 periods of the normals, 64 of the mentally defective girls, and 73 of the mentally defective boys. In the interval 27 minutes to 30 minutes fell five periods for the normals, and one each for the mentally defective girls and boys.

Table 3 presents statistical data on the analysis of play activity in terms

Table 3 Analysis of types of play activity

| Category | Total time in minutes | | | Per cent of time | | | Critical ratio | | |
	Normal children	Ment. defective Girls	Boys	Normal	Girls	Boys	NvsG	NvsB	BvsG
A	183	42	51	25	6	7	4·1	3·8	0·3
B*	498	341	286	68	47	40	3·3	4·6	1·2
C	182	308	393	25	42	54	2·8	4·9	2·0
D	47	74	37	7	10	5	1·0	0·4	1·5
E	5	7	7	1	1	1	—	—	—

*The category B here includes all constructive activity, whether or not the project is further scored A, that is, the total of B plus A as the two are described in the text.

of the categories defined earlier. Columns 1, 2, and 3 indicate the total amounts of time spent by the different groups in each type of activity; these are translated into percentages of total play time (excluding miscellaneous) in Columns 4, 5, and 6; and the critical ratios of the differences of these percentage values appear in Columns 7, 8, and 9.

The critical ratios show that the normal children spent a statistically significantly greater percentage of time on constructive activity in general (B) than did either of the mentally defective groups, and also in the higher type here called original constructive activity (A). These conclusions express, even more strikingly than the data concerning popularity of play materials, the decidedly greater preference of the normal children, in a spontaneous play situation, for activity in which they were creating something, as opposed to activity in which they were following a set pattern prescribed by the materials.

The mentally defective groups spent a significantly greater percentage of their time playing with games and toys (C). As would be expected from the chronological and mental age groups studied, the amount of time spent in manipulative activity (D) is small in every instance. The time falling under observation and inspection (E) is insignificant for all groups.

Data on the number of children engaging in each type of play activity show the same trends as the data on the percentage of total time. Fourteen of the twenty-five normal children, four of the feeble-minded girls, and five of the feeble-minded boys did original constructive work (A); 23 normals, 19 mentally defective girls, and 20 mentally defective boys showed constructive activity (B); 19 normals, 21 mentally defective girls, and 23 mentally defective boys played with the games and toys.

Discussion

The authors are fully aware that the unanswered questions concerning the play situation here presented are many. The effect of the presence of an adult in the playroom cannot be stated. Observation of the changes in play behaviour when two children are allowed to play together would provide an interesting follow-up study. The effects of the institutional environment of the mental defectives as compared with the home environment of the normal children remain unmeasured. This difference in environment is accompanied by differences in socio-economic status, most of the institution children having come from the lower socio-economic class, the normals from the middle class.

Perhaps most important are questions concerning the play materials. The wide differences in chronological age created a problem in the choice of materials suitable for all ages involved. That this problem was met fairly satisfactorily is evidenced by the fact that only two of the seventy-five children asked to leave the playroom before the period was ended. An obvious question centres around the relative familiarity of the different groups with the various play materials. This question cannot be answered positively, but the use of the blocks provides an interesting commentary. The blocks were identical with a set used and reported popular in the cottage of the mentally defective boys; blocks as a plaything were relatively unfamiliar to the mentally defective girls; the experiences of the normal children with building blocks were varied. Yet they were the outstanding choice of the normal children, and were quite unpopular with both groups of mental defectives.

The greater superiority of the normals in terms of spontaneous creative activity seems to be clearly demonstrated by the data. The implications of this fact are several. Theoretically, it implies that mental defectives and normals of the same mental age, that is, of the same quantitative developmental level, react differently in the face of a situation which allows the choice of an exercise of ingenuity or a stereotyped response to familiar objects.

Educationally, it would seem to emphasize the need for specificity in the training of feeble-minded children, that is, a programme in which the child is trained in the specific skills and attitudes which his vocational and social status will demand, rather than a generalized programme in which he himself is responsible for the application and transfer of his knowledge. This does not, of course, diminish the importance of a broad programme of activities in meeting problems of recreation and adjustment.

(From *The Journal of Genetic Psychology*, No. 61, 1942, pp. 33–46.)

Frustration and Regression

While the previous studies in this section have been concerned with intractable conditions, the present one has to do with situational factors depressing play.

In this investigation we have studied the effects of frustration upon behaviour by comparing the behaviour of children in a non-frustrating or free-play situation with their behaviour in a frustrating situation.

Every child was observed on two occasions. First, the child was placed in a standardized playroom and allowed to play without restriction. On a second occasion he was placed in the same room and with the same toys. However, on this second occasion there were also in the room a number of highly attractive, *but inaccessible*, toys. The latter arrangement was provided by replacing a temporary wall of the original room with a wire-net partition through which the subject could easily see the fine toys but through which locomotion was impossible.

Procedures

The subjects in the experiment were children (ages 25–61 months) who attended the pre-school laboratories of the Iowa Child Welfare Research Station.

Free-play situation

The arrangement of the experimental room in the free-play situation is as follows. On the floor of the room there were three squares of paper, each 24 by 24 in. A set of standardized play materials was placed on each square. On one square there were the following things: a little chair on which a Teddy bear and a doll were seated, a cup, a small truck and trailer, a saucer, a teapot without a lid, an ironing board and an iron (but nothing to iron), and a telephone receiver which squeaked when shaken. On another square were placed a box of crayons and two pieces of writing paper 8½ by 11 in. On the third square there were a small wooden motorboat, a sailboat, a celluloid duck and frog, and a fishing pole with a line and a magnet for a hook.

After entering the experimental room with the child, the experimenter approached Square 1, and picking up each toy said, 'Look, here are some things to play with. Here is a Teddy bear and a doll. Here is an iron to iron with,' etc. In proceeding this way, the experimenter named and demonstrated every toy on all three squares. Then he said, 'You can play with everything. You can do whatever you like with the toys, and I'll sit down here and do my lesson.' The experimenter then sat on the chair at the table.

The child was left to play alone for a 30-minute period. During this time the experimenter, as if occupied with his own work, sat at his table in the corner and took notes on the child's behaviour.

Pre-frustration period. – In the pre-frustration period, the partition dividing the room was lifted so that the room was twice the size it had been in the free-play situation.

The squares were in their places, but all toys except the crayons and paper had been incorporated into an elaborate and attractive set of toys in the part of the room that had been behind the partition.

In one corner there was a big doll-house (3 by 3 ft.). It was brightly decorated and large enough to admit the child. Inside there was a bed upon which the doll was lying, a chair in which the Teddy bear sat, a stove with cooking utensils, and a cupboard. The ironing board with the iron on it stood against one wall, and the telephone, this time on its base with a dial and bell, was in a corner. The house had electric lights, curtains, and a carpet.

Outside the house there was a laundry line on which the doll's clothes hung. A rubber rabbit sat near the entrance to the house, and behind it was the small truck and trailer used in the preceding experiment. Near by there was a child's table prepared for a luncheon party. On the table there were cups, saucers, dishes, spoons, forks, knives, a small empty teapot, and a large teapot with water in it.

In the other corner of the new part of the room there was a toy lake (3 by 3 ft.) filled with real water. It contained an island with a lighthouse, a wharf, a ferryboat, small boats, fishes, ducks, and frogs. The lake had sand beaches.

In all cases the children showed great interest in the new toys and at once started to investigate them. Each child was left entirely free to explore and play as he wished. During this time, the experimenter did his 'lesson'.

The pre-frustration period was designed to develop for the child a highly desirable goal which he could later be prevented from reaching. This was a prerequisite to creating frustration.

The transition from pre-frustration to frustration was made in the following way. The experimenter collected in a basket all the play materials which had been used in the free-play experiment and distributed them, as before, on the squares of paper. He then approached the child and said, 'And now let's play at the other end,' pointing to the 'old' part of the room. The child went or was led to the other end and the experimenter lowered the wire partition and fastened it by means of a large padlock. The part of the room containing the new toys was now physically inaccessible but visible through the wire netting.

Frustration period. – With the lowering of the partition, the frustration period began. This part of the experiment was conducted exactly as the free-play experiment. The experimenter wrote at his table, leaving the child completely free to play or not as he desired. The child's questions were answered, but the experimenter remained aloof from the situation in as natural a manner as possible.

Thirty minutes after the lowering of the partition, the experimenter suggested that the child leave.

Post-frustration situation. – After the experimenter had made sure that the child wanted to leave, the partition was lifted. Usually the child was pleasantly surprised and, forgetting his desire to leave, joyfully hurried over to the fine toys.

The raw data consisted of two synchronized running accounts of the course of events, one made by an observer behind a one-way vision screen, the other by the experimenter. These separate records were combined into a single, more complete, account.

Both the free-play situation and the frustration situation produced two general kinds of behaviour: (*a*) occupation with accessible goals, and (*b*) activities in the direction of inaccessible goals. We shall call the first 'free activities' and the second 'barrier and escape behaviour'.

Type of Behaviour

Free activities. – The free activity includes play with the accessible toys and diversions with non-toy objects.

Diversions, i.e. occupation with non-toy objects, include the following: (*a*) *Activities with the experimenter* (other than those which are social attempts to reach the inaccessible toys or to escape from the experimental situation). This behaviour takes the form of conversation with the experimenter, helping him with his 'lessons', and playing with him. It has been mentioned before that every effort was made not to encourage these contacts. (*b*) *Activities at the window*: climbing upon the sill and looking out. (*c*) *'Island' behaviour*: Despite our continual vigilance in excluding any but standardized objects from the room, the children were forever finding additional material – e.g. a nail or a piece of string – or selecting for special attention some indifferent object in the room, as the light switch or a crack in the floor. Such objects not infrequently appeared to have the significance of a foreign object to the child, e.g. one not naturally connected with the rest of the situation, and as such to provide a refuge or an island of escape within the situation. (*d*) *Looking and wandering about.* (*e*) *Disturbances*: reactions to outside noises, lights failing, etc.

Barrier and escape behaviour. – Both attempts to gain access to the toys behind the barrier and attempts to leave the experimental situation may entail (*a*) actual physical approaches to the inaccessible regions, such as trying to lift or climb over the barrier or kicking the door; (*b*) social attempts by means of requests, pleadings, coaxing, threats, etc., to get the experimenter to raise the barrier or open the door; or (*c*) passively directed actions such as looking at or talking about the inaccessible toys or the outside regions.

Overlapping activities. – A subject can be involved in more than one activity simultaneously; e.g. he may ask to have the barrier raised while swinging the fish line; in these cases we speak about 'overlapping regions of activity'. A type of overlapping behaviour of special importance to us exists when play and non-play activities overlap. We will call this 'secondary play'. Primary play, on the other hand, occurs when the subject gives the play his complete attention.

Substitute behaviour. – Passive barrier and escape behaviour frequently seemed to be in the nature of a substitute for playing with the inaccessible toys or for leaving the experimental situation. This was particularly true of conversation about the inaccessible objects. Active barrier and escape behaviour also seemed sometimes to be a substitution; e.g. 'fishing' through the barrier, throwing the accessible toys into the inaccessible region, playing that the accessible portion of the room was a part of the inaccessible part, etc.

Constructiveness scale. – One can distinguish variations in the type of play on a continuum ranging from rather primitive, simple, little-structured activities to elaborate, imaginative, highly developed play. In our experiment, constructiveness was rated on a seven-point scale (2 to 8) devised to be applicable to occupations with all the toys.

To demonstrate the use of this scale, we present a few examples of various constructiveness levels with the same toy, the truck and trailer. Our remarks are not definitions of the various constructiveness levels. They are intended merely to point to some characteristics of these specific examples.

Constructiveness 2. The toys are examined superficially. Example: Sits on floor and takes truck and trailer in hand. 10 sec.

Constructiveness 3. The truck is moved to a definite place or from one place to another. Example: Phone, truck and trailer, manipulated and carried to window sill. 25 sec.

Constructiveness 4. This is a somewhat more complicated manipulation of the truck. Example: Truck and trailer backed under chair. 15 sec.

Constructiveness 5. This is definitely a more complicated and elaborated manipulation of the truck. Example: Truck and trailer unloaded, detached; pulled in circles, re-attached, detached, re-attached; pulled in circles. 45 sec.

Constructiveness 6. The truck is used as a means to haul other things. Example: Takes truck and trailer. 'More things are going to be hauled.' Puts cup, saucer, teapot on trailer. Talks to self. 'Ride along, mister.' To square 3. 60 sec.

Constructiveness 7. The meaning of the play is an extensive 'trip' or another elaborated story in which the handling of the truck is merely a part of a larger setting. Example: 'Here's a car truck, and its going out fishing, so we have to take the trailer off. First, we have to go to the gas station. Toot! Toot! Now, he's going to the gas station. Ding, ding, ding.' Gets gas. Now back for the trailer and the fish pole; child has truck and takes the motor boat. Attaches it to truck and trailer. 'Hmmmm! Here he goes.' Behind Square 2 to 1. 'Quack! Quack! Mr Ducky come' (places on truck and trailer). Goes to Square 3. 'Here's the sailboat.' 225 sec.

Constructiveness 8. Play showing more than usual originality is placed here. Example: To Square 1. Truck and trailer reattached. 'I'll bring them here.' Detaches truck, has it coast down trailer as an incline, re-attaches. 30 sec.

Table 1 Average time in seconds occupied by different activities in free play and in frustration

Activity	Mean time		Difference	Difference σ difference
	Free play	*Frustration*		
Barrier behaviour	19·50	510·50	+491·00*	11·47
Primary play	1144·17	569·83	−574·34	8·88
Secondary play	33·12	128·16	+95·04	4·00
Escape behaviour	49·67	112·67	+63·00	2·68
Diversions	177·17	204·17	+27·00	†

* + indicates increase in frustration; − indicates decrease in frustration.
† Not computed.

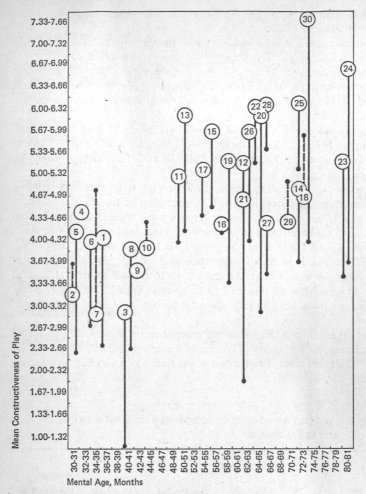

Fig. 1. The relation between mean constructiveness of play and mental age and the change of constructiveness in the frustration situation. (1) The mean constructiveness of (primary plus secondary) play in the free-play situation is indicated for each child by a circle. The number given is that of the subject. (2) The mean constructiveness of play in the frustration situation is indicated by a dot. (3) Change in constructiveness from the free-play to the frustration situation is designated by a solid line when constructiveness decreases in frustration, by a broken line when constructiveness increases. The absence of a dot indicates no change in mean constructiveness for that child.

Results

Frequency of Various Activities in Free-play and Frustration Situations. – Although the same types of behaviour occurred in both experimental situations, their frequency of occurrence changed greatly from free play to frustration. The amount of time occupied with different activities is shown in Table 1.

Average Constructiveness of Play in Free Play and Frustration. – The mean constructiveness of the play of each child in free play and in frustration is shown in the correlation chart, Fig. 1. These data include all play, both primary and secondary. The mean constructiveness of play in free play is 4.99 constructiveness points and in frustration, 3.94 points. The mean regression is 1.05 constructiveness points with a standard error of 0.24, i.e. the mean regression is 4.39 times its standard error. Stated in terms of mental-age equivalents, i.e. in terms of the regression of constructiveness upon mental age, the mean regression amounts to 17.3 months of mental age. Twenty-two of the subjects regressed in the constructiveness of their play, three did not change, and five increased.

Analysis of the results for primary play alone indicates that the mean regression in constructiveness, although less in amount, is statistically significant.

These data establish rather definitely the fact that a frustrating situation of the kind considered here reduces, on the average, the constructiveness of play below the level upon which it normally occurs in a non-frustrating, free-play situation.

(From *Child Behaviour and Development*, eds R. G. Barker, J. S. Kounin, and H. F. Wright, McGraw Hill, New York, 1943. Also in *University of Iowa Studies in Child Welfare*, Vol. 18, No. 386, 1941.)

Play and the World of Symbols

Part Four deals with play and the world of symbols. In it we reach the heart of play as distinctively human. The papers on pretend, on language, on creativity, and on civilization represent a variety of approaches ranging from the observation of higher primates, through experimental exercises on creativity, on to the deep insights of anthropologists, philosophers, and poets.*

Students of behaviour have never quite known what to do with 'make-believe' and fiction, perhaps because it is difficult to make sober sense of them. Herbert Simon's book *The Sciences of the Artificial* notes how hard it is to say what is 'real' in human affairs and what is 'make-believe'. We wake in the morning to an alarm clock marking abstract Newtonian time. Once up, we read the newspaper's selective representation of reality, and pay for its delivery each month with a slip of paper on which we have signed our name – a cheque. We scan the stock-market quotations, a consensus of man's guesses about the future. What matters is not just the symbolic act, but the consequences that ensue. And they are real – a theme explored in the paper on deep play by Clifford Geertz.

It is a chronic source of embarrassment to decide firmly what is real and what make-believe. Some of what we take to be make-believe are the most deeply serious things in our lives. How can we handle hostility? Or sexuality? Are we serious or playing a game? Philosophers have come increasingly to study the game-like rules governing our ordinary lives. Some actions can only be interpreted by their lack of any conventional code. Can we talk about them as play or as fiction? Yet fiction requires a verisimilitude to be regarded as fiction, a surrealism. Child's play too has rules of verisimilitude, as Catherine Garvey so vividly shows.

The first paper on 'Pretend Play' astonishes us; we are not the only creatures who 'make-believe'. Viki, a domesticated chimpanzee, is en

---

* Papers published after 1973 are not included in this collection. Since then, the literature on social and symbolic play has grown by leaps and bounds. Scholarly conferences have explored the theoretical importance of play and many groups such as the Preschool Playgroup Association and the Toy Library Association have been concerned with its practical relevance.

route to the world of symbols. Clyde Kluckhohn (1949) described primitive societies as a 'mirror for man', man seeing himself in different manifestations. Primate studies are a mirror as well, with a time dimension whereby we see not only our present selves but our evolutionary part.

The classic paper by Lev Vygotsky probes into the props of make-believe, the pivots that allow passage from the real to the fictive. Jean Piaget looks at the development of symbolic play in light of the twin processes of assimilation and accommodation. He considers how children assimilate reality to the schemas they form and how reality itself becomes a construction.

The remaining papers in the opening section are evocative documentations of 'pretend' in human lives. First there is Auden's recognition that even the fantasy play of children has about it a quality of necessity. So too with the liveliness – in the literal sense of live – in the character games played by Simone de Beauvoir and her sister and Dylan Thomas and his cat-hunting friend Jim.

The last paper in the section on pretend play documents the way in which one boy turned his aggressive play into an art form. Child art is 'action painting' in a very real sense and is often accompanied by sounds and actions appropriate to the theme. Here, as in the studies of monkeys, it appears that play allows, even encourages, aggressive impulses that might in uncontained form be disruptive.

The second section on 'Play and Language' tells of how language increases the range of play. For not only does it provide a means of representing reality, but makes it possible to turn reality on its head. Kornei Chukosvky illuminates the ways in which nonsense verse and riddles turn reality inside out. But meta-linguistic play is found in the crib, too, as Ruth Weir describes in her powerful study of her son's language play after the lights are out. Instead of playing with objects, he plays with words, the representations of objects. Such play is directed at the very nature of grammar. The child pushes its rules to the limit, even to producing what Nelson Goodman has called the 'counterfactual conditional' (1951) for dealing with events that might have happened. 'What would it have been like if the first man had done X?'

The roots of our ability to use language for representing the real and the totally fictive are treated in the second section. It closes with Peter Reynolds' conjecture, shared by many of us, that language and play are causally intertwined in our evolutionary past.

If play fosters make-believe, it is no surprise that it is thought to be intimately tied to creativity. Although we are all capable of recognizing the fruits of creativity, the process defies analysis, perhaps because its practice is a mix of spontaneity and novelty on the one hand and constraint on the other. The third section 'Play and Creativity' explores this mix, beginning with the most elusive element in the creative product, its surprise. Arthur Koestler next comments on the processes that produce the ordinary association that ties things together as opposed to bisociation that drives them into new corners of novelty, surprise and delight. It is probably fair to say, despite Koestler's brave and challenging effort, that creativity not only defies explanation, it defies description too.

The essays in the final section on 'Play and Civilization' explore how civilization itself may reflect the manner in which man's play forms his conceptions of reality and leads him to shape institutions in support of that formation.

References

GOODMAN, N. (1951), *The Structure of Appearances*, M.I.T. Press.
KLUCKHOHN, C. (1949), *Mirror for Man*, McGraw-Hill.
SIMON, H. *The Sciences of the Artificial*, M.I.T. Press.

A Pretend Play

The Imaginary Pulltoy

Viki was a young chimpanzee raised in a human family from early infancy. Her surrogate mother kept careful record of her development, noting especially her more human achievements.

The singular events which I am about to relate find no parallel in chimpanzee literature or in the experience of my friends who work with apes. This story might better be told by a writer of detective fiction, or a psychiatrist, but since it must be told by me, only a bewildered mother, I shall tell it straight with no attempt to analyse, explain, or further confuse an already baffling mystery.

It all started on an unseasonably warm day in January. I was dozing over a book in the big chair while through the open bathroom door I watched Viki at play. She was supposed to be sitting on her potty, but while not yet completely trained, she always reaches the potty in time and so is permitted to play in the vicinity with her pants off when action is .expected. She swings from the towel racks, bangs the door of the medicine cabinet, and snuggles into the wash basin. Most frequently of all she runs in circles around the toilet.

On the sunny afternoon our story begins, I sat lulled by the bird song and the sunshine when suddenly I became aware that Viki's monkey-jungle activity had stopped. She seemed to be absorbed in a brand-new game. Very slowly and deliberately she was marching around the toilet, trailing the fingertips of one hand on the floor. Now and then she paused, glanced back at the hand, and then resumed her progress.

'What are you doing, Viki?' I called, and was instantly sorry that I had. For she stopped short with a rapid look of guilt and embarrassment. Then she pretended to be very busy examining a knob which juts out from a pipe behind the toilet.

During the next couple of days Viki often played this new game, but now she paused frequently to make sure that I was not watching her. She has always practised games on the sly, permitting no one to join her or even to watch until she has attained considerable skill or established the rules of the game.

Watching her cautiously so as not to be apprehended, I thought at first that she might merely be enjoying the vibrations from her fingertips as they scratched along the linoleum. But gradually I remembered where I had seen her act this way. Viki was at the pulltoy stage when a child is for ever trailing some toy on a string, when everything with a string attached becomes a pulltoy. Dragging wagons, shoes, dolls, or purses, her body assumed just this angle. She trudged along just this busily on two feet and one hand, while the other arm extended backward this way to pull the toy. Viki had an imaginary pulltoy!

No sooner had I arrived at this amazing deduction than she interrupted the sport one day in turn and make a series of tugging motions. That is, they would have been called tugging had there been a rope to tug, which of course there was not. She moved her hands over and around the plumbing knob in a very mysterious fashion; then placing both her fists one above the other in line with the knob, she strained backward as in tug of war. Eventually there was a little jerk and off she went again, trailing what to my mind could only be an imaginary pulltoy. This incident had convinced me that my hypothesis was correct.

Still I was reluctant to believe what I had seen until Viki found a new game to play with her imaginary toy. She dearly love to 'fish'. Standing on the furniture, she pulls up from the floor any plaything with a string tied to it. Now from the potty she began to raise the 'pulltoy' hand over hand by its invisible rope. Then she lowered it gently and 'fished' it up again.

As a mother I had to face it. Was this the beginnings of imaginative genius, or a budding psychosis? Imagination or hallucination?

Soon the movements took place all through the day, whether or not I was watching, with either hand or in either direction. She often transferred the 'rope' to the other hand, and reversed direction as she ran. But it never happened except around the toilet.

Early in February the thing reached a climax in what was to date the oddest event of our life together. It remains in my memory as a symbol of the affectionate rapport between us and the tragedy of the language barrier which separates us.

It was one of those days when Viki loves me to distraction. All day long she had pestered me to hold her. She had pattered along in my shadow and cuddled close when I came to rest. At every little crisis she called for 'mama', and was very much the helpless baby. Late in the afternoon I was combing my hair before the bathroom mirror while Viki dragged the unseen pulltoy around the toilet. I was scarcely noticing what had become commonplace, until she stopped once more at the knob and struggled with the invisible tangled rope. But this time she gave up after exerting very little effort. She sat down abruptly with her hands extended as if holding a taut cord. She looked up at my face in the mirror and then she called loudly, 'Mama! Mama!'

Suddenly I was frightened by the eerie quality of the whole business, but I felt that I must play along for the sake of our future harmony. I said with a smile, 'Here, let me help you.'

Acting out an elaborate pantomine I took the rope from her hands and, with much pulling and manipulation, untangled it from the plumbing. I dared not meet her eye until I held out to her the rope which neither of us could see (I think). 'Here you are, little one,' I said.

Then I saw the expression on her face. In a human mute it might have been called a look of sheer devotion, of appreciation for understanding. In addition a tiny smile played on her lips. And her whole face reflected the wonder in children's faces when they are astonished at a grown-up's enthusiastic escape into make-believe. I have heard children say, 'It isn't really true, you know. It's just a game.'

But perhaps Viki's look was just a good hard stare.

In any event it was only there for a spellbound second. Then her funny little face crinkled into a grin and she tore off around the toilet faster than every before, dragging her imaginary toy behind her. I just stood there, feeling very eccentric indeed.

After this I decided to get into the fun. One day as she played on the couch in a confusion of toys, I began to walk up and down the room, trailing a ghostly pulltoy of my own. But my toy had sound effects. It went 'clackety clackety' on the bare floor, had to be hoisted on to the rug, and there it went 'squush squush'. In a little while Viki began to stare at me. She jumped off the couch and came running, not to me but to my toy. I stopped and she stopped also, at exactly the spot my invisible rope met my imaginary pulltoy. She stared transfixed and then uttered her awestruck 'Boo!'

The final episode occurred the very next day. Once again I was pulling my toy across the floor while Viki played on the couch. She noticed me and seemed about to come down. Then she began to worry, flopping prone on the couch and rocking nervously. I went on walking, glancing back, and going 'clackety clackety' and 'squush squush'. Finally her eyebrows came together in great anxiety and she cried, 'Oo oo, oo oo,' as distressed as I have ever seen her. When I passed close by, she made a flying leap into my arms.

Had she had enough of a good thing? Did she resent my usurping of her game? Was she frustrated by my unique ability to produce sound effects? Did she recognize that make-believe is fun for a baby, but dangerous in a parent? Or have I misinterpreted the whole mystery? I shall probably never know, for on that day the imaginary pulltoy disappeared from our home never to be played with again.

(From *The Ape in Our House*, Gollancz, 1952.)

Play and its Role in the Mental Development of the Child

In speaking of play and its role in the pre-schooler's development, we are concerned with two fundamental questions: first, how play itself arises in development – its origin and genesis; second, the role of this developmental activity, which we call play, as a form of development in the child of pre-school age. Is play the leading form of activity for a child of this age, or is it simply the predominant form?

It seems to me that from the point of view of development, play is not the predominant form of activity, but is, in a certain sense, the leading source of development in pre-school years.

Let us now consider the problem of play itself. We know that the definition of play on the basis of the pleasure it gives the child is not correct for two reasons – first, because we deal with a number of activities which give the child much keener experiences of pleasure than play.

For example, the pleasure principle applies equally well to the sucking process, in that the child derives functional pleasure from sucking a pacifier even when he is not being satiated.

On the other hand, we know of games in which the activity process itself does not afford pleasure – games which predominate at the end of pre-school and the beginning of school age and which only give pleasure if the child finds the result interesting; these are, for example, sporting games (not only athletic sports, but also games with an outcome, games with results). They are very often accompanied by a keen sense of displeasure when the outcome is unfavourable to the child.

Thus, defining play on the basis of pleasure can certainly not be regarded as correct.

Nonetheless it seems to me that to refuse to approach the problem of play from the standpoint of fulfilment of the child's needs, his incentives to act, and his affective aspirations would result in a terrible intellectualization of play. The trouble with a number of theories of play lies in their tendency to intellectualize the problem.

I am inclined to give an even more general meaning to the problem; and I think that the mistake of a large number of accepted theories is their disregard for the child's needs – taken in the broadest sense, from inclinations to interests, as needs of an intellectual nature – or, more briefly, the disregard of everything that can come under the category of incentives and motives for action. We often describe a child's development as the development of his intellectual functions, i.e. every child stands before us as a theoretical being who, according to the higher or lower level of his intellectual development, moves from one age stage to another.

Without a consideration of the child's needs, inclinations, incentives, and motives to act – as research has demonstrated – there will never be any advance from one stage to the next. It seems to me that an analysis of play should start with an examination of these particular aspects.

It seems that every advance from one age stage to another is connected with an abrupt change in motives and incentives to act.

What is of the greatest interest to the infant has almost ceased to interest the toddler. This maturing of new needs and new motives for action is, of course, the dominant factor, especially as it is impossible to ignore the fact that a child satisfies certain needs and incentives in play, and without understanding the special character of these incentives we cannot imagine the uniqueness of that type of activity which we call play.

At pre-school age special needs and incentives arise which are highly important to the whole of the child's development and which are spontaneously expressed in play. In essence, there arise in a child of this age large numbers of unrealizable tendencies and immediately unrealizable desires. A very young child tends to gratify his desires immediately. Any delay in fulfilling them is hard for him and is acceptable only within certain narrow limits; no one has met a child under three who wanted to do something a few days hence. Ordinarily, the interval between the motive and its realization is extremely short. I think that if there were no development in pre-school years of needs that cannot be realized immediately, there would be no play. Experiments show that the development of play is arrested both in intellectually under-developed children and in those with an immature affective sphere.

From the viewpoint of the affective sphere, it seems to me that play is invented at the point when unrealizable tendencies appear in development. This is the way a very young child behaves: he wants a thing and must have it at once. If he cannot have it, either he throws a temper tantrum, lies on the floor and kicks his legs, or he is refused, pacified, and does not get it. His unsatisfied desires have their own particular modes of substitution, rejection, etc. Towards the beginning of pre-school age, unsatisfied desires and tendencies that cannot be realized immediately make their appearance, while the tendency to immediate fulfilment of desires, characteristic of the preceding stage, is retained. For example, the child wants to be in his mother's place, or wants to be a rider on a horse. This desire cannot be fulfilled right now. What does the very young child do if he sees a passing cab and wants to ride in it whatever may happen? If he is a spoiled and capricious child, he will demand that his mother put him in the cab at any cost or he may throw himself on the ground right there in the street, etc. If he is an obedient child, used to renouncing his desires, he will go away, or his mother will offer him some candy, or simply distract him with some stronger effect and he will renounce his immediate desire.

In contrast to this, a child over three will show his own particular conflicting tendencies; on the one hand, a large number of long-term needs and desires will appear, which cannot be fulfilled at once but which, nevertheless, are not passed over like whims; on the other hand, the tendency towards immediate realization of desires is almost completely retained.

Henceforth play occurs such that the explanation of why a child plays must always be interpreted as the imaginary, illusory realization of unrealizable desires. Imagination is a new formation which is not present in the consciousness of the very young child, is totally absent in animals, and represents a specifically human form of conscious activity. Like all functions of consciousness, it originally arises from action. The old adage that child's play is imagination in action can be reversed: we can say that imagination in adolescents and schoolchildren is play without action.

It is difficult to imagine that an incentive compelling a child to play is really just the same kind of affective incentive as sucking a pacifier is for an infant.

It is hard to accept that pleasure derived from pre-school play is conditioned by the same affective mechanism as simple sucking of a pacifier. This simply does not fit our notions of pre-school development.

All of this is not to say that play occurs as the result of each and every unsatisfied desire: the child wanted to ride in a cab, the wish was not immediately gratified, so the child went into his room and began to play cabs. It never happens in just this way. Here we are concerned with the fact that the child not only has individual affective reactions to separate phenomena, but generalized, unpredesignated, affective tendencies. Let us take the example of a microcephalic child suffering from an acute inferiority complex; he is unable to participate in children's groups, he has been so teased that he smashes every mirror and pane of glass showing his reflection. But when he was very young it had been very different; then, every time he was teased there was a separate affective reaction for each separate occasion which had not yet become generalized. At pre-school age the child generalizes his affective relation to the phenomenon regardless of the actual concrete situation because the affective relation is connected with the meaning of the phenomenon in that it continually reveals his inferiority complex.

Play is essentially wish fulfilment, not, however, isolated wishes but generalized affects. A child at this age is conscious of his relationships with adults, he reacts to them affectively, but in contrast to early childhood he now generalizes these affective reactions (he respects adult authority in general, etc.).

The presence of such generalized affects in play does not mean that the child himself understands the motives which give rise to the game or that he does it consciously. He plays without realizing the motives of the play activity. In this, play differs substantially from work and other forms of activity. On the whole, it can be said that motives, actions, and incentives belong to a more abstract sphere and only become accessible to consciousness at the transitional age. Only an adolescent can clearly account to himself the reason for which he does this or that.

We will leave the problem of the affective aspect for the moment – considering it as given – and will now examine the development of play activity itself.

I think that in finding criteria for distinguishing a child's play activity from his other general forms of activity it must be accepted that in play a child creates an imaginary situation. This is possible on the basis of the separation of the fields of vision and meaning which appears in the pre-school period.

This is not a new idea, in the sense that imaginary situations in play have always been recognized, but they were always regarded as one of the groups of play activities. Thus the imaginary situation was always classified as a secondary symptom. In the view of older writers, the imaginary situation was not the criterial attribute of play in general, but only an attribute of a given group of play activities.

I find three main flaws in this argument. First, there is the danger of an intellectualistic approach to play. If play is to be understood as symbolic, there is the danger that it might turn into a kind of activity akin to algebra in action; it would be transformed into a system of signs generalizing actual reality. Here we find nothing specific to play, and look upon the child as an unsuccessful algebraist who cannot yet write the symbols on paper, but depicts them in action. It is essential to show the connection with incentives in play, since play itself, in my view, is never symbolic action in the proper sense of the term.

Second, I feel that this idea presents play as a cognitive process. It stresses the importance of the cognitive process while neglecting not only the affective situation but also the circumstances of the child's activity.

Third, it is vital to discover exactly what this activity does for development, i.e. how the imaginary situation can assist in the child's development.

Let us begin with the second question, as I have already briefly touched on the problem of the connection with affective incentives. We observed that in the affective incentives leading to play there are the beginnings not of symbols but of the necessity for an imaginary situation; for if play is really developed from unsatisfied desires, if ultimately it is the realization in play form of tendencies that cannot be realized at the moment, then elements of imaginary situations will involuntarily be included in the affective nature of play itself.

Let us take the second instance first – the child's activity in play. What does a child's behaviour in an imaginary situation mean? We know that there is a form of play, distinguished long ago and relating to the late preschool period, and considered to develop mainly at school age: namely, the development of games with rules. A number of investigators, although not at all belonging to the camp of dialectical materialists, have approached this area along the lines recommended by Marx when he said that 'the anatomy of man is the key to the anatomy of the ape'. They have begun their examination of early play in the light of later rule-based play and have concluded from this that play involving an imaginary situation is, in fact, rule-based play. It seems to me that one can go even further and propose that there is no such thing as play without rules and the child's particular attitude towards them.

Let us expand on this idea. Take any form of play with an imaginary situation. The imaginary situation already contains rules of behaviour, although this is not a game with formulated rules laid down in advance. The child imagines herself to be the mother and the doll the child, so she must obey the rules of maternal behaviour. This was very well demonstrated by a researcher in an ingenious experiment based on Sully's famous observations. The latter described play as remarkable in that children could make the play situation and reality coincide. One day two sisters, aged five and seven, said to each other: 'Let's play sisters.' Here Sully was describing a case where two sisters were playing at being sisters, i.e. playing at reality. The above-mentioned experiment based its method on children's play, suggested by the experimenter, which dealt with real relationships. In certain cases I have found it very easy to call forth such play in children. It is very easy, for example, to make a child play with its mother at being a child while the mother is the mother, i.e. at what is, in fact, true. The vital difference in play, as Sully describes it, is that the child in playing tries to be a sister. In life the child behaves without thinking that she is her sister's sister. She never behaves with respect to the other just because she is her sister – except perhaps in those cases when her mother says, 'Give in to her.' In the game of sisters playing at 'sisters', however, they are both concerned with displaying their sisterhood; the fact that two sisters decided to play sisters makes them both acquire rules of behaviour. (I must always be a sister in relation to the other sister in the whole play situation.) Only actions which fit these rules are acceptable to the play situation.

In the game a situation is chosen which stresses the fact that these girls are sisters: they are dressed alike, they walk about holding hands – in short, they enact whatever emphasizes their relationship as sisters vis-à-vis adults and strangers. The elder, holding the younger by the hand, keeps telling her about other people: 'That is theirs, not ours.' This means: 'My sister and I act the same, we are treated the same, but others are treated differently.' Here the emphasis is on the sameness of everything which is concentrated in the child's concept of a sister, and this means that my sister stands in a different relationship to me than other people. What passes unnoticed by the child in real life becomes a rule of behaviour in play.

If play, then, were structured in such a way that there were no imaginary situation, what would remain? The rules would remain. The child would begin to behave in this situation as the situation dictates.

Let us leave this remarkable experiment for a moment and turn to play in general. I think that wherever there is an imaginary situation in play there are rules. Not rules which are formulated in advance and which change during the course of the game, but rules stemming from the imaginary situation. Therefore to imagine that a child can behave in an imaginary situation without rules, i.e. as he behaves in a real situation, is simply impossible. If the child is playing the role of a mother, then she has rules of maternal behaviour. The role the child fulfils, and her relationship to the object if the object has changed its meaning, will always stem from the rules, i.e. the imaginary situation will always contain rules. In play the child is free. But this is an illusory freedom.

While at first the investigator's task was to disclose the hidden rules in all play with an imaginary situation, we have received proof comparatively recently that the so-called pure games with rules (played by school-children and late pre-schoolers) are essentially games with imaginary situations; for just as the imaginary situation has to contain rules of behaviour, so every game with rules contains an imaginary situation. For example, what does it mean to play chess? To create an imaginary situation. Why? Because the knight, the king, the queen and so forth, can only move in specified ways; because covering and taking pieces are purely chess concepts; and so on. Although it does not directly substitute for real-life relationships, nevertheless we do have a kind of imaginary situation here.

Take the simplest children's game with rules. It immediately turns into an imaginary situation in the sense that as soon as the game is regulated by certain rules, a number of actual possibilities for action are ruled out.

Just as we were able to show at the beginning that every imaginary situation contains rules in a concealed form, we have also succeeded in demonstrating the reverse – that every game with rules contains an imaginary situation in a concealed form. The development from an overt imaginary situation and covert rules to games with overt rules and a covert imaginary situation outlines the evolution of children's play from one pole to the other.

All games with imaginary situations are simultaneously games with rules and vice versa. I think this thesis is clear.

However there is one misunderstanding which may arise and which must be cleared up from the start. A child learns to behave according to certain rules from the first few months of life. For a very young child such rules, for example, that he has to sit quietly at the table, not touch other people's things, obey his mother, are rules which make up his life. What is specific to rules followed in games or play? It seems to me that several new publications can be of great aid in solving this problem. In particular, a new work of Piaget has been extremely helpful to me. This work is concerned with the development in the child of moral rules. One part is specially devoted to the study of rules of a game, where, I think, Piaget resolves these difficulties very convincingly.

Piaget distinguishes what he calls two moralities in the child – two distinct sources for the development of rules of behaviour.

This emerges particularly sharply in games. As Piaget shows, some rules come to the child from the one-sided influence upon him of an adult. Not to touch other people's things is a rule taught by the mother, or to sit quietly at the table is an external law for the child advanced by adults. This is one of the child's moralities. Other rules arise, according to Piaget, from mutual collaboration between adult and child, or between children themselves. These are rules which the child himself participates in establishing.

The rules of games, of course, differ radically from rules of not touching and of sitting quietly. In the first place they are made by the child himself; they are his own rules, as Piaget says, rules of self-restraint and self-determination. The child tells himself: I must behave in such and such a way in this game. This is quite different from the child saying that one thing is allowed and another thing is not. Piaget has pointed out a very interesting phenomenon in moral development – something which he calls moral realism. He indicates that the first line of development of external rules (what is and is not allowed) produces moral realism, i.e. a confusion in the child between moral rules and physical rules. The child confuses the fact that it is impossible to light a match a second time and the rule that it is forbidden to light matches at all, or to touch a glass because it might break: all 'don'ts' are the same to a very young child, but he has an entirely different attitude to rules which he makes up himself.*

Let us turn now to the role of play and its influence on a child's development. I think it is enormous.

I will try to outline two basic ideas. I think that play with an imaginary situation is something essentially new, impossible for a child under three; it is a novel form of behaviour in which the child is liberated from situational constraints through his activity in an imaginary situation.

To a considerable extent the behaviour of a very young child – and, to an absolute extent, that of an infant – is determined by the conditions in which the activity takes place, as the experiments of Lewin and others have shown. Lewin's experiment with the stone is a famous example.† This is a real illustration of the extent to which a very young child is bound in every action by situational constraints. Here we find a highly characteristic feature of a very young child's behaviour in the sense of his attitude towards the circumstance at hand and the real conditions of his activity. It is hard to imagine a greater contrast to Lewin's experiments showing the situational constraints on activity than what we observe in play. In the latter, the child acts in a mental and not a visible situation. I think this conveys accurately what occurs in play. It is here that the child learns to act in a cognitive, rather than an externally visible, realm, relying on internal tendencies and motives, and not on incentives supplied by external things. I recall a study by Lewin on the motivating nature of things for a very young child; in it Lewin concludes that things dictate to the child what he must do: a door demands to be opened and closed, a staircase to be run up, a bell to be rung. In short, things have an inherent motivating force in respect to a very young child's actions and determine the child's behaviour to such an extent that Lewin arrived at the notion of creating a psychological topology, i.e., to express mathematically the trajectory of the child's movement in a field according to the distribution of things with varying attracting or repelling forces.

*I have already demonstrated in an earlier lecture the nature of a very young child's perception of external behavioural rules; all 'don'ts' – social (interdiction), physical (the impossibility, for example, of striking a match a second time), and biological (for example, don't touch the samovar because you might burn yourself) – combine to form a single 'situational' don't, which can be understood as a 'barrier' (in Lewin's sense of the term).

†[Editor's note: Vygotsky is probably referring to Lewin's demonstration of the great difficulty a small child has in realizing that he must first turn his back to a stone in order to arrange to sit on it.]

What is the root of situational constraints upon a child? The answer lies in a central fact of consciousness which is *characteristic of early childhood: the union of affect and perception*. At this age perception is generally not an independent feature but an initial feature of a motor affecting reaction; i.e., every perception is in this way a stimulus to activity. Since a situation is always communicated psychologically through perception, and perception is not separated from affective and motor activity, it is understandable that with his consciousness so structured the child cannot act otherwise than as constrained by the situation – or the field – in which he finds himself.

In play, things lose their motivating force. The *child sees one thing but acts differently in relation to what he sees. Thus, a situation is reached in which the child begins to act independently of what he sees*. Certain brain-damaged patients lose the ability to act independently of what they see; in considering such patients you can begin to appreciate that the freedom of action we adults and more mature children enjoy is not acquired in a flash but has to go through a long process of development.

Action in a situation which is not seen but only conceived on an imagined level and in an imaginary situation teaches the child to guide his behaviour not only by immediate perception of objects or by the situation immediately affecting him, but also by the meaning* of this situation.

Experiments and day-to-day observation clearly show that it is impossible for very young children to separate the field of meaning from the visible field. This is a very important fact. Even a child of two years, when asked to repeat the sentence 'Tanya is standing up' when Tanya is sitting in front of him, will change it to 'Tanya is sitting down'. In certain diseases we are faced with exactly the same situation. Goldstein and Gelb described a number of patients who were unable to state something that was not true. Gelb has data on one patient who was left-handed and incapable of writing the sentence 'I can write well with my right hand'. When looking out of the window on a fine day he was unable to repeat: 'The weather is nasty today', but would say: 'The weather is fine today.' Often we find in a patient with a speech disturbance that he is incapable of repeating senseless phrases, for example: 'Snow is black'; while other phrases equally difficult in their grammatical and semantic construction can be repeated.

In a very young child there is such an intimate fusion between word and object, and between meaning and what is seen, that a divergence between the meaning field and the visible field is impossible.

This can be seen in the process of children's speech development. You

* [Translator's note: In the following discussion of the role of meaning in relation to objects and actions Vygotsky uses the word *smysl*, which roughly corresponds to the range of notions covered by the English 'meaning', 'sense', and 'purport'. *Smysl* is uniformly rendered as 'meaning' in this translation.]

say to the child: 'clock'. He starts looking and finds the clock; i.e., the first function of the word is to orient spatially, to isolate particular areas in space; the word originally signifies a particular location in a situation.

It is at pre-school age that we first find a divergence between the fields of meaning and vision. It seems to me that we would do well to restate the notion of the investigator who said that in play activity thought is separated from objects, and action arises from ideas rather than from things.

Thought is separated from objects because a piece of wood begins to be a doll and a stick becomes a horse. Action according to rules begins to be determined by ideas and not by objects themselves. This is such a reversal of the child's relationship to the real, immediate, concrete situation that it is hard to evaluate its full significance. The child does not do this all at once. It is terribly difficult for a child to sever thought (the meaning of a word) from object.

Play is a transitional stage in this direction at that critical moment when a stick – i.e. an object – becomes a pivot for severing the meaning of horse from a real horse; one of the basic psychological structures determining the child's relationship to reality is radically altered.

The child cannot as yet sever thought from object; he must have something to act as a pivot. This expresses the child's weakness; in order to imagine a horse, he needs to define his action by means of using the horse in the stick as the pivot. But all the same the basic structure determining the child's relationship to reality is radically changed at this crucial point, for his perceptual structure changes. The special feature of human perception – which arises at a very early age – is so-called reality perception. This is something for which there is no analogy in animal perception. Essentially it lies in the fact that I do not see the world simply in colour and shape, but also as a world with sense and meaning. I do not merely see something round and black with two hands; I see a clock and I can distinguish one thing from another. There are patients who say, when they see a clock, that they are seeing something round and white with two thin steel strips, but they do not know that this is a clock – they have lost real relationship to objects. Thus, the structure of human perception could be figuratively expressed as a fraction in which the object is the numerator and the meaning is the denominator; this expresses the particular relationship of object and meaning which arises on the basis of speech. This means that all human perception is not made up of isolated perceptions, but of generalized perceptions. Goldstein says that this objectively formed perception and generalization are the same thing. Thus, for the child, in the fraction object-meaning, the object dominates, and meaning is directly connected to it. At the crucial moment for the child, when the stick becomes a horse, i.e., when the thing, the stick, becomes the pivot for severing the meaning of horse from a real horse, this fraction is inverted and meaning predominates, giving: $\dfrac{\text{meaning}}{\text{object}}$.

Nevertheless, properties of things as such do have some meaning; any stick can be a horse but, for example, a postcard can never be a horse for a child. Goethe's contention that in play any thing can be anything for a child is incorrect. Of course, for adults who can make conscious use of symbols, a postcard can be a horse. If I want to show the location of something, I can put down a match and say, 'This is a horse.' And that would be enough. For a child it cannot be a horse: one must use a stick; therefore this is play, and not symbolism. A symbol is a sign, but the stick is not the sign of a horse. Properties of things are retained but their meaning is inverted, i.e., the idea becomes the central point. It can be said that in this structure things are moved from a dominating to a subordinate position.

Thus, in play the child creates the structure $\dfrac{\text{meaning}}{\text{object}}$, where the semantic aspect – the meaning of the word, the meaning of the thing – dominates and determines his behaviour. To a certain extent meaning is emancipated from the object with which it had been directly fused before. I would say that in play a child concentrates on meaning severed from objects, but that it is not severed in real action with real objects.

Thus, a highly interesting contradiction arises, wherein the child operates with meanings severed from objects and actions, but in real action with real objects he operates with them in fusion. This is the transitional nature of play, which makes it an intermediary between the purely situational constraints of early childhood and thought which is totally free of real situations.

In play a child deals with things as having meaning. Word meanings replace objects, and thus an emancipation of word from object occurs. (A behaviourist would describe play and its characteristic properties in the following terms: the child gives ordinary objects unusual names and ordinary actions unusual designations, despite the fact that he knows the real ones.)

Separating words from things requires a pivot in the form of other things. But the moment the stick – i.e., the thing – becomes the pivot for severing the meaning of 'horse' from a real horse, the child makes one thing influence another in the semantic sphere. (He cannot sever meaning from an object, or a word from an object except by finding a pivot in something else, i.e. by the power of one object to steal another's name.) Transfer of meanings is facilitated by the fact that the child accepts a word as the property of a thing; he does not see the word but the thing it designates. For a child the word 'horse' applied to the stick means, 'There is a horse'; i.e., mentally he sees the object standing behind the word.

Play is converted to internal processes at school age, going over to internal speech, logical memory, and abstract thought. In play a child operates with meanings severed from objects, but not in real action with real things. To sever the meaning of horse from a real horse and transfer it to a stick (the necessary material pivot to keep the meaning from evaporating) and really acting with the stick as if it were a horse, is a vital transitional stage to operating with meanings. A child first acts with meanings as with objects and later realizes them consciously and begins to think just as a child, before he has acquired grammatical and written speech, knows how to do things but does not know that he knows, i.e. he does not realize or master them voluntarily. In play a child unconsciously and spontaneously makes use of the fact that he can separate meaning from an object without knowing he is doing it; he does not know that he is speaking in prose, just as he talks without paying attention to the words.

Hence we come to a functional definition of concepts, i.e., objects, and hence a word as part of a thing.

And so I would like to say that the creation of an imaginary situation is not a fortuitous fact in a child's life; it is the first effect of the child's emancipation from situational constraints. The first paradox of play is that the child operates with an alienated meaning in a real situation. The second is that in play he adopts the line of least resistance, i.e., he does what he feels like most because play is connected with pleasure. At the same time he learns to follow the line of greatest resistance, for by subordinating themselves to rules children renounce what they want since subjection to rule and renunciation of spontaneous impulsive action constitute the path to maximum pleasure in play.

The same thing can be observed in children in athletic games. Racing is difficult because the runners are ready to start off when you say 'ready, steady . . .' without waiting for the 'go'. It is evident that the point of internal rules is that the child does not act on immediate impulse.

Play continually creates demands on the child to act against immediate impulse, i.e., to act on the line of greatest resistance. I want to run off at once – this is perfectly clear – but the rules of the game order me to wait. Why does the child not do what he wants spontaneously at once? Because to observe the rules of the play structure promises much greater pleasure from the game than the gratification of an immediate impulse. In other words, as one investigator puts it in recalling the words of Spinoza: 'An affect can only be overcome by a stronger affect.' Thus, in play a situation is created in which, as Nohl puts it, a dual affective plan occurs. For example, the child weeps in play as a patient, but revels as a player. In play the child renounces his immediate impulse, co-ordinating every act of his behaviour to the rules of the game. Groos described this brilliantly. He thinks that a child's will originates in, and develops from, play with rules. Indeed, in the simple game of 'sorcerer' as described by Groos, the child must run away from the sorcerer in order not to be caught, but at the same time he must help his companion and get him disenchanted. When the sorcerer has touched him he must stop. At every step the child is faced with a conflict between the rule of the game and what he would do if he could suddenly act spontaneously. In the game he acts counter to what he wants. Nohl showed that a child's greatest self-control occurs in play. He achieves the maximum display of will-power in the sense of renunciation of an immediate attraction in the game in the form of candy, which by the rules of the game the children were not allowed to eat because it represented something inedible. Ordinarily a child experiences subordination to a rule in the renunciation of something he wants, but here subordination to a rule and renunciation of action on immediate impulse are the means to maximum pleasure.

Thus, the essential attribute of play is a rule which has become an affect. 'An idea which has become an affect, a concept which has turned into a passion' – this ideal of Spinoza finds its prototype in play, which is the realm of spontaneity and freedom. To carry out the rule is a source of pleasure. The rule wins because it is the strongest impulse. (Cf. Spinoza's adage that an affect can be overcome by a stronger affect.) Hence it follows that such a rule is an internal rule, i.e., a rule of inner self-restraint and self-determination, as Piaget says, and not a rule which the child obeys like a physical law. In short, play gives a child a new form of desires, i.e., teaches him to desire by relating his desires to a fictitious 'I' – to his role in the game and its rules. Therefore, a child's greatest achievements are possible in play – achievements which tomorrow will become his average level of real action and morality.

Now we can say the same thing about the child's activity that we said about things. Just as we have the fraction $\dfrac{object}{meaning}$, we also have the fraction $\dfrac{action}{meaning}$.

Whereas action dominated before, this structure is inverted, meaning becoming the numerator, while action takes the place of the denominator.

It is important to realize how the child is liberated from action in play. An action, for example, is realized as finger movements instead of real eating – that is, the action is completed not for the action itself but for the meaning it carries.

At first, in a child of pre-school age, action dominates over meaning and is incompletely understood; a child is able to do more than he can understand. It is at pre-school age that there first arises an action structure in which meaning is the determinant; but the action itself is not a sideline or subordinated feature; it is a structural feature. Nohl showed that children, in playing at eating from a plate, performed actions with their hands reminiscent of real eating, but all actions that did not designate eating were impossible. Throwing one's hands back instead of stretching them toward the plate turned out to be impossible; that is, such action would have a destructive effect on the game. A child does not symbolize in play, but he wishes and realizes his wishes by letting the basic categories of reality pass through his experience, which is precisely why in play a day can take half-an-hour, and a hundred miles are covered in five steps. The child, in wishing, carries out his wishes; and in thinking, he acts. Internal and external action are inseparable: imagination, interpretation, and will are internal processes in external action.

The meaning of action is basic, but even by itself action is not indifferent. At an earlier age the position was the reverse: action was the structural determinant while meaning was a secondary, collateral, subordinated feature. What we said about severing meaning from object applies equally well to the child's own actions. A child who stamps on the ground and imagines himself riding a horse has thereby accomplished the inversion of the fraction $\dfrac{\text{action}}{\text{meaning}}$ to $\dfrac{\text{meaning}}{\text{action}}$.

Once again, in order to sever the meaning of the action from the real action (riding a horse, without the opportunity to do so), the child requires a pivot in the form of an action to replace the real one. But once again, while before action was the determinant in the structure 'action-meaning', now the structure is inverted and meaning becomes the determinant. Action retreats to second place and becomes the pivot; meaning is again severed from action by means of another action. This is a repetition of the point leading to operations based solely on the meanings of actions; i.e., to volitional choice, a decision, a conflict of motives, and to other processes sharply separated from fulfilment: in short, to the development of the will. Just as operating with the meanings of things leads to abstract thought, in volitional decision the determining factor is not the fulfilment of the action but its meaning. In play an action replaces another action just as an object replaces another object. How does the child 'float' from one object to another, from one action to another? This is accomplished by movement in the field of meaning – not connected with the visible field or with real objects – which subordinates all real objects and actions to itself.

This movement in the field of meaning predominates in play: on the one hand, it is movement in an abstract field (a field which thus appears before voluntary operation with meanings), but the method of movement is situational and concrete (i.e., it is not logical but affective movement). In other words, the field of meaning appears, but action within it occurs just as in reality; herein lies the main genetic contradiction of play. I have three questions left to answer. First, to show that play is not the predominant feature of childhood but is a leading factor in development. Second, to show the development of play itself; i.e., the significance of the movement from the predominance of the imaginary situation to the predominance of rules. And third, to show the internal transformations brought about by play in the child's development.

I do not think that play is the predominant type of child activity. In fundamental everyday situations a child behaves in a manner diametrically opposed to his behaviour in play. In play, action is subordinated to meaning, but in real life, of course, action dominates over meaning.

Thus we find in play – if you will – the negative of a child's general everyday behaviour. Therefore, to consider play as the prototype of his everyday activity and its predominant form is completely without foundation. This is the main flaw in Koffka's theory. He considers play as the child's other world. According to Koffka, everything that concerns a child is play reality, while everything that concerns an adult is serious reality. A given object has one meaning in play, and another outside of it. In a child's world the logic of wishes and of satisfying urges dominates, and not real logic. The illusory nature of play is transferred to life. This would be true if play were indeed the predominant form of a child's activity. But it is hard to envisage the insane picture that a child would bring to mind if the form of activity we have been speaking of were to become the predominant form of his everyday activity – even if only partially transferred to real life.

Koffka gives a number of examples to show how a child transfers a situation from play into life. But the real transference of play behaviour to real life can only be regarded as an unhealthy symptom. To behave in a real situation as in an illusory one is the first sign of delirium.

As research has shown, play behaviour in real life is normally seen only in the type of game when sisters play at 'sisters'; i.e., when children sitting at dinner can play at having dinner or (as in Katz's example) when children who do not want to go to bed say, 'Let's play that it's night-time and we have to go to sleep'; they begin to play at what they are in fact doing, evidently creating associations which facilitate the execution of an unpleasant action.

Thus, it seems to me that play is not the predominant type of activity at pre-school age. Only theories which maintain that a child does not have to satisfy the basic requirements of life, but can live in search of pleasure, could possibly suggest that a child's world is a play world.

Is it possible to suppose that a child's behaviour is always guided by meaning, that a pre-schooler's behaviour is so arid that he never behaves with candour as he wants to simply because he thinks he should behave otherwise? This kind of subordination to rules is quite impossible in life, but in play it does become possible: thus, play also creates the zone of proximal development of the child. In play a child is always above his average age, above his daily behaviour; in play it is as though he were a head taller than himself. As in the focus of a magnifying glass, play contains all developmental tendencies in a condensed form; in play it is as though the child were trying to jump above the level of his normal behaviour.

The play-development relationship can be compared to the instruction-development relationship, but play provides a background for changes in needs and in consciousness of a much wider nature. Play is the source of development and creates the zone of proximal development. Action in the imaginative sphere, in an imaginary situation, the creation of voluntary intentions and the formation of real-life plans and volitional motives – all appear in play and make it the highest level of pre-school development.

The child moves forward essentially through play activity. Only in this sense can play be termed a leading activity which determines the child's development.

The second question is: how does play move? It is a remarkable fact that the child starts with an imaginary situation when initially this imaginary situation is so very close to the real one. A reproduction of the real situation takes place. For example, a child playing with a doll repeats almost exactly what her mother does with her; the doctor looks at the child's throat, hurts him, and he cries, but as soon as the doctor has gone he immediately thrusts a spoon into the doll's mouth.

This means that in the original situation rules operate in a condensed and compressed form. There is very little of the imaginary in the situation. It is an imaginary situation, but it is only comprehensible in the light of a real situation that has just occurred; i.e., it is a recollection of something that has actually happened. Play is more nearly recollection than imagination – that is, it is more memory in action than a novel imaginary situation. As play develops, we see a movement towards the conscious realization of its purpose.

It is incorrect to conceive of play as activity without purpose; play is purposeful activity for a child. In athletic games you can win or lose, in a race you can come first, second, or last. In short, the purpose decides the game.

It justifies all the rest. Purpose as the ultimate goal determines the child's affective attitude to play. When running a race, a child can be highly agitated or distressed and little may remain of pleasure because he finds it physically painful to run, while if he is overtaken he will experience little functional pleasure. In sports the purpose of the game is one of its dominant features without which there would be no point – like examining a piece of candy, putting it in one's mouth, chewing it, and then spitting it out.

In play the object, to win, is recognized in advance.

At the end of development rules emerge, and the more rigid they are, the greater the demands on the child's application, the greater the regulation of the child's activity, the more tense and acute play becomes. Simply running around without purpose or rules of play is a dull game and does not appeal to children.

Nohl simplified the rules of croquet for children, and showed how this demagnetized the game, for the child lost the sense of the game in proportion to the simplification of the rules. Consequently, towards the end of development in play, what had originally been embryonic now has a distinct form, finally emerging as purpose and rules. This was true before, but in an undeveloped form. One further feature has yet to come, essential to sporting games; this is some sort of record, which is also closely connected with purpose.

Take chess, for example. For a real chess player it is pleasant to win and unpleasant to lose a game. Nohl says that it is as pleasing to a child to come first in a race as it is for a handsome person to look at himself in a mirror; there is a certain feeling of satisfaction.

Consequently, a complex of originally undeveloped features comes to the fore at the end of play development – features that had been secondary or incidental in the beginning occupy a central position at the end, and vice versa.

Finally, the third question: what sort of changes in a child's behaviour can be attributed to play? In play a child is free, i.e., he determines his own actions, starting from his own 'I'. But this is an illusory freedom. His actions are in fact subordinated to a definite meaning, and he acts according to the meanings of things.

A child learns to recognize consciously his own actions, and becomes aware that every object has a meaning.

From the point of view of development, the fact of creating an imaginary situation can be regarded as a means of developing abstract thought. I think that the corresponding development of rules leads to actions on the basis of which the division between work and play becomes possible, a division encountered at school age as a fundamental fact.

I would like to mention just one other aspect: play is really a particular feature of pre-school age.

As figuratively expressed by one investigator, play for a child under three is a serious game, just as it is for an adolescent, although, of course, in a different sense of the word; serious play for a very young child means that he plays without separating the imaginary situation from the real one.

For the schoolchild, play begins to be a limited form of activity, predominantly of the athletic type, which fills a specific role in the schoolchild's development, but lacks the significance of play for the pre-schooler.

Superficially, play bears little resemblance to what it leads to, and only a profound internal analysis makes it possible to determine its course of movement and its role in the pre-schooler's development.

At school age play does not die away but permeates the attitude to reality. It has its own inner continuation in school instruction and work (compulsory activity based on rules). All examinations of the essence of play have shown that in play a new relationship is created between the semantic and visible fields – that is, between situations in thought and real situations. (See photo inset.)

[Translator's note: Russian uses a single word, *igra*, where English uses either *play* or *game* (cf. German *Spiel*, French *jeu*, Spanish *juego, et al.*). The resulting potential ambiguity of the original Russian should be borne in mind when encountering the words *play* and *game* in this translation.]

(From *Soviet Psychology*, Vol. 12, No. 6, 1966, pp. 62–76. The article was transcribed from a stenographic record of a lecture given in 1933 at the Hertzen Pedagogical Institute, Leningrad.)

Symbolic Play

This is a continuation of Jean Piaget's essay on the contribution of play to the child's developing intellect. (See 'Mastery Play' on pages 166–71.) Here he focuses on the earliest appearances of the ludic symbol.

The appearance of symbolism . . . is the crucial point in all the interpretations of the ludic function. Why is it that play becomes symbolic, instead of continuing to be mere sensory-motor exercise or intellectual experiment, and why should the enjoyment of movement, or activity for the fun of activity, which constitute a kind of practical make-believe, be completed at a given moment by imaginative make-believe? The reason is that among the attributes of assimilation for assimilation's sake is that of distortion, and therefore to the extent to which it is dissociated from immediate accommodation it is a source of symbolic make-believe. This explains why there is symbolism as soon as we leave the sensory-motor level for that of representational thought.

During the *fifth stage* (of the sensory-motor period) certain new elements will ensure the transition from the behaviours of stage IV to the ludic symbol of stage VI, and for that very reason will accentuate the ritualization we have just noted. In relation to the 'tertiary circular reactions' or 'experiments in order to see the result', it often happens that by chance, the child combines unrelated gestures without really trying to experiment, and subsequently repeats these gestures as a ritual and makes a motor game of them. But, in contrast to the combinations of stage VI, which are borrowed from the adapted schemas, these combinations are new and almost immediately have the character of play.

Observation 63. At 0; 10 J. put her nose close to her mother's cheek and then pressed it against it, which forced her to breathe much more loudly. This phenomenon at once interested her, but instead of merely repeating it or varying it so as to investigate it, she quickly complicated it for the fun of it: she drew back an inch or two, screwed up her nose, sniffed and breathed out alternately very hard (as if she were blowing her nose), then again thrust her nose against her mother's cheek, laughing heartily. These actions were repeated at least once a day for more than a month, as a ritual.

At 1; 0 she was holding her hair with her right hand during her bath.

The hand, which was wet, slipped and struck the water. J. immediately repeated the action, first carefully putting her hand on her hair then quickly bringing it down on to the water. She varied the height and position, and one might have thought it was a tertiary circular reaction but for the fact that the child's attitude showed that it was merely a question of ludic combinations. On the following days, every time she was bathed, the game was repeated with the regularity of a ritual. For instance, at 1; 0 she struck the water as soon as she was in the bath, but stopped as if something was missing; she then put her hands up to her hair and found her game again.

At 1; 3, with one hand, she put a pin as far away as possible and picked it up with the other. This behaviour, related to the working out of spatial groups, became a ritual game, started by the mere sight of the pin. Similarly, at 1; 4, she had her leg through the handle of a basket. She pulled it out, put it back at once and examined the position. But once the geometrical interest was exhausted, the schema became one of play and gave rise to a series of combinations during which J. took the liveliest pleasure in using her new power.

At 1; 3 J. asked for her pot and laughed a lot when it was given to her. She indulged in a certain number of ritual movements, playfully, and the game stopped there, to be taken up again the following days.

At 1; 1 she amused herself by making an orange skin on a table sway from side to side. But as she had looked under the skin just before setting it in motion, she did it again as a ritual, at least twenty times; she took the peel, turned it over, put it down again, made it sway and then began all over again.

These behaviours are curious in that they are combinations not adapted to external circumstances. Obviously there is no necessity to screw up one's nose before wiping it on mother's cheek, to touch one's hair before hitting the water, or to look under a piece of orange peel (already well known) before making it move to and fro. But does the connection seem necessary to the child? We do not think so, although later on similar rituals may be accompanied by a certain feeling of efficacy, under the influence of emotion (as we are familiar with it in the game of avoiding walking on the lines between the stones in the pavement). In the present case, there is only adaptation at the starting point of such behaviours, secondary or tertiary circular reactions. But while in the normal circular reaction the child tends to repeat or vary the phenomenon, the better to adjust himself to it and master it, in this case the child complicates the situation and then repeats exactly all the actions, whether useful or useless, for the mere pleasure of using his activity as completely as possible. In short, during this stage, as before, play is seen to be the function of assimilation extended beyond the limits of adaptation.

The rituals of this stage are then a continuation of those of the previous one, with the difference that those of stage IV consist merely in repeating and combining schemas already established for a non-ludic end, while at this stage they become games almost immediately, and show a greater variety of combinations (a variety due no doubt to the habits following tertiary circular reaction). This progress in ludic ritualization of schemas entails a corresponding development towards symbolism. Indeed, insofar as the ritual includes 'serious' schemas or elements borrowed from such schemas (like the action of wiping one's nose, of asking for a pot, etc.), its effect is to abstract them from their context and consequently to evoke them symbolically. Of course, in such behaviours there is not necessarily as yet the consciousness of 'make-believe', since the child confines himself to reproducing the schemas as they stand, without applying them symbolically to new objects. But although what occurs may not be symbolic representation, it is already almost the symbol in action.

With the *sixth stage* owing to definite progress in the direction of representation, the ludic symbol is dissociated from ritual and takes the form of symbolic schemas. This progress is achieved when empirical intelligence becomes mental association, and external imitation becomes internal or 'deferred' imitation, and this at once raises a whole set of problems. Here are some examples:

Observation 64 (a). In the case of J, who has been our main example in the preceding observations, the true ludic symbol, with every appearance of awareness of 'make-believe', first appeared at 1;3 in the following circumstances. She saw a cloth whose fringed edges vaguely recalled those of her pillow; she seized it; held a fold of it in her right hand, sucked the thumb of the same hand and lay down on her side, laughing hard. She kept her eyes open, but blinked from time to time as if she were alluding to closed eyes. Finally, laughing more and more, she cried 'Néné' (Nono). The same cloth started the same game on the following days. At 1;3 she treated the collar of her mother's coat in the same way. At 1;3 it was the tail of her rubber donkey which represented the pillow! and from 1;5 onwards she made her animals, a bear and a plush dog, also do 'nono'.

Similarly, at 1; 6 she said 'avon' (savon = soap), rubbing her hands together and pretending to wash them (without any water).

At 1; 8 and the following days she pretended she was eating various things, e.g., a piece of paper, saying 'Very nice'.

Observation 64 (b). The development of these symbols which involve representation does not, of course, exclude that of purely sensory-motor rituals. Thus J., at 1; 6, went the round of a balcony hitting the railings at each step with a rhythmical movement, stopping and starting again: a step, a pause; a blow, a step, a pause; a blow, etc.

Frequent relationships are formed between rituals and symbolism, the latter arising from the former as a result of progressive abstraction of the action. For instance, at about 1 ; 3 J. learnt to balance on a curved piece of wood which she rocked with her feet, in a standing position. But at 1 : 4 she adopted the habit of walking on the ground with her legs apart, pretending to lose her balance, as if she were on the board. She laughed heartily and said 'Bimbam'.

At 1 ; 6 she herself swayed bits of wood or leaves and kept saying Bimbam and this term finally became a half-generic, half-symbolic schema referring to branches, hanging objects and even grasses.

Observation 65. In the case of L. 'make-believe' or the ludic symbol made its appearance at 1 ; 0, arising, as in the case of J., from the motor ritual. She was sitting in her cot when she unintentionally fell backwards. Then seeing a pillow, she got into the position for sleeping on her side, seizing the pillow with one hand and pressing it against her face (her ritual was different from J.'s). But instead of miming the action half seriously, she smiled broadly (she did not know she was being watched); her behaviour was then that of J. in observation 64. She remained in this position for a moment, then sat up delightedly. During the day she went through the process again a number of times, although she was no longer in her cot; first she smiled (this indication of the representational symbol is to be noted), then threw herself back, turned on her side, put her hands over her face as if she held a pillow (though there wasn't one) and remained motionless, with her eyes open, smiling quietly. The symbol was therefore established.

At 1 ; 3 she pretended to put a napkin-ring in her mouth, laughed, shook her head as if saying 'no' and removed it. This behaviour was an intermediate stage between ritual and symbol, but at 1 ; 6 she pretended to eat and drink without having anything in her hand. At 1 ; 7 she pretended to drink out of a box and then held it to the mouths of all who were present. These last symbols had been prepared for during the preceding month or two by a progressive ritualization, the principal stages of which consisted in playing at drinking out of empty glasses and then repeating the action making noises with lips and throat.

These examples show the nature of the behaviours in which we have seen for the first time pretence or the feeling of 'make believe' characteristic of the ludic symbol as opposed to simple motor games. The child is using schemas which are familiar, and for the most part already ritualized in games of the previous types: but (1) instead of using them in the presence of the objects to which they are usually applied, he assimilates to them new objectives unrelated to them from the point of view of effective adaptation; (2) these new objects, instead of resulting merely in an extension of the schema (as is the case in the generalization proper to intelligence), are used with no other purpose than that of allowing the subject to mime or evoke the schemas in question. It is the union of these two conditions – application of the schema to inadequate objects and evocation for pleasure – which in our opinion characterizes the beginning of pretence. For instance, as early as the fourth stage, the schema of going to sleep is already giving rise to ludic ritualizations, since in observation 62 J. reproduces it at the sight of her pillow. But there is then neither symbol nor consciousness of make-believe, since the child merely applies her usual movements to the pillow itself, i.e. to the normal stimulus of the behaviour. There certainly is play, insofar as the schema is only used for pleasure, but there is no symbolism. On the contrary, in observation 64 J. mimes sleep while she is holding a cloth, a coat collar, or even a donkey's tail, instead of a pillow, and in observation 65 L. does the same thing, pretending to be holding a pillow when her hands are empty. It can therefore no longer be said that the schema has been evoked by its usual stimulus, and we are forced to recognize that these objects merely serve as substitutes for the pillow, substitutes which become symbolic through the actions simulating sleep (actions which in L's case go so far as pretence without any material aid). In a word, there is symbolism, and not only motor play, since there is pretence of assimilating an object to a schema and use of a schema without accommodation.

The connection between these 'symbolic schemata' or first ludic symbols and the deferred, representational imitation of this same sixth stage is clear. In both types of behaviour we find a representational element whose existence is proved by the deferred character of the reaction. Deferred imitation of a new model takes place after the model has disappeared, and symbolic play reproduces a situation not directly related to the object which gives rise to it, the present object merely serving to evoke an absent one. As regards imitation, on the other hand, we find in the behaviours of 64 and 65 an element which might be considered imitative. In observation 64 J. imitates the actions she herself makes before going to sleep, or the actions of washing, eating and so on, and in observation 65 L. does the same. And yet, apart from the fact that this is only self-imitation, it is not purely imitative behaviour, since the objects which are present (the fringes of the cloth, the coat collar, the donkey's tail used as the pillow, and L.'s box used as a plate, etc.) are merely assimilated, regardless of their objective character, to the objects which the imitated action usually accompanies (the pillow, the plate, etc.). There is therefore, and this is characteristic of symbolic play as opposed to mere motor play, both apparent imitation and ludic assimilation. This raises a question to which we shall return presently, but before doing so we must examine the connection between the ludic symbol and the index, the sign, the concept and the development of sensory-motor games.

It is clear, first of all, that the symbolic schemata in question in observations 64 and 65 are more complex than the sensory-motor index, which has, however, been used by intelligence in the previous stages. The index is only a part or one aspect of the object or of the causal process whose assimilation it makes possible. Being an attribute of the object, it enables it to be anticipated without mental representation, by mere activation of the corresponding schema. For instance, a child of eight or nine months can find a toy under a blanket when its presence is indicated by the rounded outline of the blanket. The symbol, on the other hand, depends on resemblance between the present object, which is the 'signifier', and the absent object symbolically 'signified', and this constitutes representation. A situation is mentally evoked, not merely anticipated as a whole from the datum of one of its parts.

The symbolic schema of play, therefore, almost reaches the level of the 'sign', since in contrast to indices, where the 'signifier' is a part or an aspect of the 'signified', there is now a sharp distinction between the two. But, as we know, the 'sign' is 'arbitrary' or conventional, while the symbol is 'motivated', i.e. there is resemblance between 'signifier' and 'signified'. Being arbitrary, the sign involves a social relationship, as is obvious in language, a system of verbal signs, while the motivation of the symbol (the resemblance between signifier and signified) may be the product of individual thought.

This is the same problem as that of deferred imitation. It so happens that at the level at which the first ludic symbols appear the child becomes capable of learning to speak, so that the first 'signs' seem to be contemporary with these symbols. We see, for instance, that J. says 'Néné' or 'Nono', which are verbal signs, while she is pretending to sleep, using the fringe of a cloth like that of her pillow. She uses similarly the signs '(s)avon' and 'bimbam'. Might we not then conclude that the symbol even in its ludic form, implies the sign and language, since like them it depends on a representational factor? This representational factor would then have to be conceived as a product of social intercourse, the result of intellectual exchange and communication. But in this case, as in the case of imitation, this explanation can be discarded if we consider the continuity between the behaviours of the sixth and the preceding stages, and also the behaviour of the anthropoids.

Firstly, the formation of such symbolism is not always accompanied by speech or contact with others. For instance, L. (observation 65), unlike J., pretends to be sleeping while smiling broadly, without saying a word and unaware that she is being watched. This by itself would of course prove nothing, since interiorized verbo-social behaviours might already exist. In conjunction with other arguments, however, it has its value.

Secondly, we find the chimpanzee playing certain symbolic games such as taking 'one of its legs in its hands', and treating it 'as something extraneous to itself, a real object, perhaps a doll, rocking it in its arms, stroking it and so on' (Koehler).

Thirdly, the most characteristic effect of the system of verbal signs on the development of intelligence is certainly that it allows of the transformation of sensory-motor schemata into concepts. The normal end of a schema is a concept, since schemata, being instruments for adaptation to ever varying situations, are systems of relationships susceptible of progressive abstraction and generalization. But in order to acquire the fixity of meaning of concepts, and in particular their degree of generality, which is broader than that of individual experience, schemata must result in inter-individual communication and therefore be expressed by signs. It is thus legitimate to consider the intervention of the social sign as a decisive turning-point in the direction of representation even though the schema at stage six is already of itself representational. But the symbolic schema of play is in no way a concept, either by its form, 'the signifier', or by its content, 'the signified'. In its form it does not go beyond the level of the imitative image or deferred imitation, i.e. the level of representational imitation characteristic of the sixth stage independently of language. In its content, it is not adapted generalization, but distorting assimilation, i.e. there is no accommodation of the schemata to objective reality, but distortion of the latter for the purpose of the schema. For example, when a donkey's tail serves as a pillow (observation 64), or a box is used as a plate (observation 65), it cannot be called adapted generalization, but merely subjective, and therefore ludic, assimilation. When, however, the same child uses a spoon to pull something towards him, the spoon cannot be considered as the ludic symbol for a stick, and the behaviour must be seen as generalizing assimilation. It is only generalizing assimilation which leads to concepts, by way of the sign, i.e. through social intercourse, while the ludic symbol continues to be egocentric assimilation, even long after the appearance of language and the most social concepts of which the child is capable.

If, then, the formation of the ludic symbol is not due to the influence of the sign or of verbal socialization, it must be explained by the previous work of assimilation. It is clear that this type of symbol, like representational imitation, cannot emerge *ex abrupto* at a given moment in mental development. Here, as in the imitative behaviours, there is functional continuity between the successive stages, even when the structures (as opposed to the functions) differ one from another as much as do those of strictly sensory-motor schemata from those of partly interiorized and partly representational schemata. From this point of view, the ludic symbol is in germ (we do not say pre-formed as a structure, but functionally prepared) in the generalizing assimilation of the second stage. When a schema is applied to objectives more and more remote from its initial object, there may be progressive separation between the action and the initial object in that both old and new objectives will be put on the same plane. There is then generalization of the schema, with a balance between assimilation and accommodation. But insofar as the new objective is considered as a substitute for the initial object, there is emphasis on assimilation, which if it were conscious or mentally interiorized, would constitute a symbolic relationship. It is, of course, not so as yet, since interiorization is not possible, but from a functional point of view, such a relationship is the forerunner of the symbol. For instance, when a baby sucks his thumb instead of the breast (far be it from us to say that this substitution takes place every time he sucks his thumb!) it would suffice that the thumb served to evoke the breast for there to be a symbol. If this evocation one day takes place, it merely continues the assimilation of the thumb to the schema of sucking, by making the thumb the 'signifier' and the breast the 'signified'. The impossibility of differentiating clearly between signifier and signified prevents us from speaking of the symbol in the second stage, and we cannot therefore accept the idea of preformation held by certain psychoanalysts who already see symbolism, conscious or unconscious, in this sensory-motor assimilation. We do, however, recognize that, functionally, the starting point of the symbol is the ludic assimilation of stages two and three.

In stages four and five there is progress towards symbolization to the extent that the development of ludic assimilation leads to a sharper differentiation between signifier and signified. In the course of ludic ritualization of schemata, the child sometimes reproduces a set of actions that he usually does in quite a different context, e.g. lies down to sleep on seeing his pillow (but only for a second, and without going to sleep), or wipes his nose against his mother's cheek (without really doing it). Such actions are certainly not yet properly symbolic, since the action is only a reproduction of itself and is therefore still both signifier and signified. But as the action is unfinished, and moreover, only done for fun, it is clear that there is a beginning of differentiation between the signifier – the movements actually made, and which are only an attempt at play – and the signified, the whole schema as it would develop if completed 'seriously'. In other words there is a kind of symbolic allusion comparable to the so-called 'fictions' or 'feelings of make-believe' which K. Groos attributed rather too generously to animals, and which are merely patterns of behaviour begun but not carried through. Kittens which fight with their mother and bite without hurting her are not 'pretending' to fight, since they do not know what real fighting is, any more than J. miming the actions of going to sleep or blowing her nose has reached the stage of representation or the symbol, since there is no interiorized fiction. But we should certainly be adopting a very prejudiced attitude if we refused to admit that these symbols, which are as it were 'played', are a preparation for representational symbols.

When, therefore, during the sixth stage, the properly symbolic schema appears by assimilation of additional objects to the played schema and its initial objective (e.g. assimilation of a donkey's tail to a pillow and to the schema of going to sleep), the new situation can be summed up as the end of the sensory-motor aspect of the progressive differentiation between 'signifier' and 'signified.' The object (the donkey's tail) chosen to represent the initial objective of the schema, and the make-believe actions done to it, then constitute the 'signifier', while the 'signified' is both the schema as it would develop if completed seriously (really going to sleep) and the object to which it is usually applied (the pillow). The actions accompanying preparation for sleep are thus not only taken out of their ordinary context and left uncompleted merely as an allusion, as in the ludic ritualizations of stages four and five. They are now applied to new and inadequate objects and are carried out with strict attention to detail although they are entirely make-believe. There is therefore representation, since the 'signifier' is dissociated from the 'signified', which is a situation which is non-perceptible and only evoked by means of available objects and actions. But this symbolic representation, like deferred imitation, is nothing but a continuation of the whole existing sensory-motor edifice.

We have already observed that, like the deferred imitation with which it is contemporary, it is related to transformations in intelligence itself, which at the sixth stage, becomes capable of using interiorized and therefore representational schemas, as opposed to external or empirical schemas. We must recall here the progress of the schemas in mobility and speed to a stage at which their co-ordinations and differentiations no longer depend on external trial and error but take place before the actions themselves. This interiorization of the schemata of intelligence thus makes deferred imitation possible, since imitation is accommodation of schemata, and its deferred character comes from its interiorization. But deferred imitation in its turn has the effect of making representation possible by facilitating the interior accommodation of schemas to the situations to be anticipated. In exactly the same way, ludic assimilation, which becomes more mobile and deferred in the sixth stage for the same general reasons, is provided by imitation with the representational elements necessary for real symbolic play.

When a donkey's tail is assimilated to a pillow, or a cardboard box to a plate (observations 64 and 65), this symbolism involves both ludic assimilation, which distorts objects and uses them at will, and a kind of imitation, since the child does the actions of going to sleep or having a meal. It is even clear that it is just by virtue of this particular kind of self-imitation that ludic symbolism becomes possible, for without it there would be neither representation of absent objects nor pretence or feeling of 'make-believe'. Generally speaking, we find in every ludic symbol this *sui generis* combination of distorting assimilation, which is the basis of play, and a kind of representational imitation, the first providing what is 'signified' and the second being the 'signifier' of the symbol.

Although the distinction between practice play and symbolic play is greater than is generally thought, since their respective origins are to be found on two quite different levels of behaviour, there is still an undeniable relationship between them: *symbolic play is to practice play as representational intelligence is to sensory-motor intelligence.* And to this correspondence at two different levels must be added one at the same level: *symbolic play is to representational intelligence what practice play is to sensory-motor intelligence,* i.e. a deviation in the direction of pure assimilation.

Representative thought as distinct from sensory-motor activity, begins as soon as the 'signifier' is differentiated from the 'signified' in the system of significations which constitutes the whole intelligence and indeed the whole consciousness. In the process of adaptation through sensory-motor schemata there are already 'signifiers'. They are the 'indices' which enable the child to recognize objects and relationships, to assimilate consciously and even to imitate. But the index is only one aspect of the object or of the situation, and is therefore not a 'signifier' which is differentiated from the 'signified'. Language, on the other hand, provides the prototype of a system of distinct signifiers, since in verbal behaviour the signifier is the collective 'signs' or words, while the signified is the meaning of the words, i.e. the concepts which at this new level take the place of the preverbal sensory-motor schemata. Verbal, properly conceptual intelligence occupies this privileged position in representational thought by virtue of the fact that verbal signs are social, and that through their use the system of concepts attains sooner or later (later than is usually supposed) a high degree of socialization. But between the index and the sign, or between the sensory-motor schema and the logical concept, the symbolic image and imaged or pre-conceptual representation have their place. As we have seen, the image is interiorized imitation, i.e. the positive of accommodation, which is the negative of the imitated object. The image is therefore a schema which has already been accommodated and is now used in present assimilations, which are also interiorized, as 'signifier' for these 'signified'. The image is therefore a differentiated signifier, more so than the index since it is detached from the perceived object, but less so than the sign, since it is still imitation of the object, and therefore is a 'motivated' sign, as distinct from verbal signs which are 'arbitrary'. Moreover, the image is a signifier which is within the scope of individual thought, while the pure sign is always social. For this reason there is in all verbal and conceptual thought a stratum of imaged representation which enables the individual to assimilate for himself the general idea common to all, and for this reason also, the nearer we get to early childhood the more important is the role of imaged representation and intuitive thought. Each image has a corresponding object (i.e. the concept of this object) which, even in the adult, serves as a representative or example of the general class of which it is a part, and which in the child is a partial substitute for the general class which is not yet constructed.

This then being the mechanism of adapted thought, which is the equilibrium between assimilation and accommodation, we can understand the role of the symbol in play, where accommodation is subordinated to assimilation. The ludic symbol also is an image, and therefore imitation, and therefore accommodation. But the relationship between assimilation and accommodation in play differs from that in cognitive or adapted representation precisely because play is the predominance of assimilation and no longer an equilibrium between the two functions. (1) In the case of the adapted image there is exact imitation, or at least imitation which aims at exactness, i.e. a one – one correspondence with the object signified. For instance, the representation of a triangle can be obtained by a real imitation (a drawing, or an indication of the figure by movement of a finger), or by a purely mental imitation (an interior image or 'intuition' of a triangle), but there is then correspondence between the parts of the drawing, those of the image and those of the object represented. But when in play one thing is symbolized by another, e.g. a cat walking on a wall by the shell moved with the hand along a cardboard box, there is a whole series of signifiers, related one to another, but further and further removed from the real situation. First there is the shell representing the cat and the box representing the wall; then there is imitation through gesture, i.e., the movement of the hand representing the cat walking; finally there is presumably the mental image of the cat on the wall, an image which may be vague and undifferentiated since it is supported by motor imitation and the symbol-object. (2) The representation of a triangle is adequate and exact insofar as the triangle raises a problem, i.e., gives rise to a need for adaptation to reality, with accommodation to the object and assimilation of the object to a system of relationships not centred in the ego, while the evocation of the cat on the wall has no other purpose than temporary satisfaction of the ego: it is a 'pathic' and not a 'gnostic' attitude, to use Buytendijk's terms, but it is at the same time egocentric and not objective. We have here the explanation of the difference seen in (1). (3) In cognitive representation the mental or material image represents a particular object whose concept (the particular class) serves as a single representative or example of the general class of which it is a part. For instance, the triangle which is drawn represents all triangles, or at least all triangles of that class. But in play, the symbol-object is not only the representative of the signified, but also its substitute (the shell becomes for the moment a cat), whether the signified is general (any cat) or particular (a definite cat). In cognitive representation, therefore, there is adaptation to the signified (i.e. equilibrium between assimilation and accommodation), while the signifier consists of images, which are exactly accommodated or imitated, and whose corresponding object is only one representative of a general class. In the symbolic representation of play, on the contrary, the signified is merely assimilated to the ego, i.e. it is evoked for temporary interest or for immediate satisfaction, and the signifier is then less exact mental imitation than imitation by means of material pictures in which the objects are themselves assimilated to the signified as substitutes, by reason of resemblances which may be extremely vague and subjective. In a word, while in cognitive representation there is a permanent equilibrium between assimilation and accommodation, in ludic symbolism there is a predominance of assimilation in the relationship between the child and the signified, and even in the construction of the signifier.

This being so, the connection between symbolic assimilation, which is the source of make-believe play, and functional assimilation, which is the source of practice play, is at once obvious. Both symbol and concept already exist, in a sense, in sensory-motor assimilation. When the baby who has learnt to swing an object swings other objects, this generalized schema is the functional equivalent of the concept, because each particular case belongs to the general class of things 'to be swung' of which it has become a representative or example. The same applies in the case of things 'to be sucked', etc. But when the baby wants to go on sucking after his meal is over, and finds compensation in sucking his thumb, the thumb is more than a representative example. It becomes a substitute, and could even be considered a symbol if it were possible for the baby to evoke his mother's breast at the same time. But in spite of the Freudians, for whom such symbols exist as early as the age of two months, and in spite of K. Groos, who sees make-believe in all practice play, in our opinion there cannot be symbolism, consciousness of make-believe, before there is representation, which begins and gradually develops at the beginning of the second year, when sensory-motor assimilation becomes mental assimilation through differentiation between signifier and signified. When J. pretended to be asleep, holding a corner of the sheet and bending her head, the sensory-motor schema thus set in motion resulted in more than mere exercise, since it served to evoke a past situation, and the corner of the sheet became a conscious substitute for the absent pillow. With the projection of such 'symbolic schemata' on to other objects, the way is clear for the assimilation of any one object to another, since any object can be a make-believe substitute for any other.

The causality of symbolic play now becomes clear, since it derives essentially from the structure of the child's thought. Symbolic play represents in thought the pole of assimilation, and freely assimilates reality to the ego. As we said earlier, it is therefore to practice play what adapted thought is to sensory-motor intelligence, and it is to adapted thought what practice play is to sensory-motor intelligence, i.e. the assimilating pole. But why is there assimilation of reality to the ego instead of immediate assimilation of the universe to experimental and logical thought? It is simply because in early childhood this thought has not yet been constructed, and during its development it is inadequate to supply the needs of daily life. Moreover, the most adapted and most logical thought of which the young child is capable is still pre-logical and egocentric, its structure being intermediate between the symbolic thought of play and adult thought.

To sum up what has already been said, symbolic play is merely egocentric thought in its pure state. The essential condition for objectivity of thought is that assimilation of reality to the system of adapted notions shall be in permanent equilibrium with accommodation of these same notions to things and to the thought of others. It is obvious that it is only by the constitution of systems of logical operations (reversibility of transformations of thought), of moral operations (preservation of values) and spatio-temporal operations (reversible organization of elementary physical notions), that such an equilibrium can be achieved, for it is only through operational reversibility that thought becomes capable of preserving its notions despite the fluctuations of reality and incessant contact with the unexpected. The reversible operation is at the same time an expression of the modifications of reality and the regulated transformations of thought, and is therefore both accommodation and assimilation. As elementary operations only begin to be 'grouped' towards the end of early childhood it is natural that in the preceding stages the child's mind should be in a constant state of flux between three states: temporary equilibrium (liable to continual 'displacements') between assimilation and accommodation, intermittent accommodation displacing the previous equilibrium, and assimilation of reality to the ego, i.e. to that aspect of thought which is still centred on itself because correlative accommodation is lacking. It follows that for the child assimilation of reality to the ego is a vital condition for continuity and development, precisely because of the lack of equilibrium in his thought, and symbolic play satisfies this condition both as regards signifier and signified. From the point of view of the signified, play enables the child to relive his past experiences and makes for the satisfaction of the ego rather than for its subordination to reality. From the point of view of the signifier, symbolism provides the child with the live, dynamic, individual language indispensable for the expression of his subjective feelings, for which collective language alone is inadequate. The symbol-object, being a real substitute for the signified, makes it actually present in a way that the verbal sign can never achieve. Since the child's whole thought is still egocentric and intuitive even in its states of maximal adaptation, and is thus linked at every intermediate stage with symbolic play, this form of play can be considered to be one of the poles of thought as a whole: the pole at which assimilation is dissociated from accommodation, or in other words, from egocentric thought in its pure state.

Symbolic play, then, is only one form of thought, linked to all the others by its mechanism, but having as its sole aim satisfaction of the ego, i.e. individual truth as opposed to collective and impersonal truth; but we are still faced by the question of why the use of the symbol as opposed to the verbal concept results in make-believe and not in belief. The natural attitude of the mind is belief, and doubt or hypothesis are complex, derived behaviours whose development can be traced between the ages of seven and eleven up to the level of formal operations, at which there is a real distinction between thought and spontaneous acceptance. But although none of the conditions for this hypothetical-deductive thought obtain in the play of very young children, they make statements for the sake of stating, without believing in the game they are playing. It is a commonplace that children make the distinction between pretence and reality very early. How, then, is pretence to be explained, and why is it that ludic symbolism is divorced from belief, in contrast to the symbolism of dreams and delirium and the religious symbolism of primitive tribes? It is a complicated question, for as Janet has shown, there are various types of belief. At the level of early childhood there are two contrasting types, the one connected with social, and more particularly adult, behaviours, the other with spontaneous and egocentric individual behaviours. The first is Janet's 'promise-belief', an acceptance of others and of the adult, and therefore adherence to the reality which is generally approved. The second is Janet's 'assertive belief', which precedes the distinction between what is certain and what is doubtful, and is linked with any impact of reality on the mind. At a later stage there is 'reflective belief', associated with the mechanism of intellectual and affective operations, as, for example, belief as a result of a deduction, or a deliberate, considered decision. When the child plays, he certainly does not believe, in the sense of socialized belief, in the content of his symbolism, but precisely because symbolism is egocentric thought we have no reason to suppose that he does not believe *in his own way* anything he chooses. From this point of view the 'deliberate illusion' which Lange and Groos see in play is merely the child's refusal to allow the world of adults or of ordinary reality to interfere with play, so as to enjoy a private reality of his own. But this reality is believed in spontaneously, without effort, merely because it is the universe of the ego, and the function of play is to protect this universe against forced accommodation to ordinary reality. There is no question, therefore, in the early stages of symbolic play, of consciousness of make-believe like that of drama or poetry.* The two- to four-year-old child does not consider whether his ludic symbols are real or not. He is aware in a sense that they are not so for others, and makes no serious effort to persuade the adult that they are. But for him it is a question which does not arise, because symbolic play is direct satisfaction of the ego and has its own kind of belief, which is a subjective reality. Moreover, as the symbol-object is a substitute for the reality it signifies, there develops, during the first stages, a kind of co-operation between the two, analogous to that between the image and the object it represents.

The question then is whether collective symbolic games result in the strengthening or weakening of belief, and the answer depends on age. In the case of very young children, collective play either has no effect on the egocentric symbolism or, when there is imitation, it enhances it. In the case of older children, in whose play the symbols are replaced by rules, it is obvious that the effect of social life is to weaken ludic belief, at least in its specifically symbolic form.

Games with rules remain to be considered in the light of what has been said above. We have seen that they mark the decline of children's games and the transition to adult play, which ceases to be a vital function of the mind when the individual is socialized. In games with rules there is a subtle equilibrium between assimilation to the ego – the principle of all play – and social life. There is still sensory-motor or intellectual satisfaction, and there is also the chance of individual victory over others, but these satisfactions are as it were made 'legitimate' by the rules of the game, through which competition is controlled by a collective discipline, with a code of honour and fair play. This third and last type of play is therefore not inconsistent with the idea of assimilation of reality to the ego, while at the same time it reconciles this ludic assimilation with the demands of social reciprocity.

The first part of this essay appears on pp. 166–71.

(From *Play, Dreams and Imitation in Childhood*, Routledge & Kegan Paul, 1951.)

* It is only after the age of seven that play really becomes make-believe in contrast to 'reflective belief'.

Some Properties of Social Play

The literature on children's play reflects a major concern with the *functions* of play in the child's individual cognitive, physical, or psycho-social development. The few empirical studies that have examined play in a social context have failed to ask how the interaction is carried out or what kinds of skills are involved in play interchanges. It is the purpose of this paper to describe the structure of spontaneous episodes of dyadic play and to suggest some of the basic competencies which underlie social play activity.

It is useful to distinguish four possible states which may obtain when two children are alone together: social non-play, e.g. both may collaborate to repair a broken toy; non-social non-play, e.g. one or both may independently explore an object; non-social play, e.g. one or both may engage in an independent imaginative activity, as when one child irons the laundry and the other builds a wall with blocks; and social play, e.g. both are mutually engaged in a housekeeping activity such as cooking and eating dinner or are driving the toy car to a family vacation.

Social play is defined here as a state of engagement in which the successive, non-literal behaviours of one partner are contingent on the non-literal behaviours of the other partner. Viewed from the standpoint of either partner, this means leaving interstices in one's behaviours for the other's acts and modifying one's successive behaviours as a result of the other's acts. Non-literal behaviour is not necessarily not serious – for play can be a serious business – but it is abstract in the sense that the primary purpose of a given behaviour is reduced to a meaning component, and its re-interpreted function in the chain of activity becomes primary. Applying these two criteria (alternating, contingent behaviours and non-literalness of those behaviours) we can contrast a very simple example of social play with a type of engagement which we would wish to exclude from this category. Two children stand close together in a playroom near a wooden car which both want to ride. One shoves the other who immediately shoves back, and simultaneous shoving occurs until one child is displaced from the area of a car. The behaviours are immediate, not spaced; neither child waits for the other to complete a behaviour. The same setting can result in social play. Both children stand near the car and one shoves the other, the second shoves back and waits, the first repeats the shove and waits for the other to shove in turn. The tempo of the activity appears to be mutually regulated. Further, neither child is displaced for the shoving is non-literal. Aggressive and defensive gestures identify the type of meaning of the play but this meaning is not primary; the re-interpreted function (marked by giggles, smiles, or exaggerated gestures) is that of moves or turns in a mock-challenge. The play episode may end with both children getting on the car or with both forgetting the car in the excitement of the interaction.

We can now examine some properties of the state of social play, analysing first the structures underlying the rhythmic, repetitive behaviours which we will call ritual play and then tracing the same structures in less stylized play episodes.

Procedures

The data on which these observations are based consisted of thirty-six fifteen- to twenty-minute videotaped play sessions. Children came in groups of three to the laboratory accompanied by their nursery school teacher. Each child formed a dyad with each of the two other members of the group. All members of the group were previously acquainted from nursery school. The children in twelve dyads fell into a younger age group (3 1/2 to 4 1/3 years); twelve into a middle group (4 1/2 to 5 years); and twelve into an older age group (5 to 5 1/2 years). In all there were twenty-one girls and fifteen boys, all from middle-class families. A dyad was left alone in a well-furnished playroom and was observed through one-way mirrors. The membership of the dyad was changed at the end of approximately fifteen minutes. The third child was occupied with a series of identification tasks in another room. Episodes of focused interaction were frequent (an average of sixty-six per cent of each session was spent in mutual engagement) and there was a good deal of talk in each session (on the average, one utterance every four seconds).

Three procedural safeguards were adopted to reduce the possibility of misinterpreting the meaning or intent of the children's verbal and non-verbal gestures. First, if an event (verbal or non-verbal behaviour of one child) was to be accepted as evidence of competence in distinguishing among modes of behaviour or as evidence of recognition of an obligation in an interaction, that event was required to be non-unique. That is, the event must have occurred in a similar context in more than one dyad. Second, in interpreting the meaning of lexical items or expressions, both the verbal and non-verbal context of events were taken into account. For example, in the text the meaning of 'pretend' was opposed to the meaning of 'really' or 'real'; that is, the meaning was defined in terms of contrast.

Further, in the instances cited, consistently different behaviours accompanied the use of these opposed terms. Third, the children's own reactions were used to interpret the significance of an event. The immediate consequence of an event was included as evidence of the meaning of that· event. For example, an assertion can be interpreted as an intended joke when the partner laughs and then is joined in laughter by the first speaker.

Using the criteria of non-literalness and alternating contingent behaviours and observing these procedural safeguards, two investigators independently identified social play episodes in the corpus. Inter-judge agreement on the identification of episodes of social play was eighty per cent. Only episodes on which the investigators agreed were used in the subsequent analysis. From these episodes the ritual play sequences were selected and classified according to the formats described below.

The ritual episodes were defined as sequences composed of repetitive and rhythmic exchanges. The investigators were able to concur on all such sequences, which are redundantly marked as social play. The alternating behaviours are closely integrated in time. Non-literalness is signalled by exaggerated intonation, by distorted tempo, and by broad or extreme gestures. Rituals which are primarily verbal are almost chanted. They are set off from their surrounding context by abrupt changes in volume, tempo, or intonation contour.

Analysis of social play formats

Recurring patterns of interaction were observed in the play sessions. The clearest examples of these patterns were found in the ritual play sequences, and we will examine these first. The structure of the inter-personal behaviours will be described in terms of the rules governing alternation of participation (turns), the substantive and formal relations of the alternating behaviours, and the manner in which sequences are built up (rounds).

Interactions may be analysed as composed of *turns* at acting. A turn is the contribution (verbal and/or non-verbal) of one participant in the interchange. The content of the second participant's turn may be the same as or different from that of the first participant. If different, the difference may be paradigmatic (a member of the same class) or syntagmatic (a member of a different class, one which has some linear or sequential relation to the first class). Using the conventions of indicating first speaker or actor as X, second speaker or actor as Y and of identifying the content of a turn by capital letters with subscript p = paradigmatic difference and s = syntagmatic difference, the basic patterns of turns can be illustrated.

In the first pattern, the rule is that all features of the second turn must be identical; relevant features appear to include rhythm, intonation, and

Turn patterns	X's turn	Y's turn
1. $A-A$	Bye, mommy.	Bye, mommy.
2. $A-B_p$	Bye, mommy.	Bye, daddy.
3. $A-B_s$	You're a nut.	No, I'm not.
4. $A-B_s$	I have to go to work.	You're already at work.
C_s	No, I'm not.	

volume. In the second pattern such features also appear to be maintained in the second turn, but the latter substitutes some component – here another term of address. The third pattern employs a sequential relation. The example is an assertion followed by a counter-assertion.

The first three patterns exemplify a *symmetrical* distribution of turns. A more complex pattern is constructed of *asymmetrical* turns, as in pattern 4, where X has two turns to Y's one.

Each of the patterns forms a *round*, which is a repeatable unit of interaction. A round may be repeated intact (R_i) or may be modified (R_m).* Returning to the patterns of turns, some of the ways in which sequences are constructed can be illustrated in two-round episodes.

Turn pattern, Round type	X's turn	Y's turn
1. R_i	Bye, mommy.	Bye, mommy.
	Bye, mommy.	Bye, mommy.
2. R_i	Bye, mommy.	Bye, daddy.
	Bye, mommy.	Bye, daddy.
3. R_m	Hello, my name is Mr Donkey.	Hello, my name is Mr Elephant.
	Hello, my name is Mr Tiger.	Hello, my name is Mr Lion.
4. R_m	I have to go to work. No, I'm not.	You're already at work.
	I have to go to school. No, I'm not.	You're already at school.

In a sequence of rounds, role assignment may be symmetrical, as in the preceding example, or asymmetrical as in the following, where roles are reversed at the beginning of the second round. (Non-verbal acts are enclosed in parentheses.)

* Round modification also may be analysed as paradigmatic or syntagmatic, but this distinction will not be made in the present discussion.

4. R_i *X.* I'll be the dragon and you be
St George that killed him.

                                         Y. (shoots the dragon, *X*)

     X. (falls dead)

                                           Y. Now I'll be the dragon.

     X. (shoots *Y*, the dragon)

                                           Y. Do it again, I'm not dead.

     X. (shoots again)

                                           Y. (falls dead)

The turn patterns and round types were grouped into formats which identify the structure of many of the play episodes observed. The formats, ranked in order of increasing complexity, are as follows:

	Turn pattern	*Round type*
Format 1:	1	R_i
2a:	1	R_m
2b:	2 or 3	R_i
3:	2 or 3	R_m
4:	4	R_i or R_m

Format 1 is, of course, symmetrical in respect to role alternation in rounds. Formats 3 and 4 may be symmetrical or asymmetrical. Format 2 occurred in the present corpus predominantly in symmetrical form.

The thirty-six dyads produced 158 clearly identified episodes of social play, which were distributed among the groups as follows: younger, forty-four; middle, fifty-eight; older, fifty-six. Of these episodes, seventy-four were instances of ritual play. No child failed to participate in at least one episode of ritual play. The distribution of the ritual play episodes among the four play formats is presented in Table 1[3]. A fifth category included in Table 1 is that of mixed formats which includes temporally cohesive sequences with a single theme which utilized successively two or more basic formats.

Table 1 indicates that ritual play episodes occurred in all age groups. It is clear that for this sample of children ritual play episodes were still a frequent type of interaction even among the older dyads. Further, the results suggest that the relative complexity of the formats as ranked corresponds to some degree to the increasing age of the three groups, although all age groups employed both simpler and more complex formats.

The final column of Table 1 indicates that younger dyads repeated the rounds of such episodes more extensively than older dyads. While the older dyads did not tend to repeat rounds more than twice the younger dyads repeated rounds on the average 3·8 times. On two occasions, younger dyads continued the sequence for ten or more rounds.

Table 1 Ritual play episodes of two or more rounds

Format	1	2(a + b)	3	4	Mixed	Total episodes	Average No. rounds per episode
Younger Group*	5	14		3	2	2	26	3·8
Middle Group*	2	6		12	3	2	25	2·5
Older Group*	1	7		8	4	3	23	2·2
Total episodes in each format	8	27		23	9	7	74	

*N = 12 dyads

Although this discussion has concentrated on the alternating, contingent behaviours of ritual interchanges, it is necessary to recall that such play episodes are also characterized by the quality of non-literalness. Thus, in the corpus from which these patterns have been abstracted, each episode was marked, often redundantly, as non-literal. For example, in the 'Bye, mommy' episodes the utterances were chanted. Further, the literal leave-taking meaning was subordinated to rhythmic echoing – neither child left or turned away. In the St George episode, non-literalness was marked by explicit preparatory role assignment, 'I'll be, you be'. That episode also illustrates another feature of the sequences, which is that a turn or round can be interrupted for clarification of rules or discussion of procedures and then resumed at the point where the break occurred. This feature supports the observation that play can be conducted seriously, i.e. that the actions must be performed in a certain way and must accomplish their intended outcome – in the St George episode, that of effectively killing the dragon.

Abilities underlying social play

Certain abilities must be postulated to account for the structures of play described above. We will discuss these abilities which are required to conduct ritual play episodes but will extend the discussion to include the non-repetitive episodes of social play.

I. Reality-play distinction

First, both participants must recognize that a state of social play obtains. In order to play with another, one must have a firm grasp of reality. Since the task of explicating what is meant by 'reality', either in the sense of Piagetian cognitive theory or in the sense of phenomenologists such as

Peter Winch, would take us too far afield, we can restate that condition: in order to play, one must have a grasp of what is not play – of what is and is not 'for real'. Although the play mode may be primarily assimilative (Piaget, 1951), that is, rather than accommodating itself to perceived (or absolute) reality it transforms and absorbs its object to previously held perceptions, the necessity of moving into or out of the mode requires a distinction between play and other activities. The children we observed gave ample evidence of making this judgement. One type of evidence is the children's use of the terms 'really' and 'pretend'. (We do not contend that the word meanings of these lexical items are, either in reference or connotation, identical with those in adult speech. However, the terms were used in a contrasting manner in the children's speech and that contrast was systematic and non-unique.) Example (1) illustrates the use of these terms.

(1) (*X* sits on three-legged stool that has a magnifying glass in its centre)
X. I've got to go to the potty.
>   *Y*. (turns to him) Really?
X. (grins) No, pretend.
>   *Y*. (smiles and watches *X*)

Since the state of play entails a suspension of literalness, the reality-play distinction appears to be essential to interpreting the partner's gesture in terms of its primary meaning or its non-literal meaning. Both partners must recognize that the state of play obtains in order to interpret and correctly respond to the other's behaviour. In fact, the participants often checked on the state in order to determine the appropriate response. In another dyad, the statement, 'I've got to go to the potty,' was followed by the partner's comment, 'So do I,' and both children immediately headed for the door. In example (1), some cue (*X*'s sitting on the magnifying stool, his expression, or both) led *Y* to check on the meaning of *X*'s announcement, and the information that *Y* received led to his subsequent response. Often the state of play was explicitly bounded. The most frequent markers opening a state of play were 'pretend', e.g. 'Pretend you called me on the telephone', or explicit role assignment, e.g. 'I'll be the mommy and you be the daddy, O.K.?' The state might end by tacit, mutual consent, or its termination might be explicitly marked, e.g. 'I'm not playing any more.'

The reality – play distinctions as made by the children themselves may be viewed as manipulations of categories and contexts, as explorations of the 'fit' of behaviours to changing definitions of situations (Bateson, 1956). Whatever the cognitive functions served by these explorations, the important point is that the distinction was often tested, even among the younger dyads. It appeared to be a relevant factor in the attitude or alignment taken, not only to objects, but to the behaviour of the partner, whose definition of the situation is critical to the continuing interchange.

II. *Abstraction of rules*

Winch (1958) has pointed out that it is only possible to talk of rule-governed behaviour when one can predict what will be done next and can recognize an error in procedure. According to these criteria, the children, often explicitly, demonstrated awareness that their social play depended on mutually accepted rules of procedure. It is necessary to make a distinction here between basic general rules for interaction and specific or local strictures applicable to a limited context. The most basic general rule which holds across both verbal and non-verbal interaction is that of reciprocity. Explicit encoding of this rule often took the form of 'taking turns', but implicit conformity to the rule was clearly apparent in the alternation of turns and their integration into rounds as exemplified in the play formats. Violations of the reciprocity rule were frequently challenged by invoking the rule, e.g. 'You go next.' Since this basic rule underlies much adult conversation, it will be useful to trace the probably simpler forms of that rule in children's play, and we will attempt to describe a portion of its development below.

The point to be made here is that the explicit invocation of a rule under similar conditions across a number of different situations indicates the ability to abstract that rule from the varied and often complex activities which it structures. It further suggests an ability to perceive actions in terms of socially distributed entities such as turns or, more complex than turns, rounds, for it is these entities rather than utterances which are apportioned to speakers in play and in conversation. An example of an interaction that reflects this ability is (2).

(2) (*X* and *Y* conduct a game that consists of *X* discovering a stuffed snake, *Y* sharing the discovery, *X* playing the straight man, and *Y* expressing fear.)

X. (holds up snake)

Y. (draws back in alarm) What's that?

X. It's a snake! (laughs at *Y's* exaggerated fear)

Y. Do it again.

X. (holds up snake)

In *Y*'s request 'it' refers to the whole round. The round was then repeated exactly as before. (Example 2, which shows asymmetrical turn structure, is classified as Format 4.)

The operation of local strictures in specific situations reveals both the orderliness and the credibility that children attribute to play episodes. One type of stricture applicable to role-centred states of play is that role behaviours and role attributes must remain consistent throughout the episode. If one partner departs from the jointly created image of the 'pretend' state, the other partner has the right to correct him. The negligent partner usually accepts the correction as in example 3.*

(3) (X, preparing to speak on telephone, addressed Y)
X. Pretend you're sick.

> Y. O.K.

X. (speaks into phone) Hey, Dr Wren,
    do you got any medicine?

> Y. Yes, I have some medicine.

X. (to Y) No, you aren't the doctor,
    remember?

> Y. O.K.

X. (speaks into phone) I need some medicine
    for the kids. Bye. (turns to Y) He
    hasn't got any medicine.

> Y. No? Oh, dear.

Y was corrected by X for misinterpreting his role. Y then accepted the correction and returned to role-acceptable behaviour.

Rules based on concepts of what behaviours and attitudes are appropriate to a particular role or activity were often stated as normative guidelines. For example, in a role-playing episode, a boy told a girl, 'Take that [holster] off. Girls don't wear things like that.' Often the children's concepts of role-appropriate behaviours were reflected in the selection of actions and objects for the co-operatively created situation. For example, in several mixed-sex dyads, the girl expressed fear of a large, stuffed snake. The boy reassured her and fearlessly killed the snake while the girl watched. Both general procedural rules (e.g. turn-apportionment rules) and rules guiding behaviour in particular situations are essential to the conduct of social play.

III. Theme and variation

Related to the ability to recognize and abstract the format of the play state is the ability to construct jointly the theme of the activity and to develop it in a manner consonant with the jointly held image of the state. Any episode of social play entails the exercise of *shared* imagination and the

---

*Two points should be made in respect to the figures in Table 1. First, we have no basis for comparison of these frequencies with other subject samples on such parameters as age, social class, or setting. Second, although a round in any play episode is potentially repeatable, we do not know what conditions influence the children to produce a ritual sequence, to choose another course of interaction, or to end the state of play.

shared development of the theme of the episode. An example of joint development of a theme by two boys, is (4).

(4) (*X* is busy cooking at the stove; *Y* watches)

X. O.K. dinner is ready. Now what do
   you want for dinner? (turns to *Y*)

       Y. Well . . . (indecisively)

X. Hot beef?

       Y. O.K., hot beef.

X. Coffee, too?

       Y. No, I'm the little boy. I'll
        have some milk.

X. O.K., you can eat now.

       Y. (moves closer to stove)

X. Kid, we're going to get some milk
   from the store. Come on in the
   dunebuggy.

       Y. O.K., I'm in the dunebuggy.

(dunebuggy is a small toy car, but
   X pushes it and *Y* moves beside it)

Neither child alone determined the course of this episode. Although *X* initiated it, *Y* contributed by adopting the role of little boy, rejecting the coffee and asking for milk. This move was then accepted by *X*, who had not explicitly identified himself as mother or father, but now addressed *Y* as 'Kid'. The move led to further integrated activity, i.e. going to get the milk.

While objects are freely transformed, e.g. stool to milk carton, to conform to the needs of the episode, consistency is maintained in respect to motives and appropriate actions for the roles adopted. The little boy drinks milk, not coffee, and as they started to bring the milk home, *X*, taking into account *Y*'s 'little boy' role, assured him that it was not too heavy for him to carry. Such explicit attention to motives and to role consonant behaviours suggests greater person-centred than object-centred concern in children of the ages observed. This would explain, in part, how the children were able so efficiently to express and perceive the subtle cues necessary to the flexible and rapid development of the themes of 'pretend' play.

In summary, we have proposed that young children distinguish between play and non-play modes of interaction and we have suggested some of the competencies that underlie the observed play episodes. We will now turn to a discussion of increasingly complex interaction structures.

Interaction structures

Taking turns implies an ability to identify a unit of social interaction, the turn or the round. In 'doing the same thing' as in a simple imitation of another's act one must be able to abstract the critical features of the act as well as its function in the structure or format of the interaction (Guillaume, 1971). The simplest forms of ritual play involve alternating repetitions as in Format 1 where the round composed of two turns can be repeated in virtually identical form a number of times. Non-verbal parallels were frequently observed. For example, one child threw a curtain into the air, smiled and waited while the other threw his curtain up. The round was repeated, with laughter accompanying each turn. Slightly more elaborate versions occur with identical turns when each round introduces a change of content as in Format 2a or when the content of the turns differs but each person repeats the content of his own previous turn in successive rounds, as in Format 2b. A still more complex format is achieved when the content of each turn in each successive round is progressively modified as in Format 3. This last type can exhibit considerable sophistication in use of words and syntax while still retaining the feature of constant intonation over each lexically varied event as in example (5).

(5) (*X* and *Y*, an older dyad, are discussing their feelings about the playroom)

X. Don't you wish we could get out of
  this place?

  Y. Yeah, 'cause it has yucky things.

X. Yeah.

  Y. 'Cause it's fishy too, 'cause it
    has fishes.

X. And it's snakey too 'cause it has
  snakes. And it's beary too 'cause it
  has bears.

  Y. And it's hatty too 'cause it has
    hats.

X. Where's the hats? (*X* ends the game.)

Although *X* slipped in a double play at his turn, the intonation of the four variant sentences was the same, and each production was greeted with an appreciative smile. *X*'s last utterance was a serious request for information. Its rapid tempo contrasted sharply with the measured rhythm of the ritual. A still more complex format can be achieved when a round is composed of asymmetrically distributed turns, as in Format 4. In this type, as in previous described formats, the turns may be verbal or non-verbal. In the following example (6) only *Y*'s turn was a verbal one.

(6) (*X* puts a toy car under the
  magnifying glass in the stool)

  Y. (looks in the glass) That's the
    biggest car I ever saw! (with
    exaggerated surprise)

(*X* looks in glass and laughs)
X then fetched a hat and placed it under glass to begin round 2, looking
   expectantly at *Y* who intoned, 'That the biggest hat I ever saw.'

The basic formats of these social play episodes form patterns of interaction from which the ritual aspects can be abstracted. An example (7) of a
conversational exchange free of ritual features is taken from an older dyad.

(7) (*X* and *Y* have just been left alone in the playroom)
X. (looks at *Y*) Hey, we have to be all
   by ourselves. But there's a good thing.
   I know how to be.

> *Y*. (approaches *X*) But there's a
> good thing. I won't cry when
> someone leaves me alone. Well,
> when I was little I always cried
> when someone left me alone. Once
> mommy and daddy both left and
> I cried and cried, and I've been
> so lonesome.

X. (attends story and nods)

The first turn is echoed and elaborated in the second turn. *Y* produced
her variant of the act produced by *X*, and *X* appeared to recognize, just
as *Y* did, that they were doing the same thing. A minimal change in content
would produce a fairly typical adult conversational exchange. Sacks (1967)
pointed out that 'doing the same thing' in adult conversation provides a
way of tacitly acknowledging the intent of the speaker's gesture by advancing and elaborating the meaning of that gesture.

Of course, many conversational and interactional structures which
reflect turn taking are based on doing a complementary thing, rather than
the same thing. Providing an appropriate complementary, or syntagmatic,
response also requires that the first gesture be correctly interpreted, since
one utterance form can often serve different conversational purposes. For
example, if the interrogative utterance, 'Can you open the door?' were
interpreted as a request for information the response, 'Yes, I can,' would
be appropriate; if it were taken as a request for action, then opening the
door, with or without a verbal accompaniment, would be an appropriate
response. In two examples (8 and 9), composed of another type of request
and its complementary response, the request was encoded in two different
ways by *X* before being correctly interpreted.

(8) (*X* and *Y* are talking while *X*, who is 'Mom', sets the table)
X. Why do brother and sister always
   laugh at me?

> *Y*. I don't know.

X. Every once a week they go
out playing and start laughing at me.

> *Y*. I know, um, that's an awful
> thing.

(9) (same dyad, same roles and activities, a few seconds later)

X. How come our house is so dirty?
Brother and sister have to make it
dirty?

> *Y*. What?

X. Brother and sister have to make my
whole nice room dirty.

> *Y*. I know, that's a horrible thing to
> do too.

Y's commiserative response to *X*'s complaints reveal that at least *X*'s second utterance in each episode was interpreted as a request for sympathy. *Y*'s final responses were instances of a conventionally appropriate complementary response (rather than an instance of doing the same thing). In example (8) it appears that *X* re-coded his first message because *Y*'s first answer, 'I don't know', did not provide the requested response. In both cases, *X* appeared to be satisfied with the final response. The request for a sympathetic response occurred frequently in social play among the older dyads. Although free of the rhythmic features characteristic of ritual play, exchanges of this type were marked by the somewhat exaggerated intonation associated with pretend and role play. We suggest that the ritual play formats which employ syntagmatically varied turns and round modification provide a basis for the acquisition of more specialized conversational exchange types.

But what might actually sustain the practice, or repetition, of these basic social formats? Why engage so often in the work of meshing or interrelating behaviours instead of simply chanting or performing some rhythmically satisfying monologue or individual game? It is reasonable to postulate that an intrinsically satisfying feature of social play, which is present for each participant, is the feature of control. Observations of the apparent satisfaction obtained in manipulating features of the physical environment or, differently stated, of the effectiveness of successful manipulation in maintaining behaviour have been made of infant behaviour (Millar, 1968, Chapter 4). Rapidly accumulating evidence on the sensitivity of young children to features of the human environment suggests that they would be ready and willing, perhaps before they were able, to attempt control of the human environment and derive satisfaction from successful control of another's behaviour. In the performances of ritual play such control is precise and knowledge of its success is immediate;

furthermore, the satisfaction derived is mutual, since each party is instrumental in eliciting and maintaining the responsive behaviour of the other. The analogy of the acquisition of basic social interaction patterns with the modularization of physical action patterns in the development of complex skills as described by Bruner (1971) is more than a suggestive metaphor.

References

BATESON, G. (1956), 'The message "This is play" ', in *Group Processes*, B. Schaffner (ed.), Macy Foundation, New York. (And see this volume, p. 119.)

BRUNER, J. S. (1971), 'The growth and structure of skill', in *Motor Skills in Infancy*, K. J. Connolly (ed.), Academic Press.

GUILLAUME, P. (1971), *Imitation in Children*, University of Chicago Press.

MILLAR, S. (1968), *The Psychology of Play*, Penguin.

PIAGET, J. (1951), *Play, Dreams, and Imitation in Childhood*, Routledge & Kegan Paul.

SACKS, H. (1967), unpublished lecture notes, The University of California at Irvine.

WINCH, P. (1958), *The Idea of a Social Science*, Routledge & Kegan Paul.

Freedom and Necessity in Poetry: My Lead Mine

What I have to say is really only a gloss on two lines by Goethe:

In der Beschränkung zeigt sich erst der Meister
Und das Gesetz nur kann uns Freiheit geben.

Most of what I know about the nature of poetry or, at least, about the kind of poetry I am interested in writing or reading, I learned long before the notion of writing poems ever occurred to me. Between the ages of six and twelve I spent a great many of my waking hours constructing a private sacred world, the principal elements of which were two: a limestone land-scape based on the Pennine Moors in the North of England, and an in-dustry, lead-mining. It was, unlike a poem, a pure private world of which I was the only human inhabitant: I had no wish to share it with others, nor could I have done so. However, I needed the help of others in procuring me the raw materials for its construction. Others, principally my parents, had to provide me with maps, guide-books, text-books on geology and mining machinery, and when occasion offered, take me down real mines. Since it was a purely private world, theoretically, I suppose, I should have been free to imagine anything I liked, but in practice, I found it was not so. I felt instinctively, without knowing why, that I was bound to obey certain rules. I could choose, for example, between two kinds of winding-engines, but they had to be real ones I could find in my books; I was not free to invent one. I could choose whether a mine should be drained by a pump or an adit, but magical means were forbidden.

Then, one day, there came a crisis. I was planning my Platonic Idea of the Perfect Concentrating Mill, and I had to choose between two types of a machine for separating the slimes, called a buddle. One type I felt to be the more 'beautiful' or 'sacred', but the other one was, I knew from my reading, the more efficient. I suddenly and clearly felt that I was faced with what I can only call a moral choice: I knew it was my duty to resist my aesthetic preference and choose the more efficient.

What, then, did I learn from this somewhat odd activity? Firstly, that the construction of any secondary world is a gratuitous, not a utile, act, some-thing one does, not because one must, but because it is fun. One is free to write a poem or to refuse to write one. However, any secondary world we may imaginatively construct necessarily draws its raw materials from the Primary World in which we all live. One cannot, like God, create *ex nihilo*. How much and how many facts one takes can vary very greatly. There are some poems, the songs of Campion, for example, which take almost nothing but the English language, so that, if one tries to translate them into another language, nothing is left of value. There are others, poems, *The Divine Comedy*, for instance, which include a very great deal from the Primary World, its history, its landscape, its theology, its astronomy, etc.

Any individual poet, however, is not completely free to choose what raw materials he will use, he can only use those which stir his imagination, those which he finds enchanting or numinous, and this is a matter outside his will to choose or change. A psychologist might, no doubt, be able to explain why, in my childhood, limestone and lead-mining so enchanted me; I only know that, in fact, they did.

Lastly, any secondary world is, like the Primary World, a world governed by laws. These may be very different from the laws of the Primary World, and may vary from one secondary world to another, but for each there are laws. Though a poet has a very wide range of choice in deciding what these laws shall be, his freedom is not unbounded, but must be suited to the contents, just as, while there are many kinds of rules for various card-games, all of them have to fit the fact of a pack of four suits of thirteen cards each ranging from the King to the Ace. To return to my buddle problem. Though, at the time, I knew I must, against my inclinations, choose the more efficient, it was only later that I came to understand clearly why. Even in an imaginary world a machine cannot escape the law of machinery, namely, that efficiency of function takes precedence over beauty of appearance. (See photo inset.)

(From 'The Place of Value in a World of Facts', *Nobel Symposium 14*, eds A. Tiselius and S. Nilsson, Almqvist & Wiksell, Stockholm, 1970.)

Character Games

The games I was fondest of were those in which I assumed another character; and in these I had to have an accomplice. We hadn't many toys; our parents used to lock away the nicest ones – the leaping tiger and the elephant that could stand on his hind legs; they would occasionally bring them out to show to admiring guests. I didn't mind. I was flattered to possess objects which could amuse grown-ups; and I loved them because they were precious: familiarity would have bred contempt. In any case the rest of our playthings – grocer's shop, kitchen utensils, nurse's outfit – gave very little encouragement to the imagination. A partner was absolutely essential to me if I was to bring my imaginary stories to life.

A great number of the anecdotes and situations which we dramatized were, we realized, rather banal; the presence of the grown-ups did not disturb us when we were selling hats or defying the Boches' artillery fire. But other scenarios, the ones we liked best, required secret performances. They were, on the surface, perfectly innocent; but in sublimating the adventure of our childhood or anticipating the future, they drew upon something secret and intimate within us which would not bear the searching light of adult gazes. I shall speak later of those games which, from my point of view, were the most significant. In fact, I was always the one who expressed myself through them; I imposed them upon my sister, assigning her the minor roles which she accepted with complete docility. At that evening hour when the stillness, the dark weight, and the tedium of our middle-class domesticity began to invade the hall, I would unleash my phantasms; we would make them materialize with great gestures and copious speeches, and sometimes, spellbound by our play, we succeeded in taking off from the earth and leaving it far behind until an imperious voice suddenly brought us back to reality. Next day we would start all over again. 'We'll play *you know what*,' we would whisper to each other as we prepared for bed. The day would come when a certain theme, worked over too long, would no longer have the power to inspire us; then we would choose another, to which we would remain faithful for a few hours or even for weeks.

However, religion, history, and mythology suggested other personages

I might play. I often imagined that I was Mary Magdalene, and that I was drying Christ's feet with my long hair. The majority of real or legendary heroines – Saint Blandine, Joan of Arc, Griselda, Geneviève de Brabant – only attained to bliss and glory in this world or in the next after enduring painful sufferings inflicted on them by males. I willingly cast myself in the role of victim. Sometimes I laid stress upon her spiritual triumphs: the torturer was only an insignificant intermediary between the martyr and her crown. And so my sister and I set ourselves endurance tests: we would pinch each other with the sugar tongs, or flay each other with the sticks of our little flags; you had to die without recanting, but I always cheated shamelessly, for I always expired at the first taste of the rod, but as long as my sister did not give in, I considered her still alive. At times I was a religious confined in a cell, confounding my jailer by singing hymns and psalms. I converted the passivity to which my sex had condemned me into active defiance. But often I found myself revelling in the delights of misfortune and humiliation. My piety disposed me towards masochism; prostrate before a blond young God, or, in the dark of the confessional with suave young Abbé Martin, I would enjoy the most exquisite swoonings: the tears would pour down my cheeks and I would sink into the arms of angels. I would whip up these emotions to the point of paroxysm when, garbing myself in the bloodstained shift of Saint Blandine, I offered myself up to the lions' claws and to the eyes of the crowd. Or else, taking my cue from Griselda and Geneviève de Brabant, I was inspired to put myself inside the skin of a persecuted wife; my sister, always forced to be Bluebeard or some other tyrant, would cruelly banish me from his palace, and I would be lost in primeval forests until the day dawned when my innocence was established, shining forth like a good deed in a naughty world. Sometimes, changing my script, I would imagine that I was guilty of some mysterious crime, and I would cast myself down, thrillingly repentant, at the feet of a pure, terrible, and handsome man. Vanquished by my remorse, my abjection and my love, my judge would lay a gentle hand upon my bended head, and I would feel myself swoon with emotion. Certain of my fantasies would not bear the light of day; I had to indulge them in secret. I was always extraordinarily moved by the fate of that captive king whom an Oriental tyrant used as a mounting block; from time to time, trembling, half-naked, I would substitute myself for the royal slave and feel the tyrant's sharp spurs riding down my spine.

(From *Memoirs of a Dutiful Daughter,* translated by James Kirkup, Penguin, 1970.)

Waiting for Cats

It was on the afternoon of the day of Christmas Eve, and I was in Mrs Prothero's garden, waiting for cats, with her son Jim. It was snowing. It was always snowing at Christmas. December, in my memory, is white as Lapland, though there were no reindeers. But there were cats. Patient, cold and callous, our hands wrapped in socks, we waited to snowball the cats. Sleek and long as jaguars and horrible-whiskered, spitting and snarling, they would slink and sidle over the white back-garden walls, and the lynx-eyed hunters, Jim and I, fur-capped and moccasined trappers from Hudson Bay, off Mumbles Road, would hurl our deadly snowballs at the green of their eyes. The wise cats never appeared. We were so still, Eskimo-footed arctic marksmen in the muffling silence of the eternal snows – eternal, ever since Wednesday – that we never heard Mrs Prothero's first cry from her igloo at the bottom of the garden. Or, if we heard it at all, it was, to us, like the far-off challenge of our enemy and prey, the neighbour's polar cat. But soon the voice grew louder. 'Fire!' cried Mrs Prothero, and she beat the dinner-gong.

(From *A Child's Christmas in Wales*, New Directions, Norfolk, Connecticut, 1954.)

Combat in Child Art

An excerpt from a study of the art-work of the author's youngest son.

During the pre-school years Douglas' art was a normal blend of non-objective and objective work, weaving the two together in the intermittent manner which typifies the art activity of young children. The representational forms that did appear were classic: mother, family members, an occasional vehicle, simple architectural forms, and the sporadic integration of letters and numbers.

Towards the end of the fourth year vehicles gained in importance and an occasional soldier or gun began to appear. By the fifth year he was well launched into representational work and had established a firm concept for a boat in battle, which provided the basis for extended manipulation and elaboration for a number of years. Eventually the boat theme became enlarged to embrace a range of potential encounters (land scenes, castle and fort sieges, etc.). Although military themes tended to dominate his interests, he sometimes extended his range of operation to include battles involving sports and athletic events. These increasingly gave way to subject matter of a technical nature, including depictions of manufacturing and scientific investigation. (See photo inset.)

Specific subject matter was less a common denominator than the general orientation and disposition of the activity, i.e. the process, the purposes it seemed to serve, the inclusion of such elements as confrontation, danger, motion, power, and co-operative effort.

What was notable about these productions was the specific approach to the 'making' process. Battle pictures were not so much akin to picture-making in its traditional sense as they were to the activity of dramatic play. Initially, Douglas would build an environment for himself, on land, sea, or within an architectural complex. Upon completion he would set about the vast task of providing the necessary men and appropriate equipment, and then when all was prepared, the encounter would begin. During this initial preparatory stage he was relatively inactive, working arduously, sometimes methodically making colour and design decisions, but once the battle began, it was quite another matter. Essentially, he entered the combat as a highly active participant, moving his body ferociously to simulate the destruction that might be imposed upon a single human being or piece of equipment, pounding with his fists ferociously . . . sometimes two or more crayons in each hand simultaneously . . . rocking and rolling, and emitting diverse, relevant accompanying sounds. It appeared that most of the time he played an important leadership role in the extravagant happenings, shouting out orders, announcing changes in tactics, and so on, although on occasion he was simply one of the many men and did his share of menial, routine work and fighting.

The actual moment of encounter, the battle itself, was the peak experience. Although violence and annihilation were obviously important ingredients, there was a lightness, a buoyancy, a sense of joy that accompanied the act and always seemed to prevail. There was no anger, no genuine fury, and if interrupted while engaged in his picture making, he was readily able to stop and join in routine communication only to return to his combat, revving up again, much as a plane does prior to take-off.

The materials with which he worked played an important role. He indicated unusual sensitivity towards them, not so much in a conscious way, but by incorporating their inherent qualities into the actuality of the experience. When working with crayon, he exploited its waxiness fully, squishing, twisting, building up layers of texture, allowing the consistency of the implement to become an integral part of the picture plane. Fluid materials such as paint or clay were allowed to follow their natural inclinations, and he magnificently merged their wetness into the specific configurations and symbols that he created. On one occasion while working on a hot summer night, a fat mosquito landed in the midst of his paper. Without pausing, he destroyed the insect with his crayons, rapidly working its remnants into the picture. There was no preoccupation with the sanctity of the paper or cardboard either. If it tore or folded, it simply became integrated, and penetrations of the surface were common.

Although in the early years two-dimensional materials dominated, as he grew older he investigated many different media, and some of his most dynamic expressive work has involved three-dimensional materials. On many occasions his initial environment has been constructed out of salvage or simple manipulative modelling materials; his men are then rapidly and expediently formed out of plasticene. Once the territory is created on the floor or table, he steps back from the field, hurls simulated gunfire and cannon-balls at the battle field and seems to derive great gratification from the actual physical changes that are engendered in the clay, the bits of fragmented wood, the overall destruction and re-alignment of this replication of reality. Acting upon the environment is paramount.

Of additional significance has been the creative fluency that has accompanied these manipulations. Materials and ideas, strong emotions, the happening, all merge into one organic total experience. There is none of the often seen preoccupation in a child of this age with whether or not a figure or an object is correctly depicted, no concern with accurate rendering or 'rightness' on a conscious primary level. The media and its potential for manipulation is simply the vehicle for some much more important expressive goal; it is to be exploited, to serve, not to impose restrictions. This is not to imply that Douglas does not involve himself in an appreciation of certain aesthetic aspects of his work; he certainly does. But this almost always takes place after the battle or encounter is completed. It is the 'egg in your beer', so to speak; it is an additional dividend, one that is nice to share with others about you, but certainly not the key motivation for creation.

This battle art was like dramatic play. It enabled Douglas to examine and identify with important occurrences, while merging a visible, concrete reality with a symbolically constructed reality. The performance was essentially one of high activity and motion, of building and destroying, one in which he could participate energetically, and one which, although potentially frightening and dangerous, was well within his ability to control. It called upon a full repertoire of intellectual, emotional, and physical activity, and was obviously of great personal significance.

Notes on the illustrations (see photo inset)

It is important to realize that each of these creations is accompanied during the making process by a succession of differentiated vocalizations, each expressing patterns and organizations of its own. Some of these are intelligible communications, many of which bespeak of incredible knowledge about the situation at hand. The following examples are extracted from a tape:

C'mon, get those rivets in there. Get that tower up. Get the engine parts in. This should almost take a day's more work; it's almost finished. Get that radar up! Hurry up with the last details on the bridge. C'mon, start making those circuits better. Hurry, we gotta get this thing on a dry dock.
Those elevators have to be checked out . . . We're going on patrol soon . . . get those guns ready for firing!

The engine room needs more help; all available men to the engine room to help. Start getting the tools in place . . . Is that P.A. system finished up yet. Get that system going! MAN YOUR POSTS!!! MEN DOWN ON THE FLIGHT DECK TO SIGNAL PLANES!! Here we go . . . all ahead flank!!!

But other sounds remain not unlike emotional scribblings, abstractions, some of which are closely akin to the emitted noises of various machinery and planes, some of which can be categorized as simply expressive, rhythmic, non-specific vocalizations.

Early efforts

Drawing 1.　　Age 3: Early scribbling, incorporating stamp fragments.

Drawing 2.　　Age 5·3: Earlier forms now appear as recognizable symbols of ship, men and equipment. The human figures at this stage have only heads, bodies and legs.

Drawing 3.　　Age 8·2: A mixed-media drawing of a land encounter, which reveals the same basic principles that are apparent in the sea pictures. In this instance men are equipped with hats and machine guns and are diminutive, affording an almost 'ant-like' impression. It becomes clear that strength is perceived as collectives, whether it be men, planes, or artillery. The ship is replaced as a centre of interest by the cannon and munitions, which appear to form a basic radical composition, not entirely unlike Douglas' schema for radar. This picture has been executed by means of three separate media: magic marker, cray-pas (a waxy chalk), and crayon. He allows them to coexist and merge, utilizing each one in the manner which best exemplifies its properties.

In all of these pre-schematic pictures colour is used with occasional deference to reality, but for the most part it is employed arbitrarily, serving the child's sense of adventure and spontaneity.

Later combat art

The transition from pre-schematic to schematic work was, as one would expect, a gradual, intermittent occurrence. By the seventh year Douglas had solidified his schema for frequently utilized subjects and was capable of greater elaboration, attention to subtleties, and a more mature approach to spatial treatments.

Drawing 4.　　Age: 9·7: This picture is typical of Douglas' mature ship pictures. Although many of these battle pictures represent fluency and a varied approach, one basic scheme has been produced perhaps over one hundred and fifty times during a five- or six-year period. I do not see this as 'being stuck' and representing fixation, but rather that the basic activity is still serving some larger need and a particular format accommodates that need in a continuing way. The same might be true for the fact that Douglas continues to represent men, planes, guns, etc., in exactly the same way over the years in these pictures. He is capable of producing forms in a more mature, representational manner, as is evidenced by some of his work; but it appears that he chooses not to utilize these other possibilities, since all that is really important is the representation of a significant perceptual symbol. The crude stick figure of man, and the efficient abbreviation of plane, gun, etc., enables him rapidly to deliver multiples that reflect the essence of the situation. Since the real task is one of creating an environment within which to act, elaboration of individual units would seem to be an extraneous undertaking.

This particular drawing, the seeds of which are firmly rooted in the earlier drawings, is basically symmetrical, employing a vertical, horizontal axis (ship), flanked on either side by converging diagonals (planes). The X-ray is still employed. Earlier compartmentalizations are now integrated into functional units, and men attend a variety of tasks in their individual cubicles; a definite purpose exists. The arrow-like schema for planes is now executed with incredible rapidity, as are the ferocious dottings and slashings which serve to reveal the shooting and explosions. Ships and small craft are placed upon the sea with reasonably appropriate size relationships, and colour is more consistently considered in terms of objective reality. Water is unquestionably blue now; fire, red, orange, or yellow; men of opposing sides, each with their own colour.

The Sense of Nonsense Verse

The eye of man hath not heard,
the ear of man hath not seen . . .
William Shakespeare, *A Midsummer Night's Dream*

A letter

I received the following letter:

'Shame on you, Comrade Chukovsky, for filling the heads of our children with all kinds of nonsense, such as that trees grow shoes. I have read with indignation in one of your books such fantastic lines as:

Frogs fly in the sky,
Fish sit in fishermen's laps.
Mice catch cats
And lock them up in
Mousetraps.

Why do you distort realistic facts? Children need socially useful information and not fantastic stories about white bears who cry cock-a-doodle-doo. This is not what we expect from our children's authors. We want them to clarify for the child the world that surrounds him, instead of confusing his brain with all kinds of nonsense.'

As I read this letter I began to feel not only depressed but also stifled.

Had my accuser had other resources than 'common sense', he would have realized that the nonsense that seemed to him so harmful not only does not interfere with the child's orientation to the world that surrounds him, but, on the contrary, strengthens in his mind a sense of the real; and that it is precisely in order to further the education of children in reality that such nonsense verse should be offered to them. For the child is so constituted that in the first years of his existence we can plant realism in his mind not only directly, by acquainting him with the realities in his surroundings, but also by means of fantasy.

Timoshka on a pussycat

So that my accuser might fully comprehend the above truth, I would converse with him even from a distance and would tell him approximately the following:

Have you noticed, my misguided friend, that in Russian folk rhymes for children – in those masterpieces of poetry which have such great educational power – seldom does anyone gallop on horseback, but more often on a cat or a hen or some other unlikely animal?

There is thunder in the glen
As Foma rides a hen;
Timoshka on a pussycat,
Fast along the crooked path.

Yes, it seems that there is no bird or animal on which human beings do not take a ride in Russian children's folk verses:

An old woman mounted a sheep
And rode up the mountain steep ...

Get on a terrier
Ride to the farrier ...

Masha left her hut so narrow
To take a ride on a tiny sparrow ...

Petya holding on to a duck's bill
Rode out to the field to till ...

Everywhere in these rhymes there is a distinct departure from the norm – from the horse. How do *you* explain such 'nonsense'? Rural youngsters 'from two to five' refuse somehow to introduce into their rhymes the horse-back rider and his horse. It was only yesterday that they assimilated the important fact that a horse exists for transportation, yet today they knowingly ascribe this function to every unlikely creature.

Along the stream, along the river
Mr Redhead rode a beaver;
He met Mr Redface not in a boat
But riding a silly-looking goat.

Children make every effort to substitute for the horse any kind of nonsensical alternative, and the more palpable the nonsense the more enthusiastically does the children's rhyme cultivate it:

The cook rode on a rickety van
Harnessed to a frying pan.

And things are carried so far as to substitute for animals that seem to the child's eye enormous (like horses), miscroscopic beetles, thus emphasizing even more strongly children's obvious eccentricity in rejecting the normal:

Tiny children
On tiny beetles
Went for a ride.

But it must be noted here that simultaneously with this extreme rejection of the normal, the child is keenly aware of the normal. No matter on what kind of beetles the heroes of these rhymes ride, the child visualizes in his mind the horse that is also present, although invisibly. At times the horse seems to be present visibly, but then it makes its appearance only so that its rejection is even more noticeable:

I harnessed the horse
But the horse did not budge;
I harnessed the gnat
And the gnat sped away
To the barn.

The consistent aversion of the child to carefully established reality is universal. There is no limit to the number of ways the folk rhyme distorts the act of riding on a horse. And even when the horse remains in the verse, other means are used to demonstrate the rejection of the norm. Either the adjectives that always describe the horse and the vehicle it pulls are interchanged:

He rode on a dappled wagon
Tied to a wooden horse,

or the rider and the place he rides by are interchanged:

The village rode
Past the peasant,

or the rider sits facing in an abnormal direction:

He sat with his back to the front
As he rode off to the hunt.

In other words, one way or another, the desired distortion will be achieved, leaving untouched those elements from which the image of the horse rider is formed.

This tendency to present objects in a deliberately incorrect juxtaposition has been borrowed from folk verse and introduced into literary published works, and has been firmly established as a genre in many favourite children's rhymes. For instance, in one such rhyme two mutually exclusive means of transportation appear simultaneously:

The old woman was riding horseback
Sprawled in a fine carriage.

Children and 'Topsy-Turvies'

There is no doubt that the lines I have just cited have been accepted and approved by countless generations of Russian children. However, although each new generation of parents, grandfathers, and grandmothers sings and recites to children both the good and the inferior, only that which best serves the children's needs and tastes remains in their memories. And when he reaches old age, everyone who heard in his childhood these folk chants passes on to his grandchildren, in his turn, the very best, the most vivid and vital. And everything that is out of tune and incongruous with the psychology of the young child is gradually forgotten and becomes extinct; thus it is not passed on to posterity and ceases to exist for the next generation of youngsters.

This has proven a most reliable method of selection, and, as a result, over the centuries Russian children have inherited a precious treasure of songs which are so superlative because they were, in a sense, perpetuated by the children themselves. What was unsuitable for them perished along a thousand-year-old road. In this way an exemplary children's folklore has come into existence – exemplary in its language and rhythm, as well as ideally suited to the intellectual needs of the young child. Thus it is one of the strongest means of using the greatness of folklore for educational purposes.

The great book that is called by the English *Mother Goose* came into being exactly the same way. Many of these rhymes were first published four or five hundred years ago. For instance, *Three Wise Men of Gotham* was already considered an old rhyme in the middle of the fourteenth century.

Why, then, we ask, does one find in these folk verses, so wonderfully adaptable to the education of children, such a large number that are so odd and outlandish and so dedicated to a constant departure from the norm? Why is it that so many typical children's rhymes, approved by millions of youngsters in the course of many centuries, cultivate with such persistence the obvious violation of reality?

I have used only one theme – the horse carrying the man. But if we examine carefully children's folk literature, we find that almost every theme within the ken of children is subjected to the same treatment, as though the idea of a strict order of things and events were intolerable to the three-year-old mind.

Many verses seem to make a special effort to transpose and throw into confusion the many experiences of children which constitute their world. Most often the desired nonsense is achieved by an interchange of the functions of objects. It was by means of this very method that tall tales became part of folklore and are now widely known among Russian children:

In the sea the corn kiln burns
While the ship runs in the cornfield.

Six things are combined in these lines in a way that is completely odd: seas and kilns, ships and fields, water and fire. A similar reversed order of typical phenomena of sea and forest is found in English folklore: 'The hermit asked me: "How many strawberries grow on the bottom of the sea?" And I answered: "As many as there are red herrings in the forest." '

Allow me to repeat and re-emphasize that to be able to respond to these playful rhymes the child must have a knowledge of the real order of things: herrings are in the sea, strawberries grow in the forest. If he does not know, for example, that there is ice only in cold weather, he will not respond to the English verse,

The child skated on the ice
On a hot summer's day.

It is important first of all to understand and to remember this: all such nonsense verses are regarded by children precisely as nonsense. They do not believe for one moment in their authenticity. The ascribing of incongruous functions to objects attracts them as a diversion.

In the minor Russian genres of folklore this playfulness takes the form of slips of the tongue:

'One and a half milks of jug . . .'
'The belt wears the peasant around its waist . . .'
'Look, the gate barks at the dog . . .'
'The peasant grabbed the dog and beat the stick . . .'
'The dough is kneading the woman . . .'

At times there is an open play on incongruities. An example of this is the following verse which becomes a favourite with every new generation of children:

The blind man gazes
The deaf man listens
The cripple runs a race
The mute cries: 'Help.'

Such verses are sometimes called fiddle-faddles or absurdities.

Listen, my children
And I'll sing you a fiddle-faddle:
'The cow sat on a birch tree
And nibbled on a pea.'

One can cite any number of such verses which testify to the inexhaustible need of every healthy child of every era and of every nation to introduce nonsense into his small but ordered world, with which he has only recently become acquainted. Hardly has the child comprehended with certainty which objects go together and which do not, when he begins to listen happily to verses of absurdity. For some mysterious reason the child is attracted to that topsy-turvy world where legless men run, water burns, horses gallop astride their riders, and cows nibble on peas on top of birch trees.

Isolating these verses in children's folklore as a special category, I have given the whole series the name 'rhymed topsy-turvies', and I have tried to ascertain their practical purpose in the context of folk teaching. I said to myself: it is unlikely that the people have so persistently, in the course of so many centuries, offered to new generations of children such a multitude of these odd poetic creations if they did not contribute to their proper psychological development.

Nevertheless, I was unable for a long time to find the reason for the attraction that a topsy-turvy world held for young children. Neither Russian nor foreign authors have written a single word about this. Then, at last, I found the explanation for this strange phenomenon, not in literature, but in life itself.

My 2-year-old daughter supplied the answer to this riddle.

For her, at that time, as for many other children of similar age, it was a source of great emotional and mental activity, although in itself seemingly insignificant, that a rooster cries cock-a-doodle-doo, a dog barks, a cat miaows.

These simple bits of knowledge were great conquests of her mind. Indelibly and forever did she ascribe to the rooster the 'kukareku', to the cat the 'miaow', to the dog the 'bow-wow', and showing off justifiably her extensive erudition, she demonstrated it incessantly. These facts brought simultaneously clarity, order, and proportion to a world of living creatures as fascinating to her as to every other tot.

But, somehow, one day in the twenty-third month of her existence, my daughter came to me, looking mischievous and embarrassed at the same time – as if she were up to some intrigue. I had never before seen such a complex expression on her little face.

She cried to me even when she was still at some distance from where I sat:

'Daddy, 'oggie – miaow!' – that is, she reported to me the sensational and, to her, obviously incorrect news that a doggie, instead of barking, miaows. And she burst out into somewhat encouraging, somewhat artificial laughter, inviting me, too, to laugh at this invention.

But I was inclined to realism.

'No,' said I, 'the doggie bow-wows.'

''Oggie – miaow!' she repeated, laughing, and at the same time watched my facial expression which, she hoped, would show her how she should regard this erratic innovation which seemed to scare her a little.

I decided to join in her game and said:

'And the rooster miaows!'

Thus I sanctioned her intellectual effrontery. Never did even the most ingenious epigram of Piron evoke such appreciative laughter in knowledge-able adults as did this modest joke of mine, based on the interchange of two elementary notions. This was the first joke that my daughter became aware of – in the twenty-third month of her life. She realized that not only was it not dangerous to topsy-turvy the world according to one's whim, but, on the contrary, it was even amusing to do so, provided that together with a false conception about reality there remained the correct one. It was as if she perceived in an instant the basic element in comedy, resulting from giving simultaneously to a series of objects an opposite series of mani-festations. Realizing the mechanics of her joke, she wished to enjoy it again and again, thinking up more and more odd combinations of animals and animal sounds.

It seemed to me at that point that I understood the reason for the passion that children feel for the incongruous, for the absurd, and for the severing of ties between objects and their regular functions, expressed in folklore.

The key to this varied and joyful preoccupation which has so much im-portance in the mental and spiritual life of the child is play, but play with a special function.

(From *From Two to Five*, University of California Press, 1963.)

Play With Language and Meta-Linguistic Awareness: One Dimension of Language Experience

Although the title speaks of play and then meta-linguistic awareness, I am going to talk about them in the reverse order – first, explain what I mean by 'meta-linguistic awareness' as a special dimension of language experience and its seeming importance in education; then describe one, and only one, conception of the function of 'play' in general and play with language in particular; and finally ask how we might encourage play with language in school.

Meta-linguistic awareness

It is intuitively obvious to us as language users that when either speaking or listening, our focal attention is not on speech sounds, nor even on larger units such as words and syntactic patterns. Our focal attention is on the meaning, the intention, of what we or someone else is trying to say. The language forms are themselves transparent; we hear through them to the meaning intended. As the Duchess rightly says in *Alice in Wonderland*, 'and the moral of *that* is – take care of the sense and the sounds will take care of themselves'.

However, it is an important aspect of our unique capacities as human beings that we can not only act, but reflect back on our own actions; not only learn and use language, but treat it as an object of analysis and evaluation in its own right. Meta-linguistic awareness, the ability to make language forms opaque and attend to them in and for themselves, is a special kind of language performance, one which makes special cognitive demands, and seems to be less easily and less universally acquired than the language performances of speaking and listening. Our concern as educators with this particular kind of language performance comes from increasing arguments that it is at least very helpful – and maybe critically important – not so much in the primary processes of speaking and hearing as in what may be considered the derived or secondary processes of reading and writing.

The idea that such awareness is related to literacy is not new. For more than ten years we have been reading in Vygotsky (1962) that literacy depends on, and in turn contributes to, making previously non-conscious or tacit knowledge more conscious. More recently, a conference resulting in the book *Language by Ear and by Eye* (Kavanaugh and Mattingly, 1972) focused directly on the differences that must exist between learning to speak and learning to read. Mattingly, in his chapter on 'Reading, the Linguistic Process and Linguistic Awareness', says:

Speaking and listening are primary linguistic activities; reading is a secondary and rather special sort of activity that relies critically upon the reader's awareness of those primary activities (p. 133) ... Linguistic awareness is very far from evenly distributed over all phases of linguistic activity (p. 139). [E.g., awareness is greater for words than syllables; for syllables than sounds; and in general for units than for rules that govern their structural arrangements.] ...

Mattingly then suggests the relationship that is the focus of this paper – the relationship to verbal play:

There appears to be considerable individual variation in linguistic awareness. Some speaker-hearers are not only very conscious of linguistic patterns, but exploit their consciousness with obvious pleasure in verbal play, e.g., punning [and versifying, solving crossword puzzles, and talking Pig Latin] or verbal work (e.g., linguistic analysis). Others never seem to be aware of more than words ... this variation contrasts markedly with the relative consistency from person to person with which primary linguistic activity is performed (p. 140) ... Our view is that reading is a language-based activity like Pig Latin or versification and not a form of primary linguistic activity analogous to listening (p. 141).

If linguistic awareness is so important, what do we know about its development?

The Soviet psychologist, Elkonin (1971) argues against the 'glass theory', which is exactly what I have been calling the transparency of language. Elkonin agrees that 'the development of awareness of the language's phonological aspect ... represents one of the most essential pre-conditions for ... learning literacy'. But he asserts that children's playful manipulation of the sounds of words, apart from their meanings, is a natural, normal part of language development itself:

Just as the mastery of objective reality is not possible without formation of activity with objects, exactly in the same manner is language mastery not possible without formation of activity with language as the material object with its concrete form (p. 141).

In other words, according to Elkonin, children, as part of their species-specific ability to learn language, will use elements of that language as the objects of one aspect of development not specific to humans – namely, play. Children may shift more easily than adults between using language forms transparently in inter-personal communication, and treating them as opaque objects in play. In other words, when the child's intention is to communicate, he – like the adult – can 'hear through' his language to that end; but it is hypothesized that the child can also intend to play with the elements of language for the very delight of self-expression and mastery, and does so more easily than the adult unless the latter is a poet. This brings us to consider more generally one function of play in development.

Play

Play, according to Peter Reynolds (1972) is the performance of segments of behaviour separated from their usual instrumental context, with the functional effect of elaborating and integrating that behaviour, and the affective effect of joy. If play is an essential part of the developmental process, then its presence or absence should make a difference. Reynolds suggests that 'What is required is an assessment of the relative survival of rehearsed versus unrehearsed performances measured in terms of the particular selective system to which the action is coupled.' In our terms, the hypothesis to be treated is that a child's play with language makes one human adaptation, literacy, easier to achieve because the child's attention has been focused on the means, the forms of language, whereas in normal communicative contexts, his attention is focused only on the end.

This hypothesis remains to be tested. Some suggestive evidence exists. Negatively, Ilse Mattick (1967), in her description of the language and cognitive development of 'children of disorganized lower-class families', specifically mentions that 'there was a lack of exploration of language and an absence of the usual play with words which facilitates increasing communicative skills and serves to extend knowledge'.

More positively, we know that many young children do play with language, and that sensitive parents and teachers value that play. Examples come from a linguist-mother, Ruth Weir (1962), a Russian listener-writer of children's stories, Kornei Chukovsky (1963), and a teacher-observer of pre-school children, Harriet Johnson (1972).

In her introduction to the reissue of Harriet Johnson's book, *Children in The Nursery School*, Barbara Biber emphasizes that Miss Johnson thought that 'learning was soundest when the environment encouraged the child in his impulse to "experiment" with the exercise of his growing powers in the widening world of experience' and she specifically included words as important objects for that experimentation. For example, Geordie, who at 24 months had a fair vocabulary, accompanied motoric activities with varied syllabication:

As he ran: Bee, bee, bee; Lee, lee, lee; Dub, dub, dub
At top of slide: Ma-wee, ma-wee, ma-wee, ma-wee, A-a.

Or Mathew, as he was being undressed:

Nolly lolly, nolly, lolly, nilly lolly, sillie Billie,
nolly lolly.

And Donald as he ran around the roof:

Up a lup a dup, Up a dup I go.

Because Miss Johnson's children had companions in their play, as Anthony
Weir did not, two children sometimes created joint chants. For example,
3-year-old Philip and Caroline in the sandbox, where meaningful communication sometimes is inserted into nonsense chant play:

Philip: 'Ees not.'
Caroline: 'Ees not.'
Philip: 'Eh.'
Caroline: 'Eh.'
Philip: 'Go 'way.'
Caroline: 'Go 'way.'
Philip: 'Go 'way ko.'
Caroline: 'Go 'way ko.'
Philip: 'Go 'way ki.'
Caroline: 'Go 'way ki.'
Philip: 'Aw dee, de wa, di geh.'
Caroline: 'Aw dee, de wa, di geh.'
Philip: 'My o ketty.'
Caroline: 'My o ketty.'
Philip: 'Ga de.'
Caroline: 'Ga de.'
Philip: 'Oh, see wain go in.'
Caroline: 'Oh, see rain go in!'
Philip: 'Ees no more holes.'
Caroline: 'Ees no more holes.'

Later, beyond the years described by Weir, Johnson and Chukovsky,
comes children's delight in puns and riddles, not just turning word meanings upside down, but playing with the effects of two meanings considered
simultaneously, or the transformations of parts of words for new effects. A
young friend of mine, John Rosenthal of Washington, D.C., knowing of
my interest in word games, has been sending me examples of the current
seven-year-old folk culture:

Q. What word has more letters than any other in the world?
A. Mailman.

Police: You can't park here.
Driver: Why not?
Police: Read that sign.
Driver: I did. It says, 'Fine for parking'.

Q. What did Tenne-see?
A. The same thing Arkan-saw.

Q. What time did the man go to the dentist?
A. Too-th irty.

And at about the same time, from about the age of seven on, children play verbal games – to be distinguished from verbal play by the existence of rules which can be described and transmitted from one player to another, such as the classification game 'categories', sequencing-memory games like 'I pack my trunk' and games of word formation and transformation like *Ghost* and *Pig Latin*. Just as children can learn about their language from word games, so can we – linguists, anthropologists, or educators – learn about children and their language-learning processes by studying their verbal play and games. (See photo inset.)

Implications for education

And so what can we suggest for education? We started out with the importance which the authors in *Language by Ear and by Eye* credited to awareness of language as critical for achieving literacy, and their hope that we could learn how to cultivate it. Elkonin suggested that language was in fact more opaque to children than to adults. Presumably our overly instrumental attitude towards language for communication has dulled our ability and interest in attending to non-instrumental language elements for the joy of it (outside of the few poets and creative punsters, and the many more who enjoy crossword puzzles or games like Scrabble). Elkonin also urged that this opaqueness be kept alive at all ages by valuing and encouraging verbal play at home and school. Finally, Reynolds gave evolutionary support to the value of play and, by implication, of play with language for human children.

I think we can encourage verbal play and I think we should – not at the expense of stimulation of language for communication, but in addition to it. The danger is that when adults intervene in play, it may lose its critical characteristics and therefore its special value. We must maintain an atmosphere of familiarity and emotional reassurance, not inhibit play by directing it, or prevent its intrinsically joyful quality through external reinforcement.

In closing, I can do no better than quote Lucy Sprague Mitchell, from the section on Form in the Introduction to her *Here and Now Story Book*:

There is no better play material in the world than words. They surround us, go with us through our work-a-day tasks, their sound is always in our ears, their rhythms on our tongue. Why do we leave it to special occasions and to special people to use these common things as precious play material? Because we are grown-ups and have closed our ears and our eyes that we may not be distracted from our plodding ways! But when we turn to the children, to hearing and seeing children, to whom all the world is as play material, who think and feel through play, can we not then drop our adult utilitarian speech and listen and watch for the patterns of words and ideas? Can we not care for the *way* we say things to them and not merely *what* we say? Can we not speak in rhythm, in pleasing sounds, even in song for the mere sensuous delight it gives us and them, even though it adds nothing to the content of our remark? If we can, I feel sure children will not lose their native use of words: more, I think those of six and seven and eight who have lost it in part – and their stories show they have, – will win back to their spontaneous joy in the play of words.

(From a paper presented at the second Lucy Sprague Mitchell Memorial Conference, *Dimensions of Language Experience*, at Bank Street College of Education, New York City, 19 May 1973.)

References

CHUKOVSKY, K. (1963), *From Two to Five*, University of California Press. (And see this volume, p. 596.)

ELKONIN, D. B. (1971), 'Development of speech', in *The Psychology of Preschool Children*, A. V. Zaporozhets and D. B. Elkonin (eds), (first published, 1964), M.I.T. Press, pp. 111–85.

JOHNSON, H. M. (1972), *Children in The Nursery School*, (first published, 1928), Agathon Press, New York.

KAVANAUGH, J. F., and MATTINGLY, I. G. (eds), (1972), *Language by Ear and by Eye: the Relationship between Speech and Reading*, M.I.T. Press.

MATTICK, I. (1967), 'Description of the children', in *The Drifters: Children of Disorganized Lower-class Families*, Little Brown, Boston, U.S.A., pp. 53–83.

MITCHELL, L. S. (1948), *Here and Now Story Book*, E. P. Dutton, New York.

REYNOLDS, P. (1972), *Play and Human Evolution*, Stanford University Medical Center. Paper presented at the annual meeting of the American Association for the Advancement of Science, 1972. (And see this volume, p. 621.)

VYGOTSKY, L. S. (1962), *Thought and Language*, M.I.T. Press. (And see this volume, p. 537.)

WEIR, R. H. (1962), *Language in the Crib*, Mouton, The Hague. (And see this volume, p. 609.)

Playing with Language

Introduction

This research deals with certain aspects of the language of a $2\frac{1}{2}$-year-old child. The investigation focuses on language, both as a skill, that is, in its distinctive function, and as a means of communication, that is, in its significative function. The child's language is studied as a self-contained system under special circumstances, namely, just before he falls asleep at night, and his linguistic system at the time can be called his own 'idiolect'.

In addition to the establishment of the child's phonemes, their patterning is studied in terms of clusters occurring in his speech. However, since the phoneme is a bundle of simultaneous articulatory features which appear in combination with each other, it must be assumed that the child learns these important sub-phonemic elements so that his phonemes can be properly actualized. It is a relevant question to ask, which of these features have been learned well by the child, which ones are still unstable, or which ones he still ignores.

The hierarchical nature of a linguistic structure imposes as the next step the study of forms and their meanings. Again, the issue revolves around the child's morphemes and words and their variants within his self-contained system, although some comparison with his day speech and the structure of forms in adult English will be made. In his morphology and vocabulary, the combinatory possibilities allow the child some freedom which had not been available to him in the phonology and he makes limited use of them, in word coinage. His selection of linguistic entities will be described in examining his linguistic system in a number of functions.

The arrangement of forms, or the syntactic constructions and sentence types, present an interesting system in the child's language, often mastered, apparently, before the forms themselves. The relative freedom of possible combinations into sentences, and the great freedom of combinatory possibilities into even larger units give the child the opportunity for a good deal of linguistic exercise.

We would, however, be remiss if we restricted our linguistic analysis to phonology and grammar, without dealing with the various functions of language. Jakobson (1960) has outlined six such functions, corresponding to the constituents of the speech events, and we will apply these to our data. In order to do that, the distinctive elements of sounds and forms must be analyzed first as the system underlying the various functions of the child's language. Freud's 'sense in nonsense' (1960) in dealing with language in the description of the joke technique is relevant to an understanding of the nature of the monologues. Just as the pleasure in a joke can be derived from play with words, so does the child enjoy play with words. But analogous to the joke, where there is sense in nonsense in the deliberate use of word play, the child's word play also makes sense. The pleasure of play is structured so that it serves as a systematic linguistic exercise.

Language functions

We often encounter reference to linguistic play in the literature on child language. Thus Chao (1951) says: 'There is occasional intentional playing with language . . . The resulting syllables are usually not expected to make sense.' Or Kaper (1959) talks of the use of words for pleasure by the young child. Ohnesorg (1947) also confirms the play with words, as do Jespersen (1922) and Stern and Stern (1928). The latter two, however, go further when they mention the child's predilection for rhythm, rhyme, and alliteration. Scupin and Scupin (1907) discuss 'Klangassoziationen', association based on recurring sounds. In our recordings, a great deal of play with the sounds of words and with the words themselves is found. Coming back to Jakobson's outline of the functions of language, we have in such instances as the primary function what he calls the *poetic* function of language. That is not to say that the child is creating poetry, just as the political slogan 'I like Ike' analysed by Jakobson is not a poem, but a poetic exploitation of the function of language with the referential function being only secondary. So there are a great number of instances in the child's monologues where play with the sounds of the language is basic in the hierarchy of language functions with other functions, be they referential or conative or metalingual, subordinated to it.

A great number of examples of the child's play with sound can be found throughout the corpus. We will quote a few simple examples. . . .

Babette
Back here
Wet

Babette is the name of an acquaintance whom the child has seen only very few times, and it is unlikely that she had made any particular deep impression on the child. However, for phonologic reasons, the name probably has appeal to him since the syllables alliterate and have rhythm. *Back* of the next line repeats the alliterating /b/, followed not only by the same phoneme /E/ as in the second syllable of *Babette*, but also by the same phonetic variant [ɛ] which again occurs in the third line, *wet*. The alveolar /t/ of the first line is changed to velar /k/ in the second, but /t/ reappears in the third line where the bilabiality of the preceding two initial /b/'s is again reflected in the glide /w/.

The sentence *Daddy dance*, formally an imperative, expressing a wish which has rarely, if ever, been granted, occurs several times non-contiguously in a paragraph, and it is a clear example of sound play where every syllable begins with the same consonant /d/, the first and third also having the same vowel phoneme /E/, giving the sentence rhythm and alliteration.

Second only to the role of sound play is the one assumed by grammatical practice. This can be subsumed under the heading of *meta-language* as the logicians have called speaking about language. In the child's monologues, it is often accomplished by the selection of a grammatical pattern where substitution occurs in one slot of the grammatical frame. The words substituted often belong to the same form class, or pronouns are substituted for nouns. The selection within the form class, in turn, can be governed either by sound or meaning associations. The paragraph:

(1) *What colour*
(2) *What colour blanket*
(3) *What colour mop*
(4) *What colour glass*

is an exercise in noun substitution. The first line is merely the frame of the pattern, the full pattern occurring in the second line, with lines three and four repeating the frame with different substitution items of the same form class as in the original pattern sentence. The items are selected phonologically, that is, on the basis of sound. The bilabiality of the initial consonant in *blanket* is repeated in the /m/ and /p/ of *mop*, as is the nasality of the original /n/ in /m/. The phonemic sequence /blE-/ of the first substitute, consisting of voiced stop plus liquid plus /E/, is reflected in the initial phonemes of *glass*, the velar stop there rather than the bilabial being an echo of the velar /k/ of *blanket*. However, the primary function of this paragraph is pattern practice, sound play being relegated only to the selections of items within the form class to be substituted.

The matter of paradigmatic selection is of great importance to the child. Vinogradov (1930) and Chukovsky (1956) in their analysis of the language patterns of children's games, nursery rhymes, and sayings have shown clearly the role played by the paradigmatic axis in this formalized aspect of children's language. The child finds great joy in practising his discovery that linguistic units can be combined freely up to a point, but subject to rules which he is exploring. In our example just given, the tautology of the noun form class is presented. We have no semantic redundancy here, no synonyms, but the characteristic of the paragraph is morphologic redundancy. Anthony is testing a list of substitution items for a particular slot. In the paradigm just given, all items fit, and the pattern is being 'overlearned' as it were. But at times the practice of a pattern starts out grammatically incorrectly and reaches the point of correct grammar in the last unit, e.g.:

Three bottle
Four bottles

where the plural is practised but the plural morpheme appears with the second occurrence of *bottle* only, not with the first one. The possessive case of the noun also forms a paradigmatic practice pattern, with a minimum of semantic content, as in:

Betsy's Mommy not home
Frica's Mommy not home
Betsy's Mommy not home.

The name of the first line reappears in the third so that only the second line contains new information as to the person who is *not home*. The semantic selection is kept at a minimum to work the paradigm.

Pronominal substitution exercises occupy the child a good deal, to be expected in view of the difficulty of tying a pronoun, a general substitute, to a specific noun. The great number of pronominal substitution exercises also point to the fact that these are genuine learning exercises rather than mere repetitions of patterns which have already been well internalized since the use of pronouns is often grammatically incorrect during his day speech. The example:

I go up there (2×)
I go
She go up there

is an exercise of substituting one personal pronoun for another with *I go* occurring as a partial echo repetition between the two pattern sentences. Both pronouns used in this paragraph have not been well learned by the child as yet; the third person singular marker is missing in the verb which also points to the imperfect learning of the pattern.

Pronouns can also be substituted for nouns or vice versa, using *it*, the best learned personal pronoun:

Take the monkey	*Stop it*
Take it	*Stop the ball*
	Stop it.

One form class is now substituted for another correctly, and the selection here has proceeded along semantic sameness, but grammatical difference. Such transformation exercises occur also with other grammatical structures. Sound play occurs again as well, but the primary function of these paragraphs is substitution exercises.

Verb substitution patterns, although not as frequent as noun substitutions, since verb designs are fewer than noun designs, like

Go get coffee
Go buy some coffee

show an example of a substitution of an unmarked verb form, whereas in

I'm fixing the door
Door's open
I'm locking

marked verb forms are the substitution items. In the next example:

Listen to microphone
Go to microphone

the different functions of *to* are equalized for substitution purposes. Here again we have grammatical sameness and semantic difference, which is also true of adjective substitution patterns which are quite frequent, particularly with colour attributes, as the following example shows:

Put on a blanket
White blanket
And yellow blanket
Where's yellow blanket.

Other noun modifiers can be substituted as well:

There's a hat
There's another
There's hat
There's another hat
That's a hat

the longest line being the most explicit one. This is also the case with the following expansion exercise:

Look through the window
Look through all the window

where the second line contains the highest numerical concept for the child, *all*, putting the sentences into a hierarchical order, arriving at the highest number gradually.

Equational sentences are also frames for substitution, and the list culminates in the longest unit, perhaps also the most important one to the child.

Monkey (3×)
That's a (2×)
That's a Kitty
That's a Fifi here
That's teddybear and baby.

This paragraph also is reminiscent of enumerations, a frequent exercise which serves as a practice of the conjunction *and*, the only conjunction well learned by the child:

You take off all the monkeys
And Kitties
And Phyllis and Humpty Dumpty
And monkey and horsie
And vacuum cleaner
And Fifi
And horsie
No house
And house (2×)
No records
And the blue blanket
This is the blue blanket.

As before, the selection of various nouns enumerated is based on sound play, but the primary function of the paragraph is grammatical practice.

Enumeration *par excellence*, counting, is another linguistic practice:

One two three four
One two
One two three four
One two three
Anthony counting
Good boy you
One two three.

Here the child even informs us what he is doing, he commends himself for the activity and counts once more for good measure. He not only produces the speech event, but discusses it as well, as if he were citing someone else. It is very doubtful that he fully understands the concept of numbers. He is learning to count as a linguistic activity, and yet usually the numbers appear in ascending order as in the example, with one culminating line.

Negatives are also practised occasionally as in:

Don't jump or *Like it*
Jump *Don't like it*
Like it Daddy

where in the second example *Daddy* was no doubt evoked by *don't* of the preceding line, but essentially this is another transformation exercise showing the transformation to and from a negative structure.

Don't ticklish
Don't do that

is an example of a somewhat different type where the negative is not contrasted with the affirmative, but occurs in both lines. Identical initial consonant phonemes in all three words also occur in the second line.

Another favourite transformation exercise is the one of question to non-question or vice versa, as exemplified by:

Step on the blanket
Where is Anthony's blanket.

Manipulation of imperative and interrogative signals is central to this paragraph. A three step operation can also be performed by the child as in:

There is the light
Where is the light
Here is the light

where he also answers the question, another exemplification of the dialogue of vocalized inner speech.

The paragraph

The best summary to characterize the nature of the paragraph or for that matter of all the material is Freud's description of the joke technique 'sense in nonsense' (1960). Just as the enjoyment of a joke can be derived from play with words, so does the child enjoy play with words, by repetitions of similar sounds, by his rediscovery of what is familiar to him. But analogous to the joke, where there is sense in nonsense in the deliberate use of word play, the child's play also has sense: the pleasure of play is structured so that it serves as a linguistic exercise. The role of content in most cases is subordinated to linguistic form, or the content serves the form, as Vinogradov (1930) pointed out. That there is linguistic structure in Nonsense has been demonstrated by Sewell's (1952) excellent analysis of the works of E. Lear and L. Carroll, and of nursery rhymes. Her definition of Nonsense as 'a collection of words which in their internal composition of letters and syllables or in their selection and sequence do not conform to the conventional patterns of language to which the particular mind is accustomed' fits exactly our set of data. Sound is what is played with, and it is done within the framework of paradigmatic and syntagmatic exercises. It is a world out of language, similar to the one described by Kaper (1959) for older children. That is not to say that secondary ludic symbolism as discussed by Piaget (1951) is not present, but our concern is primarily the overt linguistic structure of the paragraph. It is not within our province to decide whether the non-occurrence of certain past forms of the verb, for example, are due to the child's suppression of certain past events, but what we can determine is the role of the past paradigm of the verb in the structure of the monologues. It is being consciously practised, just as are other grammatical combinations and selections, so that at times we have the feeling of listening in on a foreign language lesson with extensive pattern practice. The substitution lists used by the child are very limited; the vocabulary of nouns is primarily made up of names of objects within his immediate surroundings, the crib and room, except for some 'personalized' nouns. Play with epithets, frequent in nursery rhymes, is mainly confined to colours used in substitution patterns in the monologues. Another common usage of adjectives is that of negative parallelism, but that too fits into a paradigmatic set. Paradigmatic relationships are transposed into sequences, a characteristic only of the poetic function of language with adults, but not so with the child. Paradigms, however, are not the only linguistic exercise, the exploration of combinatory possibilities and the resulting syntagmatic exercises shed still more light on the sense in nonsense. At times the combinations do lead to grammatical nonsense as well, but these are the hazards of exploration.

The selection of substitution items is not based on semantic synonymity, but on grammatical parallelism. The items either belong to the same form class, and then sound play is the basis of selection within the form class, or they are pronominal substitutes. The use of the semantically precisely defined numerals used imprecisely serves as an excellent framework for substitution in the monologues, also part of the structure of Nonsense in Sewell's analysis. The paradigmatic use of nouns as substitution items is more pronounced than that of any other form class. With verbs, grammatical markers are more frequently selected as the items to be changed in a pattern, be it the *-ing* form or the past alternating with the unmarked form.

But the selection in the paradigm and the building of longer grammatical combinations are not the only typical aspects of the paragraph construction. Paired association as described by Wallon (1945) is characteristic in either negative parallelism as already mentioned, or in associations, or in linguistic parallelism. A sentence with a noun object followed by a sentence with a pronoun object is a paired association, so typical of the thought process of the young child. Following Steinitz's classification of paired construction in folkloric poetry, we can also distinguish several pairs analogous to his: the contrastive pair which consists either of two antonyms, or of a statement and its contradiction; the varying pair which goes from the simple to the complex, or vice versa; and the enumerative pair which results in a chain. The chain complex, as a matter of fact, is most descriptive of our data. As characterized by Vygotsky, it is

a dynamic, consecutive joining of individual links into a single chain... The decisive attribute keeps changing during the entire process. There is no consistency in the type of the bonds or in the manner in which a link of the chain is joined with the one that precedes it and the one that follows it. The original sample has no central significance. Each link, once included in a chain complex, is as important as the first and may become the magnet for a series of other objects.

Anthony's paragraphs are just such a chain, and a number of functional criteria have to be applied in order to understand the structure of this unit.

In these linguistic sessions the child does not assume only the role of the student, however, for he is the other participant in the language learning situation, the model, as well. It is really inaccurate to call these soliloquies monologues, because outside of the fact that they are produced while the child is physically isolated, he becomes his own interlocutor and produces the equivalent of a dialogue spoken by a single person. He can switch roles in this interchange readily – he asks a question and provides the answer, he performs a linguistic task and commends himself on the accomplishment, he produces a linguistic event and explicitly corrects himself. The importance of the conative function as shown by the great number of imperatives, supports clearly the premise of a social aspect of this vocalized inner speech as Vygotsky (1962) has suggested it, or as Peirce (1933) has characterized thought.

Besides the conative, two other functions of language as outlined by Jakobson (1960) are particularly characteristic of our data. One, the metalingual as shown by the child's preoccupation to practise the language he is learning, and the other, the poetic, which the play with words and sounds illustrates. But there is even more of the latter structured in our nonsense than just play. Alliterations are frequent and paronomastic images emerge, often connecting the individual lines of the paragraph. That both these functions are predominant in the monologues is consistent with the nature of the language of a young child where these two functions often merge, contrary to adult speech.

However, the paragraph at times is not only delimited by a change of topic or by a change of linguistic exercise, but by a larger circular, rondo-like construction. Frequently, it ends just as it began. Moreover, smaller closed constructions occur, as part of the larger circle, and, after we have been led back to the beginning, a new round just like the completed one may be started, a structure parallel to rounds in songs. There is linguistic sense in the child's nonsense, that is our conclusion.

(From *Language in the Crib*, Mouton, The Hague, 1962.)

References

CHAO, Y. R. (1951), 'The Cantian idiolect', *Semitic and Oriental Studies*, No. II.

CHUKOVSKY, K. (1956), *Ot dvux do pjati*, Moscow.

FREUD, S. (1960), *Jokes and their Relation to the Unconscious*, Routledge & Kegan Paul.

JAKOBSON, R. (1960), 'Linguistics and poetics', in *Style in Language*, T. A. Sebeok (ed.), M.I.T. Press.

JESPERSEN, O. (1949), *Language: Its Nature, Development and Origin*, Macmillan, New York.

KAPER, W. (1959), *Einige Erscheinungen der kindl. Spracheswerbung*, Gröningen.

OHNESORG, K. (1947), *Fonetickà studie*, Prague.

PEIRCE, C. S. (1933), *Collected Papers*, Oxford University Press.

PIAGET, J. (1951), *Play, Dreams and Imitation in Childhood*, Routledge & Kegan Paul. (And see this volume, pp. 166 and 155.)

SCUPIN, E., and SCUPIN, G. (1907), *Bubi's erste Kindheit*, Leipzig.

SEWELL, E. (1952), *The Field of Nonsense*, Chatto & Windus.

STERN, C., and STERN, W. (1928), *Die Kindersprache*, Leipzig.

VINOGRADOV, G. (1930), *Russkij detskij folklor*, Irkutsk.

VYGOTSKY, L. S. (1962), *Thought and Language*, M.I.T. Press.

WALLON, H. (1945), *Les Origines de la Pensée chez l'enfant*, I, II, Paris.

Chimpanzees, Alas, Do Not Babble

At about three months, a remarkable thing happens to the human baby. Without apparent provocation, it begins to make sounds with its lips: 'm's', 'p's', and 'b's' combined with vowel sounds like 'oo' and 'ah'. Then, obviously delighted, the baby begins to play with other syllables. The stream of chatter grows more varied and more frequent. Driven by an undeniable urge, the child chatters almost constantly. His babbling includes not only the syllables of his native language, but all other known languages as well.

The importance of babbling as a basis for human speech probably cannot be overestimated. To the onlooker, the babbling baby is obviously having fun, but at the same time he is learning to use his lips, tongue and breathing in different combinations. He is gaining control of these until in time he will be able to produce whatever sound he pleases. He is developing *the motor skill of vocalization.*

When the human is about five months old, he begins repeating his simple syllables and may say something like 'mamamamam ma mah!' or 'dadadada da!' Hearing this, his parents are overjoyed and proudly celebrate 'Baby's first word'. In response to the attention it gets him, Baby may repeat the words many times, although he will not know what it means until months later. It is here that the deaf child, who has been babbling, becomes mute – when further learning depends on listening to himself and grown-ups.

The normal child learns many words by hearing people speak. By receiving praise for only certain sounds, he concentrates on his native tongue and abandons the incoherent hodgepodge of his early chatter. This then is how a child learns intelligible speech and the whole long hard struggle has its beginnings in the play behaviour called babbling.

Apes do not babble – at least not much. As an infant, Viki lay in her crib perfectly silent. If we spoke to her, she made her greeting sound and various monosyllables as well: 'poo', 'pwah', 'bra', 'bee', and 'wha', but as soon as we went away, she fell silent again. This was the first sad fact we had to face in trying to teach an ape to talk: they babble very, very little.

Once she said 'ee oo' without provocation, and repeated it several times, apparently enjoying the sound of her own baby voice. At other times she played with 'ah ho' and 'ba hoo' or simply gargled a bubble of saliva to form a continuous 'l'. We were delighted and immediately drew false hope from this. Soon Keith's first question every night was 'What did Viki say today?' And I would recite the 'ah goo's', 'pee oo's', and 'coo ee's'. Some days I had choice stories to tell, about Viki challenging her echo in Mrs Clarke's spacious living room, or how she addressed a gathering of visitors with a stream of 'uuh uh's' so varied in volume and inflection that everyone insisted that Viki was 'talking'.

But suddenly at four months of age Viki's spontaneous chatter fell off sharply. She still made the chimp noises with which she had come equipped, but we heard less and less of her 'babbling', which had never approached the human level in either quantity or variety. Now, at an age when the human child begins making every conceivable sound, Viki grew increasingly silent until in the evening, when Keith asked me what she had said during the day, I found myself replying, 'Nothing at all.'

(From *The Ape in Our House*, Gollancz, 1952.)

Play, Language and Human Evolution

The evolution of behaviour

Discussions of play always turn eventually to speculation about its function. Play has been said to be causally related to the acquisition of skills, environmental information, and adult social behaviour. Perhaps it would be more rewarding to consider play in the light of a more general proposition about the processing and flow of information. If we think of a system as operating in conjunction with other systems, so that its output serves as inputs to the others, then a system whose output is temporarily uncoupled from its normal input relations to other systems will be said to be functioning in the *simulative mode*. It can in fact be shown that play involves the simulative execution of systems at several levels of biological organization, and that the function of play must be understood in the light of the function of simulation in general.

The essential feature of the simulative mode is that the system, while functioning normally, is uncoupled from its normal consequences vis-à-vis the other systems. However, the feedback consequences within the acting system are unimpaired. It is to this feedback capability that simulation owes its current popularity in modern technology. A simulated space mission, for example, should give evidence of any unforeseen consequences deriving from the system's operation, yet at the same time it should not actually result in those consequences. The simulative mode of action is paradoxical: the system's operations should have their normal consequences, yet those consequences must at the same time be rendered inconsequential. Where exactly does this difference in the inconsequentiality of action lie? The biologist cannot resist answering: in the relative savings in the biological economies of the organisms involved. In the simulative mode of action, both the energy expenditure and the danger to the participating organisms is less.

The buffering of play behaviour from consequences is paralleled by an analogous phenomenon on the level of social interactions: play fighting does not lead to injury nor play sex to offspring. In that social play does not feed directly into the survival-oriented social activity of the species, the play group can be thought of as a simulative social system.

The function of the simulative mode resides in its informativeness or feedback capability, but the acquisition of feedback information is not restricted to the simulative mode. Actors can learn from performances before a live audience and space programmes can learn from actual moon landings. However, the simulative mode allows the feedback process to occur in the absence of the reinforcement or selective systems to which the action is to be ultimately coupled. Herein lies its advantage. The drama critic would probably maintain that unrehearsed plays close early; and the biologist would make the same argument in another way: organisms whose behavioural performances are unsatisfactory do not get another opportunity to perform. It follows then that experimental attempts to ascertain the effects of restricted opportunity to play on later skilled action or problem-solving are misguided. What is required is an assessment of the relative survival of rehearsed versus unrehearsed performances measured in terms of the particular selective system to which the action is coupled.

In cases where behaviour is already well integrated and known to be instrumental to the desired effect, simulation is *not* efficient. Pursuing the dramatic analogy still further, rehearsal of a play already in the repertory is a waste of energy. For this reason play activity only makes its appearance in animals that have a certain capacity for the ontogenetic modification of behaviour. Modifiability creates certain problems. Where the organism once had only one behavioural sequence with which to respond, he now has to choose among alternatives. External information is now required for response selection, and the integration of actions requires internal information. While both kinds of information can be acquired through simulation, there is an additional evolutionary change that must take place before a rehearsal function is possible: the young organism's survival needs must be met through parental care. Play cannot be considered in isolation but must be viewed as part of an adaptive complex involving ontogenetic plasticity in behaviour, infantile dependency, a capacity for learning from previous action, and parental care. Since there is no general term embracing all of these phenomena, I refer to them as the *flexibility complex*. Like other behavioural complexes, such as the advent of terrestrialism, it gave to living matter a whole new range of evolutionary options.

There is reason to believe that the history of man consists largely of a progressive phylogenetic elaboration of the flexibility complex. Seven main developments are involved: (a) an increased delay in maturation; (b) a greater reliance for social development on that subset of play I term the *pregame*; (c) an increased ability to manipulate objects and incorporate them into instrumental behaviour; (d) an increased reliance on observational learning for the acquisition of both behaviour patterns and environmental information; (e) the development of conventional sequences of imitated behaviour patterns; (f) a progressive complexification of the subculture of the play group; and (g) the acquisition of survival functions by play group subcultures. These changes are not independent of each other but are synergistically related.

The flexibility complex

The most conspicuous development is the phylogenetic trend towards delayed maturation in primates (Table 1). As a general rule in embryology, structures are more readily modifiable early in ontogeny than later, and behaviour is no exception. *Neoteny*, the retention of infantile characteristics into adulthood, has been suggested as an important factor in the development of hominid anatomy (DeBeer, 1958), and the theory has merits on behavioural grounds as well. By delaying maturation the organism not only has more time for learning more learned behaviour, but sexual maturity may be reached before behavioural maturity. When this happens the organism's behaviour becomes adult – if not 'mature' – by virtue of its being coupled to survival functions, and the properties of immature behaviour can be carried into adulthood.

Consider the nature of play in the following encounter between monkeys e and z: e chases z/ z chases e/ e chases z/ z chases e/ stop. While the behaviour of the two actors is asymmetrical, the net effect of the encounter is to negate the asymmetry through the alternation of roles. Sometimes the role of victim will be voluntarily assumed: one animal will touch another and then run away. In such cases, the role asymmetry of the encounter is negated by the chase-initiated action that precedes it. In other cases, the roles are already symmetrical, as when individuals wrestle or grapple.

Table 1 Delayed maturation in primates

Species	Foetal phase in days	Infantile phase in years	Juvenile in years	Total life span
Lemur	126	?	?2	14
Macaque	168	1·5	6	27–28
Gibbon	210	?2	6·5	30+
Orang-utan	233	3·5	7	30+
Chimpanzee	238	3	7	40
Gorilla	265	3+	7+	?35
Man	266	6	14	70–75

after Napier and Napier 1967

All of the above cases can be contrasted to the following in which the encounter more closely resembles serious business than a game:

t walks towards b/ b presents to t/ t mounts b and walks away.

Encounters in which role relations are symmetrical or made symmetrical through negation of role asymmetry in the course of the interaction are here termed *mutual* encounters. While mutual encounters are known from non-play contexts, such as grooming, they reach their greatest complexity in play.

Not all play encounters are necessarily mutual encounters. Often asymmetrical encounters appear to be controlled by the play system. In some unilateral chases, for example, the victim does not look fearful nor the pursuer angry. Mutual and non-mutual encounters must share the social play time of young rhesus monkeys. The mutual interaction is in fact embedded in a matrix of non-mutuality. Dominance rank is implicit in social play, and mutual encounters do not violate these differences in social rank. A long series of mutual chases, for example, while suggesting complete equality between the participants, will nonetheless conform to the tendency of dominant animals to begin encounters actively and passively end them. Equality may reign within the mutual encounter, but at its points of contact with the larger sphere of social interaction, it firmly conforms to the social structure (Table 2). This should not surprise us, for human games are typically what game theorists call *zero sum*: there is a winner and a loser. The game begins by setting the players equal, but the playing results in a new inequality.

Table 2

Monkey	Short play encounters		Long play encounters	
	Rank	Score	Rank	Score
Linus	1	0·18	1	0·25
Descartes	2	0·26	5	0·57
Broca	3	0·50	3	0·51
Tag	4	0·57	2	0·42
Edna	5	0·72	4	0·53
Zelda	6	0·76	6	0·62

Rankings and scores of 6 infant rhesus monkeys on a dominance-submission scale for long play encounters ('most playful') and short play encounters ('least playful'). The most dominant animal (Linus) is dominant in both cases and the most submissive animal (Zelda) is submissive in both cases. The middle of the hierarchy is unstable. The measure is computed by assuming that dominant animals are those that are least likely to terminate encounters by leaving and most likely to initiate encounters by approaching.

In addition to play the flexibility complex has facilitated object use. Among rhesus monkeys, objects become incorporated into social encounters on rare occasions. These animals are not particularly object-oriented when compared to man or chimpanzees. They will respond briefly to novel objects and will sometimes mouth or manipulate familiar objects in solitary play, but in social play objects are usually used only indirectly as a surface to support the action. It sometimes happens that a player will act indirectly through an object instead of directly upon another player. In these cases, the action of the objects will constitute the move in the game. Tug-of-war with a rope is one example, where a pull by one animal leads to a pull by another. Sometimes too rags and pieces of rope are incorporated into chases, where dropping the object by one player is a signal for the other player to grab and run with it. This non-instrumental object use is the only socially significant object use described for rhesus monkeys. There is little doubt that an increased capacity for object use has been fundamental to hominid evolution.

Another progressive development in the flexibility complex is the development of observational learning. There are probably two distinct but related phenomena involved here: (a) the acquisition of environmental information by observing the consequences of another's action and (b) the acquisition of a novel behaviour pattern by observing another execute it. The latter is sometimes called *imitation* or *imitative learning* (Bandura, 1962, 1965 (a), 1965 (b); Hall, 1963; Piaget, 1962).

It is suggested here that the acquisition of novel behaviour patterns is a play context phenomenon. The young ape or hominid, being more likely to be in a play state, is more likely to respond to another's behaviour with imitation. The buffering of the play context facilitates this phenomenon. The young individual, not being required to respond 'appropriately' to most actions of adults, is free to imitate them. Since the demonstrator need not himself be playing to provide information, observational learning permits the acquisition of behaviour from all of the non-play contexts.

Observational learning requires that the organisms not only acquire the behaviour patterns of others but also attend to the consequences of the behaviour *for* others. This is attested to by experiments on imitation which show that human children are more likely to imitate behaviour that is rewarded in others (Bandura *passim*) and by the vicarious reinforcement literature (Kanfer, 1965), which shows that in man the reinforcement of others is as effective in controlling behaviour (and sometimes more so) as direct reinforcement of the subject himself.

Menzel (1971) gave certain chimpanzees in a group privileged information about the location of food. Even though the location was varied from trial to trial, the other chimpanzees soon learned to follow the knowledgeable members and to anticipate the location from the direction of their walk.

Knowledge of the reinforcing properties of behaviour in others is actually knowledge of a very abstract and inferential sort. The most obvious clue to the complexity of the process is the fact that reinforcement cannot be directly observed in another. It must be inferred from information derived from the special senses and combined with prior information about the external correlates of reinforcing events. Furthermore, since complex reinforcing actions are composed of subordinate actions that are not themselves reinforcing but only instrumental, the observer must be able to relate behaviour to physical as opposed to reinforcing effects in order to understand the sequence. In other words, it is argued that the ability to acquire knowledge of the reinforcing properties of behaviour by others is no different from the acquisition of the knowledge of physical properties. The reinforcing consequences of action in others are inferred through observation of physical consequences.

This argument is an important one, for it suggests that the advent of observational learning is inextricably linked to the emergence of *formal conceptual learning* (Bruner *et al.*, 1956; Carroll, 1967; Flavell, 1970), which is the categorization of experience on the basis of physical rather than reinforcement properties. It is well known that conceptual learning is not restricted to man but has been demonstrated in mammals and birds (Bernstein, 1961; Brown *et al.*, 1959; French, 1965; Hicks, 1956; Koehler, 1950; Riopelle, 1967; Thorpe, 1963). Many kinds of animals can form relational concepts, such as oddity or size. What is learned is not a particular stimulus configuration but a rule that enables the organism to distinguish the exemplar of a concept from a non-exemplar, which can then be generalized to new instances. What is not presently known is the extent to which the conceptualization of animals is as systematic as in man. Human concepts do not exist in isolation but can be related to each other through logical operations like conjunction, disjunction and negation (Flavell, 1970). Typically they are organized into logical systems varying with age, personality, experience, culture and psychopathology. Some authors implicate language as the causative agent in human conceptual systemization, and there may be a good deal of truth in this position. Yet the wide phylogenetic distribution of conceptualization and the unique occurrence of language suggests that language evolved after the establishment in primates of at least non-systematic conceptual knowledge.

In summary, observational learning can be viewed as a joint sensorymotor process in which the conceptual encoding of sensory events leads to inferential knowledge of events and their reinforcing properties and to the formation of hierarchically organized motor control systems called schemas that enable the observer to replicate behaviour observed in others in the appropriate environmental context. Observational learning in conjunction with delayed maturation, mutual play encounters, and object use characterize the flexibility complex of contemporary anthropoid apes, particularly chimpanzees. The first effect of observational learning is to alter the nature of play.

Meta-play

The play system must be viewed as specialized for the transmission of information between the environment and the non-play systems. Behaviour patterns are transferred to play control for simulative mode execution, and information is transferred back. With the advent of observational learning, new behaviour patterns and their environmental consequences are learned in play, organized, and made available to non-play control. When the observer watches adult organisms, the behaviour learned will conform to the goal-oriented behaviour of adults. While such imitated behaviour may be playfully executed by the observer, as we see in human children, its non-play execution will conform to that of adults. If, however, imitated behaviour is acquired from the *play* behaviour of other organisms, then the schematic representation should generate behaviour structurally identical to play itself. This phenomenon I term *meta-play*. The play encounter would itself serve as a model of interaction, allowing the development of schemas capable of generating mutual play encounters. Once this development takes place, the phenomenon of meta-play can be said to be established.

Once schematic models of play interactions become possible, the play interaction can expand its original domain. Since schemas acquired in play can be transferred to non-play systems, the structure of mutual play encounters can become the model of interaction for non-play encounters as well. In addition, the possibility of cumulative transmission of play behaviour is established. In colony-housed rhesus monkeys, mutual encounters appear to arise *de novo* each generation. There is no indication that play is transmitted from older to younger animals, as is commonplace in human societies. In humans, when schemas of mutual interaction are transmitted in this way, it becomes possible to develop conventional sequences of moves. When mutual sequences are constrained by purely historical, as opposed to pragmatic or instrumental criteria, I term the encounters *pregames*. The name recognizes their affinity to the conventional rule-bound sequences of human games but takes cognizance of the fact that true games, with articulate and specifically agreed upon rules, are a later phylogenetic development.

With the advent of meta-play, the play context ceases to be just a rehearsal of adult skills, and the play group is no longer a mere simulation of adult social structure. The play group acquires a pivotal role in behavioural evolution. The situation is adumbrated in contemporary non-human primates, where play provides much of the variety needed to allow different social traditions to evolve. Poirier (1969), for example, has chronicled the adaptation of Nilgiri langurs to alteration of their habitat by agriculture. The innovation of eating the leaves of cultivated plants was introduced by immature animals to the others, and similar examples are known from other species (Kawai, 1967; Kawamura, 1963; Tsumori, 1967; Kummer, 1971). Cultural systems can operate in a similar way. In a stable environment, where the behaviour of adults is rewarded, the play subculture of the older juveniles will come to approximate more and more the adult culture. In a changing environment, much of the adult behaviour will be unrewarded, and the play subcultures will acquire successful innovations and diverge from the adult culture, eventually passing on its innovations or replacing the adult culture entirely.

Metaplay operates within this general framework, but it provides a mechanism for progressive as well as cladogenic evolution. The pregame allows the development of a positive feedback process involving conventionally constrained behaviour systems. The more complex the behavioural environment, the more complex the schemas of interaction; and the more complex the schemas of interaction, the more complex the pregame they can generate. In this way, it is possible for the play group to evolve complex forms of behaviour that have no parallel in adult culture. When transferred to non-play systems, the complication of play can complicate the adult behaviour of the species.

The characteristics of mutual play encounters, in conjunction with observational learning and some additional changes yet to be discussed, set the stage for the development of behavioural systems in the subculture of the play group that were more complex than those of the adult society. When this complication proceeded to the point where the behaviour could assume survival-oriented functions, the subculture of the play group replaced the then-current adult culture. In other words, the behavioural Rubicon of human evolution was crossed by the non-simulative execution of behaviour derived from the simulative mode.

Language

Human language has long been regarded as the largest and swiftest flowing Rubicon of all. Some authors have contended that it forms an insuperable barrier to evolutionary accounts of human behaviour. The comparative evidence seems to support this position. There are no natural communication systems intermediate in complexity between language and non-language among man's living primate relatives. The communication systems of non-human primates are no more sophisticated, and often less so, than those of other mammals, and their phylogenetic relationship is to man's paralinguistic communication – such as facial expression and intonation – not to his language (Altmann, 1967; Hinde, 1972; Ploog and Melnechuk, 1969; Reynolds, 1970; Sebeok, 1968). However, these facts are only discrepant if we *expect* to find the precursors of language in the communication of animals. Most communicative signals in animals evolve from non-communicative precursors that are initially only behavioural concomitants of certain affective states. Following this line of reasoning, we might expect a new kind of communicative system, such as language, to evolve from behaviour that was initially not communicative at all. A candidate for the status of a precursor of language would be characterized not by its achievements but by its potential.

The relevant mechanisms are changes in the behavioural system of the protohominids following the development of a capacity for increased voluntary control of the vocal tract. It is argued that this feature reorganizes the flexibility complex in such a way that referential and propositional functions can be assumed by vocal behaviour.

Lieberman and his colleagues (Lieberman, 1968, 1973; Lieberman *et al.*, 1969) have shown that man's capacity for fine movements of the vocal organs is far superior to other primates. While part of this ability doubtlessly evolved under the impetus of speech, other events, probably in part anatomical remodelling following the accession to bipedalism, must have predisposed speech towards the auditory-vocal channel before communicative specialization could have begun. The vocal behaviour of all non-human primates is innate and lacks the degree of modification available to the visual-motor channel. This is apparently due as much to meagre motor resources as to supposed mental deficiencies. It is suggested that changes in the peripheral vocal anatomy allowed the protohominids to develop vocal behaviour that was acquired as a skill. Given skilful vocal behaviour, it is likely that it would be employed as a concomitant to action by other effectors, especially in play. Contemporary chimpanzees, at least in areas where they are not heavily hunted, are among the noisiest animals in the forest. It is not unlikely that protohominids would exhibit this trait with voluntary vocalizations.

Once voluntary vocal behaviour was acquired, it would in some respects follow an evolutionary course identical to other forms of skilled behaviour. Vocal behaviour would become a 'move' in encounters with other members of the social group. The moves would become incorporated into schemes of mutual vocal interaction, and observational learning of vocal schemas would allow the development and transmission of vocal pregames. Vocal pregame schemas, developed in the play context, could be shifted to non-play control for instrumental execution. This account, while reasonable up to a point, does not consider two fundamental differences between vocal and non-vocal skilled behaviour. First of all, only the effects of vocal behaviour, not the behaviour itself, are observable to another. Hence, vocal behaviour is not exactly comparable to behaviours that can be seen. Secondly, vocal behaviour has no observable environmental effects other than sound itself. Hence, there is no point in shifting vocal schemas to non-play control because they have no instrumental utility.

Evolution, with characteristic resourcefulness, has transformed these shortcomings into virtues. As is now well known (Gardner and Gardner, 1969, 1971; Premack 1971a, 1971b), chimpanzees show a capacity to acquire and use behaviours in the visual-motor channel that are beyond their capacity in the auditory-vocal channel. Hewes (1971, 1973) has maintained that human language was preceded by a voluntary controlled visual-motor communication system on the grounds that this channel is already well developed in apes. However, it is much easier to account for language by assuming it to have been vocal from the very beginning. What is required for an incipient communication system is a behavioural channel that is not being used for any instrumental behaviour. The reason lies in the way communication is related to instrumental behaviour.

In animal communication systems, behaviour patterns such as intention movements and displacement activities that are empirically associated with a particular behavioural context can become signals of that context. Other organisms come to respond to the signals as they would to instrumental behaviour itself. Once the signals become reliable context indicators, they can be shifted to another context to re-define that context to an observer.

In a similar fashion, as the behavioural repertory of a protohominid species incorporates more imitated behaviours, they become associated with different behavioural contexts and systems by virtue of their appropriateness to the different goals to be achieved. They can also be used to redefine an ongoing context through an *intercontextual shift*, in a way analogous to change of meaning of animal signals. Since imitated behaviour patterns are acquired in play and are not restricted to a single system, intercontextual shifts of imitated behaviour can occur voluntarily in a single organism and need not wait on genetic encoding.

The difference in the communicative function can be seen in the difference between change of meaning in an animal signal and its referential analogue, the intercontextual shift. The former is akin to mimicry and hence to deception: it prompts the observer to treat one context or situation as another. The intercontextual shift, on the other hand, merely simulates one context within another. The observer is not misled into thinking of the communication as real behaviour. Referential communication, by its very nature, is not reality itself but owes its power to its capacity to bring other realities to mind. Voluntary control of the vocal tract facilitates the development of this distinction. It allows imitated behaviour in the non-instrumental vocal channel to be executed concurrently with the instrumental behaviour of the visual-motor channel. The intercontextual shift allows a discrepancy to exist between the contextual origins of the concurrent behaviour in the two channels. When this happens the observer is faced with a contradictory reality, similar in some respects to the schizophrenogenic communication discussed by Bateson (Bateson *et al.*, 1956). However, the two channels are not equally real. By being involved in the instrumental activities subserving the non-play systems, the behaviours of the visual-motor channel become linked to the reality end of the epistemological gradient demarcated by the survival-oriented values of the limbic system. By virtue of being unconstrained by the prior goals characteristic of instrumental activity, the vocal channel is free to employ the play-like schemas of vocal pregames. The presence of behaviour structurally similar to play helps to define the channel as simulation, just as behaviour patterns differing from their normal execution help to define the play context. Once the vocal channel comes to be regarded as simulative of reality itself, it can be viewed as supplementary to the ongoing context rather than as an attempt at context re-definition.

The fact that language evolved in the auditory-vocal channel is neither historical accident nor a secondary development. It follows logically from specialization of function already implicit in a non-instrumental auditory modality and a visual-motor channel weighted down with survival functions. The evolution of referential communication requires both that the real thing and its simulation become differentiated by channel and that the behaviour of the two channels be capable of being executed concurrently. Because of these factors, it is difficult to imagine language not evolving as speech.

There is another characteristic of the auditory-vocal channel that has facilitated its assumption of communicative functions: the invisibility of vocal behaviour to an observer. With the exception of the lips and the size of the oral cavity, the actual behaviour involved in vocalization is invisible to an external observer without special tools. The observer only has access to the sound waves that follow from the behaviour, not to the behaviour itself. In this respect, vocal behaviour is analogous from the observer's vantage point to a hypothetical kinds of object manipulation in which the objects are visible but the behaviour is not. Consequently, the vocal pregame is structurally equivalent to the game with objects. In the latter case, it is not behaviour *per se* that constitutes a move in the inter-action but the movement of the object. The mutual rope pulling seen in rhesus monkey play is a simple example: what is responded to by the other is the movement of the rope. If this equivalence between the vocal pre-game and the object pregame is accepted, then it becomes reasonable to assume that sound sequences and modifications of sound sequences are understood by an observer in the same way as he understands object movements and sequences of object movements.

Under certain conditions, perceptual information is assimilated to the categories of agent of action, action, and object of action. If an observer assumes that a temporal sequence of sounds is to be understood in a similar light, then he will apply the categories of causality to the auditory input. If this is the case, then the precursor of propositionality lies in the capacity to parse auditory input with causal categories. However, in man not all auditory sequences are analysed in this way. How does it happen that certain sequences of imitated sounds are assimilated to the schemas of objects while other sequences, as in music, are considered to be events unrelated to cause and effect?

The answer is that only sounds originally produced as part of a vocal pregame are so analysed. The statement previously made that vocalizations have no environmental effect is only partially true. Once vocalizations lead to responses by other organisms, they have the environmental effect of *causing* other sounds. However, since instrumental vocalization with social utility would presuppose the very system we are trying to explain, it follows that the original vocal activity must lie in the propensity towards activity for its own sake that we see in play. The vocal pregame, by making sound production significant even in the absence of social utility, was the precursor to the perception of causal relations in imitated sounds. As De Laguna (1927) pointed out long ago, the basic unit of linguistics is not the sentence but the conversation.

When the vocal imitated behaviour patterns are assimilated to the schemas of object manipulation, the mental associations of the behavioural patterns, derived ontogenetically from their contextual association, can be perceived as acting upon each other in the same way as the perceptual phenomena from which they are derived. In a similar way, it becomes possible for the observer himself to assimilate his own vocal associations of mental states to object schemas and produce vocal behaviour incor-porating the same causal relations. While the processes of conceptual understanding are not themselves understood, it becomes possible to explain the evolution of propositionality by assuming that these processes treat auditory and visual input in a similar way. The nature of propositional referential communication is thus re-defined: it becomes the assimilation of imitated vocal behaviour to the categories of cause and effect. This event begins a process of complication and intrinsic change that is far beyond the scope of this paper.

The argument developed here lends itself to experimental verification. It suggests that object play of non-human primates is the appropriate model system for the phylogenetic study of human language. Certainly the correspondence recently found between object play and language development in the human child (Greenfield *et al.*, 1972) gives reason for optimism. In addition, the hypothetical psychological equivalence between sounds and objects under certain conditions can be investigated in both man and animals. A major question following from the present account is whether the schemas underlying auditory-vocal referential communication are derived phylogenetically from the visual-motor system or from a more general capacity to interpret reality in causal terms. While there are insufficient data to answer this question at the present time, a *rapprochement* between cognition and animal studies and between biology and psychology will find the answer to this and other more fundamental questions bearing on the evolutionary precursors of human behaviour.

(Excerpts from a paper presented at the Annual Meeting of the American Association for the Advancement of Science, Washington, D.C., in December 1972.)

References

ALTMANN, S. A. (1967), 'The structure of primate social communication', in *Social Communication among Primates*, S. A. Altmann (ed.), University of Chicago Press.

BANDURA, A. L. (1962), 'Social learning through imitation', in *Nebraska Symposium on Motivation*, M. R. Jones (ed.), University of Nebraska Press.

BANDURA, A. L. (1965a), 'Vicarious processes: A case of no-trial learning', in *Advances in Experimental Social Psychology*, S. Berkowitz (ed.), Academic Press, New York.

BANDURA, A. L. (1965b), 'Behavioral modifications through modelling procedures', in *Research in Behavior Modification*, L. Krasner and L. P. Ullmann (eds), Holt, Rinehart & Winston, New York.

BATESON, G., JACKSON, D., HALEY, J., and WEAKLAND, J. (1956), 'Toward a theory of schizophrenia', *Behavioral Science*, No. 1, pp. 251–64.

BERNSTEIN, I. S. (1961), 'The utilization of visual cues in dimension-abstracted oddity by primates', *J. Comp. Physiol. Psychol.*, No. 54, p. 243.

BROWN, W. L., OVERALL, J. E., and BLODGETT, H. C. (1959), 'Novelty learning sets in rhesus monkeys', *J. Comp. Physiol. Psychol.*, No. 52, pp. 330–32.

BRUNER, J. S., GOODNOW, J., and AUSTIN, G. A. (1956), *A Study of Thinking*, Wiley, New York.

CARROLL, J. B. (1967), 'Words, meanings and concepts', *Harvard Educational Review*, No. 34, pp. 178–202.

DE BEER, G. (1958), *Embryos and Ancestors* (3rd ed.), Clarendon Press, Oxford.

FLAVELL, J. H. (1970), 'Concept development', in *Carmichael's Manual of Child Psychology*, P. H. Mussen (ed.), Vol. 1, Wiley, New York.

FRENCH, G. M. (1965), 'Associative problems', in *Behavior of Non-human Primates*, A. M. Schrier, H. F. Harlow and F. Stollnitz (eds), Vol. 1, Academic Press, New York.

GARDNER, R. A., and GARDNER, B. T. (1969), 'Teaching sign language to a chimpanzee', *Science*, No. 165, pp. 664–72.

GARDNER, B. T., and GARDNER, R. A. (1971), 'Two-way communication with an infant chimpanzee', in *Behavior of Nonhuman Primates*, A. Schrier and F. Stollnitz (eds), Vol. 4, Academic Press, New York.

GREENFIELD, P. M., NELSON, K., and SALTZMAN, E. (1972), 'The development of rulebound strategies of manipulating seriated cups: a parallel between action and grammar', *Cognitive Psychology*, No. 3, pp. 291–310.

HALL, K. R. L. (1963), 'Observational learning in monkeys and apes', *Brit. J. Psychol.*, No. 54, pp. 201–26.

HEWES, G. (1971), paper presented at American Anthropological Association Meeting, November, 1971.

HEWES, G. (1973), 'Primate communication and the gestural origin of language', *Curr. Anthrop.*, No. 14, pp. 5–24.

HICKS, L. H. (1956), 'An analysis of number-concept formation in the rhesus monkey', *J. Comp. Physiol. Psychol.*, No. 49, pp. 212–18.

HINDE, R. A. (ed.), (1972), *Non-Verbal Communication*, Cambridge University Press.

KANFER, F. H. (1965), 'Vicarious human reinforcement: a glimpse into the black box', in *Research in Behavior Modification*, L. Krasner and L. P. Ullmann (eds), Holt, Rinehart & Winston, New York.

KAWAI, M. (1967), 'Catching behavior observed in the Koshima troop – a case of newly acquired behavior', *Primates*, No. 8, pp. 181–8.

KAWAMURA, S. (1963), 'The process of sub-culture propagation among Japanese macaques', in *Primate Social Behavior*, C. H. Southwick (ed.), Van Nostrand, Princeton, New Jersey.

KOEHLER, O. (1950), 'The ability of birds to count', *Bulletin of Animal Behavior*, No. 9, pp. 41–5.

KUMMER, H. (1971), *Primate Societies: Group Techniques of Ecological Adaptation*, Aldine, Chicago.

LAGUNA, G. DE (1963), *Speech: Its Function and Development*, (1st ed. 1927), University of Indiana Press.

LIEBERMAN, P. (1968), 'Primate vocalizations and human linguistic ability', *Journal of Acoustical Society of America*, No. 44, pp. 1574–84.

LIEBERMANN, P. (1973), 'On the evolution of language: a unified view,'

presented at the IXth International Congress of Anthropological and
Ethnological Sciences, Chicago, September 1973.

LIEBERMAN, P. H., KLATT, D. H., and WILSON, W. (1969), 'Vocal tract
limitations on the vowel repertoires of rhesus monkeys and other non-human
primates', *Science*, No. 164, pp. 1185–7.

MENZEL, E. W., JR (1971), 'Communication about the environment in a
group of young chimpanzees', *Folia Primat.*, No. 15, pp. 220–32.

NAPIER, J. R., and NAPIER, P. H. (1967), *A Handbook of Living Primates*,
Academic Press, New York.

PIAGET, J. (1951), *Play, Dreams and Imitation in Childhood*, Routledge &
Kegan Paul.

PLOOG, D., and MELNECHUK, T. (1969), 'Primate communication',
Neurosciences Research Program, Vol. 7, No. 5, pp. 419–510.

POIRIER, F. E. (1969), 'Behavioral flexibility and intertroop variation among
Nilgiri langurs (*Presbytis johnii*) of South India', *Folia Primat.*, No. 11,
pp. 119–33.

PREMACK, D. (1971a), 'Language in chimpanzee?', *Science*, No. 172, pp. 808–22.

PREMACK, D. (1971b), 'On the assessment of language competence in the
chimpanzee', in *Behavior of Nonhuman Primates*, A. M. Schrier and
F. Stollnitz (eds), Vol. 4, Academic Press, New York.

REYNOLDS, P. C. (1970), 'Social communication in the chimpanzee: a review',
in *The Chimpanzee*, G. Bourne (ed.), Vol. 4, Karger, Basle.

RIOPELLE, A. J. (ed.), (1967), *Animal Problem Solving*, Penguin.

SEBEOK, T. A. (ed.), (1968), *Animal Communication: Techniques of Study and
Results of Research*, University of Indiana Press.

THORPE, W. H. (1963), *Learning and Instinct in Animals*, Harvard University
Press.

TSUMORI, A. (1967), 'Newly acquired behavior and social interactions of
Japanese monkeys', in *Social Communication among Primates*, S. A. Altmann
(ed.), University of Chicago Press.

C Play and Creativity

Squares and Oblongs

St Augustine was the first real psychologist for he was the first to see the basic fact about human nature, namely, that the Natural Man hates nature, and that the only act which can really satisfy him is the *acte gratuite*. His ego resents every desire of his natural self for food, sex pleasure, logical coherence, because desires are given not chosen, and his ego seeks constantly to assert its autonomy by doing something of which the requiredness is not given, that is to say, something which is completely arbitrary, a pure act of choice. The psychoanalyst can doubtless explain St Augustine's robbing of the pear-tree in terms of natural desire, as, say, a symbolic copy of some forbidden sexual act, but this explanation, however true, misses the point which is the drive behind the symbolic transformation in consequence of which what in its original form was felt as a given desire now seems to the actor a matter of free and arbitrary choice.

Similarly, there are no doubt natural causes, perhaps very simple ones, behind the wish to write verses, but the chief satisfaction in the creative act is the feeling that it is quite gratuitous.

In addition to wanting to feel free, man wants to feel important, and it is from the immediately given feelings with which he identifies himself that the natural man derives his sense of self-importance. In consequence he is in a dilemma, for the more he emancipates himself from given necessity, the more he loses his sense of importance and becomes a prey to anxiety.

That is why so many *actes gratuites* are, like that of St Augustine, criminal acts. The freedom is asserted by disobeying a law of God or man which gives the importance. Nearly all crime is magic, an attempt to make free with necessities.

The alternative to criminal magic is the innocent game. Games are *actes gratuites* in which necessity is obeyed because the necessity here consists of rules chosen by the players. Games, therefore, are freer than crimes because the rule obeyed in the former is arbitrary while the rule disobeyed in the latter is not; at the same time, they are less important.

But the very readiness with which we frankly discuss such matters with each other is a sign that they are not our serious concern. Underneath them our serious day-dream carries on its repetitious querulous life, and it too has its manifest and latent content. What it actually says over and over again is: 'Why doesn't my neighbour love me for myself?', but this is a code message which, decoded, reads: 'I do not love my neighbour as myself and may God have mercy on my soul.' About this, just because it is a serious matter, we quite rightly keep silent in public.

The rules of a game give it importance by making it difficult to play, a test of skill. In this, however, they betray that their importance is really frivolous, because it means that they are only important to those who have the physical or mental gifts to play them, and that is a matter of chance.

Granted that a game is innocent, the test of whether one should play it or not is simply whether one enjoys playing it or not, because the better one plays the more one enjoys it. A cripple may dream of being a star football player but he would feel miserable if he were actually compelled to play football.

Ask a talented surgeon why he is a surgeon and, if he is an honest man, he will not say: 'Because I want to benefit suffering humanity'; he will say: 'What a silly question. Because I love operating, of course.' It is perfectly possible to imagine a surgeon who hated human beings at the same time that he saved their lives, because of the pleasure he took in exercising his gift.

The only serious possession of men is not their gifts but what they all possess equally, independent of fortune, namely their will, in other words, their love, and the only serious matter is what they love, themselves, or God and their neighbour. Life is not a game because one cannot say: 'I will live if I turn out to be good at living.' No, gifted or not, I must live. Those who cannot play a game can always be spectators, but no one can be a spectator of life; he must either live himself or hang himself. And in living well, i.e. in loving one's neighbour, the pleasure-pain criterion does not apply. If the Good Samaritan is asked why he rescued the man who fell among thieves, he may answer: 'because I like doing good', but this answer will be a joking reproof to the interrogator for asking silly questions when he already knows the answer, which is that to love my neighbour as myself is an order and whether I enjoy obeying an order or not is irrelevant. If pleasure and pain were relevant, then the Good Samaritan would simply be more gifted at loving than the Levite, and the whole thing would be a game.

To hear people talk, you would think that in their free time, i.e. when not engaged either in action or directed thinking, they were concerned with nothing but sex, prestige and money.

(From *Poets at Work*, essays based on the modern poetry collection at the Lockwood Memorial Library, University of Buffalo, ed. Charles C. Abbott), Harcourt, Brace, Jovanovich, 1948.)

Surprise, Craft and Creativity

If the creative product has about it anything unique, it is its quality of surprise. It surprises, yet is familiar, fits the shape of human experience. Whether truth or fiction, it has verisimilitude.

Surprise in the creative takes three forms. One is the surprise of the fitting but unlikely, an empirical or functional surprise. 'How clever to use *that* in *that* way!' Psychologists use the principle in a 'multiple uses test' to find whether someone uses objects 'creatively'. Empirical surprise is ingenious rather than deep. Consider formal surprise, by contrast. Take hands of bridge. Any hand is equally unlikely. Some are extremely interesting – all spades, for a case. What makes such a hand interesting is not its improbability but its relevance to a rule structure. That feature is at the heart of formal surprise. Suppose one produces a solution to a mathematical problem that is within the formal constraints of the rule system, yet is both shockingly new and yet obvious (once done). Almost inevitably, such a product will have both power and beauty. The powerful simplicity of the great formulations in physics are a case in point.

Formal surprise is also to be found in music. Music has structure; composers have signatures within that structure. One can simulate Bach-like or Mozart-like music by computer. It is quite banal. Yet both Bach and Mozart used the same sort of 'programme' and produced surprises – and not just historical ones. Their nature is harder to characterize since music lacks anything by way of the truth-testability of elegant scientific formulations or the consistency tests of logic.

Finally, there is metaphoric surprise. Its shock value depends upon the structured medium of language and symbols. Metaphoric surprise opens new connections in awareness, relates where relations were not before suspected. Eliot's lines 'I should have been a pair of ragged claws/ Scuttling across the floors of silent seas' bring together furtive darkness beneath the sea with the dark agonies of depression. Why does it illuminate? What does it satisfy? The answer remains obscure.

While our three forms of surprise have creative novelty about them, they are almost always the fruit of disciplined craft. The proverb about poor workmen blaming their tools is relevant. Auden comments that a poet 'likes to hang around words'. Good painters cannot let go; neither can the good mathematician, though his hanging on (like Lewis Carroll's) may be full of fun. For the production of creative surprise demands a masterful control of the medium. It is not the product of spontaneous seizure, an act of sudden glory. Music and mathematics give gifts to the well prepared. So, too, poetry, and engineering. How curious that surprise grows in the soil of grinding work. A woman at a dinner party is alleged to have said to Alfred North Whitehead, 'We are all philosophers, you know.' 'Yes,' he agreed, 'but some of us spend all day at it.'

Association and Bisociation

A convenient definition of associative thinking is given by Humphrey (1951): 'The term "association", or "mental association", is a general name often used in psychology to express the conditions under which mental events, whether of experience or behaviour, arise.' In other words, the term 'association' simply indicates the process by which one idea leads to another.

But an idea has associative connections with many other ideas established by past experiences; and which of these connections will be activated in a given situation depends on the *type* of thinking we are engaged in at the moment. Orderly thinking is always rule-governed, and even dreaming, or daydreaming, has its own rules. In the psychological laboratory, the experimenter lays down the rule 'name opposites'. Then he says 'dark', and the subject promptly says 'light'. But if the rule is 'synonyms', then the subject will associate 'dark' with 'black' or 'night' or 'shadow'. To talk of stimuli as if they were acting in a vacuum is meaningless; what response a given stimulus will evoke depends on the rules of the game we are playing at the time – the *canon* of that particular mental skill. But we do not live in laboratories where the rules of the game are laid down by explicit orders; in the normal routines of thinking and talking the rules are implicit and unconscious.

This applies not only to the rules of grammar, syntax, and common-or-garden logic, but also to those which govern the more complex structures we call 'frames of reference', 'universes of discourse' or 'associative contexts'; and to the 'hidden persuaders' which prejudice our reasoning. In *The Act of Creation* I used the term 'matrix' as a unifying formula to refer to all these cognitive structures, that is to say, to all *mental habits and skills governed by a fixed set of rules but capable of varied strategies in attacking a problem*. In other words, matrices are *cognitive holons*. They are controlled by their canons, but guided by feedback from the environment – the distribution of the men on the chessboard, the features of the problem in hand. They range from extremes of pedantic rigidity to liberal open-mindedness – within limits. They are ordered into 'vertical' abstractive hierarchies, which interlace in 'horizontal' associative networks and cross-references.

Let me repeat: all routine thinking is comparable to playing a game according to fixed rules and more or less flexible strategies. The game of chess allows for more varied strategies than draughts, a vaster number of choices among moves permitted by the rules. But there is a limit to them; and there are hopeless situations in chess when the most subtle strategies won't save you – short of offering your opponent a jumbo-sized Martini. Now in fact there is no rule in chess preventing you from doing that. But making a person drunk while remaining sober oneself is a different sort of game with a different context. Combining the two games is a bisociation. In other words, associative routine means thinking according to a given set of rules on a single plane, as it were. The bisociative act means combining two different sets of rules, to live on several planes at once.

I do not mean to belittle the value of law-abiding routines. They lend coherence and stability to behaviour, and structured order to thought. But when the challenge exceeds a critical limit, adaptive routines are no longer sufficient. The world moves on and new facts arise, creating problems which cannot be solved within the conventional frames of reference, by applying to them the accepted rules of the game. Then the crisis is on with its desperate search for a remedy, the unorthodox improvisation which will lead to the new synthesis – the act of mental self-repair.

The Latin *cogito* comes from *coagitare*, to shake together. *Bisociation means combining two hitherto unrelated cognitive matrices in such a way that a new level is added to the hierarchy, which contains the previously separate structures as its members*. The motions of the tides were known to man from time immemorial. So were the motions of the moon. But the idea to relate the two, the idea that the tides were due to the attraction of the moon, occurred, as far as we know, for the first time to a German astronomer in the seventeenth century; and when Galileo read about it, he laughed it off as an occult fancy. Moral: the more familiar the previously unrelated structures are, the more striking the emergent synthesis, and the more obvious it looks in the driver's mirror of hindsight. The history of science is a history of marriages between ideas which were previously strangers to each other, and frequently considered as incompatible. Lodestones – magnets – were known in antiquity as a curiosity of Nature. In the Middle Ages they were used for two purposes: as navigators' compasses and as a means to attract an estranged wife back to her husband. Equally well known were the curious properties of amber which, when rubbed, acquired the virtue of attracting flimsy objects. The Greek for amber is *elektron*, but the Greeks were not much interested in electricity nor were the Middle Ages. For nearly two thousand years, electricity and magnetism were considered as separate phenomena, in no way related to each other. In 1820 Hans Christian Oersted discovered that an electric current flowing through a wire deflected a compass-needle which happened to be lying on his table. At that moment the two contexts began to fuse into one: electro-magnetism, creating a kind of chain-reaction which is still continuing and gaining in momentum.

The AHA reaction

From Pythagoras, who combined arithmetic and geometry, to Newton, who combined Galileo's studies of the motion of projectiles with Kepler's equations of planetary orbits, to Einstein, who unified energy and matter in a single sinister equation, the pattern is always the same. The creative act does not create something out of nothing, like the God of the Old Testament; it combines, reshuffles and relates already existing but hitherto separate ideas, facts, frames of perception, associative contexts. This act of cross-fertilization – or self-fertilization within a single brain – seems to be the essence of creativity, and to justify the term 'bisociation'.*

Take the example of Gutenberg, who invented the printing press (or at least invented it independently from others). His first idea was to cast letter-types like signet rings or seals. But how could he assemble thousands of little seals in such a way that they made an even imprint on paper? He struggled with the problem for years, until one day he went to a wine harvest in his native Rhineland, and presumably got drunk. He wrote in a letter: 'I watched the wine flowing, and going back from the effect to the cause, I studied the power of the wine press which nothing can resist . . .' At that moment the penny dropped: seals and the wine press combined gave the letter press.

Gestalt psychologists have coined a word for that moment of truth, the flash of illumination, when bits of the puzzle suddenly click into place – they call it the AHA experience. But this is not the only type of reaction which the bisociative click can produce. A quite different kind of response is aroused by telling a story like the following:

A Marquis at the court of Louis XV had unexpectedly returned from a journey and, on entering his wife's boudoir, found her in the arms of a bishop. After a

---

*Similar views have been put forward among others, by the mathematician Henri Poincaré, who in an oft-quoted lecture explained discovery as the happy meeting of 'hooked atoms of thought' in the unconscious mind. According to Sir Frederick Bartlett (1958), 'the most important features of original experimental thinking is the discovery of overlap . . . where formerly only isolation and difference were recognized'. Jerome Bruner (1949) considers all forms of creativity as a result of 'combinatorial activity'. McKellar (1957) talks of the 'fusion' of perceptions, Kubie of the 'discovery of unexpected connections between things'; and so on, back to Goethe's 'connect, always connect'.

moment's hesitation, the Marquis walked calmly to the window, leaned out and began going through the motions of blessing the people in the street.

'What are you doing?' cried the anguished wife.

'Monseigneur is performing my functions,' replied the nobleman, 'so I am performing his.'*

Laughter may be called the HAHA reaction. Let us briefly discuss first the logical, then the emotional, aspect of it.

The HAHA reaction

The Marquis' behaviour is both unexpected and perfectly logical – but of a logic not usually applied to this type of situation. It is the logic of the division of labour, where the rule of the game is the *quid pro quo*, the give-and-take. But we expected, of course, that his reactions would be governed by a quite different canon, that of sexual morality. It is the interaction between these two mutually exclusive associative contexts which produces the comic effect. It compels us to perceive the situation at the same time in two self-consistent but habitually incompatible frames of reference; it makes us function on two wave-lengths simultaneously. While this unusual condition lasts, the event is not, as is normally the case, perceived in a single frame of reference, but *bisociated* with two.

But this unusual condition does not last for long. The act of discovery leads to a lasting synthesis, a *fusion* of the two previously unrelated frames of reference; in the comic bisociation we have a *collision* between incompatible frames which for a brief moment cross each other's path. However, the difference is not absolute. Whether the frames are compatible or not, whether they will collide or merge, depends on subjective factors – for, after all, the colliding or merging takes place in the minds of the audience. In Kepler's mind the motions of the moon and the motions of the tides fused – they became branches of the same causative hierarchy. But Galileo treated Kepler's theory literally as a joke – he called it an 'occult fancy'. The history of science abounds with examples of discoveries greeted with howls of laughter because they seemed to be a marriage of incompatibles – until the marriage bore fruit and the alleged incompatibility of the partners turned out to derive from prejudice. The humorist, on the other hand, deliberately chooses discordant codes of behaviour, or universes of discourse, to expose their hidden incongruities in the resulting clash. Comic discovery is paradox stated, scientific discovery is paradox resolved.

Looked at from his own point of view, the Marquis' gesture was a truly original inspiration. If he had followed the conventional rules of the game,

---

*I have used this particular story in *The Act of Creation* and am using it again because of its neat pattern. Most anecdotes need lengthy explanations to make their logical structure clear.

he would have had to beat up or kill the Bishop. But at the court of Louis
XV assassinating a Monseigneur would have been considered, if not exactly
a crime, still in very bad taste; it could not be done. To solve the problem,
that is, to save his face and at the same time humiliate his opponent – a
second frame of reference, governed by different rules of the game, had
to be brought into the situation and combined, bisociated, with the first.
All original comic invention is a creative act, a malicious discovery.

Laughter and emotion

The emphasis is on malicious, and this brings us from the *logic* of humour
to the *emotional factor* in the H A H A reaction. When the expert story-
teller tells an anecdote, he creates a certain tension which mounts as the
narrative progresses. But it never reaches its expected climax. The punch-
line acts like a guillotine which cuts across the logical development of the
situation; it debunks our dramatic expectations, the tension becomes redundant and is exploded in laughter. To put it differently, laughter disposes
of the overflow of emotion which has become pointless, is denied by reason,
and has to be somehow worked off along physiological channels of least
resistance.

If you look at the brutal merriment of the people in a tavern scene by
Hogarth or Rawlinson, you realize at once that they are working off their
surplus of adrenalin by contractions of the face muscles, slapping of thighs
and explosive exhalations of breath from the half-closed glottis. The emotions worked off in laughter are aggression, sexual gloating, conscious or
unconscious sadism – all operating through the sympathico-adrenal system.
However, when you look at a clever *New Yorker* cartoon, Homeric laughter
yields to an amused and rarefied smile; the ample flow of adrenalin has been
distilled into a grain of Attic salt. Take, for instance, that classic definition:
'What is a sadist? A person who is kind to a masochist . . .' The word
'witticism' is derived from 'wit' in its original sense of ingenuity; the two
domains are continuous, without a sharp dividing line. As we move from
the coarse towards the subtler forms of humour, the joke shades into epigram and riddle, the comic simile into the hidden analogy; and the emotions
involved show a similar transition. The emotive voltage discharged in
coarse laughter is aggression robbed of its purpose; the tension discharged
in the A H A reaction is derived from an intellectual challenge. It snaps at
the moment when the penny drops – when we have solved the riddle hidden
in the *New Yorker* cartoon, in a brain-teaser or in a scientific problem.

Let me repeat, the two domains of humour and discovery form a continuum. As we travel across it, from left to centre, so to speak, the emotional
climate gradually changes from the malice of the jester to the detached
objectivity of the sage. And if we now continue the journey in the same

direction, we find equally gradual transitions into the third domain of creativity, that of the artist. The artist, too, hints rather than states, and poses riddles; and so we get a symmetrically reversed transition towards the other end of the spectrum, from highly intellectualized art forms towards the more sensual and emotive, ending in the thought-free beatitude of the mystic.

The A H reaction

But how does one define the emotional climate of art? How does one classify the emotions which give rise to the experience of beauty? If you leaf through textbooks of experimental psychology, you won't find much of it. When Behaviourists use the word 'emotion', they nearly always refer to hunger, sex, rage and fear, and the related effects of the release of adrenalin. They have no explanations to offer for the curious reaction one experiences when listening to Mozart, or looking at the ocean, or reading for the first time John Donne's *Holy Sonnets*. Nor will you find in the textbooks a description of the physiological processes accompanying the reaction: moistening of the eyes, catching one's breath, followed by a kind of rapt tranquillity, the draining of all tensions. Let us call this the AH reaction – and thus complete the trinity.

HAHA!	AHA	AH . . .

Laughter and weeping, the Greek masks of comedy and tragedy, mark the extremes of a continuous spectrum; both are overflow reflexes, but in every other respect are physiological opposites. Laughter is mediated by the sympathico-adrenal branch of the autonomous nervous system, weeping by the parasympathetic branch; the first tends to galvanize the body into action, the second tends towards passivity and catharsis. Watch yourself breathing when you laugh: long deep intakes of air, followed by bursts of exhalatory puffs – ha, ha, ha! In weeping, you do the opposite: short, gasping inspirations – sobs – are followed by long, sighing expirations – a-a-h, aah . . .

In keeping with this, the emotions which overflow in the A H reaction are the direct opposites of those exploded in laughter. The latter belong to the adrenergic, aggressive-defensive type of emotions. In our theory, these are manifestations of the *self-assertive* tendency. Their opposites I shall call the *self-transcending* emotions, derived from the *integrative* tendency. They are epitomized in what Freud called the oceanic feeling: that expansion of awareness which one experiences on occasion in an empty cathedral when eternity is looking through the window of time, and in which the self seems to dissolve like a grain of salt in a lot of water.

(From *The Ghost in the Machine*, Hutchinson, 1967.)

References

BARTLETT, F. (1958), *Thinking: an Experimental and Social Study*, Unwin.
BRUNER, J. S., and POSTMAN, L. (1949), *J. of Personality*, XVIII.
HUMPHREY, G. (1951), *Thinking*, Methuen.
McKELLAR, P. (1957), *Imagination and Thinking*, Cohen & West.

Effects of Play on Associative Fluency in Pre-School Children

Numerous writers (Almy, 1967; Jackson and Messick, 1965; Klinger, 1969; Lieberman, 1965; Slobin, 1964; Sutton-Smith, 1966, 1967; Wallach, 1970; Wallach and Kogan, 1965; Wenar, 1971) have hypothesized a connection between play and creativity. However, previous research bearing directly on this relationship is limited to only two studies. Lieberman (1965) found kindergarten teachers' ratings of children's playfulness to be significantly correlated with three divergent thinking measures adapted from Torrance and Guilford.

Sutton-Smith (1967) had kindergarten children give alternative uses for four toys with which they had become familiar during their school year. The boys in his sample gave more uses for the two toys which they preferred, while the girls gave more uses for the two toys which they preferred. However, inasmuch as Sutton-Smith apparently confounded playful experience with total exposure to the toys, we cannot necessarily conclude that it was the *playfulness* of the experience *per se* that resulted in the obtained differences.

The present study may be viewed as an attempt to provide an experimental test of the relationships explored in the Sutton-Smith investigation.

Accordingly, one group of children was permitted to play with a particular set of objects; a second group was asked to engage in an equivalent amount of imitative behaviour with those same objects; and a third group was given a 'neutral' experience not involving those objects. Following the experimental treatments, each subject was asked to suggest alternative uses for each of the stimulus objects. The selection of the alternative-uses test for the dependent measure was based primarily upon the work of Wallach and his collaborators (Wallach, 1970; Wallach and Kogan, 1965; Wallach and Wing, 1969). The tests themselves evolved from Wallach and Kogan's theory of creativity and were designed to tap an individual's ability to form associative elements into new combinations which meet certain task requirements. It was predicted that the information registered during playful activity would tend to increase a child's associative fluency as measured by the number of responses produced in an alternative-uses test.

Method
Subjects

The subjects were ninety children of middle- and upper-middle-class background, all attending either a nursery school or a nursery school day care centre in Toledo, Ohio. There were forty-five girls and forty-five boys ranging in age from 4·0 to 6·1 years (M = 5·0). Approximately 84% of the subjects were white and 16% were black. Thirty subjects were randomly assigned to each of the three treatment conditions: play, imitation, and control. Both sex and race were distributed equally across the three groups.

Stimulus materials

For the play and imitation groups, the stimulus materials included a pile of ten paper towels, a screwdriver, a wooden board (6 × 14 inches) with five screws set in it, a pile of thirty paper clips, fifteen blank cards (3 × 5 inches), ten empty kitchen-size matchboxes, and a tray containing six wet plastic cups. These materials were placed on a table, behind which stood a screen (4 × 5 feet) with a drawing of a clown and numerous abstract geometric shapes pasted on its multi-coloured background. Subjects in the control group were given four sketches, such as those found in children's colouring books, and a box of crayons.

Procedure

Every subject was seen twice, once for a rapport-building five-minute colouring session, and then one week later during the experiment proper. At the start of the second session, subjects in the play group were presented with the stimulus materials and told, 'You may play with all of these things. Do whatever you would like to do with them.' The play period lasted ten minutes.

Imitation subjects were asked to watch the experimenter as he performed four tasks (turning screws with a screwdriver, fastening cards with paper clips, wiping wet cups with a paper towel, putting small sticks in empty matchboxes). Then the subject was instructed to repeat the experimenter's actions exactly as he had seen them performed.

The control subjects were given a box of crayons and four sketches which they were permitted to colour as they wished.

The dependent measure

Immediately following the play, imitation, or colouring sessions, each subject was given an alternative-uses test by the same individual who administered the experimental treatments. All objects were removed from the subject's view. The experimenter then randomly selected one of the four experimental objects and showed it to the subject saying, 'You can use a – in lots of different ways. I would like you to tell me all of the things that you could do with it, make with it, or use it for.' Once the subject stopped responding, the experimenter would ask, 'Could you do anything else with it?'

Results

Responses were scored as standard whenever they named, or made reference to, a use for which the object had been primarily designed (e.g., for the paper towel, responses making reference to wiping, drying, washing, or cleaning were scored as standard). All other non-redundant responses were scored as non-standard.

Standard and non-standard responses were analyzed separately so as to clarify the manner in which the treatments were affecting associative fluency. It was assumed that prior experience with the four objects would result in standard uses being high-probability responses for most of the children. Thus, the three groups were not expected to differ significantly in the number of such responses they could produce.

The analysis of variance performed on the number of standard responses produced for the four objects showed that the play, imitation, and control conditions did not differ significantly on this measure (F 1). Although the main effect of objects was significant ($F = 14.63$, $df = 3/261$, $p < 0.01$) there was no significant Treatment Condition X Object interaction ($F = 1.44$, $df = 3/261$, $p < 0.05$).

Figure 1 is a representation of the mean number of non-standard responses to each of the four objects for each of the three groups. The analysis of variance for these data indicated a significant Treatment Condition X Objects interaction ($F = 2.46$, $df = 6/261$, $p < 0.05$). An analysis of variance for the simple main effects was computed and showed a significant difference between the three treatment conditions for each of the four objects (Fs 6.12, $df = 2/348$, $p < 0.01$). Pair-wise comparisons among the means shown in Figure 1 indicated that subjects in the play condition produced significantly more non-standard responses for every object than subjects in either the imitation or control conditions (using Tukey's honesty significant difference procedure (HSD), $p < 0.01$). The differences between the imitation and control conditions were all non-significant.

Discussion

The protocols of the play subjects provided numerous examples of the free combinatorial and associative activity suggested by Piaget (1951) and Sutton-Smith. Children stated that they could 'wrap (a paper towel) around a bunch of paper clips and throw it', use an empty matchbox to

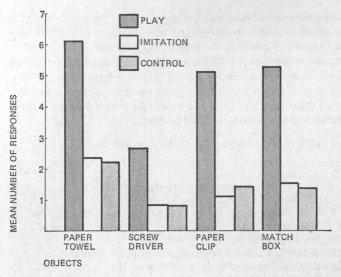

Fig. 1. Mean number of non-standard responses given by play, imitation, and control groups for four objects.

'put sand in it for a little house for ants', and use paper clips to 'make a chain out of them and tie up dogs with it'. One child suggested that he could use a matchbox to make either 'a little T.V.' (or) 'a big swimming pool'. Another claimed that 'If you turn it (a screwdriver) like this, it will be a merry-go-round.' Despite the fantastic nature of many non-standard uses, the children did tend to observe certain physical properties of the objects. For example, uses for paper towels frequently involved tearing, folding, and crumbling, but none of the uses for screwdrivers hinted at such properties. Thus it can be seen that these uses, though maybe fantastic, were generally not bizarre. Indeed, such associations might well prove to be useful to a child as he interacts with his everyday environment.

The precise manner in which the effects of the play treatment were transferred to performance on the alternative-uses task remains uncertain. Some non-standard responses were obvious reiterations of uses to which the objects had been put during the children's play sessions. The source of other responses was less apparent. Surely some associations were made which were neither verbalized nor acted upon during the play sessions. Some of the play subjects may have also brought a more 'playful' attitude to the questioning period than their imitation and control counterparts, although no differences in affect were detected by the experimenter.

Another factor which contributed significantly to the differences between the three treatment conditions was the considerable use which the play subjects made of available environmental cues. Wallach (1970) has suggested that such a disposition towards broad attention deployment is crucial for creative productivity. This disposition may have been facilitated in the present study by the relative lack of structure inherent in the play situation. The open-ended instructions given the play subjects may have stimulated an active search of the environment for cues indicating various ways in which the available objects could be used.

(From *Developmental Psychology*, No. 9, 1973, pp. 38–43.)

References

ALMY, M. (1967), 'Spontaneous play: An avenue for intellectual development', *Young Children*, No. 22, pp. 265–76.

JACKSON, P. W., and MESSICK, S. (1965), 'The person, the product, and the response: Conceptual problems in the assessment of creativity', *Journal of Personality*, No. 33, pp. 309–29.

KLINGER, E. (1969), 'Development of imaginative behavior: Implications of play for a theory of fantasy', *Psychological Bulletin*, No. 72, pp. 277–98.

LIEBERMAN, J. N. (1965), 'Playfulness and divergent thinking: An investigation of their relationship at the kindergarten level', *J. Genet. Psychol.*, No. 107, pp. 219–24.

PIAGET, J. (1951), *Play, Dreams, and Imitation in Childhood*, Routledge & Kegan Paul.

SLOBIN, D. I. (1964), 'The fruits of the first season: A discussion of the role of play in childhood', *Journal of Humanistic Psychology*, No. 4, pp. 59–79.

SUTTON-SMITH, B. (1966), 'Piaget on play: A critique', *Psych. Rev.*, No. 73, pp. 104–10.

SUTTON-SMITH, B. (1967), 'The role of play in cognitive development', *Young Children*, No. 22, pp. 361–70.

WALLACH, M. A. (1970), 'Creativity', in *Carmichael's Manual of Child Psychology*, P. H. Mussen (ed.), Vol. 1, Wiley, New York.

WALLACH, M. A., and KOGAN, N. (1965), *Modes of Thinking in Young Children: A Study of the Creativity-Intelligence Distinction*, Holt, Rinehart & Winston, New York.

WALLACH, M. A., and WING, C. W., JR (1969), *The Talented Student: A Validation of the Creativity-Intelligence Distinction*, Holt, Rinehart & Winston, New York.

WENAR, C. (1971), *Personality Development: From Infancy to Adulthood*, Houghton Mifflin, Boston, U.S.A.

D Play and Civilization

Deep Play: a Description of the Balinese Cockfight

Of cocks and men

Bali, mainly because it is Bali, is a well-studied place. Its mythology, art, ritual, social organization, patterns of child rearing, forms of law, even styles of trance, have all been microscopically examined for traces of that elusive substance Jane Belo (1970) called 'The Balinese Temper'. But, aside from a few passing remarks, the cockfight has barely been noticed, although as a popular obsession of consuming power it is at least as important a revelation of what being a Balinese 'is really like' as these more celebrated phenomena. As much of America surfaces in a ball park, on a golf links, at a race track, or around a poker table, much of Bali surfaces in a cock ring. For it is only apparently cocks that are fighting there. Actually, it is men.

To anyone who has been in Bali any length of time, the deep psychological identification of Balinese men with their cocks is unmistakable. The *double entendre* here is deliberate. It works in exactly the same way in Balinese as it does in English, even to producing the same tired jokes, strained puns, and uninventive obscenities. Bateson and Mead (1942) have even suggested that, in line with the Balinese conception of the body as a set of separately animated parts, cocks are viewed as detachable, self-operating penises, ambulant genitals with a life of their own. And while I do not have the kind of unconscious material either to confirm or disconfirm this intriguing notion, the fact that they are masculine symbols *par excellence* is about as indubitable, and to the Balinese about as evident, as the fact that water runs downhill.

The language of everyday moralism is shot through, on the male side of it, with roosterish imagery. *Sabung*, the word for cock (and one which appears in inscriptions as early as A.D. 922), is used metaphorically to mean 'hero', 'warrior', 'champion', 'man of parts', 'political candidate', 'bachelor', 'dandy', 'lady-killer', or 'tough guy'. A pompous man whose behaviour presumes above his station is compared to a tailless cock who struts about as though he had a large, spectacular one. A desperate man who makes a last, irrational effort to extricate himself from an impossible situation is likened to a dying cock who makes one final lunge at his tormentor to drag him along to a common destruction.

But the intimacy of men with their cocks is more than metaphorical. Balinese men, or anyway a large majority of Balinese men, spend an enormous amount of time with their favourites, grooming them, feeding them, discussing them, trying them out against one another, or just gazing at them with a mixture of rapt admiration and dreamy self-absorption. Whenever you see a group of Balinese men squatting idly in the council shed or along the road in their hips down, shoulders forward, knees up fashion, half or more of them will have a rooster in his hands, holding it between his thighs, bouncing it gently up and down to strengthen its legs, ruffing its feathers with abstract sensuality, pushing it out against a neighbour's rooster to rouse its spirit, withdrawing it toward his loins to calm it again. Now and then, to get a feel for another bird, a man will fiddle this way with someone else's cock for a while, but usually by moving around to squat in place behind it, rather than just having it passed across to him as though it were merely an animal.

In the houseyard, the high-walled enclosures where the people live, fighting cocks are kept in wicker cages, moved frequently about so as to maintain the optimum balance of sun and shade. They are fed a special diet, which varies somewhat according to individual theories but which is mostly maize, sifted for impurities with far more care than it is when mere humans are going to eat it and offered to the animal kernel by kernel. Red pepper is stuffed down their beaks and up their anuses to give them spirit. They are bathed in the same ceremonial preparation of tepid water, medicinal herbs, flowers, and onions in which infants are bathed, and for a prize cock just about as often. Their combs are cropped, their plumage dressed, their spurs trimmed, their legs massaged, and they are inspected for flaws with the squinted concentration of a diamond merchant. A man who has a passion for cocks, an enthusiast in the literal sense of the term, can spend most of his life with them, and even those, the overwhelming majority, whose passion though intense has not entirely run away with them, can and do spend what seems not only to an outsider, but also to themselves, an inordinate amount of time with them. 'I am cock crazy,' my landlord, a quite ordinary *aficionado* by Balinese standards, used to moan as he went to move another cage, give another bath, or conduct another feeding. 'We're all cock crazy.'

The madness has some less visible dimensions, however, because although it is true that cocks are symbolic expressions or magnifications of their owner's self, the narcissistic male ego writ out in Aesopian terms, they are also expressions – and rather more immediate ones – of what the Balinese regard as the direct inversion, aesthetically, morally, and metaphysically, of human status: animality.

The Balinese revulsion against any behaviour regarded as animal-like can hardly be overstressed. Babies are not allowed to crawl for that reason. Incest, though hardly approved, is a much less horrifying crime than bestiality. (The appropriate punishment for the second is death by drowning, for the first being forced to live like an animal.) Most demons are represented – in sculpture, dance, ritual, myth – in some real or fantastic animal form. The main puberty rite consists in filing the child's teeth so they will not look like animal fangs. Not only defecation but eating is regarded as a disgusting, almost obscene activity, to be conducted hurriedly and privately, because of its association with animality. Even falling down or any form of clumsiness is considered to be bad for these reasons. Aside from cocks and a few domestic animals – oxen, ducks – of no emotional significance, the Balinese are aversive to animals and treat their large number of dogs not merely callously but with a phobic cruelty. In identifying with his cock, the Balinese man is identifying not just with his ideal self, or even his penis, but also, and at the same time, with what he most fears, hates, and ambivalence being what it is, is fascinated by – The Powers of Darkness.

The connection of cocks and cockfighting with such Powers, with the animalistic demons that threaten constantly to invade the small, cleared-off space in which the Balinese have so carefully built their lives and devour its inhabitants, is quite explicit. A cockfight, any cockfight, is in the first instance a blood sacrifice offered, with the appropriate chants and oblations, to the demons in order to pacify their ravenous, cannibal hunger.

In the cockfight, man and beast, good and evil, ego and id, the creative power of aroused masculinity and the destructive power of loosened animality fuse in a bloody drama of hatred, cruelty, violence, and death. It is little wonder that when, as is the invariable rule, the owner of the winning cock takes the carcass of the loser – often torn limb from limb by its enraged owner – home to eat, he does so with a mixture of social embarrassment, moral satisfaction, aesthetic disgust, and cannibal joy. Or that a man who has lost an important fight is sometimes driven to wreck his family shrines and curse the gods, an act of metaphysical (and social) suicide. Or that in seeking earthly analogues for heaven and hell the Balinese compare the former to the mood of a man whose cock has just won, the latter to that of a man whose cock has just lost.

The fight

Cockfights (*tetadjen; sabungan*) are held in a ring about fifty feet square. Usually they begin towards late afternoon and run three or four hours until sunset. About nine or ten separate matches (*sehet*) comprise a programme. Each match is precisely like the others in general pattern: there is no main match, no connection between individual matches, no variation in their format, and each is arranged on a completely *ad hoc* basis. After a fight has ended and the emotional debris is cleaned away – the bets paid, the curses cursed, the carcasses possessed – seven, eight, perhaps even a dozen men slip negligently into the ring with a cock and seek to find there a logical opponent for it. This process, which rarely takes less than ten minutes, and often a good deal longer, is conducted in a very subdued, oblique, even dissembling manner. Those not immediately involved give it at best but disguised, sidelong attention; those who, embarrassedly, are, attempt to pretend somehow that the whole thing is not really happening.

A match made, the other hopefuls retire with the same deliberate indifference, and the selected cocks have their spurs (*tadji*) affixed – razor sharp, pointed steel swords, four or five inches long. This is a delicate job which only a small proportion of men, a half-dozen or so in most villages, know how to do properly. The man who attaches the spurs also provides them, and if the rooster he assists wins, its owner awards him the spur-leg of the victim. The spurs are affixed by winding a long length of string around the foot of the spur and the leg of the cock. For reasons I shall come to presently, it is done somewhat differently from case to case, and is an obsessively deliberate affair. The lore about spurs is extensive – they are sharpened only at eclipses and the dark of the moon, should be kept out of the sight of women, and so forth. And they are handled, both in use and out, with the same curious combination of fussiness and sensuality the Balinese direct towards ritual objects generally.

The spurs affixed, the two cocks are placed by their handlers (who may or may not be their owners) facing one another in the centre of the ring. A coconut pierced with a small hole is placed in a pail of water, in which it takes about twenty-one seconds to sink, a period known as a *tjeng* and marked at beginning and end by the beating of a slit gong. During these twenty-one seconds the handlers (*pengangkeb*) are not permitted to touch their roosters. If, as sometimes happens, the animals have not fought during this time, they are picked up, fluffed, pulled, prodded and otherwise insulted, and put back in the centre of the ring and the process begins again. Sometimes they refuse to fight at all, or one keeps running away, in which case they are imprisoned together under a wicker cage, which usually gets them engaged.

Most of the time, in any case, the cocks fly almost immediately at one another in a wing-beating, head-thrusting, leg-kicking explosion of animal fury so pure, so absolute, and in its own way so beautiful, as to be almost abstract, a Platonic concept of hate. Within moments one or the other drives home a solid blow with his spur. The handler whose cock has de-livered the blow immediately picks it up so that it will not get a return blow, for if he does not the match is likely to end in a mutually mortal tie as the two birds wildly hack each other to pieces. This is particularly true if, as often happens, the spur sticks in its victim's body, for then the aggressor is at the mercy of his wounded foe.

With the birds again in the hands of their handlers, the coconut is now sunk three times after which the cock which has landed the blow must be set down to show that he is firm, a fact he demonstrates by wandering idly around the ring for a coconut sink. The coconut is then sunk twice more and the fight must recommence.

During this interval, slightly over two minutes, the handler of the wounded cock has been working frantically over it, like a trainer patching a mauled boxer between rounds, to get it in shape for a last, desperate try for victory. He blows in its mouth, putting the whole chicken head in his own mouth and sucking and blowing, fluffs it, stuffs its wounds with various sorts of medicines, and generally tries anything he can think of to arouse the last ounce of spirit which may be hidden somewhere within it. By the time he is forced to put it back down he is usually drenched in chicken blood, but, as in prize fighting, a good handler is worth his weight in gold. Some of them can virtually make the dead walk, at least long enough for the second and final round.

In the climactic battle (if there is one; sometimes the wounded cock simply expires in the handler's hands, or immediately as it is placed down again), the cock who landed the first blow usually proceeds to finish off his weakened opponent. But this is far from an inevitable outcome, for if a cock can walk he can fight, and if he can fight, he can kill, and what counts is which cock expires first. If the wounded one can get a stab in and stagger on until the other drops, he is the official winner, even if he himself topples over an instant later.

Surrounding all this melodrama – which the crowd packed tight around the ring follows in near silence, moving their bodies in kinaesthetic sympathy with the movement of the animals, cheering their champions on with wordless hand motions, shiftings of the shoulders, turnings of the head, falling back *en masse* as the cock with the murderous spurs careens towards one side of the ring (it is said that spectators sometimes lose eyes and fingers from being too attentive), surging forward again as they glance off towards another – is a vast body of extraordinarily elaborate and precisely detailed rules.

These rules, together with the developed lore of cocks and cockfighting which accompanies them, are written down in palm leaf manuscripts (*lon-tar; rontal*) passed on from generation to generation as part of the general legal and cultural tradition of the villages. At a fight, the umpire (*saja komong; djuru kembar*) – the man who manages the coconut – is in charge of their application and his authority is absolute. I have never seen an umpire's judgement questioned on any subject, even by the more despondent losers, nor have I ever heard, even in private, a charge of unfairness directed against one, or, for that matter, complaints about umpires in general. Only exceptionally well-trusted, solid, and, given the complexity of the code, knowledgeable citizens perform this job, and in fact men will bring their cocks only to fights presided over by such men. It is also the umpire to whom accusations of cheating, which, though rare in the extreme, occasionally arise, are referred; and it is he who in the not infrequent cases where the cocks expire virtually together decides which (if either, for, though the Balinese do not care for such an outcome, there can be ties) went first. Likened to a judge, a king, a priest, and a policeman, he is all of these, and under his assured direction the animal passion of the fight proceeds within the civic certainty of the law. In the dozens of cockfights I saw in Bali, I never once saw an altercation about rules. Indeed, I never saw an open altercation, other than those between cocks, at all.

This crosswise doubleness of an event which, taken as a fact of nature, is rage untrammelled and, taken as a fact of culture, is form perfected, defines the cockfight as a sociological entity. A cockfight is what, searching for a name of something not vertebrate enough to be called a group and not structureless enough to be called a crowd, Erving Goffmann (1961) has called a 'focused gathering' – a set of persons engrossed in a common flow of activity and relating to one another in terms of that flow. Such gatherings meet and disperse; the participants in them fluctuate; the activity that focuses them is discreet – a particulate·process that recurs rather than a continuous one that endures. They take their form from the situation that evokes them, the floor on which they are placed, as Goffman puts it; but it is a form, and an articulate one, none the less. For the situation, the floor is itself created, in jury deliberations, surgical operations, block meetings, sit-ins, cockfights, by the cultural preoccupations – here, as we shall see, the celebration of status rivalry – which not only specify the focus but, assembling actors and arranging scenery, bring it actually into being.

In classical times (that is to say, prior to the Dutch invasion of 1908), when there were no bureaucrats around to improve popular morality, the staging of a cockfight was an explicitly societal matter. Bringing a cock to an important fight was, for an adult male, a compulsory duty of citizenship; taxation of fights, which were usually held on market day, was a major source of public revenue; patronage of the art was a stated responsibility of princes; and the cock ring, or *wantilan*, stood in the centre of the village near those other monuments of Balinese civility – the council house, the origin temple, the market-place, the signal tower, and the banyan tree. Today, a few special occasions aside, the newer rectitude makes so open a statement of the connection between the excitements of collective life and those of blood sport impossible, but, less directly expressed, the connection itself remains intimate and intact. To expose it, however, it is necessary to turn to the aspect of cockfighting around which all the others pivot, and through which they exercise their force, an aspect I have thus far studiously ignored. I mean, of course, the gambling.

Odds and even money

The Balinese never do anything in a simple way that they can contrive to do in a complicated one, and to this generalization cockfight wagering is no exception.

In the first place, there are two sorts of bets, or *toh*. There is the single axial bet in the centre between the principals (*toh ketengah*), and there is the cloud of peripheral ones around the ring between members of the audience (*toh kesasi*). The first is typically large; the second typically small. The first is collective, involving coalitions of bettors clustering around the owner; the second is individual, man to man. The first is a matter of deliberate, very quiet, almost furtive arrangement by the coalition members and the umpire huddled like conspirators in the centre of the ring; the second is a matter of impulsive shouting, public offers, and public acceptances by the excited throng around its edges. And most curiously, and as we shall see most revealing, *where the first is always, without exception, even money, the second, equally without exception, is never such*. What is a fair coin in the centre is a biased one on the side.

The centre bet is the official one, hedged in again with a webwork of rules, and is made between the two cock owners, with the umpire as overseer and public witness. This bet, which, as I say, is always relatively and sometimes very large, is never raised simply by the owner in whose name it is made, but by him together with four or five, sometimes seven or eight, allies – kin, village mates, neighbours, close friends. He may, if he is not especially well-to-do, not even be the major contributor, though, if only to show that he is not involved in any chicanery, he must be a significant one.

Of the fifty-seven matches for which I have exact and reliable data on the centre bet, the range is from fifteen ringgits to five hundred, with a mean at eighty-five and with the distribution being rather noticeably trimodal: small fights (15 ringgits either side of 35) accounting for about 45 per cent of the total number; medium ones (20 ringgits either side of 70) for about 25 per cent; and large (75 ringgits either side of 175) for about 20 per cent, with a few very small and very large ones out at the extremes. In a society where the normal daily wage of a manual labourer – a brickmaker, an ordinary farmworker, a market porter – was about three ringgits a day, and considering the fact that fights were held on the average about every two-and-a-half days in the immediate area I studied, this is clearly serious gambling, even if the bets are pooled rather than individual efforts.

The side bets are, however, something else altogether. Rather than the solemn, legalistic pact-making of the centre, wagering takes place in the fashion in which the stock exchange used to work when it was out on the curb. There is a fixed and known odds paradigm which runs in a continuous series from ten-to-nine at the short end to two-to-one at the long: 10–9, 9–8, 8–7, 7–6, 6–5, 5–4, 4–3, 3–2, 2–1. The man who wishes to back the *underdog cock* (leaving aside how favourites, *kebut*, and underdogs, *ngai*, are established for the moment) shouts the short-side number indicating the odds he wants *to be given*. That is, if he shouts *gasal*, 'five', he wants the underdog at five-to-four (or, for him, four-to-five); if he shouts 'four', he wants it at four-to-three (again, he putting up the 'three'), if 'nine', at nine-to-eight, and so on. A man backing the favourite, and thus considering giving odds if he can get them short enough, indicates the fact by crying out the colour-type of that cock – 'brown', 'speckled', or whatever.

As odds-takers (backers of the underdog) and odds-givers (backers of the favourite) sweep the crowd with their shouts, they begin to focus in on one another as potential betting pairs, often from far across the ring. The taker tries to shout the giver into longer odds, the giver to shout the taker into shorter ones. The taker, who is the wooer in this situation, will signal how large a bet he wishes to make at the odds he is shouting by holding a number of fingers up in front of his face and vigorously waving them. If the giver, the wooed, replies in kind, the bet is made; if he does not, they unlock gazes and the search goes on.

The side betting, which takes place after the centre bet has been made and its size announced, consists then in a rising crescendo of shouts as backers of the underdog offer their propositions to anyone who will accept them, while those who are backing the favourite but do not like the price being offered, shout equally frenetically the colour of the cock to show they too are desperate to bet but want shorter odds.

Almost always odds-calling, which tends to be very consensual in that at any one time almost all callers are calling the same thing, starts off towards the long end of the range – five-to-four or four-to-three – and then moves, also consensually, towards the short end with greater or lesser speed and to a greater or lesser degree. Men crying 'five' and finding themselves answered only with cries of 'brown' start crying 'six', either drawing the other callers fairly quickly with them or retiring from the scene as their too-generous offers are snapped up. If the change is made and partners are still scarce, the procedure is repeated in a move to 'seven', and so on, only rarely, and in the very largest fights, reaching the ultimate 'nine' or 'ten' levels. Occasionally, if the cocks are clearly mismatched, there may be no upward movement at all, or even a movement down the scale to four-to-three, three-to-two, very, very rarely two-to-one, a shift which is accompanied by a declining number of bets as a shift upwards is accompanied by an increasing number. But the general pattern is for the betting to move a shorter or longer distance up the scale towards the, for sidebets, non-existent pole of even money, with the overwhelming majority of bets falling in the four-to-three to eight-to-seven range.

As the moment for the release of the cocks by the handlers approaches, the screaming, at least in a match where the centre bet is large, reaches almost frenzied proportions as the remaining unfulfilled bettors try desperately to find a last-minute partner at a price they can live with. (Where the centre bet is small, the opposite tends to occur: betting dies off, trailing into silence, as odds lengthen and people lose interest.) In a large-bet, well-made match – the kind of match the Balinese regard as 'real cockfighting' – the mob scene quality, the sense that sheer chaos is about to break loose, with all those waving, shouting, pushing, clambering men is quite strong, an effect which is only heightened by the intense stillness that falls with instant suddenness, rather as if someone had turned off the current, when the slit gong sounds, the cocks are put down, and the battle begins.

When it ends, anywhere from fifteen seconds to five minutes later, *all bets are immediately paid*. There are absolutely no IOUs, at least to a betting opponent. One may, of course, borrow from a friend before offering or accepting a wager, but to offer or accept it you must have the money already in hand and, if you lose, you must pay it on the spot, before the next match begins. This is an iron rule, and as I have never heard of a disputed umpire's decision (though doubtless there must some-times be some), I have also never heard of a welshed bet, perhaps because in a worked-up cockfight crowd the consequences might be, as they are reported to be sometimes for cheaters, drastic and immediate.

It is, in any case, this formal asymmetry between balanced centre bets and unbalanced side ones that poses the critical analytical problem for a theory which sees cockfight wagering as the link connecting the fight to the wider world of Balinese culture. It also suggests the way to go about solving it and demonstrating the link.

The first point that needs to be made in this connection is that the higher the centre bet, the more likely the match will in actual fact be an even one. Simple considerations of rationality suggest that. If you are betting fifteen ringgits on a cock, you might be willing to go along with even money even if you feel your animal somewhat the less promising. But if you are betting five hundred you are very, very likely to be loath to do so. Thus, in large-bet fights, which of course involve the better animals, tremendous care is taken to see that the cocks are about as evenly matched as to size, general condition, pugnacity and so on as is humanly possible. The different ways of adjusting the spurs of the animals are often employed to secure this. If one cock seems stronger, an agreement will be made to position his spur at a slightly less advantageous angle – a kind of handi-capping, at which spur affixers are, so it is said, extremely skilled. More care will be taken, too, to employ skilful handlers and to match them exactly as to abilities.

In short, in a large-bet fight the pressure to make the match a genuinely fifty-fifty proposition is enormous, and is consciously felt as such. For medium fights the pressure is somewhat less, and for small ones less yet, though there is always an effort to make things at least approximately equal, but even at fifteen ringgits (five days work) no one wants to make an even money bet in a clearly unfavourable situation. And, again, what statistics I have tend to bear this out. In my fifty-seven matches, the favourite won thirty-three times over-all, the underdog twenty-four, a 1·4 to 1 ratio. But if one splits the figures at sixty ringgits centre bets, the ratios turn out to be 1·1 to 1 (twelve favourites, eleven underdogs) for those above this line, and 1·6 to 1 (twenty-one and thirteen) for those below it. Or, if you take the extremes, for very large fights, those with centre bets over a hundred ringgits the ratio is 1 to 1 (seven to seven); for very small fights, those under forty ringgits, it is 1·9 to 1 (nineteen and ten).

Now, from this proposition – that the higher the centre bet the more exactly a fifty-fifty proposition the cockfight is – two things more or less immediately follow: (1) the higher the centre bet, the greater is the pull on the side betting towards the short-odds end of the wagering spectrum and vice versa; (2) the higher the centre bet, the greater the volume of side betting and vice versa.

The logic is similar in both cases. The closer the fight is in fact to even money, the less attractive the long end of the odds will appear and, there-fore, the shorter it must be if there are to be takers. That this is the case is apparent from mere inspection, from the Balinese's own analysis of the matter, and from what more systematic observations I was able to collect. Given the difficulty of making precise and complete recordings of side betting, this argument is hard to cast in numerical form, but in all my cases the odds-giver, odds-taker consensual point, a quite pronounced mini-max saddle where the bulk (at a guess, two-thirds to three-quarters in most cases) of the bets are actually made, was three or four points further along the scale towards the shorter end for the large-centre bet fights than for the small ones, with medium ones generally in between. In detail, the fit is not, of course, exact, but the general pattern is quite consistent: the power of the centre bet to pull the side bets towards its own even-money pattern is directly proportional to its size, because its size is directly proportional to the degree to which the cocks are in fact evenly matched. As for the volume question, total wagering is greater in large-centre-bet fights because such fights are considered more 'interesting', not only in the sense that they are less predictable, but, more crucially, that more is at stake in them – in terms of money, in terms of the quality of the cocks, and consequently, as we shall see, in terms of social prestige.

The paradox of fair coin in the middle, biased coin on the outside is thus a merely apparent one. The two betting systems, though formally incongruent, are not really contradictory to one another, but part of a single larger system in which the centre bet is, so to speak, the 'centre of gravity', drawing, the larger it is the more so, the outside bets towards the short-odds end of the scale. The centre bet thus 'makes the game', or perhaps better, defines it, and signals what, following a notion of Jeremy Bentham's, I am going to call its 'depth'.

The Balinese attempt to create an interesting, if you will, 'deep', match by making the centre bet as large as possible so that the cocks matched will be as equal and as fine as possible, and the outcome, thus, as unpredictable as possible. They do not always succeed. Nearly half the matches are relatively trivial, relatively uninteresting – in my borrowed terminology, 'shallow' – affairs. But that fact no more argues against my interpretation than the fact that most painters, poets, and playwrights are mediocre argues against the view that artistic effort is directed towards profundity and, with a certain frequency, approximates it. The image of artistic technique is indeed exact: the centre bet is a means, a device, for creating 'interesting', 'deep' matches, *not* the reason, or at least not the main reason, *why* they are interesting, the source of their fascination, the substance of their depth. The question why such matches are interesting – indeed, for the Balinese, exquisitely absorbing – takes us out of the realm of formal concerns into more broadly sociological and social-psychological ones, and to a less purely economic idea of what 'depth' in gaming amounts to.

Playing with fire

Bentham's (1802) concept of 'deep play' is found in his *The Theory of Legislation*. By it he means play in which the stakes are so high that it is, from his utilitarian standpoint, irrational for men to engage in it at all. If a man whose fortune is a thousand pounds (or ringgits) wages five hundred of it on an even bet, the marginal utility of the pound he stands to win is clearly less than the marginal disutility of the one he stands to lose. In genuine deep play, this is the case for both parties. They are both in over their heads. Having come together in search of pleasure they have entered into a relationship which will bring the participants, considered collectively, net pain rather than net pleasure. Bentham's conclusion was, therefore, that deep play was immoral from first principles and, a typical step for him, should be prevented legally.

But more interesting than the ethical problem, at least for our concerns here, is that despite the logical force of Bentham's analysis men do engage in such play, both passionately and often, and even in the face of law's revenge. For Bentham and those who think as he does (nowadays mainly lawyers, economists, and a few psychiatrists), the explanation is, as I have said, that such men are irrational – addicts, fetishists, children, fools, savages, who need only to be protected against themselves. But for the Balinese, though naturally they do not formulate it in so many words, the explanation lies in the fact that in such play money is less a measure of utility, had or expected, than it is a symbol of moral import, perceived or imposed.

It is, in fact, in shallow games, ones in which smaller amounts of money are involved, that increments and decrements of cash are more nearly synonyms for utility and disutility, in the ordinary, unexpanded sense – for pleasure and pain, happiness and unhappiness. In deep ones, where the amounts of money are great, much more is at stake than material gain: namely, esteem, honour, dignity, respect – in a word, though in Bali a profoundly freighted word, status. It is at stake symbolically, for (a few cases of ruined addict gamblers aside) no one's status is actually altered by the outcome of a cockfight; it is only, and that momentarily, affirmed or insulted. But for the Balinese, for whom nothing is more pleasurable than an affront obliquely delivered or more painful than one obliquely received – particularly when mutual acquaintances, undeceived by surfaces, are watching – this kind of drama which tests people out is deep indeed.

This, I must stress immediately, is *not* to say that the money does not matter or that the Balinese is no more concerned about losing five hundred ringgits than fifteen. Such a conclusion would be absurd. It is because money *does* in this hardly unmaterialistic society, matter and matter very much that the more of it one risks the more of a lot of other things such as one's pride, poise, dispassion, and masculinity, one also risks, again only momentarily but again very publicly as well. In deep cockfights an owner and his collaborators, and, as we shall see, to a lesser but still quite real extent also their backers on the outside, put their money where their status is.

It is in large part *because* the marginal disutility of loss is so great at the higher levels of betting that to engage in such betting is to lay one's public self, allusively and metaphorically, through the medium of one's cock, on the line. And though to a Benthamite this might seem merely to increase the irrationality of the enterprise that much further, to the Balinese what it mainly increases is the meaningfulness of it all. And as the imposition of meaning on life is the major end and primary condition of human existence, that access of significance more than compensates for the economic costs involved. Actually, given the even-money quality of the larger matches, important changes in material fortune among those who regularly participate in them seem virtually non-existent, because matters more or less even out over the long run. It is, actually, in the smaller, shallow fights, where one finds the handful of more pure, addict-type gamblers involved – those who *are* in it mainly for the money – that 'real' changes in social position, largely downward, are affected. Men of this sort, plungers, are highly dispraised by 'true cockfighters' as fools who do not understand what the sport is all about, vulgarians who simply miss the point of it all. They are, these addicts, regarded as fair game for the genuine enthusiasts, those who do understand, to take a little money away from, something that is easy enough to do by luring them, through the force of their greed, into irrational bets on mismatched cocks. Most of them do indeed manage to ruin themselves in a remarkably short time, but there always seems to be one or two of them around, pawning their land and selling their clothes in order to bet, at any particular time.

This graduated correlation of 'status gambling' with deeper fights and, inversely, 'money gambling' with shallower ones is in fact quite general. Bettors themselves form a socio-moral hierarchy in these terms. As noted earlier, at most cockfights there are, around the very edges of the cockfight area, a large number of mindless, sheer-chance type gambling games (roulette, dice throw, coin-spin, pea-under-the-shell) operated by concessionaires. Only women, children, adolescents and various other sorts of people who do not (or not yet) fight cocks – the extremely poor, the socially despised, the personally idiosyncratic – play at these games, at, of course, penny ante levels. Cockfighting men would be ashamed to go anywhere near them. Slightly above these people in standing are those who, though they do not themselves fight cocks, bet on the smaller matches around the edges. Next, there are those who fight cocks in small, or occasionally medium matches, but have not the status to join in the large ones, though they may bet from time to time on the side in those. And finally, there are those, the really substantial members of the community, the solid citizenry around whom local life revolves, who fight in the larger fights and bet on them around the side. The focusing element in these focused gatherings, these men generally dominate and define the sport as they dominate and define the society. When a Balinese male talks, in that almost venerative way, about the 'true cockfighter', the *bebatoh* ('bettor') or *djuru kurung* ('cage keeper'), it is this sort of person, not those who bring the mentality of the pea-and-shell game into the quite different, inappropriate context of the cockfight, the driven gambler (*potét*, a word which has the secondary meaning of thief or reprobate), and the wistful hanger-on, that they mean. For such a man, what is really going on in a match is something rather closer to an *affaire d'honneur* (though, with the Balinese talent for practical fantasy, the blood that is spilled is only figuratively human) than to the stupid, mechanical crank of a slot machine.

What makes Balinese cockfighters deep is thus not money in itself, but what money causes to happen: the migration of the Balinese status hierarchy into the body of the cockfight. The more money is involved, the more things happen. Psychologically an Aesopian representation of the ideal/demonic, rather narcissistic, male self, sociologically it is an equally Aesopian representation of the complex fields of tension set up by the controlled, muted, ceremonial, but for all that deeply felt, interaction of those selves in the context of everyday life. The cocks may be surrogates for their owners' personalities, animal mirrors of psychic form, but the cockfight is – or more exactly, deliberately is made to be – a simulation of the social matrix, the involved system of crosscutting, overlapping, highly corporate groups – villages, kingroups, irrigation societies, temple congregations, 'castes' – in which its devotees live (Geertz, 1959). And as prestige, the necessity to affirm it, defend it, celebrate it, justify it, and just plain bask in it (but not, given the strongly ascriptive character of Balinese stratification, to seek it), is perhaps the central driving force in the society, so also – ambulant penises, blood sacrifices, and monetary exchanges aside – is it of the cockfight. This apparent amusement and seeming sport is, to take a phrase from Erving Goffman, 'a status bloodbath'.

The easiest way to make this clear, and at least to some degree to demonstrate it, is to summarize the matter in a formal paradigm.

THE MORE A MATCH IS...
1. Between near status equals (and/or personal enemies)
2. Between high status individuals . . .
                    THE DEEPER THE MATCH
THE DEEPER THE MATCH...
1. The closer the identification of cock and man (or: more properly, the deeper the match the more the man will advance his best, most closely-identified-with cock).
2. The finer the cocks involved and the more exactly they will be matched.

3. The greater the emotion that will be involved and the more the general absorption in the match.
4. The higher the individual bets centre and outside, the shorter the outside bet odds will tend to be, and the more betting there will be overall.
5. The less an 'economic' and the more a 'status' view of gaming will be involved, and the 'solider' the citizens who will be gaming.

Inverse arguments hold for the shallower the fight, culminating, in a reversed-signs sense, in the coin-spinning and dice-throwing amusements. For deep fights there are no absolute upper limits, though there are of course practical ones, and there are a great many legend-like tales of great Duel-in-the-Sun combats between lords and princes in classical times (for cockfighting has always been as much an élite concern as a popular one), far deeper than anything anyone, even aristocrats, could produce today anywhere in Bali.

Indeed, one of the great culture heroes of Bali is a prince, called after his passion for the sport, 'The Cockfighter', who happened to be away at a very deep cockfight with a neighbouring prince when the whole of his family – father, brothers, wives, sisters – were assassinated by commoner usurpers. Thus spared, he returned to dispatch the upstarts, regain the throne, reconstitute the Balinese high tradition, and build its most powerful, glorious, and prosperous state. Along with everything else that the Balinese see in fighting cocks – themselves, their social order, abstract hatred, masculinity, demonic power – they also see the archetype of status virtue, the arrogant, resolute, honour-mad player with real fire, the *ksatria* prince.

Feathers, blood, crowds and money

'Poetry makes nothing happen,' Auden says in his elegy of Yeats, 'it survives in the valley of its saying ... a way of happening, a mouth.' The cockfight too, in this colloquial sense, makes nothing happen. Men go on allegorically humiliating one another and being allegorically humiliated by one another, day after day, glorying quietly in the experience if they have triumphed, crushed only slightly more openly by it if they have not. *But no one's status really changes.* You cannot ascend the status ladder by winning cockfights; you cannot, as an individual, really ascend it at all. Nor can you descend it that way. All you can do is enjoy and savour, or suffer and withstand, the concocted sensation of drastic and momentary movement along an aesthetic semblance of that ladder, a kind of behind-the-mirror status jump which has the look of mobility without its actuality.

As any art form – for that, finally, is what we are dealing with – the cockfight renders ordinary, everyday experience comprehensible by pre-

senting it in terms of acts and objects which have had their practical consequences removed and been reduced (or, if you prefer, raised) to the level
of sheer appearances, where their meaning can be more powerfully articu-
lated and more exactly perceived. The cockfight is 'really real' only to
the cocks – it does not kill anyone, castrate anyone, reduce anyone to animal
status, alter the hierarchical relations among people, nor refashion the
hierarchy; it does not even redistribute income in any significant way. What
it does is what, for other peoples with other temperaments and other conventions, *Lear* and *Crime and Punishment* do; it catches up these themes –
death, masculinity, rage, pride, loss, beneficence, chance – and, ordering
them into an encompassing structure, presents them in such a way as to
throw into relief a particular view of their essential nature. It puts a construction on them, makes them, to those historically positioned to appreciate the construction, meaningful – visible, tangible, graspable – 'real', in
an ideational sense. An image, fiction, a model, a metaphor, the cockfight is
a means of expression; its function is neither to assuage social passions nor
to heighten them (though, in its play-with-fire way, it does a bit of both),
but, in a medium of feathers, blood, crowds, and money, to display them.

The question of how it is that we perceive qualities in things – paintings,
books, melodies, plays – that we do not feel we can assert literally to be
there has come, in recent years, into the very centre of aesthetic theory
(Langer, 1953; Wollheim, 1968; Goodman, 1968; Merleau-Ponty, 1964).
Neither the sentiments of the artist, which remain his, nor those of the
audience, which remain theirs, can account for the agitation of one painting
or the serenity of another. We attribute grandeur, wit, despair, exuberance
to strings of sounds; lightness, energy, violence, fluidity to blocks of stone.
Novels are said to have strength, buildings eloquence, plays momentum,
ballets, repose. In this realm of eccentric predicates, to say that the cockfight, in its perfected cases at least, is 'disquieting' does not seem at all
unnatural, merely, as I have just denied it practical consequence, somewhat
puzzling.

The disquietude arises, 'somehow', out of a conjunction of three attributes of the fight: its immediate dramatic shape; its metaphoric content;
and its social context. A cultural figure against a social ground, the fight is
at once a convulsive surge of animal hatred, a mock war of symbolical
selves, and a formal simulation of status tensions, and its aesthetic power
derives from its capacity to force together these diverse realities. The reason it is disquieting is not that it has material effects (it has some, but
they are minor); the reason that it is disquieting is that, joining pride to
selfhood, selfhood to cocks, and cocks to destruction, it brings to imaginative realization a dimension of Balinese experience normally well-obscured
from view. The transfer of a sense of gravity into what is in itself a rather

blank and unvarious spectacle, a commotion of beating wings and throbbing legs, is effected by interpreting it as expressive of something unsettling in the way its authors and audience live, or, even more ominously, what they are.

As a dramatic shape, the fight displays a characteristic that does not seem so remarkable until one realizes that it does not have to be there: a radically atomistical structure. Each match is a world unto itself, a particulate burst of form. There is the matchmaking, there is the betting, there is the fight, there is the result – utter triumph and utter defeat – and there is the hurried, embarrassed passing of money. The loser is not consoled. People drift away from him, look through him, leave him to assimilate his momentary descent into non-being, reset his face, and return, scarless and intact, to the fray. Nor are winners congratulated, or events rehashed; once a match is ended the crowd's attention turns totally to the next, with no looking back. A shadow of the experience no doubt remains with the principals, perhaps even with some of the witnesses, of a deep fight, as it remains with us when we leave the theatre after seeing a powerful play well performed; but it quite soon fades to become at most a schematic memory – a diffuse glow or an abstract shudder – and usually not even that. Any expressive form lives only in its own present – the one it itself creates. But, here, that present is severed into a string of flashes, some more bright than others, but all of them disconnected, aesthetic quanta. Whatever the cockfight says, it says in spurts.

But, as I have argued lengthily elsewhere, the Balinese live in spurts. Their life, as they arrange it and perceive it, is less a flow, a directional movement out of the past, through the present, towards the future than an on-off pulsation of meaning and vacuity, an arhythmic alternation of short periods when 'something' (that is, nothing much) is between what they themselves call 'full' and 'empty' times, or in another idiom, 'junctures' and 'holes'. In focusing activity down to a burning-glass dot, the cockfight is merely being Balinese in the same way in which everything from the monadic encounters of everyday life, through the clanging pointillism of *gamelan* music, to the visiting-day-of-the-gods temple celebrations are. It is not an imitation of the orderliness of Balinese social life, nor a depiction of it, nor even an expression of it; it is an example of it, carefully prepared.

If one dimension of the cockfight's structure, its lack of temporal direction, makes it seem a typical segment of the general social life, however, the other, its flat-out, head-to-head (or spur-to-spur) aggressiveness, makes it seem a contradiction, a reversal, even a subversion of it. In the normal course of things, the Balinese are shy to the point of obsessiveness of open conflict. Oblique, cautious, subdued, controlled, masters of indirection and dissimulation – what they call *alus*, 'polished', 'smooth' – they rarely face what they can turn away from, rarely resist what they can evade. But here they portray themselves as wild and murderous, manic explosions of instinctual cruelty. A powerful rendering of life as the Balinese most deeply do not want it (to adapt a phrase Frye has used of Gloucester's blinding) is set in the context of a sample of it as they do in fact have it (Frye, 1964). And, because the context suggests that the rendering if less than a straightforward description is nonetheless more than an idle fancy, it is here that the disquietude – the disquietude of the *fight*, not (or, anyway, not necessarily) its patrons, who seem in fact rather thoroughly to enjoy it – emerges. The slaughter in the cock ring is not a depiction of how things literally are among men, but, what is almost worse, of how, from a particular angle, they imaginatively are.

The angle, of course, is stratificatory. What, as we have already seen, the cockfight talks most forcibly about is status relationships, and what it says about them is that they are matters of life and death. That prestige is a profoundly serious business is apparent everywhere one looks in Bali – in the village, the family, the economy, the state. A peculiar fusion of Polynesian title ranks and Hindu castes, the hierarchy of pride is the moral backbone of the society. But only in the cockfight are the sentiments upon which that hierarchy rests revealed in their natural colours. Enveloped elsewhere in a haze of etiquette, a thick cloud of euphemism and ceremony, gesture and allusion, they are here expressed in only the thinnest disguise of an animal mask, a mask which in fact demonstrates them far more effectively than it conceals them. Jealousy is as much a part of Bali as poise, envy as grace, brutality as charm; but without the cockfight the Balinese would have a much less certain understanding of them, which is, presumably, why they value it so highly.

Any expressive form works (when it works) by disarranging semantic contexts in such a way that properties conventionally ascribed to certain things are unconventionally ascribed to others, which are then seen actually to possess them. To call the wind a cripple, as Stevens does, to fix tone and manipulate timbre, as Schoenberg does, or, closer to our case, to picture an art critic as a dissolute bear, as Hogarth does, it to cross conceptual wires; the established conjunctions between objects and their qualities are altered and phenomena – fall weather, melodic shape, or cultural journalism – are clothed in signifiers which normally point to other referents. Similarly, to connect – and connect, and connect – the collision of roosters with the divisiveness of status is to invite a transfer of perceptions from the former to the latter, a transfer which is at once a description and a judgement. (Logically the transfer could, of course, as well go the other way; but, like most of the rest of us, the Balinese are a great deal more interested in understanding men than they are in understanding cocks.)

What sets the cockfight apart from the ordinary course of life, lifts it from the realm of everyday practical affairs, and surrounds it with an aura of enlarged importance is not, as functionalist sociology would have it, that it reinforces status discriminations (such reinforcement is hardly necessary in a society where every act proclaims them), but that it provides a meta-social commentary upon the whole matter of assorting human beings into fixed hierarchical ranks and then organizing the major part of collective existence around that assortment. Its function, if you want to call it that, is interpretive: it is a Balinese reading of Balinese experience; a story they tell themselves about themselves. (See photo inset.)

(From *Daedalus*, No. 101, 1972.)

References

BATESON, G., and MEAD, M. (1942), *Balinese Character*, a special publication of the N.Y. Academy of Science, Vol. 2, New York.

BELO, J. (1970), 'The Balinese Temper', in *Traditional Balinese Culture*, Jane Belo (ed.), (first published in 1935), Columbia University Press, pp. 85–110.

BENTHAM, J. (1802), *The Theory of Legislation*. International Library of Psychology, London: Kegan Paul, 1931.

FRYE, N. (1964), *The Educated Imagination*, University of Indiana Press, p. 99.

GEERTZ, C. (1959,) 'Form and variation in Balinese village structure', *American Anthropologist*, No. 61, pp. 94–108.

GEERTZ, C. (1967), 'Tihingan, A Balinese village', in *Villages in Indonesia*, R. M. Koentijaraningrat (ed.), Cornell University Press, pp. 210–43.

GOFFMAN, E. (1972), *Encounters: Two Studies in the Sociology of Interaction*, Penguin.

GOODMAN, N. (1968), *Languages of Art*, Bobbs-Merrill, Indianapolis.

LANGER, S. (1953), *Feeling and Form*, Scribner's, New York.

MERLEAU-PONTY, M. (1964), 'The Eye and the Mind', in *The Primacy of Perception*, Northwestern University Press, Evanston, pp. 159–90.

WOLLHEIM, R. (1968), *Art and Its Objects*, Harper & Row, New York.

Play and Contest as Civilizing Functions

Since our theme is the relation of play to culture, we need not enter into all the possible forms of play, but can restrict ourselves to its social manifestations. These we might call the higher forms of play. They are generally much easier to describe than the more primitive play of infants and young animals, because they are more distinct and articulate in form and their features more various and conspicuous, whereas in interpreting primitive play we immediately come up against that irreducible quality of pure playfulness which is not, in my opinion, amenable to further analysis. We shall have to speak of contests and races, of performances and exhibitions, of dancing and music, pageants, masquerades, and tournaments. Some of the characteristics we shall enumerate are proper to play in general, others to social play in particular.

First and foremost, then, all play is a *voluntary activity*. Play to order is no longer play: it could at best be but a forcible imitation of it. By this quality of freedom alone, play marks itself off from the course of the natural process. It is something added thereto and spread out over it like a flowering, an ornament, a garment. Obviously, freedom must be understood here in the wider sense that leaves untouched the philosophical problem of determinism. It may be objected that this freedom does not exist for the animal and the child; they *must* play because their instinct drives them to it and because it serves to develop their bodily faculties and their powers of selection. The term 'instinct', however, introduces an unknown quantity, and to presuppose the utility of play from the start is to be guilty of a *petitio principii*. Child and animal play because they enjoy playing, and therein precisely lies their freedom.

Be that as it may, for the adult and responsible human being play is a function which he could equally well leave alone. Play is superfluous. The need for it is only urgent to the extent that the enjoyment of it makes it a need. Play can be deferred or suspended at any time. It is never imposed by physical necessity or moral duty. It is never a task. It is done at leisure, during 'free time'. Only when play is a recognized cultural function – a rite, a ceremony – is it bound up with notions of obligations and duty.

Here, then, we have the first main characteristic of play: that it is free, is in fact freedom. A second characteristic is closely connected with this, namely, that play is not 'ordinary' or 'real' life. It is rather a stepping out of 'real' life into a temporary sphere of activity with a disposition all of its own. Every child knows perfectly well that he is 'only pretending', or that it was 'only for fun'. How deep-seated this awareness is in the child's soul is strikingly illustrated by the following story, told to me by the father of the boy in question. He found his four-year-old son sitting at the front of a row of chairs, playing 'trains'. As he hugged him the boy said, 'Don't kiss the engine, Daddy, or the carriages won't think it's real.' This 'only pretending' quality of play betrays a consciousness of the inferiority of play compared with 'seriousness', a feeling that seems to be something as primary as play itself. Nevertheless, as we have already pointed out, the consciousness of play being 'only a pretend' does not by any means prevent it from proceeding with the utmost seriousness, with an absorption, a devotion that passes into rapture and, temporarily at least, completely abolishes that troublesome 'only' feeling. Any game can at any time wholly run away with the players. The contrast between play and seriousness is always fluid. The inferiority of play is continually being offset by the corresponding superiority of its seriousness. Play turns to seriousness and seriousness to play. Play may rise to heights of beauty and sublimity that leave seriousness far beneath. Tricky questions such as these will come up for discussion when we start examining the relationship between play and ritual.

As regards its formal characteristics, all students lay stress on the *disinterestedness* of play. Not being 'ordinary' life, it stands outside the immediate satisfaction of wants and appetites, indeed it interrupts the appetitive process. It interpolates itself as a temporary activity satisfying in itself and ending there. Such at least is the way in which play presents itself to us in the first instance: as an intermezzo, an *interlude* in our daily lives. As a regularly recurring relaxation, however, it becomes the accompaniment, the complement, in fact an integral part of life in general. It adorns life, amplifies it, and is to that extent a necessity both for the individual – as a life function – and for society by reason of the meaning it contains, its significance, its expressive value, its spiritual and social associations, in short, as a culture function. The expression of it satisfies all kinds of communal ideals. It thus has its place in a sphere superior to the strictly biological processes of nutrition, reproduction, and self-preservation. This assertion is apparently contradicted by the fact that play, or rather sexual display, is predominant in animal life precisely at the mating-season. But would it be too absurd to assign a place *outside* the purely physiological, to the singing, cooing, and strutting of birds just as we do to human play? In all its higher forms the latter at any rate always belongs to the sphere of festival and ritual – the sacred sphere.

Now, does the fact that play is a necessity, that it subserves culture, or indeed that it actually becomes culture, detract from its disinterested character? No, for the purposes it serves are external to immediate material interests or the individual satisfaction of biological needs. As a sacred activity play naturally contributes to the well-being of the group, but in quite another way and by other means than the acquisition of the necessities of life.

Play is distinct from 'ordinary' life both as to locality and duration. This is the *third main characteristic of play: its seclusion, its limitedness*. It is 'played out' within certain limits of time and place. It contains its own course and meaning.

Play begins, and then at a certain moment it is 'over'. It plays itself to an end. While it is in progress all is movement, change, alternation, succession, association, separation. But immediately connected with its limitations as to time there is a further curious feature of play: it at once assumes fixed form as a cultural phenomenon. Once played, it endures as a new-found creation of the mind, a treasure to be retained by the memory. It is transmitted, it becomes tradition. It can be repeated at any time, whether it be 'child's play' or a game of chess, or at fixed intervals like a mystery. In this faculty of repetition lies one of the most essential qualities of play. It holds good not only of play as a whole but also of its inner structure. In nearly all the higher forms of play the elements of *repetition and alternation* (as in the *refrain*) are like the warp and woof of a fabric.

More striking even than the limitation as to time is the limitation as to space. All play moves and has its being within a playground marked off beforehand either materially or ideally, deliberately or as a matter of course. Just as there is no formal difference between play and ritual, so the '*consecrated spot*' cannot be formally distinguished from the playground. The arena, the card-table, the magic circle, the temple, the stage, the screen, the tennis court, the court of justice, etc., are all in form and function playgrounds, i.e. forbidden spots, isolated, hedged round, hallowed, within which special rules obtain. All are temporary worlds within the ordinary world, dedicated to the performance of an act apart.

Inside the playground an absolute and peculiar order reigns. Here we come across another, very positive *feature of play: it creates order, is order*. Into an imperfect world and into the confusion of life it brings a temporary, a limited perfection. Play demands order absolute and supreme. The least deviation from it 'spoils the game', robs it of its character, and makes it worthless. The profound affinity between play and order is perhaps the reason why play, as we noted in passing, seems to lie to such a large extent in the field of aesthetics. Play has a tendency to be beautiful. It may be that this aesthetic factor is identical with the impulse to create orderly form, which animates play in all its aspects. The words we use to denote the elements of play belong for the most part to aesthetics, terms with which we try to describe the effects of beauty: tension, poise, balance, contrast, variation, solution, resolution, etc. Play casts a spell over us; it is 'enchanting', 'captivating'. It is invested with the noblest qualities we are capable of perceiving in things: rhythm and harmony.

The element of tension in play to which we have just referred plays a particularly important part. Tension means uncertainty, chanciness; a striving to decide the issue and so end it. The player wants something to 'go', to 'come off'; he wants to 'succeed' by his own exertions. Baby reaching for a toy, pussy patting a bobbin, a little girl playing ball – all want to achieve something difficult, to succeed, to end a tension. Play is 'tense', as we say. It is this element of tension and solution that governs all solitary games of skill and application such as puzzles, jigsaws, mosaic-making, patience, target-shooting; and the more play bears the character of competition, the more fervent it will be. In gambling and athletics it is at its height. Though play as such is outside the range of good and bad, the element of tension imparts to it a certain ethical value insofar as it means a testing of the player's prowess: his courage, tenacity, resources, and, last but not least, his spiritual powers – his 'fairness'; because, despite his ardent desire to win, he must stick to the rules of the game.

These rules in their turn are a very important factor in the play-concept. All play has its rules. They determine what 'holds' in the temporary world circumscribed by play. The rules of a game are absolutely binding and allow no doubt. Paul Valéry once gave expression in passing to a very cogent thought when he said: 'No scepticism is possible where the rules of a game are concerned, for the principle underlying them is an unshakeable truth. . .' Indeed, as soon as the rules are transgressed the whole play-world collapses. The game is over. The umpire's whistle breaks the spell and sets 'real' life going again.

The player who trespasses against the rules or ignores them is a 'spoil-sport'. The spoil-sport is not the same as the false player, the cheat; for the latter pretends to be playing the game and, on the face of it, still acknowledges the magic circle. It is curious to note how much more lenient society is to the cheat than to the spoil-sport. This is because the spoil-sport shatters the playing world itself. By withdrawing from the game he reveals the relativity and fragility of the play-world in which he had temporarily shut himself with others. He robs play of its *illusion* – a pregnant word which means literally 'in-play' (from *inlusio, illudere*, or *inludere*). Therefore he must be cast out, for he threatens the existence of the play-community.

A play-community generally tends to become permanent even after the game is over. Of course, not every game of marbles or every bridge-party leads to the founding of a club. But the feeling of being 'apart together' in an exceptional situation, of sharing something important, of mutually withdrawing from the rest of the world and rejecting the usual norms, retains its magic beyond the duration of the individual game. The club pertains to play as the hat to the head. It would be rash to explain all the associations which the anthropologist calls 'phratria' – e.g. clans, brother-hoods, etc. – simply as play-communities; nevertheless it has been shown again and again how difficult it is to draw the line between, on the one hand, permanent social groupings – particularly in archaic cultures with their extremely important, solemn, indeed sacred customs – and the sphere of play on the other.

The exceptional and special position of play is most tellingly illustrated by the fact that it loves to surround itself with an air of secrecy. Even in early childhood the charm of play is enhanced by making a 'secret' out of it. This is for *us*, not for the 'others'. What the 'others' do 'outside' is no concern of ours at the moment. Inside the circle of the game the laws and customs of ordinary life no longer count. We are different and do things differently. This temporary abolition of the ordinary world is fully acknow-ledged in child-life, but it is no less evident in the great ceremonial games of savage societies. During the great feast of initiation when the youths are accepted into the male community, it is not the neophytes only that are exempt from the ordinary laws and regulations: there is a truce to all feuds in the tribe. All retaliatory acts and vendettas are suspended. This tem-porary suspension of normal social life on account of the sacred play-season has numerous traces in the more advanced civilizations as well. Everything that pertains to saturnalia and carnival customs belongs to it.

Primitive, or let us say, archaic ritual is thus sacred play, indispensable for the well-being of the community, fecund of cosmic insight and social development but always play in the sense Plato gave to it – an action accomplishing itself outside and above the necessities and seriousness of everyday life. In this sphere of sacred play the child and the poet are at home with the savage.

Even if we can legitimately reduce our ideas on the significance of primitive ritual to an irreducible play-concept, one extremely trouble-some question still remains. What if we now ascend from the lower religions to the higher? From the rude and outlandish ritual of the African, American or Australian aborigines our vision shifts to Vedic sacrificial lore, already, in the hymns of the *Rig-Veda*, pregnant with the wisdom of the Upanishads, or to the profoundly mystical identifications of god, man, and beast in Egyptian religion, or to the Orphic and Eleusinian mysteries. In form and practice all these are closely allied to the so-called primitive religions even to bizaare and bloody particulars. But the high degree of wisdom and truth we discern, or think we can discern in them, forbids us to speak of them with that air of superiority which, as a matter of fact, is equally out of place in 'primitive' cultures. We must ask whether this formal similarity entitles us to extend the qualification 'play' to the consciousness of the holy, the faith embodied in these higher creeds. If we accept the Platonic definition of play there is nothing preposterous or irreverent in doing so. Play consecrated to the Deity, the highest goal of man's endeavour – such was Plato's conception of religion. In following him we in no way abandon the holy mystery, or cease to rate it as the highest attainable expression of that which escapes logical understanding. The ritual act, or an important part of it, will always remain within the play category, but in this seeming subordination the recognition of its holiness is not lost.

When speaking of the play-element in culture we do not mean that among the various activities of civilized life an important place is reserved for play, nor do we mean that civilization has arisen out of play by some evolutionary process, in the sense that something which was originally play passed into something which was no longer play and could henceforth be called culture. The view we take in the following pages is that culture arises in the form of play, that it is played from the very beginning. Even those activities which aim at the immediate satisfaction of vital needs – hunting, for instance – tend, in archaic society, to take on the play-form. Social life is endowed with supra-biological forms, in the shape of play, which enhance its value. It is through this playing that society expresses its interpretation of life and the world. By this we do not mean that play turns into culture, rather that in its earliest phases culture has the play-character, that it proceeds in the shape and the mood of play. In the twin union of play and culture, play is primary.

Naturally enough, the connection between culture and play is particularly evident in the higher forms of social play where the latter consists in the orderly activity of a group or two opposed groups. Solitary play is productive of culture only in a limited degree.

'Playing together' has an essentially antithetical character. As a rule it is played between two parties or teams. A dance, a pageant, a performance may, however, be altogether lacking in antithesis. Moreover 'antithetical' does not necessarily mean 'contending' or 'agonistic'. A part-song, a chorus, a minuet, the voices in a musical ensemble, the game of cat's cradle – so interesting to the anthropologist because developed into intricate systems of magic with some primitive peoples – are all examples of antithetical play which need not be agonistic although emulation may sometimes be operative in them. Not infrequently an activity which is self-contained – for instance the performance of a theatrical piece or a piece of music – may incidentally pass into the agonistic category by becoming the occasion of competition for prizes, either in respect of the arrangement or the execution of it, as was the case with Greek drama.

Among the general characteristics of play we reckoned tension and uncertainty. There is always the question: 'Will it come off?' This condition is fulfilled even when we are playing patience, doing jig-saw puzzles, acrostics, crosswords, diabolo, etc. Tension and uncertainty as to the outcome increase enormously when the antithetical element becomes really agonistic in the play of groups. The passion to win sometimes threatens to obliterate the levity proper to a game. An important distinction emerges here. In games of pure chance the tension felt by the player is only feebly communicated to the onlooker. In themselves, gambling games are very curious subjects for cultural research, but for the development of culture as such we must call them unproductive. They are sterile, adding nothing to life or the mind. The picture changes as soon as play demands application, knowledge, skill, courage and strength. The more 'difficult' the game the greater the tension in the beholders. A game of chess may fascinate the onlookers although it still remains unfruitful for culture and devoid of visible charm. But once a game is beautiful to look at its cultural value is obvious; nevertheless, its aesthetic value is not indispensable to culture. Physical, intellectual, moral or spiritual values can equally well raise play to the cultural level. The more apt it is to raise the tone, the intensity of life in the individual or the group the more readily it will become part of civilization itself. The two ever-recurrent forms in which civilization grows in and as play are the sacred performance and the festal contest.

The contest as one of the chief elements of social life has always been associated in our minds with the idea of Greek civilization. Long before sociology and anthropology became aware of the extraordinary importance of the agonistic factor in general, Jacob Burckhardt coined the word 'agonal' and described the purport of it as one of the main characteristics of Hellenic culture. Burckhardt, however, was not equipped to perceive the widespread sociological background of the phenomenon. He thought that the agonistic habit was specifically Greek and that its range was limited to a definite period of Greek history. According to him, the earliest type known to Greek history is the 'heroic' man, who is followed by the 'colonial' or 'agonal' man, to be superseded in his turn by, successively, the man of the fifth century, the fourth century (who have no specific names) and finally, after Alexander, by the 'Hellenistic' man. The 'colonial' or 'agonal' period is thus the sixth century B.C. – the age of Hellenic expansion and the national games. What he calls 'the agonal' is 'an impulse such as no other people has ever known'.

It is only to be expected that Burckhardt's views were limited by classical philology. His great work, published after his death as *Griechische Kulturgeschichte*, had taken shape from a series of lectures delivered at Basle University during the eighties, before any general sociology existed to digest all the ethnological and anthropological data, most of which, indeed, were only coming to light then.

Ehrenberg also follows Burckhardt in focusing 'the agonal' on the period that succeeded the 'heroic' one, conceding at the same time that the latter already had a certain agonistic complexion. He says that on the whole the Trojan War was devoid of agonistic features; only after the 'de-heroizing of the warrior-class' (*Entheroisierung des Kriegertums*) did the need arise to create a substitute for heroism in 'the agonal', which was therefore a 'product' of a younger phase of culture. All this is based more or less on Burckhardt's striking aphorism: 'A people knowing war has no need of tournaments.' Such an assumption may sound plausible enough to our thinking but, as regards all archaic periods of culture, it has been proved absolutely wrong by sociology and ethnology alike. No doubt the few centuries of Greek history when the contest reigned supreme as the life-principle of society also saw the rise of the great sacred games which united all Hellas at Olympia, on the Isthmus, at Delphi and Nemea; but the fact remains that the spirit of contest dominated Hellenic culture both before these centuries, and after.

During the whole span of their existence the Hellenic games remained closely allied with religion, even in later times when, on a superficial view, they might have the appearance of national sports pure and simple. Pindar's triumphal songs celebrating the great contests belong wholly to the rich harvest of religious poetry he produced, of which, indeed, they are the sole survivors. The sacred character of the agon was everywhere apparent. The competitive zeal of the Spartan boys in enduring pain before the altar is only one example of the cruel trials connected with initiation to manhood, such as can be found all over the earth among primitive peoples. Pindar shows a victor in the Olympic games breathing new life into the nostrils of his aged grandfather.

Greek tradition divides contests in general into such as are public or national, military and juridical, and such as are concerned with strength, wisdom and wealth. The classification would seem to reflect an earlier, agonistic phase of culture. The fact that litigation before a judge is called an 'agon' should not be taken, with Burckhardt, as a mere metaphorical expression of later times but, on the contrary, as evidence of an immemorial association of ideas, about which we shall have more to say. The lawsuit had in fact once been an agon in the strict sense of the word.

The Greeks used to stage contests in anything that offered the bare possibility of a fight. Beauty contests for men were part of the Pana-thenaean and Thesean festivals. At symposia, contests were held in singing, riddle-solving, keeping awake and drinking.

A too narrow conception of the agonistic principle has induced Ehren-berg to deny it to Roman civilization, or actually to attribute to it an anti-agonistic character. It is true that contests between free men played a comparatively small part here, but this is not to say that the agonistic element was altogether lacking in the structure of Roman civilization. Rather we are dealing with the singular phenomenon showing how the competitive impulse shifted, at an early period, from the protagonist to the spectator, who merely watches the struggles of others appointed for that purpose. Without a doubt this shift is closely connected with the pro-foundly ritualistic character of the Roman games themselves, for this vicarious attitude is quite in place in ritual, where the contestants are regarded as representing – i.e. fighting on behalf of – the spectators. Gladiatorial games, contests between wild beasts, chariot-races, etc., lose nothing of their agonistic nature even when carried out by slaves. The *ludi* were either associated with the regular yearly festivals or were *ludi votivi*, held in honour of some vow, usually to pay homage to the deceased or, more particularly, to avert the wrath of the gods. The slightest offence against the ritual or the most accidental disturbance invalidated the whole performance. This points to the sacred character of the action.

It is of the utmost significance that these Roman gladiatorial combats, bloody, superstitious and illiberal as they were, nevertheless kept to the last the simple word 'ludus' with all its associations of freedom and joyousness. How are we to understand this?

I have dealt elsewhere and at such length with the play-element in the Middle Ages that a few words must suffice here. Medieval life was brimful of play: the joyous and unbuttoned play of the people, full of pagan elements that had lost their sacred significance and been transformed into jesting and buffoonery, or the solemn and pompous play of chivalry, the sophisticated play of courtly love, etc. Few of these forms now had any real culture-creating function, except for the ideal of courtly love which led to the *dolce stil nuovo* and to Dante's *Vita Nuova*. For the Middle Ages had inherited its great culture-forms in poetry, ritual, learning, philosophy, politics and warfare from classical antiquity, and they were fixed forms. Medieval culture was crude and poor in many respects, but we cannot call it primitive. Its business was to work over traditional material, whether Christian or classical, and assimilate it afresh. Only where it was not rooted in antiquity, not fed by the ecclesiastical or Graeco-Roman spirit, was there room for the play-factor to 'play' and create something entirely new. That was the case wherever medieval civilization built directly on its Celto-Germanic past or on even earlier autochthonous layers. The system of chivalry was built in this way (although medieval scholars might find examples of it in the Trojan or other classical heroes) and a good deal of feudalism. The initiation and dubbing of knights, the enfeoffing of a tenure, tournaments, heraldry, chivalric orders, vows – all these things hark back beyond the classical to a purely archaic past, and in all of them the play-factor is powerfully operative and a really creative force. Closer analysis would show it at work in other fields as well, for instance in law and the administration of justice with its constant use of symbols, prescribed gestures, rigid formulas, the issue of a cause often hanging on the exact pronunciation of a word or syllable. The legal proceedings against animals, wholly beyond the comprehension of the modern mind, are a case in point. In fine, the influence of the play-spirit was extraordinarily great in the Middle Ages, not on the inward structure of its institutions, which was largely classical in origin, but on the ceremonial with which that structure was expressed and embellished.

Let us now cast a quick glance at the Renaissance and the Age of Humanism. If ever an élite, fully conscious of its own merits, sought to segregate itself from the vulgar herd and live life as a game of artistic perfection, that élite was the circle of choice Renaissance spirits. We must emphasize yet again that play does not exclude seriousness. The spirit of the Renaissance was very far from being frivolous. The game of living in imitation of Antiquity was pursued in holy earnest. Devotion to the ideals of the past in the matter of plastic creation and intellectual discovery was of a violence, depth and purity surpassing anything we can imagine. We can scarcely conceive of minds more serious than Leonardo and Michelangelo. And yet the whole mental attitude of the Renaissance was one of play. This striving, at once sophisticated and spontaneous, for beauty and nobility of form is an instance of culture at play. The splendours of the Renaissance are nothing but a gorgeous and solemn masquerade in the accoutrements of an idealized past. The mythological figures, allegories and emblems, fetched from God knows where and all loaded with a weight of historical and astrological significance, move like the pieces on a chessboard. The fanciful decorations in Renaissance architecture and the graphic arts, with their lavish use of classical motifs, are much more consciously playful than is the case with the medieval illuminator, suddenly inserting a drollery into his manuscript. There are two play-idealizations *par excellence*, two 'Golden Ages of Play' as we might call them: the pastoral life and the chivalrous life. The Renaissance roused both from their slumber to a new life in literature and public festivity. We would be hard put to it to name a poet who embodies the play-spirit more purely than Ariosto, and in him the whole tone and tenor of the Renaissance are expressed. Where has poetry ever been so unconstrained, so absolutely at play? Delicately, elusively he hovers between the mock-heroic and the pathetic, in a sphere far removed from reality but peopled with gay and delightfully vivid figures, all of them lapped in the inexhaustible, glorious mirth of his voice which bears witness to the identity of play and poetry.

The word 'Humanism' arouses visions less colourful, more serious, if you like, than does the Renaissance. Nevertheless what we have said of the playfulness of the Renaissance will be found to hold good of Humanism as well. To an even greater extent it was confined to a circle of initiates and people 'in the know'. The Humanists cultivated an ideal of life formulated strictly in accordance with an imagined antiquity. They even contrived to express their Christian faith in classical Latin, which lent it more than a touch of paganism. The importance of these pagan tendencies has often been exaggerated. But it is certain that the Christianity of the Humanists was tinged with a certain artifice, a certain artificiality even, something not altogether serious. They spoke with an accent, and the accent was not that of Christ. Calvin and Luther could not abide the tone in which the Humanist Erasmus spoke of holy things. Erasmus! his whole being seems to radiate the play-spirit. It shines forth not only in the *Colloquies* and the *Laus Stultitiae* but in the *Adagia*, that astonishing collection of aphorisms from Greek and Latin literature commented on with light irony and adorable jocosity. His innumerable letters and sometimes his weightiest theological treatises are pervaded by the blithe wit he can never completely do without.

Whoever surveys the host of Renaissance poets from the *grands rhetoriqueurs* like Jean Molinet and Jean Lemaire de Belges to full-blown Renaissance products like Sannazaro or Guarino, the creators of the new pastorals so much in vogue, cannot fail to be struck by the essentially ludic character of their genius. Nothing could be more playful than Rabelais – he is the play-spirit incarnate. The *Amadis de Gaule* cycle reduces heroic adventure to pure farce, while Cervantes remains the supreme magician of tears and laughter. In Marguerite of Navarre's *Heptameron* we have a strange amalgam of coprophilia and platonism. Even the school of Humanist jurists, in their endeavours to make the law stylish and aesthetic, evince the almighty play-spirit of the times.

It has become the fashion, when speaking of the seventeenth century, to extend the term 'Baroque' far beyond the scope of its original application. Instead of simply denoting a tolerably definite style of architecture and sculpture, 'the Baroque' has come to cover a vast complex of more or less vague ideas about the essence of seventeenth-century civilization. The fashion started in German scholarship some forty years ago and spread to the public at large mainly through Spengler's *Decline of the West*. Now painting, poetry, literature, even politics and theology, in short, every field of skill and learning in the seventeenth century, have to measure up to some preconceived idea of 'the Baroque'. Some apply the term to the beginning of the epoch, when men delighted in colourful and exuberant imagination; others to a later period of sombre stateliness and solemn dignity. But, taken by and large, it evokes visions of conscious exaggeration, of something imposing, overawing, colossal, avowedly unreal. Baroque forms are, in the fullest sense of the word, art-forms. Even where they serve to limn the sacred and religious, a deliberately aesthetic factor obtrudes itself so much that posterity finds it hard to believe that the treatment of the theme could possibly have sprung from sincere religious emotion.

The general tendency to *overdo* things, so characteristic of the Baroque, finds its readiest explanation in the play-content of the creative impulse. Fully to enjoy the work of Rubens, Bernini or that Dutch prince of poets, Joost van den Vondel, we must be prepared at the outset to take their utterances *cum grano salis*. This is probably true of most art and poetry, it may be objected; if so, it affords yet another proof of our main contention – the fundamental importance of play. For all that, the Baroque manifests the play-element to an altogether striking degree. We should never inquire how far the artist himself feels or intends his work to be perfectly serious, firstly because it is impossible for anybody else to plumb his feelings and intentions to the bottom, secondly because the artist's own subjective feelings are largely irrelevant. The work of art is a thing *sui generis*. Thus with Hugo Grotius, for instance. Hugo Grotius was of an exceptionally serious nature, gifted with little humour and animated by a boundless love of truth. He dedicated his masterpiece, the imperishable monument to his spirit, *De jure belli et pacis*, to the King of France, Louis XIII. The accompanying dedication is an example of the most high-falutin' Baroque extravagance on the theme of the King's universally recognized and inestimable justice, which eclipses the grandeurs of Ancient Rome, etc. His pen bows and scrapes, the enormous compliments loom larger and larger. We know Grotius, and we know the feeble and unreliable personality of Louis XIII. We cannot refrain from asking ourselves: was Grotius in earnest, or was he lying? The answer, of course, is that he was playing the dedicatory instrument in the style proper to the age.

There is hardly another century so stamped with the style of the times as the seventeenth. This general moulding of life, mind and outward appearance to the pattern of what we must, for want of a better word, call 'the Baroque' is most strikingly typified in the costume of the age. It should be noted first of all that this characteristic style is found in the men's dress rather than the women's, and particularly in the full court-dress. Men's fashions show a wide margin of variation throughout the century. They tend to deviate further and further from the simple, the natural, and the practical until, about 1665, the high-point of deformation is reached. The doublet has become so short that it comes almost up to the arm-pits; three-quarters of the shirt bulges out between doublet and hose, and the latter have become preposterously short and wide to the point of no longer being recognizable. The *rhingrave* mentioned by Molière and others had all the appearance of a little petticoat or apron and was generally interpreted as such, until some twenty years ago a genuine specimen of this article was found in an English wardrobe and proved to be a pair of breeches after all. This fantastic outfit was sewn all over with ribands and bows and lace, even round the knees; and yet, ludicrous as it was, it managed to preserve a high degree of elegance and dignity, thanks chiefly to the cloak, the hat and the periwig.

So that by a devious route we have reached the following conclusion: real civilization cannot exist in the absence of a certain play-element, for civilization presupposes limitation and mastery of the self, the ability not to confuse its own tendencies with the ultimate and highest goal, but to understand that it is enclosed within certain bounds freely accepted. Civilization will, in a sense, always be played according to certain rules, and true civilization will always demand fair play. Fair play is nothing less than good faith expressed in play terms. Hence the cheat or the spoil-sport shatters civilization itself. To be a sound culture-creating force this play-element must be pure. It must not consist in the darkening or debasing of standards set up by reason, faith or humanity. It must not be a false seeming, a masking of political purposes behind the illusion of genuine play-forms. True play knows no propaganda; its aim is in itself, and its familiar spirit is happy inspiration.

(From *Homo Ludens: A Study of the Play Element in Culture*, The Beacon Press, Boston, U.S.A., 1955 [first published in 1939].)

Play and Actuality

1

I welcome the opportunity to turn to the play of children – an infinite resource of what is potential in man. I will begin, then, with the observation of one child's play and then turn to related phenomena throughout the course of life.

In the last few years Peggy Penn, Joan Erikson, and I have begun to collect play constructions of four- and five-year-old children of different backgrounds and in different settings, in a metropolitan school and in rural districts, in this country and abroad. Peggy Penn acts as the play hostess, inviting the children, one at a time, to leave their play group and to come to a room where a low table and a set of blocks and toys await them. Sitting on the floor with them, she asks each child to 'build something' and to 'tell a story' about it. Joan Erikson occupies a corner and records what is going on, while I, on occasion, replace her or (where the available space permits) sit in the background watching.

It is a common experience, and yet always astounding, that all but the most inhibited children go at such a task with a peculiar eagerness. After a brief period of orientation when the child may draw the observer into conversation, handle some toys exploratively, or scan the possibilities of the set of toys provided, there follows an absorption in the selection of toys, in the placement of blocks, and in the grouping of dolls, which soon seems to follow some imperative theme and some firm sense of style until the construction is suddenly declared finished. At that moment, there is often an expression on the child's face which seems to say that *this* is *it* – and it is good.

Let me present one such construction as my 'text' I will give you all the details so that you may consider what to you appears to be the 'key' to the whole performance. A black boy, five years of age, is a vigorous boy, probably the most athletically gifted child in his class, and apt to enter any room with the question, 'Where is the action?' He not only comes eagerly, but also builds immediately and decisively a high, symmetrical, and well-balanced *structure*. (See Fig. 1.) Only then does he scan the other toys and with quick, categorical moves, first places all the *toy vehicles* under and on the building. Then he groups all the *animals* together in a scene beside

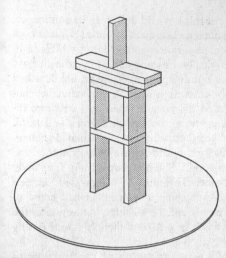

Fig. 1

the building, with the snake in the centre. After a pause, he chooses as his first *human doll* the black boy, whom he lays on the very top of the building. He then arranges a group of adults and children with outstretched arms (as if they reacted excitedly) next to the animal scene. Finally he puts the babies into some of the vehicles and places three men (the policeman, the doctor, and the old man) on top of them. That is it.

The boy's 'story' follows the sequence of placements: 'Cars come to the house. The lion bites the snake, who wiggles his tail. The monkey and the kitten try to kill the snake. People came to watch. Little one (black boy) on roof is where smoke comes out.'

The recorded sequence, the final scene as photographed, and the story noted down all lend themselves to a number of research interests. A reviewer interested in sex differences may note the way in which, say, vehicles and animals are used first, as is more common for boys; or he may recognize in the building of a high and façade-like structure something more common for urban boys. Another reviewer may point to the formal characteristics of the construction – which are, indeed, superior. The psychoanalyst will note aggressive and sexual themes not atypical for this age, such as those connected here with the suggestive snake. The clinician might wonder about the more bizarre element, added almost as a daring afterthought, that of men of authority (doctor, policeman, old man) being placed on top of the babies. Such unique terms, however, escape our comprehension in this kind of investigation, and this usually for lack of intimate life data.

In looking for a theme unique for this boy and unitary in its dominance, I would first focus on the block construction itself, 'topped' as it is by a black boy. The meaning of this configuration emerged as we listened to Robert's teachers. One said, 'Physically, this boy can compete with boys much older than he. But when he is unhappy, he becomes quite detached and dances a two-step around the classroom with his arms stretched out sideways.' As the teacher mimicked his posture, the boy's structure re-vealed itself as a body image: legs, torso, outstretched arms, and head. Another teacher gave a second clue: she had once congratulated the boy on his athletic ability, but he had responded with a despairing gesture, saying, 'Yes, but my brain is no good.' She had assured him that body and brain can learn to help each other. This must have impressed him as a formula for the solution of whatever some inner conflict had come to mean to him, or his blackness, or his age, or all three. At any rate, the theme of a dancing body with a black boy as head literally stands out by priority, prominence, and centrality.

It would take a comparison of a wide variety of such constructions to make the probable meaning of this one construction convincing. Today we must accept this one performance as an example of a five-year-old's capacity to project a relevant personal theme on the *microcosm* of a play table (Erikson, 1963).

2

Our model situation, then, owes its relevance to the observation that one child after another will use a few toys and ten to twenty minutes' time to let some disturbing fact of his life, or some life task, become the basis for a performance characterized by a unique style of representation. Let me try to give some added dignity to the matter by merely mentioning that other play constructions done by the same child over a period of time show an impressive variation as well as a continuity of themes. And if I ever doubted that such continuity is a witness of unifying trends close to the core of a person's development, I learned better when quite recently I had an opportunity to compare the play constructions done in the manner just described thirty years ago by children in their early teens with the dominant themes in their subsequent lives.* History, of course, assigned unexpected roles to many of these persons who are now in their early forties; and yet many of these constructions decades later can be clearly seen as a con-densed statement of a theme dominant in a person's destiny.

In studying such specimens, such condensed bits of life, the observer is loath to fit them into the theories to which he and others at different times and under other conditions have subordinated related phenomena. True,

* As recorded in the Institute of Human Development of the University of California.

the themes presented betray some repetitiveness such as we recognize as the 'working through' of a *traumatic* experience: but they also express a playful *renewal*. If they seem to be governed by some need to *communicate*, or even to *confess*, they certainly also seem to serve the joy of *self-expression*. If they seem dedicated to the *exercise* of growing faculties, they also seem to serve the *mastery* of a complex life situation. As I would not settle for any one of these explanations alone, I would not wish to do without any one of them.

Rather, I would now quote Piaget in order to underline one of the basic principles bequeathed by him to the Erikson Institute. Declaring that he is an 'interactionist', Piaget said:

What interests me is the creation of new things that are not performed, nor predetermined by nervous system maturation alone, and not predetermined by the nature of the encounters with the environment, but are constructed within the individual himself.

Piaget concluded by suggesting a liberating methodology in all teaching. 'Children,' he said, 'should be able to do their own experimenting and their own research.' Such experimenting, however (as I felt strongly when watching Baerbel Inhelder in Geneva induce children to be experimental), relies on some playfulness and, in fact, on an interplay of the child's inner resources with the nature of the task and the suggestiveness of inter-viewers who are 'game'. 'In order for a child to understand something,' Piaget concluded, 'he must *construct it himself*, he must *re-invent* it.'

Piaget, of course, spoke of cognitive gains. But let me suggest in passing that such play procedures as the one described may well facilitate in a child an impulse to recapitulate and, as it were, to re-invent his own experience in order to learn where it might lead. If there is something to this, then we may entertain the dim hope that some such play procedure may become an adjunct to early education rather than remain a method in the service of the clinic or of research only.

But what seems to be the *function of playfulness* in the children's responses both to Piaget's cognitive challenge and to our expressive one? The most general answer necessarily points to a quality of all things alive, namely the restoration and creation of a *leeway of mastery* in a set of developments or circumstances. The German language has a word for it: *Spielraum*, which is not conveyed in a literal translation such as 'playroom'. The word con-notes something common also for the 'play' of mechanical things, namely *free movement* within *prescribed limits*. This at least establishes the boun-daries of the phenomenon: where the freedom is gone, *or* the limits, play ends. Such a polarity also seems to adhere to the linguistic origins of the word *play*, which connotes both carefree oscillation and a quality of being engaged, committed. Language, furthermore, conveys any number of destructive and self-destructive nuances such as playing *at* something or *with* somebody, or playing oneself *out*: all these and other kinds of play connote the limits which end all play.

But if I should now make the first of a number of comparative leaps and ask where I would look for the closest analogy to our play constructions in adult life, I would point to the dramatist's job. If, in this small boy's life, the classroom and the home setting are an early equivalent of the sphere of adult actuality with its interplay of persons and institutions, then his solitary construction is the infantile model of the playwright's work: he, too, condenses into scenes of unitary place and time, marked by a 'set' and populated by a cast, the tragic (and comic) dilemma of representative individuals caught in the role conflicts of their time.

3

Before turning to the sphere of human playfulness in later life, let me touch on some of its fundamentals in man's ontogenetic beginnings. Here I can point to René Spitz's discussion of 'basic education'. He, who has given us classical studies of the tragic consequences of a restriction of sensory *Spielraum* in early childhood, now has returned to specify what that deprivation consists of. He tells us that it is the gift of *vision* which first serves to integrate the 'unconnected discreet stimulations' of taste, audition, smell and touch. To him, the maternal person, visually comprehended, is both the earliest environment and the earliest educator, who 'enables the child – all other things being equal – to achieve the capacity to learn'. She seems to do so by truly letting her face shine upon the newborn's searching eyes, and by letting herself be thus verified as one 'totality'. I would prefer to speak of wholeness rather than of totality, in order to indicate the very special Gestalt quality of that visual integration which permits the infant to extend what I have called his *auto-sphere*, and to include the inclined human face and the maternal presence in it. As Joan Erikson puts it in her essay, '*Eye to Eye*':

> We began life with this relatedness to eyes ... It is with the eyes that (maternal) concern and love are communicated, and distance and anger as well. Growing maturity does not alter this eye-centeredness, for all through life our visual intercourse with others is eye-focused: the eye that blesses and curses (Erikson, 1966).

Spitz now ascribes to organized vision the role of a first ego nucleus, anchored 'in a special sector of man's central nervous system, which permits a first integration of experience'. It will be obvious that a certain playfulness must endow visual scanning and rescanning, which leads to significant interplay as it is responded to by the mother with playful encourage-ment. This, in turn, confirms a sense of mutuality in both partners. It is such *interplay*, I would believe, which is the prime facilitator of that 'ego nucleus'.

As we proceed, I will refer to other visualized spheres endowed with a special aura. I already have mentioned the theatre. The dictionary says that the root of the word is *thea* – a sight, which, in turn, is related to *thauma* – that which compels the gaze. Maybe the 'legitimate' theatre is only a special case, a condensed version of all the imagined, depicted, and theorized spheres (yes, there is *thea* in *theory*, too) by which we attempt to create coherencies and continuities in the complexity and affectivity of existence.* And we will not forget that the late Bertram Lewin spoke af a 'dream screen' on which we experience our nightly visions.

4

But I must now ask a theoretical and terminological question. If, as we are apt to say, the maternal caretaker is the first 'object' playfully engaged by the scanning eyes, who are the 'objects' in later stages, up to St Paul's finite recognition? Are they, as some of us would be all too ready to say, 'mother substitutes'?

I would postulate that the early mother's equivalent in each later stage must always be the sum of all the persons and institutions which are signifi-cant for his wholeness in an expanding arena of interplay. As the radius of physical reach and of cognitive comprehension, of libidinal attachment and of responsible action – as all these expand, there will, of course, always be persons who are substitutes for the original mother. But that, as we know, can be a hindrance as well as a help, unless they themselves become part of that wider sphere of interaction which is essential for the increasing scope of what once was basic education. In our five-year-old's play construction we saw reflected, in addition to impulses, fantasies and familial themes, the

* I owe to Gerald Holton a number of suggestive references to Einstein's meditations on the nature of his mathematical inspiration. It is said that Einstein was not yet able to speak when he was three years old. He preferred communing with building blocks and jigsaw pieces. Later in (1945) he wrote to Jacques Hadamard: 'Taken from a psycho-logical viewpoint, this combinatory play seems to be the essential feature in productive thought – before there is any connection with logical construction in words or other kinds of signs which can be communicated to others' (Hadamard, 1945). And, again: 'Man seeks to form for himself, in whatever manner is suitable for him, a simplified and lucid image of the world (*Bild der Welt*), and so to overcome the world of ex-perience by striving to replace it to some extent by this image. That is what the painter does, and the poet, the speculative philosopher, the natural scientist, each in his own way. Into this image and its formation he places the centre of gravity of his emotional life, in order to attain the peace and serenity that he cannot find within the narrow con-fines of swirling personal experience' (Holton, 1971-2)

teacher and the school environment in the widest sense of an encounter with what can be learned. But so will, in adolescence, the peer generation and the ideological universe become part of the arena which is the equivalent of the early mother. In adulthood the work world and all the institutions which comprise the procreative and productive actuality are part of the arena within which a person must have scope and leeway or suffer severely in his ego-functioning. Thus on each step what had been 'in part' will now be recognized and interacted with in its wholeness, even as the person comes to feel recognized as an actor with a circumscribed identity within a life plan. In fact, unless his gifts and his society have on each step provided the adult with a semblance of an arena of free interplay, no man can hope to reach the potential maturity of (pre-senile) old age when, indeed, only the wholeness of existence bounded by death can, on occasion, dimly recall to him the quality of that earliest sensory matrix.

5

What we so far have vaguely called interplay can be made more specific by linking it with the problem of ritualization which was discussed on the last occasion when Konrad Lorenz and I served together on a symposium.* His subject then was the ontogeny of ritualization in animals, and mine, that in man. Julian Huxley, the chairman of that symposium, had years ago described as ritualization in animals such instinctive performances as the exuberant greeting ceremonials of bird couples, who, after a lengthy separation, must reassure each other that they not only belong to the same species but also to the same nest. This is a 'bonding' procedure which, Huxley suggested, functions so as to *exclude ambiguity* and to facilitate unimpaired *instinctive* interplay. Lorenz, in turn, concentrated on the ritualizations by which some animals of the same species given to fighting matches make peace before they seriously harm each other. It was my task to point to the ontogeny of analogous phenomena in man. But with us, so I suggested, ritualization also has the burden of *overcoming ambivalence* in situations which have strong *instinctual* components (that is, drives not limited to 'natural' survival), as is true for all important encounters in man's life. Thus the ontologically earliest ritualizations in man, the greeting of mother and baby, adds to the minimum facial stimulation required to attract a baby's fascination (and eventually his smile) such motions, sounds, words, and smells as are characteristic of the culture, the class, and the family, as well as of the mothering person.

Konrad Lorenz, the foster mother of the goose child, Martina, has

* 'A Discussion of Ritualisation of Behavior in Animals and Man', organized by Sir Julian Huxley, F.R.S. *Philosophical Transactions of the Royal Society of London*, Series B, no. 772, vol. 251, pp. 337–49.

rightly gained fame for his ability to greet animals as well as humans in a bonding manner. He has demonstrated the lost-and-found game, which in German is called guck-guck da-da and in English, peek-a-boo. Let me call all these and similar phenomena in man *ritualized interplay*. This extends from the simplest habitual interaction to elaborate games, and, finally, to ornate rituals. Today when so many ritualizations so rapidly lose their convincing power, it is especially important to remember that in this whole area of ritualized interplay the most horrible dread can live right next to the most reassuring playfulness. Little Martina was running and falling all over herself for dear survival when she pursued Konrad Lorenz, and any accidental interruption of the ritualized behaviour by which animals do away with ambiguity, can lead to murder. As to man, we only need to visualize again small children who cannot smile, or old persons who have lost all faith, to comprehend both the singular power and the vulnerability of ritualized reassurance in the human situation.

Yet, what constitutes or what limits playful ritualization in man is as hard to define as play itself: maybe such phenomena as playfulness or youthfulness or aliveness are defined by the very fact that they cannot be wholly defined. There is a reconciliation of the irreconcilable in all ritualizations, from the meeting of lovers to all manner of get-togethers, in which there is a sense of choice and ease and yet also one of driving necessity: of a highly personalized and yet also a traditional pattern; of improvisation in all formalization; of surprise in the very reassurance of familiarity; and of some leeway for innovation in what must be repeated over and over again. Only these and other polarities assure that *mutual fusion* of the participants and yet also a simultaneous *gain in distinctiveness* for each.

Consider the children who soon will enter the stage of adolescence – the stage when the young themselves must begin to offer each other traditional ritualizations in the form of spontaneous improvisations and of games – and this often on the borderline of what adults would consider the licence of youth: will they then have learned to be playful and to anticipate some leeway of personal and social development?

6

Children cannot be said or judged to be 'acting' in a systematic and irreversible way, even though they may, on occasion, display a sense of responsibility and a comprehension of adult responsibility which astonishes us. Young people, on the other hand (as we realize in our time more than ever before), are apt to continue to play and to play-act in ways which may suddenly prove to have been irreversible action – even action of a kind which endangers safety, violates legality, and, all too often, forfeits the actor's future. And, in recent years, youth closer to adulthood has begun on a large scale to usurp responsibility and even revolutionary status in the arena of public action. This has resulted in lasting consequences even where the action itself may not have been much more than a dare or a prank on a stage of imagined power. Never before, then, has it been more important to understand what is happening in that wide area where juvenile play-acting and historical action meet.

The return in adolescence of childlike and childish behaviour in the midst of an increasing anticipation of and participation in adulthood has been treated in innumerable textbooks. They point to the impulsivity of sexual maturation and of the power of the aggressive equipment and yet also to the vastly expanded cognitive horizon. There is the intensity of peer-group involvement at all costs, a search for inspiration (now often forfeited to drugs), and yet also the desperate need (yes, an ego need) for an ideologically unified universe sanctioned by leaders who would make both freedom and discipline meaningful. To all this, I have added the discussion of identity – and of fidelity.

I have emphasized fidelity because I think I have observed the fateful deficit in ego-strength resulting from the absence of such commitments as would permit youth to anchor its readiness for loyalty in social reality; and the equally fateful deficit in meaningful social interplay resulting from a state of society in which old fidelities are being eroded. I would, therefore, follow Konrad Lorenz in asserting that all through man's socio-genetic development, rites and rituals have attempted to attract and to invest that fidelity. Where and when both generations can participate in them with affective and cognitive commitment, these rites, indeed, are performing 'functions analogous to those which the mechanisms of inheritance perform in the preservation of the species'. Today, as we all agree, a deep and world-wide disturbance exists in this central area of ritualized interplay between the generations.

7

Let me now turn to a historical example. One of the most noteworthy revolutionary ritualizations of recent times has been the founding of the Black Panther Party – noteworthy in our context as an illustration of youthful political imagination on the very border of disaster. Such ritualization can go to the core of history, whether it 'succeeds' or not: it is successful if it makes an unforgettable point and if it has the flexibility to go on from there.

Much of the Panthers' history has happened in the dark of the ghetto as well as in that legal twilight which confuses and scares the 'law-abiding'.

Revolutionary activity, however, is always beset with the dilemma of defining who and what is the law, and what disruptive act, when, and where, is political rather than criminal. There may be also the proud and mocking creation of a new 'species', as attested to by the very party name, which, in the case of the Panthers, is that of an animal said to be ferocious primarily in defence, and the relentless and publicist verbal weapon of calling men of the 'legitimate' police force 'pigs'. Such debasement of the opponent is a moral violence which arouses not only murderous hate in the defamed, it can also become a retrogressive stance in the defamer. In the American Black, of course, such defamation is grounded more than in any other social group, both in a common history of daily and total defencelessness and in an explosive folk language long the only outlet for in-turned aggression – and in fact used with mocking as well as murderous abandon against other Blacks. The original imagery of the young leaders of the Black Panther movement (and I am talking about these origins of the movement and not about the tedious stance of its propagandistic habituation) surely contained, therefore, the possibility of creating a new set of roles, which often may have appeared to be all too grandiosely staged, but which did link past and future by recapitulating historical images in a radically new setting. True, certain titles of command seemed rather florid in the absence of an assured body of followers; but it must be remembered that revolutionary language – at total risk to itself – always challenges history to confirm what has already been claimed as certain. This is, of course, compounded where the revolutionaries are young, for youth and revolution both play with that theatre of action where personal conversion and radical rejuvenation confirm each other, to the point that history's agreement is taken for granted. And sometimes, history assents. Our black revolutionaries differ from others in that they are not rebelling against a father generation. Their symbol of the Establishment is 'the man'; yet, both examples given remind us to look for the adult counter-players in attempted ritualizations demanding new kinds of generational transfer. And there we often find glaring vacancies in the cast required for the fulfilment of the script – vacancies impossible to fill by excitable police or by uncomfortable judges.

8

This is the 'gap' then; Konrad Lorenz believes that what he calls 'the enmity between generations' exists not only because of a combination of historical and technological changes, but because of a misdevelopment of evolutionary proportions. He reminds us of the pseudo-tribal character of much of the present-day rebellion; and to him the widespread and truly 'bizarre distortions of cultural behavior' represent a new 'infantilism' and a regression to a primitivity which he considers analogous to a 'disturbance of the genetic blueprint'. Looking at revolutionary youth from the point of view of an evolutionary ethologist, apparently he feels that humanity has reached a critical point when the changes in social norms necessary within the period between generations have begun to 'exceed the capacity of the pubertal adapting mechanisms'.

Lorenz introduces into the discussion a term which I have used when I drew attention to the phenomenon of cultural pseudo-speciation – meaning the tendency of human groups to behave as if they were *the* chosen species. Lorenz discusses the matter vividly:

> In itself, it is a perfectly normal process and even a desirable one . . . there is, however, a very serious negative side to it: pseudo-speciation is the cause of war . . . If the divergence of cultural development has gone far enough, it inevitably leads to the horrible consequence that one group does not regard the other as quite human. In many primitive languages, the name of the tribe is synonymous with that of man – and from this point of view it is not really cannibalism if you eat the fallen warriors of the hostile tribe! Pseudo-speciation suppresses the instinctive mechanisms normally preventing the killing of fellow members of the species while, diabolically, it does not inhibit intra-specific aggression in the least.

Before coming to the implications of pseudo-speciation for youth and adulthood, however, let me ask what importance it may have for the problem of play. In the animal world, obviously the play of the young is linked with the adaptation of the species to a section of the natural environment. The play of the human child, however, must orient him within the possibilities and the boundaries first of what is imaginable and possible, and then to what is most effective and most permissible in a cultural setting. One of the playing child's tasks, then, is to try out some role pretensions within what he gradually learns is his society's version of reality and to become himself within the roles and techniques at his disposal. No wonder, then, that man's play takes place on the border of dangerous alternatives and is always beset both with burdening conflicts and with liberating choices.

At the same time, however, human play as well as adult ritualizations and rituals seem to serve the function of adaptation to the 'pseudo' aspects of human 'reality': for, as I will point out in some detail later, man, in addition to making gigantic strides in learning to know nature and the uses it can be put to, has yet also striven to maintain prejudged assumptions concerning the ordained excellence of particular versions of man. Thus, his playful imagination does not only serve all that is and could be, it also is forced to endow that which, so he is clearly taught, must be if he is to be judged sane and worthy. Youthful rebellion always attempts to create new leeway for new and potential roles in such assumed realities; but the very condition of pseudo-speciation has made man's playfulness a matter both of freedom and of bondage, both of enhanced life and of multiplied death.

Youthful play-acting and the assumption or usurpation of historical roles can border on each other. But we must now account for the fact that new ritualizations are, indeed, apt to miscarry because of the 'horrible fact that the hate which the young bear us is tribal hate'. And, indeed, it seems that the shift in the overall ecological and technological conditions of mankind has led, at least within the orbit of the American industrial world culture (which includes the World War II enemies of the United States), to a new grouping of pseudo-species: on one side all the young people across the borders of former empires and on the other the whole 'old' generation.

It is obvious enough that the young reject, above all, the insignia and the attitudes which have marked their victimization and heroification as soldiers serving one of the pseudo-species extant now. Because they carry this protest literally on the sleeve, we can now add to the subjects to be reviewed the ritual importance of human *display*, for we are reminded of the prominence, in all of classical warfare, of the resplendent uniforms, topped by animal plumage, which was intended to unite and divide the young men of the world into warriors serving either the right and godly or the wrong and evil species: that the display of physical insignia signifying human pseudo-speciation imitate those of animal speciation is only too obvious. And it begins to make sense that the rebellious youth of today is displaying, instead, an impressive array of self-contradicting insignia, often mocking all uniformity by mixing fragments of military uniforms (and even of flags) with the ornaments of relaxed brotherhood. For youth attempts to create not only new arenas for involvements and commitments, but also such new types of heroes as are essential to the emergence of a whole 'human being' representative of mankind itself – if and when the old have abrogated their pseudo-species, or have been destroyed. In the meantime, youth often seems to feel that it can enforce basic changes only by mockingly insisting on a moratorium without end and an unlimited arena of its own, and it is often only with drugs that they can aver the remaining boundaries and simulate a free territory within. This is a state of affairs open to all kinds of group retrogressions as well as personal regressions. But, then, adolescent regressions always have been, to some extent, semi-deliberate recapitulations of childhood fantasy serving the adaptive purpose of reviving what infantile playfulness was sacrificed to the established order for use on new ideological frontiers. Similarly, large-scale historical retrogressions often seem to be semi-deliberate attempts to invoke the revolutions of the past in the name of a future revolution as yet neither defined nor localized nor fixed in time. But the extremes noted here may be necessary aspects of a shift, the outcome of which can only be appraised when it will be clear where such playful trends combine with the discipline and the competence necessary for sustained change.

If one accepts the theory of a shift from the pseudo-species mentality to an all-human one, one may well see in the radical display of youth an upheaval necessary for an elemental regrouping which transvaluates past ideals of excellence and heroism in the service of a more universal speciation. To be sure, much horrible hate and much resultant paralysis is thus transferred to the inter-generational struggle where it appears to be hopelessly raw and untrained in comparison to the age-old stance and stamina of uniformed and disciplined military behaviour. This probably is the cause of occasional enactments of totally 'senseless' cruelty and of dramatic murder for the sake of a vindictive illusion of extinguishing the established.

But we may well remind ourselves of two momentous developments characteristic of the other, the adult side of playing history. The first is the fact that adult man, with the help of the most creative expansion of scientific and organizational leeway (remember Einstein's playfulness), has created a world technically ready to eliminate mankind in one instant for the sake of one nation or another that cannot stop playing empire. Is it any wonder that some of the most romantic and the most destructive behaviour in modern youth seems to mock us by anticipating the day when the nuclear holocaust *has* occurred?

The second fact is the disintegration of paternalistic dominance, both in familiar relations and in the 'minds of man'. For this again we blame primarily the anti-paternal attitude of the young. Following Freud we have obediently persisted in referring to the origins of the rebellious complex in childhood as the Oedipus Complex. But we have thus immortalized as inescapable only the behaviour of the son Oedipus, who unknowingly slew his father as the Oracle had predicted, while we have paid little attention to the fact that this father had such faith in the Oracle's opaque announcement and in his own interpretation of it, that he was willing to dispose of his son. But maybe Laius did only more openly and more dramatically what may be implicit in circumcisions, puberty rites, and 'confirmations' of many kinds. As a prize for certified adulthood, the fathers all limit and forestall some frightening potentialities of development dangerous to 'the system'. And they all strive to appropriate the new individual for the pseudo-species, marking and branding him as potentially dangerous, initiating him into the prescribed limits of activities, inducting him into a preferred service, and preparing him for being sacrificed in holy wars. Maybe they only underscore ritually what human development and the structure of human society accomplish anyway. For after having played at a variety of choices, most adults submit to so-called reality, that is, a consolidation of established facts, of acquired methods, of defined roles, and of overweening values. Such consolidation is deemed necessary not only for a style of acting and interacting, but above all, for the bringing up of the next generation of children. They, it is hoped, will, from their childhood play and their juvenile role experimentation, move right into the dominant means of production and will invest their playfulness and their search for identity in the daily necessity to work for the higher glory of the pseudo-species.

Today, Laius and Oedipus face one another in a different confrontation. For even as the youth of divergent countries begin to look, talk, and feel alike – and this whether they are rebelling against industrial civilization or are, in fact, rapidly learning the prerequisite skills – so does the older generation appear to become more and more alike and stereotyped. For they impersonate a new and universal type, the efficient member of an organized occupation or a profession, playing free and equal while being at the mercy of mass-produced roles, of standardized consumership, and of rampant bureaucratization. But all these are developments which, in fact, take the play out of work – and this not (or not only) because of a Calvinistic choice to separate the two for the sake of righteousness, but because it can't be helped. And this seems to be the message of much of the mockery of the young, that if there must be defined roles, it may be better to go on playing at choosing them, than to become their ready puppets.

9

A concluding section on play in adulthood can only be an opening section for another, a future essay. For here we enter both the twilight of what is called 'reality' and the ambiguities of the word *play* – and these two assuredly are related to each other. Even as man protests the pure truth just because he is the animal who can lie – and pretend to be natural – so he strives to be in tune with hard reality just because he so easily falls for illussions and abstractions. And both truth and reality are at issue when man must define what he means when he says he is playing – or not playing.

The poet has it, that man is never more human than when he plays. But what must he do and be, and in what context, to be both adult and playful: must he do something in which he feels again as if he were a playing child, or a youth in a game? Must he step outside of his most serious and most fateful concerns? Or must he transcend his everyday condition and be 'beside himself' in fantasy, ecstasy, or 'togetherness'?

Maybe an epigenetic view makes it unnecessary to categorize so sharply. The adult once was a child and a youth. He will never be either again: but neither will he ever be without the heritage of those former states. In fact, I would postulate that, in order to be truly adult, he must on each level renew some of the playfulness of childhood and some of the sportiveness of the young. As we have seen, the child in his play and games as well as the young person in his pranks and sports and forays into politics, protected as they both are, up to a point, from having their play-acting 'count' as irreversible action, nevertheless are dealing with central concerns both of settling the past and of anticipating the future. So must the adult, beyond playful and sportive activities specified as such, remain playful in the centre of his concerns and concerned with opportunities to renew and increase the leeway and scope of his and his fellow man's activities. Whatever the precursors of a specifically adult playfulness, it must grow with and through the adult stages even as these stages can come about only by such renewal.

At the beginning of this essay, I compared a child's solitary play construction with the function of a dramatic performance in adulthood: in both, a theme and a conflict, dominant in the 'big' world, are meaningfully condensed into a microsphere and into a spectacle and a speculum, a mirror of inner and outer conditions. The dimly lit theatre thus deals with the reflection and individual fate of all those areas of public action which occur in 'all the world', in the light of day. But if man, as pointed out, calls these spheres 'theatres', 'spectacles', and 'scenarios' one wonders sometimes which is metaphorical for what. For man endows such spheres of highest reality, too, with a ceremonial and procedural aura which permits him to get engaged with a certain abandon, with intensified loyalty, and often with increased energy and efficiency, but also with a definite sacrifice of plain good judgement.

Any observing visitor to a legislative chamber of a chief executive's mansion will not escape an occasional eerie sense of unreality in such factories of decision which must determine irreversible shifts in what will seem compellingly real to so many, and in what to generations to come will seem worth living, dying, and killing for. Most fateful for mankind as a species (we cannot say this too often) is the tendency to re-divide the political scene in such a way that those 'on the other side' suddenly appear to be changed in quality, reduced to statistical items and worthy only of 'body counts'.

I am suggesting for a future occasion, then, that we take a new good look not only at those occasions when adults claim that they are playing like children, or play-acting on the legitimate stage, but also such other occasions when they insist with deadly righteousness that they are playing for 'real' stakes and yet, sooner or later, appear to have been role-playing puppets in imaginary spheres of 'necessity'.

But the method of yesterday can also become part of a wider consciousness today. Psychoanalysis can go about defining its own place in history and yet continue to observe its traditional subject matter, namely the symptoms of repressions and suppressions – including their denial. It can study successive re-repressions in relation to historical change: there can be little doubt but that our enlightened age has set out to prove Freud wrong by doing openly and with a vengeance what he said were secret desires, warded off by inhibitions. We can learn to find out how we have contributed to such developments by our exclusive reliance (also culturally and historically determined) on the 'dominance of the intellect' which often made the acceptance of psychoanalytic theory and vocabulary the measure of man's adaptation. We know now (and the study of play confirms us in this) that the comprehension of Freud's *Wirklichkeit* must go beyond one of its meanings, namely reality, and include that of actuality (Erikson, 1964). For if reality is the structure of facts consensually agreed upon in a given stage of knowledge, actuality is the leeway created by new forms of interplay. Without actuality, reality becomes a prison of stereotyping while actuality always must retest reality to remain truly playful. To fully understand this we must study for each stage of life the interpenetration of the cognitive and the affective as well as the moral and the instinctual. We may then realize that in adulthood an individual gains leeway for himself, as he creates it for others: here is the soul of adult play.

In conclusion, we must take note of another 'gap' in our civilization which only partly coincides with the generational one. It is that between a grim determination to play out established and divisive roles, functions, and competencies to their bitter ends; and, on the other hand, new kinds of group life characterized by a total playfulness, which simulates vast imagination (often drug-induced), sexual and sensual freedom, and a verbal openness often way beyond the integrative means of individuals, not to speak of technological and economic realities. In the first area, that of habituated pragmatism, leading individuals make a grim effort at pretending that they are in full command of the facts and by no means role-playing – a claim which in fact gives them a vanishing credibility. The playful crowd, on the other hand, often seems to play all too hard at playing and at pretending that they are already sharing a common humanity, by-passing those technical and political developments which must provide the material basis for 'one world'. But man is a tricky animal; and adults playing all too hard at role-playing or at simulating naturalness, honesty, and intimacy may end up being everybody and yet nobody in touch with all and yet not close to anybody.

But we must always also be receptive to new forms of interplay; and we must always come back to the children and learn to recognize the signs of unknown resources which might yet flourish in the vision of one mankind on one earth and its outer reaches.

(*From Play and Development*, W. W. Norton, New York, 1972.)

References

ERIKSON, E. H. (1964), *Childhood and Society*, Hogarth Press.

ERIKSON, E. H. (1964), *Insight and Responsibility*, W. W. Norton, New York.

ERIKSON, J. (1966), 'Eye to eye', in *The Man-Made Object*, G. Kepes (ed.), Braziller.

HADAMARD, J. (1945), *The Psychology of Invention in the Mathematical Field*, Princeton University Press.

HOLTON, G. (1971–2), 'On trying to understand scientific genius,' *The American Scholar*, No. 41.

Acknowledgements

For Readings reproduced in this volume Acknowledgement is made to the following sources:

Introduction   Doubleday & Co. Inc.
Reading 1   American Psychological Association
Reading 2   Appleton-Century-Crofts
Reading 3   William Heinemann Ltd
Reading 4   Eyre Methuen & Co. Ltd
             Harvard University Press
Reading 5   Mr Robert Fagen
Reading 6   American Psychiatric Association
Reading 7   Cambridge University Press
Reading 8   Johnson Reprint Corporation
Reading 9   Johnson Reprint Corporation
Reading 10   Baillière, Tindall & Cassell
Reading 11   Ms Jane Egan
Reading 12   Routledge & Kegan Paul Ltd
             W. W. Norton & Co. Inc.
Reading 13   E. J. Brill
Reading 14   S. Karger A.B.
Reading 15   S. Karger A.B.
Reading 16   Mr Irwin S. Bernstein
Reading 17   Faber & Faber Ltd
Reading 18   The Zoological Society of London
Reading 19   Macmillan Journals Ltd
Reading 20   Baillière, Tindall & Cassell
Reading 21   S. Karger A.B.
Reading 22   International Universities Press
Reading 23   E. J. Brill
Reading 24   Ms Kathy Sylva, Mr Jerome S. Bruner, Mr Paul Genova
Reading 25   Baillière, Tindall & Cassell
Reading 26   The Merrill-Palmer Institute
Reading 27   Mr Jerome S. Bruner, Ms V. Sherwood
Reading 28   National Congress of Parents and Teachers
             Ohio State University College of Education
             American Orthopsychiatric Association
             Association for Childhood Education International

Ms Phyllis Levenstein and Department of Psychology,
Yale University
Family Service Association of America
Reading 29 Baillière, Tindall & Cassell
Reading 30 American Museum of Natural History
Reading 31 S. Karger A.B.
Reading 32 S. Karger A.B.
Reading 33 American Society of Zoologists
Reading 34 S. Karger A.B.
Reading 35 Weidenfeld & Nicolson Ltd
Reading 36 Royal Anthropological Institute
Reading 37 S. Karger A.B.
Reading 38 Random House Inc.
Reading 39 Ms Esther Blank Greif
Reading 40 Oxford University Press
Reading 41 Routledge & Kegan Paul Ltd
Macmillan Publishing Co. Inc.
Reading 42 Charles C. Thomas, Publisher
Reading 43 Oxford University Press
Reading 44 National Education Association
Reading 45 American Museum of Natural History
Reading 46 International African Institute
Reading 47 University of Chicago Alumni Association
Reading 48 American Museum of Natural History
Reading 49 Academic Press Inc.
Interscience Publishers
American Psychological Association
Reading 50 The Journal Press
Reading 51 McGraw-Hill Book Co.
Reading 52 McIntosh & Otis Inc.
Reading 53 International Arts and Sciences Press
Reading 54 W. W. Norton & Co. Inc., and Routledge & Kegan Paul Ltd
Reading 55 Ms Catherine Garvey
Reading 56 The Nobel Foundation
Reading 57 The World Publishing Corporation
Reading 58 J. M. Dent & Sons Ltd
New Directions Publishing Corporation
Reading 59 Ms Sylvia Feinburg
Reading 60 University of California Press
Reading 61 Agathon Press
Reading 62 Edicom N.V.
Reading 63 McIntosh & Otis Inc.
Reading 64 Mr Peter Reynolds and the American Association for the
Advancement of Science
Reading 65 Harcourt Brace Jovanovich Inc.
Reading 66 Mr Jerome S. Bruner

Reading 67   A. D. Peters & Co.
Reading 68   American Psychological Association
Reading 69   American Academy of Arts and Sciences
Reading 70   Beacon Press and Routledge & Kegan Paul Ltd
Reading 71   W. W. Norton & Co. Inc.

Photographic Acknowledgements

(*see photo inset*)

p. 1	top	Barnaby's Picture Library
	bottom	C. M. Hladik
p. 2		John Brooke
p. 3	top	Collier-Macmillan
	bottom	Collier-Macmillan
p. 4	top	J. S. Bruner
	bottom	Ron Chapman
p. 5		Caroline Tutin
p. 6	top	Dr Corinne Hutt
	bottom	Dr Corinne Hutt
p. 7	all four	Dr E. W. Menzel
p. 8		Jersey Wildlife Preservation Trust
p. 9	top	Random House Inc.
	bottom	Caroline Tutin
p. 10	top	Dr Alison Jolly
	bottom	Geoffrey Denny
p. 11		Jane Bown
p. 12	top	Fred Plaut
	bottom	Ron Chapman
p. 13		Chris Steele-Perkins
p. 14	top	Ms Sylvia Feinburg
	bottom	Ms Sylvia Feinburg
p. 15	top	Ms Sylvia Feinburg
	bottom	Ms Sylvia Feinburg
p. 16		A. M. Chitty

Author Index

Subject Index

MORE ABOUT PENGUINS, PELICANS
AND PUFFINS

For further information about books available from Penguins please write to Dept EP, Penguin Books Ltd, Harmondsworth, Middlesex UB7 0DA.

In the U.S.A.: For a complete list of books available from Penguins in the United States write to Dept D G, Penguin Books, 299 Murray Hill Parkway, East Rutherford, New Jersey 07073.

In Canada: For a complete list of books available from Penguins in Canada write to Penguin Books Canada Ltd, 2801 John Street, Markham, Ontario L3R 1B4.

In Australia: For a complete list of books available from Penguins in Australia write to the Marketing Department, Penguin Books Australia Ltd, P.O. Box 257, Ringwood, Victoria 3134.

In New Zealand: For a complete list of books available from Penguins in New Zealand write to the Marketing Department, Penguin Books (N.Z.) Ltd, Private Bag, Takapuna, Auckland 9.

In India: For a complete list of books available from Penguins in India write to Penguin Overseas Ltd, 706 Eros Apartments, 56 Nehru Place, New Delhi 110019.

A CHOICE OF
PELICANS AND PEREGRINES

☐ **A Radical Reader** Christopher Hampton   £9.95

With extracts from the writings of Wycliff, Shakespeare, Bacon, Milton, Swift, Blake, Byron, Dickens and Marx, among many others, this major new anthology spans five hundred years of radical protest from the Peasants' Revolt to the First World War.

☐ **Computer Power and Human Reason**
  Joseph Weizenbaum   £2.95

Internationally acclaimed by scientists and humanists alike: 'This is the best book I have read on the impact of computers on society, and on technology and on man's image of himself' – *Psychology Today*

☐ **Astrology** H. J. Eysenck and D. K. B. Nias   £2.50

Is astrology science or superstition? Two well-known analytical psychologists discuss the latest research and findings in a book that – for adherents of either side – will be an adventure.

☐ **The Germans** Gordon A. Craig   £2.95

'This elegant and enticing work . . . dwells not on the familiar facts of German history but on some often neglected fundamental facets of German life and culture' – *The New York Times Book Review*

☐ **Mind in Science** Richard L. Gregory   £7.95

Integrating and discussing ancient myth and philosophy, the rise of Western science, the developments of psychology and technology, and recent scientific discoveries, Gregory illuminates the nature of Mind. 'Few recent books can rival . . . its scope or its engaging enthusiasm' – *The Times Literary Supplement*

☐ **Who Cares about English Usage?** David Crystal   £1.95

Including cartoons and quizzes to stimulate the mind, this is a highly entertaining guide to English usage by David Crystal, deviser of the popular Radio 4 programme, *Speak Out*.

A CHOICE OF
PELICANS AND PEREGRINES

☐ *Know Your Own Mind*
James Green and David Lewis   £1.95

How do you *know* if you have a talent for solving problems, or creative work, or learning languages . . . ? This book contains nine assessments to help you build your own profile, discover your potential – and act on it.

☐ *The Mathematical Experience*
Philip J. Davis and Reuben Hersh   £6.95

Not since *Gödel, Escher, Bach* has such an entertaining book been written on the relationship of mathematics to the arts and sciences. 'It deserves to be read by everyone . . . an instant classic' – *New Scientist*

☐ *The Tangled Wing* **Melvin Konner**   £4.95

How far are our emotions and actions affected by our biology? This new study has been acclaimed by *The Times Higher Education Supplement* as 'a pleasure to read . . . an outstanding work of scholarship'.

☐ *The World Turned Upside Down* **Christopher Hill**   £4.50

A portrait of radical groups and ideas during the English Revolution. 'Christopher Hill has that supreme gift of being able to show us the seventeenth-century world from the inside' – Arthur Marwick in *New Society*

☐ *Exploring the Earth and the Cosmos*
Isaac Asimov   £3.95

From dinosaurs to black holes and space probes, this exhilarating book (and superb reference-source) guides us through the facts, figures, people and discoveries that have shaped our changing view of the earth and the cosmos.

☐ *Hen's Teeth and Horse's Toes*
Stephen Jay Gould   £3.95

Essays on natural history by the author of *Ever Since Darwin*. 'He has the rare gift of communicating excitement . . . he challenges one furiously to think' – *Nature*

A CHOICE OF
PELICANS AND PEREGRINES

☐ *Three Who Made a Revolution* **Bertram D. Wolfe**   £4.95

The classic historical biography of Lenin, Trotsky and Stalin. 'The best book in its field in any language' – Edmund Wilson

☐ *Montaillou* **Emmanuel Le Roy Ladurie**   £5.95

The world-famous portrait of life in a medieval French village. 'A Chaucerian gallery of vivid medieval persons' – Hugh Trevor-Roper. 'A classic adventure in eavesdropping across time' – *The Times*

☐ *The Pelican History of the World* **J. M. Roberts**   £5.95

'A stupendous achievement . . . This is the unrivalled World History for our day' – A J P Taylor

---

These books should be available at all good bookshops or newsagents, but if you live in the UK or the Republic of Ireland and have difficulty in getting to a bookshop, they can be ordered by post. Please indicate the titles required and fill in the form below.

NAME _____ BLOCK CAPITALS

ADDRESS _____

_____

_____

Enclose a cheque or postal order payable to The Penguin Bookshop to cover the total price of books ordered, plus 50p for postage. Readers in the Republic of Ireland should send £IR equivalent to the sterling prices, plus 67p for postage. Send to: The Penguin Bookshop, 54/56 Bridlesmith Gate, Nottingham, NG1 2GP.

You can also order by phoning (0602) 599295, and quoting your Barclaycard or Access number.

Every effort is made to ensure the accuracy of the price and availability of books at the time of going to press, but it is sometimes necessary to increase prices and in these circumstances retail prices may be shown on the covers of books which may differ from the prices shown in this list or elsewhere. This list is not an offer to supply any book.

This order service is only available to residents in the UK and the Republic of Ireland.